Introducing Human Resource Management

Visit the *Introducing Human Resource Management*, fourth edition Companion Website at **www.pearsoned.co.uk/foothook** to find valuable **student** learning material including:

- A variety of tests for every chapter, including multiple-choice, fill in the blank, true/false questions, crosswords and word puzzles.

- Answers are provided to help you check your understanding.

File   Edit   View   Favorites   Tools   Help

Back   Forward   Stop   Refresh   Home   History   Print   Edit

Address   http://www.pearsoned.co.uk/foothook   Go

PEARSON
Education   **Introducing Human Resource Management**
             Fourth Edition   Margaret Foot   Caroline Hook

Home   Select Resource   Welcome   Go   Site Search: Go

Welcome to the Companion Website for Introducing Human Resource Management, fourth edition.

Select the sections below, or use the drop-down menu above to navigate through the website. Use the 'Syllabus Manager' button within the sections to create and post your personalised online syllabus.

About the Book

Contains information on what you will find on this website, along with specific details about the book and its authors.

Student Resources

A multitude of helpful resources to further increase your knowledge. There are a variety of tests for every chapter, including multiple choice, fill in the blank and true/false questions, crosswords and word puzzles. Answers to the tests are also provided to help you check your understanding.

For **Instructor Resources**, visit the book catalogue page and follow the Instructor Resources link.

Copyright © 1995-2005, Pearson Education, Inc. | **Legal and Privacy Terms**

Internet

PEARSON
Education

We work with leading authors to develop the strongest
educational materials in Human Resource Management,
bringing cutting-edge thinking and best learning practice
to a global market.

Under a range of well-known imprints, including
Financial Times Prentice Hall, we craft high quality print
and electronic publications which help readers to
understand and apply their content, whether studying
or at work.

To find out more about the complete range of our
publishing, please visit us on the World Wide Web at:
www.pearsoned.co.uk

Introducing
Human Resource
Management

Fourth Edition

Margaret Foot
Caroline Hook

FT Prentice Hall
FINANCIAL TIMES

An imprint of **Pearson Education**
Harlow, England • London • New York • Boston • San Francisco • Toronto
Sydney • Tokyo • Singapore • Hong Kong • Seoul • Taipei • New Delhi
Cape Town • Madrid • Mexico City • Amsterdam • Munich • Paris • Milan

Pearson Education Limited

Edinburgh Gate
Harlow
Essex CM20 2JE
England

and Associated Companies throughout the world

Visit us on the World Wide Web at:
www.pearsoned.co.uk

First published under the Longman Group Limited imprint 1996
Second edition published under the Addison Wesley Longman imprint 1999
Third edition published 2002
Fourth edition published 2005

© Pearson Education Limited 1996, 2005

ISBN 0 273 68174 5

British Library Cataloguing-in-Publication Data
A catalogue record for this book is available from the British Library

Library of Congress Cataloging-in-Publication Data
A catalog record for this book is available from the Library of Congress

Foot, Margaret, 1946-
    Introducing human resource management / Margaret Foot, Caroline Hook.-- 4th ed.
      p. cm.
    Includes bibliographical references and indexes.
    ISBN 0-273-68174-5 (alk. paper)
     1. Personnel management. 2. Employee rights. I. Hook, Caroline, 1949- II. Title.

  HF5549.F5875 2005
  658.3--dc22
                                                 2004063549

10 9 8 7 6 5 4 3 2 1
07   06   05

Typeset by 71 in 9.5/12.5 Stone
Printed by Maten-Cromo Artes Graficas, Spain

Contents

Supporting resources

Visit **www.pearsoned.co.uk/foothook** to find valuable online resources

Companion Website for students
- A variety of tests for every chapter, including multiple-choice, fill in the blank, true/false questions, crosswords and word puzzles
- Answers are provided to help you check your understanding

For instructors
- Complete, downloadable Instructor's Manual including case study notes
- PowerPoint slides that can be downloaded and used as OHTs

Also: The maintained Companion Website provides the following features:
- Search tool to help locate specific items of content
- E-mail results and profile tools to send results of quizzes to instructors
- Online help and support to assist with website usage and troubleshooting

For more information please contact your local Pearson Education sales representative or visit **www.pearsoned.co.uk/foothook**

Guided tour of the book

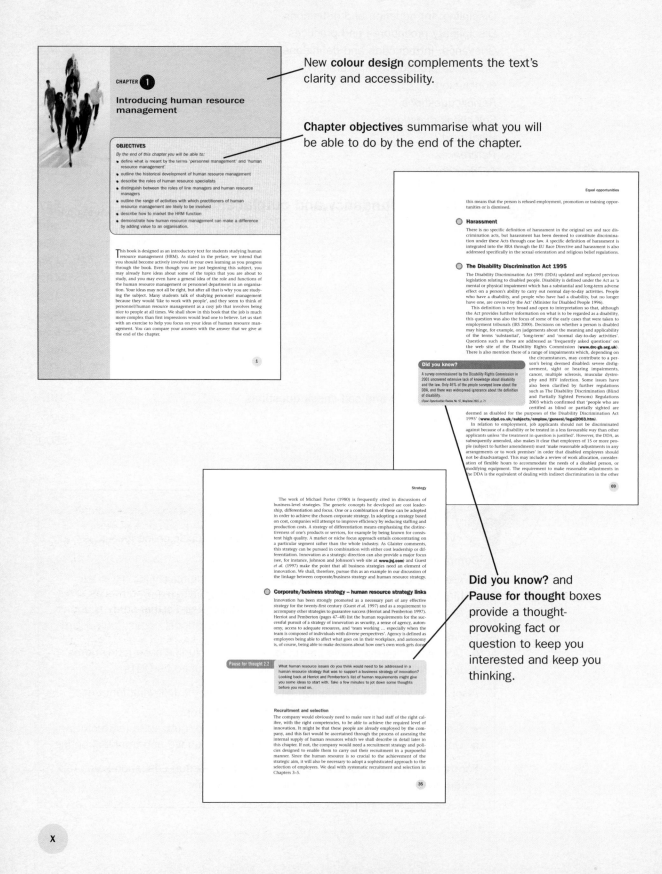

New **colour design** complements the text's clarity and accessibility.

Chapter objectives summarise what you will be able to do by the end of the chapter.

Did you know? and **Pause for thought** boxes provide a thought-provoking fact or question to keep you interested and keep you thinking.

ways in which to carry out job analysis. The usual result of job analysis is a job description, and a training specification can be written from this. In many organisations, where employees are encouraged to work towards National Vocational Qualifications (NVQs), there will already be a national standard for the employee to work towards.

Once the organisation knows the standard of work it needs from the employee, the next stage is to assess the work of the employee concerned and see the extent to which they meet those standards. This can be part of the appraisal process, where the employee and their manager have together identified an area where further work is needed. It could also be assessed by asking the person or people concerned what training they feel they need, by using questionnaires, or by an analysis of mistakes (faults analysis). If there are any gaps where they do not meet these standards then there is a possible need for training to help to close the gaps, and so a training need has been identified.

Planning the training

Once a training need has been identified, there are a number of choices to be made about how the training should be carried out. Firstly, should the training be carried out in the organisation (in-house) or by an external organisation such as a college or other training provider? Secondly, the trainer needs to consider which training techniques should actually be used and, thirdly, the training programme needs to be designed.

Internal or external training

ACTIVITY 7.4
Make up your own list in which you compare the advantages and disadvantages of providing training in-house with the possible advantages or disadvantages of using an external provider.

In-house training

Advantages	Disadvantages

External training provider

Advantages	Disadvantages

Discussion of Activity 7.4
Your lists are likely to contain several advantages and disadvantages for both approaches. Among the points you should have considered are the cost and resources available to carry out the training. It is likely that in-house training will be cheaper and will be tailored perfectly to meet your training needs. However, if the particular training need identified is very specialised and is required for

210

Activities get you applying what you're reading about to the real world.

---

to send the organisation's newsletter to past employees, and the returns in terms of morale and commitment from current employees who witness this evidence of their employer's concern for employee welfare may well repay these costs many times over.

Of course, the issue of what should be regarded as the normal retirement age is now a matter for debate. It remains to be seen how this will be affected by Government policy and the imminent regulations on age discrimination.

Conclusion

We have seen that the relationship between employer and employee consists of rights and obligations on both sides, and that these are determined by law and various other agreements. Innovations in terms, conditions and working arrangements are a sign of the times as organisations attempt to respond to increasing competitive challenges, and the expectation of further developments in European law guarantees that this will continue to be an area of change in the future.

REVIEW QUESTIONS
You will find brief answers to the review questions on page 490.

1   Peruse the 'Law at work' sections in People Management or the court cases listed in the Industrial Case Reports for the last three months or so. Select the articles or cases that are concerned with contractual issues, and review them. Summarise the major hot topics of the day. Have these issues arisen because of any changes in legislation?

2   We mentioned that employment legislation usually sets out minimum provisions for employee rights. Can you identify a number of areas where some employers are known to provide more than the minimum?

SELF-CHECK QUESTIONS
Answer the following multiple-choice and short-answer questions. The correct responses are given on page 490 for you to check your understanding of this chapter.

1   Which of the statements below best describes the psychological contract?
   (a) Managers will do nothing to destroy the relationship of trust they have with their subordinates.
   (b) Employers will do all they can to promote the mental well-being of employees, for instance by providing facilities for counselling on personal problems.
   (c) The expectations that managers and employees have of each other can lead to a relationship based on coercion, a calculation of reward for effort, or cooperation.

186

Review questions reinforce what you have learnt in the chapter. Brief answers are provided for guidance.

Self-check questions is a quick short-answer quiz to check your comprehension.

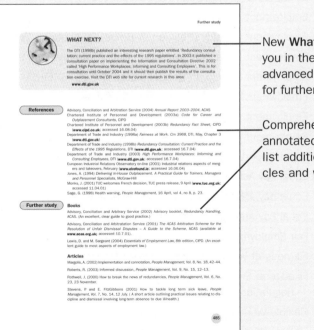

WHAT NEXT?
The DTI (1998b) published an interesting research paper entitled 'Redundancy consultation: current practice and the effects of the 1995 regulations'. In 2003 it published a consultation paper on implementing the Information and Consultation Directive 2002 called 'High Performance Workplaces: Informing and Consulting Employees'. This is for consultation until October 2004 and it should then publish the results of the consultation exercise. Visit the DTI web site for current research in this area:
www.dti.gov.uk

References
Advisory, Conciliation and Arbitration Service (2004) Annual Report 2003–2004, ACAS
Chartered Institute of Personnel and Development (2003a) Code for Career and Outplacement Consultants, CIPD
Chartered Institute of Personnel and Development (2003b) Redundancy Fact Sheet, CIPD (**www.cipd.co.uk**; accessed 16.08.04)
Department of Trade and Industry (1998a) Fairness at Work, Cm 3968, DTI, May, Chapter 3 (**www.dti.gov.uk**)
Department of Trade and Industry (1998b) Redundancy Consultation: Current Practice and the Effects of the 1995 Regulations, DTI (**www.dti.gov.uk**; accessed 16.7.04)
Department of Trade and Industry (2003) High Performance Workplaces: Informing and Consulting Employees, DTI (**www.dti.gov.uk**; accessed 16.7.04)
European Industrial Relations Observatory on-line (2001) Industrial relations aspects of mergers and takeovers, February (**www.eirofound.ie**; accessed 16.06.04)
Jones, A. (1994) Delivering In-House Outplacement. A Practical Guide for Trainers, Managers and Personnel Specialists, McGraw-Hill
Monks, J. (2001) TUC welcomes French decision, TUC press release, 9 April (**www.tuc.org.uk**; accessed 11.04.01)
Sage, G. (1998) Health warning, People Management, 16 April, vol 4, no 8, p. 23.

Further study   **Books**
Advisory, Conciliation and Arbitrary Service (2002) Advisory booklet, Redundancy Handling, ACAS. (An excellent, clear guide to good practice.)

Advisory, Conciliation and Arbitration Service (2001) The ACAS Arbitration Scheme for the Resolution of Unfair Dismissal Disputes – A Guide to the Scheme, ACAS (available at **www.acas.org.uk**; accessed 10.7.01).

Lewis, D. and M. Sargeant (2004) Essentials of Employment Law, 8th edition, CIPD. (An excellent guide to most aspects of employment law.)

Articles
Margolis, A. (2002) Implementation and connotation, People Management, Vol. 8, No. 18, 42–44.

Roberts, R. (2003) Informed discussion, People Management, Vol. 9, No. 15, 12–13.

Rothwell, J. (2000) How to break the news of redundancies, People Management, Vol. 6, No. 23, 23 November.

Stevens, P and E. FitzGibbons (2001) How to tackle long term sick leave, People Management, Vol. 7, No. 14, 12 July. (A short article outlining practical issues relating to discipline and dismissal involving long-term absence to due ill-health.)

485

New **What next?** feature points you in the direction of more advanced topics and wider reading for further study and essay writing.

Comprehensive **References** and annotated **Further study** sections list additional books, journal articles and web pages of interest.

Quick guide to employment legislation and related documents

Preface

We have written this book primarily as an introductory text for students of human resource management on a BA in HRM or on a Business Studies degree course or a Higher National Diploma in Business Studies. It will also prove very useful to students who are studying for the Chartered Institute of Personnel and Development's professional course, especially for the Management and Leadership Module. The content represents an introduction to the basic functions of human resource management and examines the following processes:

- acquiring employees
- establishing good relationships with them
- training and developing them
- retaining them.

We also consider how to deal with situations where problems develop in the employer–employee relationship and how to achive a high performance organisation.

The book is divided into 15 chapters with the intention of providing a topic each week for a modular course, although if your tutor wishes to involve you in more skills-development work or to go into these areas in more detail, the subject matter in the chapters may be spread over two semesters. Each chapter starts with a list of objectives. These are important as they are things that you should know or be able to do by the time you have finished the chapter. When you have finished the chapter, look back at the objectives and ensure that you have achieved them.

We intend that you should become involved actively in your own learning as you progress through the book, and to this end, as well as the list of learning objectives, there are activities for you to undertake, and opportunities to pause and think about issues raised in each chapter. We recommend that you have a paper and pen beside you as you read the book, so that you can complete the activities. This is important, so resist any temptation to skip them.

Discussion about specific points raised in the activities is often an integral part of the text. There are questions at the end of each chapter so that you can check your own understanding of the chapter and go back, if necessary, to points that you may not be clear about. There are also review questions and activities or sometimes longer questions designed to help you examine key learning points in more depth. Your tutor should have a further set of activities and case studies to help with the main learning points in each chapter, and you can gain further practice by trying out the exercises on the companion website at **www.pearsoned.co.uk/foothook**.

You can also take your studies to a higher level by trying out the What next? exercise at the end of each chapter.

The activities and case studies in this text are based on real-life situations, but none of the people or organisations named in them actually exists. Details have been drawn together from a number of events to create totally fictional, although realistic, situations. Real organisations are, however, mentioned in the text, particularly where they serve as examples of good practice.

Publisher's acknowledgements

We are grateful to the following for permission to reproduce copyright material: Table 8.3 from **www.qca.org.uk**, 2004 © The Qualifications and Curriculum Authority. Reproduced by permission and Table 8.4 from **www.ento.co.uk**, 2004 © ENTO Ltd. Reproduced by permission.

In some instances we have been unable to trace the owners of copyright material, and we would appreciate any information that would enable us to do so.

Introducing human resource management

This book is designed as an introductory text for students studying human resource management (HRM). As stated in the preface, we intend that you should become actively involved in your own learning as you progress through the book. Even though you are just beginning this subject, you may already have ideas about some of the topics that you are about to study, and you may even have a general idea of the role and functions of the human resource management or personnel department in an organisation. Your ideas may not all be right, but after all that is why you are studying the subject. Many students talk of studying personnel management because they would 'like to work with people', and they seem to think of personnel/human resource management as a cosy job that involves being nice to people at all times. We shall show in this book that the job is much more complex than first impressions would lead one to believe. Let us start with an exercise to help you focus on your ideas of human resource management. You can compare your answers with the answer that we give at the end of the chapter.

ACTIVITY 1.1

What do you think are the main areas in which a personnel/human resource manager is likely to be involved? Make a list of these areas. For each of the areas on the list, indicate the type of involvement of the human resource manager and whether other managers are also likely to have a role in handling this activity (use Table 1.1). We have completed the first row of Table 1.1 to start you off. Our suggestions for this Activity are given at the end of the chapter in Table 1.3.

Table 1.1   **Main activities of human resource/personnel specialists (Activity 1.1)**

Main areas of activity of human resource/ personnel specialists	Type of involvement of the human resource/ personnel specialist	Type of involvement of line manager
Recruitment and selection	Design of policies and procedure for fair recruitment and selection in order to contribute to the fulfilment of the organisation's corporate strategy. Carry out interviews or monitor and give advice on interview technique or on terms and conditions of employment.	Carry out interviews.
Training and development		

The main activities of personnel/human resource management

The areas that we would list are as follows:

- recruitment and selection
- training and development
- human resource planning
- provision of contracts
- provision of fair treatment
- provision of equal opportunities
- motivating workers to achieve improved performance
- employee counselling
- employee welfare
- payment and reward of employees
- health and safety
- disciplining individuals
- dealing with grievances
- dismissal
- redundancy
- negotiation
- encouraging involvement
- ensuring all personnel/HRM activities help to add value by helping the organisation achieve its objectives.

You may have included some slightly different activities as human resource/ personnel managers become involved in a wide range of issues and it is difficult to predict the exact nature of the job in any particular enterprise. We have selected the main topics with which we feel most human resource/personnel managers are likely to be involved.

However, for each function we have chosen it is likely that other managers will also be involved to some extent in that function. The fact that aspects of managing the human resource are an element of every manager's or supervisor's job is an important point for you to keep in mind. Some of you may be hoping to pursue careers as human resource (HR) specialists, while others may intend to obtain other posts in management and are aware that knowing how to deal with people is important to any manager's career. Many of you will find that your career may take you from line management to personnel/human resource management and then back to line management, or vice versa. The Chartered Institute of Personnel and Development (CIPD) defines personnel management both as being a function pursued by personnel/human resource managers and also as a part of every manager's job.

Pause for thought 1.1

A line manager is a person who has direct responsibility for employees and their work. Since line managers seem to have such a large part to play in human resource/personnel management, to what extent do you think they need personnel or human resource managers at all?

Obviously, we consider that line managers do need to call on the services and expertise of personnel/human resource managers. If you look at our discussion of Activity 1.1 at the end of this chapter (Table 1.3), you will see that although a great deal of work can be devolved to line managers, there is also a role for a person skilled in human resource management to establish policies, standards and procedures, to integrate these with the organisation's objectives, to provide advice and consistency, and to coordinate and provide training and development. Human resource/personnel practitioners will also often be involved in initiating company-wide programmes such as involvement, communication and consultation. The exact nature of their involvement will vary from one organisation to another, as will the range of activities covered by the human resource/personnel function. The personnel/human resource department may maintain central records on people and may provide advice and expertise for other managers to draw on. In some organisations the human resource/personnel management department may carry out all the activities listed above, while in others many or most of these functions may be devolved to other managers. Increasingly more and more aspects of the personnel function are being devolved to line managers and you will find as you work through the book that we emphasise the roles of line managers in personnel activities.

Specialist or generalist?

Even among human resource/personnel managers there will be differences in the scope of their job, with some human resource managers acting as generalists who are involved in most of these activities while others specialise, for example in training and development, reward, resourcing or employee relations. Some specialists work as consultants and are contracted to work for several organisations as and when their services are needed. There is an expectation nowadays that anyone involved in HR activities, whatever their exact role or job title, will make a difference to the organisation, adding value to it so that it can achieve its objectives.

HR consultants or HR business partners

Many people who work in the business of people management work as consultants. Some consultants are not a paid employee of any one organisation but sell their services to a number of organisations. Others may act as internal consultants within one organisation and market themselves and their services within that organisation.

Some people managers are now being called business partners. In people management most things have to be done with the cooperation of other people and the idea of partnership is important. Someone who is called an HR business partner will probably operate at a very senior level and will work with other partners, probably at board level, to provide advice, guidance and consultancy. They will be particularly concerned to ensure that HR policies are strategically aligned with other policies in the organisation so that they clearly contribute to the achievement of the organisation's strategic objectives.

The historical background to human resource management

It may help you to understand the broadness of the roles assumed by personnel and human resource managers if we look briefly at the development of the profession. A variety of names have been used to describe this area of work. It has changed in response to the social and economic conditions of the time and it is still developing dynamically. The relative importance of many of the activities has changed as circumstances have affected the needs of organisations.

⃝ Industrial welfare

The earliest activity with which the personnel practitioner was involved was welfare work. During the nineteenth century conditions of work for men, women and children in the factories were generally appalling compared to even the worst of today's standards. In 1833 the Factories Act appointed the first (male) factory inspectors, and in 1878 legislation was passed to try to regulate hours of work and conditions at least for women and children, reducing their hours of work to 60 hours per week! The trade union movement was also developing during this period, as individuals realised the strength they could gain by joining together to negotiate with employers. Collective bargaining was developing and in 1868 the first Trades Union Conference was held. In 1885 eleven trade unionists were elected to the House of Commons and demanded improvements in wages and conditions of employment.

Did you know?

Mary Wood's first day at work at Rowntree's was rather different from the type of activity you would associate with human resource managers today.

Her first morning was spent placing flowers in work-rooms — perhaps not so ineffectual a beginning as might be thought when the drabness of factories and homes at the time is remembered — and in the afternoon she went to visit girls who were sick, ordering groceries for the most necessitous cases and seeing such slums that she had never dreamt existed. Her first opportunity for making headway came during the dinner hours, when the fact that there was no supervision meant that pandemonium broke out. By degrees she brought order and discipline and before long was arranging an occasional concert or talk during the last half hour of the break. She then turned to organising games as an outlet for the high spirits of the younger girls and as a means of strengthening their physique.

(Niven 1978, p. 22)

There were, however, some enlightened employers, who wanted to try to improve working conditions for their employees and adopted schemes to improve the lot of their workforce as part of their company policy. Among these were several Quaker organisations, and it is generally held that the first personnel officer, referred to at that time as an industrial welfare officer, was Miss Mary Wood who was appointed by Rowntree's in York in 1896. She was appointed to be a type of social worker for the factory, with responsibility for ensuring the well-being of women and children in the workforce and watching over their health and behaviour.

Although Mary's first day at work over 100 years ago is very different from the type of work that we associate with human resource managers of today, welfare and the well-being of the workforce is still an area in which some personnel practitioners will be involved. Many involved in human resource management have sought to distance the profession from its early welfare image, as they feel it is no longer applicable to the modern needs of business and does not portray the right image for the profession and secure power and influence for it. However, we have included sections on welfare as the reality is that it is still of importance in many organisations today, and some organisations employ specialist counsellors or welfare officers to deal with welfare issues. Health, safety and welfare are also issues affected by legislation, and in many organisations the human resource manager will have a role in ensuring compliance.

Rowntree's, as we have seen, approached the issue of welfare by employing a specialist to deal with it. Cadbury's was another pioneering company at this time which developed a totally different approach, believing that the well-being of the workforce was the responsibility of each member of staff. Edward Cadbury spoke in 1900 of the need to 'develop the social and moral character of each worker', stating that 'the supreme principle has been that business efficiency and the welfare of employees are but different sides of the same problem' (Niven 1978, p. 23).

Although such a paternalistic approach is unlikely to be acceptable today, even in these early approaches you can see the start of the development of involvement in welfare activities for both the early personnel managers and other managers, just as in the Activity that you did earlier there was a role in most activities you listed for both personnel/human resource managers and other managers.

By 1913 the number of industrial welfare workers had grown sufficiently for a conference to be called in York by Seebohm Rowntree, with 60 people attending. At this conference the Welfare Workers Association was formed, which later, after many changes, developed into today's Chartered Institute of Personnel and Development, the professional body for those who are active in this area of work.

Recruitment and selection

The early industrial welfare workers met with great success, and Mary Wood and others were soon asked to start engaging girls, which was the beginning of the development of the role of recruitment and selection. During the First World War there was rapid development in many fields of personnel management, largely as a result of government initiatives to encourage the best possible use of people, and also because of legislation. In 1916 the Ministry of Munitions set up its own Industrial Welfare Department with Seebohm Rowntree in charge, with responsibility for introducing new welfare and personnel policies by persuasion into the factories. It became compulsory to have a welfare worker in all explosives factories, and it was strongly encouraged in munitions factories. There was also a great deal of work done, mainly by the armed forces, during this period on how to test abilities and IQ, and research was undertaken into the human factors at work.

During the inter-war years there was a pool of unemployed labour, and much that had been learnt about the need for efficient selection methods was forgotten, although a few progressive employers maintained their interest in personnel management. In 1921 the National Institute of Industrial Psychologists was established, and its members published results of studies on selection tests, interviewing techniques and training methods.

Acquisition of other personnel activities

During the Second World War the work spread from welfare to recruitment and selection and then to training; improving morale and motivation discipline, health and safety; joint consultation and often wages policies. This expansion of duties required the establishment of an adequate personnel department with trained staff.

Industrial relations

Joint consultation between management and workforce spread during the Second World War, and personnel departments became responsible for its organisation and administration. There was an increased emphasis on health and safety and a need for specialists to deal with industrial relations, so that gradually the personnel manager became the usual spokesman for the organisation in discussion with trade unions and shop stewards.

Industrial relations was also of great importance in the late 1970s, and the heated climate during that period reinforced the importance of this aspect of personnel management and saw the development of a specialist role in industrial relations negotiation. In many organisations the personnel manager had executive authority to negotiate deals about pay or other collective issues.

Legislation

During the 1970s there was a growth in the amount of employment legislation and the personnel function often took on the role of specialist adviser, ensuring that managers did not fall foul of the law and that cases did not end up at industrial tribunals, as they were then called. This is still an important role for personnel managers, particularly as a great many changes to legislation have either recently been introduced or are about to be introduced, and we have included some chapters in which we discuss their role in relation to particular aspects of law, such as employment contracts, dismissal, and health and safety.

Current issues in people management

Flexibility and diversity

In the 1990s there was a major trend for employers to seek increasingly flexible arrangements in the hours worked by employees, with a growth in the number of employees who worked part time or on temporary contracts, and an increase in distance working and working from home. This trend has continued in the early years of the new millennium. The workforce and patterns of work are becoming increasingly diverse; this will provide challenges to employers who cannot rely on their traditional recruitment practices and who will also need to develop policies in relation to managing diversity and the equal opportunities issues that managing an increasingly diverse workforce raises.

Atkinson (1984 and 1989) devised a model of the flexible firm. He identified four possible types of flexibility:

- numerical flexibility
- functional flexibility
- distancing
- pay flexibility.

Did you know?

- In the UK, 1 in 5 jobs is in financial and business services.
- Only 1 in 5 men and 1 in 10 women in the UK work in the manufacturing sector.
- There are 12.8 million men and 12.7 million women working in the UK so the numbers of men and women in employment are nearly equal.
- In the UK, 44.1% of females but only 10.1% of males work part time.

(National Statistics Online 2004)

Numerical flexibility

Many of the things Atkinson identified in his model are issues that HR managers have to deal with today. There is increasing numerical flexibility within organisations as many people are employed on short-term contracts, work for agencies or are consultants. This variety of methods of work ensures that the numbers of actual employees can be very flexible and the HR department can respond to the needs of the organisation by fairly rapidly expanding or contracting the numbers employed.

Functional flexibility

The modern worker has increasingly had to become more flexible by developing new skills or updating old skills. Traditionally people did this with the hope of progressing or being promoted within an organisation. Today organisations often have fewer layers of management so it can be more difficult to gain promotion. It is increasingly necessary for workers to update their skills or learn new skills just to remain in their jobs or to ensure their employability if the organisation they work for no longer needs their services.

Distancing

There has recently been a trend to outsource many of the non-core functions of an organisation to specialist companies or consultants. In some organisations this has extended to the management of people, so services such as payroll or learning and development are sometimes outsourced to external suppliers. This in turn raises other issues and problems for people management specialists as they try to ensure quality work and commitment to common organisational goals from people who may not be directly employed by the organisation and who may also work in remote locations.

Pay flexibility

We will discuss issues relating to pay in Chapter 10. However, it is important to note that just as Atkinson (1984 and 1989) predicted in his model, people are often paid in very flexible ways. This could be because of an element of choice in the pay and benefits package that the individual wants. However, in many organisations individuals can be employed on slightly different contracts to those working alongside them. This is likely to depend on the skills they bring to the job as well as the nature of the job itself, but poses problems relating to issues such as equity and equal opportunities for people managers.

Core and peripheral workers

Atkinson's model of the flexible firm distinguished between two groups of workers, which he called the core workers and the peripheral workers. He said that organisations would put a great deal of effort into managing and rewarding their core workers, a comparatively small group, but comprised of people the organisation would be reluctant to lose. For the peripheral workers life would be more difficult as they could be hired and fired at will and would constantly have to improve their skills to ensure their employability.

Knowledge workers will be discussed later in this chapter and to some extent current concerns about how to manage knowledge workers equates with the concern in Atkinson's flexible firm model of how to manage the core workers. However, all workers should be important to the success of an organisation and need to be motivated and managed effectively, as we will discuss later in this chapter and throughout this book. There has been a growth in flexible working and this includes growth in the number of people working as consultants. Flexibility can work in two directions and highly sought-after consultants can choose whether or not they want to work for an organisation, depending on the attractiveness of the terms and conditions offered to them. Once again it is likely that people with skills will be in short supply.

Employment in the UK

The National Statistics Office (2004) indicates that at the time of writing there are low levels of unemployment in the UK and in July 2004 only 4.8% of the workforce was unemployed. According to Berry (2004), the Recruitment Confidence Index, a measure developed by the Cranfield Business School in conjunction with the *Daily Telegraph* and *Personnel Today*, showed that 'employers' expected recruitment activity has fallen slightly since Spring 2004'. This indicates 'that the number of respondents expecting recruitment activity to increase compared to the previous quarter has decreased slightly' but 'just over a third (35%) of all organisations expect no change in activity for all staff, and 61% expect no change for managerial/professional staff.' Moreover, according to Berry in *Personnel Today* (2004) 'more than 61,000 jobs have been created across 21 key UK industries, most noticeably in the public sector.' Generally, then, the employment situation in which HR managers operate is very positive as far as employment is concerned.

The growth in the use of the Internet and moves to a 24/7 society, meant new jobs were created in e-commerce, while some jobs in more traditional areas such as shops and banks were lost. This trend created potential for people to work from home, and growing numbers of people do this, at least for part of their working week. Work goes on around the clock in the ever-increasing numbers of call centres while in some international organisations, important files and projects are e-mailed around the world, so that teams in different time zones can work on projects continuously throughout the 24-hour period. There has been a recent trend to outsource much of the non-core business of organisations to other specialist providers, sometimes including parts of the HR function itself. This poses new problems for those in HR as organisations can have problems with control of outsourced workers and with ensuring that all workers understand key issues and promote the image required of them.

These developments can create opportunities for people to work at hours that are convenient to them, but can also result in pressure on people to always be available to work, so HR managers need to look carefully at ways of effectively managing these new ways of working as issues about work–life balance and managing stress are now very important.

Employers therefore need to ensure that they provide rewarding and satisfying jobs, and to show by the policies and procedures they adopt and the way in which they treat people that they value them. Organisations need to think strategically about the issues raised, and both personnel/HRM practitioners and line managers will have important roles to play if business opportunities are not to be wasted.

⬤ Information technology

If you glance through any journal relating to human resource management nowadays, you will find countless advertisements relating to the various ways that information technology (IT) can assist those in the HR department to do their jobs. These include: systems for e-recruitment; on-line shortlisting of applicants; developing training strategies on line; psychometric testing; as well as IT systems to help with payroll; employment data; recruitment administration; references; pre-employment checks. There are even HR service centres, a type of call centre that provides HR information and deals with queries for organisations.

Pause for thought 1.2

How do you think the increased use of information technology will affect the job of the HR manager? Will it enable them to get rid of the routine jobs by delegating them to IT systems, or will it mean that more people end up in routine jobs working with computers?

It is likely that the increasing use of information technology will have both of these effects, at least to some extent. For many HR managers, using IT for routine tasks will free them from more mundane tasks, so they have more time to think strategically. Increasing use of IT will also ensure a much greater amount of information is available on which to base decisions and to plan for the future.

Teleconferencing and teleworking mean that people no longer have to be in the same place to hold a meeting or to work in the same building. E-learning means people may be able to learn at their desks. All such developments raise new issues and pose different problems about the ways staff should be managed and these will be of concern to the HR manager.

Some people will be in high value jobs using their expertise to design these labour-saving IT systems. Others may find that, perhaps for part of their career, they are dealing with completion of basic tasks using computers, or they may use their knowledge and expertise in people management to deal with HR queries from around the world, via computers or telephones.

⬤ Human capital

By 2003 several new areas were starting to be of concern to those involved in managing people. The term 'human capital' was being discussed and, in particular, ways to measure human capital was an area of concern to some employers. The government set up a strategy group to examine the concept of human capital and created the Accounting for People Taskforce to investigate it.

Professor Harry Scarborough and the CIPD Human Capital Task Force (2003) defined the term 'human capital' as 'the contribution of people [their skills and knowledge] in the production of goods and services'.

An article in *People Management* (2003) by Professor Harry Scarborough of Warwick Business School discussed the TV series *Jamie's Kitchen*, and said that 'we witnessed "human capital" in action, when a group of unemployed young people were transformed on TV into top-class chefs.' Jamie Oliver tried to pass on many of his culinary, business and professional skills to a group of unemployed 16 to 24 year olds and used a variety of methods from coaching to hectoring and pleading to achieve this. He was successful with most members of the group and created within them a desire to perform at a high level, although in the TV series it often seemed to be harder than he had imagined it would be. However, according to Scarborough 'this blending of new skills and attitudes into high performance sums up exactly what human capital can be and why it is so important to business.'

The concept of human capital also encourages organisations to move beyond just training people to do their jobs, although doing the job they are employed to do is of course still important. It is about encouraging organisations to make use of the whole range of abilities that people bring to the organisation and, as such, it is also linked to the concept of the learning organisation discussed in Chapter 8 and ideas about performance management discussed in Chapter 9. Measuring human capital is an attempt to measure the difference that people make to the organisation.

Added value

Another related concept that has gained in popularity in recent years is that of 'added value'. This is also concerned with making a difference. This concept aims to show how the HRM function or other related functions make a difference to the organisation and how they can help to shape the organisation's business strategy. Once again one of the concerns is for measurement of the difference the people initiatives have made. According to Rosemary Harrison (2002), in order to add value, HRM or human resource development (HRD) must 'achieve outcomes that significantly increase the organisation's capability to differentiate itself from other similar organisations, and thereby enhance its progress. It must also achieve these outcomes in ways that ensure, through time, that their value will more than offset the costs that they incurred.' So, they have to make a difference to the organisation but do so in a way that is also cost-effective.

Pause for thought 1.3 Do you think that Mary Wood, whom we described earlier in this chapter as the first industrial welfare worker, added value to the Rowntree organisation?

Although she wouldn't have recognised the terminology, the fact that she was seen to add value and make a difference to the effectiveness of the organisation was the main reason she was asked to take on additional duties such as recruitment and selection.

Green (1999) criticised HR professionals for not having sufficient awareness of the effects that new HR interventions would have on the organisation, and said that in order to provide added value, people professionals needed to provide three things:

- *alignment* – pointing people in the right direction
- *engagement* – developing belief and commitment to the organisation's purpose and direction
- *measurement* – providing the data that demonstrate the improved results achieved (Green 1999).

We can also use the TV series *Jamie's Kitchen* as an example of added value. In this case it was not the HRM department that introduced initiatives to add value as the organisation was too small to have an HRM department. However, Jamie Oliver added value to the trainees themselves by using a series of techniques.

Alignment

Jamie tried to point the trainees in the right direction in several ways. These included conventional on-the-job training, off-the-job training and team-building exercises on outward-bound programmes. He also used many student-centred approaches such as coaching, mentoring, counselling and sometimes cajoling, hectoring or pleading.

Engagement

Jamie tried to develop belief and commitment to the organisation's purpose and direction. He tried to instil in the unemployed youngsters some sense of purpose and the idea that they had responsibilities to themselves, the team and the organisation. He tried to point them in the right direction; in this case to become experts in culinary skills so the restaurant would be successful. He also tried to develop belief in, and commitment to, the organisation's purpose and direction so that they worked effectively together as a team to achieve the excellent standards required by what he hoped would be a top restaurant.

Measurement

In this case the measurement was partly undertaken by the TV programme itself as it provided a visual record of the developing skills of the trainees. The trainees and the viewing public could clearly see the extent to which some individuals changed, but many other measures such as restaurant reviews by food critics, numbers of bookings and repeat bookings, numbers of complaints and amount of praise also helped to measure the added value.

Jamie Oliver was successful in adding value to most of the young people he took into his kitchen. They developed from being unemployed youngsters who had very little sense of purpose into highly trained and skilled workers who were able to work together to achieve the level of cookery skills required by the organisation. In spite of the high profile nature of the experiment there were still some youngsters who did not become motivated by any of the techniques used and preferred to drop out, showing that it can be difficult to always add value in all circumstances.

Knowledge workers

There has been a decline in traditional manufacturing industry and a growth in areas of work such as the service sector or knowledge economy, where the workers are sometimes referred to as knowledge workers. The management guru Peter Drucker (1999) identified the growth and management of knowledge workers as being one of the key issues for the twenty-first century. The way organisations share and manage knowledge and motivate their knowledge workers may be a critical factor in determining the success of organisations in the twenty-first century and this is likely to be an issue for many involved in managing people. However, as we said earlier, all workers are vital for an organisation if it is to be successful and all workers should be managed in ways that will motivate them and help them to contribute to the achievement of their organisation's objectives.

There are, as you might expect, varying views about the importance of knowledge workers and how they should be managed. Peter Nolan (2001) says that 'the shift to a knowledge intensive economy won't necessarily diminish the importance of sectors producing tangible goods and services.' He claims that the new economy will only account for a tiny percentage of workers and visualises an hourglass-shaped economy where there is a growth in the numbers of knowledge workers but also a growth in unglamorous jobs as support staff.

The professional association of personnel practitioners

We have shown that the issues that face people managers change over time. In order to reflect the changing nature of the work, the institute that represented early personnel officers has changed its name several times since its formation in 1913, to reflect the changed emphasis of the work. In 1946 it changed its name yet again, this time to the Institute of Personnel Management. It retained this name until the beginning of 1995, when it merged with the Institute of Training and Development and became the Institute of Personnel and Development.

The Chartered Institute of Personnel and Development

On 1 July 2000 the Institute of Personnel and Development acquired chartered status, and changed its name again, to become the Chartered Institute of Personnel and Development (CIPD). According to Geoff Armstrong (2000), the Institute's Director General at that time, such recognition was important because it put the institute on a par with 'the premier league of professional institutes'. He felt that this was vital because of the changing nature of work and the development of an increasingly knowledge-based society. He said:

> **Did you know?**
>
> The Chartered Institute of Personnel and Development (CIPD) is the professional body that represents nearly 119,000 people who are involved in the management and development of people.
> (Kinski 2004)

> As the UK and Ireland develop into knowledge economies, people issues are becoming ever more important. The CIPD will play the leading role in defining what those issues are, how they should be addressed and how organisations, managers and other decision-makers can develop people as the primary sustainable source of competitive advantage.
>
> (Armstrong 2000)

In 2003 the CIPD gained the right to grant individual chartered status to its full members, putting it on a par with other chartered professional organisations. According to the CIPD (2004a) 'Chartered members will be recognised both within and outside the profession as being fully qualified, experienced professionals who are constantly updating their knowledge and who work to ethical standards.' The professional body has moved a long way from the original welfare workers' association we described earlier. While concern for the welfare of workers is still an issue and areas such as counselling, health, safety, welfare and stress management can be of concern to modern-day people managers, the focus is now on delivering a professional service that gets the best from all workers and makes an important contribution to achieving the objectives of organisations and ensuring they add value to it.

The CIPD's (2004a) mission statement says that 'People management professionals need to continue to demonstrate and deliver the links between people management and organisational success. We need to work with our colleagues on the board, our fellow managers and our staff colleagues at every level to boost performance through people.' This gives a very clear view of what the professional body for most people managers thinks their role should be in the future and how they will continue to work with and through other managers to achieve this level of success.

Human resource management

The concept of human resource management first appeared in the 1980s and the use of the term grew in the 1990s. Its meaning and the range of activities it encompasses have been examined and described by a large number of business writers and researchers. (Legge 1995 summarises much of the debate.) The concept has proved to be somewhat elusive, and it is not possible to find a definitive description of HRM in the literature about it. On the contrary, the achievement of a definition seems to be problematic. One approach has been to try to contrast HRM with traditional personnel management, with a number of researchers providing descriptions of the differences in tabular form, but the boundaries between the two prove to be fluid for a number of reasons (see Storey's much cited table in Storey and Sisson 1993; Guest 1987). Rather than embarking on a complex, academic, albeit fascinating, exercise of this nature, we have culled from the literature what are presented as the key characteristics of HRM. We present them here for you, followed by a brief exposition of the major difficulties that have been encountered in trying to encapsulate the essence of HRM. Our references to a number of the recognised experts in the field should provide you with a good foundation to develop a more detailed academic study of the topic should you wish to do so.

◯ Major characteristics of HRM

The major characteristics of human resource management have been identified as follows:

- The importance of adopting a strategic approach is emphasised.
- Line managers play a predominant role.
- Organisational policies must be integrated and cohesive in order to better project and support the central organisational values and objectives. Along with this, communication plays a vital role.
- An underlying philosophy is adopted that emphasises the achievement of competitive advantage through the efforts of people. This can variously be interpreted into actions that are known as hard HRM or those that are known as soft HRM (see page 17).
- A unitarist rather than a pluralist approach prevails in the relationship between managers and employees.

Focus on strategy

(handwritten: higher levels of commitment)

Throughout the 1980s and 1990s business leaders came to accept more and more that competitive advantage could be achieved only through the efforts and creativity of the people employed by them. In companies that follow through with the logical conclusions to this statement, rather than simply paying lip service to the rhetoric, developing strategies for the human resource will inevitably play a prominent role when they are formulating the corporate strategy, and senior managers will want to call on the expertise of a specialist to get the best input possible. Thus strategic activity becomes a major focus for specialists in HRM, but probably only those acting at the higher levels will be involved in board level meetings where strategic alternatives are discussed. It should also be noted that in order to have effective input into the corporate strategy, the HRM specialist will require a high level of business acumen in addition to knowledge of personnel strategies and programmes. It is this recognition that people are a resource to be managed as efficiently and effectively as any other resource that has led to the term 'human resource management.'

Role of the line manager

We have defined strategic involvement as being a key characteristic of HRM and noted that this means a focus on strategic activity for high level HRM practitioners. However, the HRM approach recognises the centrality of the human resource for all business activities, and therefore consideration of the people management aspects would be expected in the strategic planning input from managers in all business functions (e.g. production, marketing, etc). Likewise, the importance of active management of people matters becomes more clearly an integral part of every line manager's job. Line managers must combine their commitment to the technical aspects of task completion with attention to people aspects and recognise the symbiotic nature of these two elements of the managerial role.

This means that some activities that might traditionally have been undertaken by specialist personnel management staff have now been devolved to line managers. Increased line involvement in training and recruitment could be cited as areas where this has occurred. There is still, however, a substantial role for human resource specialists, as you discovered when you completed Activity 1.1, in disseminating information about evolving people management programmes to line managers, in ensuring some consistency in the treatment of employees company wide and, in general, in being supportive partners to line managers in their efforts to achieve company goals.

The pivotal role of the line manager is one of the most often cited characteristics of human resource management (see Storey's table of the take-up of HRM techniques in Storey and Sisson 1993).

Integrated policies and effective communication

Proponents of HRM emphasise that policies across the whole HR spectrum (recruitment, selection, reward, employee relations) must be fully integrated and consistent with the organisation's culture. This is logically consistent with the strategic, forward planning nature of HRM. Effective communications are a pivotal aspect of this as they constitute a means of conveying senior management's values and commitment to their goals (Legge 1995, p. 75).

Competitive advantage through people

The balanced scorecard

At this point it is appropriate to introduce the concept of the balanced score-card (BSC). This concept emanates from work done on business strategy by Kaplan and Norton (1992, 1996) in the Harvard Business School in the early 1990s, but it emphasises the role of the human resource in the achievement of business strategy. The BSC has become a well-established technique used extensively in the USA, but also worldwide, including some UK companies, for instance Tesco (see IRS 2000) and the Halifax.

The essential idea behind the balanced scorecard is the notion that businesses must measure the success of their plans in order to validate their actions, identify and evaluate their successes, and build on them for the future. Traditionally businesses have focused mainly if not exclusively on financial results to evaluate the success of their strategy, but Kaplan and Norton propose that measuring success in only one area is inadequate for a number of reasons. One argument is that financial results are always a retrospective measure of past success and do not necessarily indicate that similar actions in the future will meet with similar achievements. Also, although financial gains may be the ultimate desired outcome, it is imperative to know exactly what factors contributed to this outcome and in what way they contributed.

A more satisfactory approach to formulating strategic initiatives, and subsequently evaluating their success, is to take a more balanced approach, which is represented by the balanced scorecard. The scorecard is a flexible tool, which can be adapted according to the nature of the business adopting it, but the original model proposes four elements that should be evaluated in order to achieve a balanced overview of what contributes to a company's success:

- financial results
- customer relations
- internal processes
- learning and development.

The examination of financial results is, of course, still a necessary part of evaluating business success, but according to Kaplan and Norton, this focus needs to be balanced out by taking the other criteria into consideration. Each of the three other criteria contributes to financial success, and purposively focusing on them helps to shift managerial awareness to the role each plays. Typically, the formulation of a corporate strategy would start with a goal to increase shareholder value, and a strategy that focuses on the customer's perspective is most likely to succeed in achieving this aim (Kaplan and Norton 2000). A company must then examine its internal processes with regard to their fitness to achieve this customer strategy and adapt them where necessary. This in turn goes hand in hand with the development of the human resource that will deliver the strategy. An organisation's capacity for learning and development is regarded as being one of the key factors contributing to success in today's competitive environment, and ties in with what we say in Chapter 2 about innovation as a strategic choice.

Just as the balanced scorecard is used to formulate the overall corporate strategy and measure its success, it can also be used to plan for the component parts and measure their contribution to the achievement of company strategy. Thus, while the examination of internal processes must be carried out throughout the organisation and constitutes one component of the balanced scorecard

Human resource management

used to measure the whole company's performance, the BSC can also be used to guide and evaluate each individual's performance. That is, the development of individuals becomes explicitly tied in to the key issues addressed in the BSC at corporate strategy level, and in appraising each individual, the question is asked to what extent the individual contributed to the financial success of the company, to customer relations, to the improvement of internal processes, and to learning and growth. The Halifax is one company in the UK which uses a balanced scorecard to evaluate its employees' performance.

The adoption of the balanced scorecard by Tesco also served to strengthen and redefine the role of the stores' personnel managers. The scorecard highlighted the importance of all employees' contribution to the success of the company, and therefore the importance of people management issues. To complement this, personnel managers in Tesco stores are also expected to be fully involved in the day-to-day running of the stores, thus enhancing their business awareness and their credibility (IRS 2000).

Hard and soft HRM

The basic requirement of HRM to serve the corporate strategy and achieve corporate aims by means of a high performance workforce can be read in two ways:

- The primacy of business needs means that human resources will be acquired, deployed and dispensed with as corporate plans demand. Little regard is paid to the needs of those human resources and the emphasis is on quantitative aspects. This is known as hard HRM.
- In order to gain a competitive advantage through the workforce, regardless of whether they are full- or part-time, temporary or contract staff, all potential must be nurtured and developed, and programmes that pay due notice to knowledge about the behavioural aspects of people at work are developed. This is characterised as soft HRM.

The emphasis in our text lies mainly with soft HRM, but as Legge (1995, pp. 66–67) argues, the two are not mutually exclusive, and you will detect elements of hard HRM in the discussion of human resource planning.

Unitarist and pluralist approaches to management–employee relations

Human resource management is identified as being a unitarist rather than a pluralist approach (Legge 1995, pp. 72–73). Briefly, the unitarist stance is characterised as a senior management assumption that all members of the organisation are dedicated to the achievement of a common goal with no conflict from personal interests. Pluralism, on the other hand, recognises that within a large group of people there are inevitably a variety of interests and that these have to be managed. The adoption of one or other of these two philosophies obviously has a major impact on the way that managers treat the workforce.

We explore the concepts of unitarism and pluralism in greater depth in Chapter 13 where we come to the conclusion from observing current rhetoric that we may now be witnessing a merging of the two stances in the development of the partnership theme. This promotes the idea that managers and employees can pursue common goals while still recognising that diverging interests exist. The common purpose of the unitarists is pursued in a pluralist framework.

We refer throughout the text to the key characteristics described here and their links with specific activities. In particular, we emphasise the role of the

17

line manager in all of the activities we discuss, but in addition we focus on the theme of strategy in Chapter 2 where we examine the human resource planning activity, and the topics of unitarism, employee commitment and communication in Chapter 13.

Problems with the concept of HRM

We do not wish to confuse the issue, having presented the key characteristics of HRM, but the debate about HRM is characterised to such an extent by conflicting statements and pieces of evidence, that it seems appropriate to mention some of them briefly:

● There is no definitive agreement among researchers about what the concept includes, and at least one publication suggests that we now need to move beyond HRM as a concept to seek a new definition of the role of practitioners in this field (Sparrow and Marchington 1998).

● Some researchers attempt to categorise activities as 'hard' HRM or 'soft' HRM, but there is also some debate about whether the two are necessarily mutually exclusive.

● Even the specific concepts identified as characteristics of HRM can also be defined with different meanings, e.g. strategy is variously seen as a planned approach or something that evolves.

● Academics try to define and build models of HRM, but research on actual practice shows a multiplicity of combinations of techniques being used in some companies at one and the same time, i.e. some techniques that would be seen as part of the new HRM approach and some that would be seen as traditional personnel management run simultaneously. Hall and Torrington (1998, pp.108ff) comment on an integrated approach to human resource strategy as being an ideal, but sparsely represented in reality.

● A contingency approach to management would suggest that different circumstances call for different actions, so a rigid, prescriptive definition of HRM would in fact be counterproductive. Shaun Tyson (1995) comments on the futility of trying to pin down a definition of HRM practices when HRM is required to adapt rapidly to rapidly changing circumstances.

● Practitioners and researchers alike often use the terms 'personnel management' and 'HRM' interchangeably (Hall and Torrington 1998). However, research conducted by Hoque and Noon (2001), based on data contained in the Department of Trade and Industry's 1998 Workplace Employee Relations Survey, concluded that several HRM elements *are* more likely to be found in workplaces where the 'human resource' designation is used in preference to 'personnel'. These elements include involvement in strategic planning and greater devolution of personnel activities to line managers.

The HRM debate: a concluding statement

Karen Legge (1995) reviews the literature that has attempted to differentiate between HRM and personnel management, and highlights the problematic nature of these attempts. Because our text is an introduction to the practical work involved in HRM/personnel management, we shall not pursue this academic debate any further. What we consider to be important is not managers' titles, but what managers actually do and how they do it.

We focus mainly on applied aspects of HR practices in the workplace, and we have chosen to focus on those elements identified as soft HRM since these represent recognised good practice in employee relations today. It is, however, important to bear in mind that it is difficult, if not impossible, to designate a definitive set of best practices because the 'right' action will always depend on the contingent circumstances in which any organisation is operating.

The effective management of people

The ACAS model

As we said earlier, there is nowadays an emphasis on ensuring that HRM makes a difference within the organisation and adds value to it. The Advisory, Conciliation and Arbitration Service (ACAS) has devised a model that sets out what it feels are the key elements which will help to turn an organisation into an effective workplace. We advocate throughout this book the need for policies and procedures so that everyone knows what is supposed to be done. The exact form these policies and procedures will take will depend or be contingent on the circumstances and objectives of the specific organisation. ACAS (2004) says that having policies and procedures in place is a good start but that the way things are done is also important, an approach we have also emphasised throughout this book. The ACAS model sets out some general principles for an effective organisation and say that employers need:

1 'Ambitions, goals and plans that employees know about and understand
2 Managers who genuinely listen to and consider their employees' views so everyone is actively involved in making important decisions
3 People to feel valued so they can talk confidently about their work and learn from both successes and mistakes
4 Everyone to be treated fairly and valued for their differences as part of everyday life
5 Work organised so that it encourages initiative, innovation and people to work together.
6 An understanding that people have responsibilities outside work so that they can openly discuss ways of working that will suit personal needs and the needs of business
7 A pay and reward system that is clear, fair and consistent
8 A safe and healthy place to work
9 A culture where everyone is encouraged to learn new skills so they can look forward to further employment either in the business or elsewhere
10 A good working relationship between management and employee representatives that in turn helps build trust throughout the business
11 Formal procedures for dealing with disciplinary matters, grievances and disputes that managers and employees know about and use fairly.'
(ACAS 2004)

We discuss many of these points in specific chapters of this book and in Table 1.2 we show the main chapters to which they most clearly relate. However most of the things listed here can also relate to several topics. In organisations things are not likely to be as clearly compartmentalised as they are in chapters in a textbook. All aspects of people management should contribute to the organisation's objectives and suit its culture or way of working, and people management policies and procedures need to be integrated to achieve this.

The topics listed in the ACAS model show the importance of having HR policies about subjects such as equal opportunities, learning and development, health and safety, and pay and the organisation should also have clear strategic objectives. However, the list of topics also indicates that the way in which these HR policies are introduced and the way people are managed is important. In addition, the model is about sharing ideas, involving people and making them feel valued by the organisation so a culture that encourages good communication and everyone to feel valued is also important.

Table 1.2   **ACAS (2004) model: chapters in which main points are covered**

The main points in the ACAS (2004) model	The main chapters in this book that relate to each topic
1 Ambitions, goals and plans that employees know about and understand	Chapters 1, 2, 9 and 13
2 Managers who genuinely listen to and consider their employees' views so everyone is actively involved in making important decisions	Chapters 6, 9 and 13
3 People to feel valued so they can talk confidently about their work and learn from both successes and mistakes	Chapters 6, 7, 8, 9, 10, 11 and 13
4 Everyone to be treated fairly and valued for their differences as part of everyday life	Chapters 3, 4, 5, 6, 9 and 10
5 Work organised so that it encourages initiative, innovation and people to work together	Chapters 6, 9 and 13
6 An understanding that people have responsibilities outside work so that they can openly discuss ways of working that will suit personal needs and the needs of business	Chapters 4, 6, 9, 11 and 12
7 A pay and reward system that is clear, fair and consistent	Chapters 9 and 10
8 A safe and healthy place to work	Chapters 11 and 12
9 A culture where everyone is encouraged to learn new skills so they can look forward to further employment either in the business or elsewhere	Chapters 7, 8 and 9
10 A good working relationship between management and employee representatives that in turn helps build trust throughout the business	Chapters 9, 11, 12 and 13
11 Formal procedures for dealing with disciplinary matters, grievances and disputes that managers and employees know about and use fairly	Chapters 9, 14 and 15

The people and performance model

John Purcell and a team of researchers from the University of Bath carried out studies sponsored by the CIPD over a three-year period to try and ascertain what aspects of HRM actually make a difference to performance within organisations (Purcell *et al.* 2003).

They found that on their own, good HR policies were not sufficient to create an effective organisation. Excellent policies about recruiting, developing and retaining the people in the organisation were important. Purcell *et al.* (2003) referred to this as the 'human capital advantage'. Much of this book will address ways to achieve this type of human capital advantage. However, the other key factor that distinguished effective organisations from those that were less effective was the way they 'worked together to be productive and flexible enough to meet new challenges.' We also emphasise this approach throughout this book.

The researchers identified two vital ingredients in effective organisations. According to Purcell *et al.* (2003) these are:

- First, they had strong values and an inclusive culture.
- Second, they had enough line managers who were able to bring HR policies and practices to life.

Strong values and an inclusive culture

Purcell and his team of researchers found that organisations that developed a strong and inclusive culture usually had what they called a 'big idea'. This was always something that was clearly communicated to everyone in the workforce and that could be easily understood. This is similar to the first point listed in the ACAS model. ACAS said that it was important to have 'ambitions, goals and plans that employees know about and understand'.

The big ideas the researchers identified were ideas such as the 'pursuit of quality' at Jaguar cars, 'living the values' at Tesco and the 'principles of mutuality' at Nationwide Building Society. Everyone shared and understood these ideas and they became the foundation for all the HR policies and procedures, enabling everyone to see why they were necessary.

Line managers who could bring the policies to life

We have already mentioned the importance of line managers in the HRM approach to the management of people and here we have recent research that substantiates this view. In the research by Purcell and his team (Purcell *et al.* 2003) the line managers were found to be the other vital ingredient in making an effective organisation. The line managers had not only to see the relevance of the HR policies and procedures to themselves, but also to see how they could use them to contribute to an effective organisation. ACAS did not specifically mention line managers in its model, although it did stress the cooperative nature of work and the importance of teams. It also said that although it is important to have clear policies and procedures, other factors such as the way HR policies are implemented and the way things are done in the organisation are also very important if an organisation is to be effective.

Pause for thought 1.4

The researchers from Bath University said, 'It's better to ensure that HR policies are properly implemented than to try to develop new policies.' (Purcell *et al.* 2003) As you work through this book and learn more about HR policies and procedures, remember that the way they are introduced into an organisation is also very important and worker involvement and excellent communication are also crucial to the effectiveness of the organisation.

Marketing the human resource management function

We wish to devote a final word to the marketing of the human resource management function, as this may have a great impact on the effectiveness of the function, although it has only recently attracted attention and probably did not figure in your list of the activities that HRM practitioners should engage in.

Although we have discussed the fact that some personnel management functions may be devolved to line managers, and that this is in fact a growing trend, this section addresses the specialist HRM department and the need for HRM practitioners to advertise their services in order to maximise their contribution to corporate objectives. We have described human resource management as consisting of a complex range of functions, calling on a wide variety of knowledge and expertise. We have also explained that HRM practitioners sometimes adopt a service role in designing new initiatives, and sometimes act as an authority in enforcing obedience to the law. In the service role in particular, there is little point in the knowledge and expertise being resident in (and paid for by) an organisation if the clients are unaware of it and do not know it is there to be called on. It is very difficult in highly structured organisations for staff in one area to know, beyond a vague understanding, what staff in another area do. If HRM practitioners feel they have a valuable contribution to make to their organisations, it is incumbent on them to make sure that everyone knows what they can offer.

ACTIVITY 1.2

Imagine that you have joined the Human Resource Management department in a large company. How would you market the HRM function? List the activities you would undertake.

Discussion of Activity 1.2

Check your list of activities against the following:

- Conduct a customer survey. Companies that know what their customers require and respond to their wishes have a competitive edge. The same can be true of a functional department offering a service within a company. A survey can ascertain several things: what you do well, what you could do better, things you are not doing that your clients would like you to do.
- Expand your knowledge of the business. HRM is an integral part of the business, not a separate undertaking. The more you know about how your organisation works, the more responsive you can be in supporting it with

HRM initiatives. Demonstrate how each HR initiative contributes to the organisation's strategic aims or to its big idea.

● Be proactive and innovative in developing initiatives that will contribute to the company's success. Don't wait for problems to arise.

● Take your service to your market rather than waiting for clients to approach you:

– design leaflets, booklets, posters, intranet screens that advertise the service you offer
– emphasise the benefits your clients will gain from using your services
– be visible and approachable – have an open-door policy; visit line managers and other employees at their work stations; don't sit in your office all day
– obtain an HRM slot in briefing sessions, the company newsletter and any other information vehicles.

You will note in these suggestions that the terminology used is very much that of a business selling its products. The HRM function in any company could benefit from taking this approach, both in terms of sharpening its own definition of what it does and in ensuring that everyone in the company is able to gain the maximum benefit from what HRM can offer. Indeed, HR managers surveyed by the Industrial Relations Services (2001) identified this type of consultancy work as a major role for HR practitioners in the future. They clearly need to be able to demonstrate not only how the HR department and initiatives will add value to the organisation, but also need to enthuse line managers so that they can see why they need to get involved in these initiatives and the benefits they will gain from them.

REVIEW QUESTIONS

1 We include here a pictorial representation of this chapter in the form of a mind map (Figure 1.1). Use the key words we have included to refresh your memory of what we have covered in this chapter. Add your own key words or drawings to this mind map to reinforce your learning.

2 Go back to the objectives that we listed at the beginning of this chapter and check that you know, or can do, everything stated in the objectives.

3 Examine three advertisements for jobs in personnel management/human resource management. Make a list of the range of activities described in these job advertisements. Compare your list with the lists we have given for Activity 1.1.

Are there any differences in approach and duties shown by those advertising for human resource managers and those advertising for personnel managers? Did any of these advertisements specify that they wanted someone to work as an HR partner? How does this relate to what we said about these job titles in Chapter 1?

4 Interview a personnel manager or human resource manager about his or her job and main duties. Did this person think of themselves as a business partner in the organisation? How do your findings compare with what we said in this chapter?

5 Interview a manager about his or her job and try to establish the extent to which it also entails personnel activities. How do your findings compare with what we said in this chapter?

6 The chapters of this book will introduce you to aspects of good practice for the various activities involved in HRM. When you have studied each chapter, imagine that you are an HRM practitioner and you wish to market the function to line managers. Draft the contents of a brochure or web page for each activity. You will need to describe the service that you are offering and state how line managers would benefit from using that service.

7 Try the web addresses listed on page 31 to find out more about issues of concern to those involved in human resource management worldwide. Compare the sites listed in Britain, America and Australia. What are the main topics of concern at the moment? Are there any differences in approach shown by the professional bodies in these countries?

Figure 1.1   **Mind map of Chapter 1**

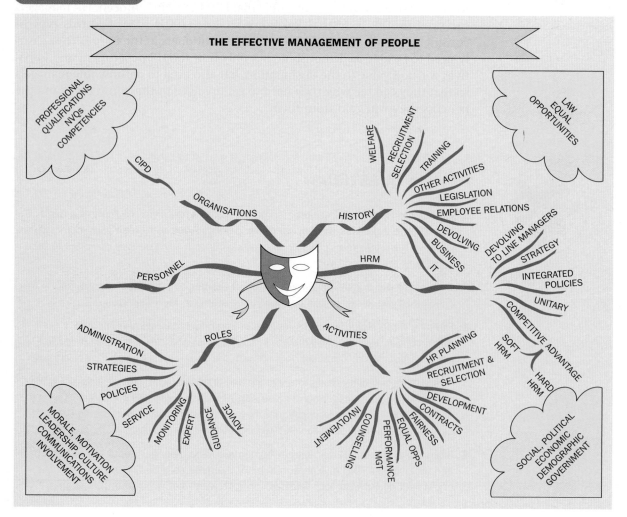

SELF-CHECK QUESTIONS

Answer the following multiple choice questions. The correct responses are given on page 487 for you to check your understanding of this chapter.

1 To which of the following do the letters CIPD refer?
   (a) The Chartered Institute of Professional Development
   (b) The Constitutional Institution for the Progress of Devolvement.
   (c) The Chartered Institute of Personnel and Development.
   (d) The Community Institute of Personal Development.

2 Which of the following activities are you NOT likely to undertake as part of the process of marketing the human resource management department?
   (a) Conduct a customer survey.
   (b) Be proactive and innovative in developing initiatives that contribute to the organisation's success.
   (c) Be reactive and wait to be approached when problems arise.
   (d) Obtain an HRM slot in briefing sessions.

3 Which of the following statements best sums up the role of the human resource manager in personnel activities?
   (a) The human resource manager is the sole person who should be involved in all personnel activities.
   (b) Both the human resource manager and line manager are likely to be involved in differing ways in a range of personnel activities.
   (c) The line manager always acts alone in all organisations in dealing with human resource management activities.
   (d) The human resource manager is only concerned with personnel activities at the tactical level.

4 Which of the following statements would be true of the human resource management approach to managing people at work?
   (a) It tackles issues in a piecemeal way.
   (b) It relies on traditional forms of communication.
   (c) There is not much involvement of the workforce in decision making.
   (d) It is strategic.

5 Which of the following sums up an underlying theme in the philosophy of HRM?
   (a) People are important whether they are full-time or part-time employees, permanent or temporary, or contract workers who are actually employed by another company.
   (b) People are important only if they are full-time, permanent employees.
   (c) People are important whether they are full-time or part-time employees so long as they are permanent and are employed by your company.
   (d) People are important whether they are full-time or part-time, permanent or temporary so long as they are employed by your company.

WHAT NEXT?

Now that you have read the first chapter and completed the exercises, you may want to go further and test your understanding. There are exercises that will help you to do this on our website at:

www.pearsoned.co.uk/foothook

In this chapter we have introduced the ideas of HRM and personnel management and indicated that these terms are still subject to a great deal of academic debate and that there are distinctions between the two approaches to managing people. Many textbooks do focus on this academic debate in more detail than we have done here, but we have chosen instead to focus on current thinking and research about HRM and the extent to which various HRM strategies contribute to the organisation being effective. You can examine some of these research studies for yourselves and details are listed below.

There have been a series of studies funded by the CIPD and conducted by the Work and Employment Research Centre at the University of Bath into the relationship between HR and performance excellence in organisations. The following study examines the issue of people and performance in relation to knowledge workers:

> Chartered Institute of Personnel and Development (2003) *People and Performance in Knowledge-intensive Firms*, CIPD

A bulletin summarising the above study is also available from the CIPD:

> Chartered Institute of Personnel and Development (2004) *People and Performance in Knowledge-intensive Firms: An Emerging Model of People Management Practices*, CIPD (**www.cipd.co.uk**; accessed 09.09.04)

A further study from the research team at the University of Bath examines case study organisations and how they achieve success when times are difficult:

> Hutchinson, S., N. Kinnie, J. Purcell, J. Swart, B. Rayton (2003) *Understanding the People Performance Link: Unlocking the Black Box*, CIPD

A summary of research in this area is also available from the CIPD:

> Chartered Institute of Personnel and Development (2002) *Sustaining Success in Difficult Times: Research Summary*, CIPD (**www.cipd.co.uk**; accessed 10.09.04)

Table 1.3 **Main activities of human resource/personnel specialists (Activity 1.1 answer)**

Main areas of activity of human resource/ personnel specialists	Type of involvement of the human resource/personnel specialist	Type of involvement of line manager
Recruitment and selection	Design of policies and procedure for fair recruitment and selection in order to contribute to the fulfilment of the organisation's corporate strategy. Carry out interviews or monitor and give advice on interview technique or on terms and conditions of employment.	Carry out interviews.
Training and development	Involved in planning training and development opportunities for the whole organisation, to meet the needs of the organisation as expressed in its strategic plan and to meet the needs of individuals. May design and organise training courses for groups and sometimes run them. May keep training records centrally and request information from line managers as part of planning exercise or to monitor success of training and development.	May also be involved in planning and provision of training and development opportunities to meet the needs of individuals and the needs of the organisation as expressed in its strategic plan, primarily for employees in his or her own department. May provide training and may also keep records of training and provide information to central personnel/HRM department.
Human resource planning	Depending on the level of appointment is likely to be involved to various degrees in contributing to the strategic plan. Collection and analysis of data, monitoring targets for the whole organisation. Providing information to managers. Conducting exit interviews and analysing reasons for leaving.	Collect information on leavers and provide information on anticipated requirements for manpower for his or her department.
Provision of contracts	Provide written statement of particulars for new employees and issue them to these employees, having checked that the detail is correct. Keep copies of all documentation relating to the employee and advise on any alterations to the contract.	Possibly issue documents and get signature of new employee.
Provision of fair treatment	Involvement in design of policies and procedures for the whole organisation to encourage fair treatment at work. Inform and train people in these policies and procedures. Monitor the success of these policies.	Responsible for fair treatment of people in his or her department to ensure all treat others in a fair way. Listen and respond to grievances as an initial stage in the grievance procedure or informally before someone gets into the grievance procedure. May contribute suggestions about design of policies.
Equal opportunities	Involvement in design of policies to encourage equal opportunities. Train and inform managers and all employees throughout the organisation in these. Monitor the effectiveness of the equal opportunities policies by collecting and analysing information.	May also be involved in, and contribute to, the design of policies. Will be responsible for ensuring that all employees for whom he or she is responsible do not suffer from any form of unfair discrimination while at work.
Motivating workers to achieve improved performance	Involvement in design and implementation of techniques to assess effectively performance of employees in a way that links clearly with the organisation's strategic plan. Train, inform and involve people in performance management techniques. Monitor the effectiveness of the procedures. May maintain central records about performance of individual employees.	Contribute to discussion of performance management techniques. Assess performance of those in own department. Involve teams and individuals in setting and agreeing targets and monitoring performance. Monitor their success and give feedback.

Table 1.3   **(contd)**

Main areas of activity of human resource/ personnel specialists	Type of involvement of the human resource/personnel specialist	Type of involvement of line manager
Employee counselling	Establish appropriate system, either in-house or by external consultants, for employee counselling. May be involved in counselling employees with problems or may have to refer them to specialised counselling service.	May be involved in the initial counselling of employees in his or her own section, or may need to suggest alternative sources of counselling if he or she does not feel qualified to deal with the situation.
Employee welfare	Establish appropriate systems for employee welfare in accordance with the objectives of the organisation. Monitor the cost and effectiveness of this provision.	Ensure the well-being of employees in his or her department and draw their attention to, and encourage use of, any provisions designed by the organisation to improve their welfare.
Payment and reward of employees	Establish appropriate payment employees and reward systems for all employees in order to contribute to the organisation's strategic plan. Monitor the success of these. Collect comparative data for other organisations in area or nationally. Deal with individual problems about pay. May be involved in negotiation about payment or reward systems. Tell individuals of their level of pay when they join the organisation or change jobs. May deal with individual problems or complaints about pay.	May be involved in, and contribute views about, appropriate systems of payment or reward to be used in the organisation. May be involved in negotiation to some extent over issues relating to own department. May deal with problems concerning pay raised by employees in his or her department in the first instance.
Health and safety	Involvement in design and implementation of the organisation's health and safety policy in order to contribute to the organisation's strategic plan. Monitor the effectiveness of this. May sit on safety committee or may have line management responsibilities for safety officer or organisation's nurse. Involvement in promotion of health and safety and encouraging the involvement of others throughout the organisation.	Responsible for health and safety of employees working in his or her department. Encourage the involvement of individuals and teams in health or safety promotion activities. Monitor activities of own staff. Carry out regular safety inspections in own department. May take initial disciplinary action against those who infringe health and safety rules.
Disciplining individuals	Design of disciplinary procedure. Monitor the effectiveness of the procedure. Give advice to line managers on disciplinary problems. Organise training for line managers and employees about disciplinary issues. Issue warnings in later stages of disciplinary procedure. Maintain central records of disciplinary action taken.	Conduct informal disciplinary interviews with own staff if necessary. Issue formal warnings as outlined in disciplinary procedure. Maintain records of warnings issued.
Dealing with grievances	Participate in the design of grievance procedure and encourage the involvement of others in this. Inform and train people in grievance handling. Monitor the effectiveness of the grievance procedure. May deal with some stages in the grievance procedure or appeals.	Deal initially with grievances raised by employees in his or her department. This may be handled informally at first or as part of the formal grievance procedure. Deal with grievances within specified time limits.
Dismissal	Review procedures for dismissal to ensure that they comply with legislation. Provide advice and guidance on fair dismissal procedure. Provide training for all who may be involved in the dismissal process. May dismiss employee.	In many organisations the actual dismissal will be handled by the personnel/HRM department with the manager being present. Nowadays managers in some organisations will also take full responsibility for dismissing an employee in their section in a fair way.

Table 1.3 **(contd)**

Main areas of activity of human resource/ personnel specialists	Type of involvement of the human resource/personnel specialist	Type of involvement of line manager
Redundancy	Is likely to be involved in consultation with appropriate people with regard to redundancy. Is likely to be involved in selection of those to be made redundant. May inform employee of redundancy and amount of pay and rights. May organise provision of more generous redundancy payment if this is in line with organisation's policy. May organise provision of outplacement facilities either in-house or by consultants.	Is likely to be involved in selection of those to be made redundant from his or her department. May be involved in telling them of the decision to make them redundant.
Negotiation	Is likely to be involved in negotiation on a wide range of organisation-wide issues.	Is likely to be involved in negotiation on a wide range of issues that affect employees in his or her department.
Encouraging involvement	Will have an extremely important role in creating a culture within the organisation in which employees are encouraged to be involved in decision making. Will be involved in designing policy and procedures to encourage employee involvement in line with strategic plan. Will also provide training to encourage employee involvement.	Will contribute to organisation's policies and will encourage involvement of employees in his or her department.
Adding value	Ensuring that all personnel/HRM activities help to add value to the organisation by helping it achieve its objectives.	Ensuring that all personnel/HRM activities help to add value to their department or section by ensuring they contribute to its objectives.

References

Advisory, Conciliation and Arbitration Service (2004) *The Acas Model*, ACAS

Armstrong, G. (2000) Institute gets its charter, *People Management*, 17 February, Vol. 6, No. 4

Atkinson, J. (1984) Manpower strategies for flexible organisations, *Personnel Management*, August, 28–31

Atkinson, J. (1989) Four stages of adjustment to the demographic downturn, *Personnel Management,* August, 20–24

Berry, M. (ed) (2004) Personnel Today's at-a-glance business data, *Personnel Today,* 14 September, 60

Chartered Institute of Personnel and Development (2004a) *Mission Statement,* CIPD (**www.cipd.co.uk**; accessed 14.09.04)

Chartered Institute of Personnel and Development (2004b) *Managing Knowledge Workers,* CIPD (**www.cipd.co.uk**; accessed 16.9.04)

Drucker, P. (1999) *Management Challenges for the Twenty-first Century*, Harper Business

Green, K. (1999) Offensive thinking, *People Management*, Vol. 5, No. 8, 27

Guest, D. (1987) Human resource management and industrial relations, *Journal of Management Studies*, Vol. 24, 503–521

Hall, L. and D. Torrington (1998) *The Human Resource Function: The Dynamics of Change and Development*, Financial Times Pitman Publishing

Harrison, R. (2002) *Learning and Development*, CIPD

Hoque, K and M. Noon (2001) Counting angels: a comparison of personnel and HR specialists. *Human Resource Management Journal*, Vol. 11, No. 3, 5–22

Industrial Relations Services (IRS) (2000) In-store personnel managers balance Tesco's scorecard, *IRS Employment Trends*, May, 13–16

Industrial Relations Services (IRS) (2001) HR in 2001: the IRS audit, *IRS Employment Trends*, 728, May, 4–10

Kaplan, R. S. and D. P. Norton (1992) The balanced scorecard – measures that drive performance, *Harvard Business Review*, January–February, 71–79

Kaplan, R. S. and D. P. Norton (1996) *The Balanced Scorecard: Translating Strategy into Action*, Harvard Business School Press

Kaplan, R. S. and D. P. Norton (2000) Having trouble with your strategy? Then map it, *Harvard Business Review*, September–October, 167–176

Kinski, M. (2004) President's message, *CIPD Annual Report 2003/4*, Chartered Institute of Personnel and Development (**www.cipd.co.uk** accessed 14.09.04)

Legge, K. (1995) *Human Resource Management: Rhetorics and Realities*, Macmillan Business

National Statistics Online (2004) *The Jobs People Do,* Office for National Statistics (**www. statistics.gov.uk**; accessed 16.09.04)

Niven, M. (1978) *Personnel Management* 1913–63, IPM

Nolan, P. (2001) Shaping things to come, *People Management*, Vol. 7, No. 25, 30–31

Office for National Statistics (2003) Labour Force Survey, *Part time working by sex,* Spring (**www.statistics.gov.uk**; accessed 16.09.04)

Purcell, J., N. Rinnie, S. Hutchinson, (2003) Open minded, *People Management*, Vol. 9, No. 10, 31–33

Scarborough, H. (2003) Recipe for success, *People Management*, Vol. 9, No. 2, 32–35

Scarborough, H. and the CIPD Human Capital Task Force (2003) Human capital: external reporting framework *The change agenda,* CIPD (**www.cipd.co.uk**; accessed 16.9.04)

Sparrow, P. and M. Marchington (1998) *Human Resource Management: The New Agenda*, Financial Times Pitman Publishing

Storey, J. and K. Sisson (1993) *Managing Human Resources and Industrial Relations*, Open University Press

Tyson, S. (ed) (1995) *Strategic Prospects for HRM*, Institute of Personnel and Development

Further study

Books

Advisory, Conciliation and Arbitration Service (1999) *Effective Organisations: The People Factor,* ACAS. (One of a very useful series of ACAS advisory booklets. This one aims to assist anyone involved in improving effectiveness of organisations through the contribution of the people who work in them.)

Hall, L. and D. Torrington (1998) *The Human Resource Function: The Dynamics of Change and Development*, Financial Times Pitman Publishing. (A research-based book that describes various aspects of human resource management and comments on its status in UK companies in the 1980s and 1990s. The strategic nature of HRM is discussed in Chapter 6, 'Involvement in HR strategy', and the marketing of the function is described in Chapter 8, 'Internal marketing of HR activities and the HR function'.)

Storey, J. (1992) *Developments in the Management of Human Resources*, Blackwell Publishers. (Examines the changing nature of people management and the development of a business perspective rather than a personnel-driven picture.)

Articles

Fowler, A. (1994) Personnel's model army, *Personnel Management*, September, 35–37. (A good guide to the history of personnel management and of the various models that have been used to illustrate its development.)

Fowler, A. (1994) The way we were 1969–1994. Rediscovering humanity in the workplace, *Personnel Management*, mid-December, 23–26. (A clear analysis of trends in personnel management.)

Hodges, C. Stockport sells its HR services, *Personnel Management Plus*, March, 24–25. (A short article that describes how the central personnel unit of Stockport Borough Council designed and marketed its services.)

Industrial Relations Services (2001) HR on the net: the IRS guide, *IRS Employment Trends, 733,* August, 7–12. (Reviews the use of the World Wide Web by HR practitioners and provides information on a number of interesting sites.)

Journals

Human Resource Management Journal (Quarterly, contains articles on a wide range of HRM issues of interest to practitioners and academics alike. Vol. II, No. 3, 2001 is a special issue devoted to various aspects of the personnel management profession, including contributions on the relationship between HR and line managers by Graeme Currie and Stephen Proctor and on the role of HR specialists as change agents by Raymond Caldwell.)

People Management (Twice-monthly journal produced on behalf of the CIPD with topical articles relating to personnel management issues.)

Personnel Review (Journal produced six times per year with in-depth articles on personnel topics.)

Personnel Today (Contains topical articles on personnel management.)

Internet

There are numerous useful sources of information from around the world relating to human resource management. We have found the following to be particularly useful:

The Advisory, Conciliation and Arbitration Service   **www.acas.org.uk**
(Useful articles, news and lists of ACAS publications.)

The American Society for Human Resource Management   **www.shrm.org**
(The web site for a US body that represents HRM managers.)

The Australian Human Resource Institute   **www.ahri.com.au**
(Many articles relating to human resource management in Australia.)

Balanced Scorecard Report   **www.hbsp.Harvard.edu/products/bsr/**
(A bi-monthly journal published by the Harvard Business School. Sample content can be viewed at the web site.)

Chartered Institute of Personnel and Development   **www.cipd.co.uk**
(The web site for the professional body that represents personnel and development professionals in the UK.)

Department for Trade and Industry   **www.dti.gov.uk**
(Many useful DTI publications, discussion documents and booklets can be found on this site.)

The Government   **www.open.gov.uk**
(Useful information site especially for the text of legislation.)

Incomes Data Services Limited   **www.incomesdata.co.uk/**
(Some very useful articles on a range of HRM topics, including a section on management pay and remuneration, plus lists of contents for IDS publications.)

People Management   **www.peoplemanagement.co.uk**
(Journal produced on behalf of the CIPD with topical articles relating to personnel management issues.)

Personnel Review   **www.mcb.co.uk**
(Journal with in-depth articles on personnel topics.)

Trades Union Congress   **www.tuc.org.uk**
(This gives the TUC's views on many current HRM issues and new legislation in Britain.)

Workforce online (US)   **www.hrhq.com/**
(Another American site that provides useful information about HRM in the USA.)

CHAPTER 2

Human resource strategy and planning

OBJECTIVES

When you have studied this chapter you will be able to:

- describe the three basic levels of strategic planning
- explain the need for human resource strategies in work organisations
- describe the stages involved in human resource planning
- identify and describe the issues that have an impact on supply and demand forecasts
- outline the types of information required as a basis for human resource planning
- understand the process of job analysis and its role in the human resource planning process
- produce job descriptions and person specifications
- use basic mathematical techniques to produce forecast supply figures.

The chapter introducing human resource management (HRM) established that a key characteristic of the HRM approach is the involvement of the personnel function at a strategic level. We will now look briefly at the different levels at which strategy can be formulated and the generic types of strategy that are encountered, and comment on the links between strategy and consideration of human resource issues. You must remember that we shall be looking at the ideal situation or models of how corporate/business strategy and HR considerations could interact. What we describe as an ideal is not always found in reality, or, indeed, the specific circumstances in which a business is operating might call for a different approach. You will find that occasionally throughout the text we refer to contingency approaches, which means that there is no one right way to manage human resources in an organisation.

Following an overview of corporate/business and human resource strategies, we shall examine the activities that underpin the strategic human resource function, namely the activities involved in human resource planning.

Strategy

Strategy can be defined as a plan of action for the future, answering the questions, firstly of *what* to do, then of *how* to do it. A strategic plan should have a long-term focus, business plans usually being developed around a five-year perspective. The aim of designing and following a strategic plan is to create a competitive advantage, and all efforts in the formulation and implementation processes will be directed towards this. As far as work organisations are concerned, strategy can be formulated and implemented at different levels, and there are recognised generic forms of strategy that organisations or sub-divisions of organisations might adopt.

Levels of strategy

The levels at which strategy is formulated and implemented are most frequently identified as corporate, business and functional or operational (see, for example, Anthony *et al.* 1996; Boxall and Purcell 2003; Greer 2001; Lynch 2003; Marchington and Wilkinson 2002).

Corporate and business strategies

Corporate strategy is concerned with the overall direction that an organisation will follow. For large corporations, this is a question of which lines of business they will choose to be engaged in. These organisations would then develop separate business level strategies for their divisions, each of which might be engaged in producing very different products or services. As Anthony *et al.* (1996) point out, corporate and business strategy would be one and the same thing for a small organisation dealing only with one line of products or services, and it follows that you will sometimes find writers using the terms interchangeably when they are discussing these two levels of strategy.

Functional strategy

The functions represented in an organisation depend on the type of business, its size and structure, but may include production, marketing, sales, finance, research and development, and human resources. Each of these functional areas needs to be following strategic plans that are consonant with the corporate and business plans adopted by their organisations. The strategic plans adopted by all these functional departments must be integrated, however, to ensure the success of the organisation; they are interdependent and cannot be formulated in ignorance of each other. Indeed, it can be stated incontrovertibly that the human resource is an integral part of every one of the above-named functions.

The strategy formulation process

You will find throughout the discussion of the strategic planning process that there is a great deal of emphasis on gathering information as a basis for decision making. There is a need to focus on relevant information, but it is also imperative to be comprehensive so you do not miss something that could have an impact. Since planning implies forecasting future actions, there is always the potential for developments that you may not have foreseen. This means that planning becomes a rolling process, and that a five-year plan developed in 2005 cannot be followed slavishly until the year 2010, but will probably need to be adjusted on an ongoing basis to account for unforeseen developments.

> **Pause for thought 2.1**
>
> What kinds of information might senior managers in a company manufacturing and distributing consumer goods need to consider in order to formulate strategic plans?

You may have considered a variety of factors and kept in mind the types of changes that businesses in general are facing. Your list may include some of the following:

- Product life cycle: Is the product or service a new one with room for development and an expanding potential market? Is the product something that is bought once or do customers replace it? Is the product mature and not likely to attract more customers? Are customers likely to look for an alternative to the product or service?
- Changing consumer tastes and requirements: How are these likely to affect the demand for the product? Are there changes in customer expectations that organisations need to respond to?
- Expansion of business into other countries: Are there opportunities to sell your product or service abroad?
- Competition: What are the threats from competitors and the opportunities to compete? What will be the impact of new issues such as the growth of global competition, for instance increasing competition from countries like China?
- Technological developments: Will new technology affect the design of products, work processes and costs?
- Legislation: What regulations are in the pipeline and what are the associated implications for costs, work processes and product standards?

These are just some of the factors that affect business planning, and you may be able to identify even more. Information about all of these factors will influence what managers see as threats and opportunities and will therefore affect the strategic choices made and formulation of the strategic plan.

Generic types of corporate and business strategy

There are a number of recognised generic types of strategies that companies may choose to follow. The overarching corporate strategies are generally cited as being growth, stability and retrenchment (Glaister 1995), but there are a number of ways of pursuing each of these. Growth can be achieved, for instance, through the development of new products, by acquiring a larger share of the market for existing products, through mergers and acquisitions. Glaister also lists internationalisation as a possible generic strategy that organisations might wish to follow. These strategic directions (i.e. growth, stability and retrenchment) are normally associated with the life cycle stages of products and markets (Johnson and Scholes 2002). The idea behind the BCG matrix put forward by the Boston Consulting Group in the 1970s is that large corporations would aim to have a balanced portfolio of businesses encompassing a range of these (see Lynch 2003).

The work of Michael Porter (1980) is frequently cited in discussions of business-level strategies. The generic concepts he developed are cost leadership, differentiation and focus. One or a combination of these can be adopted in order to achieve the chosen corporate strategy. In adopting a strategy based on cost, companies will attempt to improve efficiency by reducing staffing and production costs. A strategy of differentiation means emphasising the distinctiveness of one's products or services, for example by being known for consistent high quality. A market or niche focus approach entails concentrating on a particular segment rather than the whole industry. As Glaister comments, this strategy can be pursued in combination with either cost leadership or differentiation. Innovation as a strategic direction can also provide a major focus (see, for instance, Johnson and Johnson's web site at **www.jnj.com**) and Guest *et al.* (1997) make the point that all business strategies need an element of innovation. We shall, therefore, pursue this as an example in our discussion of the linkage between corporate/business strategy and human resource strategy.

Corporate/business strategy – human resource strategy links

Innovation has been strongly promoted as a necessary part of any effective strategy for the twenty-first century (Guest *et al.* 1997) and as a requirement to accompany other strategies to guarantee success (Herriot and Pemberton 1997). Herriot and Pemberton (pages 47–48) list the human requirements for the successful pursuit of a strategy of innovation as security, a sense of agency, autonomy, access to adequate resources, and 'team working … especially when the team is composed of individuals with diverse perspectives'. Agency is defined as employees being able to affect what goes on in their workplace, and autonomy is, of course, being able to make decisions about how one's own work gets done.

Pause for thought 2.2

What human resource issues do you think would need to be addressed in a human resource strategy that was to support a business strategy of innovation? Looking back at Herriot and Pemberton's list of human requirements might give you some ideas to start with. Take a few minutes to jot down some thoughts before you read on.

Recruitment and selection

The company would obviously need to make sure it had staff of the right calibre, with the right competencies, to be able to achieve the required level of innovation. It might be that these people are already employed by the company, and this fact would be ascertained through the process of assessing the internal supply of human resources which we shall describe in detail later in this chapter. If not, the company would need a recruitment strategy and policies designed to enable them to carry out their recruitment in a purposeful manner. Since the human resource is so crucial to the achievement of the strategic aim, it will also be necessary to adopt a sophisticated approach to the selection of employees. We deal with systematic recruitment and selection in Chapters 3–5.

Employee relations

We assume that any right-thinking company will espouse the tenets of equality of opportunity, which we deal with extensively in Chapter 3, but, as we mention there too, some companies recognise the business advantage to be obtained from pursuing a policy of diversity, which is an extension of equal opportunities. The management of diversity means obtaining innovative ideas by promoting the involvement of employees from a wide variety of backgrounds, working in teams. A strategy of pursuing diversity has implications for the recruitment strategy and policies.

The word 'involvement' was used in the preceding paragraph. You will find in Chapter 13 that we discuss types of involvement and the modern push for partnership between employers and employees. A human resource strategy of involvement and partnership would support a corporate strategy of innovation.

Training and development

A strategy of innovation implies change that will have to be managed, and requirements for new skills as new products, services or processes are developed. All of these call for skills training, as do some of the other policies outlined in this discussion, such as embarking on a partnership agreement or promoting diversity in the workforce. Training in new skills and multi-skilling can also contribute to the sense of security that Herriot and Pemberton listed as a requirement for innovation. This is because employees develop a higher level of employability through the acquisition of a wider range of skills, and so feel more secure about their future employment prospects.

Reward

After investing so much in obtaining and training employees capable of carrying a strategy of innovation, you will not want to lose them to competitors, so you will need to develop reward strategies that will motivate employees to stay with your organisation and to reach the highest levels of productivity. We investigate the different ways of paying employees in Chapter 10, but non-monetary rewards can also contribute to the retention of employees, and helping employees to develop skills can play a part in this. We examine relevant aspects of performance management and development in Chapters 7–9.

You will note from the preceding description of human resource strategies that are appropriate to a corporate/business strategy of innovation (a) that a number of facets need to be addressed, and (b) that they affect each other and need to be integrated, e.g. a recruitment policy of promoting diversity engenders training needs for those involved in the recruitment and selection processes.

We have presented these human resource strategies as if they were designed to support a previously established corporate policy of innovation. This implies that an appropriate HR strategy is being 'read off' the corporate strategy to provide the 'best fit' between the two levels of strategy (Marchington and Wilkinson 2002, pp. 215–227). Ideally, however, human resource considerations should inform the corporate strategy and affect what is included in it. The costs of pursuing these HR strategies, and the probability of being able to fulfil them in order to achieve the strategic objectives, should have been a factor in the decision to pursue this strategic goal in the first place.

Human resource planning

Whatever the strategy adopted by an organisation, it is recognised that an unrelenting and increasing rate of change is an unavoidable phenomenon of today's workplace. The implication is that tomorrow's workplace will not be the same as today's. Employment patterns are changing, as we shall discuss in more detail in the chapter on the employment relationship, and changing work methods give rise to requirements for different and new skills and for flexibility from existing employees to acquire new skills or adapt to new methods of working. This highlights the need for human resource planning which responds to this situation by taking a long-term view and works towards preparing an organisation to cope with its future requirements and achieve its strategic objectives. The information acquired through the process of human resource planning provides the foundation for the development of human resource strategies.

The rest of this chapter will examine the stages involved in the human resource planning process, the types of issues and information that need to be considered, and techniques for processing that information.

Estimating the demand for human resources

Whatever the goals of the corporate/business plan are, they can be achieved only by the application of human skill and effort. One of the primary stages in the human resource planning process is therefore to estimate what will be required in terms of skills and numbers of people to achieve the corporate goals. Let us take some examples of corporate goals so that we can envisage what this exercise might entail.

ACTIVITY 2.1

Examine the following two scenarios, and evaluate what will be required in terms of human resources in order to achieve the goals stated in each case. What factors would have to be considered in making forecasts of requirements?

1 A UK distributor of women's clothing wishes to expand its customer base into Germany, France and Spain. It intends to open a warehouse and distribution depot in France.
2 A regional building society and a national bank are set to merge.

Discussion of Activity 2.1

In order to assess the requirements for human resources in the above scenarios, you would have to envisage:

- what tasks need to be done
- the skills required to complete these tasks
- how the tasks could be grouped together to form jobs, taking the skills requirements into consideration
- how many people would be required to complete the volume of work.

Firstly, then, there is a matter of the identification of discrete work tasks, followed by the organisation of those work tasks into jobs (i.e. a collection of tasks that somehow belong together and could reasonably be carried out by one individual), and a qualitative analysis of the skill base required to perform those jobs and achieve the organisation's goals. The records that document tasks and skills in an organisation are the job descriptions (JDs) and person specifications, and the information contained in these documents is collected and organised through the processes of job analysis and job design, which are discussed later. Alternatively, an organisation might use a competency framework and create job profiles based on this (see pages 46–47). Secondly, there is the task of quantifying the numbers of people required.

In scenario 1 you will have identified the need for the staff to run the warehousing and distribution processes in the new depot in France. This will include a manager, picking and packing staff, administrative staff and drivers. You may further have considered the need for language skills among some of these staff to cope with communications with the customers in Spain and Germany and with the home base in the UK. The expansion of business into these countries might also mean adding new tasks and skill requirements to existing posts in the home base, or it may mean recruiting a new manager and/or administrative staff who have the requisite language skills and knowledge of marketing and business processes in those countries. At the very least, the expansion of business into new countries implies a need for someone to coordinate the activities with headquarters. You would need additional information about the expected volume of business to be able to calculate how many people will be required in each category of employee.

Scenario 2 requires an examination of where skills and functions overlap within the two types of business, which might imply that some duties can be merged and not all of the existing posts will be needed. Alternatively, because the new, merged organisation will cover a wider range of tasks than either of the separate organisations had, there may be a new requirement for people who can combine skills and manage tasks in both areas.

Job analysis

Job analysis is an operational function that underpins the strategic level of human resource planning (and other human resource management functions) by providing the database required for analysis and planning. It is a process of gathering together all data about each existing job, which activities are performed and what skills are needed. As far as human resource planning activities are concerned, job analysis and job design (see pages 47–48) link the tasks of calculating the demand for human resources and calculating the internal supply of human resources, since together they provide the blueprint for what is required but also document the existing complement of employees, what they are doing and what skills they are using.

Job analysis, then, results in documents that pull together information about the tasks, skills and abilities represented in the current array of work performed in the organisation. If tasks and skills needed for the future are incorporated, the process is called job modelling. The products of job analysis are job descriptions and person specifications or a job profile related to a competency framework. Because these documents form the essential basis for recruitment and selection, job analysis is most often dealt with in textbooks in relation to those functions, and we shall remind you of its importance for them in Chapters 3 and 4. We feel, however, that job analysis is an essential part of human resource planning activities which, as you will see, should precede the formulation of recruitment plans.

For the purpose of illustrating how to compose a job description, we shall be using a relatively junior position, which will probably be familiar to you all, but even this example will demonstrate that changes in the workplace can affect positions at all levels and need to be planned for. You will find our sample job description for a receptionist later, in Figure 2.1 (page 42).

Pause for thought 2.3 Can you list several activities that you might undertake in order to perform a job analysis as defined above?

Job descriptions

The first task involved in drawing up a job description is to gather information about the tasks that are performed by the postholder. The following questions need to be considered:

- Who can best provide the information?
- Who can best gather the information?
- What techniques can be used for gathering the information?
- Who should write the job description?

Who can best provide the information?

Before you read on, stop and ask yourself: 'Who knows most about any particular job?' Most people would probably respond by saying: 'The person who actually does the job.' The postholder is, therefore, a good source of information about any post. But is the postholder the best source, or the only source? The direct line manager will also know the job requirements intimately, and will probably have a better perspective on how the job fits into the wider context of the company. Gathering information from both of these individuals will create a better picture of the post than gathering information from only one of them.

Personnel specialists also develop detailed knowledge of the tasks performed throughout the company, particularly if they are involved in the human resource planning process, so they can bring an even wider perspective to the description of an individual post. To that extent they can also provide input to the job description, but their major role as far as job descriptions are concerned is not about providing information.

Information given by any person will be influenced by his or her perceptions and self-interest. Consider the pros and cons of involving the postholder and the line manager in the production of job descriptions. Your list might include the following points:

1 The postholder:
   - knows the job in detail
   - may wish to inflate the importance of certain duties as a matter of status or self-image

- may represent preferred duties as more important duties
- may have incorrect perceptions of level of authority
- may not have the specialised skills needed to gather information and compose job descriptions
- may be reluctant to spend the time necessary to develop a good job description.

2 The line manager:
- knows the job well, but not as well as the jobholder
- can give information about how the job fits in with other functions performed in the company
- may sometimes be reluctant to define which tasks his or her subordinates have full authority for
- may not have the specialised skills needed to gather information and compose job descriptions
- may be reluctant to spend the time necessary to develop a good job description.

Who can best gather the information?

This is the role that the human resource specialist can best fulfil. Although line managers may often put job descriptions to good use, most of them would not consider the production of JDs to be part of their duties, and there is no reason to assume that line managers in a wide range of functions would necessarily have the skills needed in order to produce a good job description. The human resource management function would normally provide this as a service to line management, and of course people with the requisite skills would be recruited and selected to perform this duty. Depending on the structure of the HRM division, the task could be allocated to a specialist job analyst, a recruitment specialist or a human resource management generalist.

What techniques can be used for gathering the information?

A range of techniques are available for performing job analysis, including observation, critical incident analysis and the use of questionnaires and interviews.

Observation involves shadowing employees and observing what they actually do. Obviously this can be very time-consuming and could stretch over a long period if, for instance, some tasks were performed infrequently. This technique is therefore most appropriate in the case of routine jobs with a narrow range of repetitive tasks.

Critical incident analysis involves getting a number of jobholders and their supervisors to describe events that showed successful behaviour on the job and events that showed unsuccessful behaviour. The analyst collects a large number of such anecdotes and condenses out of them a list of dimensions that represent the job. The advantage of this is seen as being that it focuses on behaviours, i.e. what people actually do, but the process is very time-consuming and may miss some of the more routine aspects of the job.

A sound approach for gathering information would involve written questionnaires and interviews. A structured questionnaire can be used to gather initial information from the jobholder, supplemented with details from the line manager. The job analyst can then interview both and obtain clarification on the details outlined in the questionnaire. The draft job description should then be submitted to the jobholder and line manager for further comment. A structured questionnaire will guide people into giving relevant and adequate information.

If you were asked to design a form in order to conduct a job analysis, what questions would you include?

The questions on a job analysis form might be dictated to some extent by the type of company you are working in. For instance, if you worked in a bank, which is closed in the evening, you would not include questions about night shift work, whereas if you worked in a chemical plant with a 24-hour process, you obviously would ask questions about shift patterns. If we ignore such differences between organisations, however, there are some basic data that you would want to include in any job analysis. These would include such details as:

- a description of the duties performed
- the most important or responsible duties
- time spent on each duty
- how often each duty is performed (daily/weekly/monthly/annually)
- levels of supervision/independence
- the skills and skill levels needed to perform each task
- any special conditions related to the performance of these tasks.

The questionnaire and interview should be designed so that information needed for each section of the job description will be obtained. If employees and their managers are asked to describe ways in which they think their jobs will change, this adds information to the job analysis beyond what is already observable about the job. When this information is incorporated into the job profile, the exercise is known as job modelling.

Although many people are happy to talk about their job, some people do not respond well to questioning or lack good powers of expression. The job analyst needs to develop good interviewing techniques to extract all the relevant information. Interviewing skills are an essential part of many aspects of human resources management and you will find more information about relevant techniques and skills development in Chapter 4 (selection) and Chapter 11 (managing employee welfare).

Who should write the job description?

Again the personnel specialist can best perform this task because of the writing skills required and the opportunity to become familiar with jobs throughout the organisation. This means that all job descriptions will be written in a uniform manner, providing an excellent database of all tasks performed within the organisation. This will facilitate the analysis of the information contained in job descriptions for human resource planning purposes.

How to write a job description

Structure and content

If a collection of job descriptions is to serve as a database of all tasks performed within an organisation, it makes sense to adopt a standard format for all job descriptions. This will ensure that the same types of information are gathered for each post, and will make the information more accessible to the reader and facilitate coding if the data are to be entered on to a computerised information system. The following elements are commonly found in job descriptions:

- job title
- reporting structure:
  – reports to
  – responsible for
- purpose of job
- major duties.

Sample job description

Figure 2.1

JOB DESCRIPTION

Job title: Receptionist

Reports to: Office Services Manager

Responsible for: Junior receptionists (2)

Purpose of post: To ensure that visitors to the company are received in a welcoming fashion, to answer routine queries and to ensure that all other queries are handled expeditiously by the appropriate staff member. To ensure that all telephone queries are handled in the same manner.

As the first point of contact for the company, the receptionist must maintain high standards of customer care.

Contacts: All customers and other visitors to deal with initial and routine queries. All members of staff to pass on queries as appropriate.

Major duties:
- Greet walk-in visitors and ascertain purpose of their visit. Handle or redirect queries as appropriate.
- Answer phone queries as above.
- Answer all initial queries about receipt of payments using the on-line payment receipts system.
- Open and sort incoming post by department. Organise delivery of post by assistant receptionists.
- Perform clerical tasks assigned by departments in agreement with the Office Services Manager.
- Supervise assistant receptionists and delegate work as appropriate.
- Perform other duties as assigned by the Office Services Manager or other authorised manager.

These are the essential elements of a job description, but you will find an assortment of other elements included in some job descriptions, for example: contacts, working conditions, salary grade, performance standards. Each organisation must decide what factors should be included in a job description, and this will depend on the nature of the business. For instance, some local authorities include a description of the contacts their employees are expected to deal with because they have complex internal structures, and contact with the public is an important part of their operation. The four elements listed above, however, are the basic information you would expect to find in any job description.

Most JDs contain a summary description of the post or, as we have called it, an outline of the purpose of the post. This is a brief paragraph encapsulating what the job is all about – what the jobholder contributes to the organisation. The major part of any JD is the list of major duties, itemising in detail the activities the jobholder undertakes and what he or she is meant to achieve.

Torrington *et al.* (2002) demonstrate the inclusion of performance standards in job descriptions. This can certainly enhance a job description by giving more information about what is expected from the jobholder. For instance, the second duty in our sample JD might read: 'Answer phone queries within three rings.'

Did you know?

An IRS (2003b) survey of 250 organisations identified that 71% of employers use jobs descriptions for all of their posts, 3% use them for most posts, and a further 9% use them for some posts.

Writing style

One important pointer when you are writing a job description is to use verbs to describe what a person is doing. For instance, the phrase 'responsible for letters' does not indicate what this employee would actually be doing. It is much better to employ a verb and say: 'writes letters'; 'sorts and distributes letters'; 'replies to letters'.

You should also, where possible, avoid the temptation to use the phrase 'assists with', as again this does not give a clear picture of what an individual employee is actually doing. Take, for example, the phrase: 'assists the manager with invoices'. It must be possible to get a clearer idea of which duties have been delegated to the employee and what activities are retained by the manager. 'Sorts the invoices by date'; 'processes invoices and forwards them to appropriate departments'; 'checks that invoices have been processed and payment made': each of these indicates a different activity and a different level of responsibility, and each is certainly more meaningful than 'assists the manager with invoices'.

Uses of the job description

It has been mentioned previously that job descriptions can be used for a number of purposes. These will be dealt with more extensively in other chapters, but it is worth pausing here to reflect briefly on what the applications of job descriptions are and whether they have any implications for how job descriptions are compiled and written. The major uses of job descriptions are as follows:

- human resource planning
- recruitment and selection
- day-to-day performance management
- long-term performance management/performance appraisal
- identification of training needs
- job evaluation.

Can one description provide all the information needed for the whole range of these activities? Some personnel managers may argue that different input is needed, for example, for the job evaluation process. More detailed information may be needed about the amount of freedom that employees have to make decisions independently, the impact their actions have on other colleagues, or the financial implications of their work. The question arises of whether a different job description is needed for the purposes of job evaluation. You can form a better opinion on this when you read about these other activities and the uses of job descriptions to support them.

ACTIVITY 2.2

1 Design a generic questionnaire that could be used to solicit adequate information from an employee to draft a job description. (It might help you if you have one or two posts in mind while you design the questionnaire: what sorts of question would you need to ask in order to elicit all the relevant information? You may also wish to work with a group of fellow students to pool your ideas about the questionnaire design.)
2 Test your questionnaire on a friend, relative or other willing volunteer, and follow up with an interview to fill in the gaps.
3 Analyse this process and make recommendations for improvement.
4 Draft the job description from the information you have gathered.

Person specifications

The person specification is a document that outlines the skills and qualities a person would need to have in order to be able to do the tasks on the job description. Drawing up a person specification requires a fair amount of judgement in assessing what level of skill is necessary. Often there is a tendency to inflate these requirements, especially with regard to academic qualifications, resulting in an unjustified rejection of skills and knowledge acquired through experience. The requirements detailed in a person specification should be the minimum standards required for a person to be able to perform the job. There should be an expectation that any person will improve performance while doing a job, and the fact that training could be provided should also be considered.

How to write a person specification

Several models of person specifications are available, those designed by Alec Rodger in 1952 and John Munro Fraser in 1978 being the most widely known. We shall briefly describe the criteria set out in these two models, with some indication of how you might interpret the recommended dimensions in modern circumstances, and then we shall apply a simplified model to our sample job description.

Rodger developed the seven-point plan which described people in terms of:

- Physical make-up   – Any particular physical requirements of the job, such as visual acuity

- Attainments   – Education and training

- General intelligence   – It is difficult to make a meaningful statement about intelligence unless you intend to test for it

- Special aptitudes — Verbal, numerical and diagrammatical abilities related to the job
- Interests — Current wisdom is that private interests are not good indicators of job performance
- Disposition — Job-related behaviours such as persuasiveness
- Circumstances — Only job-related circumstances such as availability for shift work

The criteria suggested by Fraser are known as the five-fold framework:

- Impact on others — Similar to Rodger's physical make-up and disposition
- Qualifications and experience — Education, training and skills developed through work experience
- Innate abilities — Similar to intelligence in Rodger's plan
- Motivation — Difficult to apply for human resource planning and selection purposes since differing motivational structures can lead to equally good performance
- Emotional adjustment — Relevant personality factors such as the ability to cope with stress

In essence, the person specification should cover three areas of requirements:

- knowledge
- skills
- personal attributes or qualities.

These three dimensions have long been used to create person specifications in North America where they are referred to as KSAs.

The person specification can be drawn up by examining each task in the job description and determining:

1 what each task requires in terms of knowledge, skills and personal qualities
2 how these skills, knowledge and personal qualities might be acquired.

As mentioned earlier, a high level of judgement is needed to decide on relevant criteria, and one person's judgement may differ from another's. You must be able to justify any requirement you make and be ready to explain why it is reasonable, particularly when the specification is to be used later in recruitment and selection. You should also take care to avoid meaningless clichés like 'a sense of humour', when what is really required is the ability to deal calmly with stressful situations.

Once you have a list of the criteria you are looking for, they must be arranged in a logical and understandable fashion:

- Similar criteria, e.g. all skills and knowledge involving numeracy, should be grouped
- Criteria can be designated as essential for the post or merely desirable.

The sample person specification in Table 2.1 relates to the sample job description in Figure 2.1.

Table 2.1   **Sample person specification**

Person specification		
Post: Receptionist		
Attributes	**Essential**	**Desirable**
Knowledge	Knowledge of clerical systems	Knowledge of the company
Skills	Experience of clerical work Experience in handling queries in person and over the telephone	Supervisory experience
Personal qualities	Polite manner Ability to work under pressure	

Pause for thought 2.5

One of the major requirements for the job described in Figure 2.1 has been missed out of the model person specification in Table 2.1. Can you identify it? What can you add to the person specification to cover this requirement?

The job description mentions use of an on-line system to answer queries about receipt of payment, yet there is no requirement for computer skills in the person specification. Obviously a low level of skill is required. It would not, for instance, be appropriate to ask for programming skills, but it would be reasonable to require the 'ability to extract information from a computerised database'.

ACTIVITY 2.3

Draft a person specification for the job description in Figure 2.1 using the models provided by Alec Rodger and John Munro Fraser. Compare your drafts with those of other students and incorporate the best ideas into a final version.

Competency frameworks

Competencies are work-related behaviours that have been identified as necessary for successful performance at work. Rather than designing a person specification for each post, perhaps using new vocabulary each time to describe the skills, knowledge and personal attributes required, it may be possible to design a schematic or framework of competencies that can be applied to all jobs performed in a particular company. At least it should be possible to identify a set of core competencies required of all employees, with more specialised competencies attached to the job descriptions of particular posts.

Setting up a competency framework is a complex endeavour, and organisations that wish to introduce one into their HRM systems would normally call on the services of a firm of occupational psychologists to assist in the design and implementation processes. Competency frameworks come in many shapes and sizes, and the issues that would typically need to be addressed in designing a system include the following:

- Should we adopt a framework geared towards particular categories of employee (e.g. managers) or design one that can be applied to all employees in the organisation?

- What are the competencies relevant to our enterprise? How many should we include to build a comprehensive but manageable representation of the skills, knowledge and personal qualities required in the organisation?
- Which competencies can be grouped together as clusters, how many performance levels should there be for each competency and how will these levels be described?
- How do these competency clusters, individual competencies and levels of competency relate to individual jobs in the organisation?

An example of a competency cluster, individual competency and levels of competency should help you to recognise the significance of these issues and appreciate the potential usefulness of a competency framework. Typical competencies that are required by organisations include things like communication skills, analytical abilities, ability to work in a team, leadership, and ability to plan work.

Let us take the employees in a supermarket as an example. Most of these employees would at some time come into contact with the public, so 'working with people' might well be a major area of competence which would subsume a cluster of related competencies. 'Working with people' therefore becomes a competency cluster, and the competencies included under this designation might include communication, customer service and teamwork. These competencies might be applied to all jobs in the supermarket, including managerial, supervisory, office and shop-floor employees. Obviously, different levels of these competencies would be expected from employees working in different functions and at different levels in the organisation. Thus a description of the level of competence in teamworking required of a manager would probably allude to the ability to devise and implement new structures that enhance productivity, whereas the level of competence expected of a shelf stacker would probably involve statements such as 'assists other team members when own work is completed' or 'helps other team members solve queries'. Whiddett and Hollyforde (1999) provide a more detailed sample competency framework, and the Incomes Data Services (IDS 2001) review examples of the frameworks used in a number of organisations.

ACTIVITY 2.4

The competencies we have just outlined in our supermarket example are presented in a grid in Figure 2.2. Provide descriptions of the levels of competency left blank for all the competencies, and indicate which jobs these would apply to.

Job design

When new tasks arise and new skills are required to complete them, existing jobs may have to be redesigned to incorporate these additional requirements or new posts may be created. It is important to obey certain principles when designing jobs in order to enhance the motivating potential of the job, and consequently increase the contribution of the employee to the organisation. It is beyond the scope of this text to examine the tenets of motivation theory in detail, but the major thrust of job design, according to theories such as the Job Characteristics Model, is to provide for variety, responsibility and autonomy in a person's work (Hackman and Oldham 1980). This can be effected by the mix of tasks that are combined into one job and by setting up work processes so

| Figure 2.2 | Competency framework exercise |

	LEVEL 1	LEVEL 2	LEVEL 3	LEVEL 4	LEVEL 5
WORKING WITH THE TEAM	• Demonstrates willingness to help other members of the team complete their work • Uses knowledge to help other team members solve problems			• Designs and implements new team work structures to improve efficiency and effectiveness	
CUSTOMER SERVICE					
COMMUNICATION SKILLS					

that individuals have responsibility and autonomy. A recognised way of achieving this is to design jobs so they can be done by teams of employees. This incorporates the motivational elements noted above and is recognised as good HR practice (Marchington and Wilkinson 2002). You can find a fuller explanation of motivation and job design in Rollinson and Broadfield (2001) and the ACAS (2003) advisory booklet, *Teamwork: Success Through People*, is also a good source of information on this topic.

Applying job analysis data to human resource planning

The documents produced from the processes of job analysis and job design – JDs, person specs, competency profiles – may be used to support recruitment, selection, job evaluation, training needs analysis and performance appraisal. For human resource planning purposes, where an overview of the whole workforce is needed, it is evident that computerisation of these data will be advantageous even for medium-sized organisations, so that alternative scenarios can be set up and analysed and the impact of change can be assessed by running 'what if' scenarios. Database systems for HRM functions are commonly known as computerised personnel information systems (CPIS) or human resource information systems (HRIS). For the information obtained from job analysis to be computerised, the elements of the job description and person specification would need to be standardised across jobs, and some coding, for example, of categories of employee, would be necessary. If an organisation-wide competency framework is used instead of individually drafted person specifications, this would provide the standardised terminology for a computerised database. The description of the human requirements for all jobs using a common terminology is regarded as one of the advantages of using the competency approach. We can look further at the sorts of data that are needed for human resource planning when we look at how to estimate the supply of human resources later in this chapter.

It may seem as if job analysis is a major, time-consuming task to carry out for an organisation of any size and that this might slow down the development of strategic plans. This thought is confounded by two arguments:

● The planning process cannot take place without a proper database of information to work on.
● Once the database of job descriptions and competency profiles/person specifications is established, job analysis becomes a matter of reviewing these documents to incorporate new tasks and skill requirements. This is not as onerous as starting from scratch.

Quantitative aspects of estimating demand

Having worked out what is required in terms of tasks to be done and skills needed to do those tasks, an analysis is required of how many people are needed for the volume of work.

Pause for thought 2.6

Imagine you are a manufacturer who is going to export clothes to mainland Europe. You have estimated that you will require sewing machine operators to produce an additional 10,000 blouses in the first year. What methods could you use to estimate how many people you would need for this task?

If you have no previous measures of how much work is produced by your employees, you can engage in work study techniques. This involves determining how the task can be performed most efficiently and timing the operation. You would then calculate how many blouses can be sewn at this rate in one year by one operator and divide your production target of 10,000 by this number to get the number of employees required.

If prior data do exist, you can use past production figures and calculate the ratio of operatives to the number of blouses produced by taking the total figure of blouses produced divided by the total number of operatives engaged in this or similar work. You might also apply managerial judgement by basing your calculations on a task that is similar to producing a blouse.

Another historical ratio employers might use is the ratio of various categories of personnel to the volume of sales or the number of customers. For instance, if a distribution company has one invoice clerk for every 10,000 customers, and it intends to increase its customer base by 10,000, the historical ratio indicates a need for one additional invoice clerk.

Did you know?

HRP is alive but is it well? Working on the basis of what it would ideally like to see in place, Swansea NHS Trust forecasts a need for an additional 1,236 employees, including 800 nurses by 2008. Recognising that lack of funding and skills shortages were likely to make this unachievable, senior managers raised the question of why the Welsh National Assembly requires the submission of plans based on the ideal situation. The Trust plans to estimate its future demand on a more realistic basis from 2005 on.

(*South Wales Evening Post*, 31 July 2004)

You would need to take account of the fact that new employees might not work at full capacity until fully trained, or you might envisage savings from economies of scale or from changing work methods or the technology used. In other words, even when statistical methods are used to calculate the demand for human resources, managerial judgement will also be a factor.

Estimating the internal supply of human resources

As with estimating the demand for human resources, you will need qualitative as well as quantitative data to assess whether the requisite resources will be available. The organisation's collection of job descriptions for existing posts represents a database of tasks that are currently being performed, and the person specifications/competency profiles are a partial database of existing skills.

Pause for thought 2.7

Why do you think it was stated above that an organisation's collection of person specifications/competency profiles is a partial database of the supply of existing skills?

A fact that employers often forget is that people frequently have skills that their employer may not have required them to use in their current post. These could include facility in foreign languages, computer knowledge, training skills and interpersonal skills. In order to have a full picture of skills available from the current workforce the organisation needs to develop a skills inventory in addition to JDs and person specs, and these should be recorded on the personal records of employees, which will form part of the organisation's HRIS. The skills inventory should list skills that are available but not being used in addition to those that are being used.

A properly designed HRIS will also provide data on the numbers of employees in various categories of posts, and personal data that may have an impact on how long they are likely to be with the organisation. There are some simple statistical techniques that enable employers to forecast fluctuations in their workforce numbers. The basic figure that most employers calculate is the labour turnover rate, sometimes referred to as the wastage rate or the separation rate, which represents the proportion of employees who leave in a given period of time, usually a year or a quarter. This figure is calculated as a percentage by dividing the number of leavers by the total complement of staff and multiplying this figure by 100. If the requirements for staff vary during the time period, the total complement can be calculated as an average of the number required at the beginning of the period and the number required at the end. This would give an overall turnover rate for an organisation, but it is usually more useful to calculate the rate for specific categories of staff such as secretarial staff, systems analysts, employees in specified production areas, etc.

For example, if a company requires 50 machinists throughout the year, and 5 of these have left in one year, then the turnover rate is $(5/50) \times 100 = 10\%$. The average turnover rate experienced over a period of time can be used as a trend to forecast requirements for the future. For instance, if the turnover rate for machinists in our example company has been fairly stable at about 10% over the past three years, then this employer knows that it is likely to be necessary to recruit five machinists next year to maintain his or her supply. If the demand forecast implies that additional machinists will be needed over the next few years, the 10% turnover rate should be factored into the recruitment calculation.

ACTIVITY 2.5

At the end of 2005, the employer in question decides that she will require 10 additional machinists in each of the next three years. They are to be recruited at the beginning of each year. How many machinists will she have to recruit during each year to maintain the workforce?

Discussion of Activity 2.5

These figures are best calculated by tracking the base figure required each year, the increase in personnel required, and an adjustment for the expected turnover. As you can see, the manufacturer needs not only to recruit the additional 10 employees each year, but also to cover the turnover on the new base figure. In 2006, five of the original employees may leave, and perhaps one of the new employees. The figures are presented in Table 2.2.

Table 2.2 **Estimated recruitment figures adjusted for labour turnover**

	Number of machinists required	Increase over previous year	Projected turnover during year	Number to recruit
End of 2005	50			
2006	60	10	6	16
2007	70	10	7	17
2008	80	10	8	18

Another calculation that can be made is known as the stability index. This also gives an indication of turnover, but provides information additional to the base turnover figure and is calculated as follows: (Number of people currently employed with one year or more of service/number of people employed one year ago) × 100.

ACTIVITY 2.6

This is a simple activity that will help you to focus on the information that can be gleaned by analysing the same data in different ways.

1 You are asked to perform a simple calculation for each of three situations.
   (a) Your organisation has 20 drivers. In one year, 5 of these drivers leave and have to be replaced. Calculate the turnover rate.
   (b) Your organisation has 20 drivers. At the end of one year, you still have 19 of those drivers with you, but you have had to recruit 5 times to keep your staff complement up to 20. Calculate the turnover rate and the stability index.
   (c) Your organisation has 20 drivers. In one year, 5 drivers leave. Each of them had 2–5 years of service. You have had to replace each of them and your new recruits are still with you. Calculate the turnover rate and the stability index.

2 What do these turnover and stability index figures tell you?

Discussion of Activity 2.6

You should have calculated a turnover figure of 25% for each of these circumstances. On its own, the turnover figure reveals nothing about the underlying causes of turnover, and this is emphasised by the fact that you have the same figure for the two very different circumstances described as (b) and (c) above. The turnover rate on its own becomes meaningful only if you can compare it with rates experienced by your organisation in the past or by other organisations in your industry for similar categories of staff. Then you can deduce whether you are performing in a competitive way in terms of retaining staff, or whether there are problems you need to investigate.

The stability index figures, 95% in scenario (b) and 75% in scenario (c), are much more revealing. The similarity among all three scenarios in the exercise is that there have been five recruitment actions in each case; the stability index, however, reveals that the situations are different and the reasons for the vacancies differed. The higher figure, which means that the turnover is not occurring among the longer-serving employees, indicates that there is a problem with retaining new recruits. The lower figure indicates that the problem lies with the retention of longer serving employees. Each problem requires different action to remedy it, and this will be very important when you arrive at the stage of formulating human resource management action plans.

Pause for thought 2.8

In the discussion of Activity 2.6, we mentioned that comparing your turnover to that experienced by your competitors might prompt you to analyse retention problems. If your turnover rate was unfavourable in such a comparison, what might some of the problems and remedies be?

Some of the problems and remedies associated with excessive turnover are represented in Table 2.3.

Table 2.3   **Labour turnover: causes and remedies**

Cause	Remedy
Poor handling of new recruits	Design and implement induction process
Unfavourable salary/terms and conditions of employment	Revise reward strategies
Job dissatisfaction	Improve job design
Low morale	Organisational culture change Employee involvement Employee opinion surveys
Recruits not equipped for work demands	Improve recruitment and selection practices Improve training

There are some other factors that have an impact on the turnover rate. These might be reflected in long-term trends or they may cause occasional fluctuations. One such factor is the age of employees. Retirement may account for a certain percentage of leavers on an ongoing basis, but it also sometimes happens that an organisation has a large number of people due to retire at the same time, which will temporarily increase the turnover rate.

Did you know?

The IDS (2004) reports the following labour turnover figures from a variety of surveys:

- 16% – the overall labour turnover figure for the UK
- 10.3% – the figure for voluntary labour turnover, i.e. one that excludes turnover related to redundancies and dismissals
- 10% – in the transport and communication sectors
- 26% – in the retailing sector.

The last two figures reflect the lowest and highest rates reported.

These factors need to be taken into consideration in forecasting the supply of human resources and when adjusting the estimates to reflect the effects of labour turnover. The HRIS should be set up so that it can provide this information.

In addition to information about numbers, the analysis of various aspects of the workforce can highlight a range of problems or issues that deserve consideration. Some of the analyses that could be obtained are:

- the male/female distribution of personnel across the whole workforce or in each category of employee
- the distribution across the workforce or by employee category of members of specified ethnic minority groups
- age profiles
- length of service for each of the above.

These analyses could help managers to see where new approaches or policies are needed to help the organisation reach its goals.

Assessing the external supply of human resources

At the same time as analysing their internal supply of human resources, employers need to be aware of the availability of potential employees externally in case the internal supply falls short of what is required. If the internal supply of employees cannot meet the demand, managers must know whether there are problems with the availability of employees from outside the organisation. Indeed, the Industrial Relations Services (2001) report that competition for new recruits is likely to be a major problem for employers throughout the first decade of the twenty-first century. The ongoing problems with skills shortages, reported later in this chapter, indicate that this has in fact proved to be the case.

The labour force is defined as the number of people aged 16 and over, and who are either in employment or available for work. As such, those members of the labour force who are not currently employed by a particular employer constitute that employer's external labour market. Sometimes separate figures are given for people of working age, but since some people continue working past the state retirement age, figures for persons in their late sixties and seventies are included in estimates of the total labour force. Current debate about the state retirement age also suggests that it is likely to be raised before 2010.

Pause for thought 2.9

There are many factors that have an impact on:
- the size of the labour force in general
- the availability of employees from the labour force to any particular employer.

Before you go on to read about these factors, make a list of as many of them as you can think of. You may also wish to consider what employers might have to do to counteract any problems you identify.

Size and composition of the labour force

British labour force projections for the years 1998–2011, as reported in *Labour Market Trends* (Armitage and Scott 1998), included the following data:

- Between 1997 and 2011 the labour force is set to increase by 1.8 million persons from 28.0 million to 29.8 million.
- Of this increase, 1.3 million will be women.
- In 2011, women will represent 46.1% of the labour force (44.2% in 1997).
- The number of people in the labour force aged under 35 will decline by 0.7 million while the group aged 35 and over will increase by 2.4 million.

Changes in the numbers of people in the labour force are caused by a combination of population effects and activity rate effects. The largest population effect is the variation in the number of births. There was a peak birth rate around 1964 which accounts for some of the increase in the 35 and over age group in the projection period, and the birth rate was particularly low in the years 1973–1979. Economic activity rates also affect the size and composition of the labour force. Increasing numbers of young people are choosing to study full time which, together with birth rate effects, accounts for the lower numbers of people in the lower age groups available for work. However, this may be counteracted by an increase in the numbers of students who work on a part-time basis.

The growing proportion of women in the labour force is attributed in part to socio-economic influences such as the greater availability of part-time work and the social acceptability of women in employment. All of the factors discussed in this section have implications particularly for employers who have a traditional view of whom they might employ, for instance in positions thought of as being suitable for school leavers. The changing demographic structure of the external labour market may oblige employers to adopt more open approaches to recruitment and to consider the necessity of providing training.

The figures provided by surveys of the national labour force are important in providing a broad indication of factors to be considered in human resource planning. There are, however, some limitations on their usefulness. The statistics are only estimates, projections of the numbers of people expected to be economically active in the future. As such, they have to be predicated on some basic assumptions linked with patterns of economic activity observed at the time the analysis is performed. Obviously, unexpected events can occur which may have a sizeable impact on the validity of the projected figures. The IDS study, *The Future Workforce* (1996), provides some useful guidelines on how to interpret statistical data culled from workforce surveys.

The ageing of the workforce

One of the demographic phenomena that has attracted much comment in the early years of the twenty-first century is the expected ageing of the workforce. One of the reasons for this is the lower birth rate mentioned previously, which means smaller numbers of younger workers coming into the labour market at various times. The other reason is the expectation that more of the older employees will wish to extend their participation in the workforce until a later age, many of them for financial reasons such as poor pension provision. Some of the figures reported are: 'by 2010 the proportion of working-age people between 50 and 64 years old will be greater than at any time since the mid-1970s'

(Dixon 2003, p. 68); the population of under-16 year olds decreased from 24% in 1951 to 16% in 2001 while the population of 60+ year olds increased from 16% in 1951 to 21% in 2001 (**www.agepositive.gov.uk**; accessed 25.02.03); there will soon be more people aged over 40 in the UK labour market than people aged under 40 (**www.peoplemanagement.co.uk**; accessed 02.01.03).

The important issue from the point of view of analysing the external labour market is the extent to which employers are noting this shift and adjusting their recruitment strategies in response. As will be seen later, skills shortages are a continuing challenge for employers, and if the people available in the labour market are increasingly more mature, this may call for different strategies in attracting them, a different approach to training may be required, and older employees may have different requirements with regard to flexibility in their working arrangements.

> **Did you know?**
>
> The ageing of the workforce is a phenomenon that is not restricted to the UK. The IRS (2003c) reports that employers in the USA are also facing similar developments. The Society for Human Resource Management there has expressed concerns that US employers are not preparing adequately for this demographic shift.

Unemployment

Rates of unemployment and the prevalence of redundancies have an obvious impact on the numbers of people looking for work. This does not necessarily mean, however, that meeting one's requirements for human resources is automatically easier in times of high unemployment. One example of this is the numbers of coal miners made redundant by the closures of coal mines in the early 1990s. Coal miners may have a range of skills, but not necessarily in the areas required by other employers. There is also resistance among newly redundant people to accepting a large immediate drop in earnings. The existence of large numbers of unemployed or newly redundant people, therefore, does not equate directly with a ready supply of human resources.

Skills shortages

Skills shortages are broadly defined in terms of the proportion of posts that employers report having difficulty in filling. Some of these difficulties may be attributed to factors other than an actual lack of skill, factors such as an organisation's reputation as an employer, poor recruitment practices or low pay. Based on two government-funded surveys conducted in 1999, the Industrial Relations Services (2000) reported that employers in the UK were facing difficulties in filling some 50% of advertised vacancies. Discounting the other factors that might affect recruitment, the IRS states that 20% of vacancies are unfilled because of true skills shortages. Continuing headlines such as 'No end in sight to employers' resourcing problems' (IRS 2003) confirm the persistence of these difficulties.

The surveys identified craft and technical occupations as being the area where most skills shortages occurred (40% of the instances of skills shortage), followed by personal service and sales jobs (25%). These shortages affect the manufacturing and retail sectors, but all sectors continue to be affected by a shortage of managerial skills.

> **Did you know?**
>
> A number of employers have turned to new sources of overseas workers to combat skills shortages. One example is the transport company, First, which is reported to have recruited a number of Polish nationals as bus drivers, following the accession of Poland to the EU (Campling 2004). Hurstfield and Pearson (2004) point out that refugees also represent a source of potential employees.

Other potential or actual skills shortages that have been reported in a number of sources, including news broadcasts on TV and radio, include nurses (Cottell 2004; IRS 2004), teachers, police officers, and a range of jobs in the hospitality industry. Skills shortages have also been reported in construction (Pandya 2004) and plumbing (Steiner 2004).

Assuming that employers follow a systematic process as described in Chapter 3 and thus advertise only vacancies that need to be filled, these skills shortages in the external labour market must have a detrimental impact on their operational effectiveness. The IRS (2000) reports that one major result of recruitment difficulties, together with the problem of skill gaps identified in internal staff, is a poorer level of customer service. Lost business and an inability to develop new products as planned are also identified as consequences of skills shortages and skill gaps. These business repercussions highlight the effect of skills shortages on strategy formulation.

Opportunities for education and training

In connection with the concern over skills shortages, employers will be interested in Government plans for youth training, what is taught in schools, and how well people are prepared for employment. Many employers develop links with educational institutions to improve the likelihood of relevant skills being available to them. Asda is one example of a company that has developed a scheme to provide part-time employment to students with the aim of creating a pool of graduate applicants with relevant work experience in the future.

Competition

The presence of competitors in an employer's locality, who also need people with the same skills, will obviously influence the availability of human resources. This may have a direct impact on recruitment and pay strategies as employers try to attract the best people in direct competition with other companies. For the purposes of human resource planning, it will be important to assess the likelihood of new competitors arriving on the scene.

Geographical considerations

The distribution of the labour force across the country is affected by the availability of housing and transport and by patterns of migration. Changes in the availability of public transport might mean you can no longer depend on obtaining workers from a particular geographical area, so it is important for employers to be aware of the plans of privatised transport companies and developments in the infrastructure.

The type of job you wish to fill will influence whether you consider availability of resources in your locality (junior, low-paid work) or whether it makes sense to broaden your horizons. There could be a problem if you wish to recruit large numbers of low-paid employees locally and they are not available. This would have a direct impact on your strategic plan and might entail relocation to an area where the resources are available. Alternatively, you might consider turning to the global labour market to have computerised work done. Information technology systems have broken down geographical boundaries for work that can be sent across the world. A number of financial services companies in particular are reported to have moved call centre jobs to India, and are expected to increase their offshore facilities (Crabb 2003; Selb 2004; Simms 2004).

Summary

All the factors that affect the labour force are important to employers. Up-to-date information is the key to effective human resource planning, and managers need to be aware of local, regional, national and global trends and be able to integrate this knowledge into their strategic plans. Knowledge of the key issues will enable organisations to assess the threats and opportunities in their environment, and to evaluate their ability to respond with their existing and available resources.

Comparing demand and supply forecasts

A comparison of your expected demand for human resources and your expected supply will identify what you need to accomplish in your human resource plans in order to achieve your corporate goals, or, as already mentioned, there may be an indication that the corporate/business plan needs some adjustment. You can be faced with a number of situations:

- internal supply = demand
- internal supply > demand
- internal supply < demand
- internal plus external supply < demand.

Since there are so many changes affecting organisations, as we have already discussed, and since this is likely to continue for the foreseeable future, internal supply is not likely to equal demand. This is more likely to occur in very stable conditions. If internal supply is greater than demand, human resource plans will need to focus on eliminating the surplus through redeployment or redundancy or through other adjustments to working arrangements. When supply is less than demand, an organisation will be involved in recruitment or other methods of acquiring the necessary skills.

Developing and implementing human resource strategies

In Chapter 1 we described the major personnel management functions as resourcing, development, reward and relations. It is useful to refer to these categories to identify the areas in which it is necessary to develop human resource strategies and action plans.

Resourcing

If demand exceeds supply, the organisation will have to develop plans to acquire the additional skills it needs. This may involve recruitment activities, but there may also be a need for career and succession planning for existing employees, and the organisation may consider subcontracting work. If internal supply exceeds demand the organisation may have to release staff, but consideration should first be given to redeployment and to providing the training that this might entail.

Figure 2.3   **Model of the human resource planning process**

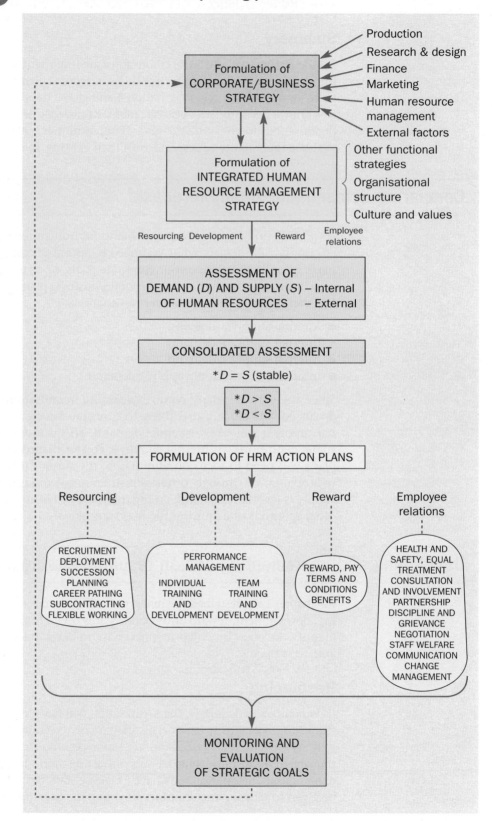

Development

If the skills the organisation needs are not present in its current workforce, it should make plans to develop those skills through training, team and individual development, and performance management.

Reward

A review and restructuring of the reward system might enable an organisation to attract and retain the required complement of human resources. The organisation should examine its pay levels and the attractiveness of its benefits packages and terms and conditions compared with those of competitors. Action plans should also address the issue of linking rewards properly to the achievement of corporate goals.

Employee relations

Improvements in the contribution that employees make to their employing organisation can often be achieved through developing better employee relations. Areas to consider include consultation, communications, employee welfare, employee involvement and the development of a partnership approach.

Conclusion

All of the functional areas mentioned briefly above are discussed in greater depth in the chapters that follow. The major aspects of the strategic human resource planning process are captured in the model presented as Figure 2.3. You should be able to track the elements of this model back to the discussion contained in this chapter.

A final word should be said about the evaluation of the effectiveness of human resource strategies and the planning process. Organisations should develop systems to review and evaluate their performance in all activities and to ensure that there is feedback from this assessment into the corporate/business strategies. The human resource strategy is interpreted into action plans in a variety of functions, as outlined above, and each of these needs to be monitored and evaluated. You can read more about this in the other chapters of this text.

REVIEW QUESTIONS

You will find brief answers to these review questions on pages 487–488.

1 Describe the different levels of strategy found in organisations, and comment on their interconnecting nature.

2 Describe the process of job analysis, and comment on the contribution it can make to an organisation's systems and goals.

3 Outline the major stages of the human resource planning process, and comment on the major considerations at each stage.

4 'Information is crucial as a basis for decision making in the human resource planning process.' Comment on this statement, and describe the sources of information available to management.

SELF-CHECK QUESTIONS

Answer the following multiple-choice and short-answer questions. The correct responses are given on page 488 for you to check your understanding of this chapter.

1 Name the three major generic strategies available at the corporate level.

2 Name the three business level strategies described by Porter.

3 Which of the following is NOT a factor listed in Rodger's seven-point plan?
  (a) intelligence
  (b) job-related competencies
  (c) physical make-up
  (d) circumstances.

4 List the five elements usually included in a job description.

5 Name five uses of job descriptions other than human resource planning.

6 What phrase is used to describe a job analysis exercise when information about potential developments in the job is incorporated into the resulting job profile?

7 A local supermarket employs 50 sales assistants on a part-time basis. Over the past year the personnel department has had to recruit 25 new employees to keep the establishment full. Of the assistants who were hired over a year ago, 40 are still working with the supermarket in the same positions. Calculate the turnover rate.

8 Calculate the stability index for the situation in question 7.

9 What does the stability index indicate?

10 Which stage has been left out of the following brief description of the human resource planning process?
  ● development of corporate strategy
  ● estimation of the demand for human resources
  ● formulation of human resource management plans.

WHAT NEXT?

In this chapter we have looked at how an organisation might go about calculating its own demand for human resources depending on its strategic plans for the future. This *Labour Market Trends* article takes a look at the effects of demand for human resources on a national basis, including the impact on wages, and contrasting situations encountered in

London and the North East. The article is a good starting point to develop a deeper under-standing of the statistics used in analysing the labour force and the possible applications of these statistics:

Williams, R. D. (2004) The demand for labour in the UK, *Labour Market Trends*, August, 321–330

References

Advisory, Conciliation and Arbitration Service (2003) *Teamwork: Success Through People*, ACAS

Anthony, W. P., P. L. Perrewe and K. M. Kacmar (1996) *Strategic Human Resource Management*, 2nd edition, Harcourt Brace

Armitage, B. and M. Scott (1998) British labour force projections: 1998–2011, *Labour Market Trends*, June, 281–291

Boxall, P. and J. Purcell (2003) *Strategy and Human Resource Management*, Palgrave Macmillan

Campling, K. (2004) Why our new bus drivers will have extra Polish, *Huddersfield Daily Examiner*, 11 August, 3

Cottell, C. (2004) Candles light career path for young Asians, *The Guardian (Jobs and Money: Work)*, 18 September, 27

Crabb, S. (2003) East India companies, *People Management*, 20 February, 28–32

Dixon, S. (2003) Implications of population ageing for the labour market, *Labour Market Trends*, February, 67–76

Fraser, J. M. (1978) *Employment Interviewing*, 5th edition, Macdonald and Evans

Glaister, K. (1995) Introduction to the strategic management process, in C. Clarke-Hill and K. Glaister (eds) *Cases in Strategic Management*, 2nd edition, Pitman Publishing

Greer, C. R. (2001) *Strategic Human Resource Management: A General Managerial Approach*, 2nd edition, Prentice Hall

Guest, D., J. Storey and W. Tate (1997) *Innovation: Opportunity through People. Consultative Document*, Institute of Personnel and Development, June

Hackman, J. R. and G. R. Oldham (1980) *Work Redesign*, Addison Wesley

Herriot, P. and C. Pemberton (1997) Facilitating new deals, *Human Resource Management Journal*, Vol. 7, No. 1, 45–56

Hurstfield, J. and R. Pearson (2004) Accessing the talent pool, *Personnel Today*, 7 September, 36–38

Incomes Data Services (1996) *IDS Focus: The Future Workforce*, No. 80, December, IDS

Incomes Data Services (2001) *IDS Study 706: Competency Frameworks*, April, IDS

Incomes Data Services (2004) *IDS HR Studies Update 769*, IDS

Industrial Relations Services (IRS) (2000) Responding to the challenge of skills shortages, *Employee Development Bulletin 130*, October, 4–9

Industrial Relations Services (IRS) (2001) Be prepared: forecasts for recruiters' needs to 2020, *Employee Development Bulletin 139*, July, 5–7

Industrial Relations Service (IRS) (2003a) No end in sight to employers' resourcing problems, *IRS Employment Review 775*, 9 May, 12–14

Industrial Relations Service (IRS) (2003b) Setting the tone: job descriptions and person spec-ifications, *IRS Employment Review 776*, 23 May, 42–48

Industrial Relations Service (IRS) (2003c) US employers face old age question, *IRS Employment Review 782*, 15 August, 16

Industrial Relations Service (IRS) (2004) Great Ormond Street Hospital rises to the challenge, *IRS Employment Review 801*, 4 June, 45–48

Johnson, G. and K. Scholes (2002) *Exploring Corporate Strategy*, 6th edition, Financial Times/Prentice Hall

Lynch, R. (2003) *Corporate Strategy*, 3rd edition, Financial Times/Prentice Hall

Marchington, M. and A. Wilkinson (2002) *People Management and Development – Human Resources Management at Work*, 2nd edition, Chartered Institute of Personnel and Development

Pandya, N. (2004) Are men a hard hat to follow? *The Guardian (Jobs & Money: Work)*, 8 May, 21

Porter, M. E. (1980) *Competitive Strategy*, Free Press

Rodger, A. (1952) *The Seven Point Plan*, National Institute of Industrial Psychology

Rollinson, D. and A. Broadfield (2001) *Organisational Behaviour: An Integrated Approach*, 2nd edition, Financial Times Prentice Hall

Selb, C. (2004) NU sends thousands more jobs to Asia, *The Times*, 23 September, 44

Simms, J. (2004) Home or away? *People Management*, 3 June, 35–39

Steiner, S. (2004) To the spanner born, *The Guardian (Weekend)*, 5 June, 58–59

Torrington, D., L. Hall and S. Taylor (2002) *Human Resource Management*, 5th edition, Prentice Hall

Whiddett, S. and S. Hollyforde (1999) *The Competencies Handbook*, CIPD

www.agepositive.gov.uk; accessed 25.02.03

www.jnj.com; accessed 5.10.04

www.peoplemanagement.co.uk; accessed 02.01.03

Further study

Books

Advisory, Conciliation and Arbitration Service (2004) *Absence and Labour Turnover*, ACAS (available at **www.acas.org.uk**; accessed 20.09.04).

Advisory, Conciliation and Arbitration Service (2004) *Recruitment and Induction*, ACAS (available at **www.acas.org.uk**; accessed 20.09.04).

Bramham, J. (1994) *Human Resource Planning,* 2nd edition, IPD.

Cascio, W. F. (1998) *Applied Psychology in Human Resource Management*, 5th edition, Prentice Hall. (A good introduction to the benefits of, and techniques used for, job analysis and human resource planning is provided in Chapter 9, 'Analyzing jobs and work', and Chapter 10, 'Strategic human resource planning'.)

Incomes Data Services (IDS) (2004) *IDS HR Studies 765: Improving Staff Retention*, IDS. (Looks at various methods of calculating labour turnover, what the implications of the resulting figures might be and ways of improving retention, and provides case studies of six organisations.)

Articles

Cornish, A. (2003) How to form a resourcing strategy, *People Management*, 4 December, 44–45. (One of *People Management's* 'How to …' series: concise overviews of topical issues.)

Hewitt, G. (2003) Come together, *People Management*, 23 October, 36–38. (Addresses the HR role in business strategy.)

Industrial Relations Services (IRS) (2000) Benchmarking labour turnover 2000/01, *Employee Development Bulletin 131*, November, 4–20. (This article provides useful guidance on the reasons for analysing labour turnover, techniques for calculating it, a review of recent trends in various employment sectors and a list of sources of further information.)

Industrial Relations Service (IRS) (2003) A coherent approach to tackling staff turnover, *IRS Employment Review 777*, 6 June, 42–48.

Industrial Relations Service (IRS) (2003) Effective retention strategies, *IRS Employment Review 773*, 4 April, 32–38. (Two reports on retention strategies used by a variety of employers.)

Labour Market Trends (A monthly journal. Contains statistical analyses of various facets of the workforce, and articles and news items about issues of current interest. Essential reading for keeping up to date.)

Pearn, M. and R. Kandola, (1993) *Job Analysis: A Manager's Guide,* 2nd edition, IPD, Chapter 3: 'The ten most useful JTR methods'. (The information in this chapter builds on the simple approaches to job analysis which we have described.)

People Management (Produced for the Chartered Institute of Personnel and Development, this magazine is aimed at keeping HR practitioners informed, and frequently contains articles on HR strategy. A good source of case studies.)

Tyson, S. (ed). (1997) *The Practice of Human Resource Strategy*, Pitman Publishing. (Provides case studies of human resource strategies in action in companies in a number of countries.)

CHAPTER 3

Recruitment

OBJECTIVES

When you have read this chapter you will be able to:

- explain the aims of recruitment and describe how specified policies and procedures contribute to these aims
- understand the role of human resource managers and line managers in the recruitment process
- describe the legislative framework that affects recruitment activities
- describe and design support documentation for the recruitment process – job description, person specification, job advertisement, application form, letters to applicants
- evaluate and draft recruitment policies and procedures.

The processes of recruitment and selection are closely linked. Both activities are directed towards obtaining suitably qualified employees, and recruitment activities lay the groundwork for the selection process by providing the pool of applicants from whom the selectors may choose. However, although the two activities are closely connected, each requires a separate range of skills and expertise, and may in practice be fulfilled by different staff members. The recruitment activity, but not normally the selection decision, may be outsourced to an agency. It makes sense, therefore, to treat each activity separately. This chapter will deal with recruitment actions, policies and procedures which, of course, should be designed to meet the strategic objectives of the organisation.

Recruitment can be defined as:

- all activities directed towards locating potential employees
- attracting applications from suitable candidates.

The aims of recruitment

Organisations do not operate in a vacuum, and recruitment drives are one of the times when an organisation has direct contact with the outside world. Other factors affecting recruitment are the framework imposed by legislation and the fact that no organisation will want to spend money on unnecessary activities. In light of this and the definition of recruitment given above, the aims of recruitment are:

- to obtain a pool of suitable candidates for vacant posts
- to use a fair process and be able to demonstrate that the process was fair
- to ensure that all recruitment activities contribute to organisational goals and a desirable organisational image
- to conduct recruitment activities in an efficient and cost-effective manner.

These statements intimate that a number of judgements have to be made about how recruitment is carried out. What is meant by a 'suitable candidate', and who decides this? Does the organisation have a process for evaluating the need to fill a post? What is a fair recruitment process and in what terms can fairness be evaluated or demonstrated? What recruitment actions can contribute to, or damage, an organisation's image? What are the costs involved in recruitment and how can they be managed to maximise the efficiency of the process? Acting as an umbrella to all of these considerations is also the need to tailor recruitment action to the corporate strategic plan, which itself should have incorporated factors in the environment such as skills shortages, technological advances, etc. Figure 3.1 is a mind map of some of the factors that need to be considered in a systematic recruitment process. (Can you add any more?)

Most human resource management issues can be analysed in terms of legal, moral and business considerations. With reference to the stated aims of recruitment, these considerations could be said to be:

- *legal* – to comply with anti-discrimination legislation
- *moral* – to avoid unfair discrimination for moral reasons as well as legal reasons
- *business* – to ensure that all efforts are directed towards achieving corporate and not personal goals.

To achieve all these aims, and because recruitment is likely to involve a wide range of people within an organisation, it is important to have a systematic approach so that all steps of the recruitment and selection process are conducted in line with:

- the organisation's human resource strategy
- equal opportunities goals.

The first step towards ensuring that the recruitment process achieves these aims in a coordinated manner is to develop and implement appropriate policies and procedures.

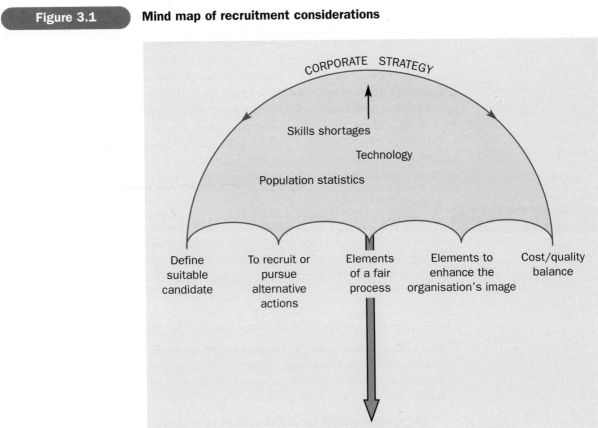

Figure 3.1 **Mind map of recruitment considerations**

Recruitment policies

A policy is simply a statement of intent on the part of an organisation; it outlines the approach everyone is expected to adopt and the standards they should achieve. A recruitment policy enables all employees involved in the process to direct their efforts towards achieving the organisation's goals and to know that they are acting in the spirit intended by the organisation.

A basic recruitment policy should at the very least include statements about the organisation's stance on:

- the overall goal of recruitment
- equal opportunities.

To show that they value their employees, wish to retain them and want to provide them with every opportunity to develop, organisations may also adopt a policy of giving preference to suitably qualified internal applicants over external applicants, and this too would need to be stated explicitly in the organisation's recruitment policy. Such a policy would have implications for the way that recruitment procedures are developed.

One argument that is sometimes raised against internal recruitment policies is that they may lead to entrenching any equal opportunities problems that exist. That is, if the organisation has not previously hired from a particular ethnic group, then it will not improve its record by hiring from within. A counter-argument to this is that if current employees are moved to new positions, presumably they eventually leave a vacancy that must be filled by external candidates. Organisations following good equal opportunities policies would be able to address any problems at this stage.

Organisations that wish to take the human resource management approach to enhancing the contribution and commitment of their employees should certainly consider adopting a policy on internal recruitment.

Pause for thought 3.1

Imagine you are in a company that has decided to formulate a recruitment policy which reflects its commitment to equality of opportunity along with an intention to give preference to internal candidates. Before you read on, consider what might be included in a recruitment policy for this company.

The following is an example of how such a policy might be worded:

> This company aims to employ the person best suited for each post without regard to sex, marital status, racial origin, disability, sexual preference, religion, age or any other factor that cannot reasonably be construed as being related to a person's ability to do the job.
>
> The company values the contribution of its employees and so will seek wherever possible to help employees develop new skills so that they may be considered for promotion opportunities. The company will advertise vacancies externally only if there are no suitably qualified internal candidates for transfers or promotions.

Since equality of opportunity plays such an important role in all recruitment activities, we shall now examine this issue and the relevant legal framework before returning to the discussion of the processes involved in recruitment.

Equal opportunities

Legislation exists in the UK to protect the interests of groups of people who have historically been discriminated against in terms of employment and services. However, in spite of the existence of legislation providing protection against sex and race discrimination for more than a quarter of a century, both types of discrimination are still rife in the UK and, particularly in the case of racial discrimination, continue to make headline news. Sir William Macpherson, investigating the handling of the Stephen Lawrence murder case, found evidence of institutional racism in the police force and in his report of the inquiry in 1999 made 70 recommendations on action to break down institutionalised racism. Naaz Coker (2001) of the King's Fund reported on racism found in the NHS, and racial tensions in the community resulted in violent outbursts in Oldham and Bradford in 2001. These occurrences highlight why it is still essential to actively promote equality, and in fact as a result of the Macpherson inquiry report, new legislation was promulgated to strengthen the Race Relations Act 1976 in the form of the Race Relations (Amendment) Act 2000.

The Acts that provide protection against unfair discrimination, together with just a selection of the major recent amendments, and the areas they cover are summarised in Table 3.1.

Because of historical developments in Northern Ireland, certain statutes apply there that differ from the rest of the UK. These are outlined in a separate section later in this chapter.

The Sex Discrimination Act 1975 and the Race Relations Act 1976

The Sex Discrimination Act (SDA) and the Race Relations Act (RRA) address unfair discrimination in similar ways. Both referred originally to three kinds of discrimination:

- direct discrimination
- indirect discrimination
- victimisation.

Direct discrimination occurs when someone is treated less favourably for a reason directly to do with his or her sex, marital status (i.e. being married), race or racial origin, etc. Examples of this would be to refuse a woman a job as a truck driver simply because she is a woman, and to refuse a Chinese person a job in a school kitchen simply because all the other employees are white European and the employer fears that a person from a different racial background will not 'fit in'.

Table 3.1 **Anti-discriminatory legislation**

Act	Areas covered
Sex Discrimination Act 1975	Sex and marital status (the latter referring specifically to persons who are married)
Sex Discrimination (Gender Reassignment) Regulations 1999	Persons who intend to undertake a sex change, are currently in the process of doing so or have completed treatment
Race Relations Act 1976	Race, colour, nationality, national or ethnic origins
Race Relations (Amendment) Act 2000	The duty of public authorities to take positive action to promote good race relations
Disability Discrimination Act 1995	Disabled persons
Disability Discrimination Act (Amendment) Regulations 2003	Removal of the exemption for employers of fewer than 15 people; shift in the burden of proof
Employment Equality (Sexual Orientation) Regulations 2003	Orientation towards persons of the same sex, of the opposite sex, of both the same sex and the opposite sex
Employment Equality (Religion or Belief) Regulations 2003	Religion or similar belief
Equal Pay Act 1970	Male and female pay for like work, work rated as equivalent, and work of equal value
Rehabilitation of Offenders Act 1974	Persons with spent convictions
Human Rights Act 1998	Prohibition of forced labour and slavery; right to respect for private and family life (*inter alia*)

A European Court ruling in 1996 specified that sex discrimination laws also apply to transsexuals, and this protection has been further strengthened by the Sex Discrimination (Gender Reassignment) Regulations 1999. This means that employees are protected if they suffer less favourable treatment than other employees because they have undergone, are undergoing or intend to undergo a change in gender.

Indirect discrimination occurs when someone is treated unfairly because of some requirement or condition that would disproportionately exclude the particular group that person belongs to, and when the requirement cannot be objectively justified. For example, if you wished to hire someone to clean the windows in your building, and you stipulated that applicants must be six feet tall, could this requirement be justified in terms of the skills and abilities required to do the job? Which groups might such a requirement discriminate against? Fewer women than men, for instance, are six feet tall. This requirement therefore discriminates indirectly against female applicants.

The European Union Directives on equality have brought about some changes in the definition of indirect discrimination, including replacing the phrase 'requirement or condition' with the phrase 'provision, criterion or practice'. As the IRS (2003d) point out, this terminology broadens the sphere of potential indirect discrimination to include informal practices.

ACTIVITY 3.1

Can you think of any other instances of indirect discrimination and identify which groups might be affected by them?

Look through the records of cases heard by employment tribunals and you will find some examples. To find reports of such cases you can use several sources:

● A number of human resource management journals have a section that gives updates on the law and describes recent cases. Look, for instance, in *People Management* and *Personnel Today*.
● You can look in the subject index of the *Legal Journals Index*, for instance under the heading 'sex discrimination'. This will give a brief summary of the major points of the case, and refer to a journal in which you can read more about the case.
● There are also numerous cases reported in the *Equal Opportunities Review* and some issues of the *IRS Employment Review*.

You may wish to compare the instances you find with those found by others in your class.

Victimisation occurs when someone is treated less favourably because that person has made a complaint or indicated an intention to make a complaint about sex or race discrimination. An example of this might be a woman who has complained to the Equal Opportunities Commission about lack of promotion in comparison to similarly qualified men and who is subsequently dismissed unfairly.

The legislation also stipulates that this unfair treatment must be to the disadvantage of the person so treated. In the case of employment

Did you know?

In most cases an employee needs to have completed a one-year qualifying period of employment to take a complaint of unfair dismissal to an employment tribunal. This qualifying period does not apply if the complainant feels that the reasons for the unfair dismissal were connected to any of the types of discrimination covered by legislation. You can read more about this in Chapter 15.

this means that the person is refused employment, promotion or training opportunities or is dismissed.

Harassment

There is no specific definition of harassment in the original sex and race discrimination acts, but harassment has been deemed to constitute discrimination under these Acts through case law. A specific definition of harassment is integrated into the RRA through the EU Race Directive and harassment is also addressed specifically in the sexual orientation and religious belief regulations.

The Disability Discrimination Act 1995

The Disability Discrimination Act 1995 (DDA) updated and replaced previous legislation relating to disabled people. Disability is defined under the Act as 'a mental or physical impairment which has a substantial and long-term adverse effect on a person's ability to carry out normal day-to-day activities. People who have a disability, and people who have had a disability, but no longer have one, are covered by the Act' (Minister for Disabled People 1996).

This definition is very broad and open to interpretation so that, although the Act provides further information on what is to be regarded as a disability, this question was also the focus of some of the early cases that were taken to employment tribunals (IRS 2000). Decisions on whether a person is disabled may hinge, for example, on judgements about the meaning and applicability of the terms 'substantial', 'long-term' and 'normal day-to-day activities'. Questions such as these are addressed as 'frequently asked questions' on the web site of the Disability Rights Commission (**www.drc-gb.org.uk**). There is also mention there of a range of impairments which, depending on the circumstances, may contribute to a person's being deemed disabled: severe disfigurement, sight or hearing impairments, cancer, multiple sclerosis, muscular dystrophy and HIV infection. Some issues have also been clarified by further regulations such as The Disability Discrimination (Blind and Partially Sighted Persons) Regulations 2003 which confirmed that 'people who are certified as blind or partially sighted are deemed as disabled for the purposes of the Disability Discrimination Act 1995' (**www.cipd.co.uk/subjects/emplaw/general/legal2003.htm**).

In relation to employment, job applicants should not be discriminated against because of a disability or be treated in a less favourable way than other applicants unless 'the treatment in question is justified'. However, the DDA, as subsequently amended, also makes it clear that employers of 15 or more people (subject to further amendment) must 'make reasonable adjustments in any arrangements or to work premises' in order that disabled employees should not be disadvantaged. This may include a review of work allocation, consideration of flexible hours to accommodate the needs of a disabled person, or modifying equipment. The requirement to make reasonable adjustments in the DDA is the equivalent of dealing with indirect discrimination in the other

> **Did you know?**
>
> A survey commissioned by the Disability Rights Commission in 2001 uncovered extensive lack of knowledge about disability and the law. Only 46% of the people surveyed knew about the DDA, and there was widespread ignorance about the definition of disability.
>
> (*Equal Opportunities Review*, No. 97, May/June 2001, p. 7)

pieces of equality legislation. Employers are compelled at least to consider these matters seriously and be prepared to justify their decisions with regard to their reasonableness. Anyone who feels that they have suffered discrimination because of a disability has the right to take their case to an employment tribunal.

The DDA not only applies to employment, but also affects any organisation which provides a service to the public. Under the Act, such an organisation must make reasonable adjustments to their premises or to the way in which they provide services in order to accommodate the needs of disabled people.

The DDA was criticised for its restriction to organisations which employ 15 or more employees and this provision was removed with effect from October 2004.

Employment Equality (Sexual Orientation) Regulations 2003

These regulations state that persons should not be treated unfavourably because of their sexual orientation, i.e. orientation towards persons of the same sex, of the opposite sex, of both the same sex and the opposite sex. Note that the legislation addresses sexual orientation and not sexual practices, where existing law continues to apply. Sexual orientation refers to gay and lesbian preferences, heterosexuality and bisexuality. Issues such as consensual versus non-consensual sex, paedophilia, etc. are not covered by the equality regulations. The regulations apply to recruitment and selection and to treatment in the workplace, such as opportunities for training and promotion.

Did you know?

The RAF's first recruitment drive to be specifically targeted at gays and lesbians was widely reported in the news media in August 2004 when the RAF recruited at a gay pride festival.

As with the SDA and the RRA, employers need to guard against direct and indirect discrimination, harassment and victimisation. Harassment is defined as unwanted conduct that intimidates or humiliates an individual, affecting their dignity or creating a hostile work environment. The behaviour in question can be verbal or physical, and it is important to note that the target individual's perception of the effect of the conduct can contribute to the behaviour being deemed to be harassment. Remarks about a person's family members or friends with regard to their sexual orientation can also constitute harassment.

It may be possible to identify a genuine occupational requirement (GOR) for some posts, in which case a particular sexual orientation may be specified during recruitment. For instance, an organisation that offers support and advice on relationships to bisexual persons may wish to recruit bisexual counsellors who may be more able to empathise with their clients. Employers must carefully evaluate whether a position merits a GOR. If anyone interested in such a post feels that they have been unfairly excluded on this basis, they can challenge the GOR at an employment tribunal, which is the ultimate arbiter of the acceptability of GORs.

Employment Equality (Religion or Belief) Regulations 2003

The Employment Equality (Religion or Belief) Regulations 2003 outlaw discrimination based on religion or similar philosophical beliefs. Whether a set of beliefs is recognised under these regulations will be for employment tribunals to decide. For example, humanism would be recognised as a set of beliefs similar to a religion, but political beliefs normally would not be covered. The regulations work in a similar way to the sexual orientation regulations in terms of types of discrimination (direct, etc.) and the possibility of a GOR for certain positions. There may, however, be some complex cases of interpretation between these two sets of regulations as it may be permissible to discriminate against persons of a particular sexual orientation if this is necessary to 'avoid conflicting with a significant number of followers' strongly held religious convictions' (Acas 2004b, p.29).

Many commentators agree that the key challenge to employers in dealing with religious discrimination will probably be in the area of harassment (ACAS 2004a; Higginbottom 2003). It will be necessary to make it clear to all employees that so-called banter can be regarded as offensive by individuals and should be avoided. Communications with employees and the creation of a culture of tolerance and acceptance of diversity will become even more important.

Genuine occupational qualifications/requirements

In exceptional circumstances there may be a requirement for an employee to be of a particular sex, racial background, religion or sexual orientation. These are known as genuine occupational qualifications (GOQs) or genuine occupational requirements (GORs). GOQ is still the term used with reference to the SDA; the 2003 regulations refer to GORs; the RRA refers to GOQ with reference to colour and nationality and to GOR with regard to race and ethnic or national origins. The adoption of the GOR terminology coincides with the amendments to legislation that have occurred since 2003 to bring UK legislation into line with the relevant EU Directives. Since the race Directive refers only to race and ethnic or national origins, and not specifically to colour or nationality, this accounts for the difference in the terminology used in the UK in different instances of racial discrimination.

Such requirements and qualifications are acceptable in instances where authenticity is required, say in entertainment, modelling (for instance male or female fashion clothes) or serving food in ethnic restaurants to create a specific ambience, and where privacy and decency in the provision of personal services are concerned. An example of a genuine occupational qualification would be to advertise for a female care attendant to provide personal services to a female stroke victim.

Note that the word 'genuine' is used. It is a term that is meant to be narrowly defined and not regarded as a loophole to avoid compliance with the legislation. Employers could be challenged by a person who thought she or he had been unfairly excluded from selection because of a GOR or GOQ, and it would be up to an employment tribunal to decide whether or not the GOR/GOQ was justified.

Employers are not the only participants in the recruitment process who are bound by the terms of the equality legislation. Publishers of advertisements also have a duty to ensure there is no unlawful discrimination in the advertisements they print. If a person of a particular sex, member of a particular racial group or person with a particular sexual orientation or religion is required, the publisher must also ensure that a reference to the relevant section of the legislation is included. For example, an advertisement for a female project leader to provide personal support to young homeless women might carry the statement 'section 7(2)(E) of the Sex Discrimination Act applies'.

Note that the presence of a GOR means not only that persons from the specified group are being invited to apply, but also that such a person will be selected. This is often confused by less informed job-seekers with encouragement for members of under-represented groups to apply for vacancies so they can be considered along with all other qualified applicants in the selection process. You can read more about the recruitment of under-represented groups later in this chapter, under the heading 'Targeted recruitment'.

The equality commissions

The Sex Discrimination Act 1975 established the Equal Opportunities Commission (EOC) and the Race Relations Act 1976 established the Commission for Racial Equality (CRE) to promote and monitor equality of opportunity. As part of that duty, the EOC produced a code of practice in 1985 and the CRE produced a code of practice in 1984.

The codes provide guidelines to employers and employees on the meaning of the relevant legislation, on practical measures that can be taken to eliminate discrimination and on techniques that can be used to promote equality of opportunity. These guidelines refer to all phases of employment, including the recruitment and selection stages. The commissions also give advice to employers as well as dealing with complaints from those who feel they have encountered discrimination. The commissions may decide to take a complaint to an employment tribunal.

The EOC and CRE can also issue a non-discrimination notice against employers if they investigate a complaint and find that there is evidence of discrimination in an employer's actions, whether intentional or unintentional. A non-discrimination notice may oblige an employer to inform the EOC and CRE about changes it has initiated to bring its employment practices more in line with the codes of practice.

As with the SDA and the RRA, a commission was set up to promote the implementation of the provisions of the Disability Discrimination Act, albeit after some delay. The Disability Rights Commission (DRC) commenced its work in April 2000, and a number of articles reviewed its progress after one year in operation (IRS 2001b; Massie 2001). Bert Massie, the chair of the DRC, reported on the work of the Commission in setting up operations in London, Manchester, Cardiff and Edinburgh, establishing a service offering policy advice to commerce and government, the development of 'a range of new services, including an independent conciliation service' launched in March 2001, and the provision of direct assistance to disabled enquirers.

Did you know?

The Disability Rights Commission's helpline dealt with more than 60,000 calls in its first year of operation.
(IRS 2001b, p. 6)

Like the EOC and the CRE, the DRC provides assistance to legitimate claimants in taking their case to an employment tribunal, and is engaged in producing various codes of practice which address a number of aspects of the DDA.

During the 1990s there was some discussion about rationalising the work of the various equality commissions, but this debate became more focused in the early years of the twenty-first century with the advent of increasing amounts of equality regulations. The Commission for Equality and Human Rights (CEHR) was founded by the Department of Trade and Industry in 2004 with a mandate to consolidate the work of the three existing commissions and establish a unified body to deal with all aspects of equality, but the new commission is not expected to be fully operational until 2006: **(www.womenandequalityunit.gov.uk).**

The proponents of the other commissions expressed some doubts about whether their constituents would be best served by a unified commission, with claims that their designated groups had needs which differed from those of the other groups and which might not be addressed adequately by a non-specialist organisation. In particular, the DRC and the CRE were reported to have reservations about the development of a single commission to deal with all aspects of discrimination.

Good practice in equal opportunities

Essentially, to operate within the spirit of the equality legislation, all actions and documents involved in the recruitment process must be free of any criteria that could be interpreted as being discriminatory within the terms of the legislation. As ACAS (2004a and 2004b) points out, the existence of an up-to-date equality policy signals an organisation's intention to follow good practice with regard to all discrimination issues covered by the law. A good policy establishes a framework that enables current employees to know how they are expected to behave with regard to these issues and that they themselves will be treated fairly. Prospective employees may also be attracted to an organisation that demonstrates its intentions to treat employees fairly. It must be noted, however, that the mere existence of an equality policy is not enough to signify that an employer is serious about equal opportunities. Communication of the policy and training of line managers in implementing it are crucial.

Advertisements, job descriptions and person specifications must not include anything that could be construed as an intention to discriminate on an unlawful basis. Except in the case of a GOQ or GOR as described earlier, advertisements should not include words that might indicate a preference for hiring females rather than males, or vice versa. For example, it is not lawful for a restaurant to advertise for waitresses as this would imply that men could not apply for these posts. This would be direct discrimination on the basis of sex. The same stricture applies to the other groups protected or about to be protected by legislation.

Did you know?

It is interesting to note that it is generally regarded as unacceptable to request an applicant to attach a photograph to a job application in the UK, whereas this is still common practice in France and Germany. Such a requirement would conflict with the spirit of the UK legislation, as a photograph can only provide information about sex and racial background and not about skills and knowledge. The use of such input can be seen as unfair discrimination.

The existence of a good person specification can help an employer to avoid inadvertent sex, race or other unlawful discrimination. The design and use of person specifications was discussed more fully in Chapter 2 and will be addressed again with specific reference to recruitment in the section on procedures. Direct discrimination is rarely overtly expressed ('We really don't think a woman can do this job'). The intention to discriminate can be inferred from various events, and introducing new criteria after the person specification has been agreed is one such event. If a post involves a GOR or GOQ, this should be decided before the post is advertised and made clear to everyone through the person specification and the job advertisement.

Positive action is allowed under the discrimination legislation in terms of providing assistance to underprivileged groups to enable them to compete on a more level playing field. This might involve assistance with the completion of application forms or the provision of training for specified groups. Final hiring decisions must, however, be made on the basis of each individual's ability to do the job.

Organisations that wish to promote equality of opportunity can also introduce complaints procedures, so that applicants who feel they may have been discriminated against can appeal in the first instance to the organisation concerned. This would normally mean that at least one staff member would be designated as responsible for the promotion of equal opportunities, so that applicants felt they were approaching a disinterested person.

As indicated in Table 3.1, the Race Relations (Amendment) Act 2000 also strengthens the RRA by imposing a duty on public authorities to actively promote improvements in race relations. Some local authorities have done this by forging relationships with community groups to examine what their problems and requirements are. Monitoring of job applications to check on racial equality is compulsory under this amendment, but not under the other equality statutes. It is, however, regarded as good practice and will be revisited later in this chapter when we review recruitment procedures.

Burden of proof in discrimination cases

From 2001, a number of regulatory amendments introduced a shift in the burden of proof into the equality legislation, meaning that the burden of proof is shared between the complainant and the respondent employer. Once a tribunal is satisfied that an applicant has provided prima facie evidence of discrimination (that is, it considers that on the balance of probabilities, discrimination may have occurred), it is then up to the employer to provide positive evidence that it did not discriminate, and that its decision was based on factors that had nothing to do with the sex, race, etc. of the applicant. Such evidence could include copies of the documentation used throughout the recruitment and selection processes, including equality policies, non-discriminatory job descriptions and person specifications, and evidence that only non-discriminatory questions were used during interviews. Further evidence to support an employer's claim to have acted in a non-discriminatory fashion might include notes made during interviews, the results of non-biased tests, analysis of data collected for monitoring purposes, evidence of how the position was advertised and a description of equality training that is provided to managers and others involved in the selection process.

As the European Commission (2003) points out, it is the managers making decisions who have the full information behind why a particular decision was made and who are therefore best placed to demonstrate that it was made on a non-discriminatory basis.

Updating the equality legislation

As with the issue of GORs and GOQs, the shift in the burden of proof with regard to the RRA refers to cases involving race and ethnic or national origins, and not to those emanating from perceived discrimination based on colour or nationality (IRS 2003d). This seeming anomaly has arisen because the amendment was made specifically to integrate elements of the EU race directive into UK law. The government has maintained the general approach of the EU directives in the 2003 regulations and intends to do the same with the imminent age legislation (IRS 2003c). It will no doubt take some time for legislative review to iron out any inconsistencies within the various equality laws. For practical purposes, however, it is not sensible to believe that any form of discrimination would be acceptable in any case, and followers of good practice in general should not need to worry about these subtle differences.

Equal Pay Act 1970

Most problems related to issues covered by the Equal Pay Act and its subsequent amendments tend to arise once people are in employment and can compare their pay with that of other employees in the same organisation. The Act provides for members of one sex to claim equal pay with a member of the opposite sex who is doing like work, or work of a different nature which can be shown to be similar in terms of the requirements for skill and effort, i.e. work of equal value. The Equal Pay Act is dealt with in more detail in Chapter 10, which examines payment systems and the evaluation of jobs. The major point here is that it would be unlawful to advertise different pay rates for men and women doing the same work, or to offer employees of one sex disadvantageous terms and conditions.

Rehabilitation of Offenders Act 1974

The Rehabilitation of Offenders Act 1974 stipulates a range of time periods after which convictions for various offences are regarded as being spent. This means that a past offender should not be expected to reveal his or her offence once the conviction is spent, and should not be denied employment because of this previous offence. An offence that attracts a sentence of life imprisonment or a sentence of more than 30 months' imprisonment is never spent. The time periods over which convictions do become spent vary, and include 7 years for imprisonment for less than 6 months, 10 years for a prison sentence of 6 to 30 months, 1 year for a probation order (longer if the order covers a longer period) and the period of a disqualification for a driving offence. A number of exceptions to these rules about spent convictions apply to people who in the course of their jobs have unsupervised access to minors or other groups of vulnerable people, meaning that for this category of employee certain convictions can never be regarded as spent. Issues relating to employer access to criminal records will be explored more fully in Chapter 5.

> ### Did you know?
>
> The crime reduction charity Nacro, which is dedicated in part to the rehabilitation of ex-offenders, worked together with KPMG, the management consultancy firm, on a campaign to promote better understanding and attitudes amongst employers to ex-offenders. In July 2001, the unemployment rate for ex-offenders was 60%.
> (*Guardian Society*, 4 July 2001, p. 12)

The Human Rights Act 1998

The Human Rights Act 1998 (HRA) implements the provisions of the European Convention on Human Rights, and came into force in October 2000. The Act has direct effect on public authorities (which are deemed to include employment tribunals), so employees of those organisations have direct recourse to the courts if they feel their rights have been infringed under the HRA. However, the courts are also bound to interpret other national law with reference to the meaning of the HRA, so in that way, all employers in the UK are affected by the HRA.

Some of the rights guaranteed under the HRA are covered well by existing legislation in the UK, such as the right to freedom from discrimination based on sex or race.

Age discrimination

In 2000, the Council of Ministers of the European Union adopted the Employment Directive based on Article 13 of the Treaty of Amsterdam. This imposed on member states a duty to create legislation protecting people against discrimination based on disability, religious belief, age and sexual orientation with the objective of promoting similar levels of equality across the European Union by the end of 2006. The one remaining area of new legislation from this directive in the UK relates to age, and the relevant legislation will be introduced by October 2006.

Age discrimination has been a subject of discussion for many years in the UK, but even without legislation, there is a good business case for avoiding it. The CIPD confirms its commitment to the elimination of age discrimination 'because it is wasteful of talent and harmful to both individuals and organisations. The use of age, age bands and age-related criteria reduces objectivity in employment decision-making and increases the likelihood of inappropriate decisions' (CIPD 2003a).

Pause for thought 3.2

Setting age limits such as 17–28 or a maximum age of 35 for applicants could prove to constitute indirect sex discrimination against women. Why is this so?

Setting upper age limits for applicants can be indirect sex discrimination, as women are more likely to take a career break for reasons of maternity in their twenties and early thirties and are therefore likely to progress through their careers at a different rate. This means that women of this age are less able to apply for more senior posts than men of this age.

It should also be noted that companies such as B&Q have had success through deliberately hiring older workers and benefiting from their particular expertise.

ACTIVITY 3.2

Mrs Meninder Patel applied for a post as a careers adviser with a local authority. The advertisement and person specification for the post had listed three years' experience in careers advice as one of the criteria being sought, and Mrs Patel had worked as a careers adviser in local schools for four years. The careers service received a number of good applications and the selection panel had difficulty in shortlisting a small number of applicants to call for interview. After some deliberation they decided that they would interview those candidates who had experience dealing with adults, because the careers service was going to expand into this area and the panel decided that this specific experience would be valuable. Mrs Patel was not one of the applicants called to interview. She felt that she was well qualified for the post according to the advertisement and the job description and person specification that had been sent to her. Mrs Patel felt that she must have been discriminated against unfairly and decided to pursue the matter.

Comment on the equal opportunities implications of this case. Why might Mrs Patel feel that she has been the victim of unlawful discrimination? What should the local authority do?

Discussion of Activity 3.2

In times of high unemployment it is common to find large numbers of people applying for vacancies. It is difficult to achieve the correct balance between a tight person specification and one that excludes people unnecessarily. However, introducing criteria after applications have been submitted could be seen as an attempt to exclude people for covert reasons, for example to exclude women or certain racial groups. Depending on who was ultimately hired for this post, Mrs Patel could believe that she had been discriminated against because of her sex, marital status or ethnic origin.

Let us assume that there was no discriminatory intent on the part of the selection panel and that they were merely seeking a device to enable them to carry out the shortlisting exercise. The case points out the importance of developing a good person specification in the first place, and the equal opportunities implications that this can have.

The local authority should ensure that there is an adequate internal mechanism for dealing with Mrs Patel's query. The fact that an employer tries to address any problems of this nature in a sincere fashion would be recognised by the equality commissions as part of good equal opportunities practice.

The employer should also ensure that training is provided to all employees involved in recruitment and selection to ensure that they understand the importance of each element of the process.

Fair employment in Northern Ireland

Although regulations relating to discrimination on the basis of religion or belief were only introduced to the rest of the UK in 2003, legislation banning religious discrimination in the workplace has existed in Northern Ireland since 1976. The special issue of sectarian discrimination between Protestants and Roman Catholics was originally addressed in the Fair Employment (Northern Ireland) Act 1976, updated in an Act of the same name in 1989 and updated again in 1998 by the Fair Employment and Treatment (Northern Ireland) Order 1998. These Acts also address political beliefs.

Like the rest of the UK, Northern Ireland is expected to comply with the European Union Race and Equality Directives. The province has similar structures in general to deal with a range of discriminatory issues similar to those dealt with in the rest of the UK, but with different agencies and nomenclature. For instance, there was a Fair Employment Commission set up to deal with complaints under the relevant legislation named above, but this has now been replaced by an Equality Commission which also deals with complaints lodged under race, sex and disability discrimination legislation. It is notable that race discrimination legislation was only introduced into Northern Ireland in 1997. The Labour Relations Agency in Northern Ireland undertakes functions similar to those of ACAS.

Unlike in the rest of the UK, monitoring of the composition of the workforce and of job applicants with regard to religious belief is compulsory in Northern Ireland. Employers are required to review a wide range of their practices with regard to fair employment opportunity, including recruitment and selection, provision of training, promotion, and redundancy (**www.cfrlawonline.com**). A further example of the difference in approach engendered by the circumstances in Northern Ireland is provided in a *People Management* article (Johnson 2003) about the Police Service of Northern Ireland (PSNI, formerly the Royal Ulster Constabulary or RUC). In order to redress the imbalance of Catholic and Protestant police officers in the force, the responsible authorities had to apply a quota system during recruitment, for which they needed special dispensation from the European Union. They called this 50–50 recruitment (Johnson 2003, p. 32), which meant that from every pool of qualified applicants, an equal number of Protestants and Catholics would be selected. The need for such drastic measures is perhaps understandable when one considers that 92% of the staff in the RUC were Protestant (Johnson 2003, p. 31). It must be remembered, however, that this recruitment action is an exceptional case and the pursuit of quotas is not a normal aspect of the fair employment initiatives in Northern Ireland.

On its website (**www.equalityni.org**), the Equality Commission for Northern Ireland lists 'the main pieces of equality legislation in Northern Ireland' as follows:

- Equal Pay Act (Northern Ireland) 1970 (as amended)
- Sex Discrimination (Northern Ireland) Order 1976 (as amended)
- Race Relations (Northern Ireland) Order 1997 (as amended)
- Fair Employment and Treatment (Northern Ireland) Order 1998 (as amended)
- Disability Discrimination Act 1995
- Equality (Disability, etc.) (Northern Ireland) Order 2000
- Employment Equality (Sexual Orientation) Regulations (Northern Ireland) 2003
- Northern Ireland Act 1998

Managing diversity in the workplace

Some organisations go much further than mere compliance with legislation as they are keen to promote the concept of diversity in the workplace. According to the CIPD, managing diversity means 'that people should be valued as individuals for reasons relating to business interests, as well as for moral and social reasons. It recognises that people can bring fresh ideas and perceptions which can make the way work is done more efficient and products and services better' (Institute of Personnel and Development (IPD) 1997).

Pause for thought 3.3

In what ways is managing diversity different to the legislative approach to equal opportunities? How would this approach manifest itself within an organisation?

Discussion of Pause for thought 3.3

There are some quite fundamental differences in this approach. Firstly, all ferences are recognised, not just the differences identified in legislation such as race, sex or disability, etc. These include differences such as academic or vocational qualifications, social background, accent and political views. There is also another fundamental difference in approach in that the differences are perceived as positive; there is recognition that everyone is different and as each person is unique they also bring a unique range of talents to the organisation, from which the organisation will benefit. The organisation, therefore, needs to develop a culture that is supportive of individual differences so that creativity and innovation will flourish. Workplace policies and procedures also need to be continuously reviewed to ensure that they are not inadvertently providing barriers to opportunities.

In order for diversity management to work there must be involvement from a wide range of people, from the chief executive and the board through to the human resource manager and the line managers. According to the CIPD, 'Managing diversity needs to become a mainstream issue which influences all employment policies and working practices' (IPD 1997).

Recruitment procedures

The description of recruitment procedures has been preceded by the discussion of equal opportunities issues because these issues should guide your actions at every stage of the recruitment process.

The first step in the recruitment process is to decide that you have a vacancy you wish to fill. The vacancy may be a new post that has been identified through the corporate strategic plan, or it may have arisen because an employee has resigned, retired or been dismissed. The latter are sometimes referred to as replacement posts to distinguish them from new posts. You may also decide to recruit a job-share partner for an established employee who no longer wishes to work full time.

The planning process that precedes the creation of new posts was described in Chapter 2. A planning process should also precede recruitment for replacement posts; they should not be filled automatically. When a jobholder leaves, HR and line managers should take the opportunity to examine the work done and consider whether it can be covered in another fashion. Here are some of the factors that could be considered:

- Are all the tasks necessary?
- Can some tasks be incorporated into another post?
- Should the job be redesigned to include more interesting and challenging work?
- Can some tasks be completed in other ways, e.g. by machine, by computer?
- Can the work be done on a part-time, flexi-time or job-share basis?
- Is there a permanent need for the output of the post or should it be filled on a temporary basis or even contracted out?

Recruitment procedures include:

- preparation of all supporting documents such as job descriptions and person specifications or competency profiles
- guidelines on actions to be taken such as writing and placing advertisements, and administrative procedures related to contacting prospective candidates.

Job descriptions and person specifications/competency profiles

In organisations that engage in human resource planning there will be ongoing work dedicated to producing and maintaining job descriptions and person specifications/competency profiles, since these documents contain much of the information required for the planning process. The process of job analysis which is followed to produce these documents was therefore described in Chapter 2. However, even in organisations that do not engage fully in human resource planning, it is essential to produce job descriptions and person specifications/competency profiles for all existing posts as a basic framework for recruitment activities. These documents contain the information around which the job advertisement and the assessment of candidates will be structured. If you have not read the section on job analysis in Chapter 2, you should read it now.

The job description in the recruitment context

We have seen already (page 42) that the four basic elements of the job description are: the job title; the reporting structure, i.e. the job title of the person to whom the postholder reports and the number and categories of the people the postholder is responsible for; a statement of the purpose of the post; and a description of the major duties. Taken together, they should provide a job applicant with a good idea of what the job entails.

The job title, such as sales assistant, warehouse supervisor, marketing department manager or nurse, already contains a lot of information about the position. In choosing a job title you should be careful not to inflate the level of the job, for instance by the inappropriate use of words such as executive or director, and you should avoid any potentially biased language such as waitress and foreman.

The information given in the sections on reporting structure enables applicants to see where the job fits into the organisation's structure and whether the post has any supervisory responsibilities. If there are particularly pertinent details about terms and conditions, such as shift work or a requirement to work on Sundays, they should also be included since this will enable candidates to judge whether they are willing to take on such responsibilities.

The person specification/competency profile in the recruitment context

The very fact that an employer draws up a person specification/competency profile demonstrates an attempt to introduce some objectivity into what can otherwise be a very subjective process. Rather than relying on instinctive personal judgements about the knowledge, skills and qualities the successful candidate should possess, the employer with a person specification/profile is following a much more methodical and reasoned process. It is also a much more open process, since the specification is a written record of what the employer is basing his or her selection decision on. These written records can be requested by employment tribunals should anyone complain of unfair treatment, but many employers now share this information openly with applicants for posts, so applicants also know in detail what the employer is looking for in a candidate.

Care should therefore be taken that no one is unfairly excluded from being considered for a position because the requirements were set unnecessarily high. This could constitute indirect discrimination, as certain disadvantaged groups may have more difficulty in acquiring some qualifications or competency levels. Care should also be taken that none of the criteria set are directly unlawfully discriminatory.

The information about skills, knowledge and personal qualities should be summarised and included in advertisements for the post.

As mentioned above, the person specification/competency profile can be included with the information sent to candidates to give them more details about requirements. It is an excellent practice to design and send to candidates a form showing each requirement and how it will be assessed, for example from information included on the application form, at the interview or from references. Table 3.2 shows an example of this, based on the person specification for a receptionist which is given in Chapter 2 (Table 2.1).

Job advertisements

Once you know you have a vacancy to fill, you must decide what is the best way to let people know about it. The following are some methods of advertising the existence of vacancies:

- on-site noticeboards
- local/national newspapers

Table 3.2   **Assessment of person specification criteria**

Post: Receptionist

Attributes	Criteria	How assessed
Knowledge	Knowledge of clerical systems	Application form Interview Work sample test
	Knowledge of the company	Interview
Skills	Experience of clerical work	Application form Interview Work sample test
	Experience of handling queries in person and on the telephone	Application form Interview
	Ability to extract information from a computerised database	Application form Interview
	Supervisory experience	Application form Interview
Personal qualities	Polite manner	Interview
	Ability to work under pressure	Interview

- professional journals
- minority group newspapers and magazines
- recruitment agencies
- university/college/school careers centres
- job centres
- radio/television (including text pages)/cinema
- Internet sites
- set up a stall at a recruitment fair or exhibition.

Deciding where to place an advertisement

You will need to assess the available advertising methods in terms of their appropriateness for a particular vacancy. Considerations will include: the likelihood of finding people with particular skills in a particular geographical location; the type of qualifications you are seeking and which publications people with those qualifications are likely to read; salary level and whether you are likely to be able to attract someone to move to your area for the salary you are offering. Obviously some judgement is required to make these decisions, but one should always be wary of making assumptions about what people will do given their personal circumstances, and one should strive to keep recruitment open and fair. It may be unfair, for example, to restrict applications to your geographical area as there may be good candidates who would be willing to move to your area for the sake of the job. That should remain the personal decision of the prospective candidate.

> **Did you know?**
>
> Suffering from a shortage of school teachers, the Department for Education and Employment (as it was then called) launched a series of advertisements in cinemas and on television in the late 1990s. Designed to catch the attention of young people making career direction decisions, the advertisement used sound-bites from well-known personalities (e.g. Tony Blair, Stephen Hawking, Joanna Lumley) naming teachers who had had a positive influence on them, and ending with the catchphrase: 'No one forgets a good teacher.'
>
> As the teacher recruitment and retention difficulties persisted into the twenty-first century, the Government followed up the earlier campaign with one focusing on the slogan 'Those who can, teach' and then 'Use your head: teach!'.

The costs of advertising are also a factor. You may be more willing to spend a large portion of your advertising budget on a senior post than on a junior one. However, you may have a relatively junior post that requires skills not readily available in your locality, or you may have a large number of low-paid posts and the need to fill these posts may call for the willingness to spend more on advertising.

Word-of-mouth advertising is often listed in textbooks as a possible method of recruitment, and it is used to varying extents in some organisations. It is mentioned here for clarification but excluded from the recommended list because of its potentially discriminatory effects. Organisations that recruit heavily by word of mouth run the risk of perpetuating the gender and ethnic make-up of their workforce. In general, employees tend to recommend people like themselves from among their family and friends. For example, in general, if an organisation's workforce were all white Europeans, word-of-mouth recruitment would tend to bring in more white Europeans. A commitment to equality of opportunity means that this cycle has to be broken, and one way of doing this is to advertise in the ethnic press.

> **Did you know?**
>
> Some of the companies quoted as using on-line recruitment successfully include Woolworth's, B&Q, PricewaterhouseCoopers, GlaxoSmithKline and British Gas.
> (Smethurst 2004)

As the twenty-first century progresses, the use of the Internet to advertise posts and deal with recruitment processes is becoming ever more well-established (IRS 2001a and 2001c). Vacancies for a wide range of posts are listed by some organisations on their own web site, in other cases by recruitment agencies and on the jobs pages of newspapers and journals. The CIPD (2003b) reported, however, that companies appeared to be decreasing their usage of job board sites (down to 14.7% in 2003 from 28.9% in 2002) in favour of their own company web sites (up to 71.5% in 2003 from 51.7% in 2002).

The numbers of job-seekers on-line reportedly continues to grow apace. Between 2000 and 2001, the numbers grew from 4 million to 5.4 million. Both Tulip (2003) and Smethurst (2004) report some 11 million on-line job-seekers in the UK in 2003/04. Tulip (2003), however, reports that some employers may not be using systems to their full capability, and that they need to become more involved in on-line assessment to deal with the volume of applications in order to benefit fully from the expected advantages of on-line recruitment, such as minimising the time from receipt of application to hiring decision. Corporate sites in particular are reportedly not making full use of the technical capabilities of systems such as acceptance of applications on-line and initial sifting of applications. This is obviously an area of flux and change, so it will be interesting to observe how the use of on-line recruitment develops in the future. Human resource managers need to be aware of these issues and developments to maximise the effectiveness of their recruitment process.

ACTIVITY 3.3

One advantage of using a web site for recruitment purposes is that organisations can provide easy access to a lot of information for prospective candidates. You can easily find some current job advertisements that include an Internet address. Visit a selection of these web sites to see for yourself how employers are using the World Wide Web for recruitment.

Designing recruitment advertisements

First consider what the objectives of a job advertisement are, and what techniques might be used to achieve those objectives. The overall aim of the advertisement is to secure sufficient applications from suitably qualified persons with the end result that the employer will find 'the best person for the job'. Note that advertisers wish to obtain a reasonable number of applications, and not an overwhelming number. The first principle of writing job advertisements is therefore to *give sufficient information about the post so that suitable candidates will apply* but also so that *unsuitable candidates will be discouraged from applying.*

What will attract good applicants to a post? Consider these factors and also consider how they should be incorporated into an advertisement to achieve maximum impact. For example, is salary a major selling point for your organisation? Should salary figures be included or excluded? Should they be displayed at the top of the advertisement, in the body of the text or at the end? A job advertisement is an opportunity to tell people what you can offer as well as what you require. The following are some suggestions of the kind of factors you may wish to include in a job advertisement:

- organisation name and information
- job title and major duties
- qualifications, skills and experience required
- opportunities and challenges
- salary and benefits
- statement of policy on important issues such as equal opportunities and smoking in the workplace
- how to apply.

Organisation name and information

Obviously people need to know which organisation they are applying to. Information about the organisation's prospects and what it can offer as an employer can be a selling point.

Pause for thought 3.4 Where will you find a record of the information you should include relating to the job title, duties, skills and experience?

Job title and major duties

The job title should be the one used in the job description, and the main duties should be summarised for the advertisement.

Qualifications, skills and experience required

The person specification/competency profile will provide a good basis for summarising the qualifications, skills and experience you are looking for.

Opportunities and challenges

The tasks in a job can be described as requirements, but it is much more appealing to most people if you emphasise the opportunities a job will offer them to use their skills and feel a sense of achievement, and the challenges that will provide them with a chance to develop.

Salary and benefits

Every organisation will have records of the salary ranges and benefits that are attached to each job. An organisation might have a particularly attractive range of benefits that could be the deciding factor for someone deliberating on whether or not to apply for a position. You can read more about salaries and benefits in Chapter 10.

How to apply

A range of possibilities exist, and the most appropriate will depend on the particular post being filled, the volume of applications expected or desired, and the systems and capabilities of the department receiving the applications. You may request interested applicants to do any of the following:

- call in person
- attend an open day interview event

- phone/leave a message on a 24-hour answer machine
- write a letter applying for the post
- contact a particular person
- request and return an application form
- request further information
- send a curriculum vitae (CV) and covering letter
- send a CV or acquire and return an application form by computer
- apply by a certain date.

Information packages

Information packages are usually prepared for more senior posts, and contain brochures and other documents that give a range of information about the post, the organisation and possibly the attractions of moving to the geographical location in which the organisation is situated.

ACTIVITY 3.4

1 Draft a letter to accompany a requested application form.

2 Design a recruitment package for a real or imaginary organisation of your choice.

Discussion of Activity 3.4

You will find a model letter in Appendix 3.1 to compare with your draft. Designing a recruitment package is a major undertaking. You may wish to work with a group of fellow students to pool your resources. You could choose a currently advertised vacancy to base your recruitment package on, and use the resources of your library or visit the Internet to find out more about the organisation.

Style of writing

The style of writing that is appropriate for a job advertisement depends on the nature of the position. Traditionally, advertisements were written in a very formal style, using phrases like: 'The successful candidate will possess a university degree and two years of directly related work experience.' In recent years, most advertisements have been written in a less formal and more direct style, using 'you' as if the recruiter were speaking directly to the prospective applicant.

Other techniques that have been used to attract the reader's attention are the use of questions and bold or controversial statements such as:

> **Are you looking for your next challenge and an opportunity to develop your project management skills?**

or

> **You'd have to be crazy to take on this job!**

or

> **We can offer you long hours and tiring days … but plenty of rewards too.**

These are acceptable techniques for producing job advertisements, but care should be taken that they are not overused, thereby losing their freshness and impact. A list of questions at the start of an advert can become tedious. Once you have caught your reader's attention, you should proceed swiftly to giving information. You should also avoid using hackneyed phrases, clichés or essentially meaningless phrases. Most employers would like to employ enthusiastic, intelligent, well-motivated and outgoing people. However, since practically no one is likely to admit to not being any of these, it seems pointless to include them as criteria in a job advertisement as they help neither qualified persons to identify themselves nor unsuitable persons to screen themselves out.

Job advertisements: whose responsibility?

In Chapter 2, we considered who should participate in writing job descriptions. Now consider who should be responsible for producing job advertisements.

Is the post of a routine nature, with simple duties or a job description that has not changed much? Does a previous advert exist that can be used without much change? A junior member of the HRM department could handle this or the administrative staff in any unit where this activity has been devolved to line management.

If the post is new or has changed considerably, the line manager should be more involved in deciding the content, and more expertise in composing advertisements will be needed so someone with more experience in this area and well-developed writing skills should take on the task.

If the post is difficult to recruit for (maybe due to a local skills shortage), you may consider using the specialised skills of a recruitment advertising agency. The additional cost of this would be a factor to weigh against the cost of unsuccessful recruitment attempts.

If you have *any* doubts about your writing ability, get help! Advertisements are very expensive and very public, and can contribute to the public image of your organisation. If the requisite skill is not available within your organisation, you may have to consider using the services of an advertising agency.

Targeted recruitment

The equality Acts and Regulations described earlier in this chapter are designed to protect specified groups against unfair discrimination in employment. What they do not prescribe is affirmative action such as deliberately hiring a quota of members of any specific group to redress any imbalances. Targeted recruitment is a method of encouraging previously disadvantaged groups to apply for vacancies but, in keeping with the intention of equal opportunities legislation, any subsequent selection must be based on merit only.

Targeted recruitment can take several forms:

- A statement that encourages under-represented groups to apply for a post, for example: 'We welcome applications from people with disabilities, women, and members of black and ethnic minority groups as they are under-represented in the company in positions at this level.'
- Photographs and text that show people in non-traditional roles, thus emphasising an employer's desire to receive applications from groups that do not traditionally apply for particular posts.
- An assurance that qualified candidates with a disability will be invited to interview.
- Photographs showing a mix of men, women and members of various racial groups.

Employers who engage in targeted recruitment have recognised that good, able people have become discouraged from even applying for certain jobs because of a history or perception of discrimination. A number of such companies were profiled in a *Personnel Management* article (Paddison 1990). The experience of these companies was that targeted recruitment attracted a much greater pool of suitable candidates, and not only from the specified groups. There was an overall improvement in the quality of applications. Targeted recruitment, then, speaks loudly about an organisation's level of commitment to equal opportunities, but a side-effect is that it also attracts applications from better candidates in general.

ACTIVITY 3.5

Review a number of job advertisements from a variety of sources, and comment on what you regard as poor and good factors with regard to the elements described in this chapter. For example:

- What caught your eye?
- How complete is the information about tasks, skills requirements, salary, etc.?
- Does the advert appropriately assist the reader in self-selection?
- Are important aspects of organisational culture presented, such as equal opportunities policies?

You may wish to discuss your findings with others in your class in small groups, and present your combined findings to the whole class.

Application forms

Once you have provided people with information about your vacancy, you must decide on the best way for interested candidates to present information about themselves. The major choices are:

- application form
- curriculum vitae (CV) ⎫ submitted on paper or electronically
- letter of application ⎭
- handwritten/typed submission
- personal call.

Many organisations prefer to use their own application form because of the advantages this can offer. Application forms can be designed to elicit information specific to the types of work done in your organisation. The information can be arranged so that very important information is seen first, for example, academic qualifications or membership of professional bodies without which a person could not be considered for particular posts. One advantage of application forms over CVs is that the organisation controls the information that is given, not the applicant. In this way the organisation can ensure that the same types of information are gathered from all applicants, the information is relevant to the work the organisation can offer, and information that could potentially lead to unlawful discrimination is excluded.

The application form is a bridge between the recruitment process and the selection process. Once a completed form has been received, it can be used as a basis for the initial selection exercise, but until this occurs, it is part of the recruitment process and its design should be subject to recruitment considerations. A poorly designed form – one, for example, that requests inappropriate information – could alienate potential applicants and discourage some from applying.

When deciding which information to obtain from job applicants, you can submit your queries to two tests:

1 Will this query result in information that can be construed as discriminatory in a way that is unlawful according to employment legislation?
2 Will this query elicit information that is strictly related to the applicant's ability to do the job as reflected in the skills, qualifications and personal qualities outlined in the person specification/competency profile?

If your query passes these two tests, you can be assured that you are not infringing the equal opportunities laws and that you are on the way to recruiting in a fair manner. This issue will be of great importance once you are involved in the selection processes, but it needs to be kept in mind at all stages of the recruitment process and may, for example, influence the way you design your application form.

Pause for thought 3.5
Can you think of any kinds of information that some managers might be tempted to find out, but which are considered as inappropriate in terms of equal opportunities legislation?

Many managers feel that they need to know details about a candidate's personal circumstances in order to judge whether or not the candidate will be able to fulfil the requirements of the job. They want to know, for example, whether a person is married, especially in the case of a young woman. The implication is that a young woman may become pregnant and either leave or have to be temporarily replaced. They may also wish to know how old a person's children are. Again this information can be interpreted in a fashion that is discriminatory against women, as there is an assumption that they will be responsible for child care, and that any problems such as a child being ill will lead to the woman taking time off work. Application forms should not request details about dependants or marital status.

You should consider the following criteria when designing an application form:

● The layout should be clear and simple, be easy to fill in, provide adequate space for information, make it obvious where details are to be entered.
● The language used should be clear and unambiguous.
● The form should be capable of acquiring a range of information about qualifications and skills for a variety of jobs.
● Applicants should not have to repeat details.
● You should be aware of equal opportunities implications – ask only for relevant information; do not ask for potentially discriminatory information.
● You should provide applicants with an opportunity to give all relevant information supporting their application.
● Applicants should not feel confused or irritated by questions on the form.
● You should ensure that the purpose and use of equal opportunities monitoring information is clear.

Although we have presented the advantages of using an application form, there are some advantages to using CVs too. If an advertisement required all applicants to submit a CV, the organisation would have eliminated the step, and therefore the cost, of sending out application forms. It must be remembered, however, that designing a CV requires a fairly good standard of writing skills, so it would not be appropriate to require this for all positions. Many advertisements for managerial posts request interested candidates to apply by sending in a CV.

ACTIVITY 3.6

1 Choose an employer and design an application form that could be used for all posts with that organisation. Check that your form elicits all relevant information from applicants. Consider the design and layout of your application form: is it easy to complete; is it easy for selectors to locate relevant information?

2 Compare your application form with the sample form given in Activity 4.3.

Equal opportunities implications

In order to promote access to jobs, employers may wish to assist those with poor language skills in completing application forms. There are many posts where the duties to be performed do not require the levels of reading, writing and language ability that are necessary for a person to be able to complete an application form. Positive measures to ensure that such people are not unfairly excluded from such posts would be an example of good practice and could lead to an organisation acquiring committed employees.

Equal opportunities monitoring

Many application forms now contain an equal opportunities monitoring section so that employers can evaluate their success in attracting applications from qualified members of designated groups, and also monitor the handling of these applications at all stages of the selection process. The information on this form should be used only to provide feedback to the organisation that it is operating in a non-discriminatory fashion, and should not be used as part of the selection process. It is essential that candidates are informed about why the information is being requested and how it will be used. It is best if the monitoring form can be detached from the application form so that it is clear to applicants that the monitoring and selection processes are completely separate. Monitoring forms usually request information about factors which are directly addressed in the legislation on discrimination. You will find a sample monitoring form on the final page of the application form in Figure 4.2, where you will notice that we have also decided to monitor age as a matter of good practice in advance of the expected legislation. ACAS (2004a and 2004b) recommends that employers give a great deal of thought to whether and how they introduce new categories of information into their monitoring forms as many people may feel sensitive about issues such as sexual orientation and religious belief and regard any queries about these as an invasion of privacy. It is also regarded as good practice to invite applicants to specify any special requirements that may need to be met to enable them to attend an interview (e.g. avoidance of a clash with timing of a religious festival or time of religious observance).

Administrative procedures

The final aspect of the recruitment process we need to consider is how you are going to handle applications. You will need to design administrative procedures that address the following issues:

- accepting applications by phone/walk in/electronically
- sending forms/information
- acknowledgement of applications received.

In deciding on the appropriate administrative procedures you will need to address questions about what you want to achieve, but also the question of cost. There is a public relations element in every recruitment exercise, as your organisation will have contact with many people who will not become employees, but who may be potential customers and will certainly relate to others how you treated them. You will want to create a good impression with every applicant, but the desire to do this must be tempered by the question of cost. Many organisations are now alerting potential applicants that they will not receive an acknowledgement of receipt of their application form due to rising postal costs and the number of applications expected (IRS 2003a). A sample letter can be found in Appendix 3.1, but one alternative is to include a statement on the application form as you can see on the sample form in Activity 4.3.

Conclusion

This chapter has discussed the aims of recruitment and examined the impact of legal, moral and business issues on decisions made about the recruitment process. The particular importance of equality of opportunity in employment has been explained.

We have reviewed the range of policies and procedures involved in effective recruitment and emphasised the need for a methodical approach, using job descriptions, person specifications/competency profiles and well-designed advertisements and application forms to support the process. The next two chapters will examine the processes and techniques involved in making a selection from the applications you receive.

REVIEW QUESTIONS

You will find brief answers to review questions 1, 3 and 5 on page 488.

1 Outline the major legislative factors that affect the recruitment process. What can an organisation do to ensure it is an equal opportunities employer?

2 Choose five current advertisements for job vacancies from different sources. Comment on the structure, content and placement of the adverts, evaluate their effectiveness and suggest improvements.

3 Describe the uses of the job description and person specification/competency profile in the recruitment process.

4 Interview someone about his or her job. Draft a job description, person specification and advertisement for the post.

5 Comment on the approaches to recruitment an employer can adopt in order to create and project a positive public image.

SELF-CHECK QUESTIONS

Answer the following multiple-choice and short-answer questions. The correct responses or page references are given on page 488 for you to check your understanding of this chapter.

1 Which of the following are laws that protect groups against unfair discrimination in Britain?
   (a) Equal Opportunities Act; Disability Discrimination Act; Race Relations Act.
   (b) Disabilities Act; Race Relations Act; Equal Opportunities Act.
   (c) Sex Discrimination Act; Race Relations Act; Disability Discrimination Act.
   (d) Anti Sex Discrimination Act; Disabilities Act; Racial Discrimination Act.

2 Which of the following is not an example of a GOR?
   (a) An Indian person to wait on tables in an Indian restaurant.
   (b) A man to cut hair in a men's hair stylist's shop.
   (c) A woman to provide personal care to a woman with multiple sclerosis.

3 Which of the following does the Race Relations (Amendment) Act 2000 do?
   (a) It corrects the list of ethnic groups that may not be discriminated against.
   (b) It imposes a duty on public authorities to actively engage in the promotion of good race relations.
   (c) It authorises affirmative action, i.e. the ability to give preference to people in employment decisions because they belong to an ethnic minority.

4 Which of the following is not covered by the Employment Equality (Religion or Belief) Regulations 2003?
   (a) Being a Roman Catholic.
   (b) Being a member of the Labour Party.
   (c) Being a Muslim.
   (d) Being a humanist.

5 You have interviewed a 25-year-old man called John Brooker for a position as a truck driver delivering goods from a soft drinks manufacturer to major retail outlets in England and Wales. Because you are concerned about the potential for theft, you asked during the interview, 'Do you have any criminal convictions?', to which he replied 'No'. You consider that he is well qualified and able to do the job. On the morning that you are going to phone and offer him the job, a colleague stops by your office and says, 'By the way, did you know that Johnny Brooker

91

was once put on probation for stealing somebody's welfare cheque? I think he was about 19 at the time.'

(a) Will you still offer the job to John?

(b) Was John dishonest in denying that he had a criminal conviction?

6 List three things you would consider when deciding whether or not a vacancy exists.

7 Name three standard methods of advertising vacant posts.

8 List the major components you would include in a job advert.

9 Does targeted recruitment mean that members of under-represented groups will be selected in preference to other candidates? YES or NO

10 Everyone involved in selecting candidates should see the equal opportunities monitoring form. TRUE or FALSE?

WHAT NEXT?

Now that you have mastered the introductory level of information presented in this chapter, you may wish to take your studies to a higher level. The article cited below is a research-based assessment of a particular aspect of recruitment. Read the article and draw out from it what you consider to be the major points the researchers are making. Does this article suggest to you any further issues that could be researched with regard to the effectivesness of recruitment activities?

Allen, D. G., J. R. van Scotter and R. F. Otondo (2004) Recruitment communication media: impact on prehire outcomes, *Personnel Psychology*, 57, 143–171

References

Advisory, Conciliation and Arbitration Service (2004a) *Religion or Belief and the Workplace: A Guide for Employers and Employees*, ACAS

Advisory, Conciliation and Arbitration Service (2004b) *Sexual Orientation and the Workplace: A Guide for Employers and Employees*, ACAS

Chartered Institute of Personnel and Development (2003a) *Age and Employment*. (**www.cipd.co.uk/subjects/dvsequl/agedisc/ageandemp.htm**; accessed 17.02.04)

Chartered Institute of Personnel and Development (2003b) *Recruitment and Retention 2003: Survey Report,* CIPD

Coker, N. (ed) (2001) *Racism in Medicine: An Agenda for Change*, King's Fund

European Commission (2003) *Annual Report on Equality and Non-Discrimination 2003: Towards Diversity*, Office for Official Publications of the European Communities

Higginbottom, K. (2003) More than lip service, *People Management*, 4 December, 14–15

Industrial Relations Services (IRS) (2000) Disability discrimination: the current state of play, *Industrial Relations Law Bulletin 649*, September, 2–12

Industrial Relations Services (IRS) (2001a) All aboard the online express, *Employee Development Bulletin 134*, February, 5–10

Industrial Relations Services (IRS) (2001b) DRC puts carrots before sticks, *IRS Employment Trends 729*, June, 6–10

Industrial Relations Services (IRS) (2001c) Moving ahead in online recruitment, *Employee Development Bulletin 137*, May, 15–16

Industrial Relations Services (IRS) (2003a) Labour saving devices, *IRS Employment Review 774*, 18 April, 34–40

Industrial Relations Services (IRS) (2003b) New guidance on burden of proof in sex discrimination claims, *IRS Employment Review 779*, 4 July, 59–62

Industrial Relations Services (IRS) (2003c) Setting the tone: job descriptions and person specifications, *IRS Employment Review 776*, 23 May, 42–48

Industrial Relations Services (IRS) (2003d) Unlawful discrimination – a new era, *IRS Employment Review 781*, 1 August, 50–64

Institute of Personnel and Development (1997) *Managing Diversity: An IPD Position Paper*, January, IPD

Johnson, R. (2003) Bill of rights, *People Management*, 9 October, 28–35

Macpherson, W. (1999) *The Stephen Lawrence Inquiry: Report of an Inquiry by Sir William Macpherson*, HMSO

Massie, B. (2001) 'Barking or biting' – the DRC's first year, *Equal Opportunities Review*, No. 97, May/June, 19–21

Minister for Disabled People (1996) *The Disability Discrimination Act, Employment DL70: Disability on the Agenda*, Department for Education and Employment

Paddison, L. (1990) The targeted approach to recruitment, *Personnel Management*, November, 54–58

Smethurst, S. (2004) The allure of online, *People Management*, 29 July, 38–40

Tulip, S. (2003) A flying start, *People Management*, 7 August, 38–43

www.cfrlawonline.com. *Fair Employment in Northern Ireland* (accessed 06/05/04)

www.cipd.co.uk/subjects/emplaw/general/legal2003.htm *Legal Developments in 2003 and Expected Changes in 2004* (accessed 17/02/04)

www.drc-gb.org.uk. *Disability Rights Commission* (accessed 09.09.04)

www.equalityni.org. *Equality Law* (accessed 31.08.04)

www.womenandequalityunit.gov.uk. *Fairness for All: A New Commission for Equality and Human Rights* (accessed 09.06.04).

Further study

Books

Advisory, Conciliation and Arbitration Service (2004) *Recruitment and Induction,* ACAS. (One of the advisory booklets that provide succinct advice on good practice. Available at **www.acas.org.uk**; accessed 09.09.04.)

Advisory, Conciliation and Arbitration Service (2004) *Tackling Discrimination and Promoting Equality – Good Practice Guide for Employers,* ACAS. (One of the advisory booklets that provide succinct advice on good practice. Available at **www.acas.org.uk**; accessed 09.09.04.)

Cascio, W. F. (1998) Recruitment and initial screening, in *Applied Psychology in Human Resource Management*, 5th edition, Prentice Hall.

Chartered Institute of Personnel and Development (2003) *Recruitment and Retention 2003: Survey Report*, CIPD. (Can be downloaded from the CIPD web site. The CIPD surveys a large number of employers to report on recruitment and selection practices, and comments on trends and key issues.)

Commission for Racial Equality (1984) *Code of Practice for the Elimination of Racial Discrimination and the Promotion of Equality of Opportunity in Employment*, CRE. (Also look at the CRE web site for information on updated codes.)

Courtis, J. (1994) *Recruitment Advertising. Right First Time*, IPD. (Courtis writes in a humorous style, and this book is based on many years of experience as a recruitment and selection consultant. He makes many interesting points worth noting and considering.)

Department of Employment (1995) *Equality Pays: How Equal Opportunities Can Benefit Your Business. A Guide for Small Employers*, Department of Employment. (An excellent booklet that crystallises the benefits for small enterprises of good practice in equal opportunities.)

Equal Opportunity Commission (1985) *Code of Practice for the Elimination of Discrimination on the Grounds of Sex and Marriage, and the Promotion of Equality of Opportunity in Employment*, EOC. (Also see the EOC's web site for up-to-date advice on various aspects of the legislation.)

Incomes Data Services (2003) *IDS Studies: Recruitment Practices* No. 751, June, IDS. (A concise overview of the basic range of both recruitment and selection practices with case studies of six employers, including Surrey Police and 3, a mobile telecommunications company.)

Industrial Relations Services (2000) *Managing Disability. IRS Management Review 18*, IRS. (Various chapters deal with the position of disabled people as part of the workforce, recruitment and retention, the Disability Discrimination Act 1995, employer case studies, and resources for employers and employees.)

Macdonald, L. A. C. (2004) *Equality, Diversity and Discrimination*, CIPD. (A practical guide on how to avoid discrimination and benefit from diversity.)

Minister for Disabled People (1996) *A Brief Guide to the Disability Discrimination Act, DL40: Disability on the Agenda*, Department for Education and Employment.

Selwyn, N. (latest edition) *Law of Employment,* Butterworth. (This is an excellent reference book on employment law. The book is updated fairly frequently, so you should always make sure you are working with the latest edition.)

Articles

Cooper, C. (2003) Minority support, *People Management*, 4 December, 25–27. (Cooper provides an interesting overview of the state of play in a number of organisations in the week that the new regulations on religious discrimination were introduced. There are a number of interesting articles on this and the sexual orientation regulations in this issue of *People Management*.)

Edwards, C. (2004) Assister act, *People Management*, 2 September, 26–30. (An update on developments with regard to the Disability Discrimination Act 1995.)

Fredman, S. (2001) Equality: a new generation? *Industrial Law Journal*, Vol. 3, No. 2, June, 145–168. (A very readable overview of the then current and planned status of equality legislation in the EU and its implications for the UK. Still valuable as an interesting discussion of the values underpinning attitudes towards equality though subsequent changes in the law should be kept in mind when reading this article.)

How to develop a dyslexia-friendly workplace (2004) *People Management*, 16 September, 50–51.

Industrial Relations Services (2003) Labour saving devices, *IRS Employment Review 774*, 18 April, 34–40. (An overview of what employers are doing to make their recruitment processes cost-effective.)

Industrial Relations Services (2003) Sentence served: recruiting ex-offenders, *IRS Employment Review 779*, 4 July, 42–48. (A concise review of issues to be considered.)

Industrial Relations Services (2003) Unlawful discrimination – a new era, *IRS Employment Review 781*, 1 August, 50–64. (A detailed review of changes to be introduced into equality legislation during and after 2003.)

Ingham, J. (2003) How to implement a diversity policy, *People Management*, 24 July, 44–45. (The 'How to . . .' series provides very useful summaries of the major considerations in a range of human resource management activities. See also the entries under 'Jackson' and 'Wilkinson'.)

International Labour Review (2003/04) Vol. 142, No. 4. (Entire special issue on equality at work.)

Jackson, R. and N. Osmond (2003) How to recruit and retain older staff, *People Management*, 15 May, 46–47.

Wilkinson, A. (2004) How to use recruitment advertising agencies, *People Management*, 15 January, 44–45.

Internet

Many recruitment agencies are now using the Internet and many newspapers also have pages on it. Interesting sources of information on the Internet that we have checked include the following:

Age Posi+ive   **www.agepositive.gov.uk**
(A web site dedicated to 'tackling age discrimination and promoting age diversity in employment'.)

BBC World of Opportunity   **www.bbc.co.uk/jobs**
(The BBC is one example of a large corporation that regularly advertises job vacancies on its company web site.)

Chartered Institute of Personnel and Development   **www.cipd.co.uk**
(The CIPD web site contains a wealth of information on various aspects of recruitment, equality and the law.)

Commission for Racial Equality   **www.cre.gov.uk**
(Good explanations of the law as well as other aspects of race relations.)

Disability Rights Commission   **www.drc.org.uk**
(The DRC's web site provides information on the commission and its work, the Disability Discrimination Act and frequently asked questions about the rights of the disabled.)

Employers' Forum on Disability   **www.efd.org.uk**
(A fount of information for employers, including guidelines and factsheets, information on events and awards, and links to many more sites.)

Equal Opportunities Commission   **www.eoc.org.uk**
(The EOC web site provides a wealth of information on equality related to sex discrimination and equal pay, including a review of the essential steps to take in order to become an equal opportunities employer. Provides a checklist specifically designed for line managers on handling situations that might arise during the recruitment process, including the production of a person specification and advertising the vacancy. Go to the main site and search for the equality checklists.)

Monster Board   **www.monster.co.uk**
(A worldwide professional employment and job search agency.)

Nacro   **www.nacro.org.uk**
(A charitable organisation dedicated to the rehabilitation of ex-offenders. The web site provides information on numerous leaflets available from Nacro for prisoners, ex-offenders, their families and potential employers.)

Race issues in Britain   **www.guardian.co.uk/race**
(Provides links to *Guardian* news items, other reports and the scripts of TV news reports.)

Total Jobs   **www.totaljobs.com** and **www.jobability.com**
(The main site acts as a recruitment agency, but also has interesting profiles of a number of organisations (NHS, Carlsberg-Tetley, easyJet) and their use of the Internet. The company has also developed a site at 'jobability' specialising in information for the disabled applicant.)

Northern Ireland sites

Department for Employment and Learning   **www.delni.gov.uk**
(Supplies information about employment rights in NI.)

Equality Commission   **www.equalityni.org**
(Provides a good overview of the equality legislation in NI.)

Appendix 3.1   **Sample letter to accompany application form**

XYZ Company
1 Company Lane
Companytown
XY1 1YZ

Mr D White
3 Candidate's Close
Everytown
EF3 4GH

March 18, 2005

Dear Mr White

Thank you for your query about the post of Marketing Assistant. Please complete the enclosed application form and return it to us by April 8, 2005.

We regret that we are unable to acknowledge receipt of applications. However, if you wish to enclose a self-addressed and stamped postcard or envelope, we would be pleased to return this to you to indicate that your application has been received.

The selection committee will complete its review of all applications within three weeks of the closing date, and selected candidates will then be notified of an interview date. We intend to hold interviews in the week of May 9, 2005.

If you have not heard from us before May 3, 2005, you should assume that you have not been successful on this occasion.

Yours sincerely

N Barkley
Human Resource Manager

Selection: shortlisting and interviews

OBJECTIVES

When you have studied this chapter you will be able to:

- explain the aims of the selection process
- name and describe the steps that can be taken in the selection process
- identify typical interviewer errors and explain how to avoid them
- plan an interview process and formulate appropriate questions
- conduct an interview, assess the candidates and record your evaluation
- justify your decision and provide feedback to unsuccessful candidates.

A successful recruitment campaign will have resulted in a good number of applications from people who are suitably qualified for your vacancy, and the next task is to select the most suitable person from this number. Employers must consider who should be involved in this task and provide support in terms of policies, procedures and training. This chapter will examine these factors as well as discussing the expertise needed to participate successfully in the selection process.

Aims and objectives of the selection process

The ultimate goal of selection is usually expressed as 'to choose the best person for the job'. Selectors attempt to predict performance on the job, but they also need to ensure that the candidates fully understand all major aspects of the job so that new recruits are not likely to become disillusioned and leave within a short period of time. The objectives of the selection process, which will lead to the fulfilment of the main goal, are as follows:

- gather as much relevant information as possible
- organise and evaluate the information
- assess each candidate

in order to:

- forecast performance on the job

and

- give information to applicants

so that

- they can judge whether or not they wish to accept an offer of employment.

Collecting information

Gathering and evaluating information in order to make the selection decision can be done in a number of stages. The most common methods used include:

- shortlisting from information on application forms and CVs
- interview
- tests
- biographical/extended application form
- assessment centre
- references.

This chapter will deal with shortlisting and interviewing as these two processes tend to be used in almost all cases. Alternative or supplementary methods of gathering information for the selection decision and methods of providing information will be discussed in Chapter 5.

Policy and procedures

It is amazing how many managers still claim to be good judges of character and ability based on very short acquaintance. These managers will tell you that within a few minutes they can tell whether they are going to get on with someone, and whether that person will do well in the job. This kind of over-confidence is a major contributing factor to the low validity of interviews as a selection method. The concept of validity will be discussed in more detail later in the chapter, but it can be stated here that the HRM approach would suggest that employees are too valuable a resource to be selected or rejected in such a subjective and uninformed manner.

Every effort should be made to design a methodical and objective system for selecting employees. Personal factors and perceptions cannot be totally eliminated, but having objective policies and procedures in place can help to obviate any potentially harmful effects of individual persuasions. Good selection policies and procedures provide guidance and support to line managers and others involved in the selection process to carry out this duty successfully, confident that they are following the tenets of best practice.

Selection policies, like recruitment policies, are a statement of an organisation's intentions and should normally address such issues as equality of opportunity, maybe giving information about targeted groups. A selection policy might read as follows:

The objective of the selection process is to obtain employees who will be productive and committed members of staff, working and developing to their full potential. This organisation will select employees on the basis of merit only. Internal and disabled applicants who have the required knowledge and skills are guaranteed an interview.

Selection procedures should address the following issues:

- the stages and techniques that should be used
- who is to be involved in assessing candidates
- administrative processes.

Several factors would be decided on for each of these issues, and relevant guidelines provided. The procedures documentation might, for example, indicate that a shortlist must be prepared and interviews conducted for each vacancy; guidelines might be given on who is to prepare the shortlist and conduct the interviews, and what methods should be used to accomplish these tasks. Further issues to be addressed in selection procedures include: guidelines on non-discriminatory questioning; the appropriateness of testing; whether references should be taken up and when. All these issues will be addressed in this and the following chapter.

Shortlisting

As mentioned earlier, most employers will wish to interview a number of applicants before offering a position. In many instances, however, a successful recruitment campaign will attract more applicants than it would be possible to interview. The first step is therefore to reduce the applications to a manageable number, a process known as shortlisting. The shortlisting of applicants is, then, a selection procedure that may be performed purely on the basis of the written information that applicants have supplied or which may involve the acquisition of additional information about candidates, for example by conducting a telephone interview.

Screening written applications

Often candidates for a post give information in their applications which is not required for making a selection decision, and which could lead to accusations of unfair discrimination if it were taken into consideration. For example, candidates might describe their family situation in order to explain a gap in their employment record. Applicants also, obviously, have to give their name so that the organisation can communicate with them. A name, however, can reveal information that is not apropos to the selection process, such as gender and racial origin. A useful technique to avoid being influenced by such information is to assess the application and make notes that refer only to relevant selection criteria. Furthermore, if these notes refer to the candidates only by their initials, any information that might indicate gender or racial origin is eliminated. If the persons shortlisting refer to these notes instead of the original applications when drawing up the shortlist, they will be greatly assisted in eliminating any unconscious biases.

As well as avoiding criteria that have been designated as unlawfully discriminatory, selectors should take care to avoid considering any other criteria that are not strictly related to the candidate's ability to do the job.

Before you read on about poor practices in selection, can you suggest a methodical approach to shortlisting that would be fair and effective? That is, how would you decide on the 'relevant selection criteria' referred to above?

Selectors have been known to introduce a wide range of criteria that reflect their own preconceived ideas about people's circumstances and how people are likely to act in those circumstances. This is a matter of imposing one's own assumptions on other people. Some examples of this are selectors who exclude applicants who do not live locally, assuming they will frequently be late for work or will not wish to relocate; selectors who exclude applicants who are currently earning more than the vacancy offers; selectors who exclude people who are currently unemployed. You should even think twice before rejecting an application simply because the writing is difficult to read. Medical practitioners notoriously have poor handwriting (although this is a stereotypical image and as such should be questioned), yet they hold responsible, professional jobs.

So what is the right way to shortlist applicants? If you have read the chapter on recruitment (Chapter 3), you will remember that certain documents should be available to support the whole of the recruitment and selection process. The person specification or competency profile, in particular, plays an important role throughout the selection process. Applications should be assessed certainly against the skills and knowledge requirements listed on the person specification, and where possible against the personal qualities, although it may be more practical to assess the latter at the interview stage. Selectors should note where candidates meet the requirements of the person specification/competency profile and where they lack the required skills and knowledge. Each application could be scored with a series of + and − signs or with numerical grades if you wish to weight the criteria you have selected. To provide you with an example, the application form that appears later in this chapter, in Activity 4.3, has been assessed in relation to the receptionist person specification in Chapter 2 (see Table 4.1).

Table 4.1　**Assessment of application form (with reference to person specification)**

Post: Receptionist

Attributes	Essential	Desirable
Knowledge	Knowledge of clerical systems +	Knowledge of the company −
Skills	Experience of clerical work + Experience in handling queries in person and over the telephone ? Ability to extract information from a computerised database −	Supervisory experience −
Personal qualities	Polite manner ? Ability to work under pressure ?	

Why do you think some of the skills and personal qualities listed in the person specification in Table 4.1 have been marked with a question mark?

A preliminary evaluation of most of the skills of the applicant can be made at the shortlisting stage, but in this particular instance it is not possible to judge the applicant's personal qualities, for instance, based on the information contained in the application form. Assessment of these elements will have to be made later in the selection process, and the question marks merely indicate that no assessment can be made at present.

If possible, at least two people should undertake to shortlist from the applications received, and they should do this independently of one another. After the initial selection they can then compare their evaluations of applicants, discuss any discrepancies in their judgements and justify the decisions they have made. If the two shortlisters are following the same objective process, there should be a fair amount of agreement about suitable candidates, but the involvement of two people increases the objectivity of the process and helps to eliminate the effects of individual biases. The shortlisters should end up with a ranked list of candidates using the number of pluses and minuses given to each candidate. Typically they will try to obtain six suitable candidates to be invited for interview for a single vacancy, but this number will vary according to circumstances.

Did you know?

Some organisations were beginning to use the Internet in their shortlisting process for graduates in the late 1990s. By getting students to complete on-line career and personality questionnaires which are matched against identified competencies, it is claimed that organisations can filter out as many as 90% of applications at a very early stage in the selection procedure.

(Jilly Welch reporting on graduate recruitment, *People Management*, 28 May 1998, p. 14)

A shortlisting checklist

- At least two people to shortlist applications independently.
- Note where applications meet and fall short of the person specification/competency profile.
- Separate all applications according to agreed criteria: suitable/possible/unsuitable.
- Rank the suitable applications.
- Shortlisters to confer on person specification/competency criteria only and select suitable number to call for interview.

Telephone interviewing

The CIPD (2004) points out that telephone interviewing as an initial part of the recruitment and selection process has become more popular, particularly with the growth of call centres. For these employers, telephone skills will be an essential requirement for many jobs, and the telephone interview can be used as a legitimate method of testing the telephone manner of applicants. The Institute cautions, however, that telephone interviews should be just as structured and focused as face-to-face interviews and not be allowed to degenerate into 'just a chat over the phone'.

Interviewing

Almost every employer includes a face-to-face interview as part of the selection process. The initial selection interview might be delegated to a recruitment agency or a local job centre, but most employers would be reluctant to take on new employees without having met them first in person. The interview continues to be the most popular and frequently used method of selection, even though research studies have found interviews to be poor predictors of future performance in a job (Makin and Robertson 1986). This is referred to as low validity. The poor validity of interviews means that they do not test what they purport to test, i.e. ability to perform a job well. The reasons for this mainly lie with the interviewer concerned. A number of interviewer errors contribute to the low validity of interviews, and awareness of these is one step towards eliminating them or at least reducing their impact.

Interviewer errors

Interviewer errors arise because of the perceptual process we all use to deal with the world around us. From myriad stimuli that surround us, we select those to which we will pay attention. This process is known as perceptual selection, and what we select is determined by our own experience, personality and motivation. This means that we focus on certain aspects of our environment and ignore others. Our own experience might lead us into focusing on inappropriate stimuli in some circumstances and ignoring information that is in fact apposite. A number of such perceptual errors have been identified, and those most relevant to the selection process are described here.

The halo effect

Some candidates for interview make a very strong impression on the interviewers as soon as they enter the room. They may be well dressed and attractive, have a firm handshake and a very confident manner. Research has shown that if interviewers form an initial good impression of a candidate, this has two effects. Firstly, this good impression tends to influence positively their interpretation of everything else that happens in the interview. Secondly, the interviewers will seek more positive information to confirm their initial judgement. This is known as the halo effect, but it can also happen with an initial negative impression. This is sometimes referred to as the horns effect and can be detected when interviewers start to seek negative information to confirm their first impressions.

Making snap decisions

It is often said of interviewers that they make up their minds about a candidate in the first five minutes and then do not change their assessment of that person's suitability. In terms of the perceptual process this means that interviewers are responding to a limited range of stimuli and not taking the opportunity to elicit a wide range of information.

Hiring people like oneself

There is an innate human tendency to identify with people who are like us and share several of our characteristics. An outgoing person may feel more comfortable with other extroverts and the opposite is true for a more reserved person. These characteristics do not, however, necessarily equate with the ability to perform a job, and it is probably detrimental to an organisation to have only like-minded people on its staff. If interviewers fall prey to this tendency, they are said to be hiring in their own image.

Stereotyping

Allowing one's stereotyped images of people to influence selection decisions is probably the most dangerous of the perceptual errors, and could very often equate to some form of unlawful discrimination. Stereotyping occurs when a person is identified primarily with some group that he or she belongs to and then is assumed to have a range of characteristics that are thought to be common to all members of that group. Some examples of stereotypes are: that Scots are frugal; that all students are irresponsible and lazy; that Americans are brash and loud. It is not possible for all members of a group to have the same characteristics, and we should all guard against forming biases of this nature.

Making assumptions

The halo effect, making snap decisions and stereotyping are all specific forms of assumptions based on limited information, but making assumptions can also be a more generalised fault. There are many instances where interviewers are willing to impose their own personal view of how they would act in particular circumstances, instead of ascertaining how the interviewee would act. One example of this is assuming that women will bear the major responsibility for child care, or that women are less likely to move their families to take up a new post.

Gathering insufficient or irrelevant information

Again, all the specific perceptual errors discussed in this section could be attributed to gathering insufficient or irrelevant information. Interviewers obviously need to be aware of this as a general fault and make sure they use proper techniques to counteract it.

The contrast effect

Imagine yourself in the following scenario. You are a final year student and you have been asked by one of your lecturers to judge presentations being made by students in the first year of your course. You are using a scale of 1–5, with 1 being poor and 5 being excellent. You watch one presentation and the student makes a really poor job of it. The presentation is boring, too long and the student uses no visual aids. You rate this presentation as poor and give it a score of 1. The next student gives a presentation which is somewhat better, and it is a relief to you that this presentation is not as boring. The contrast between the two presentations is likely to have an effect on your judgement, and you will probably rate the second presentation higher than you would have done on some objective measure. If the presentation actually merits a 3, you may rate it as a 4 because of the contrast with the preceding poor presentation. This is known as the contrast effect. It means that candidates at interview may be rated more highly than they merit by interviewers because they were preceded by a poor candidate, and by contrast they appear to be better than they are in reality.

Interviewer errors: summary

- Making snap decisions.
- Gathering negative/positive information to support first impressions.
- Hiring in one's own image.
- Stereotyping.
- Making assumptions; imposing one's personal view of how one would act in other people's personal circumstances.
- Gathering insufficient/irrelevant information.
- Contrast effect.

Eliminating interviewer errors

As stated earlier, the very fact that you are aware of interviewer errors can help you to eliminate them if you wish to do so and if you make a conscious effort while you are interviewing. There are also some techniques that you can consciously employ to diminish the effects of interviewer errors.

Gather sufficient information

This is a general rule that will help to eliminate most interviewer errors. The interviewer should not decide early in the interview that a candidate is unsuitable and then fail to pursue the whole range of information necessary to make a proper decision. Interviewers who persist in gathering information even when a candidate has initially made a poor impression are achieving several goals that may contribute to better decisions:

- They are resisting the halo/horns effect.
- They are making an effort to gather the full range of information.
- They are giving candidates every opportunity to present themselves.

Structured interviews

Conducting interviews in a structured fashion will also contribute to the aim of gathering sufficient information on all candidates. Structured interviews involve the following steps:

- Design a set of questions to elicit information relevant to the selection decision.
- Provide all candidates with an opportunity to answer this set of questions.

Pause for thought 4.3 How would you go about designing a relevant set of questions? Why should you ask all of the questions of each candidate?

The way to design the basic set of questions for a structured interview is, of course, to refer to the person specification/competency profile and the job description, and to create questions related to the tasks, knowledge, skills and personal qualities listed there. The quality of the information gained will be influenced by the types of question asked, and this is dealt with later in this chapter.

Asking all candidates the same questions means that you will have a similar profile for each candidate which you can compare and use to assess each candidate against the others. Notice that the structured interview gives you a basic set of comparable details; you may wish to supplement this with individualised information on each candidate, clarifying particular details of their experience, etc. In other words, the structured interview guarantees that you will collect certain information, but it is not a straitjacket that restricts you to that information. As well as preparing and using the questions for the structured interview, the interviewer must be adept at using probing questions, as described later.

Giving all candidates an opportunity to respond to a set of questions can also help to diminish the halo effect and gives a nervous candidate time to relax and do better as the interview proceeds. Preparing a set of questions in advance also means that interviewers:

● can relax during the interview and concentrate on the candidates' responses, rather than be thinking about what to ask next
● are less likely to inadvertently ask questions that may be construed as discriminating illegally.

More than one interviewer

In general, the one-on-one interview is not regarded as best practice for selection purposes. One reason for this is to do with equal opportunities; the interviewer errors that arise because of individual perceptions are less likely to occur if more than one person is involved in interviewing. Since human resource management specialists often hold responsibilities for an organisation's equal opportunities programmes, they often participate in the interviewing process.

Obviously, line managers know most about the work that needs to be done and can judge whether candidates have the appropriate knowledge, skills and personal qualities. Consideration can also be given to involving others affected by the post, such as co-workers or members of other departments. Acceptance of the new employee can be increased if others are involved in the selection process, but this must be balanced against unwieldiness and, of course, everyone involved in interviewing must be trained.

Only trained people involved in interviews

Although the people involved in interviews may have different interests, they should all be working towards the same outcome, i.e. to select the best person for the post in a fair and objective manner. Training for interviewers usually includes an awareness of equal opportunity issues and development of questioning skills.

Allow sufficient time for interviews

Line managers often see interviewing as a disruption to their normal work, and wish to minimise the amount of time devoted to interviews. It is up to the HRM specialist to resist this pressure. Ten minutes is not long enough to find out sufficient detail to base such a decision on. In 1995 the BBC broadcast a series of programmes showing the recruitment processes followed by a number of organisations; one of the managers who took part in these programmes commented on the length of a courtship that precedes the decision to marry compared with the length of a selection interview on which one will base the decision about someone one may be working with on a daily basis for many years. He expressed a great sense of unease about the need to make such an important decision on such short acquaintance.

Eliminating interview errors: summary

- Gather sufficient information.
- Allow adequate time.
- Structured interviews: gather the same information from all candidates.
- More than one interviewer.
- Only trained people involved in interviews.

ACTIVITY 4.1

George, the Personnel Manager, and Ruth, one of the personnel assistants, were both conducting preliminary interviews of candidates for the post of PR assistant in the busy public relations department of a large organisation. The PR assistant would have to deal directly with the general public, sometimes with extremely irate people, and would also have to communicate with the press. George and Ruth had decided to interview the candidates separately and then get together to compare their impressions. Ruth was rather inexperienced at interviewing as she was new to the personnel office. She was a quiet person who liked to approach work in a calm, methodical manner.

Ruth particularly liked one of the candidates, Jane Marsden. Jane seemed somewhat tense at the beginning of the interview, and Ruth empathised with this as she had recently gone through a number of interviews herself before she got her current job. Ruth got Jane to relax by talking about her interests, and her feeling that Jane was an interesting person was confirmed by the discovery that they shared interests in learning languages and travelling abroad. Ruth went on to tell Jane a little about the job, and Jane said she thought it sounded very interesting. Ruth also confirmed that Jane had actually dealt with customer complaints in previous positions.

Ruth noted the following points in her assessment of Jane:

- turned up for the interview well dressed and looking professional
- showed enthusiasm for the job
- has relevant experience.

She also wrote: 'Jane makes a good impression. I'm sure she'll be good at the job.' Ruth reflected that the other two candidates she'd seen that morning hadn't seemed as enthusiastic as Jane, weren't as smart in appearance and hadn't been very expansive about their experience.

When they got together to discuss the candidates afterwards, Ruth recommended Jane to George, but George responded by saying: 'Well, when I asked her to describe her experience of dealing with an irate customer, she told me that she had always worked in offices dealing only with correspondence. I think some of the other candidates have more suitable experience.'

1 Identify the perceptual errors that may have occurred in this case.
2 Suggest what George might do to help Ruth to avoid such errors in the future.

Discussion of Activity 4.1

The perceptual errors you identified may have included the following:

- *Identifying with the candidate/focusing on irrelevant details*. Ruth seems to pay undue attention to similarities between herself and Jane, and much of the interview seems to have focused on matters other than Jane's knowledge, skills and work-related qualities.
- *Halo effect*. Jane makes a positive first impression by being well dressed and looking professional. It may be that Ruth seeks evidence to support this impression.
- *Collecting inadequate information*. The fact that Jane had dealt with customer complaints proved to be insufficient to judge her abilities for the current post. Rather than accepting a superficial answer to the question about relevant experience, Ruth should have probed for more detailed information.
- *Contrast effect*. Jane seems to be a better candidate than she is because Ruth is comparing her with other candidates she has assessed as being poor.

The techniques for eliminating interviewer errors listed before this Activity could serve as guidelines for George in helping Ruth to develop better interviewing skills. He could discuss with her the need to gather appropriate information, and help her to structure her questions in preparation for interviews. If they interviewed together, Ruth could probably learn about good techniques by observing her more experienced manager: she would witness the use of more expert questioning techniques and also be privy to the information they elicit from candidates. Finally, George could arrange some further off-the-job training for Ruth.

Interviewer skills

In addition to the techniques you may wish to employ to avoid common interviewer errors, there is a range of skills you can develop to ensure your effectiveness as an interviewer. Since we have established that both HRM specialists and line managers should be involved in selection interviews, these skills are important to both. The skills are presented below, followed by a more detailed discussion:

- Carry out thorough planning and preparation for the interview.
- Put candidates at their ease.
- Remain detached: don't send signals to candidates.
- Ask a range of relevant questions.
- Encourage the candidate to talk.
- Record the information.
- Respond to candidates' questions.
- Close the interview.
- Evaluate information and reach a decision.
- Record and justify the decisions.

Planning and preparation

The list of interview skills could almost double as a list of interview stages, and indeed the planning stage entails thinking through and planning the whole process, especially if you are responsible for coordinating it. This includes:

- arranging for the reception of candidates
- ensuring you have a private room available where you will not be interrupted
- reviewing the application forms so that you are properly informed about candidates
- reviewing the job description and person specification/competency profile so you are properly informed about the requirements of the position
- preparing the interview questions
- ensuring everyone knows what role he or she is to play in the process.

Put candidates at ease

It is widely acknowledged that most job applicants feel nervous about interviews, and this anxiety may be increased if the candidate is faced by a panel of interviewers or a series of interviews with different people. In some cases, interviewers deliberately subject candidates to stress, arguing that they wish to test the person's ability to handle stress in the job (see Figure 4.1).

A counter-argument to this is that the interview situation is stressful enough anyway, so there is no need to induce stress artificially. If one of the main objectives is to acquire as much information as possible from candidates, it is probably better on balance to try to get candidates to relax and talk freely. It is also worth remembering that for every candidate who eventually joins your organisation, there may be five or more for whom the interview is their only contact with you. It is better for an organisation's public image if these five leave the interview feeling they were treated properly.

Pause for thought 4.4   Make a list of three things you could do to help put interviewees at ease.

| Figure 4.1 | How not to put candidates at ease |

The techniques you might use to help put candidates at ease include:

● making introductions and explaining the interview process so that candidates have a chance to settle in before they have to respond
● engaging in small-talk about the traffic difficulties, how the candidate travelled to your location, etc.
● starting the interview with easy questions that entail straightforward description rather than opinion or interpretation, for example: 'What are your major duties in your current post?' rather than 'How do your current duties make you qualified for this position?'

Remain detached: don't send signals to candidates

It is important that interviewers do not influence candidates during interviews by indicating whether or not the candidate is doing well. This is especially so if a candidate starts out with weak responses, as any sign of impatience or boredom on the part of the interviewer will no doubt make the candidate more nervous, contributing to the horns effect.

Questioning techniques

In addition to using a variety of types of question, there is another component of effective questioning technique that is probably just as important as asking the right questions. That is *listening*.

It is difficult to concentrate for prolonged periods of time, and often recruiters will find themselves involved in a series of interviews stretching over many hours or even a number of days. Interviewers need to become practised in the techniques of active listening to ensure that they maintain their concentration and gather as much information from the interviewee as possible. You will find a fuller discussion of active listening in Chapter 11; it will suffice for now to highlight some of the techniques of active listening:

- Maintain good eye contact with the interviewee.
- Look interested; do not yawn or look bored.
- Make encouraging remarks such as 'Yes, I see'; 'That's interesting'; 'Do go on'.
- Summarise what the interviewee has said to check your understanding: 'So you are saying that you prefer to work in an office on your own?'

Actively practising these techniques will help the interviewer to stay alert and concentrate on what the interviewee is saying. A further effect of active listening is that the interviewee is constantly reassured of your attention, which makes him or her more comfortable with the process.

Types of question

There are a number of ways of phrasing a question, and each will have an effect on the likely response. In choosing which type of question to ask, you should consider what the purpose of the question is. What type of information do you wish to elicit from the candidate?

The three basic forms of question are the closed question, the leading question and the open question. The closed question invites a response of 'yes' or 'no'; the leading question indicates to the interviewee what kind of response is expected; the open question is phrased in such a way that the interviewee is encouraged to speak freely and give information about himself or herself. Here are some examples of each type of question, together with a comment on what sort of response might be expected.

Closed questions

- Did you work with a computer at XYZ Ltd?
- Have you had sales experience?

Comment

Each of these questions could be answered by a simple response 'yes' or 'no'. If the interviewer is trying to elicit as much information as possible, these questions are not very useful. Closed questions can, however, be useful for checking the correctness of information. An example might be: 'Did you use Excel on the computer at XYZ Ltd?'

Pause for thought 4.5
Before you go on to read about leading questions and open questions, stop to rephrase the two closed questions in the example above as open questions. That is, how would you put these questions so that an interviewee would be encouraged to speak more freely?

Leading questions

- You do enjoy working with the computer, don't you?
- You have had sales experience, haven't you?

Comment

The phrasing of these questions implies that an affirmative response is expected of the candidate. At the very least this will destroy the confidence of a candidate who answers in the negative. It could also induce a nervous candidate to give false information on the spur of the moment. It is so easy just to answer 'yes' to questions like those above.

Open questions

- What experience have you had of working with a computer?
- Tell me about your experience working with a computer.
- What did you like about working in sales?
- How did you decide to take up a career in personnel management?

Comment

None of these questions can be answered with a one-word answer, neither do they indicate what the questioner expects to hear. Open questions usually start with words like what, why or how. Alternatively, the interviewee can simply be asked to talk about something: 'Tell me about . . .'

It should be obvious that the majority of the questions in an interview should be phrased as open questions, with relatively few closed questions to check facts. Leading questions are not very useful and should be avoided.

> **Did you know?**
>
> According to the CIPD survey of recruitment and selection processes published in 2003, there was a marked increase in the number of employers using competency-based interviews to improve their selection decisions. The percentage of respondents using these rose from 25.8% in 2002 to 58.7% in 2003.
> (CIPD 2003)

Situational and patterned behaviour description questions

It is a fairly straightforward task to gather information about qualifications and skills by careful questioning and listening and by using a variety of tests. Assessing attitudes and interpersonal skills is more difficult. Situational and behavioural questions are suitable for this purpose, as well as for assessing skills and how these would be translated into behaviour in the workplace. Research also indicates that the use of these two types of question improves both the reliability and the validity of selection interviews (Latham *et al.* 1980; Weekley and Gier 1987).

More recently, the IRS (2003) has reported on employers' attempts to improve the effectiveness of their selection processes by using competency-based questions. These are essentially behavioural or situational questions based on a competency framework where such a framework is in place.

Both types of question require an analysis of critical incidents in the job. Interviewers can ascertain what would be critical incidents in the post using methods like those used to draw up a job description or to develop criteria on which to appraise a person's performance or evaluate a post. You will be able to read about the last two issues in Chapters 9 and 10. For the purposes of selection, you will need to design questions that will get candidates to talk about their performance in these areas and the competencies they would call upon.

Pause for thought 4.6   Can you list some of the methods used to gather information for writing a job description? Jot down a few ideas and then check them against what was said in Chapter 2, pages 39–41.

Situational interview questions

The interviewee is presented with a situation that represents a typical incident in the job for which he or she is being interviewed, and is then asked to describe what he or she would do in this situation.

The responses to a situational interview question need to be assessed carefully in order to achieve increased reliability between interviewers. There should be prior agreement on what constitutes a poor, an acceptable and a good answer to the question. A model of each type of answer should be designed, and points can be assigned to each level of response. Each interviewer then grades the actual answers of interviewees accordingly.

Gary Latham and his colleagues (1980) describe a fairly complex manner of designing the graded responses to situational questions, involving knowledge of what was said by previous candidates who turned out to be poor, average or good performers. For most interview situations in practice it is probably adequate for managers to suggest the type of behaviour that they would regard as poor, average and good performance.

An example of a situational question and graded answers for the receptionist post described in Chapter 2 is shown on page 113.

Patterned behaviour description interview questions

These questions are similar to situational questions in that the interviewee is presented with a situation that represents a typical incident in the job for which he or she is being interviewed. The interviewee is then asked to recount what he or she did in a similar situation in a past position. Although this is a very useful approach, there are disadvantages compared to situational interview questions:

- Candidates who do not have any previous experience of the specific incidents will be at a disadvantage. Interviewers will have to decide whether it is the previous experience that is important or the way people would behave in a given situation.
- It is not possible to design and rank expected answers, as candidates may respond with reference to a wide range of examples of when they encountered similar situations. It should be possible, however, to identify the range of skills and competencies you would expect candidates to allude to in their answers.

An example of a behavioural question for the receptionist post is: 'Tell us about an incident when you had to deal with several things at the same time.'

Example

Critical incident

Dealing with several customer enquiries simultaneously, maintaining a customer-centred approach and a friendly manner.

Situational question

One of the junior receptionists has just gone to the cafeteria for his 15-minute coffee break and the other one is working in a nearby office on some invoices that have to be cleared this morning. You have just answered the phone and the caller has a query to which you don't know the answer. Suddenly a number of people come to the reception desk at the same time, so you have a queue of people wanting assistance. How would you handle this situation?

Ranked answers

3 (poor performance)
- Ask the caller to call back in the afternoon.
- Deal with the people at the reception desk.
- Find out the answer to the phone query.

4 (average performance)
- Ask the caller to hold.
- Deal with the people at the reception desk.
- Find out the answer to the phone query and deal with the phone caller.

5 (good performance)
- Explain the need to find out data to the phone caller, and offer to call back.
- Apologise for the delay to the people at the reception desk, and recall the junior receptionist to the reception area. Deal with the customers together.
- Find out the answer to the phone query and call the customer back.

ACTIVITY 4.2

1 Choose a job and design a situational and a behavioural question for it. The job could be one you have experience of or know something about, or one for which you have found an advert in the press.

2 Try out your questions on members of your class. Judge the usefulness of the responses in terms of making a selection decision.

Probing questions

Interviewers need to get over their inhibitions about pursuing information, and practised interviewers often go back to clarify what candidates have said before. The interview is essentially a one-time-only opportunity for both the interviewer and the candidate, and if candidates seem evasive, they may legitimately not realise what you want to know. It is fairer to do all you can to gather relevant information than to superimpose your own assumptions; you should find some polite but insistent way of doing it. It is better to reject some-one for something you know than for an assumption made because informa-tion was missing.

Within this context it should be noted that interviewers will have to ask individualised questions to obtain clarification related to individual appli-cants. The set of questions designed for the structured interview is not meant to inhibit the collection of relevant information.

Questions to be avoided

In spite of what we have said about relating interview questions to the job description and person specification for the post, you will still no doubt encounter many interviewers who ask questions that do not seem to have been designed in this way. Some very general questions have almost become stan-dard fare in interviews, such as:

- What are your strengths and weaknesses?
- Where do you see yourself in five years' time?
- Tell me about yourself.

Such questions might elicit relevant information, but they are vague, and given the time constraints of the interview process, it is better for the inter-viewer to focus more narrowly on essential information.

There are other questions that do not overtly contribute much to the selec-tion process, apart perhaps from attempting to relax a nervous candidate by asking easy questions. These include questions like 'What were your favourite subjects at school?' or 'What do you do in your spare time?' In the limited time available for an interview, there are job-related questions that can be answered in a straightforward fashion which can be used to help candidates relax and which will contribute more to the proceedings. Such a question might be: 'Tell me what you do on a typical day at work.'

It should also be borne in mind that questions about what an applicant does outside of work may be regarded as an infringement of a person's right to respect for their private and family life under the Human Rights Act 1998. Candidates may also feel pressured by such questions into giving information that could potentially be perceived as unlawfully discriminatory, for example if a person is heavily involved in a religious group in his or her spare time or participates in gay rights campaigns. The widening scope of equality legisla-tion reinforces the fact that employment interviews should focus on work issues and not personal matters. Indeed, the ACAS guidelines on how to imple-ment the sexual orientation regulations recommend the avoidance of ques-tions on a person's social life and the guidelines on the religion and belief regulations recommend the avoidance of questions on communal involve-ment (ACAS 2004a and 2004b).

A third variety of questions of dubious merit consists of those that seem intended to put candidates on the defensive, including statements such as 'You seem to think very highly of your interpersonal skills.'

All these questions should be judged against what they are meant to achieve. Better results are achieved by interviewers who concentrate on formulating questions related to the job and the skills, knowledge and qualities needed to perform well in the post. It bears repeating here that your questions should be linked to the job description and person specification/competency profile, that you should be able to demonstrate that this is the case and that you should be able to justify why every question is being asked.

Questions for candidates with little or no work experience

We have firmly established that it is best practice to acquire work-related and job-specific information from applicants to make good selection decisions. However, we must concede that a modified approach may be necessary when dealing with individuals who have no work experience, little work experience or no recent work experience. Typical examples we can identify include:

- school leavers
- students graduating from college and university
- the long-term unemployed.

Pause for thought 4.7

Review what we have said about questioning techniques, and consider how you might have to adapt your approach if you were interviewing an applicant in this category.

Asking open questions about work experience related to the tasks involved in the vacancy would obviously not be very productive with this group of applicants. However, it should still be possible to ask about relevant transferable skills. The interviewer might need to give fuller explanations about the requirements of the organisation before asking about the applicant's related knowledge and abilities. You should have identified that situational questions are suitable for people with little experience, so it would make sense to develop such questions in this case rather than patterned behavioural questions. In addition, interviewers faced with people who are not currently accustomed to the working environment might recognise the potential for increased nervousness, and therefore decide to spend more time at the commencement of the interview on putting the applicant at ease.

Discriminatory questions

If you conduct structured interviews with a planned set of questions that have been designed on the basis of a properly constructed person specification, you are unlikely to ask any questions that are discriminatory in terms of the SDA, the RRA or any of the other equality regulations. The implication behind your questions is that if you ask the question, you intend to use the information to make your decision. Avoid any question that would result in your acquiring information on things the legislation or your policies have said would constitute unfair discrimination, for example marital status, race, age of dependants.

One procedure that is often recommended to avoid accusations of unfair discrimination under the SDA is to ask the same questions of all candidates, both male and female. This will supposedly preclude any suspicion of an intention to discriminate against female applicants. However, in today's society there is still generally an expectation that women bear more responsibility for child care than men. If a young woman said she had two children under the age of five, and a young man said the same thing, most people would draw different conclusions about the relative impact of this.

These assumptions are based on each individual's experiences and are not necessarily true for other people. It is best practice, therefore, simply to avoid questions about personal circumstances unless there is some specific element of the job, such as the ability to undertake shift work, where personal circumstances are in fact relevant. Even then, candidates can be asked whether something like shift work will cause them any problems, rather than the interviewer's imposing his or her own view of whether or not the applicant should undertake such work. The Equal Opportunities Commission provides further advice on discriminatory questions on its web site (**www.eoc.org.uk**; accessed 10.09.04).

Before we leave this discussion of the interviewer's questions, we should once again emphasise that it is more important for the candidate to talk than the interviewer. Interview questions are designed as keys to unlock information, and sometimes a pause to allow the candidate time to reflect can be more effective than jumping in with a new question.

Encourage candidates to talk

Proper formulation of questions should ensure that the candidate does most of the talking and not the interviewers. However, it is worth repeating that allowing candidates to talk to obtain the information you need is the objective of the interview, and interviewers should practise due restraint.

For all questions, you should decide in advance what it is you are trying to find out with the question; you can then rephrase and probe if the candidate does not respond with the expected information.

Record the information

You could simply note how each candidate scored on the criteria you are using to assess applicants, but it is much more helpful to have a record of what the candidate actually said. This means that it is necessary for someone to take notes during the interview. It is difficult to take notes, pay attention to what the candidate is saying and keep a normal flow of conversation going, but interviewers develop this skill with experience. Alternatively, roles/tasks can be shared among a panel of interviewers by pre-arrangement. It is also best to explain to candidates what you are doing and why.

ACTIVITY 4.3

As Office Services Manager, you have received the completed application form shown in Figure 4.2 for the position of receptionist described in Chapter 2. The personnel trainee has prepared three sets of questions, and asked you which set you would like to use in the interviews.

1 Review the following sets of questions and choose the one that you feel would get the best results. Give reasons for your choice and state why you rejected the other two sets.
2 Develop any further questions you would like to ask.

3 Use the chosen, revised set of questions as a basis for mock interviews with members of your class, using the data on the application form as the interviewee's background. Evaluate whether or not you have obtained sufficient information to make a selection.

Interview questions

Set 1

1 I see you've been with Marvel Appliances for a year. Do you like working there?
2 How do you think your past work experience has prepared you for this job?
3 Can you tell us of a time when you had to deal with several things at the same time?
4 One of our junior receptionists is male and he's older than you. Do you think you'd have any problems being his supervisor?
5 What do you think contributes to good customer care?

Set 2

1 I see you've been with Marvel Appliances for a year. Can you tell me a little about what you do there on a typical day?
2 How do you think your past work experience has prepared you for this job?
3 I'd like to describe a typical situation you might encounter in this post, then ask you how you would respond to it.

   One of the junior receptionists has just gone to the cafeteria for his 15-minute coffee break and the other one is working in a nearby office on some invoices that have to be cleared this morning. You have just answered the phone and the caller has a query to which you don't know the answer. Suddenly a number of people come to the reception desk at the same time, so you have a queue of people wanting assistance. How would you handle this situation?
4 Can you describe any supervisory experience you have had?
5 What do you think contributes to good customer care?

Set 3

1 I see you've been with Marvel Appliances for a year. Why do you want to leave?
2 How do you think your past work experience has prepared you for this job?
3 Can you tell us of a time when you had to deal with several things at the same time?
4 What kinds of hobbies do you have?
5 If we employed you, how long do you think you would stay with us? What about your personal plans for the future?

Candidates' questions

It is good practice in an interview, usually at the end, to allow candidates an opportunity to ask questions about the post. Remember that both parties can benefit from the interview being a two-way process; it is important that prospective employees find out about the job and the organisation so that they can make an informed decision if offered the post. This may help to avoid the situation where someone is hired, only to decide after a short while that

Figure 4.2 Example application form: receptionist

XYZ Company

XYZ is striving to become an Equal Opportunities Employer. All appointments are made in keeping with our Equal Opportunities Policy.

APPLICATION FOR EMPLOYMENT

POST Receptionist   LOCATION Manchester   REF NO R101/HO

Please type or write clearly in black ink. Give all details in full.

SURNAME *Reives*

FORENAME *Joan*

ADDRESS *23 Burns Street*
Dorton, Manchester, M16 0BF

TELEPHONE HOME: *0161-000-000*   WORK: *0161-000-000*

Do you hold a current driving licence? (YES)/ NO

EMPLOYMENT EXPERIENCE

PRESENT OR MOST RECENT EMPLOYMENT

NAME & ADDRESS   JOB TITLE: *Junior Receptionist*
OF PRESENT EMPLOYER   START DATE: *July 2004*
Marvel Appliances   END DATE: *Still there*
10 Dean Street   (if applicable)
Stalybridge   PRESENT SALARY: *£12,000*
MIN 19 2QF   PERIOD OF NOTICE
                              REQUIRED: *Two Weeks*

DUTIES:

I welcome visitors to the company and call the person they want to see to the reception desk. I operate the switchboard and I transfer phone calls to other employees.

PREVIOUS EMPLOYMENT (START WITH MOST RECENT POST)

FROM MONTH/YEAR	TO MONTH/YEAR	EMPLOYER	JOB TITLE AND BRIEF DESCRIPTION OF DUTIES	FINAL SALARY
July 2003	*Sept 2003*	*Allgood's Department Store*	*Sales Assistant Assisted customers to choose purchases and completed cash or credit card transactions*	

EDUCATION AND TRAINING

SCHOOL/COLLEGE/UNIVERSITY/OTHER	QUALIFICATION	FROM	TO
Stalybridge High School	*3 'A'-Levels*	*2002*	*2004*
	6 GCSEs	*2002*	*2002*

MEMBERSHIP OF PROFESSIONAL ASSOCIATIONS

Figure 4.2 (contd)

ADDITIONAL INFORMATION

Please state why you are interested in the position you are applying for, and explain how your qualifications and work experience relate to this post. Please supply any additional information you feel may assist the selection panel in evaluating your application for this post. You should include any unpaid or voluntary work experience or any leisure activities where you feel you have developed relevant skills.

I have lots of experience as a junior receptionist and working with customers. I am ambitious and hardworking and I know I could do a good job as a receptionist. I think I am ready for a promotion.

REFERENCES

Please give the names, addresses and telephone numbers of two referees. One of these should be your current or most recent employer. Please indicate if you wish to be consulted before we contact your current employer. (YES)/NO

1 Name: *Mr Willis*

Address: *Marvel Appliances*
10 Dean Street
Stalybridge
MN19 2YF

Tel No: *0161-000-000*
Position: *Manager*

2 Name: *Mrs Green*

Address: *Allgood's Dept. Store*
The Crescent
Manchester
MS3 9MN

Tel No: *0161-000-000*
Position: *Manager*

DECLARATION

I certify that the information provided in this form is correct and accurate to the best of my knowledge. I understand that any misrepresentation makes me liable to disqualification or dismissal should I be engaged.

Signature *J Reives*   Date *15/9/2005*

Thank you for completing this form. Please return it to:
Director of Human Resource Management
XYZ Company
Ourtown
Ourcountry
PC1 6YZ

We regret that we are unable to acknowledge individual applications. If you wish to have confirmation that your application has been received, please enclose a stamped, addressed envelope. If you have not heard from us within three weeks, you should assume that your application has been unsuccessful on this occasion.

EQUAL OPPORTUNITIES MONITORING INFORMATION

This information is collected ONLY to assist us in monitoring equal opportunities in our company. We are asking you to provide the information on this tear-off strip so that it can be retained in the Human Resource Management department before your application is circulated to other managers. The details given here will NOT be considered as part of the selection process.

If you choose not to complete this section, this will not affect your application.

Surname: *Reives*

Forename: *Joan*

Date of Birth: *3.8.86*

Male [ ]   Female [✓]

Do you consider yourself to be disabled? YES (NO)

If so, what is the nature of your disability?

How would you describe your ethnic origin?

Afro Caribbean [ ]   Asian [ ]

UK Afro Caribbean [ ]   UK Asian [ ]

UK European [✓]   Other European [ ]

he or she is not suited to the job. As well as responding to candidates' questions, organisations can employ other techniques to supply information to applicants. Some of these, such as supplying job descriptions and organisational literature, are relevant to the recruitment process, and others, such as realistic job previews, usually take place during the selection process. Realistic job previews are discussed more fully in the next chapter. Company web pages are also an excellent source of information for candidates.

Close the interview

To close the interview, the interviewer should thank the interviewee for attending and inform him or her of what to expect next. This may include a second stage of interviews for selected candidates, a variety of tests, the time frame for the decision and details about how candidates will be informed about the outcome.

Evaluate information

Even if the interview has been carefully structured, with the involvement of several interviewers and the use of a range of well-designed questions, there is still a temptation at this stage to revert to making a decision based on gut feeling or the overall impression that candidates have made. In order to achieve a more objective evaluation of the mass of information that has now been gathered, it is possible to devise a scoring system, either for the answers to interview questions or for the elements of the person specification. Marks can be allocated to each question and questions can be weighted according to their relative importance. It would also be possible to stipulate that a candidate should achieve a passing mark on a question of particular significance in order to be considered further. For example, candidates for a personnel position might be rejected for giving an unacceptable answer on a sex or race discrimination issue, no matter how well they performed in the rest of the interview.

A numerical score for each candidate will allow the interviewers to create a ranked order of candidates following an agreed method. Another system that could be used is quite simply to mark the person specification/competency profile for each candidate, + for the criteria that have been met, and – for those that have not. The use of essential and preferred categories implies some weighting of elements.

Record and justify decision

The methodical approach described in the previous section means that it should be easy for the selection panel to justify why they have selected the chosen candidate and why the others have been rejected. All reasons for the decisions reached should be expressed in terms of where candidates did or did not meet the criteria stipulated in the person specification/competency profile.

It is important to keep a written record of these factors for several reasons:

● To be able to present evidence of a proper and fair procedure should a candidate decide to pursue a case under any aspect of the equality legislation.
● To be able to provide feedback to candidates who request it. Increasingly,

applicants for posts do this in their quest to make a good impression and to improve their chances of finally securing a post. As you will read in the next chapter, there is an obligation to provide information to candidates who have completed psychometric tests, but it is part of an organisation's good image to be able to respond to requests of this nature from rejected applicants in any case.

● To ensure that interviewers follow a rigorous and methodical process.

Monitoring for equal opportunities purposes

On a longer-term basis, it is important for the human resource management department to monitor the selection process in order to ensure that no unlawful or unfair discrimination is taking place, to keep managers informed of the organisation's performance in terms of equal opportunity and to initiate appropriate programmes should any issues need to be addressed. Monitoring involves analysis of the information gathered on the equal opportunities monitoring section of the application form, and would normally relate to different stages of the recruitment and selection process:

● who applied for the position
● who was called for interview
● who was selected after the interview, either to be hired or to proceed to further stages.

Monitoring during the selection process, then, continues the monitoring process that should commence during the earlier recruitment stages, as described on page 89. Monitoring for equality is regarded as good practice in general, but it is actually a legal requirement of public sector organisations with regard to racial equality under the Race Relations (Amendment) Act 2000. It may also provide relevant information should an employer need to respond to an accusation of discrimination in an employment tribunal, as described in Chapter 3 in the section on the burden of proof.

Administrative procedures

The interview may represent the end of your recruitment and selection process. If so, you would proceed at this stage to offer the post to the successful candidate and to inform those who had not been successful. However, you may decide to incorporate additional stages in your selection process, such as a number of tests. These are discussed in the next chapter, and you will find more information about closing the selection process at the end of that chapter.

ACTIVITY 4.4

Recruitment and selection case study: The Fabric Brothers' Recruitment Drive

Thomas and Edward Fabric founded a small clothing manufacturing company in the early 1960s in the North of England. Over the years the company has grown and recently the Fabric brothers won a new contract to manufacture dresses for a catalogue company. This has necessitated their taking on 10 new sewing machine operators.

Edward's son, John, has taken care of recruitment since he joined the family enterprise in 1978 when he was 20 years old. The company had functioned very much as a small, family-owned business for many years, and John developed a paternalistic attitude which has never been challenged. He let the 'girls' in the sewing room know that he was looking for some additional employees, and he posted a notice on the factory gates, advertising the vacancies as a good opportunity for, as he put it, 'ladies looking to make some extra money while your children are in school'.

John interviewed a few people who dropped in to ask about the job, and he was able to fill his 10 vacancies with no bother. He was very surprised a few weeks later to get a letter from the Commission for Racial Equality stating that two Asian women, who had applied for the post and been interviewed but not selected, felt that they had been discriminated against on the basis of race. Talking it over with his father, John said: 'Well, I did ask them questions about how long they had been in England and whether they felt their English was good enough for the job, but surely that's not racial discrimination?'

John was actually quite upset because he did not think of himself as a racist. Of course, all the girls in the sewing room were white, but that's just the way things had worked out. Imagine his surprise, then, when a few days later he received a similar letter from the Equal Opportunities Commission stating that a man he had rejected had complained that he had been rejected on the basis of sex. This man had once worked as a tailor, so he felt he could not have been rejected on the grounds of competence.

John knows that you have some background in personnel issues, so he has turned to you to explain to him how all this could have happened and to give him some advice about what to do both now in response to these complaints, and in handling recruitment and selection in the future.

REVIEW QUESTIONS

You will find brief answers to these review questions on pages 489–490.

1 Describe the aims of the selection process and comment on a methodical approach that can be used to achieve these aims.

2 Explain the terms 'validity' and 'reliability' with reference to employment interviews.

3 What factors contribute to the low validity of employment interviews and how can this be overcome?

4 Critically assess the value of different types of questioning in employment interviews.

SELF-CHECK QUESTIONS

Answer the following multiple-choice and short-answer questions. The correct responses are given on page 490 for you to check your understanding of this chapter.

1 Which of the following questions is an open question?
   (a) Did you get here by train?
   (b) Don't you enjoy working with computerised files?
   (c) What experience have you had in dealing with after-sales support services?
   (d) So you worked with your last employer for three years?

2 Is the following statement true or false? Of all the selection methods available to employers, interviews have been found to have the highest validity.

3 Which of the following is the best definition of validity?
   (a) A method of assessment that gives the same results when it is applied by a number of different people.
   (b) A method of assessment that measures what it sets out to measure.
   (c) A method of assessment that uses a wide range of techniques.
   (d) Interviews conducted by more than one person.

4 An interviewer is very impressed by the smart appearance and confident manner of a candidate. The interviewer tends to seek positive information from this candidate and readily overlooks any negative information. This is known as:
   (a) stereotyping
   (b) the contrast effect
   (c) closed questioning
   (d) the halo effect.

5 The validity of an interview can be increased by:
   (a) being aware of potential interviewer errors
   (b) structuring interviews to obtain the same information from all candidates
   (c) having interviews conducted by more than one interviewer
   (d) all the above
   (e) none of the above.

6 Which of the following is the best definition of (i) a situational interview question, (ii) a patterned behaviour description interview question?
   (a) The interviewee is asked to describe a situation in which he or she has performed well.
   (b) The interviewee is presented with a situation that represents a typical incident in the job for which he or she is being interviewed. The interviewee is asked to recount what he or she did in a similar situation in a past position.
   (c) The interviewee is presented with a situation that represents a typical incident in the job for which he or she is being interviewed. The interviewee is asked to describe what he or she would do in this situation.
   (d) The interviewee is presented with a situation that represents a typical incident in the job for which he or she is being interviewed. The interviewee is asked to describe what the ideal behaviour would be in this circumstance.

7 Which of the following best defines how to assess the responses to a situational interview to achieve increased reliability?
  (a) Decide in advance what could be regarded as a good, an adequate and a poor response. Assign points to each level of response. Each interviewer grades answers accordingly.
  (b) Each interviewer reviews responses from all candidates after the interviews. Each interviewer ranks the responses according to acceptability and compares the results with the other interviewers.
  (c) The interviewers as a group review the responses from all candidates after the interviews. The interviewers as a group rank the responses according to acceptability.
  (d) Decide in advance what could be regarded as a good, an adequate and a poor response. Assign points to each level of response. Interviewers as a group grade responses accordingly.

8 Is the following question a situational question or a patterned behaviour description question? 'Can you tell us about a situation where someone approached you with a problem that was affecting his or her work?'

9 What is the term that is used for analysing recruitment and selection data to ensure that no unfair or unlawful discrimination is taking place?

WHAT NEXT?

Now that you have mastered the introductory level of information presented in this chapter, you may wish to take your studies to a higher level. The article cited below is a research-based assessment of a specific aspect of selection. It looks in depth at a particular aspect of interviewee behaviour (impression management) and how this might affect interviewers' perceptions of the candidate. Read the article and draw out from it what you consider to be the major points the researchers are making. Does this article suggest to you any further issues that could be researched with regard to the effectiveness and management of interview processes?

Kristof-Brown, A., M. R. Barrick and M. Franke (2002) Applicant impression management: dispositional influences and consequences for recruiter perceptions of fit and similarity, *Journal of Management*, Vol. 28, No. 1, 27–46

References

Advisory, Conciliation and Arbitration Service (2004a) *Religion or Belief and the Workplace: A Guide for Employers and Employees*, ACAS

Advisory, Conciliation and Arbitration Service (2004b) *Sexual Orientation and the Workplace: A Guide for Employers and Employees*, ACAS

Chartered Institute of Personnel and Development (2003) *Recruitment and Retention 2003: Survey Report*, CIPD

Chartered Institute of Personnel and Development (2004) *Telephone Interviewing*, CIPD (**www.cipd.co.uk**; accessed 28.09.04)

Industrial Relations Services (IRS) (2003) Sharpening up recruitment and selection with competencies, *IRS Employment Review 782*, 15 August, 42–48

Latham, G. P., L. M. Saari, E. D. Pursell and M. A. Campion (1980) The situational interview, *Journal of Applied Psychology*, Vol. 65, No. 4, 422–427

Makin, P. and I. Robertson (1986) Selecting the best selection techniques, *Personnel Management*, November, 38–40

Weekley, J. A. and J. A. Gier (1987) Reliability and validity of the situational interview for a sales position, *Journal of Applied Psychology*, Vol. 72, 484–487

www.eoc.org.uk; accessed 10.09.04

Further study

Books

Black, J. S., H. B. Gregersen, M. E. Mendenhall and L. K. Stroh (1999) *Globalizing People through International Assignments*, Addison Wesley. (Although its focus is specifically on HR aspects of dealing with international employees, this book contains some interesting information about recruitment and selection which could have wider applications, including some good examples of open and behavioural questions on the competency areas of perseverance and delegation.)

Chartered Institute of Personnel and Development (2003) *Recruitment and Retention 2003: Survey Report*, CIPD. (An overview of what employers are currently doing in recruitment and selection, based on survey evidence. Highlights what employers consider to be the main issues affecting the sourcing and retention of employees.)

Cook, M. (2004) *Personnel Selection: Adding Value through People*, Wiley. (A thorough review of selection methods and issues, including interviews, tests, assessment centres and validity.)

Incomes Data Services (2003) *IDS Studies: Recruitment Practices*, No. 751, June, IDS. (A concise overview of the basic range of both recruitment and selection practices with case studies of six employers, including an NHS trust and Loop Customer Management.)

Roberts, G. (1997) *Recruitment and Selection: A Competency Approach*, IPD. (A general introduction to various aspects of HRM including chapters on screening and interviewing.)

Smith, M. and I.T. Robertson (1993) *The Theory and Practice of Systematic Personnel Selection*, 2nd edition, Macmillan. (A thorough discussion of all the stages involved in selection, and of issues such as ethical considerations, discrimination and validity of selection methods.)

Articles

Jenks, J. M. and L. P. Zevnik (1989) ABCs of job interviewing, *Harvard Business Review*, July–August, 38–42. (This article discusses how to formulate questions and gives practical guidelines.)

Judge, T. A., D. M. Cable and C. A. Higgins (2000) The employment interview: a review of recent research and recommendations for future research, *Human Resource Management Review*, Vol. 10, No. 4, Winter, 383–406. (Presents interesting findings on both interviewer and interviewee behaviours. With its focus on research, this article is a good starting point for anyone wishing to undertake an academic study of the interviewing process.)

Latham, G. P., L. M. Saari, E. D. Pursell and M. A. Campion (1980) The situational interview, *Journal of Applied Psychology*, Vol. 65, No. 4, 422–427. (This article describes research into the validity of situational interviewing, and provides an example of a question used for manual employees.)

McDaniel, M. A., D. A. Whetzel, F. L. Schmidt and S. D. Maurer (1994) The validity of employment interviews: a comprehensive review and meta-analysis. *Journal of Applied Psychology*, Vol. 79, 599–616. (Provides a good review of the results of a wide range of research into the validity of employment interviews. An excellent starting point, both because of its content and the extensive list of references, for anyone wishing to compile an academic report on this topic.)

Weekley, J. A. and J. A. Gier (1987) Reliability and validity of the situational interview for a sales position. *Journal of Applied Psychology*, Vol. 72, 484–487. (This article describes research into the reliability and validity of interviews, particularly interviews using situational questions. A sample question is provided, together with suggestions on how to assess responses.)

Internet

The Chartered Institute of Personnel and Development   **www.cipd.co.uk**
(Browse the CIPD's web site to find information related to recruitment and selection. The referenced document on telephone interviewing also contains good information on interviewing in general.)

Equal Opportunities Commission   **www.eoc.org.uk**
(Provides a checklist specifically designed for line managers on handling situations that might arise during the shortlisting and interview processes. Go to the main site and search for the equality checklists.)

information so that they too can make an informed decision about the suitability of the post for them. Ways of giving this information may be included in your list. One of these is known as the realistic job preview, which is described later in this chapter.

Your list may include some of the following activities:

- psychological tests
  - ability
  - intelligence
  - interests
  - motivation
  - personality
- work sample
- role play; demonstration
- observation at work
- assessment centres
- references
- medical examination
- criminal record check
- drug use check
- lie detector test
- graphology
- phrenology
- astrology
- realistic job preview
- company tour
- opportunity to meet prospective colleagues.

Some of these are obviously *not* to be recommended, so the rest of this chapter will review some of the available selection methods and conclude with an overview of the activities that need to be undertaken to complete the selection process.

Supplementary selection techniques

Note that we are using the term 'supplementary' and not 'alternative'. In spite of reservations about the effectiveness of interviewing, interviews are not likely to be replaced as a selection method. You will need to choose which methods to use to complement the information gained from interviews, and integrate these additional measures into your selection and decision-making processes. The description of supplementary techniques in this chapter should enable you to do this.

The essential criterion in choosing supplementary methods is that they should provide information that is directly related to performance on the job. This should be the guiding principle both in choosing off-the-shelf tests and in designing exercises tailor-made for a particular workplace. In their review of what they call personnel testing, Murphy and Davidshofer (2001) stress that better results are obtained the more closely a test, such as a work sample test, resembles things that are actually done in the job concerned. A related issue is that candidates can easily see the point of a test that requires them to do something they know will be done on the job. This increases the face validity of the test, making it more acceptable to the candidates. This, in turn, may affect the candidates' willingness to take the test seriously and their motivation to perform the task to the best of their ability. Face validity is therefore something that should be taken into consideration when choosing or designing a test.

Psychological testing

Psychological testing is sometimes referred to as psychometric testing, and is a method of acquiring objective information about a range of individual abilities and traits. Psychological tests are defined as having the following characteristics:

- They are professionally developed and checked for reliability and validity.
- They are administered and scored in a standardised manner.
- They test maximum performance and habitual performance.
- They result in scores that can be compared to norms for relevant populations.

These characteristics will be explained more fully as we examine the various issues surrounding the uses of psychological tests.

The characteristics of psychological tests listed above indicate that their inclusion in the selection process will:

- add an element of objectivity
- increase the predictive validity of selection decisions
- measure some factors that cannot be assessed through the application form and interview.

The standardised administration of tests means that all applicants answer the same test questions in the same conditions, and objective scoring means that the scores are not open to individual interpretation as is the case with interview responses. There is a vast amount of research that underpins the development of commercially produced tests, including proofs of their reliability and validity. If this is properly documented, the user of the tests can rest assured that the tests will improve the validity of the selection process.

Because psychological tests are such complex instruments, they should be used only by people who have had specific training in how to administer them and how to interpret the results, and in fact reputable test providers will only supply commercially developed tests to properly accredited persons with appropriate training. The British Psychological Society (BPS) has approved the standards of training needed to administer and interpret tests at various levels and to give feedback to test takers, and this training is available from various sources, including the suppliers of tests, who also provide additional training in the use of their own products. The basic level of training, which qualifies persons to use ability tests, is the BPS Certificate of Competence in Occupational Testing (Level A). This training takes approximately five days. Further training of approximately five days with a follow-up day some time after the initial training is necessary to be able to use personality questionnaires. There is a cost implication in this for employers, but the cost of training staff and of staff time for administering tests may be offset by the improved validity of selection decisions. An alternative to having a trained member of staff is to use the services of an occupational psychologist on a consultancy basis when the use of psychological testing seems to be appropriate. A controversial issue that attracted attention in 2001 (*People Management*) was the use of the Internet to conduct psychological tests, and this continues to be an issue where pros and cons need to be closely examined (Pickard 2004).

The IPD *Guide on Psychological Testing* (1997) outlines what to consider when deciding whether to use a test. Firstly, the test should be directly relevant to requirements specified in the personnel specification/competency profile. There is a very wide selection of tests to choose from, and test suppliers provide brochures outlining the sort of information each test will provide and what types of job each test might be appropriate for. Tests are designed with different groups of people in mind, and test suppliers offer advice about who the tests are suitable for. Some examples of designated groups for whom tests are available are middle to senior managers, administrative/supervisory employees, skilled operatives and staff who have direct customer contact. Secondly, test suppliers should provide evidence that the test is reliable, valid, and free of racial or sex bias. Thirdly, ease of administration and interpretation should also be considered. Further indicators of when to use psychometric tests and questionnaires are:

- when a wrong hiring decision would be extremely costly, for example for very senior positions or when employee errors could render employers liable for high financial outlay
- when the selection ratio (the ratio of applicants to the number of positions to be filled) is high and additional information is needed so that the number of candidates can be reduced.

Psychological tests cover a range of human characteristics and may assess:

- intelligence
- ability
- interest
- motivation
- personality.

Intelligence tests

General intelligence tests assess ability in a range of skills such as verbal, arithmetical and diagrammatical reasoning, producing an overall score.

Ability tests

Ability tests focus on specific mental abilities and produce separate scores for the different skills. Sometimes a distinction is made between tests of attainment and tests of aptitude, but in fact it is not always easy to distinguish between the two. Attainment tests assess skills and knowledge that have been acquired through experience and learning, and aptitude tests measure individuals' potential to develop ability. The results of an attainment test, say after learning a foreign language, might also be an indicator of aptitude for learning that language. Since both kinds of tests examine verbal, arithmetical and diagrammatical skills, it is probably more helpful to think of them under the general heading of ability tests.

Work sample tests or school exams are examples of attainment tests, and the use of these would not require the special training outlined above. There are aptitude tests for specific occupations such as word processing, and test batteries that produce a profile of the candidate over a range of abilities.

Tests of interest and motivation

The relationship between interests and motivation and successful performance is not a straightforward one. For this reason these tests are not used for selection (Smith and Robertson 1993), but interest tests can be used for career guidance and counselling, and motivation tests can be used for decisions about how best to manage people and enhance their performance by responding to what motivates them.

Personality questionnaires

The expression 'personality questionnaire' has been used in preference to 'personality test', because in terms of measuring personality characteristics there are no right and wrong answers as would be the case in questions of verbal or arithmetical reasoning. Ability tests are examples of tests of maximum performance, meaning that they reflect the best performance an individual is capable of at that point in time in the skill being tested. Personality questionnaires are indicators of habitual performance, meaning that they reflect stable traits that are likely to be revealed in typical behaviour. Of all the assessments that are carried out in the workplace, personality questionnaires are probably the most contentious, especially with regard to acceptance by candidates. For this reason, it is particularly important to explain to applicants how the test is related to performance on the job concerned and to provide feedback on the results. Test users should also monitor results to ensure that tests do not discriminate unfairly.

Personality questionnaires examine aspects of personality that have been shown through research to correlate with performance at work. Murphy and Davidshofer (2001) refer to evidence that some personality characteristics are related to job performance in general, including agreeableness, conscientiousness and openness to experience. Together with extraversion and neuroticism these traits are known as 'the big five', which are the focus of much interest in current psychological research (Robertson 2001).

Most personality questionnaires are of the self-report variety, where applicants are asked to record how they see themselves on a range of characteristics or traits. Some items may be open-ended questions asking about preferred activities, and some items may be a choice from a number of statements, asking applicants to choose which statement most resembles them or is most unlike them. These measures usually result in a profile of the person on a range of personality dimensions. One of the most well known of these instruments is Cattell's 16 Personality Factor test (16PF). The 16PF is based on Cattell's work in isolating a range of 16 elements which he believed could be used to describe the whole spectrum of an individual's personality. Cattell's personality dimensions include reserved–outgoing, tough minded–sensitive, conservative–experimenting and relaxed–tense.

Other established tests include the Saville and Holdsworth Occupational Personality Questionnaire and the Myers-Briggs Type Indicator. The Myers-Briggs test is most often used within the framework of training to identify personality types and examine their impact on personal interactions. There are also questionnaires that measure characteristics that predict success in specific occupations.

One of the reasons why personality tests are sometimes regarded with some scepticism is that in self-reporting, candidates may try to give the answers they think are expected. It is also recognised that the situation can affect the responses that people make, so personality test results are not always reliable.

This leads to a very important point with regard to the use of psychological tests in general: they should never be the sole means of assessing candidates, but should always be used as part of a wider process. Information about suppliers of psychological tests is available from the CIPD to its members and Toplis *et al.* (2004) provide a brief description of the whole range of available tests.

Work sample tests

As the term suggests, a work sample test consists of getting a candidate to perform some task or element of a task that forms part of the job. You can gain a better understanding of work sample tests by working through the design process using a familiar example.

How to design a work sample test

Let us take an example of a job with which you are all familiar, that of a university or college lecturer. If you were invited to design a work sample test to be used in hiring a new lecturer in human resource management, what preliminary issues would you consider? How would you approach the task?

The first consideration is that a work sample test makes sense only if it demonstrates abilities that are a major and integral part of the job. A critical incident analysis and selection of a critical task are therefore the first step in designing a work sample test. Remember that you can perform a simplified critical incident analysis by interviewing a number of lecturers and heads of department, and asking them what they consider to be the most important activities that contribute to success in the job. Without doubt most lecturers would identify the ability to conduct a seminar as a critical task.

A second consideration ought to be how the performance of the work sample will be assessed, as this will affect the way the exercise is designed, and it may influence the instructions that are given to candidates.

Pause for thought 5.2   List the criteria on which you would assess a candidate's performance in delivering a seminar.

In deciding on your assessment criteria, you will no doubt have identified the lecturers you regard as being excellent in their seminar delivery, and then you will have identified the competencies and techniques that are part of that excellence. If you have worked with a group of colleagues you may have discussed what each of you considers to be important and agreed on a list. Your criteria will include some of the following:

- choice and relevance of topic
- knowledge of subject; integration of current material
- style of delivery

- use of materials
  - content
  - variety
  - visual aids
- ability to stimulate participation/discussion
- adequacy of preparation
- ability to handle questions.

For some of these criteria, you may also have outlined how each would be judged. Adequacy of preparation, for instance, might be judged by the absence of hesitation, well-ordered notes and materials, observable structure, control of physical equipment.

Some work samples, such as typing tests, can be assessed on an objective basis using a mathematical formula, but assessment of activities like delivering a seminar will still be subjective. It is important to have assessment guidelines to provide some level of standardisation and consequently to improve reliability among the assessors. Assessment criteria should obviously be related to what is regarded as superior performance on the job. This being the case, documentation relating to performance appraisal should be a good source of material to be used when designing work sample tests.

ACTIVITY 5.1

Make a list of the factors on which you would judge the criterion 'style of delivery'. Discuss your list with a group of fellow students and devise a set of assessment criteria for this performance criterion.

Since acceptability of the test to the candidate is an important factor, it may improve the face validity of the test to inform candidates how they will be assessed. You should consider incorporating this into the instructions to be given to candidates. For example, the instructions on conducting a seminar might be phrased as follows:

> As part of the selection process you are requested to conduct a seminar in your subject area. The seminar should last one hour and be appropriate for a foundation-level course. Your performance will be judged in terms of the appropriateness of your material, the style of delivery and your ability to stimulate participation.

Assessing performance in the work sample exercise

The assessment criteria will already have been established in the process of designing the work sample. What remains is to ensure that all the assessors involved are fully cognisant of the criteria, and that there is some agreement on what represents acceptable standards of performance. This goal can be facilitated in two ways:

- the involvement of line managers both in the design of the work sample test and in the selection process
- the use of a scoring sheet listing the assessment criteria.

An example of a scoring sheet for the lecturer's work sample test is given in Table 5.1.

We can now summarise the steps you have just worked through to design a work sample exercise:

● Identify key critical factors of performance.
● Choose factors that can be tested appropriately by a work sample.
● Identify assessment criteria.
● Design the work sample exercise.
● Write instructions for the candidate.
● Design the assessment form.
● Train the assessors.

Integration of work sample tests into the selection process

Work sample tests can easily be included in a selection process to provide additional information without necessarily developing a fully fledged assessment centre approach as described in the next section. A written work sample can, for example, be requested along with submission of the application form. This is especially useful if you are expecting a large number of applications for a particular post. One example of an organisation that has done this is a local authority in Yorkshire which requested applicants for a personnel manager position to submit a report along with their completed application forms at the time when compulsory competitive tendering was the order of the day. This process obliged departments to examine certain activities and determine whether they should be delivered in-house or outsourced. Applicants were

| Table 5.1 | **Work sample assessment record** |

Post: Lecturer in HRM; delivery of a seminar

Assess each of the following criteria on a scale of 1–5, where 1 = poor performance, 3 = acceptable performance, 5 = outstanding performance. An indication of factors you might consider is given for some of the criteria.

	Candidate 1	Candidate 2	Candidate 3	Candidate 4
Choice and relevance of topic				
Knowledge of subject: up-to-date issues included				
Style of delivery: ability to attract and keep attention; use of humour; movement about room				
Use of materials: content; variety; visual aids				
Ability to stimulate participation/discussion				
Adequacy of preparation: absence of hesitation; well-ordered notes and materials; observable structure; control of physical equipment				
Ability to handle questions				
Total				

given the following instructions: imagine that you are approached by a departmental manager who asks for advice about making a number of people redundant in readiness for the compulsory competitive tendering of services provided by his department. The manager wishes to make an in-house bid for the contract for these services and feels that the only way to make a competitive bid is to reduce costs by reducing staffing levels. Prepare a report recounting how you would advise this manager.

Pause for thought 5.3

What factors was the local authority attempting to measure with this work sample test? In what ways could this device supplement the application form to assist the authority in its selection process?

By asking applicants to submit a written report along with their application form, the authority was potentially gaining a vast amount of additional evidence about applicants' capabilities beyond what it would be able to glean from the application form alone. This includes evidence of:

- knowledge – more so than the assumption of knowledge because of academic qualifications and related experience
- report-writing skills
- ability to deliver work under the pressure of deadlines
- attitudes and abilities reflected in the content of the report – did the candidate assess the whole situation or merely respond with information on how to handle redundancies; how much consideration was given to the consultation and involvement of affected parties?

If these factors were included in the job specification, this information would have greatly assisted the authority in its shortlisting task. The exercise no doubt also brought the additional advantage of discouraging any applicants who were not seriously interested in the post or not willing to make the effort to complete the assignment. Such tests can easily be updated to reflect current requirements such as the pursuit of 'best value' in local authorities or designed to incorporate the critical requirements of various posts in any organisation.

ACTIVITY 5.2

Think of three occupations and decide on a job sample test that could be used prior to shortlisting or that could be run within the context of an interview day. Describe the test and explain how it would provide information that could be used to assess a person's suitability for the job.

When you have compiled your own list of three jobs, get together with two other students to compare your lists. Select the best three examples and present these to the rest of the class.

Assessment centres

As Woodruffe (2000) points out, an assessment centre is a method rather than a place, although some employers, particularly large organisations, might have premises dedicated to assessment, especially if they use them for both selection and development purposes. Since an assessment centre is a method, it can be used flexibly by all employers. Each organisation can decide how many or how few of the assessment methods to use, but a range of techniques would have to be used to classify a selection event as an assessment centre and usually the number of methods used would mean that the process would stretch over two or three days.

Basically, an assessment centre approach means that a number of people are assessed together by a number of assessors, using a variety of selection techniques. This enables the collection of a range of information and observation and evaluation of how individuals interact with other people. The basic assumption underlying the validity of assessment centres is that the behaviours displayed will be carried over into the workplace. Incomes Data Services (2002) point out that assessment centres are likely to lead to better results if they are designed around competencies that are used right through the recruitment and selection process. Also, the more the assessment exercises reflect aspects of what people would actually be doing in the job, the better the results are likely to be. In this way, assessment centres can also deliver a sort of realistic job preview to the candidates.

The range of activities that can make up an assessment centre include:

- work simulations
  - work samples
  - in-tray exercises
  - role plays
- group exercises and discussions
- psychological tests
- interviews
- peer assessment and self-assessment.

Makin and Robertson (1986) identified group discussion as the kind of exercise most used in assessment centres and the IDS (2002) state that all six of the companies in their study use some form of group exercise, often involving group discussion.

Work simulations

As the phrase suggests, work simulations entail engaging candidates in performing tasks that would actually be done on the job. These exercises can be performed by individuals, as in the in-tray and role-play exercises described below, or in groups if, for example, one of the tasks is to contribute to inter-departmental meetings. One issue to keep in mind when deciding what kinds of exercise to use is that individual exercises such as role plays are more demanding in terms of assessor time, since one assessor will have to be assigned to one individual rather than a group.

Work sample tests are an example of simulation, and have already been discussed in detail. In-tray exercises and role plays should be developed in the same way as we outlined for work samples in terms of isolating critical tasks, setting the assessment criteria, designing the exercise and assessing it. A typical in-tray exercise is to present a candidate for a managerial post with a number of different tasks that a manager would encounter at the beginning of the day, with instructions to prioritise the issues, write memos, make phone calls, etc. A role play could be used in situations where the employee would have to deal with customer complaints, and it would be usual for one of the assessors to take on the role of the customer.

Group exercises

A variety of tailor-made tests or exercises have been devised by various employers to assess leadership qualities that cannot easily be judged from application forms or straightforward questioning. These tests may be used in designated assessment centre days, but some of them can also be integrated into interview days if a number of candidates are called together. The following are some examples of the kinds of exercises that are used, together with some examples of employers that are known to have used them:

● A group of applicants sit around a table; four or five assessors sit around the room behind the applicants. The lead assessor explains that he or she has four or five topics (depending on the number of candidates), which will be read out one at a time. When a topic has been announced, one candidate must volunteer to take that topic and conduct a discussion on it. Five minutes will be allowed for the discussion, and the discussion leader will be alerted when four minutes have elapsed. No further information is given to the candidates regarding what is expected of them. (A metropolitan police force; civilian post.)

● Round table interview. The participants are candidates who have passed a preliminary interview. Candidates introduce themselves, and contribute to a discussion of what a manager's job entails. This is followed by a team exercise with instructions to devise an employment strategy for a new store. (A retail outlet selling toys; trainee manager.)

● Candidates engage in teamwork to get equipment across a stream with limited physical resources, sometimes with a designated leader, sometimes as a leaderless group. (The Army; officer.)

As with work sample tests, candidate performance can only be judged fairly if assessors have agreed in advance which competencies and job-related behaviours they are looking for.

Pause for thought 5.4

Look again at the exercise used by the Metropolitan Police Force. What competencies and qualities do you think they were trying to assess?

The assessors would be looking for evidence of negative and positive behaviours: domination of the discussion, assertiveness, who has good ideas, ability to get people discussing a range of ideas, sensitivity to conflicting ideas, ability to incorporate conflicting views.

Issues

Woodruffe (2000) identifies a number of issues that must be considered when deciding to use the assessment centre technique, in designing it, running it, and assessing its effectiveness. Some of the major issues will now be discussed briefly.

As with any other selection technique, all the exercises used in the assessment centre must be designed to identify and measure specific competencies needed in the vacant post. There is a need to involve managers and others such as current postholders in identifying what the critical competencies are. The activities involved in designing assessment centre exercises should be directly linked with the activities performed in the context of job analysis that you read about in Chapter 2.

Since assessment centres are very demanding in terms of time and effort, the need for acceptance of the centre by all parties becomes crucial. Line managers are being asked to give their time to the development and the assessment of exercises and to accept that the use of assessment centres will lead to better selection. Line manager acceptance is increased if they are involved at all stages. There is also a need for candidates to feel that the assessment methods used represent a relevant process, especially as the assessment centre is more demanding in terms of their time and energy than a simple interview would be. This can be achieved partly by proper design of the exercises and partly by providing feedback.

We should also briefly consider the pros and cons of assessment centres. Certainly there are identifiable costs associated with assessment centres. These include: the training of a number of assessors; the design of exercises and line manager time devoted to this; arrangements for facilities; the time needed to organise the events and coordinate group activities with individual activities, particularly when one assessor is needed per candidate as in role-play exercises; additional expenses for candidates; time spent giving feedback. The argument for assessment centres is that these costs are balanced by the acquisition of additional information, the opportunity to evaluate several candidates together and the increased validity of selection decisions.

Whenever a number of assessment techniques are used there is a need to assign a weight to each technique. This is addressed later in this chapter after all assessment methods have been considered.

⊙ Biodata

To a certain extent biographical details (biodata) are available to selectors from application forms, CVs and interviews, and are inevitably incorporated into the decision-making process, even if they are not directly connected with factors specified in the personnel specification. This occurs when, for instance, a selector takes into account factors such as how many posts an applicant has had within the past five years, how long the applicant has stayed with each employer, whether there is an obvious progression in the person's career. More detailed application forms or biographical questionnaires can be developed so that biographical data can be used in a more formalised manner and assessed more methodically. The underlying assumption is that biographical factors give rise to certain personality traits that are interpreted into behaviours that affect work performance.

The use of extended biodata, however, presents something of a conundrum. On the one hand there are claims that decisions based on biodata have a high validity (Gunter *et al.*, 1993), and yet the types of information that are routinely mentioned in descriptions of what biodata to collect are contra-indicated by the tenets of good practice in the area of unfair discrimination. For example, it has been suggested that prospective employers might gather such details as age and marital status (Smith and Robertson 1993), number of dependants, parents' occupations (Gunter *et al.* 1993), and family background and upbringing (Graham and Bennett 1998).

The evaluation of biodata is also a problem. The simplest approach is to identify groups of current employees who perform successfully and groups who perform less successfully. Examination of biographical data from each group leads to identification of factors that are present in the successful group and not in the unsuccessful group and vice versa. These factors could then be compared with biographical details of applicants to determine who is likely to be successful in the job and who is likely to be less successful. This kind of empirical approach could only be used in larger organisations with large cohorts of people performing the same job and with the capacity and expertise to perform the requisite statistical analyses. Another problem with this approach is that it does not attempt to explain the causal link between biographical characteristics and work performance. The potentially most serious problem, however, is that if the successful group happens, for example, to be all male, this could lead to unlawful discrimination against females.

References

References are another method of gathering information on applicants, and a number of surveys indicate that the popularity of references as part of the selection process comes second only to the interview (Makin and Robertson 1986; Newell and Shackleton 1991). This is so in spite of the reference's poor showing in the validity league table. In their analysis of the accuracy of selection methods, Anderson and Shackleton (1994) found that references rated a correlation coefficient of only 0.13 (0 being equivalent to chance and 1.0 being the equivalent of perfect prediction). These facts seem to suggest that you will find the acquisition of references to be a part of most selection processes you will be involved in, but that great care is needed in their interpretation.

Pause for thought 5.5

At what stage in the selection process should a reference be solicited? Which candidates would you solicit a reference for?

There are no hard and fast rules that provide an answer to these questions, except that it is usual to solicit a reference only for a selection of applicants. There are various circumstances to consider, and this is another area where policy should be formulated to provide guidance to managers.

Most employers recognise that there are costs to providing references, so they would not wish to impose an unnecessary burden on other employers. This means restricting requests for references to an essential minimum. This would imply asking for references at a late stage in the process, after candidates have been assessed using a variety of other techniques. A further argument in support of this approach is that candidates on the whole prefer their current employer not to be approached unless there is a serious possibility that the candidate will be offered the post. The disadvantage of this view is, of course, that some time may elapse before a reference is received and the prospective employer will not want to delay in making the decision.

Some organisations use all their other assessment techniques and make a job offer subject to receipt of a supportive reference. It must be remembered, however, that references are given in confidence, and in this instance, if a job offer is retracted, then the applicant will know it is because of his or her reference. This may have an impact on the extent to which referees are prepared to be truthful. Every organisation needs to think through these implications, design a policy, and stick to it.

In addition to the questions of when to secure a reference and for whom, there are considerations about what information to request, how to interpret the information supplied, and indeed what information to supply to those requesting a reference from you.

Part of the reason for the low validity of references lies in the perceptions and skill of the person writing them or in hidden agendas that may influence what is or is not said. The effects of perceptions that may occur here are similar to the interviewer errors that were discussed in Chapter 4 in that our opinions of people, even when we have known them for some time, are influenced by our own perceptual set. Lukewarm descriptions of people's abilities may also be due to inadequate powers of expression or reserve on the part of the writer.

Because of the low validity of references, employers are sometimes advised to use them to check factual information only, but references may indicate some serious problem that should be pursued for further clarification or some discrepancy in factual information such as dates of employment which should also be pursued. References should obviously, therefore, be used with caution, and human resource specialists should find ways to improve the quality of the information their organisation receives in response to requests for references.

Requesting a reference

What could you do to improve the quality of references you have solicited?

Referees are able to respond better if you indicate what areas you would like feedback on, such as skills and personal qualities. Since you are seeking information on these as they relate to performance on the job, it would be useful to provide a job description or a brief outline of critical tasks. You might also consider supplying a referee with documents and checklists you will be using to evaluate candidates, such as the person specification or checklists of competencies and behaviours.

Some employers provide a questionnaire to guide the referee and help him or her to save time when composing a reference. This, together with a covering letter explaining your request, shows courtesy to referees and may contribute to the probability of your receiving a useful response.

Supplying references

Although you are not involved in making the selection decision when you provide a reference, it is worth considering the responsibility of the referee at this stage. In giving a reference to a potential employer, referees owe a duty of care to the receiving organisation. That is, referees would render themselves culpable if they knowingly deceived another organisation and misled it into hiring a person whom they knew to be unsuitable. In the case of *Spring* v. *Guardian Royal Exchange* (1994), the House of Lords also ruled that an employer has a duty to the employee to provide a reference composed with due care and may be held liable for losses due to negligent mis-statement.

The laws and regulations on discrimination also apply to actions that might be taken subsequent to employment, for example the provision of references. It is, therefore, unlawful to make discriminatory statements in references, for example with regard to a person's sexual orientation or religious belief (ACAS 2004a and 2004b).

Criminal record checks

You may remember that the Rehabilitation of Offenders Act was mentioned in Chapter 3. Essentially this Act outlines offences that are spent and protects offenders from having to reveal these spent offences. There are, however, some offences that are never spent, and some positions for which those guilty of particular offences will not be suitable. For example, any person who has been found guilty of assaulting a child would not be considered suitable for a position working in a school where unsupervised contact with children might occur. Such positions are excepted from the Rehabilitation of Offenders Act, and there are arrangements for organisations such as local authorities to obtain a check of criminal records for individuals applying for posts such as these.

Criminal Records Bureau

The Criminal Records Bureau (CRB) was set up under Part V of the Police Act 1997 to supply three levels of information relevant to individuals' suitability for certain types of employment or volunteer activities. The levels of certificate available are basic, standard and enhanced. The main characteristics of each, as described on the CRB-linked web site **www.disclosure.gov.uk**, are:

Basic

- All convictions that are not spent.
- Certificate is sent to the individual applicant.

Standard

- All convictions and cautions including spent convictions.
- Available when people apply for work or volunteer activities with children or vulnerable adults.
- Available only for positions excepted under the Rehabilitation of Offenders Act 1974 (Exceptions) Order 1975.
- The individual's application form is countersigned by the representative of a registered body.
- Certificate is sent to the individual applicant and a copy to the registered body.

Enhanced

- All convictions and cautions including spent convictions as for the standard certificate, but with additional information on non-conviction incidents recorded in local police records.
- Available where people will have substantial, unsupervised access to children and vulnerable adults.
- Available only for positions excepted under the Rehabilitation of Offenders Act 1974 (Exceptions) Order 1975.
- The individual's application form is countersigned by the representative of a registered body.
- Certificate is sent to the individual applicant and a copy to the registered body.

In the case of standard and enhanced certificates, information will also be included from lists of people barred from working in schools or deemed unsuitable for work with children or vulnerable adults by the responsible government authorities. There are charges for organisations which wish to register with the Bureau and for the issue of certificates. The fee structure is available on the disclosure web site.

Employer access to records

The reason for the establishment of the CRB was to provide a safer environment for vulnerable groups such as children, the elderly sick and the disabled, and to set up a system for handling the growing number of requests for information on those wishing to work with these groups. It should be noted that employers requiring a certificate that reveals spent convictions, i.e. a standard or enhanced certificate, must register with the Bureau, supplying it with evidence that such requests are for a legitimate purpose. In essence, this means employers referred to in the Rehabilitation of Offenders Act 1974 (Exceptions) Order 1975.

Flaws in the system became apparent during the investigation of the Soham murders when it became evident that information about Ian Huntley, the murderer of the two schoolgirls, had not been passed on by the police force concerned, enabling him to obtain a position as a school caretaker. The subsequent inquiry recommended the formation of a national registration scheme to ensure that information relevant to such positions, but which might not have led to a criminal conviction, would be shared on a national basis (Griffiths 2004).

A different source of potential difficulty lies with the basic certificate. Employers are entitled to ask potential employees the question: 'Do you have a criminal record?' Ex-offenders are protected by the Rehabilitation of Offenders Act 1974 from having to reveal *spent* convictions, but, as the CIPD (2001) highlights, they may experience a dilemma when faced with having to declare *unspent* convictions to a potential employer. It is an accepted fact that obtaining employment is a major factor in rehabilitation and preventing recidivism, so it is socially desirable that every opportunity to secure suitable employment should be obtainable for ex-offenders. The CIPD therefore urges employers to ask questions about criminal records only where it is relevant to the job, and to handle any information provided with sensitivity. An individual could theoretically and of their own volition provide a basic certificate to explain any gaps in employment, but the Data Protection Act 1998, s 56 makes it an offence to *require* anyone to provide such a record.

Graphology, phrenology, astrology, lie detector tests

These tests have been grouped together because of their somewhat dubious predictive validity, and none of them is used to any great extent in the UK, if at all. Graphology refers to the analysis of handwriting, phrenology to the examination of bumps on the head and astrology to the influence of the stars. Lie detector or polygraph tests involve the measurement of physical reactions that supposedly reveal whether a person is lying or telling the truth when answering a set of questions. Polygraph tests are known to identify correctly people who are lying, but they also sometimes identify as lying people who are telling the truth.

Health checks

Most positions require only general good health, and the completion of a routine questionnaire should suffice to judge a candidate's suitability. Information about absence records can also be specifically requested as part of the reference from former employers. If medical evidence is required from an applicant's general practitioner, the applicant's consent must be obtained first.

Making the final selection

In the two chapters on selection we have described a number of techniques for your consideration. An important issue to identify and emphasise at this stage is the need to use *all* the information that has been gathered.

There is a tendency to focus on the last stage of the process one has engaged in and to forget prior information, or at least to attribute undue weight and importance to the last stage. For instance, it will often happen that a person who is well qualified on paper but has poor interview skills is eliminated. Is the possession of polished interview skills really a critical success factor for the post in question? Is it wise to allow the interview to be so influential, given the evidence on the reliability and validity of interviews? If you are using a variety of selection techniques, you must decide in advance what each method is going to contribute to the overall assessment. Some things will carry more weight than others, and this should be decided in advance and each component appropriately weighted. Some things will be designated as essential prerequisites, and the lack of other things may be balanced by the presence of something else. For a post managing an accounting unit, for example, good writing skills may be allowed to balance a lack of polished presentation skills, but mathematical ability will be essential. You must decide what to do if there is conflicting evidence, for example if someone performs well in the interview but not in the ability tests or vice versa.

Scoring and ranking

It is, then, important to find some methodical approach to evaluating the information you have gathered, enabling you to rank the candidates in order of preference. There are several approaches to this and a variety of issues to consider:

- Decide on the cut-off percentage score a candidate must achieve in order to be considered.
- Decide which criteria must be met and which can be traded off against each other.
- Use ticks and crosses to record the assessment of candidates.
- Decide on the relative weight of each assessment criterion and assign points accordingly to each factor, amalgamating scores from the various assessment methods. Calculate a total score for each candidate.

Table 5.2 is a sample form to record and tabulate results.

After all the selection activities have been completed, all the selectors should compare their rankings of the candidates and decide on the best candidate. If there are discrepancies in the ratings, these discrepancies can form the basis of discussion and, if necessary, of further information seeking.

| Table 5.2 | **Sample candidate assessment form** |

Key for individual scores: 5 = excellent, 3 = good, 1 = acceptable	POST: _____

Minimum acceptable scores
   Job knowledge: 38.4/64 (60%)
   Total score: 74.5/149 (50%)
	ASSESSOR: _____

	Job knowledge Weight factor: 0.8	**Organisational ability** Weight factor: 0.6	**Experience** Weight factor: 0.5	**Ability to persuade** Weight factor: 0.6
Application form Weight factor: 4	3 × 4 12		4 × 4 16	
Interview Weight factor: 6	4 × 6 24		3 × 6 18	3 × 6 18
Work sample test Weight factor: 6	4 × 6 24	5 × 6 30		
Ability test Weight factor: 4		3 × 4 12		
Personality questionnaire Weight factor: 4				4 × 4 16
Weighted criterion totals	48	25.2	17	20.4

Candidate total score: 110.6

Candidate ranked against others: 2nd of 6

Explanatory notes

The form indicates weightings that would be agreed on some justifiable basis. In this case, job knowledge is weighted higher than the other criteria, and more weight is given to the interview and work sample test than the other assessment methods.

The line under the scores would appear on the blank form to indicate which factors are to be scored under each assessment method.

Any score that fell below the agreed minimum could be ringed on the form to draw attention to the fact that the candidate is no longer to be considered.

Providing information

It is often forgotten that applicants for a post also have a decision to make about whether or not they wish to accept the offer of employment. It is risky to assume that merely applying for a job means the applicant will ultimately want the post. If new employees leave shortly after being hired, this can hardly be considered to be successful selection. Just as the selectors gather information on which to base their decision, so the applicants should gather or be given information so that they too will make the right decision.

One obvious way of giving applicants information is to encourage them to ask questions during the interview. In this way you know that you have clarified any points that are important to individual applicants, and these may of course differ from one person to the next. Also, if your interview questions and work sample tests are properly constructed to obtain job-related information from applicants, these questions and tests will have imparted a wealth of information to the interviewee, albeit obliquely. Applicants may, however, still be unaware of certain aspects of the job, and it is incumbent on the selectors to make sure that applicants know about any factors that might influence their decision, and in particular the likelihood of their remaining with the organisation for a reasonable length of time if they do accept an offer of employment.

Very often the factors that cause rapid turnover among new employees are to do with unpleasant working conditions. If recruitment and selection were just about getting people to accept employment with your organisation, it would make sense to hide information about the negative aspects of your workplace. Many organisations have realised, however, that there is a greater likelihood of retaining new recruits if they are open and honest about the less pleasant aspects of their work environment. Offering interviewees information of this nature is known as a realistic job preview. Realistic job previews can take the form of oral information given by interviewers either to individual interviewees or in a group session before the interviews, or written documentation provided to candidates, for example statements about the working conditions included in job descriptions. There are, however, some more innovative ways of providing this kind of information.

Did you know?

Asda is one of the companies reported to use a form of realistic job preview in its graduate recruitment. The company uses a video showing applicants the size of their first desk (small!).

(Graduate recruiters urged to tell the naked truth. Has your employer given you the wrong impression? *Guardian Rise: Next Moves for Graduate Professionals*, 21 July 2001, r 5)

In 1995 students in the Transport and Logistics department at the University of Huddersfield created a short video film for a distribution company that wanted to alert applicants to the fact that the jobs in its warehouse involved cold, uncongenial working conditions, as most of the work took place in refrigerated areas. This film was made available in job centres so that people who did not wish to work in such conditions would not even apply in the first instance. Realistic job previews can, then, be provided at any stage in the recruitment and selection process, but they are probably most useful at the interview stage, when there is an opportunity to discuss and clarify details.

Additional activities that could be undertaken with the specific purpose of giving information to candidates include a tour of the organisation's premises, which gives applicants a first-hand look at the environment they would be working in and an opportunity to meet prospective colleagues. Letting applicants chat unattended with prospective colleagues means that managers have no control over the kinds of information that will be exchanged; it is rather akin to using the 'sitting at Nellie's Knee' method of training you will read about in Chapter 7. However, the exercise would make additional information available to potential employees, and it is worth considering the inclusion of such an opportunity in your selection process.

Administrative procedures

Once you have completed your selection process and made a decision about the successful candidate, there are a number of things you need to do to close the process:

- The successful candidate
  - offer the position to the successful candidate
  - secure his or her acceptance of the position

- agree the details of the appointment
- confirm the details in writing
- check essential qualifications
- initiate new employee processes.
- The unsuccessful candidates
  - inform the candidates of the outcome
  - provide feedback if appropriate.
- Prepare adequate records.
- Monitor the process.

Offer the position and agree details of appointment

Many employers prefer the personal touch of using the telephone to speak directly to the person they hope will be joining their organisation. Some organisations still prefer to make the initial offer in writing. Important details that need to be agreed at this stage include the start date, the starting salary and details about salary progression.

Confirm details in writing

Although an oral agreement can be regarded as a contract, most employers and employees feel more secure about the arrangement if it is put in writing. Usually the employer will write to the candidate to confirm the appointment and in turn require written confirmation of acceptance from the candidate. There is also a legal obligation to give a statement of terms and conditions to most employees, and this is discussed in more detail in Chapter 6.

Check essential documents

If specific qualifications are required for the post, for example, a degree, a driving licence or professional certification, the selected candidate should be required to present the documentation as proof that he or she does in fact possess the relevant qualifications.

A further, general requirement that applies to all employees is, of course, that they are legally entitled to work in the UK. The Asylum and Immigration Act 1996 reinforced the employer's responsibility for ascertaining that every new employee has the appropriate status. If employers selectively check only those applicants who, because of their appearance or a foreign-sounding name, arouse doubts about their citizenship status, such action could be deemed to be unlawful racial discrimination. To avoid this and at the same time fulfil the section 8 requirement to check employees' status, employers need to audit the documentation of all new employees at some stage in the selection process. A record of documented evidence of a person's national insurance number, such as a pay slip issued by a former employer, was originally deemed to be adequate proof of the fact that an employer had carried out this duty, but this was changed with effect from 1 May 2004 with regard to all persons hired from that date on. Section 8 now requires that employers check and copy either one document from a given list or a specified combination of two documents from a second list. An example from the first list (one document only required) is 'a document showing that the holder is a national of a European Economic Area country or Switzerland. This must be a national passport or identity card.' (**www.ind.homeoffice.gov.uk**;

accessed 09/09/04.) An example from the second list, where specified combinations of two documents are required, is a work permit issued by Work Permits UK plus 'a letter issued by the Home Office confirming that the person named in it is able to stay in the United Kingdom and can take the work permit employment in question.' (**www.ind.homeoffice.gov.uk**; accessed 09/09/04.) These are just examples of the types of documentation employers are responsible for checking and copying; more detailed guidance is available from the Home Office web site.

Initiate new employee processes

In addition to the appointment letter and check of credentials, there are a number of administrative details that need to be attended to for each employee. These include such things as acquiring details on pension arrangements, ascertaining preferences with regard to benefits (if a cafeteria system of benefits is in place, and employees can choose some benefits in preference to others), acquiring personal details such as bank account data for payroll purposes, and determining whether the person wishes union dues to be deducted from salary if a check-off system is in place. These administrative details will vary from one workplace to another, and it is sufficient here to note that they need to be planned and administered.

Inform the unsuccessful candidates of the outcome

Unsuccessful candidates should be treated with courtesy and informed as soon as possible of the outcome of the selection process, usually as soon as the preferred candidate has accepted the post. We have mentioned before that there is a public relations element in the way that recruitment and selection are performed. It is probably one of the few times that outsiders are invited into your organisation and are able to observe at first hand how you treat people. You will usually reject more people than you hire, and these people could be customers or even still potential employees whom you would not wish to alienate. Most candidates who have made it through the interview stage are serious about wanting the post, and inevitably will be disappointed that they have not succeeded. The rejection message needs, therefore, to be delivered with some sensitivity and, if possible, to avoid implying that these candidates have failed or are of inferior calibre.

ACTIVITY 5.3

Compose a standard letter that could be used for informing applicants that they have not been selected for a position. A model letter is given in Appendix 5.6 for you to compare with your proposed letter.

Feedback to candidates

Usually employers do not take the initiative in offering feedback to rejected candidates unless psychological tests have been used, in which case it is considered to be good practice to do so. However, some candidates are aware that asking for feedback can make a good impression with potential employers and that honest feedback might assist them in their further job search. Proper assessment of candidates should enable employers to be ready to give feedback to candidates in a sensitive manner.

Record keeping

The assessment record can form part of the recorded justification of why candidates were selected or rejected. In addition, preparing a summary statement of the reasons for the decisions, i.e. a statement of why the selected candidate was the preferred candidate and why the unsuccessful candidates were rejected, adds some rigour to the process. It is also necessary to keep such records to be able to provide evidence of good practice in case any applicant feels he or she has been subjected to unlawful discrimination and takes a complaint to an employment tribunal. The burden of proof, which means that employers, when challenged at a tribunal, must provide positive evidence of non-discrimination, is described in more detail in Chapter 3. Since the time limit for presenting a claim of discrimination to an employment tribunal is three months, it would seem sensible to keep detailed records of selection decisions for at least that period of time, and indeed the CIPD (2003) recommends keeping them for one year.

Monitor the process

The selection process should be monitored for several purposes:
- to ensure that selection is being conducted within the framework of the organisation's policies and discrimination legislation
- to examine the validity of selection decisions
- to ensure there is an acceptable level of reliability among assessors and interviewers.

A statistical analysis of the candidates who proceed through the various stages of selection will identify trends and provide feedback about how various groups fare throughout the selection process. The data could be analysed in terms of groupings of internal vs. external candidates, male vs. female, age profiles, racial groups and the disabled etc. Remember that public sector employers are obliged by law to carry out monitoring of their recruitment and selection processes with regard to racial equality. Monitoring of other aspects of equality and monitoring by private sector employers is not prescribed by legislation but is regarded as good practice and may be helpful if decisions are challenged in an employment tribunal.

Another important consideration is whether the selection process results in the acquisition of high performing employees. Data from performance appraisals and information about promotions could be cross-referenced with the ratings awarded to candidates in the various selection exercises to show whether assessment during the selection process correlates with performance on the job.

The ratings arrived at by individual interviewers and assessors can be compared and the reasons for discrepancies investigated. This information can be used to identify the training needs of those involved in selection.

ACTIVITY 5.4

Consider whether you would make any changes to the monitoring form in our sample application form as shown in Appendices 5.2 and 5.4 to reflect changes in the equality laws. You may wish to consult the advice on monitoring given on their web sites by ACAS, the CIPD, the EOC and the CRE to help you to make an informed decision. Would you make any changes? Why or why not? If you answered in the affirmative, what would those changes be? What would be the effect of having made those changes?

Conclusion

Now that you have done all you can to find a person who is going to be a productive colleague, you must turn your thoughts to what you can do to help integrate this person into your organisation as quickly and smoothly as possible. You will find a discussion of induction activities in Chapter 8. You should find the case study at the end of this chapter a useful exercise in putting together and applying all you have learned about recruitment and selection in this chapter and in Chapters 2, 3 and 4.

SELF-CHECK QUESTIONS

Answer the following multiple-choice questions. The correct responses are given on page 490 for you to check your understanding of this chapter.

1 What kind of exercise did Makin and Robertson identify as being used most in assessment centres?
   (a) handwriting tests
   (b) group discussion
   (c) work sample
   (d) information technology skills.

2 A good selection technique predicts success on the job. Is this validity or reliability?

3 Interviews, according to Makin and Robertson, are used more than psychological tests. Is this because they have a higher validity? YES or NO

4 Psychological tests are most useful when the selection ratio is high. TRUE or FALSE?

5 Which of the following tests is regarded in the UK as being the least acceptable?
   (a) personality questionnaires
   (b) leaderless group test
   (c) graphology
   (d) attainment test.

6 Applicants for teaching posts are often asked to conduct a seminar in their subject as part of the selection process. This is an example of:
   (a) a leaderless group exercise
   (b) a job sample test
   (c) a personality test
   (d) an attainment test.

7 Is the following statement true or false? The benefit of a realistic job preview is that it persuades people to join the organisation by presenting positive information about the job.

8 Which of the following statements best describes an assessment centre?
   (a) An assessment centre is a location where groups of candidates can be assessed by a number of assessors using a range of tests and exercises.
   (b) An assessment centre is a method of collecting information where groups of candidates are assessed by a number of assessors using a range of tests and exercises.

9 References are one of the most valid techniques of acquiring information about candidates. TRUE or FALSE?

10 When an activity has face validity, it means that it:

  (a) tests what it purports to test

  (b) resembles the activity it is testing for

  (c) includes a one-on-one interview together with written tests.

MAJOR ASSIGNMENT: RECRUITMENT AND SELECTION

Background information

You are the Head of Personnel Management at the headquarters of the Recovery Insurance Group. The group has 40 branch offices based in the North of England. The Regional Head Office is in Leeds, and this is where you are based. You determine company personnel policy for the region. You normally have three personnel assistants who report to you, but there is a vacancy in one of these posts which you hope to fill soon. Each personnel assistant is responsible for the day-to-day personnel activities in a group of about a dozen branch offices which are generally between 15 and 20 miles apart from each other, but some of these are located 100 miles or so away from Leeds. Because the responsibility for some of the branches requires more travelling than others, the custom has been to rotate the allocation of branches among the personnel assistants on an annual basis.

You have been with the Recovery Group for just over one year. You are professionally qualified yourself. You undertook a BA in Business and Finance before getting your first job as an administrative assistant in a personnel department in a bank. While you worked there, you studied part time for your CIPD qualifications (though it was still the IPD at that time) and progressed to being one of the personnel officers for the bank. Since then you have worked for a further two years for another insurance company in the South of England before taking up your present post as Head of Personnel at Recovery.

The company operates a performance appraisal scheme and at present has a manual system for keeping personnel records. You have been particularly concerned by the fact that the system seems unable to provide information about employee time-keeping and absences. However, the senior managers in the company have decided to introduce a computerised personnel and payroll system in the future, and during your first year with them you have had the responsibility for leading a team which chose and recommended the purchase of a system called PersPay. Now one of your major responsibilities will be to ensure the successful implementation of this system.

You have persuaded the senior managers of Recovery to upgrade the vacant personnel assistant post, as you will need to have someone to help with the development of the computerised operations. This person will have to work closely with members of the payroll office as some parts of the system will be linked, for example, the entry of salary figures, and start and termination dates. Relations between the payroll and personnel offices have been good, but each department is facing increasing workload demands with no possibility of acquiring extra staff, so there may be some difficulty in agreeing the assignment of duties between the two departments.

Incidentally, you have also secured the agreement of the senior managers that you may rename your department and call it the Department of Human Resource Management to reflect the change in approach you wish to bring to the management of employees at Recovery.

Your tasks

1 One of the first things you want to do is fill the vacancy for the personnel assistant. You find a job description on file (see Appendix 5.1), but you feel it could be better written and needs to be updated. Produce the new job description.

2 Produce a person specification to accompany the job description.

3 Design an advertisement, and say where you will place it and why.

4 Outline the selection process you intend to follow, including any techniques you will use to supplement the interview.

5 Prepare a set of questions to be asked at interview. Write a brief rationale for these questions.

6 Among the applications you receive are four included here as Appendices 5.2, 5.3, 5.4 and 5.5. Assume for this part of the exercise that you are willing to accept CVs as well as completed application forms. Evaluate these four applications, and explain whom you would invite for interview, giving your rationale for reaching these decisions.

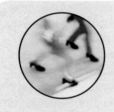

WHAT NEXT?

Now that you have mastered the introductory level of information presented in Chapters 4 and 5, and formed a good idea of what is regarded as a systematic approach to selection, you may wish to take your studies to a higher level. The article cited below is a research-based assessment of selection processes in a particular sector: hotels. It challenges the notion of best practice being applied universally and examines factors that may influence the effectiveness of selection methods in this particular sector. Read the article and draw out from it what you consider to be the major points the researchers are making. Does this article suggest to you any further issues that could be researched with regard to the effectiveness of selection processes?

Lockyer, C. and D. Scholarios (2004) Selecting hotel staff: why best practice does not always work, *International Journal of Contemporary Hospitality Management*, Vol. 16, No. 2, 125–135

References

Advisory, Conciliation and Arbitration Service (2004a) *Religion or Belief and the Workplace: A Guide for Employers and Employees*, ACAS

Advisory, Conciliation and Arbitration Service (2004b) *Sexual Orientation and the Workplace: A Guide for Employers and Employees*, ACAS

Anderson, N. and V. Shackleton (1994) Informed choices, *Personnel Today*, 8 November, 33–34

Chartered Institute of Personnel and Development (2003) *Retention of Personnel and Other Related Records* (**www.cipd.co.uk**; accessed 17/02/04)

Chartered Institute of Personnel and Development (2004) *Employing People With Criminal Records* (**www.cipd.co.uk/subjects/dvsequl/exoffenders**; accessed 16.02.05)

Graham, H. T. and R. Bennett (1998) *Human Resources Management*, 9th edition, Pitman

Griffiths, J. (2004) Inquiry calls for new register, *People Management*, 30 June, 7

Gunter, B., A. Furnham and R. Drakely (1993) *Biodata: Biographical Indicators of Business Performance*, Routledge

Incomes Data Services (2002) *IDS Studies 735: Assessment Centres*, September, IDS

Institute of Personnel and Development (1997) *IPD Guide on Psychological Testing*, IPD

Makin, P. and I. Robertson (1986) Selecting the best selection techniques, *Personnel Management*, November, 38–40

Marchington, M. and A. Wilkinson (2002) *People Management and Development: Human Resource Management at Work*, 2nd edition, CIPD

Murphy, K. R. and C. O. Davidshofer (2001) *Psychological Testing: Principles and Applications*, 5th edition, Prentice Hall

Newell, S. and V. Shackleton (1991) Management selection: a comparative survey of methods used in top British and French companies, *Journal of Occupational Psychology*, Vol. 94, 23–36

People Management (2001) Frames of mind, 14 June, 26–37

Pickard, J. (2004) Testing times, *People Management*, 29 January, 43–44

Robertson, I. (2001) Undue diligence, *People Management*, 22 November, 42–43

Smith, M. and I. T. Robertson (1993) *The Theory and Practice of Systematic Personnel Selection*, 2nd edition, Macmillan

Toplis, J., V. Dulewicz and C. Fletcher (2004) *Psychological Testing*, 4th edition, Chartered Institute of Personnel and Development

Woodruffe, C. (2000) *Development and Assessment Centres: Identifying and Developing Competence*, 3rd edition, CIPD

www.ind.homeoffice.gov.uk; accessed 09/09/04

Further study

Books

Advisory, Conciliation and Arbitration Service (2004) *Recruitment and Induction,* ACAS. (A concise overview of good practice in recruitment and selection, available at **www.acas.org.uk**.)

Ballantyne, I. and N. Povah (2004) *Assessment and Development Centres*, 2nd edition, Gower/Personnel Today Management Resources. (A practically orientated overview of the various aspects of assessment centres with detailed chapters on their design and implementation.)

Cook, M. (2004) *Personnel Selection: Adding Value through People*, Wiley. (A thorough review of selection methods and issues, including interviews, tests, assessment centres and validity.)

Graham, H. T. and R. Bennett (1998) *Human Resources Management*, 9th edition, Pitman. (This volume provides definitions and concise descriptions of major human resource management concepts.)

Gunter, B., A. Furnham and R. Drakely (1993) *Biodata: Biographical Indicators of Business Performance*, Routledge. (An in-depth examination of biodata instruments, their construction and their uses.)

Incomes Data Services (2000) *IDS Study Plus: Psychological Tests*. IDS. (Good information on psychological testing in a concise format.)

Incomes Data Services (2003) *IDS Studies: Recruitment Practices*, No. 751, June, IDS. (A concise overview of the basic range of both recruitment and selection practices with case studies of six employers, including B&Q and Marks & Spencer.)

Institute of Personnel and Development (1997) *IPD Guide on Psychological Testing*. IPD. (A concise guide to the issues involved in choosing to use psychological tests and advice on how to use them in a professional manner.)

Murphy, K. R. and C. O. Davidshofer (2001) *Psychological Testing: Principles and Applications*, 5th edition, Prentice Hall. (Chapter 19, 'Psychological measurement in industry', presents a good overview and evaluation of the uses of a variety of employment selection tests.)

Roberts, G. (1997) *Recruitment and Selection: A Competency Approach*, IPD. (A readable overview of all aspects of the recruitment and selection processes.)

Smith, M. and D. George (1994) Selection methods, in C. L., Cooper and I. T. Robertson (eds) *Key Reviews in Managerial Psychology*, Wiley. (An overview of research conducted on selection techniques, this chapter will be useful to anyone wishing to write an academic report.)

Toplis, J., V. Dulewicz and C. Fletcher (2004) *Psychological Testing*, 4th edition, Chartered Institute of Personnel and Development. (Provides an excellent overview of everything managers need to know about psychological testing in the workplace in order to be able to make informed decisions.)

Articles

Anderson, N. and V. Shackleton (1994) Informed choices, *Personnel Today*, 8 November, 33–34. (A brief overview of the popularity and accuracy of various selection methods and a comment on patterned behaviour description and situational interviews.)

Drury, B. (2001) How to assess criminal convictions, *People Management*, 22 March, 52–53. (A succinct summary of the law and the system for accessing criminal records, and recommendations for good employment practice.)

Fowler, A. (1998) How to create effective job simulations, *People Management*, 11 June, 52–55. (The 'How to . . .' series provides very useful summaries of the major considerations in a range of human resource management activities. See also McHenry (2003) below.)

Industrial Relations Services (2001) Checking out new recruits, *Employee Development Bulletin 135*, March, 11–16. (Reviews the reasons for pursuing references, their usefulness, the legal position, and advice on how to structure reference requests.)

Industrial Relations Services (2001) Monitoring for equality, *IRS Employment Trends 720*, January, 4–16. (Reviews the importance of monitoring in terms of equal opportunity and the issues raised for a number of organisations from such analysis of data.)

Lynch, B. (1985) Graphology: towards a hand-picked workforce, *Personnel Management*, March, 14–17. (A review of some personal responses of various individuals to an analysis of their handwriting.)

McHenry, R. (2003) How to make use of psychometrics, *People Management*, 17 April, 52–53

Internet

British Psychological Society   **www.psychtesting.org.uk**
(Offers information about psychological tests to test takers and test users, as well as general information and pages on current issues. Check out the interesting frequently asked questions.)

Chartered Institute of Personnel and Development   **www.cipd.co.uk**
(The CIPD site provides useful information on psychological testing and other aspects of recruitment and selection.)

Criminal Records Bureau   **www.crb.gov.uk** and **www.disclosure.gov.uk**
(Two web sites that describe the work of the CRB and provide recommendations on good practice.)

Equal Opportunities Commission   **www.eoc.org.uk**
(Provides a checklist specifically designed for line managers on handling situations that might arise during the selection process, including the use of tests. Go to the main site and search for the equality checklists.)

Immigration and Nationality Directorate   **www.homeoffice.gov.uk**
(This site will give you very detailed information about employers' responsibilities with regard to the Asylum and Immigration Act 1996.)

Recovery
Insurance Group

JOB DESCRIPTION

Job title:	personnel assistant
Responsible to:	personnel manager
Responsible for:	no one reports to this position directly, but can request work from the word-processing pool and personnel records clerks
Main purpose:	to provide a day to day advisory service to branch managers on personnel policy and procedures
Duties:	to monitor application for employment forms submitted by branch managers for candidates selected by them
	to agree salary details (in accordance with company pay scales) with branch managers
	to pass rejected applications to word-processing for standard rejection letters and check and sign those letters
	to enter agreed salary, contract, job title and joining details on selected applications and pass to word-processing for documentation
	to sign joining documentation on behalf of company
	to advise branch managers on the interpretation and implementation of the company's disciplinary procedure
	to advise branch managers on the interpretation and implementation of the company's sick pay scheme
	to advise branch managers on the interpretation and implementation of relevant legislation - including Employment Protection, Race Relations, Rehabilitation of Offenders, Disabled Persons, and Health and Safety at Work
	to pursue references, by letter and telephone, for selected applicants
	to provide references, by letter and telephone, for past employees
	to advise branch managers on current employees' salary entitlement, according to company incremental scales
	to advise branch managers on the purpose and use of the company's performance appraisal scheme
	to visit branches to advise on problems in any of the above areas, as necessary
General circumstances:	Recovery Insurance Group has divided its business into four areas for administrative purposes, each containing about 12 branches. The branch managers are all experts in insurance, not necessarily in staff matters. As all are at different locations in the north of England, much of the communication with the personnel department is by telephone, although about one day per month is normally spent visiting branch offices.

RECOVERY INSURANCE GROUP

The Recovery Insurance Group is striving to become an Equal Opportunities
Employer. All appointments are made in keeping with our Equal Opportunities Policy.

APPLICATION FOR EMPLOYMENT

POST Personnel Assistant   LOCATION Leeds   REF NO HRM 05-048

Please type or write clearly in black ink. Give all details in full.

SURNAME Paulson

FORENAME Jenni

ADDRESS 9 Queens' Way
Harrogate, HA4 5SC

TELEPHONE   HOME: 01423-000-000   WORK: _____

Do you hold a current driving licence? (YES) / NO

EMPLOYMENT EXPERIENCE

PRESENT OR MOST RECENT EMPLOYMENT

NAME & ADDRESS   JOB TITLE: Personnel Coordinator
OF PRESENT EMPLOYER   START DATE: 1996

Hartley Building Society   END DATE: 2000
Regents Road   (if applicable)
Cheltenham   PRESENT SALARY: Final salary was £25,000
Glos.   PERIOD OF NOTICE
                            REQUIRED:

DUTIES:

I was responsible for overseeing all personnel operations for the SW region of the building
society. This included recruitment and selection, advice on policy and procedure to managers,
and coordination of training.

PREVIOUS EMPLOYMENT (START WITH MOST RECENT POST)

FROM MONTH/YEAR	TO MONTH/YEAR	EMPLOYER	JOB TITLE AND BRIEF DESCRIPTION OF DUTIES	FINAL SALARY
Sept 1993	July 1996	Hart, Fleet and Burthorne Legal Group	Assistant Personnel Manager Recruitment of office staff, induction and training	£18,000

EDUCATION AND TRAINING

SCHOOL/COLLEGE/UNIVERSITY/OTHER	QUALIFICATION	FROM	TO
Hillingdon Girls School	9 GCSEs A Level English German Maths	1981	1988
University of London	BA (Hons) 2.1 English	1988	1991
University of Nottingham	MA in Industrial Relations	1991	1993

MEMBERSHIP OF PROFESSIONAL ASSOCIATIONS

Chartered MCIPD (1995)

Appendix 5.2 (contd)

ADDITIONAL INFORMATION

Please state why you are interested in the position you are applying for, and explain how your qualifications and work experience relate to this post. Please supply any additional information you feel may assist the selection panel in evaluating your application for this post. You should include any unpaid or voluntary work experience or any leisure activities where you feel you have developed relevant skills.

I have 7 years' experience in responsible personnel management positions and excellent academic qualifications. I have experience in all areas listed in your job description and feel sure I would enjoy the work at Recovery and be a very capable employee.

During my career break since 2000 I have organised a mother and toddler group and I have been active at my local church.

REFERENCES

Please give the names, addresses and telephone numbers of two referees. One of these should be your current or most recent employer. Please indicate if you wish to be consulted before we contact your current employer. YES/NO

1 Name:	Mr Peter White	2 Name:	Reverend Mark Aston
Address:	Hartley Building Society	Address:	St. Nicholas Church
	Regents Road		Parkes Road
	Cheltenham		Harrogate
	Gloucestershire		
	CH4 9TS		
Tel No:	01242–000–000	Tel No:	01423–000–000
Position:	Personnel Director	Position:	Vicar

DECLARATION

I certify that the information provided in this form is correct and accurate to the best of my knowledge. I understand that any misrepresentation makes me liable to disqualification or dismissal should I be engaged.

Signature *Jenni Paulson*   Date 10.4.05

Thank you for completing this form. Please return it to:

Head of Personnel Management
Recovery Insurance Group
Capital Square
LEEDS
LX1 1YZ

We regret that we are unable to acknowledge individual applications. If you wish to have confirmation that your application has been received, please enclose a stamped, addressed envelope. If you have not heard from us within three weeks, you should assume that your application has been unsuccessful on this occasion.

EQUAL OPPORTUNITIES MONITORING INFORMATION

This information is collected ONLY to assist us in monitoring equal opportunities in our company. We are asking you to provide the information on this tear-off strip so that it can be retained in the Human Resource Management department before your application is circulated to other managers. The details given here will NOT be considered as part of the selection process.

If you choose not to complete this section, this will not affect your application.

Surname: *Paulson*

Forename: *Jenni*

Date of Birth: *14.4.1970*

Male [ ]   Female [✓]

Do you consider yourself to be disabled? YES/NO

If so, what is the nature of your disability?

How would you describe your ethnic origin?

Afro Caribbean [ ]   Asian [ ]
UK Afro Caribbean [ ]   UK Asian [ ]
UK European [✓]   Other European [ ]
Other ....

Appendix 5.3

43 Jackland Road
Newcross
Huddersfield
HD9 5CK

Head of Personnel Management
Recovery Insurance Group
Capital Square
LEEDS
LX1 1YZ

9 April 2005

Dear Ms Jones

Please accept the enclosed CV as my application for the position of Personnel Assistant with the Recovery Insurance Group.

I have had a number of years of experience in personnel jobs, working first as a secretary in a personnel office and then moving into administrative posts. I have attended a few IT courses and used a range of computer packages. I was made redundant when Dywell was taken over by another company in 2004, and I have been working in temporary posts since then.

I am very interested in this post and would appreciate the chance to discuss my application with you at an interview.

Yours sincerely

A Walters

Amanda Walters

Amanda Walters
43 Jackland Road
Newcross
Huddersfield
HD9 5CK
Tel: 01484 000 000

PERSONAL DETAILS

Date of Birth: 25 August 1959
Marital Status: Divorced with one adult son

QUALIFICATIONS

1980 Secretarial Course. Typing 80 w.p.m
Shorthand 120 w.p.m

Short courses in word processing, databases and spread-sheets, including software for Windows.
Short courses in health and safety, supervisory skills, equal opportunities, and presentation skills.

EMPLOYMENT

1981–1992   Secretary to General Manager, Dyason's Cleaning Products.

1992–1994   Office Manager, Dywell Clothing Company.

1994–1997   Personal Assistant to the Director of Personnel, Dywell Clothing Company.

1997–2004   Assistant Personnel Officer, Dywell Clothing Company.

2005   Temporary jobs for Ace Recruitment Agency.

REASONS FOR APPLYING FOR THIS POST

I have worked for ten years in a personnel department and I have a wide range of experience including recruitment and selection, administration of personnel records, and running short courses in health and safety and supervisory skills. I am a trained secretary and have kept up my typing skills as well as updating my skills in office software. I feel that with my experience and background in personnel I have a lot to offer in a personnel position.

INTERESTS

I enjoy travelling abroad in the holidays, walking my two dogs, and I am also a member of the operatic society. I have taken part in several productions in recent years.

Appendix 5.4

RECOVERY INSURANCE GROUP

The Recovery Insurance Group is striving to become an Equal Opportunities Employer. All appointments are made in keeping with our Equal Opportunities Policy.

APPLICATION FOR EMPLOYMENT

POST *Personnel Assistant*   LOCATION *Leeds*   REF NO *HRM 05-048*

Please type or write clearly in black ink. Give all details in full.

SURNAME *Hamid*

FORENAME *Karim*

ADDRESS *5 Merton Road*
Coldfield
Leeds LS14 3BD

TELEPHONE   HOME: *0113-000-000*   WORK: _____

Do you hold a current driving licence?   (YES) NO

EMPLOYMENT EXPERIENCE

PRESENT OR MOST RECENT EMPLOYMENT

NAME & ADDRESS   JOB TITLE: *Personnel Assistant*
OF PRESENT EMPLOYER   START DATE: *2003*
Metham Office Supplies   END DATE: *March, 2005*
The Causeway   (if applicable)
Bradford   PRESENT SALARY: *£13,500*
BD1 6XY   PERIOD OF NOTICE
    REQUIRED:

DUTIES:

I created personal files for all new starters and kept the files up to date. I sent all details to the payroll office. I placed adverts for all positions and organised the applications and interviews for the managers.

PREVIOUS EMPLOYMENT (START WITH MOST RECENT POST)

FROM MONTH/YEAR	TO MONTH/YEAR	EMPLOYER	JOB TITLE AND BRIEF DESCRIPTION OF DUTIES	FINAL SALARY
Oct 2001	*Feb 2003*	*Metham Office Supplies*	*Wages Clerk Recorded hours worked by part-time staff and calculated wages.*	

EDUCATION AND TRAINING

SCHOOL/COLLEGE/UNIVERSITY/OTHER	QUALIFICATION	FROM	TO
High School	*4 GCSEs A Level History Business studies*	*1994*	*2001*
Metropolitan University of Leeds	*Professional Management Foundation Programme (1st stage of CIPD programme)*	*2003*	*2004*

MEMBERSHIP OF PROFESSIONAL ASSOCIATIONS

Appendix 5.4 (contd)

ADDITIONAL INFORMATION

Please state why you are interested in the position you are applying for, and explain how your qualifications and work experience relate to this post. Please supply any additional information you feel may assist the selection panel in evaluating your application for this post. You should include any unpaid or voluntary work experience or any leisure activities where you feel you have developed relevant skills.

I am very interested in continuing my career in personnel. I feel I can use the skills I learned at Meltham Office Supplies. I have successfully completed stage one of the CIPD qualification and I hope to continue with this in the near future.

REFERENCES

Please give the names, addresses and telephone numbers of two referees. One of these should be your current or most recent employer. Please indicate if you wish to be consulted before we contact your current employer. YES/NO

1 Name:	*Mrs Briggs*	2 Name: *Dr Meyer*

Address:	*Meltham Office Supplies*
	The Causeway
	Bradford
	BD1 6XY

Address: *Metropolitan University of Leeds Leeds LS5 7JS*

Tel No:	*01274-000-000*
Position:	*Personnel Manager*

Tel No: *0113-000-000*
Position: *Lecturer*

DECLARATION

I certify that the information provided in this form is correct and accurate to the best of my knowledge. I understand that any misrepresentation makes me liable to disqualification or dismissal should I be engaged.

Signature *Karim Hamid* Date *11th April 2005*

Thank you for completing this form. Please return it to:

Head of Personnel Management
Recovery Insurance Group
Capital Square
LEEDS
LX1 1YZ

We regret that we are unable to acknowledge individual applications. If you wish to have confirmation that your application has been received, please enclose a stamped, addressed envelope. If you have not heard from us within three weeks, you should assume that your application has been unsuccessful on this occasion.

EQUAL OPPORTUNITIES MONITORING INFORMATION

This information is collected ONLY to assist us in monitoring equal opportunities in our company. We are asking you to provide the information on this tear-off strip so that it can be retained in the Human Resource Management department before your application is circulated to other managers. The details given here will NOT be considered as part of the selection process.

If you choose not to complete this section, this will not affect your application.

Surname: *Hamid*

Forename: *Karim*

Date of Birth: *10 March 1983*

Male [✓]   Female [ ]

Do you consider yourself to be disabled? YES/NO

If so, what is the nature of your disability?

How would you describe your ethnic origin?

Afro Caribbean [ ]   Asian [ ]   UK Asian [✓]
UK Afro Caribbean [ ]
UK European [ ]   Other European [ ]
Other ....

Appendix 5.5

CURRICULUM VITAE

NAME   Arthur Jackson

ADDRESS   19 Craigley Road
                        Eastleigh
                        Hants.

TELEPHONE   Eastleigh 000000

EDUCATION

1983–1988   Eastleigh Comprehensive School, Eastleigh.
                        Obtained 4 GCSEs.

WORK EXPERIENCE

1988–1994   Office Clerk, Bilton Insurance Company, Eastleigh.
1994–1996   Assistant Supervisor, Bilton Insurance
Company.
1996–1997   Assistant Training Officer, Bilton Insurance Company.
1999–2000   Temporary Office Worker, Eastleigh Council.
2000–2002   Insurince Salesman, Staywell Insurance,
Portsmouth.
2002–2004   Personnel records clerk, Staywell Insurance.
2004–2005   Personnel Assistant, Stay well Insurance.

I would like this job because all my jobs have been in insurance companies
and i have lots of experience in personnel and training.

Appendix 5.6

Company name and logo
Company address
Town
PC1 1XX

Ms C Candidate
1 Named Street
Candidtown
PC1 1XX

1 June 2005

Dear Ms Candidate

I regret to inform you that the selection panel has selected another candidate for the position of Human Resource Assistant. I would like to thank you for the time and effort you put into your application for this post and for your participation in our selection process. The panel was impressed with the calibre of the candidates and had a difficult decision to make.

Please do not hesitate to apply again for any suitable position with Company Name.

Yours sincerely

A Barker
Director of Human Resources

CHAPTER 6

The employment relationship

OBJECTIVES

When you have read this chapter you will be able to:

- understand and describe the rights and obligations of both parties to the employment relationship
- understand the basis of the contract of employment and describe the terms that should constitute a basic contract of employment
- describe the main employment rights provided by legal statute
- describe a variety of flexible working arrangements and assess their usefulness and impact for both employers and employees
- describe the issues to be considered when an employee leaves an organisation.

The relationship between employers and their employees can be described in many ways. To get a clear picture of what this might entail, think first of any relationship between people, including personal relationships between friends, life partners and relatives; that is, think about relationships, but not necessarily in the context of employment. Any relationship is formed within a context of rights, expectations and obligations on the part of each party to the relationship. These rights etc. may be individualised for each pair of individuals as in marital relationships, or it may be that a group of people see themselves as forming one party to a relationship and that they therefore have shared interests that they wish to see represented on a collective basis. Some of these rights, expectations and obligations are unspoken: you assume that your close friends will not purposely do anything to harm you, but you do not feel that this needs to be said explicitly. In other things, you may need to negotiate and reach agreement: in spite of the much heralded concept of the 'new man', the division of labour in the household can still be a contentious area in heterosexual relationships. Beyond what individuals agree among themselves, both implicitly and explicitly, there is a legal framework that imposes obligations and guarantees rights, such as the division of possessions when a marital relationship fails. Relationships are also affected by cultural norms, custom and practice, views on what is and is not acceptable and the balance of power. These influences may be relatively stable for long periods of time, but the twentieth century was recognised as a period of great and rapid change, a phenomenon which will no doubt continue in the twenty-first century.

Stop to consider the last two sentences in the preceding paragraph. Can you identify examples of these issues either in your own life or in those of people you know? What are the determinants of power in personal relationships? What changes in these areas can you identify? Discuss this with a group of fellow students, and you will probably identify a surprising number of influences and changes.

If you accept that this complex framework applies to personal relationships, it should not come as any surprise that the employment relationship is governed by a complex mix of individual and collective agreements, implicit and explicit understandings, and rights and obligations enshrined in legal statutes, and that other influences such as culture and the balance of power apply to it too. This chapter will attempt to give an overview of the many threads that weave together to create the canvas of the employment relationship, and will also look at how trends within it can be monitored. In particular we shall examine the legal aspects of the employment relationship, together with some cultural and psychological factors and the concept of flexibility in working arrangements. We shall also look briefly at what happens on the termination of the employment relationship.

Rights and obligations of the two parties

 ### Balance of power

The extent to which one party in a relationship has rights and the extent to which that party has obligations depend in some measure on the balance of power between the two parties.

Put aside for the moment the notion that as a proponent of the HRM approach you would be seeking to develop a workforce that shared a common purpose with management and with which there was therefore little conflict. If you regard an individual employee or a group of employees as having some areas of conflict with a manager, who would you judge to have more power than the other? List your reasons. What are the implications of this balance of power for the relationship between workforce and managers?

In spite of legislation that protects a range of employee rights, the general feeling in the industrial relations arena in the 1990s was that the balance of power lay with the employer. These sentiments had been fuelled by legislation throughout the 1980s and early 1990s which progressively curtailed the powers of the trade unions, and by high levels of unemployment and frequent redundancies which undermined many employees' sense of job security. There was also a large number of redundancies in the early years of the twenty-first century, many attributed to the global effects of the slowdown in the American economy.

The implications of this for the relationship between employees and their managers lie in the areas of trust, openness, willingness to cooperate and amenability to different points of view. Where there is an imbalance of power, these areas of a relationship can suffer or at least they can be difficult to maintain. In the workplace this means that managers will have to find ways of reassuring employees that they will be treated as equal partners in the relationship. Managers will attempt to do this of their own volition if they believe that an employee relationship based on partnership is in fact a contributory factor in the success of their organisation. We shall explore this belief more fully in our examination of employee involvement in Chapter 13.

The Labour Government, first elected in 1997, produced a programme of employment measures emphasising the development of fairness at work and a partnership approach to the relationship between employer and employee. Some of its original proposals, such as improved regulations on union recognition and enhanced rights to time off work or flexible working arrangements, have subsequently been enshrined in the Employment Relations Act 1999 and other regulations. As the new rights become established, they will no doubt affect the nature of employee relations. The implementation of EU legislation on consultation and information is also shifting the focus more firmly towards employees' rights. We shall return to this theme in Chapter 13 where we provide a more detailed discussion of partnership and employee involvement.

Expectations of the two parties: the psychological contract

The concept of the psychological contract aroused much interest amongst observers of HRM in the late 1990s, even to the extent that the IPD National Conference adopted it as its major theme in 1996. Attributed initially to Argyris (1960), the concept was further developed by Schein (1978), among others. It concerns the expectations that each party holds with regard to the other, and is recognised as having an impact on the way people behave in the workplace. The psychological contract is akin to the implied terms in a legal contract, i.e. much of it will be assumed and unspoken. It includes factors that result in feelings such as loyalty and perceptions of fair treatment, and many intrinsic factors that affect motivation. Much of the debate in the 1990s was about feelings of job security as an element of the psychological contract and the extent to which organisations could or could not continue to offer reassurance with regard to job security. Guest and Conway (1997) refer to the new psychological contract where the focus has shifted to employment security or employability rather than job security. This means that if employees can no longer expect their employer to guarantee them a job for life, they might instead expect their employer to support their development to make them more employable.

The nature of the psychological contract and the motivation of the individual can be influenced by the culture of an organisation and its predominant management style, and can be seen as coercive, calculative or cooperative (Handy 1985). Coercion, where people are motivated to expend effort in order to avoid punishment, is generally regarded as unproductive and inappropriate for today's work organisations. A calculative contract will come into being where the connection between effort and reward is explicit, and each employee can calculate the value to him or herself of expending extra energy on the organisation's behalf. The cooperative contract arises when individuals identify with the goals of their organisation. The latter is the kind of psychological contract one would expect to find in an organisation that espouses the human resource management approach towards maximising the contribution of its employees.

The cooperative contract implies a more participative style of management and greater employee involvement in decisions in the workplace. Individuals differ, however, in what they perceive as motivating, as Handy points out, and he goes on to say that managers may sometimes be disappointed at a lack of response when they try to change from, say, a calculative contract to a cooperative contract. However, if an organisation is run on participative lines, it is likely to engender positive attitudes in new employees, and perseverance with new techniques may help to alter attitudes among existing staff. The renewed emphasis of the late 1990s on fairness at work and partnership between employers and employees tied in well with this concept of a cooperative contract, and the work by Guest and Conway (1997) also highlights the link between a climate of employee involvement and a positive psychological contract. You will read more about partnership and the techniques that can lead to a cooperative psychological contract in Chapter 13.

The legal framework

Contract and common law

Contract and common law, the latter being law established by judges' decisions rather than by statute, are important components of the legal framework that delineates the employment relationship. The first question that arises is whether or not a person is regarded in the eyes of the law as being an employee in the first place, and this has implications for a person's ability to claim the right to the protections provided by statutory employment law.

As with many legal questions, there are instances where there is no straightforward answer to the question of whether two parties have the relationship of employer and employee, and it is up to the courts to interpret the law and come to a decision. There is also no single definitive test that will give a conclusive answer, but some combination of the following factors can be considered in order to conclude whether a person is rendering services as an employee or on a self-employed basis. In deciding on the relationship between two parties, the courts will subject the relationship to a number of tests, including whether:

- the employer is entitled to exercise control over what the employee does and how he or she does it
- the employee is integrated into the structure of the organisation
- there is a mutual obligation to supply and accept work.

A person who is performing work for someone on a self-employed basis is not entitled to the rights enshrined in statutes such as the Employment Rights Act 1996 since such a person is not an employee in the eyes of the law.

The situation is further complicated, however, by the use of another term, i.e. 'worker'. Willey (2003) explains that a worker may be under some sort of contract, but may fail on one or more of the tests applied to determine whether the person can be classed as an employee. In a table showing the entitlements of employees and workers, Willey (2003, p. 89) indicates that both workers and employees would be covered by certain pieces of legislation (for example the Working Time Regulations and the statutory minimum wage), but that workers would not have all of the statutory rights that can be claimed by those classed as employees (such as basic maternity leave and the right to return to work). Willey further indicates that the law is developing in such a way as to provide a fuller range of rights to 'workers', a fact which is confirmed by the DTI (**www.dti.gov.uk**; accessed 4.10.04).

The contract of employment

It is a common misapprehension that the letter offering employment or the written documentation supplied by an employer to an employee constitutes the contract of employment. A contract is basically an agreement, and despite the saying that 'an oral contract is as good as the paper it is written on', if a person offers you employment over a cup of coffee in a restaurant and you accept the offer, you have a contract with each other. The written statement is evidence or proof that a contract exists, but it is not a contract per se; it is a statement of what has been agreed.

Implied and express terms

Contracts are made up of express terms and implied terms. As the phrases indicate, an express term is something that is regarded as important enough to be dealt with specifically and agreed on. Some terms may be assumed and not stated explicitly. For example, it may be stated how much notice an employee is to give if he or she wishes to terminate the contract of employment, but if it is not explicitly stated, the implied term would be whatever is customary in that particular industry or line of work. There is a statutory minimum as far as the amount of notice that an employer should give is concerned, so if there is no explicit mention of this in the contract, the statutory minimum will be the implied term.

On the whole it is best for employers to be explicit about any terms they require, for example with regard to mobility. If you are likely to require an employee to work at various locations, particularly if you already have establishments in various locations, it is advisable to include this requirement as an express term in the contract. Even then, the enforcement of such contract terms is not without difficulties; you have to be able to show that the term is justified. In a case involving a British Council requirement of its employees to work anywhere in the UK on promotion to a certain grade, *Meade-Hill* v. *British Council*, it was held that this could amount to indirect sex discrimination unless the broadly stated requirement could be justified. Such a clause could be seen as indirect discrimination because fewer women would be able to comply with it than men.

Implied terms include:

- on the part of the employer
  - the duty to maintain mutual trust and confidence
- on the part of the employee
  - the duty to obey lawful and reasonable orders
  - the duty of fidelity
  - the duty to work with due diligence and care.

The duty of fidelity can be explained as the obligation to act in good faith in dealings with an employer or on behalf of an employer. For example, submitting a tender for a contract that your employer is pursuing could be construed as breaching the implied duty to give faithful service. The employee also has an implied duty not to disclose confidential information, and a duty to cooperate with the employer, i.e. not to deliberately cause disruptions.

Variation of the terms of a contract

An employer must give written notice to an employee of any intended changes in the terms of the contract. The employer does not, however, have the right to vary unilaterally the terms of the contract, but must consult with employees and if possible obtain their agreement to the changes. If an employer tries to enforce a change without the agreement of an employee, this can be taken as a fundamental breach of contract which has the effect of repudiating the contract. In these circumstances, the employee can resign, claiming constructive dismissal, and pursue compensation at an employment tribunal. An example of a variation of terms would be insisting that a person who had been contracted to work an evening shift should start working the day shift.

Employment law

A variety of employee rights are protected by legal statute, but it is beyond the scope of this text to provide a comprehensive description of employment law. We shall give a brief explanation of how European Union law affects UK legislation, and then focus on some of the issues that have been of recent interest and that you are likely to be asked about as either a line manager or a human resource practitioner. Remember that the law can be very complex and its interpretation most difficult. A number of professional journals, for instance, publish regular briefings which help employers to interpret the law, especially in the light of new decisions on tribunal or court cases. We shall be looking at some aspects of employment law in greater detail, but remember that if you are in any doubt about an employee's or worker's rights, it is best to consult a solicitor. You should also keep in mind the fact that the law usually states the minimum entitlement of an employee, and in most circumstances employers can decide to enhance the legal entitlement with more generous contractual provision. Enhancing entitlements may be a way of attracting and retaining employees with superior abilities, and so may be a consideration in pursuing the corporate strategy, particularly one of growth or innovation. All employees and workers should ensure that they are aware of their contractual provisions, but as a line manager or personnel practitioner, you are likely to be asked for explanations.

We have dealt with certain employee rights in other chapters, so we shall not repeat that information here. You will find a discussion of the equality legislation in Chapter 3, certain aspects of the right to consultation and information in Chapter 13, dismissal and redundancy rights in Chapter 15 and health and safety regulations in Chapter 12. Our discussion here will focus on:

- the statement of particulars of employment
- notice of termination of employment
- employee rights to time off work
- guarantee payments
- the written statement of reasons for dismissal
- maternity and other parental rights
- the rights of part-time staff
- working hours
- protection of employee data.

In addition to the issues we have chosen to address, readers should be aware of the Transfer of Undertakings (Protection of Employment) Regulations 1981 (TUPE). The regulations protect the terms and conditions of employees in cases of a transfer of ownership of a trade or business, and state that dismissal because of the transfer is unfair. This is a very complex area of legislation, so much so that publications like *People Management* provide frequent articles on new interpretations brought about by judgments in court cases.

The European Union (EU) and UK employment law

EU law takes effect in a number of ways, the most important being regulations that have direct effect in member states (i.e. they override domestic law) and directives that have to be implemented through national legislation. Some directives, for example those that encourage improvements related to health and safety, can be adopted by qualified majority voting, which means that they must be enacted by all member states, including the minority that voted against them. An example of this is the European Working Time Directive which was adopted in 1993 with dissension from the then Conservative Government of the UK. As the directive was considered to be a health and safety measure, the UK was obliged to accept and implement it. This contrasts with directives concerning the social rights and interests of employees, which require unanimity and from which individual member states can opt out. For example, the Conservative Government in the UK opted out of several social measures that were adopted by the rest of the EC at the time of the Treaty on European Union 1992 (the Maastricht Treaty). Since then, however, the Labour Government has signed up to the Social Chapter which is now integrated into agreements made in the Treaty of Amsterdam 1997.

Employees in the public service sector can rely upon the direct effect of directives, i.e. if the directive has not been implemented, this group of employees can take their case to the European Court. National courts also take account of the purpose of directives when interpreting national legislation. This gave rise, for example, to the House of Lords finding in 1994 that the two-year threshold to be able to claim a range of employment protection rights should apply to all employees irrespective of the number of hours worked, in spite of the fact that this was not stated explicitly in UK law at the time of the finding. (See the later section in this chapter on part-time employees for more detail, and note that this two-year threshold was itself later reduced to a one-year qualifying period.)

Written statement of particulars of employment

Although the documentation referred to in this section does not constitute a contract as such, an employer is bound by law to issue a statement of terms and conditions to most employees, and the content of these documents serves as proof of the existence of a contract and evidence of the terms that were agreed. The legislation covering this statement is to be found in part I of the Employment Rights Act 1996. This Act consolidates various individual employment rights which had previously been enshrined in a number of pieces of legislation, including the Employment Protection Consolidation Act 1978, the Employment Protection (Part-Time Employees) Regulations 1995 (both of these now completely replaced by the Employment Rights Act 1996), and parts of the Trade Union Reform and Employment Rights Act 1993 (TURERA).

The Employment Rights Act sets out what kinds of information employees are entitled to receive about their contract with their employer, and the time frame within which this should be issued, i.e. within two months of the commencement of employment. This entitlement includes all employees contracted to work for one month or more irrespective of the number of hours worked. Parts of the documentation may be given in instalments within that two-month period.

Pause for thought 6.3

The information to be included in a statement of particulars of employment is indicated in the Employment Rights Act 1996. What would you expect to be included in this list?

The statement should contain certain details and at least refer to other documents so that employees are aware of their existence and know where they may examine them. The details to be made explicit in the statement are:

- the names of the parties to the contract
- date of commencement of employment
- date of commencement of period of continuous employment
- hours of work
- location of the workplace and an indication if there could be a requirement to work elsewhere
- details about pay – rate of pay or how it is calculated; frequency of payments (weekly, monthly, etc.)
- job title or a brief description of the duties
- holiday entitlements
- arrangements about sick pay and sick leave
- details about any company pension plan
- entitlement to receive notice of termination of employment and obligation to give notice
- date employment ends if the contract is for a fixed term
- any terms of a collective agreement that affect working conditions.

Employees are entitled to be notified in writing of any changes to be made to any of these terms.

Details about sick pay, notice periods and pension arrangements may be given to employees by referring them to other documents, but again any subsequent changes in these documents must be notified directly to individual employees.

Employees should also be referred to documents outlining the disciplinary rules, procedure, named person or position of person to whom appeals against decisions can be made, grievance procedures and name or position of person to whom a grievance should be referred in the first instance.

Notice of termination of employment

Employers may have their own schedule of the notice they require from employees and are prepared to give to employees, but the statutory rights of employees as stated in part IX of the Employment Rights Act are:

- 1 week's notice after 1 month and up to 2 years' service
- 2 weeks' notice after 2 years and up to 3 years' service, continuing to increase by one week for every completed year of service to a maximum of 12 weeks' notice.

Employee rights to time off work

The Employment Rights Act provides for employees to have a right to time off work in various circumstances. This may be unpaid or paid, depending on the circumstances, and includes time off for:

- union officials, in a union recognised by the employer, to complete certain duties such as taking part in negotiations with the employer (paid)
- members of a recognised union to participate in certain activities (unpaid)
- public duties such as acting as a justice of the peace (unpaid)
- employees selected for redundancy to look for work or make arrangements for training (paid; 2 years' service required)
- antenatal care (paid).

This is not a comprehensive list, but gives you some idea of existing entitlements to time off. The phrase that is applied to the entitlement to time off is that it should not be unreasonably refused, and in some circumstances, for example those related to the performance of public duties, employers are entitled to give consideration to business needs in assessing what a reasonable amount of time off work would be.

The Employment Relations Act 1999 also introduced rights to time off which had been addressed in the *Fairness at Work* White Paper (1998): revised maternity rights and rights to paternity leave (both dealt with later in this chapter), and entitlement for all to time off for dependants, i.e. unpaid leave in cases of emergency to arrange for care for any person who is dependent on the employee to do so. In its website guidance, the DTI includes an elderly neighbour in its definition of dependants as well as family members, but explicitly excludes tenants or boarders (**www.dti.gov.uk/er/faqs.htm**; accessed 29.09.04).

Guaranteed pay

Under the Employment Rights Act, employees are entitled to five days' pay within any three-month period for workless days if the employer cannot provide work as contracted.

Written statement of reasons for dismissal

Employees with one year of service are entitled to receive a written statement of reasons for dismissal on request. As noted in the following section, however, different rules apply to anyone dismissed during pregnancy or maternity leave.

Maternity and other parental rights

Support for family life whilst enabling people to continue working is an issue that is evidently of continuing importance to the Government, so HR professionals need to ensure they are aware of the latest developments. What follows is a summary of parental rights as they stand at the time of writing (September 2004), but since this is an area of continuing change, any practitioner responsible for interpreting related rules and policies will need to study this area in more depth and check for the latest status of the regulations.

Beginning with the Maternity and Parental Leave etc. Regulations 1999, a number of additional enhancements in maternity and other parental rights have come into effect in the years since 1999. Also, the employment rights of pregnant employees is a complex area and one in which there will be many individual circumstances to take into account. Note that we have simplified matters by using the terminology relating to birth parents, but a broadly similar range of rights to leave and pay (standard rate as described below) apply to adoptive parents. The Department of Trade and Industry web site pages on maternity and parental rights are a good starting point for more detailed information (**www.dti.gov.uk/er/workingparents**; accessed 30/04/04). The key points are as follows.

Antenatal care

As mentioned earlier, pregnant employees have a right not to be unreasonably refused paid time off work for antenatal care, regardless of length of service and hours worked.

Dismissal or selection for redundancy

Dismissal for a matter related to pregnancy or childbirth is automatically unfair. There is no qualifying period of employment or threshold of hours worked attached to this right. It is also unlawful to select a woman for redundancy on grounds of pregnancy or childbirth.

Written statement of reasons for dismissal

An employee dismissed during pregnancy or maternity leave is entitled to receive a written statement explaining the reasons for the dismissal. The employee does not have to request the statement in these circumstances, and again there is no qualifying length of service or number of hours worked.

Maternity leave

All pregnant employees are entitled to 26 weeks of ordinary maternity leave, regardless of length of service or hours worked. They are also entitled to return to work at the end of this leave period. Additional maternity leave is available to women with qualifying service of at least 26 weeks by the qualifying week (i.e. the fifteenth week before the week of expected childbirth). Additional maternity leave can take the leave period up to 52 weeks.

Maternity pay

An employee on ordinary maternity leave continues to benefit from all the terms and conditions of her contract except for remuneration. This means, for example, that she continues to accrue holiday entitlement, payments into the pension scheme should continue, and the maternity leave period counts as continuous service. The contract of employment continues during additional maternity leave, but some issues, such as pay and contributions to pension, may depend on contractual agreements (Willey 2003).

All qualifying pregnant employees are entitled to 26 weeks of statutory maternity pay (SMP). The qualifications are that they have worked for their employer for at least 26 weeks by the qualifying week (i.e. the fifteenth week before the week of expected childbirth) and their average weekly earnings are relevant for national insurance contributions. SMP is 90% of the employee's average weekly earnings during the first six weeks of the maternity leave, and the remaining weeks are paid at the standard rate, which was £102.80 from 4 April 2004 (or 90% of the employee's weekly earnings if this is a smaller amount). Additional maternity leave is unpaid.

Employers can recoup 92% of the SMP they have paid out, and small employers can recoup 104.5% if they qualify for Small Employer's Relief. More information on this is available from the employers' information pages on the web site of the Inland Revenue (**www.inlandrevenue.gov.uk**; accessed 30.09.04). Pregnant employees who do not qualify for SMP may be eligible for the maternity allowance paid by the Department for Work and Pensions.

Did you know?

The rights to paternity leave bring the UK more into line with some of the traditionally more generous EU member states like Sweden and Denmark. Norway continues to be the most generous, with 4 weeks' paternity leave paid at 100% or 80% of the mother's salary.

(*European Industrial Relations Review 331*, August 2001, p. 16)

Paternity leave

The spouse or partner of a new mother has an entitlement to 2 weeks of paternity leave, paid at the SMP rate, during the 2 months following the birth of a child. This entitlement applies to unmarried as well as married partners, and to same-sex as well as opposite-sex partners. ACAS (2004b) suggests that it might be better to think of 'paternity leave' as 'maternity support leave'. Organisations might consider using such non-discriminatory terminology in their policies. An additional criterion applied to employees requesting this type of leave is that they must, in addition to the mother's responsibilities, have the main responsibility for the upbringing of the child.

Did you know?

ACAS reports that in little over one month in early 2003, it offered advice to 12,700 employers and employees on the right to request flexible working and other aspects of parental rights.

(ACAS, *Annual Report and Accounts 2002/03*)

Parental leave

Parents of children under the age of five are entitled to 13 weeks of unpaid parental leave or 18 weeks for disabled children under the age of eighteen. This leave may be taken up until the fifth, or respectively eighteenth, birthday of the child, but there is a qualifying period of 1 year of service for this entitlement. The leave can be taken in blocks of 1 week up to a maximum of 4 weeks per year or in blocks of 1 day in the case of a disabled child, and the leave must be for the purpose of taking care of the child.

Right to request flexible working arrangements

Parents of children under the age of 6 (or 18 for a disabled child) have the right to request flexible working arrangements so they can give adequate attention to their family responsibilities while continuing to work. Qualifying employees with at least 26 weeks of service are entitled to request a change in the hours they work or in their place of work. Employers must give such requests serious consideration, but they are entitled to deny a request if there is a valid business reason for doing so, including the cost involved, the impact on the organisation's ability to meet its customers' needs, structural issues such as the potential for re-distributing the employee's work to others or the availability of recruits with the appropriate skills and knowledge. These rights and obligations were introduced in the Employment Act 2002, supplemented by the Flexible Working (Procedural Requirements) Regulations 2002 and the Flexible Working (Eligibility, Complaints and Remedies) Regulations 2002.

The IRS (2004) give a detailed overview of this legislation and its implications, explanations of how to put it into practice, and what issues need to be considered.

ACTIVITY 6.1

The IRS article cited above lists other relevant pieces of legislation for employers to keep in mind when applications for flexible working are made under these regulations and responses are delivered, and maybe when changes to the employee's contract are initiated. Think about the processes involved and which other pieces of legislation might be relevant and require some action or thought, and compare your ideas to those listed in the article.

Part-time employees

The treatment accorded to part-time employees in the UK was traditionally inferior to that given to full-time employees. However, as employers came to depend more on employees to be flexible, and to recognise the benefits organisations can gain from employing people on non-standard contracts, they also had to recognise the necessity of addressing the needs of these employees and treating them fairly. The statutory rights of part-time employees were strengthened in the mid-1990s by a ruling from the House of Lords, and subsequent legislative developments have also bolstered their position.

Prior to 1994, part-time employees had to work for considerably longer than full-time employees to acquire the employment protection rights then enshrined in the Employment Protection Consolidation Act 1978. In March 1994 the House of Lords held that the UK had been in breach of Article 119 of the Treaty of Rome and the Equal Pay and Equal Treatment Directives. The existence of differing thresholds to obtain a variety of employment protection rights amounted to indirect sex discrimination since the majority of part-time employees are women. The right of part-time employees to claim statutory protection against unfair dismissal and redundancy should be the same as that of full-time workers, i.e. a two-year qualifying period at that time. In response to this judgment, the government implemented the Employment Protection (Part-Time Employees) Regulations 1995 (now incorporated into the Employment Rights Act 1996) which created equality between full- and part-timers in terms of statutory employment rights. The qualifying period with regard to unfair dismissal was subsequently reduced to one year.

Part-time staff also have rights to membership of pension schemes as outlined in the Pensions Act 1995 ss 62–66 and Occupational Pension Schemes (Equal Treatment) Regulations 1995. Their rights have been strengthened more

recently by the adoption of the EU Part-Time Work Directive which was implemented on 1 July 2000. The Part-Time Workers (Prevention of Less Favourable
Treatment) Regulations 2000 give part-timers equal rights to the full array of
contractual terms, including rights to staff discounts, and access to training and
promotion opportunities. A major aspect of the regulations is that it is unlawful
to discriminate against a person because of his or her part-time status; cases of
discrimination against part-time employees will no longer have to be presented as sex discrimination, though the IRS (2000) argue that it may still be expe-
dient to do so.

Working time

The Working Time Regulations 1998 came into force in October 1998. The key
features are described here in brief.

Working hours

Essentially the regulations provide for a maximum of 48 weekly working hours
averaged over a period of 17 weeks. It should be noted that there are provisions
in the regulations for employers and employees to reach agreement to work
longer hours while the legislation protects employees from being *obliged* to
work longer hours. The IRS (2001, p. 2) reported that 'a significant minority of
workers are opting out of the maximum 48-hour working week'. This provision
has been the subject of much debate at EU level, and some observers expected
that it would be rescinded in a subsequent review of the regulations. At the time
of writing, however, it has been allowed to stand in the most recent proposals
for amendment of the Working Time Regulations (Jameson 2004), but with the
introduction of a proviso that a recognised union could veto an individual's
agreement to work longer hours. Arrowsmith (2004) points out that basic working hours in the countries that joined the EU in 2004 were in general longer
than the European average, resulting in a sudden change to the overall picture,
which may have accounted for the less decisive approach of the European
Commission to this issue. The averaging period is to be extended to one year.

Rest breaks

Employees should have 11 consecutive hours of rest in any 24-hour period, and
a 24-hour rest in every seven days. There is also an entitlement to a 20-minute
break if the work day exceeds 6 hours.

Annual leave

Until the advent of this legislation there was no legal obligation for employers
to provide paid annual leave for their employees, other than arrangements for
statutory holidays. Of course, the vast majority of employers did make such
provision, and annual leave has often been part of collective bargaining agreements between employers and trade unions. Even now, many employers will
provide more than the basic entitlement, but at least this legislation guarantees a basic entitlement, which was three weeks in the first year that the legislation was introduced and four weeks after November 1999.

Derogations and subsequent amendments

There were some groups of workers who were not originally covered by these regulations, including workers involved in air, sea and road transport, junior hospital

doctors and people who have autonomous decision-making powers, such as senior managers. In 2003, this opt-out was rescinded with reference to 'non-mobile workers in road, sea, inland waterways and lake transport, railway and offshore sectors, and all workers in aviation who are not covered by the sectoral Aviation Directive' so that workers in these areas were included in the terms of the regulations with effect from 1 August 2003 (**www.dti.gov.uk**; accessed 30.09.04). Regulations limiting the working hours of junior hospital doctors were also put into effect, but not until 1 August 2004.

Data protection

Employers gather and keep a wide range of personal information about employees, and employees have a right to expect that those data will be kept confidential and that a high standard of accuracy will be maintained. The Data Protection Act 1984 provided for some assurances with regard to computerised information, and since 1 March 2000, when the Data Protection Act 1998 came into effect, information relating to individuals which is kept on paper, or in any other format, is also covered. Whistleblowers have also gained some protection via the Public Interest Disclosure Act of 1998, while the Human Rights Act 1998 applies to aspects of an individual's privacy. The Freedom of Information Act 2000 provides a statutory right of access to 'recorded' information held by public authorities and this Act must be brought fully into force by 30 November 2005. The Information Commissioner has responsibilities for providing an integrated role relating to both the Freedom of Information Act 2000 and to the Data Protection Act 1998.

The Data Protection Act 1998

The Data Protection Act 1998 covers all the stages involved in gathering data, from collection, safe storage, use and disclosure to destruction. The Act applies to personal information used in recruitment and selection, employment records, employee monitoring and medical testing, and applies to any private filing systems kept by managers as well as to centralised HR record systems.

The Information Commissioner has produced a set of codes related to employment practices as follows:

> *The Employment Practices Data Protection Code Part 1: Recruitment and Selection*
> *The Employment Practices Data Protection Code Part 2: Employment Records*
> *The Employment Practices Data Protection Code Part 3: Monitoring at Work*
> *The Draft Employment Practices Data Protection Code Part 4: Information about Workers' Health*

The codes will come into force when all four parts are published, but as at November 2004, Part 4 was still presented as a draft on the Information Commissioner's web site. The codes are designed to enable employers to better understand their obligations under the Data Protection Act 1998.

The provisions of the Data Protection Act 1998 were applied in stages, but since 24 October 2001 they have applied to all manually stored records that have been collected since 24 October 1998, and also to all computerised record systems. The Act includes eight principles:

- Data must be handled and processed in a fair and lawful manner.
- The reasons for obtaining these data must be legal and have been clearly specified. The data must only be used for the reasons specified.
- Data collected must be sufficient and relevant for the specified purpose. There should be no excessive collection of data.
- Any data collected must be accurate and be updated regularly.
- It should not be kept for any longer than is necessary, so data need to be regularly reviewed so that out-of-date information is removed.
- Data should be processed in accordance with the rights of individuals.
- The data must be kept secure.
- Data may only be transferred to countries that have adequate data protection.

We said earlier that this applies to personal data held by all managers, not just HR managers, and consequently most organisations need to complete an audit to establish exactly what data is kept and by whom. Lots of managers have their own private filing systems and may store out-of-date personal data. Someone in the organisation, possibly from within the HR department, has to take on the role of data controller and ensure that managers who keep personal data also comply with the eight data protection principles.

Data subjects have the right to know what information is kept about them and can ask to see the data. Employers can charge a fee for this, but must supply the information within 40 days. The person identified as data controller may be liable if there are breaches in the security of information, or if losses occur as a result of such a breach.

Statutory rights: a concluding statement

As well as understanding the rights and obligations of both employers and employees already established in law, it is essential to be aware that this is an area where issues develop and change very rapidly. These changes can arise, as we explained earlier, from formal consideration of statutes in Parliament or because new understanding of various circumstances arises when judgments are handed down on cases in the courts. In 1995 the Walker case, among others, focused attention on employer obligations with regard to the mental health of employees. Lobbying on behalf of disabled people engendered changes in the mid-1990s in statutory law regarding their rights to equal opportunity in employment. You will find more information on these two issues in the recruitment and employee welfare chapters (Chapters 3 and 11). One way of staying informed about developments in employment law is to read the legal update articles that appear in journals such as *People Management*, *Personnel Today*, *Equal Opportunities Review* and *Industrial Law Journal*.

It is essential to review and update policies and practices to reflect the law as new requirements come into effect. The willingness of employers to offer employees more than the minimum that is required by the law might also contribute to improved employee relations and so enhance the contribution that employees are willing to make.

ACTIVITY 6.2

The Employment Law at Work section on the CIPD web site has links to frequently asked questions on a wide range of topics such as family-friendly working, maternity, paternity and adoption leave and pay, and working time regulations. Look at some of the FAQs and formulate your own response before checking out what the CIPD says. Go to **www.cipd.co.uk/EmploymentLaw/FAQ** (accessed 16.04.04).

Flexible working arrangements

Many people still have an image of traditional working patterns that involve spending Monday to Friday in a workplace with contractual provisions for a 36–40 hour work week and something like four weeks' holiday. There are, however, many new patterns evolving to suit the changing requirements of businesses. These include the increased prevalence of part-time employment; contracting-out of work; arrangements for flexi-time; and contracts based on annual or even zero hours. Supermarkets now open on Sundays, and the once restrictive Sunday licensing hours for public houses have also been relaxed. Some people are working fewer hours to provide flexibility, and some are working more to cope with the pressures of work. All this variety and change suggests that for some part of your working life you are as likely to be working under flexible conditions as in a supposedly traditional arrangement.

Did you know?

Men in Britain are more likely to work longer hours than their counterparts in the rest of Europe.
(TUC figures quoted in 'Yardstick', *Personnel Today*, 28 March 1995)

Even the traditional idea of a hierarchical structure with well-defined roles and responsibilities has been subject to much change. Charles Handy (1989) outlined his ideas about new organisations by drawing an analogy with the shamrock leaf. The basic concept is that within an organisation there would be a core of employees consisting of the specialists and managers dedicated to the essential business of the organisation. These are the people who are likely to be working longer hours than the standard 40 or even 48 per week. In fact, some contracts even contain clauses that mention 'the number of hours necessary to fulfil the requirements of the job'. Other types of work that are needed to keep the organisation going, but are not a part of the organisation's central work, are contracted out to others who specialise in them. This contracting-out of work is the second leaf of the shamrock. The third group consists of part-time and temporary employees who are hired on a flexible basis as required. If everyone in an organisation is a full-time employee, the inevitable fluctuations in business needs imply that you will have slack times when you are paying people to do little work, and times when overtime is required. The mix of working arrangements that Handy identified means that you have the flexibility to call on people's services only when you need them. The emphasis is on developing arrangements to increase flexibility and the organisation's ability to respond rapidly and well to changing requirements.

Can you think of examples where organisations may be employing people to perform tasks that are peripheral to the organisation's core activities, and where services could therefore be contracted from outside providers specialising in those areas?

Your examples may have included some of the following. As we have already mentioned in Chapter 5, compulsory competitive tendering was in place in local government for several years. Services for which external providers were able to bid included refuse collection, school dinner services and some professional services, including parts of HRM. In commerce, third-party provision of transport for the distribution of goods from manufacturers to wholesalers and retailers is well established, and many manufacturers contract out the distribution of their goods rather than maintaining their own fleet. The provision of counselling by outside agencies is discussed in Chapter 11, and external provision of outplacement services is mentioned in Chapter 15. Cleaning or cafeteria services are often bought in, and payroll services can be provided by banks.

If an organisation intends to look to external provision of services such as these, rather than creating posts and having its own employees perform this work, then the relationship changes from employer–employee to client–service provider. This relationship requires a different set of skills of managers, who must ensure that a service is delivered to their satisfaction rather than managing employees. Usually, service contracts with exact specifications of the required standards are drawn up, and performance is measured against these.

As we have just presented it, many employers are developing new working arrangements in order to meet business requirements, but sometimes these meet the needs of individual employees too. In fact, meeting the needs of business can be synonymous with meeting employee needs if an organisation wishes to retain valuable staff, whether they are members of the core staff or more peripheral workers. Since the late 1990s there has been growing recognition of the importance of achieving a good balance between work and private commitments. A good work–life balance can meet both employer and employee needs in terms of stress management, health, productivity and, of course, employers must respond to the right of eligible parents to request flexible working arrangements as described earlier. We shall review some of the important developments, looking specifically at annual hours contracts, job sharing, fixed-term contracts and teleworking.

Annual hours

Instead of contracting employees to work, say, a 40-hour week regularly throughout the year, which might entail periods of under-employment and periods of overtime for which the employer pays at an enhanced rate (usually one and a half times or double the normal rate), the employer estimates the number of hours he or she will need an employee over the period of a year, and contracts the employee to work those hours at the standard rate but according to an agreed, irregular pattern that corresponds better to fluctuating business needs. This means that, subject to agreed arrangements, the employer can call on the services of employees when they are needed, and most importantly does not pay employees for their presence at times when they are not needed. Employees are guaranteed payment for the hours that they have been contracted for, and normally the salary would be paid in equal amounts spread over the year.

Terms that would usually need to be imposed on this arrangement would be agreements on things such as the maximum number of hours an employee could be expected to work in a given number of days, entitlement to a consecutive number of days off, notice of a call in to work. The arrangements should be such that employers are able to cover both scheduled and unscheduled requirements.

A number of organisations have found that annualised hours work to their advantage. One company that has used this innovative approach is Welsh Water. Managers from Welsh Water presented their system as a case study to the IPM conference in November 1993. Employees were scheduled for new shifts which included some weeks with 40 hours of work and some with 48, weekend and on-call requirements were covered, and employees were also rostered to have one week in six off. The company saw improvements in productivity and a more controlled use of overtime. As this example shows, annual hours arrangements reduce the need for overtime working and strengthen management's ability to control them, but an element of flexibility to use overtime when needed has to remain.

Incomes Data Services (2004) reported more recently on 36 organisations that have implemented annual hours systems for specified employees. These include Boots Manufacturing–Strepsils manufacturing facility (on which the IDS provide a full case study), British Gypsum, the Gleneagles Hotel and Tesco Stores (distribution support).

Job share

The concept of having two people share the tasks designated as constituting one post probably grew out of the recognition that some women did not wish to return to full-time work after maternity leave but would prefer to continue in their careers, working a reduced number of hours. Some employers developed job-sharing schemes partly to accommodate this desire, but also because they recognised that this was one way of retaining scarce talent and benefiting from the investment they had made in employees who no longer wished to work full time. As we explained in the section on parental rights, it has also become increasingly clear that there is an obligation on all employers to at least consider the viability of such arrangements.

Job sharing requires additional arrangements to ensure coordination between partners, which has implications for the managers of job-share partners, but there are numerous benefits: it can bring additional flexibility in terms of availability of staff when required for extra work; it shows that the employer is willing to consider new arrangements that accommodate staff needs; the talents and ideas of two people are applied to one job; and it is good for morale. In fact, it is an arrangement that can clearly bring mutual benefit. Also, although we stated earlier that the arrangement probably grew out of the wishes of women returning from maternity leave, job share is not just of benefit to women. Men can also have responsibilities as the primary care givers in their families and welcome the opportunity to work part time, and job share is also attractive to people who wish to combine a steady income with consultancy activities.

Fixed-term contracts

Fixed-term contracts are addressed specifically in part XIII, s 197 of the Employment Rights Act 1996, but other sections of the Act also apply, such as the need to issue a written statement of employment particulars to anyone hired for longer than one month. Fixed-term contracts obviously offer some flexibility to employers in terms of adjusting the numbers of employees at different times to suit fluctuating business needs. There has been some concern about the rights of employees on fixed-term contracts, however, and the European Directive on Fixed Term Work required the member states to address these issues. The Fixed-term Employees (Prevention of Less Favourable Treatment) Regulations 2002 came into effect on 1 October 2002 and provided extra protection for employees on such contracts. The issue of consecutive fixed-term contracts to an employee is now limited to a period of 4 years, after which the position must be made permanent. Employers are also not entitled to include a redundancy waiver in the terms of a fixed-term contract.

The major features of fixed-term contracts are as follows:

- They state the maximum period of the contract, giving the date on which the contract will end.
- Non-renewal at the end of a fixed-term contract is a dismissal.
- A contract for a specific purpose is now included in the definition of a fixed-term contract.
- Service over a series of fixed-term contracts can be aggregated to constitute continuity of service.

Teleworking/homeworking

The work arrangements we are referring to as teleworking are not to be confused with the kind of low-paid piece work that involves activities such as stuffing envelopes. Teleworking has evolved with the rapid developments in information technology and telecommunications. With the advent of fax and e-mail, people do not need to be in the same building to transmit written documents and reports instantaneously. Distance working is also used as a term for employees who no longer need to go into an office to do their work, 'tele' being the Greek root meaning 'far'. In other words, the term can be used for people who mainly use technology to produce reports, but also for people out on the road seeing customers. Orders can be relayed using information technology, and often it is more sensible for such employees to use their home as their base rather than an office in a town centre. Jobs are no longer equated with a desk in the office.

Pause for thought 6.5   Make a list of what you think the advantages and disadvantages of teleworking are. For every disadvantage you identify, suggest a solution.

Advantages

- A wider range of people can be gainfully employed, for instance those who have care duties and cannot leave home for prolonged periods of time but who can organise their time at home to include periods of work.

- Flexibility in working hours: some people like to work at three in the morning while others sleep, and teleworking gives them the opportunity to do so.
- Working at home cuts down on travelling time and on costs of office accommodation and furniture.

Disadvantages

- Social factors may be the source of disadvantages, but that simply means that the social system needs to be managed properly. Teleworkers may suffer from isolation and a feeling of not being part of an organisation. An antidote for this is to arrange training sessions and regular briefing sessions when employees can get together and review common problems, and to use communication channels to keep people in touch. If some isolation cannot be avoided, recruiters should attempt to select people who will be suited to the type of work.
- Some managers, particularly those who adopt a control style, may be uncomfortable supervising teleworkers. It is possible to institute regular reporting mechanisms and control the volume of work done in a period of time, but on the whole the development of teleworking calls for a different style of management and a higher level of trust. The emphasis is definitely on the fact that the work gets done rather than on imposing controls on when and where it is done.

Employers who develop teleworking arrangements should be aware of their duties with regard to the health and safety of employees. They will need to conduct a risk audit of the employee's home-based workplace – information about this is readily available from the Health and Safety Executive (see Chapter 12 for information about access to HSE information).

ACTIVITY 6.3

Your class will conduct a survey to establish what kinds of working patterns are in existence and whether these meet the needs of the employees concerned. You should decide who your target population will be. For example, you may wish to survey only local businesses and residents, or to include the friends and relatives of students to extend your geographical coverage. You may wish to target a particular industry, for example, the manufacturing sector or retail outlets. You should probably exclude full-time students from your survey, as they have an obvious need to work only part time.

1 Work out in class what you want to find out and what questions you need to ask to gather this information. You will want to include some of the following issues. Establish what basis each person is employed on: part time, permanent, temporary, etc. Establish whether they are satisfied with this or would prefer some other arrangement. What are the main reasons for their levels of satisfaction or dissatisfaction?

2 Each student will conduct a survey of 5 to 10 people who have some sort of employment and make an analysis of this small sample. Compare your findings with those of others in your class.

3 Work in groups of five and compile an analysis of your pooled information. Report your results to the class and compare your results with those of the other groups in your class.

▶

4 Establish which patterns of employment and employee attitudes have emerged.

5 Discuss how this information might be used by employers to improve their human resource management practices.

The concept of flexible working arrangements is directly connected with the HRM approach in that these innovations lead to empowerment (as must be the case with teleworkers), and the flexibility that is necessary to become a high performance organisation.

Termination of employment

Employees leave their organisations in a variety of ways and a number of circumstances, and for a number of reasons. Stop for a moment and make a list of as many of these circumstances as you can think of.

In making your list you may have categorised the reasons for employee exit into those that signify voluntary exit and those that are involuntary. Voluntary reasons include:

- to take up another post
- retirement or voluntary early retirement (although not everyone welcomes retirement at the normal retirement age and the concept of forced retirement at a particular age may become a thing of the past when age discrimination legislation is introduced)
- voluntary non-employment, often due to a change in circumstances including parenting or studying.

The involuntary reasons you have listed may include:

- redundancy, or early retirement as an option to redundancy
- dismissal, including dismissal due to ill-health.

For each of these reasons for exit, there is a range of circumstances that apply, except perhaps for retirement, which usually occurs for everyone at the organisation's normal retirement age (but note the caveat above about expected legislation). People taking up another post, for example, may be doing so for a number of reasons, such as:

- personal reasons for moving to another geographical area
- because they have been offered more pay or better conditions for doing the same work with another employer
- opportunities for promotion
- to escape from uncongenial managers or colleagues
- a desire for a change of career.

If you have read the chapter on human resource planning (Chapter 2), you will realise that it is essential for employers to understand why people leave their organisations so that appropriate recruitment and retention plans can be devised to maintain the workforce necessary for them to achieve their goals. For this reason, many employers gather information from staff who are leaving for voluntary reasons by conducting an exit interview with them.

Exit interviews and employee opinion surveys

It is important to gather data on any problems connected with aspects of the employment relationship so that employers can take action to remedy any arrangement that might potentially cause more valuable employees to leave. The areas usually covered in an exit interview include:

- the reason for leaving, particularly if the person is going to another job – is it for pay/opportunity/some other benefit?
- relationships with supervisors and co-workers
- working conditions in general and specific ones that might be problematic, such as shift work.

With the expansion of equality legislation, ACAS (2004a and 2004b) suggest the inclusion of questions about whether a person has ever felt harassed in the workplace with regard to any of the types of harassment covered in the regulations.

Exit interviews are usually conducted by someone in the human resource management department since employees, even when they are leaving an organisation, may be more willing to talk about problems with a person who does not work directly with them. The interviewer should ensure confidentiality and explain that information gained from exit interviews is used to identify trends rather than to act on information from any individual. These reassurances can make people open up. A good process will include a form that the employee can complete in advance of the interview, and the interview can then be used to clarify details. You will find a similar process recommended for appraisal interviews in Chapter 9.

ACTIVITY 6.4

Design an exit interview form and process, either generic or for an organisation of your choice. Try to apply the questioning techniques you have learned from studying Chapter 4.

Employee opinion surveys can be used to assess the levels of satisfaction within an existing workforce in a variety of work conditions. It is well recognised that management must demonstrate a willingness to take action on the issues raised, or at least respond to these issues in some way, if they wish to retain the trust of their employees and have employees take any subsequent surveys seriously.

Retirement

One of the benefits that employers can offer their employees is preparation for retirement through some kind of formal pre-retirement programme. Moving from working life to retirement requires a big adjustment, and can be achieved more successfully with careful planning, in terms of coping with a changed financial situation as well as increased leisure time. Financial advice on pensions is a complex subject beyond the scope of this text. It is sufficient to note that this is another area that can be affected by changing legislation.

Employers can further consider programmes for keeping in touch with people who have retired from employment with them. It can be a low-cost benefit to arrange occasional social gatherings for past and present employees and to send the organisation's newsletter to past employees, and the returns in terms of morale and commitment from current employees who witness this evidence of their employer's concern for employee welfare may well repay these costs many times over.

Of course, the issue of what should be regarded as the normal retirement age is now a matter for debate. It remains to be seen how this will be affected by Government policy and the imminent regulations on age discrimination.

Conclusion

We have seen that the relationship between employer and employee consists of rights and obligations on both sides, and that these are determined by law and various other agreements. Innovations in terms, conditions and working arrangements are a sign of the times as organisations attempt to respond to increasing competitive challenges, and the expectation of further developments in European law guarantees that this will continue to be an area of change in the future.

REVIEW QUESTIONS

You will find brief answers to the review questions on page 490.

1 Peruse the 'Law at work' sections in People Management or the court cases listed in the Industrial Case Reports for the last three months or so. Select the articles or cases that are concerned with contractual issues, and review them. Summarise the major hot topics of the day. Have these issues arisen because of any changes in legislation?

2 We mentioned that employment legislation usually sets out minimum provisions for employee rights. Can you identify a number of areas where some employers are known to provide more than the minimum?

SELF-CHECK QUESTIONS

Answer the following multiple-choice and short-answer questions. The correct responses are given on page 490 for you to check your understanding of this chapter.

1 Which of the statements below best describes the psychological contract?
   (a) Managers will do nothing to destroy the relationship of trust they have with their subordinates.
   (b) Employers will do all they can to promote the mental well-being of employees, for instance by providing facilities for counselling on personal problems.
   (c) The expectations that managers and employees have of each other can lead to a relationship based on coercion, a calculation of reward for effort, or cooperation.

2 Explain the difference between implied and express terms in a contract.

3 Name the terms that are implied in an employment contract on the part of an employee.

4 Joe Biggins has worked for Actwell Company for nine years. There is nothing in his contract about how much notice he should get if his job is terminated. The company is now moving to another location and, following appropriate consultation, has had to dismiss all its employees. How much notice should Joe receive?

5 Annie Creston has been with Actwell for only two months. How much notice should the company give her?

6 Which piece of legislation contains the duty of an employer to supply employees with a written statement of their particulars of employment?

7 How many weeks' maternity leave constitutes the basic entitlement of pregnant employees?

8 A woman needs to have two years of service before the expected birth in order to qualify for the 26 weeks of additional maternity leave. TRUE or FALSE?

9 An annual hours contract means that employees are not allowed to work overtime. TRUE or FALSE?

10 What major problems were identified related to teleworking?

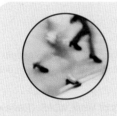

WHAT NEXT?

The Joseph Rowntree Foundation supports research on a wide variety of aspects of social policy. A report on research into attitudes towards flexible working was published in 2003 on behalf of the foundation (details below), but related findings can also be found on the foundation's web site. Take a look at the web site or the published report, and summarise the major issues addressed there. If you wish to take your research on flexible working even further, you might search out other web sites and research articles and reports to find out whether the issues discovered in this report are confirmed elsewhere:

Houston, D. M. and J. A. Waumsley (2003) *Attitudes to Flexible Working and Family Life*, The Policy Press

www.jrf.org.uk/knowledge/findings/socialpolicy/d53.asp *(Attitudes to Flexible Working and Family Life)*

References

Advisory, Conciliation and Arbitration Service (2004a) *Religion or Belief and the Workplace: A Guide for Employers and Employees*, ACAS

Advisory, Conciliation and Arbitration Service (2004b) *Sexual Orientation and the Workplace: A Guide for Employers and Employees*, ACAS

Argyris, C. (1960) *Understanding Organisational Behaviour*, Dorsey Press

Arrowsmith, J. (2004) Counting the hours, *People Management*, 16 September, 37–41

Fairness at Work (1998) Government White Paper, HMSO, May (The Paper can be viewed on the Internet at **www.dti.gov.uk**/er/fairness: accessed 10.11.04)

Guest, D. and N. Conway (1997) *Issues in People Management No 21: Employee Motivation and the Psychological Contract*, IPD

Handy, C. (1985) *Understanding Organizations*, 3rd edition, Penguin

Handy, C. (1989) *The Age of Unreason*, Hutchinson

Incomes Data Services (2004) *IDS HR Studies 767: Annual Hours*, IDS

Industrial Relations Services (IRS) (2000) The Part-time Workers (Prevention of Less Favourable Treatment) Regulations 2000, *Industrial Relations Law Bulletin 646*, IRS, August, 2–8

Industrial Relations Services (IRS) (2004) Flexible working – avoiding the legal pitfalls, *IRS Employment Review 801*, 4 June, 51–60

Information Commissioner (2002) *The Employment Practices Data Protection Code Part 1: Recruitment and Selection*, Information Commissioner
(available at **www.informationcommissioner.gov.uk**; accessed 15.11.04)

Information Commissioner (2002) *The Employment Practices Data Protection Code Part 2: Employment Records*, Information Commissioner
(available at **www.informationcommissioner.gov.uk**; accessed 15.11.04)

Information Commissioner (n.d.) *The Employment Practices Data Protection Code Part 3: Monitoring at Work*, Information Commissioner
(available at **www.informationcommissioner.gov.uk**; accessed 15.11.04)

Information Commissioner (n.d.) *The Draft Employment Practices Data Protection Code Part 4: Information about Workers' Health*, Information Commissioner
(available at **www.informationcommissioner.gov.uk**; accessed 15.11.04)

Jameson, A. (2004) Industry to challenge EU over working hours, *The Times*, September 23, 50

Schein, E. H. (1978) *Career Dynamics: Matching Individual and Organisational Needs*, Addison Wesley

Willey, B. (2003) *Employment Law in Context: An Introduction for HR Professionals*, 2nd edition, Financial Times/Prentice Hall

www.dti.gov.uk; accessed 30.09.04

www.inlandrevenue.gov.uk; accessed 30.09.04

Further study

Books

Advisory, Conciliation and Arbitration Service, *Annual Report*. (The annual reports contain a section outlining the legislation that has been created in that year, together with a comment on its likely impact.)

Advisory, Conciliation and Arbitration Service (2003) *Changing Patterns of Work*, ACAS. (Reviews a number of ways of structuring hours of work, including annual hours and job sharing.)

Advisory, Conciliation and Arbitration Service (2003) *Effective Organisations: The People Factor*, ACAS.

Advisory, Conciliation and Arbitration Service (2003) *Personnel Data and Record Keeping*, ACAS. (An advisory booklet, this reviews the types of information an employer may need to obtain from employees, and explores ways of storing the data.)

Aikin, O. (2001) *Drawing up Employment Contracts*, CIPD. (An excellent reference book for anyone who needs more practical information about various forms of employment contracts.)

Incomes Data Services (2001) *IDS Focus 98: The New Agenda*, IDS, Summer. (Reviews the HR policy and legislative issues likely to be on the agenda for the Government from 2001 on.)

Incomes Data Services (2002) *IDS Studies 729: Teleworking*, IDS. (A review of the types and prevalence of teleworking with case studies from four organisations.)

Incomes Data Services (2003) *IDS Studies 755: Maternity and Parental Leave*, IDS. (A useful overview, but check for later IDS publications or relevant web sites to ensure you are informed about any later developments.)

Selwyn, N. *Law of Employment*, Butterworth. (An excellent source of information on employment law. Make sure you refer to the latest edition available.)

Your Rights at Work: A TUC Guide (2003) 2nd edition, Kogan Page/TUC. (Covers issues such as contracts, working time, parental leave, discrimination, etc.)

Articles

Adams, M. (2004) How to tackle the long hours culture, *People Management*, 30 September, 56–57.

Gartshore, A. (2004) How to introduce homeworking, *People Management*, 2 September, 44–45.

Human Resource Management Journal (1997) Vol. 7, No. 1. (This issue contains several articles on the psychological contract.)

Industrial Relations Services (2001) Maternity, paternity and parental benefits across Europe – part one, *European Industrial Relations Review 329*, June, 21–27.

Industrial Relations Services (2001) Maternity, paternity and parental benefits across Europe – part two, *European Industrial Relations Review 330*, July, 15–18.

Industrial Relations Services (2001) Maternity, paternity and parental benefits across Europe – part three, *European Industrial Relations Review 331*, August, 13–17.

Industrial Relations Services (2003) Home comforts, *IRS Employment Review 779*, 4 July, 22–23.

Industrial Relations Services (2003) Not just another day at the office, *IRS Employment Review 780*, 18 July, 8–15. (Two of a number of articles on teleworking provided by the IRS. The second one provides an overview of a number of employers using teleworking and what they regard as the advantages and disadvantages.)

'Law at work' is a regular feature in *People Management*. (The authors offer readable interpretations of employment laws and regulations, addressing specific issues that are of current concern to HR practitioners and line managers.)

McCartney, C. (2004) How to make flexible working work, *Personnel Today*, 7 September, 33–35. (Provides some brief case studies of organisations that have benefited from improved flexibility with tips on how to implement them.)

Syrett, M. and J. Lammiman (1994) Developing the peripheral worker, *Personnel Management*, July, 28–31. (Examines the importance of the contribution of flexible workers and the need to provide them with developmental opportunities.)

Internet

There are many Internet sites that can give you access to legal information. We have listed only a selection here for you to try. Most of them have numerous linked sites that you can click on to get more specific information.

Chartered Institute of Personnel and Development   **www.cipd.co.uk/Employment Law**
(The Employment Law subject area links to many interesting and informative pages. The CIPD provides a succinct summary of how UK law is made, including an explanation of Statutory Instruments (SIs), how to find the most recent court decisions and how to cite case law. There are also lists of forthcoming employment statutes and regulations, SIs in force etc., and a list of law-related factsheets and surveys. The pages on records also address which ones have to be kept to fulfil statutory obligations and for how long.)

Community Legal Service   **www.justask.org.uk**
(A source of information on a variety of legal issues.)

Department of Trade and Industry   **www.dti.gov.uk**
(A fount of information on employment matters with links to other sites. Extensive guidelines for both employers and employees on maternity and other parental rights, including a 120-page guide to maternity rights which can be downloaded at the site.)

Equal Opportunities Commission   **www.eoc.org.uk**
(Provides a checklist specifically designed for line managers on handling situations that might arise related to maternity rights and flexible working arrangements. Go to the main site and search for the equality checklists.)

Trades Union Congress   **www.tuc.org.uk**
(Know your rights and work SMART. Free leaflets to download, information about publications and helpful links to other sites.)

CHAPTER **7**

Introduction to the learning process

OBJECTIVES

By the end of this chapter you will be able to:

- state what is meant by learning
- describe the relevance of various theories of learning to training and development
- describe the systematic training cycle
- identify when to use a variety of training techniques
- identify your own preferred learning styles and use various techniques to improve your learning.

In any organisation there are a great many things that the people employed need to learn in order to become competent in their jobs. They learn some of the things they need to know unconsciously, such as the way people speak to each other and the acceptable style of dress or behaviour. At its simplest they are learning about the common view within that organisation of 'the way we do things around here' – the organisation culture.

Anyone who leaves one organisation and goes to work in another will appreciate that things are done differently in different organisations, and people sometimes suffer a feeling of culture shock if behaviour that had been acceptable in their previous organisation is not viewed in the same way in the new one. The new person picks up clues from the behaviour of others as to what is acceptable and what is not. Supervisors and managers will be seen to praise certain types of behaviour but will frown on others.

Managers and supervisors will be keen that the new employee learn certain aspects of their job, and may use a variety of approaches to encourage this learning to occur. They need to be aware, however, that you cannot make people learn, but, by the same token, you cannot stop them; people are learning all the time, even if they do not appreciate it. When people join an organisation and learn in an informal way what behaviour is acceptable, the speed with which they learn depends on their motivation, their perceptiveness in picking up clues as to what is acceptable and the examples they see around them. Unfortunately, this may also result in learning bad habits or having incorrect perceptions of situations at work.

Although employees will learn a great deal in this informal way, it is also a good idea for organisations to try to ensure that they have the opportunity to learn things that will enable them to perform to their best ability. This will mean that the organisation will need to:

- assess what it thinks people need to learn
- plan opportunities to facilitate learning experiences
- evaluate what has worked well, and what has been less successful.

Before we actually start to consider what people need to learn we shall examine some of the ways in which people learn. The ways in which people learn have been a subject of interest for thousands of years, and many theories seek to explain how people actually learn. In a knowledge-based economy, where there is constant change and where people are regularly required to develop new knowledge and skills, perhaps the most useful skill of all is knowing how to learn. Recently there has been increasing interest in the learning process as some organisations have realised that having a knowledgeable workforce who keep learning and updating their skills is likely be the key to becoming and remaining a successful organisation. A basic understanding of the learning process is also important in order for us to be able to provide appropriate training techniques which will enable people to learn most effectively. In this chapter we shall examine different learning theories and the contribution that they have made to our understanding of the learning process. A range of training techniques will then be discussed as well as some approaches to learning, which may also help you to learn more efficiently.

The next chapter is closely linked to this one, and in it we shall discuss methods of assessing training needs and examine some specific groups and the training that they require.

Learning theories

In order to appreciate more fully the most effective methods to use in training and development, and in order to understand current debates in education or training, it is a good idea to also know a little about learning theories.

Definitions of learning

There are in fact innumerable definitions of learning, and few are likely to satisfy everyone. Some of the different theories of learning are, however, reflected in the way we use the word 'learning', and these are shown in the following definitions.

The *Shorter Oxford Dictionary* defines learning as:

> 1. The action of the verb TO LEARN.
> 2. What is learnt or taught.
> 3. Knowledge . . . got by study.

This dictionary definition seems to indicate that learning is a process in which people are involved, and that they will somehow end up with a certain degree of knowledge as a result of this. Bass and Vaughan (1966), in a definition that has become widely used, said that:

> Learning is shown by a relatively permanent change in behaviour that occurs as a result of practice or experience.

This definition sees learning as being shown by a change in behaviour which has resulted from activities or experiences in which the individual has been involved.

In the view of Honey and Mumford (1992), learning has occurred when someone:

- knows something they did not know earlier, and can show it
- is able to do something which they were not able to do before.

The last of the three definitions implies that learning could be about acquiring knowledge, which could be tested, or it could be about acquiring a new skill, which similarly could be demonstrated.

These three definitions of learning serve as a useful starting point to examine some of the major theories of learning. They illustrate three differing approaches to learning. The first definition implies that learning is about acquiring knowledge; we call this approach 'cognitive'. The second implies that it is about changing behaviour, so we refer to this perspective as 'behaviourist'. The third definition describes learning as being about both knowledge and behaviour; we might refer to this as an 'experiential approach'.

Cognitive theories

Cognitive theorists would say that learning occurs within the mind. Ancient scholars such as Plato and Aristotle saw that the exercise of mental faculties, such as reason, memory and willpower, were important to the development of the individual. From this came the notion of the importance of the trained mind. Much education and training in Europe and the United States, especially in the first half of the-twentieth century, was based on this approach. This meant that learning was structured, teaching methods tended to be by telling and directing (didactic), and the subject matter was perceived to be important in its own right, with memorising facts and learning rules seen to be of great importance. This resulted in the 'chalk and talk' approach to learning, with formal classrooms and lectures where information went from the teacher to the pupil.

This traditional approach to learning can still be seen at work much of the time, and you will see later in this chapter that it relates closely to some people's preferred style of learning. It can, however, be criticised as being too theoretical, and lacking in stimulus for learners of a practical bias. It was in the search for a more practical, active form of learning that the following modern developments in cognitive theory took place. The approach that follows came to be known as discovery learning.

Relatively recent cognitive theorists have been concerned to discover how we solve problems: whether this is by trial and error, by deductive reasoning, by seeking more information or help from someone, or by using a mixture of all these approaches. Sometimes the solution comes with a flash of sudden insight, as in the case of Archimedes' discovery of how to find the weight of irregularly shaped objects when he realised that he himself displaced by his presence a certain amount of bath water and that the amount of displaced water could be measured.

In fact, you do not have to be a genius to have moments of insight. Köhler in 1925 studied how an ape would solve the problem of getting a banana, which was just outside its cage but which was just beyond its reach. The initial attempts by the ape resulted in it stretching its arms as far as possible towards the banana, and of course failing in its task. After a short period of time, however, it reached through the bars of its cage to grasp a short stick and with the aid of the stick brought the banana into its cage. In a later experiment the banana was placed even further out of reach. This time the ape reached through the cage for the short stick which was within its reach and then used this stick to drag a longer stick, which was previously not within reach, into its cage. Then, using the longer stick, the ape was able to reach the banana and drag it into its cage. This showed that the ape was discovering how to use the sticks to get the reward of the banana (Köhler 1959).

Pause for thought 7.1

If apes can have flashes of insight, so can you. Can you give an example of a time when you had a sudden flash of insight and realised that you had learnt something new?

Köhler's approach to learning relates clearly to discovery learning, where students or trainees are given tasks to achieve but have to find clues or stimuli to show them how to proceed. They learn by working through a process of trial and error to see what does and what does not work. This method aims to provide a means of unassisted learning in which appropriate experiences are provided and by which the student or trainee will gain insights into the best method of achieving the task. This is a very powerful method of learning, as an individual is usually quite rightly proud of what they have learnt, especially since they have been actively involved in discovering for themselves the solution to a problem.

This method, although very effective, cannot always be used. Time can be a constraining factor, as it takes time to allow people to make discoveries for themselves. There is also the related problem of costs. Can an organisation afford for all of a group of trainees to waste valuable materials in order to discover for themselves something that their manager could have told them about more quickly and cheaply? There is also the problem of safety to consider: it is not always practicable to allow people to experiment with equipment or materials, even if this is a very powerful aid to learning, if they endanger themselves or others in the process.

Behaviourist theories

The work of cognitive psychologists that we have examined so far focused on what was going on in the brain, and how we learn and memorise things. In contrast, many learning theorists felt it important to focus on observable behaviour, as they believed it impossible to study the workings of the mind in a scientific manner. The behaviourists like Pavlov generally studied the behaviour of animals in order to gain insights into how people learn; they were concerned with studying changes in behaviour and said that learning occurred if you could see such a change. The behaviourists made no assumptions about what the animal was thinking or what was going on in its mind; they were concerned only with behaviour that they could see.

Pause for thought 7.2

Look again at the definitions of learning given earlier. Which of these definitions reflect the behaviourist view of learning?

The definition by Bass and Vaughan (1966) – 'Learning is shown by a relatively permanent change in behaviour that occurs as a result of practice or experience' – would seem to reflect the behaviourist view of learning. This definition focuses on the change in behaviour. It does not relate to what the person might be thinking, and unlike the definition from the *Shorter Oxford Dictionary*, it contains no reference to the idea of acquiring knowledge. This latter definition seems to reflect a cognitive approach, while the definition of Honey and Mumford (1992) shows that both gaining knowledge and demonstrating a change in behaviour can be important in the learning process. Their definition encapsulates very neatly elements from both the cognitive and the behaviourist school of thought.

Behaviourist concepts

Although work with pigeons and dogs may not appear at first sight to be very relevant to training that occurs within organisations, this work does, in fact, raise a great many important issues, of which trainers should be aware.

Early in the last century Pavlov (1927) trained dogs to salivate when he rang a bell. He noticed that dogs salivated naturally as a reflex response when food was put in front of them. For his experiment he rang a bell every time the dogs were fed; after a time, the dogs would salivate when the bell was rung, whether there was food or not (Figure 7.1). He deduced that the dogs had learnt to salivate by associating the bell with the food, and came to see the learning process as the development of responses to the new stimuli given by the world. He called them conditioned responses, as opposed to the unconditioned or natural responses that came before. His term for the process of learning was 'conditioning'.

Later, Skinner (1953) took the theory further. The limitation of Pavlov's work was that it showed that animals (or people) could learn to apply instinctive responses to new sets of circumstances, but it did not show how totally new responses could be learnt. Skinner in fact succeeded in teaching pigeons to play ping-pong by a process that he called operant conditioning. In this process, the pigeons were watched for any patterns of behaviour that might be useful when playing ping-pong, and whenever they performed one they were

| Figure 7.1 | Pavlov's dogs |

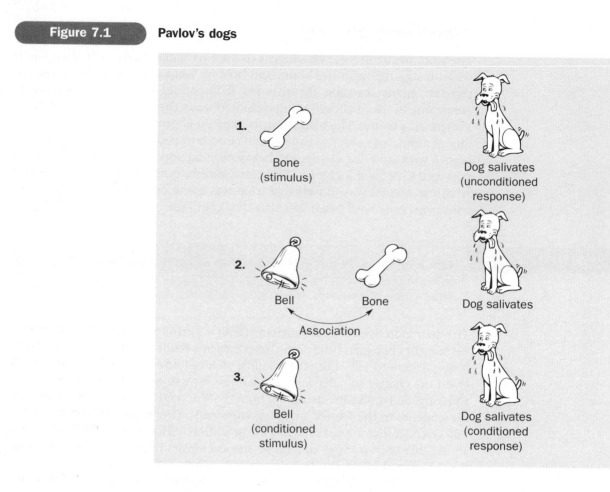

rewarded with food. Not surprisingly, the birds soon learnt to do certain move-
ments, and they retained their learning better if the reward was repeated regularly, a process Skinner called 'reinforcement'. In human learning, Skinner
believed, reinforcement mainly took the form of feedback – information
telling the learner whether he or she is getting the task right.

Skinner believed that all learning took place in this associative manner, and
that all complex patterns of behaviour, such as learning ping-pong or learning
to speak, could be broken down into small steps that could be taught one by
one in a simple fashion. He applied this theory both to training workers and to
the education of his own children, and his work is still very influential. It obviously makes sense to break down routine tasks into their component parts, and
to provide methodical training to cover them. In addition, his emphasis on the
visible or objective side of learning led to the practice of setting learning objectives or statements of what a learner had to achieve in terms of action.

On the other hand, you might be wondering whether Skinner's account of
the pigeons' learning process was complete. Did insight play no part in their
grasp of the rules of the game? In human learning insight often seems to
enable people to cut the corners on the road to knowledge, and experience of
behaviouristic attempts to teach complex matters suggests that they can lead
to a slow, mechanical set of activities. Many psychologists have challenged
Skinner's view, particularly with regard to the learning of complex behaviour
such as speech.

Scientists such as Pavlov and Skinner referred to the instinctive need that led to learning as 'the drive'. In animals this was normally provided by a desire for food, but in people the drive or motivation might be to pass an exam or just the satisfaction derived from mastering something new. This aspect of their work is important in itself, in that it points to the importance of considering people's motivation to learn. If we can find out what makes them want to learn, we will be able to tailor our instruction better.

ACTIVITY 7.1

Make a list of a range of situations where you feel that you have learnt something.

● In each case consider what was your drive, or motivation, to learn.
● Was there a stimulus to increase your drive to learn? What was this?
● Was there any form of reinforcement of your learning? What was this?

Discussion of Activity 7.1

People are motivated to learn by a variety of things, so you may have listed quite a few drives to learn. These may take the form of incentives, encouragement or rewards. Some people may be motivated by the need to do well in an examination or they may perhaps be motivated to learn a new skill because it may provide an improved opportunity for getting a better job or more pay. In other cases the motivation may be the pleasure of learning something new for its own sake or for the respect that other people may feel towards you when you have learnt something impressive. Other people may be motivated to learn by a sense of curiosity or by anxiety and fear of failure.

The tests and exercises should help you to prove to yourself that you are learning. They are one way in which you can show your response to learning. Your response shows what you have learned by giving you the opportunity to demonstrate a new skill, or by your acquisition of new knowledge on which you could be tested.

Programmed learning and computer-based training courses were developed from the behaviourists' work: in them the correct response is immediately rewarded by praise from the manual or computer and you are told that you have given the correct answer or pressed the correct key and may progress to the next stage.

Reinforcement and feedback

The behaviourists used reinforcement to indicate a correct behavioural response. The reinforcement could be negative or positive. Rewards such as food for animals or praise for people are positive forms of reinforcement of the desired behaviour, while punishments aim to eliminate incorrect behaviour. Research tends to suggest that positive reinforcement is generally more effective than negative reinforcement in gaining a change in behaviour in the long term, as with negative reinforcement the desired change often occurs only as long as there is the threat of punishment. When this threat is withdrawn then behaviour often reverts to the original behaviour.

Reinforcement of your learning could occur by your reading or viewing something and being tested on this and praised by your tutor for your efforts, or by your completing a self-check exercise and giving yourself a pat on the back if you have done well. This will reinforce correct behaviour or show you that you have the right answers, but won't necessarily give you any detailed understanding of what you have done well or of what you did wrong. For that you also need knowledge of results or feedback.

Knowledge of results or feedback is important if we are to learn effectively. In a training situation this could be by the trainer giving comments on the person's progress, or perhaps by a manager appraising the work of one of their staff. Giving feedback successfully is a very important skill to develop. Feedback is a way of learning more about ourselves and the effect that our behaviour has on others. If feedback is given in a constructive manner it should result in the individual becoming more self-aware, being aware of differing options and feeling encouraged to develop and grow. Feedback could be given in a destructive way, in which case the individual would end up feeling bad about themselves, with a feeling of hopelessness that there were perhaps no alternatives available to them, and a sense of failure.

When giving constructive feedback one should start with the positive, and focus first on the behaviour that has been done well before giving feedback about behaviour that has been done less well. Feedback about incorrect behaviour, if given skilfully, is extremely important; it doesn't have to be destructive, and here it is important to focus on specific aspects of behaviour that can be changed. General statements such as 'that was awful' are much too vague to be helpful in changing behaviour. It would be easy for the person receiving the feedback to feel that they are just being criticised unless the person who is giving the feedback also suggests alternative ways of behaving. For example, you might say 'The fact that you seemed preoccupied with your paperwork when Rosalind walked into the room, and took some time before you greeted her, seemed a very unwelcoming start to an interview. I think that if you had acknowledged her presence immediately and got up and walked towards her to greet her, it would have been a much more welcoming start to the interview, and would have been likely to have made Rosalind feel much more at ease.'

Feedback is, as we have shown, a very important part of the learning process. The saying 'Practice makes perfect' could well be modified to 'Practice with appropriate feedback makes perfect', since without the feedback the person could just carry on with the same inappropriate behaviour over and over again.

Experiential learning

Behaviourist and cognitive theories are useful, but each tells only part of the story. Other theories try to use elements of both to produce a more holistic view of the learning process. Such an approach is taken in the work of Kolb *et al.* (1974) in America, and of Honey and Mumford (1992) in Britain. They have focused on learning from experience – experiential learning – and have recognised the importance of both behaviourist and cognitive theory and integrated these into the learning cycle shown in Figure 7.2. Their theory also suggests that different people may have different preferred styles of learning.

The learning cycle

People learn in a variety of ways, and over the years may develop certain learning habits which enable them to benefit from certain types of experience more

Figure 7.2 **The learning cycle**

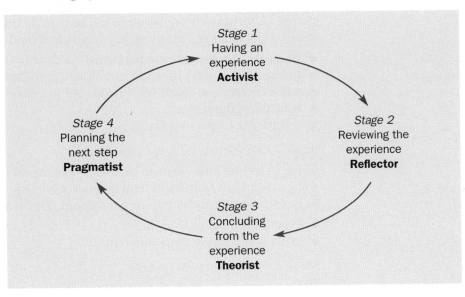

than other types. Students in college and people learning in the workplace are both likely to meet a range of different learning opportunities. Most students nowadays will work to supplement their student loan and will themselves have a range of work experiences from which they can learn. Some will be mature students who have already worked for a number of years, some will be part-time students combining study with a career, and yet others will be on sandwich course degrees where they have the opportunity of gaining work experience in a placement for a period of time. Knowing about their own learning style preferences may help them to understand and they may become more efficient in learning from these experiences.

Stage 1 – Having an experience

Most people have plenty of experiences from which they could learn, but age does not necessarily mean that people have learnt more. Some people do not use the experiences that they have. One way of learning is to let experiences come to you (reactive), and the other is to deliberately seek out new experiences (proactive). Trainers need to provide suitable experiences from which their trainees can learn (in the form, for example, of case studies, role plays and other simulations), but trainees also need to appreciate the need to be proactive and seek for themselves suitable experiences from which to learn. The use of suitable individuals who are willing to act as mentors, or forming a supportive study group of friends, can assist in this process by:

- helping to identify suitable experiences from which to learn
- reviewing with individuals what they have actually done and helping to draw out what they have learnt
- encouraging the individual to be proactive and to seek for themselves suitable learning experiences.

Stage 2 – Reviewing the experience

If we are to learn from an experience it is important to review what has happened. Unfortunately we are often too busy to do this, and some people never develop the habit of reflection. The individual should be encouraged to:

- think about what actually happened
- think of other ways in which the situation could have been handled
- make comparisons with what happened in other similar situations
- read about the subject
- compare theory and practice.

Stage 3 – Concluding from the experience

There would be little point in reviewing the experiences unless we then drew some conclusions from them. This involves scanning the raw material for lessons to be learned and reaching some conclusions. The individual should be asking:

- What have I learnt from this?
- What could I have done differently?

Stage 4 – Planning the next stage

Having reached a conclusion, it is important to try to do things better next time. To be able to do this we need to be able to plan, and this involves translating at least some of the conclusions into a basis for appropriate action next time. The individual should be encouraged to:

- state what they would actually do next time
- draw a plan of action for handling such a situation again.

The four stages in the process of learning using experiences are mutually dependent. The whole process is summarised in the learning cycle (Figure 7.2).

Learning styles

Most people only use one or two learning styles. Honey and Mumford have developed a questionnaire so that individuals can establish their preferred learning style. They developed this approach as a result of their work with managers, as they became concerned to discover why one person will learn from a particular experience but another does not appear to learn anything from the same experience. Further details of their approach are given in the recommended reading. They say that there are four types of people with differing learning styles that clearly link with the four stages of the learning cycle: activists, reflectors, theorists and pragmatists. These will now be discussed in turn.

Activists

Activists like to get fully involved in whatever is happening. They seek out new experiences and tend to be enthusiastic about new ideas and new techniques. They tend to be open minded and not sceptical, and are often enthusiastic about novelty. They tend to act first and then consider the consequences later. Their days are filled with activity and they often tackle problems by brainstorming.

Reflectors

Reflectors prefer to stand back and observe experiences from different perspectives. The thorough collection and analysis of data are important to them, so they try to avoid reaching definite conclusions for as long as possible. They would rather take a back seat in meetings and discussions and get the drift of the discussion before making their own points. When they act it is as part of a larger picture which includes the past as well as the present and takes into account other people's observations as well as their own.

Theorists

Theorists tend to adapt and integrate observations into complex but logically sound theories. They think problems through in a vertical, step-by-step, logical way. They assimilate disparate facts into coherent theories, and tend to be perfectionists who will not rest easy until things are tidy and fit into a rational scheme. They value rationality and logic.

Pragmatists

Pragmatists are keen to try out new ideas, theories and techniques to see if they work in practice. They positively search for new ideas and take the first opportunities to experiment with applications. They are the type of people who return from a training course full of ideas that they want to try out immediately. They like to get on with things and act quickly and confidently on ideas. They hate long ruminating discussions.

Individuals' barriers to learning

We all know of people who say that they have years of experience but really seem to have had the same experience over and over again for many years and not to have learnt much from it. Age or length of service does not guarantee that any greater learning has occurred for these people than for someone who has worked for a much shorter period of time, as some people create their own barriers to learning, and are not willing to try anything new or even slightly different.

> **Did you know?**
>
> Henry Ford said, 'Anyone who stops learning is old, whether at 20 or 80. Anyone who keeps learning stays young. The greatest thing in life is to stay young.'

Some of the barriers that individuals create for themselves to prevent themselves from learning at each of the stages of the learning cycle are discussed next:

- People may be afraid that they will lose face or be laughed at if they do something wrong, so they justify their unwillingness to experiment to themselves by saying that the old ways are the best and have always worked well enough in the past – so why change now? In this case, fear of making a mistake will prevent them from using the activist approach.
- In order to learn, people need to allow themselves time for reflection. Some people are too busy coping with crisis after crisis to stop and reflect on what they have learnt, and so they are unable to prevent the next crisis from occurring. If this is the case then they will not be using the reflective style of learning.
- Some people think that they are unable to learn from books and are unwilling to sit down quietly and try. They may have had bad experiences at school and may reject this as an approach to learning. These people are unlikely to be theorists or to see benefits in this approach to learning. They are unlikely to make connections between theory and practice.
- Other people enjoy studying theories but are less interested in whether they will actually work in practice, and so do not ever try to learn in this way. Since they are not interested in what happens in practice the pragmatist approach to learning will not be for them.

An understanding of which learning style seems to work best for you will give you the opportunity either to choose experiences that enable you to learn effectively using your preferred learning style, or enable you to decide to practise and develop the use of other learning styles and so increase the range of ways in which you learn. Using Honey and Mumford's learning questionnaire will help you to identify your preferred learning style or styles: how you then use this knowledge is up to you, but it is a useful starting point in learning how to learn.

ACTIVITY 7.2

1 Read the description of the four learning styles again.

2 From the descriptions given, which learning style do you think you use most frequently?

3 List the barriers that prevent you from learning using other learning styles.

4 Take this opportunity to practise using all four learning styles. Look at the references at the end of this chapter. Be pragmatic and try out these ideas in a practical way. You could do this by testing whether your view of the way in which you learn matches an analysis of your learning style by using Honey and Mumford's questionnaire. This will involve you in being an activist and seeking out a new experience by finding and answering for yourself Honey and Mumford's learning style questionnaire.

Then, see for yourself whether your analysis of your preferred learning style matches what you discover by using their questionnaire. Reflect on your findings.

Examine the theory by rereading the description of the styles outlined earlier. You might want to look at a more detailed account of how people learn, and this will also reinforce what you have already learned. Further readings to encourage you to do this are included at the end of this chapter.

Then, once you have established your preferred learning style or styles, you can be a pragmatist again and look for practical opportunities to learn in differing ways or seek out more opportunities to learn using your preferred learning style or styles.

You might take your studies further and complete the same exercise using Kolb's learning style inventory (see Kolb *et al.* 1974), the original learning style questionnaire from which Honey and Mumford developed their work, and then compare your results on the two questionnaires.

Discussion of Activity 7.2

You may have discovered that you are equally at home learning in each of these styles. Two per cent of the population use all four styles. The majority of the population – 70% – tend to prefer to use just one or two learning styles. You can use the understanding that you have gained about your learning styles in various ways. You might choose to seek out opportunities to use the learning styles that you generally use less often, and in this way you may become a more rounded learner who is able to make use of a wider range of learning opportunities.

You might, on the other hand, choose to make use of the learning styles that you know you prefer to use, so that if learning opportunities are presented to you in ways that you don't like, you may look for alternative ways to learn about the topic which are more in line with your learning style preferences.

Other approaches to learning styles and methods

There are many different ways of analysing approaches to learning. We have already mentioned the Honey and Mumford learning styles inventory and that of David Kolb *et al.*

However, other approaches are used. For example, are you a visual, auditory or kinaesthetic learner? If you like to visualise, seeing things in colour and using pictures such as mind maps, then you are probably a visual learner. If you prefer to listen to the sounds of things then you are probably an auditory learner, and if you like to move around while learning and link learning with movement then you could be a kinaesthetic learner. Do you associate other senses such as smell with particular things you have learned? Are you more of a left-brain (logical) or right-brain (creative) type of learner?

Summary

Whenever we are designing training for individuals or groups, we need to consider learning theory and build into the training as many conditions as we can to ensure effective learning. Not only is it important when learning from experiences for the individual learner to be aware of their preferred learning style, it is also important that the trainer should be aware of differing training styles in order to provide a learning experience which will be congruent with the way in which each individual trainee will learn best.

Practical issues relating to learning

We have examined some of the theories about learning, and will now consider some practical issues relating to learning which may be of some use to you in improving your own learning and your understanding of how to learn.

Learning curves

Many people think that if they keep working solidly at something that they are trying to learn they will master it. They are convinced they will continue to learn at the same pace as long as they are persistent. This approach is generally counterproductive, as people do not continue to learn at the same rate all the time. The learning curve shown in Figure 7.3 illustrates the main stages that may occur in the learning process. Each person's curve is likely to be different, but will display many of the same features. These ideas fit well with the current trend towards bite size learning, which will be discussed later in this chapter.

The learning curve illustrated here shows the rate at which someone mastered a physical task in a factory environment. At first there was no output at all, as the initial training was being undertaken (a). This means not that learning wasn't actually happening, but that at that stage it could not be demonstrated by any

Figure 7.3   **The learning curve**

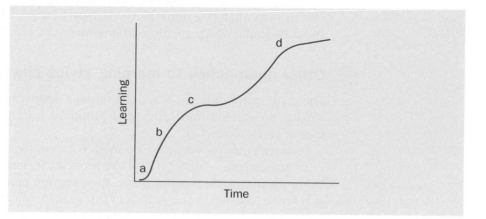

output. After a short time the learning that occurs is rapid (b), but then it seems to reach a plateau where little learning occurs (c). The rapid learning that occurs initially shows an initial mastery of the training. Learning could still be occurring when the plateau is reached, but it is not shown by an increase in output. It could be as a result of moving on to mastering a more difficult stage of the production process, or it may just reflect a need to consolidate what has been learnt. Once this has been achieved the learning is likely to be rapid for a short time before slowing down (d).

In the above case the learning that has occurred can be demonstrated by the level of output produced. The learning that a student or a trainee does, if they have to learn a certain amount of information, may reflect a similar pattern. For a short time the learning may be rapid, but it does not continue at this pace. There may be a stage where the student or trainee seems to reach a plateau and feels that they are not learning anything more. This may be because they need to master more difficult concepts, and once again it does not mean that no learning is occurring. Once this stage has been mastered the student or trainee may progress to learning more rapidly again. This can also be demonstrated using computer games. After some initial confusion where the person may seem to make little progress with the game, there is usually a stage where progress is rapid and mastery of the game seems assured. Progress to a new level, however, may introduce new skills to be mastered or new ideas to think about, and a plateau in the learning may occur.

Effective learning

If we are trying to learn a set of information, we tend to learn most effectively at the beginning of the learning period when we are fresh. We may also find that we can recall most easily things that we learnt at the beginning as well as the most recent things that we learnt at the end of the learning period. There may be a great deal of information that we thought we learnt in the middle of the learning session which we cannot recall.

It is not possible to keep learning at the same pace all the time, and besides reaching a plateau where they feel that they are not progressing, people also need to have breaks from the concentration involved in learning. It will be more effective to have a short break after studying for about half an hour than to continue to try to work at the same pace, as this will mean that when they return to study they will be fresh again and should learn rapidly once again for a short period of time. If the students keep trying to learn without taking any breaks, their increase in learning is likely to be extremely slow and their concentration will probably lapse so they may have to learn everything all over again.

Forgetting

With a physical task in a factory the trainee can demonstrate what they have learnt by their improvement in output. Since they are normally using what they have learnt again and again in the course of their job, it is unlikely that they will forget what they have just learnt. Their learning will be reinforced as they will be repeating the learned action again and again, and it will be reinforced by praise or recognition from their supervisor, or just by the fact that the right quality of product is produced. On the other hand, if knowledge or skill is not used for a long time then there is a danger that what had been learnt will be forgotten. This does not mean that this has vanished from their minds forever, just that they may have a problem in recalling it.

Figure 7.4 shows how we often seem less able to recall something that we have learnt a few days after the learning period. The diagram shows that recall is excellent just after we have learnt something, but that the amount we can recall then drops rapidly and we may be unable to recall as much as 80% of the information we had learnt.

This means that we need not only to pay attention to how we learn, but also to practise recalling what we have learnt. If the individual does not go over the material again there is a danger that they will gradually forget what they have learnt. Going over material that has been learnt later that day and then on the following day, and also a few days later, is likely to minimise this effect and to reinforce what has already been learnt.

Figure 7.5 shows how recall of what has been learnt can be improved by recalling it at different times (reviews) so that it becomes easy to remember the information. This could involve the students testing themselves on what they can recall by rewriting what they have learnt in different words and then going over the information again.

Figure 7.4 **The forgetting curve**

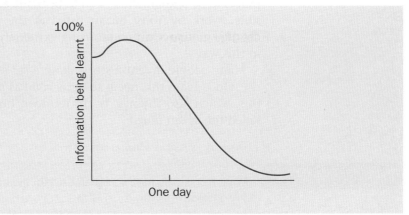

Figure 7.5   **Ways of improving recall**

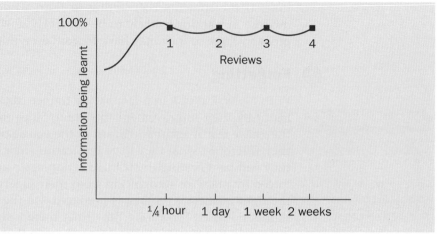

Techniques to improve learning and recall

The way in which people were traditionally taught or trained tended to value memorising many facts. It is still important in some circumstances today. In some examinations you may need to recall factual information accurately. This subject will be considered briefly here, but further guidance on how to improve learning and recall can be found in the recommended reading.

Some people use special techniques to help them to learn effectively and to improve their ability to recall what they have learnt. Mnemonics, number rhymes and stories can all help here.

Mnemonics provide a system for remembering lists of information by associating each word with a key letter and creating a word which you would find easy to remember from this. A simple example of this is the term SWOT analysis. This stands for Strengths, Weaknesses, Opportunities and Threats, and is a way of examining an organisation or department under these four headings.

Number rhymes can also prove to be very effective ways of remembering a list of words. In this case you have a rhyming word for each number in the list, which you then associate with the word that you are trying to remember, e.g. 1 = gun, 2 = shoe, 3 = tree. In each case the rhyming word and the word that is to be remembered need to be made as memorable in your mind as possible. Work by Tony Buzan listed at the end of the chapter will provide detailed guidance on memorising extremely large lists of factual information in this way.

Many people invent a story about a set of words that they need to memorise. Once again this needs to be as vivid as possible. A well-known example of this, which also rhymes, is: 'In fourteen hundred and ninety-two Columbus sailed the ocean blue.'

Pause for thought 7.3   What techniques have you been using in memorising what you have been reading in this book?

Mind mapping techniques

Psychologists are finding out more about the ways in which we think and learn. Some psychologists have studied which part of the brain governs logic and rationality and which side of the brain uses creativity. Psychologists now say that our minds work in patterns and that several ideas can be developing at once. The brain then goes through a process of integrating ideas, but this doesn't necessarily happen in a linear order.

Did you know?

It is generally believed that the two sides of the brain are used for different things. The left side of the brain is used mainly for analysis, words, planning and dealing with things in a logical, rational way. The right side of the brain is better at the synthesis of ideas, presenting information in pictorial form, spatial competencies, and creativity and the generation of new ideas.

Tony Buzan (1982) developed the idea of mind maps to allow people to express themselves freely and encourage creativity, without being necessarily governed by the linear form. Many people, when presenting information in the form of a mind map, show a very detailed grasp of the subject which they were not be able to demonstrate in a traditional written form. The mind maps (some examples are used as chapter summaries in this book) start with the central subject, which can be presented pictorially. Lines then lead from this subject to other connected topics. This gives more freedom for ideas to appear without worrying at first about the connections, and it allows for several links to be made between related parts of a topic.

The mind map shown in Figure 7.6 illustrates our view of the key points with which this chapter has been concerned so far. Mind maps encourage creativity, and if they are to be used in a way that helps someone to remember and learn effectively then they should be very visual. The central topic should be written clearly, preferably in capital letters, and underlined. A pictorial representation of that topic is also useful, as it encourages easier recall. Lines should then be drawn from this key word, and the main areas relating to the subject area should be drawn.

Further diagrams or pictures can be useful to make the mind map of the topic memorable. Further lines and words should branch from each of these, and the pattern is then developed. Groups of ideas can be linked by the use of different colours. Links can be made easily, by using arrows or lines, between related topics. Relationships and links with other subjects can also be made and identified at the edges of the mind map.

ACTIVITY 7.3

The mind map in Figure 7.6 is incomplete, since it is being used part-way though this chapter. When you have read the rest of this chapter, complete the remainder of the mind map in a way that will make it memorable for you. Draw links with other subjects or topics around the edge of the mind map.

Discussion of Activity 7.3

You should have included further sections on:

- the systematic training cycle
- the role of the organisation
- the value of learning theories for training and development
- techniques to improve learning.

Figure 7.6   **Partial mind map of the chapter**

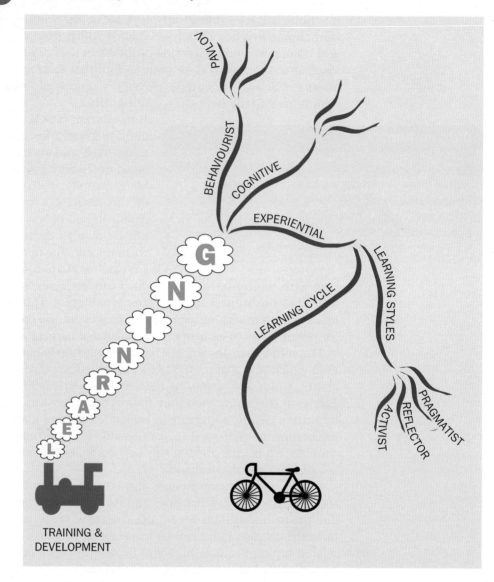

You may have included other things that you considered relevant such as e-learning, bite size learning and blended learning. You should certainly be able to introduce some very visual and memorable images for each of these, and in order for it to be useful and memorable you should have made the mind map as visually attractive as possible. Further links could also be made with the next chapter to draw connections with:

- the learning organisation
- recent developments in education and training
- training for specific groups.

Training

We have examined briefly some of the ways in which people learn, and will now move on to consider how they should be trained and the various training techniques or strategies that may be used.

The systematic training cycle

All the people who are involved in training and development at work need to be aware of the key stages in the training process. This is often referred to as the training cycle. The training cycle is shown in Figure 7.7, and each of the stages will now be discussed in more detail.

Assessing training needs

[handwritten: — a need for training — training gap (recognised)]

It is important, as we said earlier, for organisations to plan the training that employees may need. While there is much to be gained from training in terms of improved skills and productivity for the workforce, it is nevertheless a costly activity, so it is important to provide training of the right type for the people who need it. An understanding of how the individuals or groups learn, and their preferred styles of learning, is important here, but it is even more important to identify first whether training is needed at all. There is little point in designing a programme that will suit the individuals' learning styles if there is not a need for training.

This stage of the training cycle is referred to as assessing training needs. Training needs can be assessed in many ways, but one of the easiest ways is to examine the job that has to be done and the knowledge, skills or competencies needed to do it. Job analysis needs to be undertaken to establish what is involved in the job. Refer back to Chapter 2 to refresh your memory of the

*[handwritten marginal notes: * What is involved (Job training) for aspects people learn * How individuals learn styles of learning (of the individuals) suit & match]*

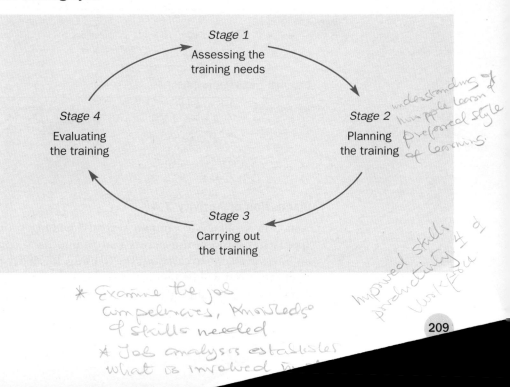

Figure 7.7   **The training cycle**

Stage 1
Assessing the
training needs

Stage 2
Planning
the training

Stage 3
Carrying out
the training

Stage 4
Evaluating
the training

[handwritten notes near Stage 2: understanding of how people learn, preferred style of learning]

[handwritten notes bottom right: improved skills & productivity of workforce]

*[handwritten notes bottom: * Examine the job competencies, knowledge & skills needed * Job analysis establishes what is involved in...]*

ways in which to carry out job analysis. The usual result of job analysis is a job description, and a training specification can be written from this. In many organisations, where employees are encouraged to work towards National Vocational Qualifications (NVQs), there will already be a national standard for the employee to work towards.

Once the organisation knows the standard of work it needs from the employee, the next stage is to assess the work of the employee concerned and see the extent to which they meet those standards. This can be part of the appraisal process, where the employee and their manager have together identified an area where further work is needed. It could also be assessed by asking the person or people concerned what training they feel they need, by using questionnaires, or by an analysis of mistakes (faults analysis). If there are any gaps where they do not meet these standards then there is a possible need for training to help to close the gaps, and so a training need has been identified.

Planning the training

Once a training need has been identified, there are a number of choices to be made about how the training should be carried out. Firstly, should the training be carried out in the organisation (in-house) or by an external organisation such as a college or other training provider? Secondly, the trainer needs to consider which training techniques should actually be used and, thirdly, the training programme needs to be designed.

Internal or external training

ACTIVITY 7.4

Make up your own list in which you compare the advantages and disadvantages of providing training in-house with the possible advantages or disadvantages of using an external training provider.

In-house training

Advantages	Disadvantages
Cheaper Knows d pple	take HR/themes for granted

External training provider

Advantages	Disadvantages
More hands on	Costly

Discussion of Activity 7.4

Your lists are likely to contain several advantages and disadvantages for both approaches. Among the points you should have considered are the cost and resources available to carry out the training. It is likely that in-house training will be cheaper and will be tailored perfectly to meet your training needs. However, if the particular training need identified is very specialised and is required for only one or two people, or if there is no one available able to carry out the training, then it may be better and more cost-effective for them to join a course run by an external training provider. This, although it may not be tailored to meet the organisation's specific needs, will have the advantage of providing a wider experience and opportunities to find out how other organisations do things.

In the past when people were trained they were often just made to sit next to someone and told to do what they did. This is often referred to as 'sitting at Nellie's knee', and the effectiveness of the training depended on how good Nellie was at her job. If she was good at it, and a naturally good instructor, then it could work well, but there was always a danger that the trainee would learn faults as well as good practice. This was one of the main disadvantages of using 'on-the-job' training. In more recent times the emphasis in a great many organisations has switched back to on-the-job training with the introduction of NVQs. This time, however, the person who does the training and assesses what has been learnt is trained themselves, and there are national standards to work towards, so there should be much greater consistency in approach. This aims to harness the benefits of on-the-job training, in terms of low cost and relevance to the organisation, while ensuring that standards are high and consistent. In this case using on-the-job training could be beneficial, as the training has been planned, there is a trainer who knows how to train, and a qualified person will test whether the individual is competent in that job. NVQs will be discussed in more detail in the next chapter.

Training techniques

We stated earlier that once the decision has been made about where the training is to take place, it is also important to decide on the most appropriate training techniques to use. The training method used must be chosen to be appropriate for the particular training need that has been identified. Table 7.1 lists some of the available training methods, with suggestions as to training situations in which they might be suitable.

E-learning

As well as the more traditional approaches to learning, trainers and individual learners now have a choice also of using e-learning techniques. There is some confusion about what exactly constitutes e-learning but it can include computer-based training and learning, technology-based training and learning and web-based training and learning. It may be integrated alongside traditional learning as a support mechanism, or be used separately as part of a distance learning or open learning course. Some university degrees, post-graduate qualifications and training packages are delivered totally by e-learning methods and this makes them easily accessible to people in any part of the world at any time.

One major advantage is that individuals, so long as they have access to the technology, should be able to choose when, where and what they learn and this should increase opportunities for learning. Support can be provided by chat rooms, discussion groups and on-line tutoring with everyone involved able to respond at a time that is convenient. Threaded discussions can be initiated by the trainer about a particular topic, and groups can have their say on that topic. Alternatively, approaches such as virtual classrooms, audio-visual conferencing and two-way live satellite broadcasts provide immediate feedback so trainers and trainees can interact with each other almost as quickly as they would in a more traditional classroom situation.

ACTIVITY 7.5

How do you feel about e-learning as an approach to learning? Is it a method you enjoy or is it an approach you dislike?

ACAS provides some excellent opportunities for you to experience e-learning on its website at **www.acas.org.uk** (accessed 19.11.04). It is developing a range of e-learning resources and you can undertake short e-learning courses and learn about several topics covered in later chapters of this book, such as discipline and grievance, consultation and involvement, and absence management.

Other training techniques

> **Did you know?**
>
> I hear, I forget
> I see, I remember
> I do, I understand.
> (Old Chinese proverb)

Many other training techniques could also be used and we have summarised the suitability of some of these in Table 7.1. From your reading in this chapter so far, use the blank spaces in the table to assess the suitability of on-line discussion groups and audio or video conferencing. Spaces have also been left at the end of Table 7.1 for you to add your own suggestions for different training techniques.

Table 7.1   Training techniques and their suitability

Training technique	Suitability
Lecture	This is suitable when a large amount of information needs to be given to a large number of people at the same time. The information can be prepared in advance but a disadvantage is the lack of participation from the audience.
Role play	Here a small group of people have the chance to act as if they were in a real work situation. They have a problem or situation to deal with which would be similar to a situation that they might experience at work. They can practise their responses and receive help and support from the trainer and from the others in the group. This can help in developing awareness of interpersonal skills and can give confidence, as there is an opportunity to practise skills in a protected environment where it does not matter if mistakes are made. There can sometimes be a problem if the role play is not taken seriously or if trainees are too nervous or embarrassed to perform their roles.
Group discussion	This can lead to a free exchange of knowledge, ideas and opinions on a particular subject among the trainees and the trainer with the opportunity to air various viewpoints. It can be useful when there are varying opinions about an issue, or a range of ways in which a situation could be handled. There is a danger that the trainees may wander too far from the subject if it is not handled skilfully by the trainer, and that important points may not be discussed.
Video or film	These can be used to show a real situation and differing ways of handling that situation, or to give information to several people at once. They can show examples of good and bad use of interpersonal skills to a large number of people at once and be used as the basis for a group discussion. They do not demand much involvement from the audience, although the trainer could add to this by use of discussion or questions after each showing.
Project	Normally a task is set by the trainer which will give an individual or group general guidelines to work to, but will also leave a great deal of scope for them to show creativity or initiative. This is a good way of stimulating creativity or initiative but, in order to do so, the project has to be about something that will interest the trainee.
Case study	A case study is a history of some event or situation in which relevant details are supplied for the trainee to get an overall picture of the situation or organisation. Trainees are then asked to diagnose

Table 7.1 (contd)

Training technique	Suitability
	the problems or suggest solutions. A case study provides the opportunity to examine a situation in detail yet be removed from the pressures of the real work situation. This allows for discussion and provides opportunities to exchange ideas and consider different options. Since a case study can limit the number of factors or issues that should be discussed, it may sometimes seem too easy and trainees may not fully appreciate that in the real-life situation there may be other more complex issues to take into account.
Computer-based training	This allows the trainee to work at their own pace through a series of questions or exercises using a computerised training program. The trainees get immediate feedback from the computer program and can cover a range of work in a short space of time, going back over exercises if necessary and learning at a time that is convenient for them. Trainees can learn without the need for a trainer to be present, although since some trainees may be nervous of the technology or may experience difficulties, it is normally useful to have easy access to help or advice at least via a telephone.
Guided reading	A series of recommended reading is provided on a topic, perhaps graded according to difficulty. The trainee is able to work at their own pace through this. Since the reading has been selected by someone else to highlight points on that subject, this can save the trainee time, since they know that the materials will be relevant to the subject. It does not encourage the trainee to research further around the subject or seek materials for themselves.
In-tray exercise	Trainees are given a series of files, memos and letters similar to those that they might have to deal with in a real work situation. They need to decide on the appropriate action to take and the priority for action. This gives an opportunity for trainees to experience the sort of issues that can arise, but it is important that the contents of the in-tray are realistic.
On-line discussion groups	
Audio or video conferencing	

Some of these training methods are much more participative than others, and it is a good idea to use a variety of techniques to avoid the trainee becoming bored and also to give opportunities to practise skills if a skill is being taught. This will also mean that if you are training a group of people and you utilise a variety of techniques, you are likely to use the preferred learning styles of different individuals at various times. Learning is an active process, and even if it is a list of facts that needs to be learnt, most people learn more effectively when they test themselves, or rewrite information in their own words. This also improves their recall of the information.

These points emphasise the importance of providing some opportunities for the trainee to practise what they are supposed to be learning, and underline the value for you of completing the exercises as you go through this book so that you continue to learn effectively.

ACTIVITY 7.6

Consider each of the training techniques listed in Table 7.1. Make four new lists as shown below, naming the training techniques you think will suit activists, reflectors, theorists and pragmatists. (Some of the techniques may suit more than one style of learning.)

Training techniques to suit people who prefer each of the four learning styles

Activist	Reflector	Theorist	Pragmatist

Discussion of Activity 7.6

Your list is likely to include a variety of different training techniques, some of which we listed earlier and some that you have added for yourselves. We will consider in turn each of the preferred learning styles.

Activist

The training techniques that allow activists to participate fully in the learning experience will be the ones that appeal most to them. These could include: role play, group discussion, project work, case studies, computer-based learning and in-tray exercises. The role play is especially likely to appeal to the activist, as it provides plenty of opportunity for them to become involved in a leading role. Activists are likely to be bored by the lack of involvement required from them in techniques such as lectures, videos or films.

Reflector

Reflectors are likely to appreciate learning techniques where they are presented with information that they can then think about, so lectures, films, videos and guided reading are likely to appeal to them. They will probably also appreciate to some extent group discussions and case studies, as long as they do not have to take too active a part and have plenty of time for reflection afterwards. Computer-based training courses, in which they can progress at their own speed and go back to examine again points that they want to look at in more detail, may also prove popular.

Theorist

Theorists welcome opportunities to examine new theories and compare them with other points of view. Lectures and guided reading are likely to appeal most to them as training techniques. Lectures with a fairly academic content are preferred, so that ideas gained can be compared with other ideas and theories. If the guided reading covers a suitable range of material this could also be useful to a theorist, although if the material is not extensive or theoretical enough for them, they are likely to want to delve further into other areas.

Pragmatist

The pragmatist wants to know how things will really work in practice, so they are likely to find training techniques that are close to reality useful. Case studies, role plays and in-tray exercises will appeal to them if they think that they are realistic and of immediate use to them at work.

New approaches to learning and development

Before we examine the design of training programmes it is worth mentioning two new approaches to learning and development that have been gaining in popularity recently. These are bite size learning and blended learning.

Bite size learning

This sounds like it should be just smaller chunks of training, but fans of the approach say that it goes much further than this. Octavius Black, managing director of the Mind Gym (2004) says that:

> People often thought that the more time they spent on learning, the better their knowledge would be. In fact, they could learn equally effectively – if not more so – in short bursts. Research shows that we remember and apply much more knowledge when we learn little and often than when we learn lots in one go.

This fits very well with what we said earlier about remembering information. You are likely to be more successful in remembering information if you are frequently spending small amounts of time going over what you have learned.

However, Black also says delivering training in bite size chunks means that one must adapt to the needs of individuals and provide short, focused training that suits their needs and lifestyle. He says we need to think of employees as customers and think about what they want to get from the training. It may be, according to Black (2004), that:

> They want to get the boss off their back, feel less stressed or get out of the rut they are in. Ideally they would like a magic wand that would sort these problems out. But since this is not available, they would be happy with something that gave them the skills to meet these challenges with minimum disruption to the rest of their lives. This is where a fast paced workshop focusing on specific skills and lasting between 90 minutes and two hours has appeal. The bite size workshop can give people the same two or three insights they are likely to get from a two day course – and it can be more fun.

According to Crofts (2004), one of the most common barriers to training cited by CIPD members is the amount of time it takes and as workers in the UK work increasingly long hours, bite size training certainly fits a need. However, trainers are likely to need to develop different skills to deliver material in a fast paced way, with exercises taking only a few minutes to complete.

Blended learning

Another type of learning and development that is currently proving popular is the concept of blended learning. According to Allison Rossett and Felicia Douglas (2004):

> A blend is an integrated strategy for delivering on promises about learning and performance. It involves a planned combination of approaches as varied as coaching by a supervisor, participating in on-line class, self-assessments, and in on-line attendance in workshops and in on-line discussions.

We have already advocated that there should be a mix of learning and development methods to suit the needs of the learners, and blended learning seems to involve planning this into the learning in ways that will suit the needs of particular groups.

It is too early to comment on how successful this approach is, although some studies (Rossett and Douglas 2004) suggest that those involved with learning through a planned blend of learning methods tend to learn more and at greater speed than those using other methods. However, there is a need for far more studies to show whether this is really the case. In many instances, on-line learning forms part of the blend and cuts down the need for time spent on classroom-based learning, but every organisation has to reach its own blend of learning and development ingredients to suit the needs of the organisation and the participants in the learning and development programme.

Designing the training programme

It is not enough just to choose the training techniques to be used and hope that these will develop into a course. When you are designing a training programme you should have in mind clear objectives for the course. What do you want the trainees to be able to do and what do you want them to know by the end of the course?

Pause for thought 7.4

- What were the objectives for this chapter?
- What should you know by the end of the chapter?
- What should you be able to do by the end of the chapter?
- What opportunities were provided for you to practise things you learnt?

The objectives for this chapter were stated at the beginning. By the end of the chapter you should know something about all five objectives. You should be able to demonstrate this by stating various definitions of learning. You should also be able to describe the relevance of various theories of learning to training and development by being able to discuss these. You should be able to describe the systematic training cycle and show that you can identify when to use a variety of training techniques, even if you have not yet had an opportunity to use them. You will also have had opportunities to identify your own preferred learning styles and to experiment with various techniques to improve your learning.

A variety of opportunities have been provided for you to achieve these objectives. Firstly, you have had the opportunity to read the text itself. Secondly, opportunities have been provided for you to undertake exercises to practise some of the things you have read about. In one exercise you covered every stage of the learning cycle, and you have been encouraged to be actively involved in learning and to reflect on what you have learnt. The Pauses for thought also provide the opportunity for you to be actively involved in your own learning process and to practise recall of information.

Once you have decided your objectives for the course, you are then able to plan a programme that uses a variety of training techniques in order to achieve this aim in the most effective way. The next chapter will focus on the provision of training courses, but first we need to discuss briefly the other stages in the training cycle.

If the training is to be effective it cannot be left to chance and a great deal of planning needs to happen first. Who are the people that you are going to involve in this training? Will you do all the training yourself or will you involve managers from other departments? When you have decided these points you need to decide on the most logical order for the training and plan the course. Will it be a traditional learning or development programme over several days or bite size learning? Will you use e-learning or more traditional approaches, or a combination in the form of blended learning? Some parts of the course will be obvious – for example the introduction, perhaps stating your objectives for the course, is likely to be at the beginning – but you have considerable freedom after that, although you will be constrained by the amount of time each part of the course takes and also, of course, by cost. Some examples of the design of specific training programmes will be discussed in the next chapter. Remember that people do need to have breaks, as their attention spans are not limitless and they will learn more when they are refreshed, so you should timetable tea, coffee and lunch breaks if the course runs for full days. Remember also to give opportunities for people to be actively involved in their own learning, and to allow time to practise skills and time to go over points so that recall is enhanced. Specific training programmes for particular groups of workers will be considered in the next chapter.

Carrying out the training

You need to ensure that everyone is aware of the training course in plenty of time. Letters should have gone to the course participants, people involved in running the course, and the supervisors and managers of those who will be on the course so that there is time to arrange cover for their absence from work, if necessary. Those who are to carry out the training should themselves have some training in running training programmes. Although specialised training officers or human resource managers with responsibility for training will be trained in training techniques, line managers or other members of staff will often be involved in actually training individuals. Everyone at some time has the experience of showing a new employee what to do in a job. At the very least an appreciation of what is involved in giving job instruction on a one-to-one basis is useful. The techniques required to instruct on a one-to-one basis will be described fully in Chapter 8.

Evaluating the training

This is an extremely important stage in the training cycle, and one that is often neglected by organisations. According to Findlay (2004) it is still true to say that 'many training and development professionals do not evaluate the outcomes of their work – beyond handing out "happy sheets" at the end of courses. These provide feedback on whether the learners have enjoyed a course or other learning interventions but do little to measure its impact.' If no evaluation of training is carried out at all then the organisation does not know whether the training has been enjoyed or successful, or even whether the training objectives have been met, so it may waste money and resources on training that was not very effective.

Very little has actually changed in the way training is evaluated. Donald Kirkpatrick set out the general principles in 1956 in an article 'How to start an objective evaluation of training' (see Findlay 2004). He basically argued that there should be four levels of evaluation. First, at the end of the training course, the course participants should be asked their views on the effectiveness of the training. This could be done by means of a simple questionnaire to the course participants, which will at least give clear views as to whether the people concerned liked the course, what they felt would be useful and what they felt was less useful. Consequently it should yield a great deal of valuable material, which the manager responsible for the design of the course should be able to incorporate usefully in the next course.

However, this only establishes what the participants say they feel about the course. It may also be useful to establish what they have learnt on the course, and so both knowledge and skills may be tested at the end of the training.

It is also useful to find out what effect the training has on the person when they actually get back to work. This can be done by questionnaires or with interviews the course participants and their supervisor a few weeks later, or by a review of the person's work and the effect that the training has had on him or her. In Kirkpatrick's levels, the happy sheets we mentioned earlier equate to level one evaluation. Level two evaluation is concerned with how much the person has learnt and this is often undertaken by tests for knowledge and skills at the end of the training.

Sometimes, however, people may seem to do well in a learning situation but when they return to their normal work area they revert to their usual behaviour. Level three evaluation aims to test whether transfer of learning has taken place and whether the learning that has occurred has successfully transferred to the workplace. Essentially this level of evaluation aims to measure changes in job behaviour.

Kirkpatrick's fourth level of evaluation relates to whether the learning and development activity has made a difference to the bottom line in an organisation. Has it succeeded in making a difference to the organisation or added value? According to Martin Sloman (2004), 'If you focus your training on the organisation's learning requirements, you won't need to get hung up on assessment.'

According to Ian Thomson (2004), 'Evaluating training is a way of combining the assessment of the impact of training and development, while raising the profile and influence of HR and training functions.' Therefore it is in the interest of these departments to evaluate at all levels, not only to ensure that the learning objectives have been met, but also to demonstrate to the rest of the organisation that they have been successful in adding value to the organisation by making a difference in key strategic areas.

The role of the organisation in learning

Some organisations do not seem to encourage learning. They put up barriers at different stages of the learning cycle. If people are to learn from experience then sometimes they will make mistakes. An organisation that does not tolerate some mistakes will not encourage learning to take place, as people will be too frightened to take risks and will not experiment with the way they do things. There are also organisations where the emphasis is on practical experience and where life is so action packed that there is no time to stop and reflect on what has been learnt.

In some organisations the culture is one where management pride themselves on having got on without the benefit of much education, so that people who enjoy referring to books or theoretical ideas are looked down upon. In others the reverse may be true and only academic approaches are valued.

A culture where there is a preference for distance and detachment is unlikely to encourage people to be active in their learning style, whereas an organisation in which people are secretive or mistrustful, or with an emphasis on living for today, will be unlikely to encourage a reflective style of learning:

Organisational barriers to learning

Although it is true to say that individuals can create their own barriers to learning, as illustrated above, it is also true that the organisations in which we work may hinder us from learning because of their culture. According to the CIPD

(2004), when it conducted an on-line poll at the HRD conference and exhibition area of its web site:

> 48% of the 973 people taking part cited time pressures, while 31% said that the main barrier was lack of support from their line managers. These results were in sharp contrast to the number of people claiming motivation was a problem – just 12%. And only 9% felt that poor quality training offerings were to blame.

While this is not a very large number of people and provides just a snapshot, it is, according to Martin Sloman (2004), CIPD Advisor Learning and Development, in line with the findings from other more detailed studies. In other research 'we have emphasised that the important thing is to create a supportive culture of learning in the workplace.'

Conclusion

We have tried in this chapter to provide a brief account of several different learning theories and to show how knowledge of learning theory is important for trainers and individuals alike in order to understand the way in which people learn, and in order that they provide appropriate training which is geared to the employees' needs. Although no one theory provides all the answers to the question of how people learn, the various theories we have discussed suggest a variety of ways of helping people to develop knowledge, skills and competencies more effectively.

Feedback on how a person is performing is necessary in training and development, and individuals need to know how they are doing in order to continue to learn effectively. Computer-based training uses some of the ideas of the behaviourist school of learning, and rewards a correct behaviour such as pressing the correct key with praise or by allowing you to progress to the next stage.

We have also shown that people learn in a variety of ways and that they often have one or two preferred learning styles. In order to cope with groups of trainees with varying learning styles and to help individuals develop and use other styles, a variety of training techniques need to be used, and we have considered when different approaches would be appropriate.

Learning can be improved by breaking the learning periods up into short sessions with breaks. There are also techniques, such as mnemonics and number rhyming systems, that can help when it is necessary to memorise facts. Recall can be improved by going over the information at regular intervals.

Rationality and logic are not the only important qualities, and people should also be encouraged to develop creativity and to use the right side of their brain more. For many people the use of mind mapping techniques provides an opportunity to display knowledge that they have not always been able to demonstrate using traditional approaches to learning. Mind maps also give the opportunity to plan topics in a creative way, and can make it easier to remember the key points of a topic.

We have examined the stages in the training cycle, training techniques and the design of training programmes. The next chapter will consider approaches to developing training courses for specific groups, and will also consider some recent developments in learning and development.

REVIEW QUESTIONS

1 Plan a series of learning activities to develop your own ability to learn using a learning style that is not normally one of your preferred styles. Then, working in pairs, get a friend/colleague to suggest additional learning activities for you so that you can further develop this learning style, while you suggest and plan a variety of learning activities for them.

2 Get further ideas for developing your learning styles from the suggested reading at the end of the chapter.

3 Plan a revision session for one topic in this book by designing your own mind map to cover the key points.

4 Try out for yourself the effects of bite size learning by dividing the chapter into small chunks for revision purposes. Compare your level of success using this approach with trying to revise a whole chapter at once.

SELF-CHECK QUESTIONS

Answer the following multiple-choice questions. The correct responses are given on page 491 for you to check your understanding of this chapter.

1 The illustration in Figure 7.8 shows what happens when Caroline makes a cup of tea. She often chooses to feed the cats at the same time as putting the kettle on. Thus the kettle and the tin of cat food being opened are linked in the cats' minds. Sometimes she puts the kettle on but doesn't open a tin of cat food. However, the cats now appear when they hear the sound of the kettle.
  (a) What is this effect known as?
  (b) According to Pavlov, how should we label the cat food in diagram 1?
  (c) According to Pavlov, what is the link between the kettle and the cat food known as? Label diagram 2.
  (d) According to Pavlov, what should the kettle be labelled in diagram 3?

2 According to Honey and Mumford:
  (a) Learning has occurred when knowledge has been acquired by study.
  (b) Learning has occurred when a person knows something that they did not know earlier and can show it, or is able to do something that they were not able to do before.

Figure 7.8   **Caroline's cats**

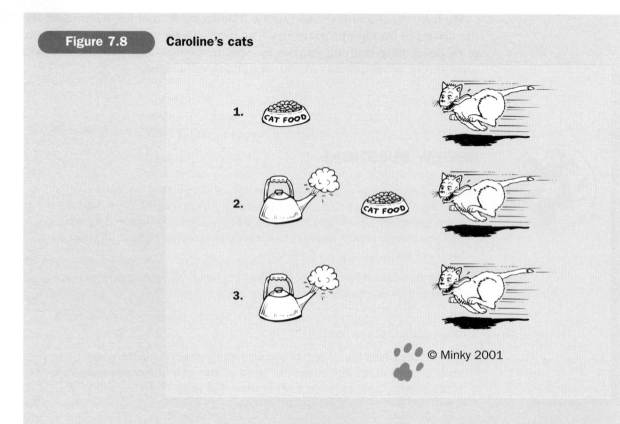

© Minky 2001

(c) Learning has occurred when a person knows something that they did not know earlier but can't show it, or is able to do something that they were not able to do before.

(d) Learning is shown by a relatively permanent change in behaviour that occurs as a result of practice or experience.

(e) Learning is shown by a change in behaviour which occurs just as a result of experience.

3 Which of the following terms best describes Köhler's approach to learning?
   (a) experiential learning
   (b) experimental learning
   (c) discovery learning
   (d) holistic learning
   (e) cognitive learning.

4 The *Shorter Oxford Dictionary* defines learning as: '1. the action of the verb TO LEARN. 2. What is learnt or taught. 3. Knowledge . . . got by study.' This definition is an example of which of the following views of learning?
   (a) cognitive
   (b) behaviourist
   (c) experiential
   (d) holistic
   (e) experimental

5 According to Honey and Mumford, a pragmatist is someone who:
   (a) seeks out new experiences and is open minded, not sceptical, and enthusiastic about novelty
   (b) integrates and adapts observations into logically sound theories
   (c) thinks problems through in a step-by-step, logical way
   (d) collects data in a very thorough way and analyses them
   (e) is keen to try new ideas, theories and techniques to see if they work in practice.

6 Which of the following is NOT one of the stages in the training cycle?
   (a) assessing training needs
   (b) having an experience
   (c) planning the training
   (d) evaluating the training
   (e) carrying out the training.

7 Computer-based training and programmed learning were developed from the work of which of the following schools of thought?
   (a) cognitive psychology
   (b) experiential psychology
   (c) the holistic school of thought
   (d) behaviourist psychologists
   (e) the pragmatic school of thought.

WHAT NEXT?

For a thorough review of how we learn read the following research report from the CIPD:

Reynolds, J., L. Caley and R. Mason (2002) *How do People Learn? Research Report*, CIPD

A second piece of research, details below, takes a rather different approach. The various forms of learning styles have all been accepted for a number of years and many people are fans of particular approaches. However, recent research from a team based at Newcastle University does cast some doubt on the reliability of these measures. They assessed 13 different learning style instruments and found only one, the cognitive styles index by Allinson and Hayes, that they felt gave statistically meaningful and consistent results. They also found two others that seemed to work well, even though they have not been fully tested through independent research. These are Apter's motivational style profile and Vermunt's learning style inventory. Examine the research for yourself and decide what you think about the different approaches to learning and whether learning styles are of use to you. The full research report is available at:

http://www.lsda.org.uk/files/pdf/1543.pdf

For something completely different on the possible future of learning, read the following article which discusses pioneering work to link a person's brain, nervous system and a computer and uses thought communication. This is no longer the realm of science fiction!

Warwick, K. (2004) Mind blending, *People Management*, Vol. 10, No. 7, 32

References

Bass, B. M. and J. A. Vaughan (1966) *Training in Industry – the Management of Learning,* Tavistock Publications

Black, O. (2004) The future's bite, *People Management,* Vol. 10, No. 8, 25

Buzan, T. (1982) *Use Your Head,* BBC

Chartered Institute of Personnel and Development (2004) Bite size learning takes off. HRD 2004 conference report, *People Management,* Vol. 10, No. 9, 15

Crofts, P. (2004) Support key to success, *People Management,* Vol. 10, No. 11, 55

Findlay, J. (2004) Evaluation is no white elephant, *People Management,* Vol. 10, No. 6, 50

Honey, P. and A. Mumford (1992) *The Manual of Learning Styles,* 3rd edition, Peter Honey Publications

Köhler, W. (1959) *The Mentality of Apes,* Vintage Books

Kolb, D., I. M. Rubin and J. M. McIntyre (1974) *Organizational Psychology: An Experiential Approach,* Prentice Hall

Pavlov, I. (1927) *Conditioned Reflexes,* Oxford University Press

Rossett, A. and F. Douglas (2004) The house blend, *People Management,* Vol. 10, No. 8, 36

Skinner, B. F. (1953) *Science and Human Behaviour,* Macmillan

Sloman, M. (2004) Evaluation and evolution, *People Management,* Vol. 10, No. 14, 50

Thomson, I. (2004) The power and the impact, *People Management,* Vol. 10, No. 8, 15

Further study

Books

Advisory, Conciliation and Arbitration Service (2003) *Induction Training,* ACAS. (Available at: **http://www.acas.org.uk**; accessed 2.09.04.)

Advisory, Conciliation and Arbitration Service (2003) *Recruitment and Induction,* revised edition, ACAS. (Available at: **http://www.acas.org.uk**; accessed 2.09.04.)

Bee, F. and R. Bee (2003) Learning *Needs Analysis and Evaluation,* CIPD. (This is excellent at linking training needs and the needs of the business and discusses how corporate strategy must be developed.)

Boydell, T. and M. Leary (1996) *Identifying Training Needs,* IPD.

Bramley, P. (2003) *Evaluating Training,* 2nd edition, CIPD.

Buzan, T. (2000) *Use Your Head,* BBC.

Buzan, T. (2000) *The Mind Map Book,* BBC.

Fowler, A. (1999) *Induction,* Institute of Personnel and Development.

Gough, J. (2000) *Developing Learning Materials,* Beekman Publications.

Hackett, P. (1997) *Introduction to Training,* IPD.

Hardingham, A. (1996) *Designing Training,* IPD.

(The above all form part of the CIPD's Training Essentials Series and each covers in some detail the stages in the training cycle described in this chapter.)

Harrison, R. (2002) *Employee Development,* 3rd edition, Institute of Personnel and Development.

Honey, P. and A. Mumford (2000) *The Learning Styles Helper's Guide,* Peter Honey Publications.

Honey, P. and A. Mumford (1992) *The Manual of Learning Styles,* 3rd edition, Peter Honey Publications. (The learning style questionnaire comes as part of this package and provides a useful start to establishing your preferred learning styles.)

Honey, P. and A. Mumford (1990) *The Opportunist Learner,* Peter Honey Publications. (This guide complements the manual of learning styles and is written for the use of learners.)

Honey, P. and A. Mumford (1986) *Using your Learning Styles,* 2nd edition, Peter Honey Publications. (Gives clear information about ways to improve effectiveness of particular learning styles. Useful mainly for those concerned with designing training programmes.)

Kirkpatrick, D. (1998) *Evaluating Training Programs*, Pfeiffer Wiley.

Kolb, D., I. M. Rubin and J. M. McIntyre (1974) *Organizational Psychology: An Experiential Approach*, Prentice Hall. (This contains the American test that led Honey and Mumford to develop their version of the learning style questionnaire. It also relates clearly to the stages of the learning cycle.)

Reid, M., H. Barrington and M. Brown (2004) *Human Resource Development*, 7th edition, CIPD.

Siddons, S. (1997) *Delivering Training*, IPD.

Simmonds, D. *Designing and Delivering Training*, CIPD.

Skapinker, M. (2002) *Knowledge Management*, Change Agenda Series, CIPD.

Sloman, M. and J. Rolph (2003) *E-learning: The Learning Curve*, Change Agenda Series, CIPD.

Articles

Bee, F. (2000) How to evaluate training, *People Management*, Vol. 6, No. 6, 16 March.

Chartered Institute of Personnel and Development (2004) *Induction*, CIPD. (**www.cipd.co.uk**; accessed 2.9.04.)

Industrial Relations Services (IRS) (2003) The best conditions for the start of a beautiful friendship, *IRS Employment Review*, No. 771, 34–40.

Industrial Relations Services (IRS) (2003) Induction to perfection: the start of a beautiful friendship, *IRS Employment Review*, No. 772, 34–40.

Mumford, A. (1998) Sources for courses, *People Management*, Vol. 4, No. 40, 14 May, 48–51.

Spurling, M. and E. Trolley (2000) How to make training strategic, *People Management*, Vol. 6, No. 8, 13 April.

Thomas, H. C. (2003) How to design induction programmes, *People Management*, Vol. 9, No. 9, 42–43.

CHAPTER 8

Learning and development programmes

OBJECTIVES

By the end of this chapter you should be able to:

- explain the meaning of the terms training, education, human resource development and learning and development

- describe the role of the human resource manager, line manager and learning and development manager in training and developing the people in the organisation

- demonstrate the importance of induction training

- design a simple training programme to meet the needs of a particular group of employees

- instruct a person in a particular skill by training on a one-to-one basis

- describe recent developments in learning and development.

The last chapter introduced you to some of the ideas in the area of learning. We discussed definitions of the term 'learning', each of which reflects the view of a particular school of thought and makes a useful contribution to our understanding of the learning process. We showed how some understanding of the learning process is necessary to trainers and to those being trained. In this chapter we shall examine some aspects of learning and development in more detail, but before doing so it would be useful to define four important terms: learning and development, human resource development, education and training.

Learning and development

We have chosen to call this chapter learning and development as this term has gained in popularity in recent years as organisations increasingly recognise that in order to stay competitive they must utilise and develop the knowledge of their workers as fully as possible and as the focus of their activities switches from training to learning. According to the CIPD (2003):

> New business forces demand a different approach to the development of employees. Capable and committed people have become the critical source of competitive advantage. Emphasis must be shifted from training as a series of top-down interventions to a focus on individual learning.

The term learning and development has been defined in the CIPD research report *How do People Learn*? (see Reynolds *et al*. 2002) as follows:

> Learning is the process by which a person constructs new knowledge, skills and capabilities, whereas training is one of several responses an organisation can undertake to promote learning.

This puts the process of learning very clearly under the individual's ownership and, as we said in the previous chapter, people do learn in all sorts of ways, some of them planned and some totally unplanned. Organisations want to get the best from people in order to gain competitive advantage, so need to suggest a range of interventions to achieve this.

The concept of learning and development implies that learning and development occurs in all sorts of situations, not just in the more traditional, formal training opportunities, although we hope that learning will occur there too. Learning and development includes other less formal approaches to learning such as coaching, mentoring, work shadowing and job swaps.

A move from training to learning does demand a different approach to that used previously. However, although this change in emphasis is undoubtedly occurring, you will still find other terms are used, so we have included some definitions of some of the more frequently used terms here.

Human resource development

Human resource development (HRD) is a term frequently used to describe training and development needs both within and outside organisations. There are clear links with human resource management since in both, one of the key features is that a strategic approach is adopted. The term appears to reflect the reality of the changing nature of many workplaces today. Many people work in increasingly flexible and varied ways, with many temporary workers being employed by agencies, volunteers working in schools or charities, consultants working on short-term contacts or special tasks, or work being outsourced. No longer is it an adequate approach just to concentrate on developing employees since other workers, who are not actually employees of the organisation at all, may play an important role within the organisation and may need development opportunities too.

According to Reid *et al.* (2004), most definitions of HRD:

> attempt to stress the HRD function's aim to enhance learning for individuals, groups and organisations in line with the organisation's business objectives. It does this in a number of ways, but is fundamentally concerned with learning and with creating circumstances to encourage learning.

Education

Education has been defined as:

> activities which aim to develop the knowledge skills, moral values and understanding required in all aspects of life rather than a knowledge and skill relating only to a limited field of activity.
>
> (Manpower Services Commission 1981 in Reid *et al.* 2004, p. 2)

Although this definition seems to relate primarily to young people and implies that education is a preparation for life, education is not solely the preserve of the young and many people embark on degree programmes or other traditional educational routes throughout their life.

Training

According to Rosemary Harrison (2000):

> Training is a narrower concept and usually involves planned instructional activities, or other developmental activities and processes.

An earlier definition of training from the former Manpower Services Commission (MSC) is:

> Training is a planned process to modify attitude, knowledge or skill behaviour through learning experience to achieve effective performance in an activity or range of activities. Its purpose, in the work situation, is to develop the abilities of the individual and to satisfy the current and future needs of the organisation.
>
> (MSC 1981 in Reid *et al.* 2004, p. 2)

Comment

Although there appear to be clear distinctions between education and training, with education being a general foundation for life and training being specifically related to work, it is not in fact as simple as that. Learning opportunities are nowadays provided in a wide range of places, in differing formats and for all age groups. It is not always easy to distinguish whether a particular learning opportunity is education or training. Some adults may decide to improve their education later in life, and may take courses, for example in languages, that might be regarded as education. If their language course is relevant to their need to speak another language for their job, then this might be viewed as training. Some young people who are in the mainstream educational system may study for vocational courses such as General National Vocational Qualifications (GNVQs), which could have large elements that we would consider to be training.

Education and training can no longer be regarded as being in watertight compartments, and there is often considerable overlap between the two. Learning and development and human resource development are concerned with utilising all learning opportunities whether they are regarded as education or training, or some combination of both. There are a wide range of ways in which this may be brought about, and besides formal education and training there are many sources of developmental opportunities which will be discussed later in this chapter. Human resource development also concerns all employees and not just human resource or training and development managers.

Education, training, learning and development and human resource development all involve creating conditions in which it is possible for people to learn. As we stated in the previous chapter, people do learn all the time and you cannot stop people learning. Sometimes learning occurs in a very random and ad hoc way but these four definitions all imply a sense of purpose. In the rest of this chapter we shall examine first some learning and development interventions which are designed to achieve specific purposes. Later we shall discuss some of the organisations and government initiatives involved in encouraging better education, training and human resource development and also examine qualifications and new training initiatives.

While it is important for students of this subject to be aware of the changing emphasis that is occurring in the move towards learning and development, it is not always helpful to use these terms with managers. They are not usually interested in the subtle distinctions between different terms. What they want is something that will work for them. Ian Cunningham (2001) says that 'Mentioning learning, training or any other related term can put off busy managers. Rather than becoming instant converts to the latest idea they can become averse to the attempts at selling from trainers and HRD professionals.'

Strategic learning and development and the people involved

People are an organisation's most precious resource, and so it is extremely important that they work to their optimum level of performance. Learning and development makes an important contribution to this, but in order to be most effective it should be part of the strategic plan for the organisation and must very clearly relate to the organisation's objectives. In this way the contribution of all those involved in employee development will be seen to be aimed at specific organisational objectives, thus making a vital contribution to organisational effectiveness rather than, as has sometimes been the case, being viewed just as an expensive luxury. Too often in the past, training has been regarded as an unnecessary expense rather than as an integral part of achieving organisational effectiveness.

ACTIVITY 8.1

With reference to any organisation of your choice, examine the organisation's strategic objectives and list the ways in which learning and development might help contribute towards the achievement of these objectives.

Discussion of Activity 8.1

This will obviously depend on the organisation chosen and its objectives, but may include, for example, the provision of language training for marketing managers for an organisation which aims to diversify into new European markets, or the provision of training about information technology for supervisors, where the stated aim is to improve efficiency by introducing new technology.

It may be that the strategic level of activity described above is performed by someone at director level. Others involved may include the human resource manager, the training specialist, the line manager and the individuals themselves.

Many human resource managers will be directly responsible for the learning and development of the people in their organisation, though this does not, of course, mean that they necessarily provide all the learning interventions themselves. It may be that all the records of learning and development are held within the human resource department, or there may be a separate learning and development section with a learning and development manager or human resource development manager as head of department. If there is a separate department there will need to be strong links between the two departments, as they need to work very closely together. Since the merger of the Institute of Personnel Management and the Institute of Training and Development in July 1994, all their members have become members of the same institute and a joint qualification has been developed. This merger emphasises the closeness of learning and development to human resource management, together with the importance to the organisation of learning and development and the need for both human resource management and learning and development to work together, if they are separate.

Besides the human resource manager there may also be, as we have already seen, learning and development officers or human resource development officers. They are trained in the same way as human resource managers, but are likely to have chosen to specialise in learning and development. It is unlikely that even they will do all the learning or development work within the organisation, as line managers have an increasing role to play in developing their own staff. Human resource managers and learning and development officers are, however, likely to provide specialist courses and advice and also to ensure that managers are trained adequately to carry out the level of training required for their own staff.

Not only are line managers likely to be involved in employee development for their own staff and to be trained and encouraged to seek a range of suitable developmental opportunities, but the staff themselves will also be encouraged to actively seek opportunities for their own development. In organisations where there is often little room for promotion, and where the future of the organisation itself is insecure, it is in workers' own interests to keep themselves as up-to-date as possible and to seek out new opportunities for developing new skills or new knowledge. *for employability (external labour mkt*

Getting line managers involved in learning and development is essential. There is a great deal of research evidence nowadays that suggests that learning and development makes a huge difference to the profitability of organisations, but it can be difficult to get line managers to see how it will make a difference to them and how it will enable them to contribute to the organisation's strategic objectives.

Ian Cunningham (2004) offers 10 top tips for getting managers interested, but first you should remember the tip we mentioned earlier: it is better not to use the language of learning and development at all, but rather to focus on the issues that matter to the line manager. Cunningham's first tip for getting line mangers actively involved is:

> *Tip 1.* Managers are usually interested in getting solutions to their problems – not your problems. . . The simple rule is 'start with live problems and then find solutions for them' as opposed to supply-led training which says 'we have a solution; let's see if we can bend your problem to fit it.'

Further tips from Cunningham (2004) include:

- finding out what is important to the line managers
- not overselling the training and development
- not always accepting someone else's view of what needs to be done without exploring further
- accepting that managers make decisions on their own terms
- spotting the best moment to involve them in learning and development; only introducing a maximum of four concepts at any one time
- tackling only what should be potentially achievable problems
- structuring presentations to make the business case
- linking the learning to the business.

In this way Cunningham (2004) argues that line managers will want to be involved in the learning and development activities as they will be able to see the benefits both for themselves and for the organisation.

We emphasised in the previous chapter the importance of identifying learning needs. A learning need is often viewed as the difference between what a person knows or is able to do, and what his or her job description indicates he or she should know or be able to do. Clearly, the identification of a gap between these two might indicate a learning need. In this case a carefully chosen learning intervention would be needed to bring the person's work up to the standard required. Employee development could also be about ensuring that people are not only able to do the jobs that they are employed to do, but also developing in ways to meet future organisational needs and to cope with the pace of change today.

Learning and development for particular groups of employees

Although all employees are likely to have learning needs, and should be concerned to develop themselves fully to meet future needs and the pace of organisational change, there are also likely to be many groups whose needs may be met by some traditional training interventions. These groups include new employees, women returning to work after a break, supervisors and managers, and people who are taking up an appointment in another country. This section will focus on one group who have particular development needs, namely new employees.

New employees

New employees are each likely to have their own individual learning needs and establishing what these are during the induction process is important. Starting individual personal development reviews during the induction period and setting times for individual interviews to review progress regularly is important. However, they all have to learn certain things about the organisation and its culture. This could be even more important if the person is working in another country or using a second language. Intervention to help awareness of cross-cultural differences or in language skill may also be needed as part of the induction as we explain in Chapter 16. New employees need to learn a great deal of information when they join an organisation. This can be learned informally, but this may take a long time and the employee may learn the wrong things. Consider the following example.

ACTIVITY 8.2

Read the following story about a student, Ros, who hoped to improve her language skills and earn some money for university by working as a waitress in a hotel in France for the summer. She has just started work as a 'stagiaire' or trainee and is telephoning her mother, a few days after her arrival.

Read the story and answer the questions at the end of it.

Ros   Hello Mum. I got here in the end and I've survived the first day, but it has been quite difficult. I'm not sure how long I will stay.

Mum   Oh dear! What has happened? Was the journey OK? Were you met by someone with a car from the hotel, as they had arranged?

Ros   No, the hotel car didn't turn up. I had to get a taxi and it was miles from the airport, so it cost a fortune. The human resource manager took me to my accommodation, but no one else seemed to be expecting me. I'm living in an apartment with about another eight people, but they were just going out when I arrived and no one had told them that I was also going to be joining them in their accommodation. They were really nice but had trouble finding a bed for me and the only spare bed is in the kitchen and it's broken.

Mum   Well, I expect you felt better when you found out what your job was and got your uniform.

Ros   Well, I'm still not sure what is happening. I got up early yesterday morning, because no one had told me when to start work, but when I got to the office I was told that I was not on duty until today so I'm still not sure what hours I'm actually working. I thought it would be 35 hours a week but some of the others told me that this can be averaged over a few weeks so it may be more.

I haven't got a uniform yet either, as the only one the HR manager had left was extra large, so was much too big for me. He suggested I wore a black skirt and white blouse until they can get a uniform in a small size for me. I spent the day on the beach with some of the other stagiaires, so at least that was good, but I had to borrow some clothes for work as the airline has lost my luggage.

Mum Oh dear! Have you reported it? I hope your luggage will turn up soon. You'll feel a lot more positive when you have your own things.

Ros Yes, I reported it at the airport and it will be sent here when they find it, but I wonder if I'll still be here by then. Everything is different to what I expected.

The HR manager told me that I would be joining the receptionists rather than the waitresses. Then when I turned up for work again this morning, I was placed in the marketing department. Another girl, who had been working there, has been moved to help at another hotel this week, because the Tour de France is going through the town. Consequently that hotel is full, so a lot of the temporary staff have been moved there to help for the week.

Mum You should get plenty of opportunities to improve your French working in marketing.

Ros My boss in marketing is really nice and I have been phoning French and English hotels to check on competitors' prices and I'm going to be helping to do a customer satisfaction survey in both French and English. Mind you, they really need a staff satisfaction survey!

Mum Well, at least the job sounds interesting.

Ros Yes, my boss says she wants to keep me in the marketing department, as she has plenty of work for me to do, even when the other trainee returns. The HR manager was talking about me helping to clean chalets next week, so I'm still very confused about the job I'll be doing. I want to come home.

Mum You're bound to feel unsettled for the first few days, but I'm sure you'll feel better when you get a bit more established and when you have your luggage. Have the meals been good? At least you get your board and lodging provided on top of your wage.

Ros I hope I'll feel better soon, but today I missed meals so I've only had a baguette.

Mum Oh dear! Why was that? I thought free meals were part of your payment and in France you would expect them to be good, even for the staff.

Ros The office staff have breaks at a different time to the people working in the restaurant and the hotel, so there was no food left when I arrived. I'll have to buy something later. I thought I was being paid weekly in cash, as it said in the letter that I was sent. The others say we get paid at the end of the month and that I'll need to set up a French bank account for myself as we get paid by cheque. I hope my euros will last until I get paid. It is proving much more difficult than I thought. All the information I was sent has been wrong.

Questions

1 Comment on what happened.
2 What information should she have received before she left England?
3 How could her first few days have been made easier?
4 What differences are there in the hours of work between Britain and France?

Discussion of Activity 8.2

Ros was in a foreign country, speaking a different language and was having a difficult time during her first few days of her summer job. Being in a different country may have added to the problems as she may have experienced some culture shock, but you also could have similar experiences in a job in this country and some of you may have had bad experiences when starting a temporary or even a permanent job.

Ros did not know who to ask for information and had been sent incorrect and inadequate information before she left England. She ended up feeling more lost and confused because of this lack of information and this may have added to any culture shock she may have experienced. All organisations need to take care to ensure that people have a better work experience than this, as some students may go home immediately, and this type of experience does not enhance the reputation of the hotel to their families and friends.

A more structured approach is needed, with individuals being clear about the information a new starter needs and also who is going to give them this information. A clear induction programme, which starts before they commence in the job, is needed. A pack of information should have been sent to her beforehand and an induction to the organisation on arrival would have helped to make the first few days a better experience. There are differences in all organisations about the way things are done. These are likely to be even greater since the organisation is in France and some differences in law, such as the 35-hour working week, would also need to be explained.

Induction

We define induction as the process of helping a new employee to settle quickly into their job so that they soon become an efficient and productive employee. The actual process of induction starts before the person's first day at work, and generally starts as part of the recruitment and selection process. The impression the interviewers create about the organisation, and the letters and information sent to the prospective employee, can all be regarded as part of the induction process.

ACTIVITY 8.3

Imagine that you are the learning and development manager at the hotel in France where Ros had her summer job.

Design an induction course for Ros, and the other students at this hotel.

- What will be your objectives for the induction programme?
- What would you want Ros to know at the end of the programme?
- What do you want her to be able to do by the end of her induction programme?

Discussion of Activity 8.3

You are likely to have listed some of the following points and your objectives, in terms of knowledge, are likely to include the following.

At the end of the induction period the trainee will:

1 Have accurate information about her conditions of employment such as the accommodation, hours of work and job title.
2 Understand the basis of the payment system and the pay periods.
3 Know the layout of the hotel in which she works including entrances and fire exits, toilet and washroom areas, restaurant areas and actual place of work.
4 Know the names of her supervisor and the other people who will be working in the same department.
5 Know the names of other senior managers within the organisation.
6 Have accurate information about the organisation's dress code and uniform if necessary.
7 Know about the hotel's first aid facilities for staff and customers.
8 Understand the hotel's rules about health, safety and hygiene.
9 Understand the company's disciplinary rules and grievance procedures.
10 Know the hotel's rules on sickness and how to report an absence.
11 Know how and where to find more information, whether on notice boards, in a staff handbook, by e-mail, on the company intranet or by word of mouth.
12 Have some understanding of cross-cultural differences in France and how these may affect working in an international hotel.

You are also likely to want her to be able to do certain things, such as:

13 Find her way unaided around the main working areas.
14 Carry out aspects of her job, such as answering the telephone or dealing with customer complaints, in a specified manner, in French or English as appropriate.
15 Record time sheets accurately.

As we said earlier, in many organisations as well as identifying general learning needs for all new starters and dealing with these during the induction period, an individual personal development interview or review might also be completed. At this review, any specific individual learning needs identified during the induction period would be discussed. These learning needs may have been identified by the learning and development specialist or by the individual themselves and agreement should then be reached about how they could be addressed using specific leaning and development interventions tailored to suit the individual. A series of individual development review interviews could also be set up at regular intervals.

In this case, Ros was starting a temporary vacation job, so there may not have been the time or money to set up a full personal development programme for her, but it would certatinly be appropriate for workers who were going to be there longer.

Ros' first day at work was far from successful and many employees who felt as badly as she did in those first few days would be on the next flight home. Even without the problems of language and a different culture, many employees who had a similar experience in this country would probably not return. This would be a very expensive waste of resources, which human resource managers should be concerned to eliminate. The loss of employees soon after they start work is known as the induction crisis.

In order for Ros to settle quickly into her new work environment there was a great deal of information she needed to know. An induction course would have helped. As we have said, induction actually starts before the first day at work and it would have been very helpful to Ros to receive information prior to starting work. This would have included information such as:

- transport arrangements to the hotel
- details of whom to contact on arrival
- information about where to report for work
- payment details and information about meals
- uniform details
- information about accommodation
- information about hours of work
- job title and brief description of the job
- an introduction to workplace culture and customs in France.

When she started work an induction course would also have been useful as she would still need to have information about:

- the layout of the hotel and the hotel's 'big idea' such as the provision of excellent service
- the managers and their responsibilities
- the actual duties involved in her job
- common cross-cultural differences/issues which might arise in an international hotel
- health, safety and hygiene
- discipline and grievance handling, etc.

This would have provided her with opportunities to ask questions and not feel foolish. You may also have identified other information that you think Ros should be given. It is important to consider how much information to give, and the appropriate timescale for giving this information. Although Ros had suffered, in this example, because of lack of information, too much information may also be problematic as there is a danger that some will be forgotten or the person will become bored and not listen.

An induction programme must be designed to meet your objectives and you should decide what information the new person is required to know, over what timescale, the length and training methods to be used, and the role of the line managers and human resource staff in the programme. Some information needs to be given immediately, such as layout of the building, names of work-mates and supervisors, and points about safety. Other information may be necessary later, such as pension rules or details of the sports and social clubs.

Other staff need to be prepared and aware of their roles, so for example in the case of Ros, the hotel driver would need to know the time he should collect her from the airport. Normally a receptionist or security person would need to know of the arrival of the new member of staff and who to inform about it. The HR manager, or their deputy, should not only have been available to greet the new person, but also to ensure that basic information was given and questions and problems were dealt with. A 'buddy', perhaps of a similar age, could be allocated to help the new person find their way around and could answer any questions that he or she had been too nervous to ask the managers about. Managers, supervisors and trainers should also be aware of their own roles in the person's induction.

Induction training

As we have just shown, there is a need for induction training to help new members of staff settle into their new job as quickly as possible. Induction also helps to create a favourable image of the organisation in the mind of the new employee, and is therefore also a valuable public relations exercise. Part of the induction process starts at the time of interview, with the information and impression of the organisation that is given at that stage. Any letters or booklets given after this also form an important part of the induction process.

When new employees actually start work, they will need to get to know the people with whom they will be working, become familiar with their surroundings, learn about their new job and learn about the organisation in which they will be working. Although there is a great deal of information to impart to the new employee, not all of it is needed immediately and in fact there is a danger of overloading the individual with information if it is all given at once. If formal induction courses are run for all new starters then these could be spread over parts of several days, imparting the most urgent information, such as the geography of the building, canteen arrangements and introductions to supervisors and work colleagues, first. It may be that the formal courses do not even need to start on the first day, especially if recruitment is sporadic. Small groups of employees may be gathered, perhaps once a month, for the formal induction course, providing of course that their immediate induction needs such as information on safety rules have been adequately covered.

A formal induction course is useful, as several new starters can be given information at the same time. However, the new employees are likely to be starting different jobs in various departments, so that there is still an important role for their line managers to play in their induction, particularly in carrying out personal development reviews and then tailoring individual learning and development initiatives to meet the specific learning and development needs of the individual in that department. A checklist indicating which topics will be covered, when they will be covered and who will cover them is also extremely useful. This can be signed by the employee when he or she has gone through all the topics and then stored with his or her training records. It also provides a useful reminder to all of the need to cover these topics.

Table 8.1 gives an indication of the type of things that need to be covered during an induction period. It is useful to indicate who is responsible for dealing with each topic and when it should be covered. A section for the trainee to sign to say that she or he has completed each topic would also be useful.

Table 8.1   **Sample induction checklist**

Topic	Person responsible for covering this topic	Day 1	First week	First month
Reception	Human Resource Manager	★		
Documentation and introduction to manager	Human Resource Manager	★		
Hours, clocking on, flex-time, lunch breaks, overtime	Human Resource Manager	★		
Layout of department, outline of function and introduction to staff	Supervisor	★		
Tour of main work areas, staff restaurant, toilets, fire exits	'Buddy' or person delegated by the supervisor to look after and befriend the new starter	★		
Health and safety rules	Supervisor	★		
The organisation – products, services, the organisation's handbook	Training Officer			★
Rules and procedures – discipline and grievance	Human Resource Manager		★	
Payment, holiday pay and sickness pay	Human Resource Manager		★	
Communication and consultation	Training Officer			★
Training and development	Training Officer			★
Performance appraisal and set-up of personal development plan and reviews	Training Officer			★
Pensions	Training Officer			★
The trade union	Shop Steward			★

Some of the information will need to be given in a written form, perhaps in a handbook. Although much of this information may also have been given verbally in the formal induction course, it is useful to have a source of reference for things such as what to do when you are ill. This might not have seemed particularly relevant to a new starter, and indeed may not be needed for a year or two, by which time it may have been largely forgotten unless there is a handbook to refer to.

Since it is important not to give too much information, as the new starter may feel overwhelmed, it is better to spread the information over a period of time and alternate with periods where the person is introduced to his or her new job and given a chance to settle into this. After all, that is the reason they have joined the organisation. In some organisations new recruits are asked to arrive later than the rest of the workforce on their first day, so that those who will be involved in their induction can get things organised and deal with any crises that may occur, and then have time to spend on the new recruit.

If the new employee comes from another country, or if the work is in an international organisation where workers come from many different countries, there is also likely to be a need to deal with cross-cultural issues to encourage greater understanding and increase tolerance of different ways of working. The induction period would provide a useful foundation for this and progress could be reviewed during subsequent personal development reviews.

Job instruction on a one-to-one basis

Managers, supervisors and experienced members of the workforce, as well as human resource professionals and learning and development specialists, are all likely to be involved in training at some time. Even if they are not specialists in this area, many people are asked to give introductory instruction to others in a new skill, so a basic understanding of the process is likely to be useful to everyone. In this section we shall discuss ways in which you can be more effective if you have to instruct someone in a simple task.

Once again, there have to be systematic stages that the instructor works through relating clearly to the training cycle and you should go through stages 1–4 described in the last chapter (see Figure 7.7).

Stage 1: Assessing the training needs

Pause for thought 8.1 The first stage should, as always, be to assess the training needs of the individual. What methods might you use to assess the training needs here? (Refer back to the previous chapter if you cannot remember.)

◯ Stage 2: Planning the training

1 Agree objectives.
   - State what the trainee must be able to do.
   - State the standard they must achieve.
   - State any time limits in which this must be achieved.
   - Agree with the trainee exactly what they need to learn and the time and quality standards that are appropriate.

2 Break the instructions down into key stages.
   - Do the job or rehearse the subject yourself.
   - Divide the job into stages.
   - Select the main or key points for each stage of the instruction.

3 Get everything ready and material and equipment organised before you start to instruct.
   - Pay attention to layout.
   - Have the correct materials.
   - Have all the correct equipment working properly.
   - Decide on training aids you will use: charts, diagrams, overhead transparencies, videos, lap-top computer and projection facilities.
   - Decide where the training will take place.

4 Make a training plan.
   - How will the trainee's absence from the job be covered?
   - What standards of performance are required?
   - Do any targets have to be reached?
   - Select who is to be trained.
   - Arrange a date for completion of training.
   - Use the trainee's abilities to best effect.
   - Keep the plan up to date.

◯ Stage 3: Carrying out the training

1 Prepare the trainee for instruction.
   - Put him or her at ease.
   - State clearly the job or subject.
   - Check the existing knowledge of the trainee.
   - Create an interest in learning the skill.
   - Discuss and agree with the trainee their learning objectives for the session.
   - Ensure that the trainee is positioned correctly to see and hear all your instructions.

2 Present the training material.
   - Tell, show and demonstrate the task one step at a time.
   - Emphasise key points, especially points about safety or quality.
   - Give instructions clearly and patiently.
   - Encourage the trainee to ask questions.

3 Allow the trainee to try to complete the task by themself.
   - Get the trainee to show and explain each stage of the task to you.
   - Ensure that you correct errors as they occur.

- Check the trainee's understanding of the key points as they demonstrate them.
- Continue until satisfied that the trainee has mastered all stages.

4 Put the trainee to work.
- Ensure that they are aware of targets and safety.
- Tell them who will help them if they have a problem.
- Encourage questions.
- Check at intervals that progress has been maintained.
- Check that the trainee is meeting the agreed learning objectives.

Pause for thought 8.2

What should the fourth and final stage of the training cycle be? (Refer back to the previous chapter (Figure 7.7) if you are unable to remember.)

Throughout this process of instructing on a one-to-one basis we have emphasised the need to break the task down into small manageable sections and to go through them in a systematic manner, giving clear instructions and giving the trainee opportunities to practise the new task for themselves.

ACTIVITY 8.4

Think about a simple task that you can do well. It might be a part of a sport or hobby. Prepare to instruct someone else in this task. As part of your planning for instruction, break the task down into stages using the columns below.

Stage	Step	Key points

Discussion of Activity 8.4

Even a fairly simple task usually has several stages. The following example gives the stages that one might go through when instructing a person in the simple task of refilling a stapler.

This shows an example of a simple task being broken down into stages. It is important to provide an overview at the beginning so that the person knows how this particular task fits into the wider context of the job and fits with their learning objectives and personal development plan. This may help to prevent them from making obvious mistakes, as they will have some understanding of why they are doing the task and of its importance.

Stage	Step	Key points
Overview	1. Describe equipment	• used everyday • take care not to get fingers trapped as staples are sharp
	2. Point out parts	• base • arm • striking plate • staple track • staples • spring
Loading	1. Open stapler	• Hold lower part near the base plate in left hand with thumb and index finger (if right-handed). With right hand grasp top firmly and pull up until you hear the click. BE CAREFUL.
	2. Insert staples	• With your right hand, slide back the metal plate attached to the spring to create room for the new staples on the track. Insert the required number of staples on the track with their points facing down. Allow the spring to slide back gently into position so that the staples are held in place. Ensure they are straight and slide them to the front of the track.
	3. Close	• With your left hand move the upper section of the stapler upwards and then downwards, rotating it on its hinge. Push down gently so that it engages with the staple track and clicks into place.
Using	1. Decide on style of stapling	• Turn the stapler upside down and locate a screw under the base plate. Push down on this and then swivel the base plate into the required position depending on whether you require temporary or permanent staples.

ACTIVITY 8.5

When you have chosen a task for yourself and broken it down into stages like this, you can practise instructing someone in the task you have chosen. Sometimes, as in the example above, it may be necessary to check whether the person is right- or left-handed before you start to instruct. In the example of refilling a stapler, even though staples are sharp, there are not a great many safety points to pay attention to. Make sure in your example that you stress important factors such as safety or quality.

Recent developments in learning and development

Although the human resource is the organisation's most important resource and consequently its full development is essential for the organisation's future success, many have traditionally not been very good at developing it and this has resulted in various Government-led initiatives to encourage employers to train their staff. In the 1960s and 1970s there were Industrial Training Boards which aimed to encourage this. They imposed a levy on organisations depending on their size, which could be repaid to the organisation fully or in part depending on the amount of training that they did. Some of these became bureaucratic and most were disbanded. Then the government encouraged Training and Enterprise Councils (TECs) or, in Scotland, Local Enterprise Councils (LECs) to take responsibility locally for encouraging training and development. TECs and LECs administered the Youth Training and Employment Training schemes in their areas but were also able to develop local training initiatives with employers, often in partnership with them. They in turn were replaced in 2001 by the Learning Skills Council (LSC) and the Local Learning Skills Councils (LLSCs).

The Learning and Skills Council and Local Learning Skills Councils

The Learning and Skills Council was established in April 2001 to cover learning and skills development in a wide range of areas. This includes work-based training for young people, further education and adult and community learning. The Council also aims to help with the development of the workforce, provide information and guidance for adults and establish links between business and education. It has responsibility for funding and planning education and training for anyone over 16 years of age in England. According to its Chairman, Bryan Sanderson:

> The Learning and Skills Council is here to improve education and training. We want to increase national productivity by providing the skills that businesses need. And, just as importantly, we want to provide greater opportunities to help people achieve their full potential through learning. There can be few more important goals for the health and well-being of our country.
>
> (See Learning and Skills Council 2004.)

In this statement Bryan Sanderson emphasises not only the need for improved skills and learning and development to meet the needs of businesses and the country, but also states that individuals have much to gain by learning. His view is that the Learning and Skills Council is acting as a catalyst for change in improving skills for everyone so the country in turn becomes increasingly able to be more competitive. Its primary aims are summed up in its vision and mission statements quoted next (see Learning and Skills Council 2004).

> *Our vision*:
> By the year 2010 young people and adults in this country will have the knowledge and skills to match the best in the world.
>
> *Our mission*:
> To raise the number of people leaning new skills – and gaining qualifications – by providing high quality education and training that puts people first.

There are 47 Local Learning and Skills Councils throughout England and these also include representatives from local employers and other learning providers such as community groups.

The national targets for education and training

The Learning and Skills Council consulted widely with the Local Learning Skills Councils and in effect carried out a nationwide analysis of learning needs. They produced national targets for education and training throughout England. They aim to work with partners, such as colleges and other providers of education, at local and regional levels to achieve these. The most recent targets available at the time of writing and the success rates in achieving these are shown in Table 8.2.

The Qualifications and Curriculum Authority (QCA)

The Qualifications and Curriculum Authority came into being on 1 October 1997 and brought together the work which had previously been undertaken by the National Council for Vocational Qualifications (NCVQ) and the School Curriculum and Assessment Authority (SCAA). It is sponsored by the Department for Education and Skills (DfES) and is governed by a board whose members are selected by the Secretary for State for Education and Skills. It is run on a day-to-day basis by an executive team. The QCA aims to be pivotal in helping the UK to become one of the most dynamic knowledge-based economies in the world.

In the previous chapter we showed how often in Britain training and education have been treated in differing ways with newer competence-based qualifications sometimes suffering lack of parity of esteem when compared

Table 8.2   **National learning and development targets**

The targets	Performance levels in 2002–03
16-18 year olds	
The target for the end of 2004 was to have 80% of this age group participating in learning.	By the end of 2002, 76.4% of this age group were participating in learning so this is likely to be achieved by the end of 2004.
Adult basic skills	
The target for the end of 2004 was to train 750,000 in basic skills.	By April 2004, 510,000 adults had improved their basic skills and received recognition for this.
Modern apprenticeships	
The target for 2004–05 was to have 175,000 of 16–21 year olds (28% of this age group) in modern apprenticeship schemes.	On target.
Employer training pilots	
The target was to involve 10,000 employers and to enrol up to 50,000 employees for basic skills or level 2 qualifications by Autumn 2004.	Within the first six months of this scheme, 2,100 companies and 10,000 employees enrolled so this is also likely to achieve its target.

(Adapted from the Learning and Skills Council's Annual Report and Accounts 2002–03; www.lsc.gov.uk; accessed 24.08.04)

with more traditional academic qualifications. This can be traced back, as we said in Chapter 7, to the underlying theories of learning such as cognitive or behaviourist, but it resulted in the creation of two education and training systems in Britain. The creation of the QCA was a move to integrate these two education and training systems and end the academic/vocational divide.

The QCA is responsible for establishing a comprehensive qualifications framework. This means everything ranging from the curriculum for those of pre-school age, to the National Curriculum, GCSEs, AS and A levels, NVQs and GNVQs, through to higher-level vocational qualifications. It is also involved in providing an international dimension to England's qualification and curriculum system by undertaking European and international research into these areas and by becoming involved in a worldwide exchange of information about qualifications, education and training. The QCA has recently reviewed the national qualifications framework and introduced a new framework with nine levels to be used from September 2004. This is entry level plus eight further levels, and this has been changed in order to include within it links to qualifications in higher education and to enable smooth progression.

According to QCA (2004) the national qualifications framework aims to:

- promote access, motivation and achievement in education and training, strengthening international competitiveness
- promote lifelong learning by helping people to understand clear progression routes
- avoid overlap and duplication of qualifications while making sure all learning needs are covered
- promote public and professional confidence in the integrity and relevance of national awards.

The new qualifications framework is designed to provide clear and easy guidance for everyone from the learners themselves to employers. The indicators have been expressed in a way that shows the types of 'learning and achievement that happen at each level and show how the skills and knowledge relate to job roles. The indicators are not intended to be precise or accurate, they are working guides' (QCA 2004). The framework is outlined in Table 8.3.

The Employment National Training Organisation (ENTO)

There are currently about 30 national training organisations. They were originally developed by the Department for Education and Employment to replace lead bodies and other organisations involved in establishing standards in learning and development such as National Vocational Qualifications (NVQs) in England and Scottish Vocational Qualifications (SVQs) in Scotland.

The Employment National Training Organisation (ENTO) has a governing council and represents those involved in training and development, trade unions, health and safety and personnel and human resource management.

Table 8.3   **The national qualifications framework 2004**

Framework level	Level indicators	Examples of qualifications
Entry	Entry-level qualifications recognise basic knowledge and skills and the ability to apply learning in everyday situations under direct guidance or supervision. Learning at this level involves building basic knowledge and skills and is not geared towards specific occupations.	Qualifications are offered at Entry 1, Entry 2 and Entry 3, in a range of subjects
Level 1	Level 1 qualifications recognise basic knowledge and skills and the ability to apply learning with guidance or supervision. Learning at this level is about activities which mostly relate to everyday situations and may be linked to job competence.	NVQ 1; Certificate in Plastering; GCSEs Grades D–G; Certificate in Motor Vehicle Studies
Level 2	Level 2 qualifications recognise the ability to gain a good knowledge and understanding of a subject area of work or study, and to perform varied tasks with some guidance or supervision. Learning at this level involves building knowledge and/or skills in relation to an area of work or a subject area and is appropriate for many job roles.	NVQ 2; GCSEs Grades A*–C; Certificate in Coaching Football; Diploma for Beauty Specialists
Level 3	Level 3 qualifications recognise the ability to gain and, where relevant, apply a range of knowledge, skills and understanding. Learning at this level involves obtaining detailed knowledge and skills. It is appropriate for people wishing to go to university, people working independently, or in some areas supervising and training others in their field of work.	Certificate for Teaching Assistants; NVQ 3; A levels; Advanced Extension Awards; Certificate in Small Animal Care
Level 4	Level 4 qualifications recognise specialist learning and involve detailed analysis of a high level of information and knowledge in an area of work or study. Learning at this level is appropriate for people working in technical and professional jobs, and/or managing and developing others. Level 4 qualifications are at a level equivalent to Certificates of Higher Education.	Diploma in Sport & Recreation; Certificate in Site Management; Certificate in Early Years Practice
Level 5	Level 5 qualifications recognise the ability to increase the depth of knowledge and understanding of an area of work or study to enable the formulation of solutions and responses to complex problems and situations. Learning at this level involves the demonstration of high levels of knowledge, a high level of work expertise in job roles and competence in managing and training others. Qualifications at this level are appropriate for people working as higher-grade technicians, professionals or managers. Level 5 qualifications are at a level equivalent to intermediate Higher Education qualifications such as Diplomas	Diploma in Construction; Certificate in Performing Arts

Table 8.3 **(contd)**

Framework level	Level indicators	Examples of qualifications
	of Higher Education, Foundation and other degrees that do not typically provide access to postgraduate programmes.	
Level 6	Level 6 qualifications recognise a specialist high level knowledge of an area of work or study to enable the use of an individual's own ideas and research in response to complex problems and situations. Learning at this level involves the achievement of a high level of professional knowledge and is appropriate for people working as knowledge-based professionals or in professional management positions. Level 6 qualifications are at a level equivalent to Bachelors, degrees with honours, graduate certificates and graduate diplomas.	Certificate or Diploma in Management
Level 7	Level 7 qualifications recognise highly developed and complex levels of knowledge which enable the development of in-depth and original responses to complicated and unpredictable problems and situations. Learning at this level involves the demonstration of high level specialist professional knowledge and is appropriate for senior professionals and managers. Level 7 qualifications are at a level equivalent to Masters, degrees, postgraduate certificates and postgraduate diplomas.	Diploma in Translation; Fellowship in Music Literacy
Level 8	Level 8 qualifications recognise leading experts or practitioners in a particular field. Learning at this level involves the development of new and creative approaches that extend or redefine existing knowledge or professional practice.	Specialist awards

(The Qualifications and Curriculum Authority 2004; **www.qca.org.uk**; accessed 25.08.04)

The mission statement of the ENTO (2004) says that its primary purpose is:

the enhancement and the improvement of the performance of people involved in the development, management, health and safety and representation of people in the workplace.

In order to do this it provides impartial advice, information, and support and support products for those who use National Occupational Standards. It is responsible for developing standards in the following areas:

- personnel
- managing work-related violence
- recruitment consultancy

- counselling
- learning and development
- trade unions
- health and safety
- advice, guidance and advocacy
- mediation
- assessment and verification
- modern apprenticeships in related areas.

Since the focus of this chapter is on learning and development, this is the part of the ENTO qualification structure that we shall examine next. The qualification structure in learning and development has six NVQs at levels 3, 4 and 5. These are shown in Table 8.4. There are nine further qualifications at certificate level that can be awarded in areas that relate specifically to learning and development.

Table 8.4   **NVQs in learning and development**

Level	Title
3	Learning and Development
3	Direct Training and Support
4	Management of Learning and Development Provision
4	Co-ordination of Learning and Development
5	Learning and Development

(Employment National Training Organisation 2004; **www.ento.co.uk**; accessed 25.8.04)

ENTO regards itself as having a unique role as its customers include trainers from many other industry sectors who complete the 'D' units, which are the units in assessment and verification. Therefore in many ways ENTO's influence goes far beyond its own industry sectors.

Pause for thought 8.3

There has been constant change over many years in national vocational education and training, and in education in general. It is always said that these changes are to improve standards.

To what extent do you think these changes have been successful? Do we still need more change in order to encourage everyone to learn throughout their lives? Note down your thoughts.

Some of you may be working towards these qualifications yourself, perhaps as part of your own career plan to enhance your competencies in these areas or to help towards gaining Graduate Membership of the CIPD. You will notice once again the importance of training and development strategy for those working towards the level 5 qualification. Remember that people operating at level 5 should be able to demonstrate substantial personal autonomy, responsibility for allocation of resources and for the work of others. They are likely to be operating at a fairly senior managerial level and so must be able to demonstrate that they are competent in thinking strategically and developing training and development strategies.

The Investors in People award (IiP)

This initiative aims to improve the quality of British training and development practices by setting national standards for good practice and by linking these to the achievement of business goals. Since training and development is closely linked to the organisation's objectives it will result in people being trained and developed in ways which exactly suit the organisation's requirements and this should enable the value of training and development activities to be clearly demonstrated.

The national standard was originally developed during the 1990s but has subsequently been revised every three years in order to ensure the award is accessible and relevant to a range of organisations, particularly small organisations which might not have an HR expert. The standard aims to provide a national framework which will help to improve business performance and competitiveness and which will add real value to an organisation. It does this by providing a planned approach to establishing and communicating the business objectives of an organisation and to achieve these by developing the people within that organisation. Once again, learning and development activities are perceived to be vital in making an organisation competitive.

The Investors in People Standard was revised in 2005. According to the CIPD (2005) the three key principles of IiP are:

- **Developing strategies to improve the performance of an organisation** – an Investor in People develops effective strategies to improve the performance of the organisation through its people.
- **Taking action to improve the performance of an organisation** – an Investor in People takes effective action to improve the performance of the organisation through its people.
- **Evaluating the impact on the performance of the organisation** – an Investor in People can demonstrate the impact of its investment in people on the performance of the organisation. (CIPD fact sheet Investors in People, revised January 2005)

The standards have been simplified and these three principles now form the basis of the IiP cycle and are in turn broken down into 10 indicators. Any organisation wanting recognition as an Investor in People will now be assessed against these three principles and ten indicators.

The focus of the new standards has shifted and is now on employee involvement, a topic we cover in more detail in , and on maximising worker potential to achieve high performance working. Organisations are further encouraged to involve their employees in decisions about learning and development initiatives.

The earlier version of the Investors in People standard had focussed on gaining commitment from the top to learning and development, and making clear the strategic links so learning and development clearly supported the organisation's strategic objectives. IiP seems to have been largely successful in achieving this.

The new revised standards recognise that all managers, at whatever level, have a vital role to play in the development of their workers. As we said earlier in this chapter, it has often been difficult to get the commitment of line managers to spending time and money on the learning and development of their workers. These new standards emphasise this vital role and are likely to have quite an impact in this area. Achieving the IiP award is not the final stage as the organisation will then need to continue to encourage continuous improvement in order to get even better at developing its people and in order to meet the requirements of the standard again in future years.

Many organisations have demonstrated commercial benefits from achieving the standards and there are benefits for their workforce too, not only in being part of a thriving organisation but also in improvements in their own training and development.

National Vocational Qualifications (NVQs) and Scottish Vocational Qualifications (SVQs)

NVQs, and the Scottish equivalent SVQs, are qualifications designed specifically for people who are at work, giving them opportunities to continue to train and develop while also working towards a nationally recognised qualification. NVQs are also part of the movement away from pure classroom-based learning as they promote learning as an ongoing process which also occurs at work and which can and should continue throughout life as lifelong learning. They fit within the national qualifications framework and provide a vocational route to achieve qualifications. Access to NVQs/SVQs may also sometimes be available via colleges and in these cases work-based learning facilities would be provided.

The National Training Organisations for each industry or occupational sector developed national occupational standards for their sectors, so the qualifications are relevant to those industries. There are 11 NVQ/SVQ occupational areas. These are:

1 communicating
2 construction
3 developing and extending knowledge and skill
4 engineering
5 extracting and providing natural resources
6 manufacturing
7 providing business services
8 providing goods and services
9 providing health, social care and protective services
10 tending animals, plants and land
11 transporting.

Within these sectors there are over 800 NVQ titles so individuals should be able to find an NVQ/SVQ relevant to their job and to the competencies which they want to develop.

In order to gain an NVQ/SVQ the individual must complete the mandatory units for that NVQ, and also any optional units that they have selected. There is not a specified time limit for this so people can repeat units if necessary. To demonstrate competence in the workplace the individual will be observed in the work situation by an assessor who is qualified to do the assessment. The assessor will also discuss certain points with him or her and may also examine evidence of the work or products that the individual has produced. Statements from people with whom he or she works may also be taken into account before the assessor decides whether or not to award the NVQ. The assessor will usually observe the individual doing their job and will also ask him or her questions about it. When the assessor is fully satisfied that the worker has demonstrated the appropriate standard of work, they will 'sign off' each unit that has been achieved.

There are five levels of NVQ that can be achieved within work. According to the Department for Education and Skills (DfES 2004) these are:

Level 1 – Foundation skills in occupations
Level 2 – Operative or semi-operative occupations
Level 3 – Technician, craft, skilled and supervisory occupations
Level 4 – Technical and junior management
Level 5 – Chartered, professional and senior management occupations

In order to maintain the quality of NVQs those involved as either assessors or verifiers also need to have qualifications. These units were previously known as the 'D' units but are now referred to by the initial 'A' for assessment or 'V' for verification. These are not full NVQs/SVQs but are nevertheless national standards and anyone involved with the assessment or verification process for NVQs/SVQs must have completed the appropriate 'D' unit. These assessment and verification units now have unit reference numbers as follows:

Unit	Title
A1	Assess candidates using a range of methods
A2	Assess candidates' performance through observation
V1	Conduct internal quality assurance of the assessment process
V2	Conduct external assessment of the quality assurance process

(Employment National Training Organisation 2004)

Pause for thought 8.4

What do ENTO, NVQ and CIPD stand for? (Look back earlier in the chapter to find the answer if you are unsure.)

Apprenticeships and advanced apprenticeships

Apprenticeships were launched in 1995 as part of the attempt by the Government to revitalise education and training. They were originally known as modern apprenticeships, to differentiate them clearly from old-style apprenticeships. They were later divided into two different types of modern apprenticeship known as foundation modern apprenticeships and advanced modern apprenticeships. Recently they have been re-branded and are now known as apprenticeships and advanced apprenticeships. They are usually aimed at those under 25, although the Government is currently reviewing whether to extend them to people over 25 as well. They are available in over 80 different work sectors. They provide opportunities for young people to develop skills and gain qualifications while working. Apprenticeships exist at two levels: apprenticeships and advanced apprenticeships. Advanced apprenticeships provide the young person with the chance to gain qualifications at NVQ level 3 plus key skills and a technical qualification. The advanced apprenticeships normally last for two years. Apprenticeships normally take at least one year to complete and enable the apprentice to gain an NVQ at level 2, key skills and usually a technical certificate.

Since NVQs are national standards they allow the young person to gain important transferable skills and a qualification highly regarded by employers, which will still be relevant if they move to another organisation in the same sector.

Employers who hire an apprentice are normally involved in working with the LSC or with a training provider to decide the exact form of the training and to establish a training plan in consultation with the apprentice and designed to meet their specific learning needs within that organisation. Employers were involved in developing the national standards, so these are geared to the requirements of each industry sector, but there can be some flexibility in the training plan to meet special requirements for an individual business. There may also be funding available to employers to help to pay for the training they provide, but this depends on the industry sector and the type of training provided.

New Deal

New Deal was originally a scheme for 18–24 year olds but this has since been extended to other groups. The New Deal schemes form part of the Government's Welfare to Work strategy and aim to help those who are unemployed not only to get work, but also to develop many of the skills employers need. While it is not solely a training scheme, there are nevertheless important training provisions within it, originally called 'the Gateway', an introduction to, and intensive preparation for, work which clients undertake before they go to an employer. There is also a requirement for training to be provided either by the employer or by a third party to bring the person up to the required standards.

The mandatory New Deal schemes

There are now six versions of the New Deal scheme for those who are long-term unemployed. These are:

● New Deal for Young People (18–24)
● New Deal for 25 plus.

There are subsidies available to employers who take people from these two mandatory programmes to help towards the cost of their wages, for a period of time, and also to help with the costs of training.

The voluntary New Deal schemes

There are also six voluntary New Deal programmes which have been designed to help people who are claiming benefits but who want to work. These are:

● New Deal 50 plus
● New Deal for Lone Parents
● New Deal for Disabled People
● New Deal for Partners of Unemployed People.
● New Deal for Self-Employment.
● New Deal for Musicians.

These have been targeted to meet the needs of specific groups who have sometimes found it difficult to get back into full-time employment.

Sector-specific training: the ambition programmes

Other newer initiatives are also in place to help people to find jobs in sectors which face particular skills shortages but where the employers would not normally consider recruiting jobless people. The first of these ambition programmes covered jobs in the information technology sector. The ambition programmes established so far are:

● Ambition: Information Technology March 2001
● Ambition: Retail in April 2001

- Ambition: Construction in October 2001
- Ambition: Energy in June 2002

In this type of programme there is a great deal of consulation with key employers in the industries concerned to ensure the relevance of the programmes to the needs of the industry.

New Deal does provide individual help for eligible job-seekers from a personal advisor, so individuals are supported while they prepare for work, find the job and undergo relevant training. There is an initial interview at a Job Centre, where a review of the person's experience, skills and job aspirations takes place. This is part of the assessment of the individual's training needs to ensure any gaps in skills or knowledge, which might prevent the person achieving their chosen job, are identified and a plan is developed to help them. The gaps may be filled by a range of different measures including: the provision of subsidised employment; work experience with employers; or training in areas such as basic skills. They may also require specific help in areas such as interview practice.

The individual should benefit from the training and development opportunities as well as by getting the chance of employment. Employers benefit not only from a motivated worker, but also by subsidies for employing the person and a grant for specified training costs.

The learning organisation

Another popular recent idea is the idea of the learning organisation. In some ways the term is confusing, since people actually do the learning, but it is good that people have started to see learning within organisations as being of importance. According to Jones and Hendry (1992), the term at its simplest means an organisation where there are 'a lot of people learning' and according to Pedler *et al.* (1988) it means 'an organisation which facilitates the learning of all its members and continuously transforms itself'.

If an organisation is to encourage learning to occur, then it must develop a culture which recognises that people learn in different ways and must provide a range of experiences from which they may learn. Many organisations, as we have already shown, create situations where people learn all the things that the managers don't want them to learn. In the learning organisation, human resource managers and learning and development specialists have an important role in ensuring that the organisation develops in a way which facilitates the learning that the organisation does want to occur, and that a suitable environment is created in which continuous improvement is actively encouraged. Line managers also need to be involved in encouraging learning to occur, and the organisation should try to minimise barriers that may hamper learning and development and encourage individuals to seek learning opportunities for themselves. The training and development that occurs should clearly link with the objectives of the organisation, and its efficiency and effectiveness should be regularly evaluated.

> **Did you know?**
>
> 'Toy workers are killed in factory fires in the Far East, children work for a pittance in India unprotected from damaging chemicals.' (Roger Cowe 1998)
>
> Many big-name manufacturers have excellent policies, procedures, training and quality standards for their staff in Western countries, but have still been exposed for profiteering from the exploitation of workers in developing countries.

◯ Approaches to training adopted by learning organisations

Specific training techniques have been discussed both here and in the previous chapter. But even within specific training programmes such as apprenticeships, or the training element within New Deal, there is an emphasis on learning and development and of identifying and agreeing the learning needs with the people concerned. All programmes also emphasise the difference that learning and development can make to an organisation by adding value to that organisation. A few others, which might be used by an organisation that wants to encourage the culture of a learning organisation, will be discussed here.

Trade union learning representatives

As part of the shift from training to learning, and in order to promote learning at all levels and within all organisations, the Employment Act 2002 established a new group known as learning representatives. These learning representatives are appointed by trade unions and have several statutory rights. These include the right to time off work in certain circumstances in order to:

- analyse learning and training needs
- provide information or advice relating to any learning or training issues
- organise specific learning or training
- consult with the employer about learning and training issues
- participate themselves in training for their role as a learning representative.

The ACAS (2003) *Code of Practice on Time off for Union Duties and Activities* gives further details of these rights.

Union members also have the right to time off to discuss issues or attend learning activities organised by trade union appointed learning representatives, although they do not have to be paid for this.

Pause for thought 8.5

Compare the role of the union representative with the role of the trainer within an organisation. To what extent do the roles differ? To what extent do the roles overlap?

Learning representatives are appointed by the trade unions and they are there to facilitate learning and development. Although a great deal of the emphasis has shifted to the learner they are not always in a strong position to initiate the learning that they require by themselves, so learning representatives can help with this.

We have already argued that there is a clear business case for learning and development in the workplace as this can add value to the organisation by helping it to achieve its objectives, but not all organisations see things in this way. Historically many organisations have just perceived learning and development activities as a cost, rather than an investment in their human resources. Moreover, traditionally some organisations have only focused their training activities on certain groups of workers such as managers or graduates. If lifelong learning is to become a reality then learning representatives should help to kick-start some learning and development activities for all workers.

Sometimes it can be a question of attitude: the employer is willing to fund learning and development but workers or their supervisors do not see the relevance to them and do not participate fully. Once again the learning representatives have a role to play in fostering a positive attitude towards learning and development and increasing motivation to learn.

It has also been claimed that large numbers of workers lack basic skills in numeracy and literacy but have successfully hidden this from their employers for many years. In many organisations HR and HRD departments are now working with learning representatives to get to groups of workers who have not traditionally participated in learning and development and who may have poor basic skills which could be holding back their career progression.

There are many benefits to be gained by having learning representatives within an organisation as they should help to increase awareness of the learning and development that is available and also provide a valuable additional set of resources so all groups can get involved in lifelong learning.

Mentors

Rather than just leaving learning experiences to chance, many organisations now use mentors to help individuals to learn. Mentors need to be prepared to guide and suggest suitable learning experiences for their protégé. They may encourage reflection on these learning experiences by asking for reports, and may suggest books to read on the subject. They may also sometimes provide opportunities for the individual to demonstrate what he or she has learnt by, for example, reviewing a presentation before the learner makes it to the target audience. While their main aim is to encourage individuals to learn, mentors are also likely to learn a great deal themselves by their involvement in this learning experience. In effect, mentors will be encouraging the individual to learn in different ways according to their development needs and to practise using different learning styles and different stages of the learning cycle.

Coaching

This is another approach to learning and development that has been gaining in popularity. Coaches help individuals or groups to perform better, rather like a sports coach. According to Sol Davidson (2002), there are three types of coaching: traditional, transitional and transformational:

- Traditional coaching is closely related to training and involves a coach who is an expert in a subject helping to improve the skills and knowledge of an individual or group.
- Transitional coaching is useful where large changes are about to be made in an organisation. Here the coach does not necessarily know all the answers, but will help the group to find successful new ways of working.
- Transformational coaching is targeted at senior management but is aimed at helping the whole organisation move to new ways of working. It could be appropriate when an organisation is faced with a great deal of change.

Learning logs

Another way in which individuals may be encouraged to learn from their experiences is by the use of a learning log. A learning log is a way of keeping track of a person's development, with emphasis on unstructured, informal activities. This is likely to involve individuals in describing events that they feel are important for their own development process. They would then need to comment on what they had learnt from the experience and how, if a similar situation were to arise again, they would handle that situation. The idea is that because individuals have to write up their learning experiences, they will be likely to do things better in the future. Learning also ceases to be a haphazard process, as it becomes conscious and increasingly learner centred. This means that the individual will have used several of the stages of the learning cycle.

Keeping a learning log should encourage activists to be more reflective and encourage reflectors/theorists to take action and to do things after reflecting on them. This could be undertaken with a mentor or as a totally self-directed method of gaining insights into your own learning processes. This method is very subjective but tends to encourage an analytical approach to problems. It can also be therapeutic to get a problem sorted out on paper, with clear targets for how you would handle a similar situation in the future.

The main headings likely to be used for a learning log will be:

- Description of a significant learning experience.
- What actually happened.
- What you concluded/learnt from this experience.
- What action you will take now or how you would handle a similar situation in the future.

In order to ensure that all stages of the learning cycle are covered, a further section could be added:

- How what you learnt relates to the theory on this subject.

Continuing professional development

Nowadays the pace of change is rapid and people who studied 20 years ago, or even a couple of years ago, may find that their skills and knowledge are outdated. In order to update their members, many professional groups have introduced the concept of continuing professional development (CPD).

The Chartered Institute of Personnel and Development also encourages CPD and strongly encourages the use of a form of learning log as a means for members to continue to update their professional knowledge. This is to ensure that individuals will stay up-to-date not only on facts but also on opinions and skills. The CIPD aims to ensure that the reputation of its members remains high, that they aspire to high levels of performance, and that its members devise and manage learning methods appropriate to their needs and the circumstances in their own organisation.

The CIPD acknowledges that continuing professional development opportunities will take many forms, but suggests a balanced mix which includes professional work-based activities, courses and seminars and self-directed informal learning. Not all professional bodies emphasise the same mix of activities as being appropriate for CPD and some other professional groups do not include the less formal self-directed methods which the CIPD allows.

The CIPD emphasises the fact that what is important is the outcome rather than the quantity of the input. The Institute promotes the key principles of CPD which it says are:

- Professional development is a continuous process that applies throughout a practitioner's life.
- Individuals are responsible for controlling and managing their own development.
- Individuals should decide for themselves their learning needs and how to fulfil them.
- Learning targets should be clearly articulated and should reflect the needs of employers and clients as well as the practitioner's individual goals.
- Learning is most effective when it is acknowledged as an integral part of all work activity rather than an additional burden (CIPD 2000).

This list provides for both formal and informal learning opportunities. Evidence of continuing professional development is required for changes in grade of CIPD membership. The CIPD suggests that all its members keep a personal record of their professional development, and CIPD branch meetings and national conferences provide the participants with forms to complete a record of what they have learnt on each occasion.

The CIPD suggests that individuals should develop their own personal development plan and also that they keep a record of what they have achieved. The personal development plan should be a record of what the individual thinks they want to be doing, or where they want to be, by the end of a specified period. Megginson and Whittaker (2004) say there are four stages to the CPD cycle. These are:

1 Self-assess.
2 Plan and prioritise.
3 Do.
4 Review.

This basically provides a framework which is very similar to the training cycle but involves the individual doing this for themselves. They analyse their own skills and knowledge then decide what they want to achieve and where they want to be in the future. They can then identify gaps which could be filled by additional learning and development and then plan, prioritise and undertake the learning and development in order to get to where they want to be. This cycle provides a structure for individuals to plan their own learning and development in order to achieve their own ends. Like the training cycle, it then allows for a review and for the individual to set themselves new targets to work towards to meet their goals. The development plan could be recorded in various ways but is likely to include a statement of what they need to learn, how they will go about learning this and the resources they will need. Target dates and performance criteria may be additional features. This is basically intended to get the individual thinking about and taking charge of their own development and their career.

Records of learning are also needed if the CPD record is going to be used for purposes such as upgrading membership. In order to upgrade membership the

CIPD requires a record of CPD activities for one year and an action plan for a further year, but other professional bodies have different requirements.

The CIPD suggests that individuals should devote between 5 and 30 days to their own development per year.

Conclusion

In this chapter we have provided an introduction to learning and development and what this means today. We have focused on the training needs of new employees and also discussed techniques of training on a one-to-one basis which you will probably find some opportunities to apply, whatever environment you work in. We then examined some of the recent changes affecting learning and development today. This is a constantly changing area where many new developments and Government-led initiatives are occurring, and we have outlined some of these. If you want to explore these areas further then newspaper or journal articles and Internet sites will provide you with the most up-to-date information. Learning and development is a very important subject for human resource managers today, as it is vital if we are to be competitive with other nations that we find ways to help people and organisations to work at their optimum levels. Learning and development activities also play an important role in multinational organisations in helping individuals to understand differing cultures and traditions. Further useful materials are listed at the end of this chapter as suggestions for you to use if you want to examine particular areas in more detail.

REVIEW QUESTIONS

You will find brief answers to these review questions on page 491.

1 Find out the current national targets for training and education and establish the extent to which they are likely to be met.

2 Use the Internet, Government publications or your local Learning Skills Council to find out more about one of the following topics: Investors in People, apprenticeships, New Deal. Using this information, describe how you would persuade a sceptical line manager of the benefits to be gained from introducing the initiative into an organisation of your choice.

3 Interview a manager about his or her organisation's strategic plans and objectives and try to assess the extent to which learning and development in that organisation contributes to the achievement of those strategic plans.

4 Many organisations do not provide an adequate induction programme for new employees. Comment critically on the benefits to be gained from implementing a good induction programme, and outline what should be contained in that programme.

5 Evaluate the relative effectiveness of on-the-job training and off-the-job training.

SELF-CHECK QUESTIONS

Answer the following multiple-choice questions. The correct responses are given on page 491 for you to check your understanding of this chapter.

1 Does the definition we have quoted from Rosemary Harrison define human resource development in the following way? YES or NO

Human resource development should be separate from the organisation's overall human resource strategy and as such there should be skilful provision and organisation of learning experiences in the workplace in order that performance of individuals can be improved.

2 Should employees themselves be involved in determining the context of human resource development? YES or NO

3 When there are very few new recruits to an organisation, should induction be left for several months until there are sufficient to form a group? YES or NO

4 Do the initials ENTO stand for Employing National Training Officers? YES or NO

5 Does NVQ award qualifications? YES or NO

6 Is an NVQ a statement of competence clearly related to work, intended to facilitate entry or progression into further education or training? YES or NO

7 Are mentors always training managers? YES or NO

8 Does CPD stand for continuing personal development? YES or NO

WHAT NEXT?

Learning and development is a topic that is constantly changing as every Government seems to frequently introduce new initiatives. It is therefore very useful to regularly review developments on the Department for Education and Skills site and particularly to examine the government's strategy for the future of learning and development.

www.dfes.gov.uk

Another useful organisation is the Learning Skills Development Agency. This focuses on research and development in learning and development for those aged over 16. Examine its new research at:

www.lsda.org.uk

References

Advisory Conciliation and Arbitration Service (2003) *The Code of Practice on Time Off for Union Duties and Activities*, ACAS (**www.acas.org.uk**; accessed 31.08.04)

Chartered Institute of Personnel and Development (2000) *Continuing Professional Development*, CD-ROM Pack

Chartered Institute of Personnel and Development (2003) *The Change Agenda: Focus on the Learner*, CIPD (**www.cipd.co.uk**; accessed 31.0.04)

Chartered Institute of Personnel and Development (2004) *The Change Agenda: Trade Union Learning Representatives*, CIPD (**www.cipd.co.uk**; accessed 31.0.04)

Chartered Institute of Personnel and Development (2005) *Fact Sheet: Investors in People.* CIPD (**www.cipd.co.uk**; accessed 5.2.2005)

Cowe, R. (1998) Code breaks the ethics ploys, *The Guardian*, 13 June, 30

Cunningham, I. (2004) How to get managers' support for learning, *Members' Resource: Topics for Trainers*, CIPD (**www.cipd.co.uk**; accessed 19.11.04)

Davidson, S. (2002) How to choose the right coach, *People Management*, Vol. 8, No. 10, 54–55

Department for Education and Skills (2004) *How are NVQs Achieved?* DfES (**www.dfes.gov.uk**; accessed 31.08.04)

Employment National Training Organisation (2004) *Mission Statement*, ENTO (**www.ento.co.uk**; accessed 31.08.04)

Harrison, R. (2000) *Employee Development*, 2nd edition, CIPD

Jones, A. M. and C. Hendry (1992) *The Learning Organisation: A Review of Literature and Practice*, HRD Partnership

Learning and Skills Council (2004) *Annual Report and Accounts 2002–3*, LSC (**www.lsc.gov.uk**; accessed 31.08.04)

Megginson, D. and V. Whittaker (2004) *Continuing Professional Development*, CIPD

Pedler, M., J. Burgoyne and T. Boydell (1988) *The Learning Company Project*, Training Agency

Qualifications and Curriculum Authority (2004) *Codes and Criteria*, QCA (**www.qca.org.uk**; accessed 31.08.04)

Reid, M., H. Barrington and M. Brown (2004) *Human Resource Development*, 7th edition, CIPD

Reynolds. J. (general editor), L. Caley and R. Mason (2002) *How do People Learn? Research Report*, CIPD

Further study

Books

Advisory, Conciliation and Arbitration Service (2003) *Recruitment and Induction*, ACAS. (A very useful guide to this subject.)

Fowler, A. (1999) *Induction*, CIPD. (Extremely useful on the subject of induction training.)

Harrison, R. (2002) *Learning and Development*, CIPD. (An excellent textbook for those who wish to study the subject of employee development in more depth.)

IDS Study 649 (1998) *Employee Development Initiatives*, Income Data Services, June. (This examines company-sponsored employee development schemes, open learning and provision for lifelong learning.)

IDS Study 679 (1999) *Training Strategies*, Income Data Services, November. (This study examines the way in which six organisations use training as a vital feature of business success.)

Ollin, R. and J. Tucker (2004) *The NVQ Assessor and Verifier Handbook,* Kogan Page. (A clear guide to assessment processes for those who want to be involved in the assessment of NVQs.)

Parsloe, E. (1999) *The Manager as a Coach or Mentor*, Training Extras Series, CIPD. (Another book in the CIPD Training Extras series, designed to cover specific management skills. In this book the similarities and differences between coaching and mentoring are explored by the author, who uses a lively, easy-to-read style.)

Reid, M., H. Barrington and H. Brown (2004) *Human Resource Development,* CIPD. (Another excellent textbook for those wishing to explore more fully the whole subject of worker development.)

Articles

We have covered a wide range of issues relating to training and development in this chapter, and there are innumerable articles published on these topics. We include a selection of articles that you may find useful if you want to start to discover more about a particular aspect of training and development.

Beardwell, I. (1998) On the record, *People Management*, Vol. 4, No. 8, 16 April, 43–46. (An account by three senior personnel practitioners of their learning experiences and the completion of their CPD record.)

Boyatzis, R. A. Howard, B. Aspisarda and S. Taylor (2004) Target practice, *People Management*, Vol. 10, No. 5, 26–32. (This describes some methods of executive coaching which involve focusing on positive goals.)

Carrington, L. (2004) Mentors make their marks, *Training Magazine*, March, 25. (This examines a formal mentoring programme at Marks & Spencer which is driven by the business.)

Chartered Institute of Personnel and Development (2004) Learning and training: a summary, *Research*, CIPD (**www.cipd.co.uk/research**; accessed 2.9.04). (A useful summary of recent research conducted by the CIPD in the area of learning and development.)

Chartered Institute of Personnel and Development (2004) Training: a short history, *Factsheet*, CIPD (**www.cipd.co.uk**; accessed 2.9.04). (This provides a useful summary of the history of training and in particular of Government interventions in national vocational education and training.)

Fowler, A. (1990) How to plan an induction programme, *Personnel Management Plus*, September, 20–21.

Foxwell, S. and R. Johnson (2000) A welcome departure, *People Management*, Vol. 6, No. 8, 13 April. (An article about the use of CPD to develop training staff at Cathay Pacific.)

Gill, V. (2003) National Skills Strategy: developing the National Skills Strategy and delivery plan, *CIPD Response to the DfES Proposed Strategy May 2003*, CIPD (**www.cipd.co.uk/about/_natskills.htm?IsSrchRes**; accessed 2.9.04). (Comments from the CIPD on the Government's plans for improving levels of skills nationally.)

Greene, M. and A. Gibbons (1991) Learning logs for self-development, *Training and Development*, February, 30–32.

Honey, P. (1991) The learning organisation simplified, *Training and Development*, July, 30–33.

Lee, G. and L. Pick (2004) How to buy coaching, *People Management*, Vol. 10, No. 5, 50. (A description of a process that helps anyone responsible for buying coaching for an organisation to meet not only the organisation's needs but those of the individuals too.)

Lees, J. (2004) How to be your own career coach, *People Management*, Vol. 10, No. 9, 42. (An outline of ways to assess one's own strategies for career development that suit the twenty-first century.)

Pickard, J. (1998) A slice of the action, *People Management*, Vol. 4, No. 40, 14 May, 36–43. (A detailed account of the role of the new NTOs.)

Pickard, J. (1998) New training bodies focus on skill gaps, *People Management*, Vol. 4, No. 40, 14 May, 15. (A brief analysis of the role of the new NTOs.)

Rana, E. (2000) IiP revamp aims to cut back on bureaucracy, *People Management*, Vol. 6, No. 8, 13 April. (A brief description of the changes in IiP standards.)

Sparrow, S. (1997) The right chemistry, *Training: The Personnel Today Magazine for Training Professionals*, May, 12–13. (An interesting account of BP Chemicals' experiences of NVQs and of the need to develop similar training schemes for older workers.)

Spurling, M. and E. Tolley (2000) How to make training strategic, *People Management*, Vol. 6, No. 8, 13 April.

Welch, J. (1998) National firms raise team spirit to offset local bias, *People Management*, Vol. 4, No. 8, 16 April, 14–15. (A description, from the perspective of several large employers, of experiences of the Government's New Deal.)

Internet

Apprenticeships (England and Wales)	www.realworkrealpay.info
Apprenticeships (Scotland)	www.scottish-enterprise.com/modernapprenticeships
Chartered Institute of Personnel and Development	www.cipd.co.uk
Department for Education and Skills	www.dfes.gov.uk
The Employment National Training Organisation	www.empnto.co.uk
The Information Network on Education in Europe	www.eurydice.org
Investors in People UK	www.iipuk.co.uk
Learn Direct	www.learndirect.co.uk
Learn Direct Scotland	www.learndirectscotland.com
The Learning and Skills Council	www.lsc.gov.uk
The National Academic Recognition Information Centre for the UK	www.naric.org.uk
New Deal	www.newdeal.gov.uk
Qualifications and Curriculum Authority	www.qca.org.uk
21st century skills: realising our potential (White Paper)	www.dfes.gov.uk/skillsstrategy

CHAPTER

CHAPTER 9

Performance appraisal and performance management

OBJECTIVES

By the end of this chapter you will be able to:

- state what is meant by the terms 'performance management' and 'performance appraisal'
- explain the differences between these terms
- give examples of techniques used in the management of performance at work
- design a simple performance appraisal system.

It is always important for managers and supervisors to get the best performance from their workforce in terms of levels of production and quality of output. They are concerned to motivate and encourage their employees to work effectively in pursuit of the strategic objectives of the organisation, and one way of trying to achieve this involves managers in designing systems to give employees feedback about their performance. We have discussed the importance of feedback in Chapter 7, and in this chapter we shall be looking at a specific way of giving feedback, called 'performance appraisal'.

Although, as we have said, it is important to motivate employees, this is often difficult to achieve, and if the organisation or manager handles the complex process of performance appraisal in an inappropriate way, then instead of feeling motivated, the employee may end up feeling totally demotivated by the experience. We aim to show in this chapter how to avoid the main pitfalls associated with the introduction of performance appraisal, so that the organisation and manager get it right.

We shall examine what is meant by 'performance management', a relatively new term for a sphere of management activity that began to take shape in the 1980s and steadily increased in popularity during the 1990s. It is widely held to have grown out of performance appraisal, and also to have absorbed some of the newer techniques used in performance appraisal such as emphasis on setting objective standards of performance and competence-based appraisals. Like performance appraisal, performance management is concerned to get the best performance from the individual, but goes further in that it also aims to get the best performance from the team and from the organisation as a whole. While performance appraisal will

263

form part of the performance management approach there is more to it than this, and each of the topics covered in this book also makes a contribution towards performance management. Simply initiating a new performance appraisal scheme or introducing a new form of performance management will not in itself bring about the desired motivation of workers. These schemes need to be part of a wider process that is undertaken within the organisation. In Chapter 1 we referred to the ACAS (2004) model and said that this gave an outline of what ACAS feels are the necessary steps to turn an organisation into an effective workplace. We have advocated throughout this book the need for policies and procedures so that everyone knows and shares a common understanding of what is supposed to be done. ACAS (2004) says that this is a good start, but that the way things are done is also important. This is an approach we also emphasise throughout this book. The way organisations manage performance can impact on most of the areas listed in the ACAS (2004) model and consequently can impact on workplace effectiveness.

In Table 1.2 in Chapter 1 we showed links between most aspects of the ACAS model and performance appraisal and performance management. We did not make a strong link between performance and a safe and healthy place to work, but this is something that does need to be in place if all the other things are going to happen. As indicated in Maslow's hierarchy of needs, workers are not likely to be motivated about their work if basic requirements relating to health and safety are not in place. Health and safety issues could in those circumstances form part of the performance appraisal discussion.

In Table 1.2 we did show a link between performance management and appraisal and the formal procedures for dealing with disciplinary matters, grievances and disputes. Although it is true that disciplinary and grievance issues should be dealt with separately and not as part of the appraisal procedure, performance management is about trying to get improvements in performance, so things like attendance monitoring or disciplinary procedures could be part of a performance management system.

In Chapter 1 we also referred to the research carried out by Professor John Purcell and his team at the School of Management at the University of Bath (Purcell *et al.* 2003). Their people and performance model also showed the interrelationship of different HR policies. However, while traditional HR policies and procedures were important in this, the other area that they said really made a difference in organisations was 'the way people work together to be productive and flexible enough to meet new challenges'. They found in the organisations they studied that the organisation first had to have strong values and an inclusive culture and, second, have sufficient line managers to be able to bring the HR policies and practices to life. Both elements fit well with the view of performance management shown in the following definition.

> Performance management is a process for sharing an understanding about what needs to be achieved and then managing and developing people in a way that enables such shared objectives to be achieved.

Purcell and his team found that in the organisations that were most successful at managing performance, everyone did share common values. There was generally what the researchers called 'a big idea' that was meaningful to everyone in the organisation (Purcell *et al.* 2003). This could be about the importance of customers to the organisation or the pursuit of quality, but in all cases it was an idea that everyone could relate to. Whatever it was, they all shared the idea and then managed the performance of people accordingly.

The other important strand in Purcell's effective performance model was the line managers. We shall examine some of the issues and suggestions for involving line managers in performance management and performance appraisal later in the chapter.

Performance appraisal is often one of the techniques used to encourage, motivate and help employees improve their performance. This chapter will examine first what is meant by performance appraisal and the development of different systems of performance appraisal before going on to examine the topic of performance management itself.

Definitions

Before going any further it would be useful to define exactly what we mean by the terms 'performance appraisal' and 'performance management'.

Performance appraisal

We have already said that performance appraisal is one way of giving employees feedback about their performance at work. According to ACAS 2003:

> Appraisals regularly record an assessment of an employee's performance, potential and development needs. The appraisal is an opportunity to take an overall view of work content, loads and volume, to look back on what has been achieved during the reporting period and agree objectives for the next.

This definition clearly shows that the employee does get feedback about his or her past performance, but indicates that in performance appraisal there is the opportunity to assess or judge various aspects of an employee's work performance by looking back at how they have performed in the past and then by looking forward to agree future objectives or workload.

Fletcher and Williams (1985) have gone further than this in their definition of appraisal, and have said that the assessment of people is not the only thing that we do when we appraise a person's work performance. They feel that there are in fact two conflicting roles involved in appraisal – those of judge and helper.

We shall consider each of these facets of appraisal in turn. Firstly, we all act as judges when we make informal judgements about the way people talk, what they wear and how they behave. These informal judgements may be objective or subjective and we may not even be aware that we are making them. They may not have much effect on people in everyday life, as we don't normally have any right to try to change these things in others, and we don't usually have any power to influence the way people behave. If we start to judge people in a work situation in this informal way with regard, for example, to the way they dress, we are likely to be accused of being too subjective and we might, quite rightly, be accused of treating people unfairly according to our own whims and prejudices. This sort of appraisal is not likely to encourage people to feel motivated about work. In this sense the term 'appraisal' means judging the worth, qualities or value of something, and in a work situation especially it is important that any judgements are fair and are based on objective job-related criteria.

Secondly, the term 'appraisal' is also used in another way, as Fletcher and Williams (1985) have indicated. When we appraise people in the work situation, we not only judge them but we usually also try to help them to improve aspects of their performance. We may suggest alternative ways of behaving, or suggest training courses or provide developmental opportunities in order to help employees improve their performance and assess their own developmental needs.

Performance appraisal is therefore about giving feedback to the employee, but also involves the appraiser in being both judge and helper to an individual employee. The performance appraisal interview represents the organisation's provision of a formal opportunity in which to give feedback and be both judge and helper to that employee.

As we said earlier in the chapter, performance appraisal can help an organisation become the type of organisation advocated in the ACAS (2004) model, but this does need to be part of a wider process undertaken within the organisation.

Performance management

Armstrong and Baron (1998) define performance management as:

> a process which contributes to the effective management of individuals and teams in order to achieve high levels of organisational performance. As such, it establishes shared understanding about what is to be achieved and an approach to leading and developing people which will ensure it is achieved.

They further emphasise the fact that it is:

> a strategy which relates to every activity of the organisation set in the context of its human resource policies, culture, style and communication systems. The nature of the strategy depends on the organisational context and can vary from organisation to organisation.

With these definitions it is easy to see why we earlier said that performance appraisal and performance management link clearly with all areas of the ACAS (2004) model. As we demonstrated, performance appraisal ties in with some of the areas, but performance management goes even further and helps to integrate all aspects of the HR systems together.

In earlier editions of this textbook we used a definition of performance management taken from Michael Armstrong (1994). At that time Armstrong defined performance management as 'a process which is designed to improve organisational, team and individual performance and which is owned and driven by line managers.' Ten years after this definition we can see that performance management is still about involving the individuals, teams and the whole organisation to achieve improved performance in line with the organisation's strategic objectives. However, in recent definitions of performance management there is no mention of the process being owned and driven by line managers, and this was originally supposed to be a key feature which differentiated this process from performance appraisal. It is certainly true that line managers have taken increased responsibility for many areas in relation to managing their staff, but it is disappointing to note that in some organisations they still suffer from some of the familiar problems associated with performance appraisal, and do not always see the necessity for performance management. We will discuss the issue of getting increased commitment from the line managers later in the chapter.

Performance management is a much broader concept than performance appraisal, which as we have seen has traditionally been concerned with judging the individual's performance, giving the individual feedback about this performance and helping that individual to improve by systematically trying to motivate them to work harder or more effectively. Performance management is concerned with improving not only the performance of the individual, but also the performance of the team and the organisation. Some traditional appraisal schemes have been accused of being run for the benefit of personnel managers or top managers, with many other people in the organisation not really understanding or appreciating what the performance appraisal scheme was trying to achieve. This may be true of some poorly designed schemes, but is a rather harsh judgement on many excellent appraisal schemes and personnel managers and on the contribution they make to their organisations' effectiveness. In order that the same criticisms cannot be made of performance management, there is an increased emphasis on the role of the line manager and on the involvement of teams and individuals. Performance management forms part of the human resource management approach to managing people, and performance is basically a shared process between managers, individuals and teams in which objectives are agreed and jointly reviewed and which aims to integrate corporate, individual and team objectives. It is also strategic in nature and is about broad issues and establishing long-term goals.

According to Armstrong and Baron (1998) performance management should be a device or tool to ensure that managers do manage effectively. The managers should ensure that the people or teams they manage:

- know and understand what is expected of them
- have the skills necessary to deliver on these expectations
- are supported by the organisation to develop the capacity to meet these expectations
- are given feedback on performance
- have the opportunity to discuss and contribute to individual and team aims and objectives (Armstrong and Baron 1998).

Some of these things can be achieved by using the techniques of performance appraisal or by performance development reviews.

Since performance appraisal schemes form part of the techniques used in a performance management system, and are still perhaps more widely known, we shall start by examining performance appraisal systems and discussing other types of performance review before going on to consider performance management in detail. Learning and development is also a key tool that many organisations use to improve organisational performance. We discussed this in detail in Chapters 7 and 8 so in this chapter we shall include it where appropriate and show how it contributes to performance management.

Performance appraisal schemes

Performance appraisal schemes may be used for a wide range of reasons, some of which may conflict with each other, but the main reasons are likely to include the following:

- to improve current performance
- to provide feedback
- to increase motivation
- to identify potential
- to identify training needs
- to aid career development
- to award salary increases
- to solve job problems
- to let individuals know what is expected of them
- to clarify job objectives
- to provide information about the effectiveness of the selection process
- to aid in career planning and development
- to provide information for human resource planning
- to provide for rewards
- to assess competencies.

Randell *et al.* (1984) suggest that for most employers there are three main uses for appraisal reviews *performance, potential* and *reward*. All the reasons listed above fall into one of these three categories, and we shall examine each category in turn.

Performance review

Managers seek to review an individual's past performance and assess strengths, level of effort and areas where further development would be useful. Here the focus is on what the employee has actually done in the past, and an attempt is made to build on the employee's strengths and make improvements in other areas so that the employee can perform more effectively in the future. Many managers claim that they give this sort of feedback all the time informally, and if they do this well there may indeed be no need for a formal appraisal scheme. However, it is unlikely that all managers in a particular organisation will appraise their staff constantly and effectively. It is more likely that without a formal system and proper training, many managers will be appraising infrequently or not at all, using subjective criteria or not appraising fairly, so a formal appraisal system is necessary. Improvements in performance are most likely to occur if most of the factors in the ACAS (2004) model are in place in the organisation. If an individual's performance is to improve then they must know what is expected of them and how this fits with the organisation's plans. This relates to the first of the points in the ACAS (2004) model, that there should be within the organisation 'ambitions goals and plans that the employees know about and understand'. The performance appraisal interview provides a perfect opportunity to link the performance of the individual to the performance required by the organisation and show how this contributes to the organisation's goals and objectives.

If the performance of the individual is to improve then they also need to be able to discuss both successes and failures. In relation to the ACAS (2004) model, there also has to be a feeling that the 'managers will listen to the employee's point of view so everyone is involved in the decision making' and that 'people feel valued so they can talk confidently about their work and learn from both successes and failures.' As we said in Chapter 8, people sometimes have to learn from mistakes and they learn better in an environment in which there is not a blame culture, rather than in one where they are too afraid to admit to mistakes or learn from them.

People should also feel 'that everyone will be treated fairly and valued for their differences' and that work is organised so 'that it encourages initiative, innovation and people to work together'. Once again, performance appraisal can do a great deal to reinforce values of fairness, and discussions within a performance appraisal interview can do a great deal to foster a positive 'can do' culture.

Everyone is different and differences should be valued so that managers should be able to 'discuss ways of working that will suit personal needs and the needs of business' within a performance appraisal interview.

So far we have linked the idea of performance to the first six points in the ACAS (2004) model described earlier.

Objectives or competencies

There are basically two different approaches that can be used by employers when assessing performance. The first is concerned with outputs from the employee: it uses objectives and sets targets for the employee to work towards. The alternative approach is to examine the input that the employee makes to the organisation and determine the level of competence that the employee must achieve in their job.

In organisations where job descriptions based on competence are used, and where staff are used to working towards the achievement of NVQs, the second approach is likely to be favoured. Whichever approach is used there will still be a need to develop a method of assessing the employee's performance using some form of rating scale.

If the first of these approaches is to work well, then clearly the organisation needs to have 'ambitious goals and plans that employees know about and understand' – point 1 of the ACAS (2004) model.

If the focus is on the employee's level of competence, then 'people will need to feel valued so they can talk confidently about their work and learn from both successes and failures' – point 3 in the ACAS (2004) model.

Potential and development review

From an examination of past performance many employers wish to identify as part of their human resource planning process, or for individual career development, individuals with potential to take up new or more responsible or challenging positions within the organisation. The concern here is not just with what the person has done in the past, but with trying to predict the level and type of work that employees will be capable of doing in the future, and then helping them to reach their full potential, so that the organisation can also benefit fully from their talents and abilities.

In order for this approach to appraisal to work, an organisation would have to create 'a culture where everyone is encouraged to learn new skills so they can look forward to further employment either in the business or elsewhere' and where there is a 'good working relationship between management and employee representatives that in turn helps build trust throughout the business'. Points 9 and 10 in the ACAS (2004) model are likely to be particularly important if the focus of the appraisal scheme is on future potential. One might expect that the organisation would be working towards becoming a learning organisation, as discussed in Chapter 8, and that it would use lots of both formal and informal approaches to encourage learning. Working with trade union-appointed learning representatives to encourage those who traditionally had not participated in the learning process would also be important.

Reward review

This use of performance appraisal basically entails trying to reward employees for their past work, while hoping that the incentive of a reward will encourage other employees also to strive to work harder in the future. In recent years many organisations have sought to motivate their employees by linking rewards, using a system like performance-related pay, to excellent performance at work.

If this is one of the main purposes of the appraisal scheme then the organisation must, as ACAS (2004) says, create 'a pay and reward system that is clear, fair and consistent'. There is really no hope of this type of appraisal system working if people feel others are rewarded because of unfair bias from managers or if they do not understand what they need to do to be rewarded. We will return to the subject of reward, and discuss in more detail ways to create fair reward systems, in Chapter 10.

Many organisations try to get too much from one appraisal scheme, and try to use one scheme to fulfil all three purposes. This is unlikely to work, and usually results in the scheme falling into disrepute.

Problems

A number of problems may prevent the appraisal schemes from being as effective as they should be as not all organisations follow the ACAS model and some try to create an appraisal scheme that does not fit with the normal culture of their organisation. These problems include:

- the organisation not being clear about the purpose of the appraisal system and consequently trying to use the appraisal scheme to fulfil too many different purposes
- links with pay preventing open discussion of problems or of areas where improvement could be made
- keeping information secret from the employee
- the appraiser attacking the appraisee's character
- being too subjective in judgements
- using appraisal as part of the disciplinary process.

Did you know?

It is often suggested that as many as two-thirds of all appraisal schemes are abandoned or altered substantially within two years of their creation. This, to a very large extent, is due to organisations not being aware of, or not paying enough attention to, a range of problems that can be avoided with sufficient forethought and planning, and to trying to make one scheme serve too many incompatible purposes.

Lack of clarity

We have already shown that most appraisal schemes fall into one of three categories, i.e. they are concerned with performance, potential or reward. An organisation should not attempt to use one appraisal scheme to fulfil all three categories. The particular objectives of an appraisal scheme should be clarified before the scheme is designed in detail, and should have been discussed with employees and other workers, trade unions and managers in order to take account of their views and to gain their commitment to the new appraisal scheme. Everyone should then be clear what the particular scheme is trying to achieve. Any scheme, however good the design, is unlikely to succeed if the managers and the workforce are suspicious of the reasons for its introduction and are opposed to making it work effectively.

While there are good reasons why employers should seek to appraise performance potential or give rewards to good employees, problems can also occur if employers try to achieve too much from their performance appraisal scheme. It is difficult, if not impossible, to devise a scheme that will appraise successfully all three areas, and there is a grave danger that the performance appraisal scheme will be rejected if it fails to live up to all that is claimed for it. This can easily happen if the scheme is poorly designed or if the managers show a reluctance to impart critical assessments, or if people are not trained properly in the appraisal process.

Linking appraisal with pay

In particular, it is difficult to imagine that a person being appraised is likely to admit to any developmental need, or be willing to accept any help in their performance, if their salary increase depends on a good appraisal. It is therefore recommended that employers should in general try to keep reward considerations separate from the other areas of appraisal.

In spite of this advice and research evidence which suggests that performance-related pay (PRP) does not always motivate everyone in a workforce, many employers think that the offer of an incentive or reward is the only way to motivate employees to work harder, and this is often their main reason for introducing performance appraisal. The motivational aspects of pay will be discussed in more detail in Chapter 10, but the important point is that great care needs to be taken if appraisal systems are linked to pay. It will be especially important to ensure that the criteria being appraised are objective and free of unfair bias, and that there are genuine opportunities for all employees to be rewarded for their efforts. In many organisations financial constraints mean that the number of people who are awarded PRP is severely restricted and there is a serious danger that if the vast majority of the workforce do not feel they have any opportunity to receive a reward, they may feel much more demotivated than they did before the appraisal scheme was introduced. Only the select few who receive the reward will then feel positive about the experience and about the organisation, and even they will not necessarily be motivated to work harder.

It is quite common for appraisal linked to pay to be part of the performance management process, but in that case there will be other regular development reviews or performance reviews which provide the opportunities for discussion of both good and bad performance. These reviews are often kept separate from the review at which reward is discussed. Consequently they do not provide such an immediate deterrent to discussion of any weaknesses or aspects of poorer performance since their focus should be on past and future performance and the development needs of the individual. However, although this approach does weaken any direct link between pay and performance and learning, it would be foolish to think that it breaks the connection entirely. Employees may still feel reluctant to fully discuss their development needs unless they feel confident it will not affect their pay, even if that review is held at a different time of year. On the other hand, they may take the view that discussion of areas of their performance in which they have done less well are worthwhile if this means that they gain access to more learning and development opportunities which may ultimately result in them getting more pay or being more employable.

Keeping information secret from the employee

Appraisal involves, as we have already said, being both a judge and helper for an individual employee. In order that we can help the individual it is also important that they know about the judgements that have been made about them and that they receive feedback about these. Therefore if people are to be helped to develop, there must be discussion about problem areas, and any judgements made about employees should not be kept secret from them. Obviously the appraisal interview and reports of it do need to be confidential from other employees, but not so confidential that they are a secret from the employee concerned.

Subjectivity or attacks on the appraisee's character

If the person doing the appraising feels insecure about his or her own performance, there could be a tendency to try to ensure that the employee being appraised doesn't become a threat to them by focusing solely on the aspects of the job that have not been handled well and failing to show recognition for jobs that have been done well. In some cases, subjective judgements may be made because there are no clear criteria on which to appraise the employee, and the appraiser may resort to attacking aspects of the person's character that the person cannot do anything about. In the past many appraisal schemes were based on assessing personality traits that were thought to be important to a particular job, but that in fact were very broad categories that could only be judged subjectively. These included personality traits such as enthusiasm, application, intelligence and resourcefulness.

Pause for thought 9.1

How would you feel if one of your tutors said that you lacked integrity or that your intelligence was inadequate?

We imagine that you would not feel very happy with comments about your lack of integrity or poor level of intelligence, and would want to know on what criteria these comments were based.

If appraisal schemes are to be credible to employees, great care must be taken that judgements made are objective and have some basis that can be discussed with the employee. Integrity is likely to mean slightly different things to different people, and judgement of a person's integrity is likely to be fairly subjective. Rather than focusing on subjective topics such as this or on aspects of an individual's personality which they cannot alter, it is better to examine aspects of the job that the person actually does, and make an objective judgement about the person's effectiveness at carrying out each aspect of the job or their success in meeting their objectives.

Appraisers should also concentrate on seeking to help to bring about an improvement in areas of the employee's work where the appraisee can do something to make an improvement. Criticising someone for not being intelligent enough is similar to criticising them for being too short. There is really not much that they can do about it, so it is pointless to judge them on it and impossible to help them to change.

Appraisal as part of the disciplinary process

We have already said that appraisal is partly about making judgements about an employee's performance, and that areas where performance is not as effective as it should be need to be discussed. However, this does not mean that disciplinary matters should be saved for several months to be dealt with at the appraisal interview. If a disciplinary offence occurs, then it should be dealt with immediately and not saved for discussion at the time of the appraisal interview. The appraisal interview should be about seeking to motivate employees, not an opportunity to discipline them although, as we shall show later, dealing with poor performance should be part of the performance management process.

◯ The manager in performance appraisal

Traditionally the people who are involved in the appraisal process are most likely to be the person who is to be appraised and his or her immediate manager. This has the advantage that the managers or supervisors should know their subordinates and should also know about each subordinate's job and the way in which the subordinate carries out his or her duties. Managers and their subordinates will see each other every day but may be too busy to discuss performance. The performance appraisal interview provides the time for the individual and the manager to sit down together to discuss the individual's progress. This should enable the manager to feel that he or she is helping the career of one of the staff, and prove to be a motivating experience for the employee, who has the undivided attention of the manager listening to his or her views and focusing attention on his or her development.

There can, however, be some disadvantages in having the employee's immediate manager carry out the appraisal, especially if there is a conflict of personalities or if the manager perceives the employee to be a threat and is therefore unwilling to look for positive aspects of the employee's performance. If the appraisal scheme allows a high degree of subjectivity in comments made by the manager, then there is a danger that more will be learnt about the manager's attitudes to work and managing employees than about the employee's performance. Training in performance appraisal techniques is obviously extremely important here. We shall return to this subject later in this chapter.

ACTIVITY 9.1

In spite of these problems, the appraisee's immediate supervisor or manager is usually the person most involved in the appraisal process, although in some organisations other people may be involved. Using Table 9.1, write a list of people who you think might be involved in the appraisal process. For each of them, list the advantages and the disadvantages of their involvement.

Table 9.1	People involved in the appraisal process	
People who may be involved in the appraisal process	Advantages	Disadvantages

Discussion of Activity 9.1

Table 9.2 **People involved in the appraisal process**

People who may be involved in the appraisal process	Advantages	Disadvantages
The appraisee's manager's immediate manager	Often used as well as the appraisee's manager to check that the manager is being fair. When used as sole appraiser there is the possible advantage of being more objective about employee's work and of not being directly threatened by their success.	Not likely to know the appraisee well and likely to have to obtain information about the individual's performance from their immediate manager.
The personnel manager	Often used as a check that the manager is being fair and as a monitor of consistency of approach throughout the organisation. Personnel managers are sometimes used as sole appraiser for reasons of fairness and consistency and because they are not perceived to be a threat to the manager.	Not likely to know the appraisee well and likely to have to obtain information about the individual's performance from their immediate manager.
Colleagues	This can be especially useful where teamwork is important or in an organisation with a matrix organisation structure where the individual may report to more than one manager. The main advantage is that colleagues are likely to have a clear idea of how effective the individual is at working with them and the views of several people are likely to provide a balanced perspective.	The colleagues concerned may not know about all aspects of the individual's job. They may be reluctant to express an honest opinion about a colleague, and may be influenced by whether they have a good or poor relationship with that person, or by jealousy or rivalry.
Subordinates	People who work for the individual who is being appraised will certainly have a different view of that individual's abilities and performance and can therefore provide valuable information about the person's performance.	They may be too frightened to express their real opinion, if they feel that their manager might hold this against them at some future date. The person being appraised may be reluctant to accept the views of his or her subordinates.
Self-appraisal	Often used as part of the appraisal process, as in many systems the appraisers and the appraisee complete forms independently of each other and then use them as the basis of discussion. The individual will have a more detailed knowledge of the standard of their own work performance than their manager. Since individuals should be encouraged to take a great deal of responsibility for their own development, this increased self-awareness will be useful.	Some people may find it difficult to analyse their own work performance and may have unrealistic views of how well they have actually done. They may not be willing to admit to weaknesses, although in many cases the opposite is true, and people are more critical of themselves than their manager would be.
360° appraisal (not actually a person, but gathers information from all the people mentioned so far)	This form of appraisal gathers information from all the above sources to gain an all-round view of the person's performance. This is extremely thorough and will provide information on different aspects of the individual's performance, so that it is possible to compile a total picture of the person's job performance.	It can be very time-consuming to collect information from so many people, and may not always be cost-effective. It is also subject to all the disadvantages listed above.

Table 9.2   **(contd)**

People who may be involved in the appraisal process	Advantages	Disadvantages
540° appraisal (not actually a person but gathers information from all the people mentioned so far, as in 360° appraisal, but also gathers and uses customers additional information from people outside the organisation, such as customers or clients)	Once again an extremely thorough way of gathering information as those outside the organisation, such as clients or customers, may be able to provide very valuable insights into how an individual is performing.	This can be difficult to organise as customers or clients may not wish to spend time participating in questionnaires and cannot be coerced into doing so. Many employers will also be hesitant to use this approach as they may not wish to give their clients or customers any cause to think that they, or any of their employees, might ever provide a less than perfect service or product.
Assessment centres (not actually a person, so you may not have included assessment centres in this list, but we include them as they form yet another important way of assessing performance)	Individuals undertake a battery of tests to measure: aspects of personality; verbal, numerical and reasoning skills; and ability to lead and work in a team. This provides an all-round view of the person's talents and abilities. Particularly useful when assessing future potential and in the appraisal of potential supervisors or managers.	Expensive and time-consuming to carry out for all employees.

Although, as we said earlier, line managers are the most frequent group to be involved in conducting appraisal interviews, they do not always relish this part of their job or see its importance. Terry Gillen (2004) says that managers see appraisal as a low priority for two reasons and that it is necessary to understand their viewpoint on this in order to be able to convince them of the relevance of appraisal to them and to their department. According to Gillen (2004) the first reason why it can be difficult to get managers to conduct performance appraisal interviews is because they prefer to spend their time doing things rather than managing things or managing and leading people. Gillen (2004) says that generally most managers went into their jobs, not to manage, but to do things, for example to build things, to teach things or to sell things. They did not specifically go into the job to manage either things or people and often consider that these parts of their job mean they spend less time on what they enjoy. They therefore tend to put off doing them because they do not see the immediate relevance to them or to their department of initiatives such as performance appraisal.

According to Gillen (2004) the second reason is because managers perceive some specific problems related to appraisal. These will vary from organisation to organisation but are likely to result in line managers saying or feeling some of the following:

1 I've got enough to do without also having to fill in forms for Personnel.
2 The appraisal process is 'divorced' from the realities of my 'business cycle'.
3 Appraisal is inherently unfair.
4 Appraisal is amazingly time-consuming.
5 Giving staff feedback on their performance during an appraisal interview is uncomfortable (Gillen 2004).

Some of these statements are undoubtedly true. As we said, it can be difficult to give staff feedback on their performance and sometimes managers struggle to remember their employee's key achievements, particularly those that occurred some months earlier. Appraisal can seem quite time-consuming and may appear to be organised to suit someone else's time schedule.

Some of the other statements are less easy to justify and may result from the line manager's false perception of the situation. If an organisation has established a performance appraisal scheme in the ways we will describe, then it should certainly not be perceived as 'inherently unfair' and managers who feel that the appraisal process is undertaken just to please the personnel or HR department have not had the process properly explained to them.

Whatever the reasons for these negative perceptions of performance appraisal, they do need to be overcome if the scheme is to be successful. Gillen (2004) suggests various ways to erase these misconceptions and to help line managers appreciate the benefits of appraisal. One useful idea he suggests is that line managers should be made aware of the three main elements to their job: doing things, managing things, and managing and leading people, and that they should be involved in a discussion about which of these they enjoy most. After a discussion in which he establishes that performance requirements in a job are generally getting harder and that people do not want to work even longer to achieve them, he then draws a parallel with lifting a heavy load using a lever and explains that this becomes easier if one uses a longer lever. He says that for managers, using performance appraisal and working on the managing and leading element of their job is the equivalent of using a longer lever. It is about working smarter and not harder.

Design of documentation

In most appraisal systems it is necessary to have some type of documentation to record what has been agreed. At its simplest this could just be blank sheets of paper for both the appraiser and appraisee, on which they both assess the performance of the appraisee. This provides a means for jotting down ideas and views on performance which can then be used as a basis for discussion at the time of the performance appraisal interview. The disadvantage of this system is that there may be little basis for agreement about the topics to be discussed.

In order to provide for a systematic and consistent approach to performance appraisal, many organisations design an appraisal form. In this case, the manager and the person being appraised both complete a form prior to the appraisal interview. They then exchange forms and at the interview use both the forms as a basis for discussion. This has the advantage of both parties having focused on similar topics and saves time at the interview, as both should have already done quite a bit of preparation for the interview. When designing such a form, there should be clear guidelines explaining what is meant by each section, and the points already discussed in the section on problems must be borne in mind. The criteria to be appraised should not be subjective and should be fair. They should relate to things that employees could improve, and there should be opportunities for the employee to see the appraiser's comments and a section in which to respond to those comments. There should also be a right of appeal. The guidelines should indicate what should then happen to the appraisal forms. Where will they be kept? Who will ensure that action is taken on key points?

The actual content of such a form will be influenced by the type of appraisal scheme adopted by the organisation. This will now be discussed.

Types of performance appraisal

Management by objectives (MBO)

We have already said that appraisal schemes are most likely to succeed if the criteria to be appraised can be assessed objectively rather than subjectively, and that the appraisal of aspects of a person's personality should be avoided. One way of achieving this is to set clear objectives for the employee to achieve before the next appraisal, and then to focus the discussion at the appraisal interview on the extent to which these objectives have been achieved. An appraisal interview also provides an opportunity to look forward, so the next stage would be to set and agree objectives for the next review period.

One way in which to achieve this would be to look first at the job description and then agree specific objectives for each of the main tasks. This has the additional advantage that the objectives can be linked very clearly to the organisation's strategic goals, so that the individual can see exactly what to do to help the organisation to meet its objectives. A sample form for this type of performance appraisal is shown in Figure 9.1.

In this example there is an opportunity to look at past objectives and consider the extent to which they have been achieved, and also a chance to look forward and agree future objectives. Here the appraisee has an opportunity to write comments, as do the manager and countersigning manager. This type of appraisal can also link with overall organisational objectives, and is often used as part of a performance management system, as we shall show later.

Rating scales

This is another form of performance appraisal scheme that seeks to encourage objectivity by focusing on aspects of the employee's job and then indicating by graded statements how successfully the employee has fulfilled each of the main duties listed in his or her job description. The statements would be linked to the job description, and the team of writers would provide a series of statements for each category of the job description, indicating levels of performance or level of competence required in that duty, ranging from excellent to poor. The appraiser would discuss the person's performance using these scales during the appraisal interview, and would then tick the statement that he or she and the appraisee agreed best summed up the appraisee's performance or which matched their level of competence.

Figure 9.1   **Sample form for performance appraisal using management by objectives**

NAME . . . .   JOB TITLE . . . .

DATE OF APPRAISAL . . . .   DEPARTMENT/SECTION . . . .

JOB DESCRIPTION (To be agreed with employee)

REVIEW PERIOD . . . .

    1. Objectives agreed for this last review period. (This should include special tasks, personal training and development.)

    2. To what extent have these objectives been achieved?

    3. Were there any other major achievements?

    4. Were there any obstacles which prevented achievement of agreed objectives?

    5. What steps need to be taken to overcome these obstacles?

    6. What training development and education were undertaken during the review period?

NEXT REVIEW PERIOD . . . .

    1. What specific objectives have been agreed for the next review period?

    2. What training development and education should be undertaken during the next review period?

    3. What follow-up action is needed?

COMMENTS OF APPRAISER

Signed . . . .(Appraiser)

COMMENTS OF APPRAISEE

Signed . . . .(Appraisee)

COMMENTS OF COUNTERSIGNING MANAGER

ACTIVITY 9.2

Do you remember the job description which we gave in Chapter 2? The main duties for this are listed in Figure 9.2. For each of these duties, write a series of statements to indicate the possible degrees of success of someone who is working in this job. It is intended that these statements will form the basic information with which the individual's performance in that job is compared by the appraiser. We have started this for you by suggesting some graded statements for the first row.

Figure 9.2   **Job rating (Activity 9.2)**

Name of job holder: _____

Job title: <u>Receptionist</u>

Date of appraisal: _____

Main duties	Appraiser's comments	A (Well ahead of standard performance)	B (More than satisfactory, slightly above job requirements)	C (Less than satisfactory, needs slight improvement)	D (Requires constant supervision)
Greet walk-in visitors and ascertain purpose of their visit. Handle or redirect queries as appropriate.		Always quick to greet visitors and ascertain purpose of visit, dealing with queries extremely rapidly and effectively so visitors are always highly satisfied.	Greets visitors, ascertains purpose of visit and deals effectively with queries.	Normally greets visitors promptly and ascertains purpose of their visit; sometimes slow to redirect queries.	Slow to notice walk-in visitors, does not always greet them promptly, and is not always able to deal with queries or redirect them to the appropriate place.
Answer phone queries as above.					
Answer all initial queries about receipt of payments using the on-line payment receipts system.					

Figure 9.2 (contd)

Main duties	Appraiser's comments	A (Well ahead of standard performance)	B (More than satisfactory, slightly above job requirements)	C (Less than satisfactory, needs slight improvement)	D (Requires constant supervision)
Open and sort incoming post by department. Organise delivery of post by assistant receptionist.					
Perform clerical tasks assigned by department in agreement with the Office Services Manager.					
Supervise assistant receptionists and delegate work as appropriate.					
Perform other duties as assigned by the Office Services Manager or other authorised manager.					

Comments of appraiser

Signature...(Appraiser)

Comments of appraisee

Signature...(Appraisee)

Comments of countersigning manager

Signature...(Manager)

Discussion of Activity 9.2

This gives a simple way of rating the employee's behaviour in the job that is clear and easy to use, as the appraiser simply ticks the box containing the comment that most nearly reflects the actual performance of the employee. It also means that there is a common standard which all appraisers would use when appraising a person doing that job. In this case, examples of four types of behaviour had to be provided for each aspect of the main duties listed in the job description. This was because many appraisers tend to rate employees as average just to avoid upsetting people or to avoid giving too much praise: by not allowing a middle category, they are encouraged to be more decisive. There may still be a tendency to go for the middle two boxes (and for many employees this will be highly appropriate), but appraisers must be encouraged by training to use the full range of categories if and when this is needed.

In this Activity you were the only person to choose the descriptions for the criteria to be rated, so there could still be some degree of subjectivity involved, as you may have described the performance of each duty in a different way to other people. It would be more usual to involve a team of people to provide the descriptors for each main duty and to get consensus about the descriptors to be used.

Behaviourally anchored rating scales (BARS)

If this appraisal system were to be introduced in a large organisation, it would not rely on just one person's ideas of a suitable range of categories. In the first section of the ratings exercise we have used the following terms as descriptors of the first of the major duties listed in the job description:

- Always quick to greet visitors and ascertain purpose of visit, dealing with queries extremely rapidly and effectively so visitors are always highly satisfied.
- Greets visitors, ascertains purpose of visit and deals effectively with queries.
- Normally greets visitors promptly and ascertains purpose of their visit; sometimes slow to redirect queries.
- Slow to notice walk-in visitors, does not always greet them promptly, and is not always able to deal with queries or redirect them to the appropriate place.

These were purely our own subjective choices, and we had not checked whether or not other people would describe this aspect of the job in the same way. You could find other descriptors that may be more effective than these. We may have chosen terms to describe each level of performance that are different from the way in which other people would describe the same task.

One way to try to get round the subjectivity of having just one person writing the descriptions of behaviour is to use a newer technique, known as behaviourally anchored rating scales. In this case a group of other raters would also be asked to suggest descriptions for a range of behaviour for each aspect of the main duties, so that a wide range of behavioural examples could be collected.

These descriptions are then collated and returned to the sample raters, but this time there is no indication of the scale point for which they were suggested. The sample raters are asked to indicate a scale point from A to D, where A represents excellence and D represents bad work, to which they think each descriptor most aptly relates. The descriptors that are consistently located at the same point of the scale are then used in the final version of the behaviourally anchored scale. This is intended to remove the subjectivity inherent in the simpler rating method and ensure that descriptions used are likely to mean the same thing to most people.

ACTIVITY 9.3

What do you see as the main advantages and disadvantages of this system of behaviourally anchored rating scales? Make a list.

Discussion of Activity 9.3

Compare your list of advantages and disadvantages with the following list.

Advantages

- Objective rating of each of the main duties listed in job description.
- Agreement over suitable descriptors for each category of behaviour.
- Easy to use.
- Useful if lots of people have the same job descriptions so that the amount of time involved in designing the system will be repaid.

Disadvantages

- Time-consuming, as it takes a long time to get agreement on descriptors for each job.
- Only takes account of existing job performance; does not allow for discussion of future potential.

Behavioural observation scales (BOS)

These form another way of rating performance in a job. These scales are also developed as a result of lengthy procedures, and indicate a number of dimensions of performance with behavioural examples for each. Job analysis is used to identify the key determinants of performance and the performance dimensions are once again related to the job description, but in this case the appraiser is asked to indicate a point on a scale by a numerical value.

An example of such a scale in relation to selected aspects of a lecturer's job is given below. The appraisers simply circle the number that they think relates most closely to the usual behaviour of the appraisee.

ACTIVITY 9.4

You can try this for yourself by selecting a lecturer you know well and assessing him or her on this scale. Circle the number that most closely relates to the lecturer's normal behaviour.

1 Provides clearly structured lecture that is easy to follow

| Almost never | 5 | 4 | 3 | 2 | 1 | Almost always |

2 Provides up-to-date and interesting material in lectures/tutorials

| Almost never | 5 | 4 | 3 | 2 | 1 | Almost always |

3 Explains to students exactly what is expected of them when they complete written work

| Almost never | 5 | 4 | 3 | 2 | 1 | Almost always |

4 Is willing to give advice and guidance

Almost never   5   4   3   2   1   Almost always

5 Gives detailed and helpful feedback concerning written work that students have completed

Almost never   5   4   3   2   1   Almost always

Discussion of Activity 9.4

We hope that you were fair in your assessment and were not influenced by personality or past grades given to you! In this case you were assessing the lecturer from the position of a student, and you are likely to have a very different view of his or her work performance to the lecturer's manager or the human resource manager. You may not, however, be able to assess all aspects of the lecturer's job such as his or her ability to carry out research, or an individual's administrative capabilities, but this exercise is similar to assessment by a person's subordinates which we mentioned earlier. It has the same type of limitations that we discussed then, but it gives you some idea of the way in which different points of view can be important and shows that if this were combined with appraisal from other perspectives, as in a system such as 360° or 540° appraisal, it could contribute to developing a full picture of a person's effectiveness and provide valuable feedback.

The appraisal interview

Interviews have already been discussed in some detail in Chapters 4 and 5, and the points made there with regard to selection interviews also apply to appraisal interviews. Preparation, privacy and confidentiality, good questioning technique, avoidance of bias, good records and attention to the style of interview will also be important in the appraisal interview.

Preparation

There is a need, as we explained in Chapter 4, for careful preparation before any interview and employees should be given adequate notice of the date of the appraisal interview to allow them time to prepare. In the appraisal interview this is also likely to mean that care needs to be taken with the layout of the room, so that the person being appraised will not be intimidated by a formal set-up with barriers such as a big desk, and so that he or she feels comfortable and at ease. There is also a need to avoid interruptions and to ensure that telephone messages are taken elsewhere and that there are no unnecessary distractions.

If the person has been appraised in the past, then the last appraisal record will need to be read to check what objectives, if any, were agreed for the current appraisal period. The individual's job description will also need to be checked and the training and development records examined to discover what training and development has occurred since the last interview. In some cases, if the person who is to be appraised works for several people, it may also be necessary to obtain information from other managers, or in the case of other types of performance appraisal, from subordinates or peers.

It is also useful for both parties in the appraisal to prepare for the meeting, and both the appraiser and appraisee need to have received training so that they know what to expect in order that they can both skilfully handle what is potentially a difficult interaction. A constructive approach used by many organisations is to give both the appraiser and appraisee a form to complete prior to the appraisal interview. In some organisations these are then exchanged, and this has the advantage of focusing the attention of appraiser and appraisee on common issues. In other organisations these forms are simply used as an aide-memoire for the individuals concerned, but if they are exchanged prior to the interview, they can help to clearly identify areas where there is broad agreement so that more time can be allowed to discuss other topics where there are differences of opinion.

Privacy and confidentiality

We have already indicated that the appraisal is an important way of giving feedback to the employee about his or her work performance. In the past some organisations did not allow the appraisee to see the records of their appraisal, but we feel that this misses a valuable opportunity for providing feedback from which the employee could learn. On the other hand, the appraisal form and interview have to be kept confidential from other people as there will probably be very personal information on the form, and no one who feels that half the department can hear every word of the conversation is likely to feel willing to discuss his or her performance openly.

Good questioning technique

The appraisal interview has, as we have already said, much in common with all other types of interviews. Once again the type of questions asked will be important. As this is an opportunity to provide feedback to the employee there will perhaps be slightly more opportunity for the interviewer to do more talking than in some other forms of interview, but this should be treated with caution. It is certainly not the time for the appraiser to do all the talking.

There should be an introductory phase where the interviewer tries to put the person being appraised at ease. It is generally better to follow this with a discussion of the employee's strong points and then try to get information, especially about any areas of perceived weakness, from the employee by asking open questions and teasing out the information. Areas of weakness need to be raised and discussed fully, and open questions are important here. If the interviewer uses closed questions that merely need yes or no answers, he or she will end up doing most of the talking. Leading questions, which put words in the appraisee's mouth or indicate what the appraiser wants him or her to say, should also be avoided.

Appraisers should also take great care not to be unduly influenced by a high assessment in one particular area, and should not allow this to cloud their judgement so that they rate all other areas of the employee's performance highly, even though these may not deserve such a high rating. This is known as the 'halo' effect. Similarly, care should be taken to avoid being unduly influenced by one very poor assessment. This is known as the 'horns' effect.

The contingency approach to interviews

While it is fair to say that the style of interview that is generally recommended for appraisal interviewing is a joint problem-solving approach which involves the appraiser and appraisee equally, it is also possible that some other styles of interview may be appropriate in certain circumstances. For example, if the person being appraised is new to the department they may have less to say than someone who has been there longer and so it may be appropriate for the appraiser to do a little more of the talking. If, on the other hand, the person being appraised is very experienced and has worked for the organisation for many years then they may hold many views about their own performance and have clear ideas for improving it. In this case it is possible that the person being appraised might be allowed to do slightly more of the talking. The contingency approach means that the most appropriate style of interview will depend on the circumstances at the time: the approach will be contingent on the circumstances.

The choice of style depends on factors such as the manager's own style, the organisation's culture and the behaviour of the appraisee themselves. In an autocratic organisation where people are not used to having their views considered, there may be a high degree of suspicion if at the time of the appraisal interview the manager suddenly adopts a joint problem-solving approach and actually asks for the views of the employees. This can be a problem for many organisations, because if the organisation normally conducts its affairs in such a way that the employees don't trust the managers to treat them fairly, then it is going to be extremely difficult, if not impossible, for the employees suddenly to start trusting the person who is conducting their appraisal, and to talk in an open and honest way to them. This shows that appraisals should not be used just as an isolated technique to try and motivate the workforce. They need to be an integral part of the way the organisation treats people, and fundamental issues such as the culture of the organisation and its normal style of management also need to be addressed.

Performance management

Although the aim of performance appraisal is undoubtedly to improve individual and consequently organisational performance, in poorly designed systems this may not be as effective as it should be. We shall now examine the topic of performance management, and establish the extent to which it differs from traditional performance appraisal.

Armstrong and Baron's (1998) definition of performance management, which we used at the beginning of this chapter, says that it is 'a process which contributes to the effective management of individuals and teams in order to achieve high levels of organisational performance'.

We said earlier that performance appraisal should not be used just as an extra technique to be attached to an organisation's systems when the organisation wants to try to motivate employees, but that rather it needs to be integrally linked with the whole ethos and culture of the organisation. Performance management attempts to do just this, and highlights the use of performance appraisal as a central activity in the good management of employees. A good system of performance appraisal is therefore still important as a part of performance management. Figure 9.3 shows the way in which performance appraisal contributes to performance management.

Figure 9.3 Performance management: a dynamic approach

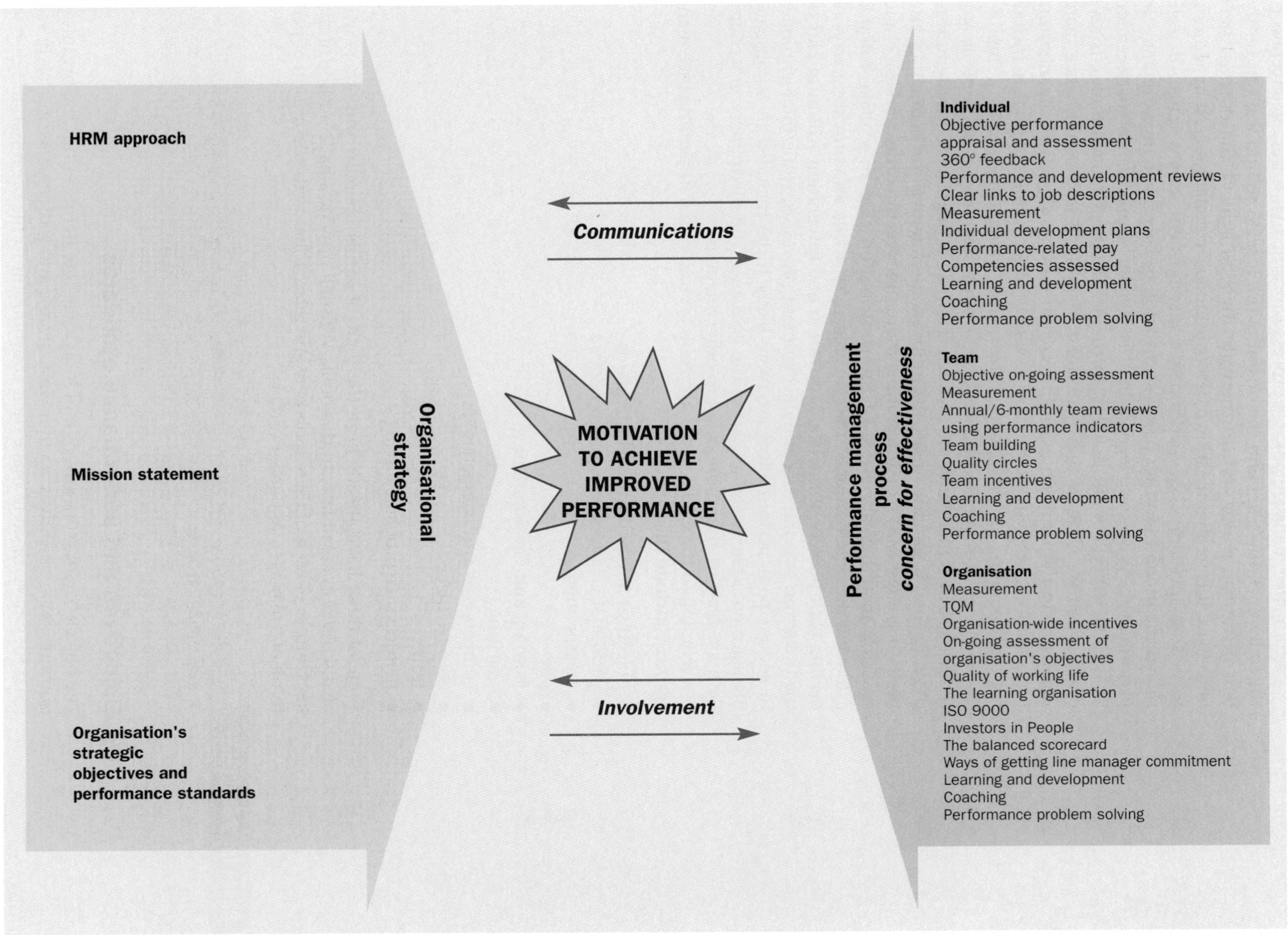

Individual
Objective performance appraisal and assessment
360° feedback
Performance and development reviews
Clear links to job descriptions
Measurement
Individual development plans
Performance-related pay
Competencies assessed
Learning and development
Coaching
Performance problem solving

Team
Objective on-going assessment
Measurement
Annual/6-monthly team reviews using performance indicators
Team building
Quality circles
Team incentives
Learning and development
Coaching
Performance problem solving

Organisation
Measurement
TQM
Organisation-wide incentives
On-going assessment of organisation's objectives
Quality of working life
The learning organisation
ISO 9000
Investors in People
The balanced scorecard
Ways of getting line manager commitment
Learning and development
Coaching
Performance problem solving

**Performance management process
concern for effectiveness**

Communications

MOTIVATION TO ACHIEVE IMPROVED PERFORMANCE

Involvement

Organisational strategy

HRM approach

Mission statement

Organisation's strategic objectives and performance standards

Performance management is a process concerned with the effectiveness of the individual, the team and the organisation. It seeks to find ways to get the best performance from all, to motivate them to achieve the organisation's objectives. It is frequently shown as a continuous, circular process. In addition to performance appraisal, performance management uses a range of techniques mentioned in other parts of this book to encourage improvements in performance. As we said earlier in this chapter, performance management links to all aspects of HR practice. In the ACAS (2004) model of an effective organisation we showed that performance appraisal and performance management clearly contribute to the creation of an effective organisation. Performance management uses a wide variety of techniques to do this, including team building, quality circles, total quality management (TQM), improving quality of working life, and working towards the Investors in People award. It must also be remembered that while performance management systems seek to get the best from individuals and motivate them to perform better, they also need to address ways of integrating the employee into the workforce and ensuring that they are aware of the contribution that they make towards achieving the organisation's strategic objectives, while also providing ways of dealing with poor performance. Motivation and integration will form part of the induction and training and development processes, while the techniques to address poor performances are more likely to be included in an absence management system and as part of the grievance and disciplinary procedure. Both are dealt with in more detail in other chapters.

According to the CIPD (2004), the tools typically used in performance management include the following:

- objectives and performance standards
- performance and development reviews
- measurement
- pay
- learning and development
- coaching
- competences and competencies
- 360° feedback
- teams
- performance problem solving.

Some of these have already been the topic of earlier chapters and others will be discussed in detail later in this book. We shall provide a basic outline of the key features of each of these tools here and relate them to the definition of performance management given earlier.

Pause for thought 9.2   How did Armstrong and Baron (1998) define performance management? Read their definition again.

⬤ Objectives and performance standards

The objectives for work groups and individuals are derived from the organisation's strategic objectives, so that work groups and individuals can clearly see what they have to do to make their contribution to the organisation's overall effectiveness. In addition to individual performance, the team is also considered to be important here and will have clear objectives which the members will help to set. Team achievements can also be assessed in the same way as individual performance. The objectives need to be clear and measurable and should be agreed after discussion between the team, the individual and the manager concerned. In this way the goals of the team and of the individual are both clearly related to those of the organisation. Both good communications and involvement are extremely important aspects of performance management, as the organisation's objectives and mission need to be clearly communicated to all employees in order that they can participate in setting objectives and contribute to the fulfilment of the organisation's objectives. Moreover, communication should not just be from top to bottom within the organisation, but should also provide for upward and lateral communication so that everyone can make a real contribution to the achievement of the organisation's objectives.

The objectives for the individual, which are derived from the organisation's strategic objectives, will be jointly devised by the appraiser and the appraisee and will have clear, measurable targets intended to contribute to the individual's development needs by providing a challenge, as well as contributing to the achievement of the needs of the organisation as a whole.

The team or work group may also have objectives to achieve, and the individual must be aware of the need to play a part in these. Performance indicators may be used for an office or team, to set standards and to measure the team's effectiveness in meeting those standards. The following is an example of some possible performance indicators for the operational staff in a human resource department:

1 A staff presence will be provided in the human resource department between 8.30 a.m. and 5.00 p.m. (Monday to Friday).

   Percentage achieved =

2 All telephone calls will be returned within two working days, and all callers will be allocated a time or date to be contacted or to call again.

   Percentage achieved =

3 The answer machine will be switched on outside normal office hours, and all messages will be cleared from it by 9.30 a.m. each day.

   Percentage achieved =

4 All urgent letters will be dealt with within two working days.

   Percentage achieved =

5 All non-urgent letters will be dealt with within five working days.

   Percentage achieved =

It might be agreed with the team that standards 1, 2 and 3 should be achieved 100% of the time, but, perhaps because of staffing difficulties, performance standards 4 and 5 should be achieved 90% of the time during the first six months, with the aim of being able to meet them 100% of the time.

Performance and development reviews

Organisations which do not use the performance management approach have traditionally used performance appraisal as their main tool in assessing performance. We discussed appraisal systems and the problems involved in getting them right earlier in this chapter. One issue we focused on then was the problem of getting supervisors and other line managers to participate fully in appraisals and to see their value. Because of these sorts of problem, some organisations have moved away from only using traditional performance appraisal. The extent to which they have done this varies, and for some it is still an important part of performance management.

For example, some organisations that have adopted the performance management approach still use a performance appraisal system as part of this approach, but supplement it with other, more regular reviews such as personal development reviews. However, because of the type of problems with performance appraisals we described earlier, many organisations now prefer to use just personal development reviews. In organisations where appraisal was traditionally seen as a 'top-down' process, where managers did the talking and the appraisers listened, adopting the performance management approach has the advantage of breaking away from this tradition and puts the review on a very different basis. Of course, as we said before, performance appraisal interviews should not be conducted as a top-down process.

Organisations that adopt a performance management approach still have to provide individuals with an opportunity to do the things that are traditionally associated with a good performance appraisal scheme. They still need to provide a means for the individual to reflect on their past performance and use this as the basis for agreeing targets for the future. They still need a forum in which to discuss any gaps in skills or knowledge, and to identify future learning and development needs. The performance development review provides the opportunity to do these things, but according to the CIPD (2004), performance and development reviews must also be 'constructive, and various techniques can be used to conduct the sort of open, free-flowing and honest meeting needed, with the reviewee doing most of the talking'.

As a result of the regular performance development review, each individual will have an individual development plan which is designed to give detailed goals and provide for activities to enable that individual to achieve his or her goals. This may start at induction and continue throughout their career. The plan is jointly designed by the manager and the employee, and the manager will provide support and coaching to help the employee to meet his or her goals. This relates very closely to the idea of the organisation being a learning organisation, discussed in Chapter 8, where everyone is encouraged to learn and to develop themselves so that the organisation will also change and develop over a period of time.

Measurement

We have already discussed the importance of setting standards and objectives and holding performance development reviews to discuss how these can be achieved. In order to make the performance development review as useful as possible, clear objective measures of past performance and future performance are also required.

The CIPD (2004) says that it is critical here to identify what should be measured because measuring the wrong things or having too many confusing measures in place could bring the performance management scheme itself into disrepute. It suggests that it might be appropriate to measure a senior manager's performance by assessing their success in meeting their objectives, but that it might be more relevant to assess a production worker by the outputs they achieve or by the levels of competency achieved. The important point here is that whatever measures are selected, they need to be appropriate to the individual's position in the organisation and to the type of job they do.

Pay

Performance-related pay is an important component of many performance management schemes. However, there are also some organisations that adopt a performance management approach but which choose not to link pay to performance because of the problems involved.

In a performance management system, the annual performance appraisal, if used, is often linked with pay and is intended to reward those who have done well in meeting their objectives. Relating assessment to pay results in the same problems as other forms of performance appraisal scheme, in that there is a potential conflict between the need for employees to talk frankly about their performance and a reluctance to do so because it would jeopardise their pay award. Performance development interviews and performance reward interviews are consequently often held separately in order to try to minimise this effect.

Decisions about whether or not to make the link between performance and pay do depend to a large extent on whether the organisation and its top management think that pay motivates, or whether they feel other factors are more likely to motivate their workers. The performance management approach is about trying to motivate workers to perform, so the issue of what will motivate particular workers is important here.

Some organisations adopt a different approach and link pay to the competence level of the worker. Organisations that use this approach have to have a clear competency framework in place and be able to measure the competence levels of workers against this; problems can occur when trying to measure levels of competence. The topic of performance-related pay and motivation will be explored in more detail in the next chapter.

Learning and development

In Chapters 7 and 8 we emphasised the importance of learning and development for modern organisations and made a business case for learning and development adding value to the business. Organisations that adopt a performance management approach are most likely to view learning and development as crucial to improving performance and are likely to adopt a wide variety of learning and development methods to promote individual, team and organisational learning. They are likely to adopt many of the characteristics of a learning organisation. In particular they will probably, as far as is possible within their particular type of organisation, adopt a blame-free culture where they use mistakes as learning opportunities. They are also likely to use the performance review itself as a learning event and encourage individuals to commit to their own development by planning their own future learning and development activities and identifying the help they might need with this. Some organisations may even have separate performance reviews and development reviews to ensure that development needs and performance are given equal priority.

Coaching

Coaching is an important learning and development intervention that we discussed in Chapter 8. The CIPD (2004) says that it is an important tool in performance management as it is a way of developing an individual's skills and knowledge so that their performance improves. It is a student-centred approach to learning and development that can be on-going and carried out at any time of the year and so it fits well within the performance management cycle.

Competences and competencies

In Chapter 2 we defined competencies as 'work-related behaviours that have been identified as necessary for successful performance at work' and briefly discussed the use of competency frameworks. Although not all organisations use competences and competencies as an integral part of the performance management process, there are many that do. The CIPD (2004) says:

> Competences describe what people need to be able to do to perform a job well (the descriptions in National Vocational Qualifications are examples of competences). Competencies (more helpfully 'behavioural competencies') are defined as dimensions of behaviour that lie behind competent performance.

Employees need to be able to operate in a competent way and to possess behavioural competencies that reinforce their technical skills. If an organisation adopts this approach then competence will be measured and this then gives a useful way of comparing actual levels of competence with required levels. This can obviously provide a useful tool for measurement of performance and consequently for the performance management process.

360° feedback

We showed earlier in this chapter that 360° appraisal is a useful tool. In some organisations that have adopted the performance management approach, the 360° idea is used in all forms of feedback rather than specifically with appraisal. As we said earlier, collecting data from a wide range of sources does provide a very thorough picture of how an individual's performance is viewed and can be an extremely powerful tool in analysing performance and acting as a catalyst for change.

Margaret Kubicek (2004) says that:

> To have any genuine value or meaningful impact, 360° feedback must be far more than a standalone activity. It should involve managing the individual's expectations, aligning questionnaires to competency frameworks, setting goals to integrate the exercise into personal development plans and providing feedback from trained facilitators. The process surrounding the 360° process itself is complex, and how well HR and learning managers plan that process will determine what impact it will have.

This shows that while 360° feedback is not an easy process to introduce into an organisation, it does nevertheless provide a powerful tool that fits well with the performance management approach.

However, recent research by Beverley Alimo-Metcalfe (see Kubicek 2004), the Chief Executive of Leadership Research and Development, suggests that 360° feedback is sometimes adopted by organisations as a fad, with insufficient support provided for the development needs that are identified. She sounds a note of caution and says 'what organisations should be doing is not introducing 360 until they're absolutely committed to the development that needs to follow.' As we said, performance management is a process that integrates all aspects of HR practice, so just adopting one aspect of it without sufficient integration with other areas is unlikely to work. Alimo-Metcalfe also describes some other familiar problems that organisations face when introducing 360° feedback. She says 'the other reason for failure is line managers don't follow up, and the individuals themselves don't go back (to the results) regularly'. This describes the same problem that we discussed earlier in this chapter of the line managers not being fully involved in the process and not seeing the relevance of it to themselves or their department. Any organisation that is introducing 360° reviews must spend time ensuring that line managers and the individual workers understand the benefits to them if it is going to be an effective part of the performance management process.

Teams

The performance management approach does not focus just on individual performance. In many organisations people work in teams and performance management is equally concerned with motivating teams to work effectively. Many of the tools we have discussed already will also be applied to teams. For example, there should be clear team objectives or targets, regular team reviews, plans for team development and objective measures of team performance. The teams will be encouraged to identify their learning and development needs and may be coached to improve team performance. They may also have team bonuses.

Performance problem solving

Performance management should not only be concerned with constantly getting increased levels of performance from individuals, teams and the whole organisation, but should also include ways of dealing with poor performance if it occurs. Counselling and employee assistance programmes are approaches that may be used as part of this approach. Absence management, discipline procedures and grievance schemes may also be a necessary part of performance management.

The balanced scorecard

In Chapter 1 we explained that some organisations have adopted an approach, developed originally from work by Kaplan and Norton (1992 and 1996), known as the balanced scorecard (BSC). You will remember that Kaplan and Norton took the view that organisations often focused too heavily on financial measures, without paying sufficient attention to other aspects of performance. The balanced scorecard is a way of translating an organisation's mission and strategy into a set of measures for organisational performance. Organisational performance is measured on four dimensions:

- financial results
- customer relations
- internal business processes
- learning and development.

While financial performance is still an important aspect of the BSC, this approach also provides a very clear rationale for measuring the performance of employees and shows that investing in people and providing them with skills and knowledge is also vital for the organisation to achieve its strategic objectives. It is particularly important as we move further towards a fast-moving, knowledge-based economy where the knowledge and skills of employees are vital for innovation and growth of an organisation.

Performance management summarised

Performance management derives from the human resource management approach as a strategic and integrated approach to the management and development of people. It emphasises the important role of line managers to take responsibility for the management of the performance of the people in their department. With its emphasis on the need for continuous performance review, performance management also relates clearly to the ideas of continuing development and the learning organisation discussed in Chapter 8. It uses the techniques of performance appraisal but prefers to use the more objective types, such as management by objectives. It does, however, go further than performance appraisal as what is appraised is clearly derived from the strategic plan and both individuals and teams are involved in setting objectives for themselves and in evaluating their success in achieving these objectives. Line managers also have responsibility to review progress and development throughout the year, not just at the time of the annual appraisal interview. Both individual and team objectives are clearly derived from the corporate strategic objectives, and everyone is aware that management of performance is the concern of all in the organisation, and not just personnel management or the senior management team. Performance management is above all a process for sharing an understanding about what needs to be achieved, and then managing and developing people in a way which will facilitate this so that excellent communications, in all directions, and employee involvement are also extremely important. As we showed earlier in this chapter, performance appraisal and performance management are important tools that can contribute to an organisation being effective. The ACAS (2004) model list 10 main steps which can help to turn an organisation into an effective organisation. We have shown that performance appraisal and performance management, if carried out correctly, in a way that fits with the organisation's culture, can contribute to most, if not all, of these steps.

REVIEW QUESTIONS

You will find brief answers to these review questions on pages 491–493.

1 From your knowledge of organisational behaviour, what would you say are the main motivation theories that influence and underpin the ideas of performance management?

2 'It (appraisal) has a long history of being damned for its ineffectiveness at the same time as being anxiously sought by people wanting to know how they are doing. It is difficult to do, it is frequently done badly with some serious results, but on the occasions when it is done well it can be invaluable for the business and literally life-transforming for the individual' (Torrington and Hall 1998). Discuss this statement.

3 Performance appraisals are intended to motivate employees towards greater productivity and improve communication/relations between managers and their team members. Explain why performance appraisals often fail to achieve this goal, and comment on the skills that managers need to make performance appraisal work.

4 Performance management is described by Michael Armstrong as a 'systematic approach to the management of people, using performance, goals, feedback and recognition as a means of motivating them to realise their full potential'. Explain how performance appraisal systems operate as a performance management technique in terms of this definition.

5 Describe three different approaches to performance appraisal, and comment critically on the benefits to be gained from these systems.

SELF-CHECK QUESTIONS

Answer the following multiple-choice and short-answer questions. The correct responses are given on page 493 for you to check your understanding of this chapter.

1 Which of the following is stated in this chapter as being least likely to contribute to an organisation becoming an effective workplace?
  (a) Policies and procedures that everyone knows about and understands.
  (b) Effective health and safety policies and procedures.
  (c) Line managers who perceive performance appraisal as totally separate from the realities of their business cycle and their business objectives.
  (d) Line managers who perceive performance appraisal as an important aspect of their job that they need to spend time on so they develop their staff and then meet their business objectives.
  (e) An organisation with a 'big idea' that everyone knows about and understands.

2 According to ACAS, performance appraisal is
  (a) an assessment of an employee's performance, potential and disciplinary needs

(b) an assessment of an employee's performance, potential and development needs

(c) an assessment of an employee's personality, potential and development needs

(d) an assessment of an organisation's performance, potential and development needs

(e) an assessment of an organisation's performance, potential and disciplinary needs.

3   In this chapter we said that when we appraise someone there are three key, but sometimes contradictory, roles. Which of the following are the three roles to which we referred?
(a) Giving feedback and being friend and helper.
(b) Giving feedback and being judge and source of discipline.
(c) Giving feedback and being judge and helper.
(d) Giving a subjective assessment of performance and being judge and helper.
(e) Giving feedback and being judge and critic.

4   Which of the following is a good reason for organisations to introduce a performance appraisal scheme?
(a) to improve current performance
(b) to provide a check on their staff's integrity
(c) to check on the honesty of their employees
(d) to clarify the employee's contract
(e) to discipline individuals.

5   Appraisal schemes may not be as effective as they should be because of a number of problems. Which of the following is not one of the problems associated with the introduction of performance appraisal schemes?
(a) The organisation is not clear about the purpose of its appraisal scheme.
(b) The performance appraisal scheme is too objective in the judgements made.
(c) Information is kept secret from the employee.
(d) The performance appraisal scheme is too subjective in the judgements made.
(e) Appraisal is used as part of the disciplinary process.

6   Which of the following best describes what is meant by the term 'performance management'?
(a) A process which contributes to the effective management of individuals and teams in order to achieve high levels of organisational performance.
(b) A process which contributes to the effective management of the HR department in order to achieve high levels of departmental performance.
(c) A process which contributes to the effective management of teams in order to achieve high levels of team performance.
(d) A process which contributes to the effective management of individuals in order to achieve high levels of individual performance.
(e) A process which contributes to the effective management of individuals and teams in order to improve the personnel department's performance.

WHAT NEXT?

Now that you have read this introductory chapter on performance appraisal and performance management, and have completed all the exercises, you may feel ready to progress further. If you would like more opportunities to test your own learning on this subject then you can go to the student web site that accompanies this book:

http://www.pearsoned.co.uk/foothook

If you feel ready to examine this subject in more depth then there have been several research studies that could help you to further your understanding of how organisations achieve improvements in performance. Some of the CIPD-sponsored studies were referred to at the end of Chapter 1 and include:

Chartered Institute of Personnel and Development (2003) *People and Performance in Knowledge-intensive Firms*, CIPD

A bulletin summarising this study is also available from the CIPD:

Chartered Institute of Personnel and Development (2004) *People and Performance in Knowledge-intensive Firms: An Emerging Model of People Management Practices*, CIPD (**www.cipd.co.uk**; accessed 9.9.04)

A further study from the research team at the University of Bath examines case study organisations and how they achieve success when times are difficult:

Hutchinson, S., N. Kinnie, J. Purcell, J. Swart, B. Rayton (2003) *Understanding the People Performance Link: Unlocking the Black Box*, CIPD

A summary of research in this area is also available from the CIPD:

Chartered institute of Personnel and Development (2002) *Sustaining Success in Difficult Times: Research Summary,* CIPD (**www.cipd.co.uk**; accessed 10.9.04)

Income Data Services conducts regular reviews of various HR issues. The following study by Income Data Services examines five case study organisations in relation to performance management:

Income Data Services Limited (2003) *Study 748: Performance Management*, IDS

References

Advisory, Conciliation and Arbitration Service (2003) *Employee Appraisal*, ACAS

Advisory, Conciliation and Arbitration Service (2004) *The ACAS Model*, ACAS (**www.acas.org.co.uk**; accessed 9.9.04)

Armstrong, M. (1994) *Performance Management*, Kogan Page

Armstrong, M. and A. Baron (1998) *Performance Management: The New Realities*, Institute of Personnel and Development

Chartered Institute of Personnel and Development (2004) *Fact Sheet: Performance Management*, CIPD (**www.cipd.co.uk**; accessed 9.9.04)

Fletcher, C. and R. Williams (1985) *Performance Appraisal and Career Development*, Hutchinson

Gillen, T. (2004) *Topics for Trainers* 'Appraisal: getting managers' buy-in', CIPD (**www.cipd.co.uk**; accessed 9.9.04)

Kaplan, R. S. and D. P. Norton (1992) The balanced scorecard — measures that drive performance, *Harvard Business Review*, January–February, 71–79

Kaplan, R. S. and D. P. Norton (1996) *The Balanced Scorecard: Translating Strategy into Action*, Harvard Business School Press

Kubicek, M. (2004) Turning appraisals around, *Training Magazine* produced by *Personnel Today*, September, 20–22

Purcell, J., N. Rinnie, S. Hutchinson (2003) Open minded, *People Management*, Vol. 9, No. 10, 31–33

Randell, G. A., P. M. A. Packard, R. L. Shaw and A. J. P. Slater (1984) *Staff Appraisal*, IPM

Torrington, D. and L. Hall (1998) *Human Resource Management*, 4th edition, Prentice Hall Europe

Further study

Books

Advisory, Conciliation and Arbitration Service (2002) *Teamwork: Success through People*, ACAS. (This booklet concentrates on one very important aspect of performance: teams.)

Advisory, Conciliation and Arbitration Service (2003) *Appraisal-Related Pay*, ACAS. (Another excellent guide, this time to the complex task of linking performance appraisal to pay.)

Advisory, Conciliation and Arbitration Service (2003) *Effective Organisations: The People Factor*, ACAS. (This booklet focuses on getting the best from people and this is what performance management is all about. It examines a wide range of measures that may contribute to an improvement in the organisation's performance.)

Advisory, Conciliation and Arbitration Service (2003) *Employee Appraisal*, ACAS. (An excellent, clear guide to performance appraisal.)

Armstrong, Michael. *Performance Management,* Kogan Page, 2000. (A very thorough examination of the whole topic of performance management.)

Armstrong, M. (2002) *The Performance Management Audit: An Eight-stage approach to help Analyse, Develop and Improve Performance Management Processes so that the Organisation Achieves its Business Goals*, Cambridge Strategy Publications

Armstrong, M. and A. Baron (2004) *Performance Management: The New Realities,* CIPD.

Brown, D. and M. Armstrong (1999) *Paying for Contribution: Real Performance-Related Pay Strategies*, Kogan Page.

Fletcher, C. (2004) *Appraisal and Feedback: Making Performance Review Work*, CIPD.

Income Data Services (2003) *Study 748: Performance Management*, IDS, April. (This study provides an overview of the performance management process and explores the link between performance appraisal, pay and development opportunities. It examines five case study organisations.)

Randell, G. A., P. M. A. Packard, R. L. Shaw and A. J. P. Slater (1984) *Staff Appraisal*, IPM. (A classic work on how to manage staff appraisal effectively.)

Articles

Beagrie, S. (2003) How to conduct an appraisal, *Personnel Today*, 8 July, 25. (A succinct one-page summary of key points to remember when conducting a performance appraisal interview.)

Gillen, T. (2003) Expert's view: Terry Gillen on appraisals, *Personnel Today*, 8 July, 25. (A review of common failings in performance appraisal and the qualities and characteristics that make for good appraisers.)

Goodge, P. (2000) How to manage 360-degree feedback, *People Management*, Vol. 6, No. 4, 17 February, 50–51. (Provides a checklist and suggestions for best practice in 360° appraisal.)

Hobbs, N. (2004) How to appraise board members, *People Management*, Vol. 10, No. 10, 42–43. (The Combined Code on Corporate Governance means that listed companies have to evaluate the performance of their board members. This article describes ways to achieve this.)

Johnson, R. (2001) Double entente, *People Management*, Vol. 7, No. 9, 3 May, 38–39. (A fascinating account of how the newly merged pharmaceutical company Alliance UniChem used a multilingual 360° appraisal scheme as a way of harmonising cultures.)

Purcell, J., N. Kinnie and S. Hutchinson (2003) Open minded, *People Management*, Vol. 9, No. 10, 31–33. (The first in a series of articles in this edition of *People Management* in which a research team from the School of Management University of Bath explore how effective people management results in excellent performance and competitive advantage.)

Purcell, J., N. Kinnie and S. Hutchinson (2003) They're free, *People Management*, Vol. 9, No. 10, 34–35. (The second article in this series relating to Selfridges.)

Purcell, J., N. Kinnie and S. Hutchinson (2003) The multipack scan, *People Management*, Vol. 9, No. 10, 36–37. (The third article in this series describes research into management behaviour in four Tesco stores.)

Rose, M. (2000) Target practice, *People Management*, Vol. 6, No. 23, 23 November, 44–45. (This makes the argument against rigid performance objectives in performance appraisal and performance management and argues that a model of continuous improvement is more appropriate to today's fast-changing world.)

Swinburne, P. (2001) How to use feedback to improve performance, *People Management*, Vol. 7, No. 11, 31 May, 46–47. (Provides a guide to providing balanced feedback to help people to learn.)

Towner, N. (2004) Turning appraisals 360 degrees, *Personnel Today*, 17 February, 18. (An article describing the positive effects of 360° appraisal at AAH Pharmaceuticals.)

Watkin, C. (2003) How to review leadership talent, *People Management*, Vol. 9, No. 11, 42–43. (An article explaining how some organisations review the performance of their top leadership teams.)

Internet

Council for Excellence in Management and Leadership   **www.managementandleadershipcouncil.org**

The Performance Management Network   **www.pmn.net/index.html**

CHAPTER **10**

Payment systems

OBJECTIVES

By the end of this chapter you will be able to:

- explain the main factors that influence the choice of a particular payment system
- describe the relationship between motivation theories and pay systems state the advantages and disadvantages of different types of payment systems
- explain the process of job evaluation
- explain how to use a particular job evaluation system
- identify issues relating to payment systems in international organisations.

We have indicated in previous chapters that human resource management is concerned that people should work as effectively as possible for the organisation, and that one of the ways in which the organisation attempts to achieve this is by using an appropriate system of payment to encourage and reward them. The payment system that is adopted must, as stated in Chapter 2, be in line with and support the key elements of the strategic plan.

In this chapter we shall be examining a variety of payment systems and discussing the philosophies on which they are based, and the links with motivation theory, as well as the circumstances in which particular payment systems may prove appropriate.

Definitions

Before we proceed, it will be useful to define some of the words we shall use throughout this chapter. Several words are commonly used to refer to the wages or salaries paid to people at work, and these include the terms 'compensation', 'remuneration', 'reward' and 'pay'. We shall examine these definitions and then define other terms used in connection with payments, such as'harmonisation' and 'job evaluation'. We shall then examine the different types of payment system that are available for an employer to use.

Compensation is frequently used to refer to payment, but implies that the employee somehow has to be compensated for a loss or injury caused through work, rather than that they are actually being paid to work. This seems to reflect a theory X viewpoint on work (see Did you know below), and to imply that people do not enjoy work and so have to be compensated for working at all.

Reward is frequently used nowadays to refer to payment systems, especially since many payment systems try to motivate people to work harder and then reward them for their extra effort. The word 'reward' is useful in this sense, and could apply to either monetary or non-monetary award, but it also implies that something special is being rewarded. While it is true that many payment schemes do seek to reward extra effort, this is normally only one part of the payment system. The term 'reward' also seems to have theory X overtones, as it implies that it is always necessary to dangle a carrot in order to get good work from an employee.

Remuneration means broadly the same as payment system, but is a more cumbersome term to use (and more difficult to spell!).

Payment is the most straightforward of the four terms, and seems to us to be the most appropriate term to use. It can include monetary or non-monetary payment. This is therefore the term we shall use in general throughout this chapter. We include under this heading various types of both monetary and non-monetary payment, as well as sickness pay, maternity pay and pension arrangements.

Although distinctions between wages and salaries are decreasing as many organisations move towards harmonisation of terms and conditions for different groups of workers, it is also useful to define the differences that do still exist.

Wages tend to be paid weekly and may be based on an hourly rate of pay, with possible deductions for lateness or absence, and this hourly rate is often the rate that is referred to in negotiations. Wage-earners are often still paid in cash and are less likely to have fringe benefits such as luncheon vouchers, company cars or expenses. Organisations paying wages expect short-term thinking from their employees, and incentives for wage-earners are also usually quick and precise. There has traditionally been less job security for wage-earners than for salaried employees, and the emphasis is on a short-term relationship with the employing organisation. The peak of wage-earners' earning capacity is comparatively early, perhaps while they are still in their twenties. Wage-earners perceive themselves as doing a totally different type of job from management, and expect jobs to be short term, with some degree of insecurity.

Salaries tend to be paid monthly, and these monthly payments are normally expressed as an annual salary, this being the figure that is normally referred to

---

Did you know?

Douglas McGregor (1960) stated that the way managers perceived work and employees would affect the way in which the employees actually carried out their work. He said that there were two contrasting assumptions that managers made about the behaviour of employees, which he called theory X and theory Y.

Theory X

A manager who adopts the theory X viewpoint would tend to assume that the average worker will dislike work and avoid it if they can, and will only be made to work by a mixture of control and threats. A 'carrot or stick' approach is what is generally seen to be appropriate here. The use of the words 'compensation' and 'reward' would seem to fit this perspective, and to lead to the idea of management needing to provide either control or incentives to motivate the employee to work effectively.

Theory Y

Theory Y assumes that work is a natural and welcome activity which need not be controlled by the manager, as the employee will seek responsibility and will be motivated by the work itself. Managers who hold a theory Y view are not going to be particularly interested in providing control or incentives, and so the words 'reward' and 'compensation' seem less appropriate for them. Instead these managers are more likely to be concerned with having a fair, easy-to-understand payment system and are also more likely to involve workers in the design of this.

in negotiations on salary. Those who are salaried normally have their salaries paid directly into a bank or building society and they are also likely to have several fringe benefits, such as company cars, extra payments for additional qualifications, or luncheon vouchers. Some salaried workers get immediate incentives added to their incomes, but generally the most widely held incentive is supposed to be a much longer-term consideration, that of good prospects. Salaried employees either are in managerial posts or tend to identify very closely with management, and they perceive themselves to be on a lengthy career progression with the peak of their earning power achieved relatively late in life. In addition, until fairly recently they have expected to have long-term job security.

Harmonisation

There are differences in organisations' attitudes towards those paid wages and those paid salaries, but as mentioned earlier, many organisations have tried to get away from the problems that this sometimes causes, and have moved towards a common system of payment with the harmonisation of terms and conditions of employment for both groups of workers. This means that there is an expectation that all employees can be treated in the same way and will expect the same benefits. In these organisations, everyone is paid a monthly salary rather than a weekly or hourly rate of pay, and everyone gets the same sick pay and redundancy arrangements, works the same hours and eats in the same canteen.

Nowadays there is also much less job security, and career progression for salaried employees and promotion or even job security cannot be regarded as automatic, as many organisations in which salaried jobs were normally secure have moved to remove whole strata of managers. The growing trend towards the acquisition of a flexible workforce with increasing numbers of part-timers and contract workers has also led to a blurring of distinctions between the two groups.

The term may also be used to refer to the harmonisation of wages and conditions of employment in different countries. Since 2002, when countries within the euro zone adopted the euro as their common currency, workers in these countries have been able to compare their wages with workers doing a similar job in different countries. This increased level of transparency may result in wages and conditions of employment in different countries becoming increasingly similar, or harmonised.

Job evaluation

A further term that is relevant to payment systems and will be discussed fully later in this chapter is 'job evaluation'. ACAS (2003) defines job evaluation in the following way:

> The aim of job evaluation is to provide a systematic and consistent approach to defining the relative worth of jobs within a workplace, single plant or multiple site organisation. It is a process whereby jobs are placed in a rank order according to overall demands placed upon the job holder. It therefore provides a basis for a fair and orderly grading structure. Job evaluation does not determine actual pay. That is a separate operation, normally the subject of negotiation between management and employees or their trade union representatives. Only the job is evaluated, not the person doing it.

As you can see here, job evaluation does not actually determine rates of pay that any individual employee should receive, but it can be used as a systematic basis for determining differences in jobs and subsequently the different pay levels for those jobs. As such it seems to us to be an appropriate topic to discuss in this chapter.

The main influences on payment systems

What the organisation decides to pay staff will depend on many factors, some of which are under the control of the organisation and some of which are external.

ACTIVITY 10.1

We have provided you with a selection of job titles and you have to decide how much to pay these staff. You are to consider who you think *ought* to be paid the most rather than considering what actually happens in reality.

(a) Put the jobs listed below in order of importance, i.e. with number 1 being the job that you judge should be paid the most.

(b) List the factors that will influence how much you will pay these staff.

Waiter or waitress	_____
Nurse	_____
Sales assistant (clothes shop)	_____
Car park attendant	_____
Office cleaner	_____
Accountant	_____
Police officer	_____
Receptionist	_____
Teller (bank)	_____
Warehouse supervisor	_____
University lecturer	_____
Truck driver	_____
Secretary	_____
Traffic warden	_____
Security guard	_____
Safety officer (manufacturing company)	_____
Warehouse picker	_____
Doctor	_____
Personnel manager	_____
Church minister	_____
Ambulance driver (paramedical)	_____
Transport manager	_____
Computer services officer	_____
Lawyer	_____
Undertaker	_____
Professional football player	_____
IT consultant	_____

(c) Compare your order with others and try to reach agreement about a list of factors that should be taken into account when you are making these decisions.

Discussion of Activity 10.1

The relative worth of these jobs is likely to vary according to the type of organisation, and your ranking is likely to vary compared with that of your colleagues because you have been highly subjective. You should think about what influenced your choice of each job's worth. Did you have knowledge of some jobs? Did you most value strength, skill, level of responsibility or a caring response, or were you influenced by people you know who do some of these jobs, or by your own career aspirations? There will be many highly subjective influences on your decision.

Many other factors may influence the relative worth of jobs. Your list is likely to include at least some of the following:

- what the organisation can afford to pay
- what other organisations in the area are paying for similar jobs
- national or international rates of pay within the organisation
- legislation and the minimum wage
- trade unions' or employee demands
- Government initiatives
- the scarcity of particular skills
- the state of the economy
- the introduction of new technology
- the relative worth of jobs as rated by a job evaluation exercise
- the actual performance of the person in the job.

As you can see from this list, an organisation does not have a completely free hand when it decides how to pay someone. Many factors influence the decision of how and what to pay, and we shall discuss these more fully in turn.

What the organisation can afford to pay

Obviously, no organisation can afford to put itself out of business by paying more than it can afford, so this has to be one of the first factors that influence how much an organisation will pay.

What other organisations in the area are paying for similar jobs

Most organisations will at least take account of the rates that other local organisations are paying. The organisation may refer to published pay surveys or do its own survey of the local area to establish rates that others are paying for similar jobs. If it can afford to, and if it wants to be able to select the best employees, it may choose to pay slightly more than the going rate. This can cause a spiral of wage increases as other employers retaliate by increasing their wages. When labour is scarce this is one way in which many employers will behave.

Even when employing people on a small scale, the rate of payment can have quite an effect locally. Sometimes people from London, or perhaps those moving to or buying second homes in countries such as France or Spain, may have an effect on local wages when they employ a local gardener or cleaner and pay much more than the local rate. Those with second homes will probably be able to afford to pay good wages, particularly if they are used to paying for similar services in a more expensive area such as London. When they pay these same rates to local cleaners they obviously attract good staff, but are then accused by other locals of poaching their cleaners and of setting rates that the locals cannot afford to match. In this situation the second home owners get excellent cleaners but may not make many friends.

National or international rates of pay within your organisation

If the organisation is part of a larger organisation, there may be national or international agreements that will affect what is actually paid, and the human resource manager also needs to assess these rates.

Nowadays as travel to other countries is easier and quicker than in the past, pay rates often have global implications. In recent years poor pay for nurses in Britain, and the subsequent staff shortages, meant hospitals and NHS trusts increasingly had to search further afield for qualified nurses. Many carried out recruitment drives which attracted nurses from countries such as the Philippines to Britain. Poor pay and working conditions for teachers have also resulted in many education authorities conducting recruitment drives in countries such as Russia and South Africa.

> **Did you know?**
>
> It is claimed that Sol Campbell of Arsenal was the first footballer to earn £100,000 per week, including bonuses.
> (*Guardian*, Editorial, Thursday, 16 August 2001)

What is considered poor pay in one country may seem a fortune to an individual coming from a poorer country. Individually they gain an opportunity to travel and broaden their own experience and may even be able to save money to send home to their families. This may in turn create skills shortages for those countries losing people and consequently some Governments have requested that Britain does not carry out recruitment drives in their country. The global effects of pay rates are not all in one direction. In the 1960s and 1970s there was talk of a 'brain drain' from Britain and more recently similar problems have arisen as many senior academics and scientists go to America in search of better pay and working conditions and for better research facilities.

Legislation

All organisations are affected by the law of the country in which they operate. In Britain they will also be affected by European Union legislation. The legislation that will have most effect on payment or reward systems is:

- The Equal Pay Act 1970
- The Equal Pay Amendment (Regulations) 1983
- The Employment Rights Act 1996
- National Minimum Wage Act 1998

The Equal Pay Act 1970

The Equal Pay Act 1970 actually came into effect in December 1975, at the same time as the Sex Discrimination Act 1975, which is discussed in Chapter 3. It was part of a two-pronged attack on inequality and specifically aimed to ensure that men and women who were doing the same job, or jobs that were broadly similar in nature, would receive the same pay. Consequently it is now illegal to pay men and women doing the same or broadly similar jobs different amounts of pay.

Under the Equal Pay Act 1970 it is also illegal to pay different rates to men and women who do different jobs, but whose jobs have been rated the same under a job evaluation scheme. The whole topic of job evaluation and problems of fairness and equality within job evaluation will be discussed later in this chapter.

The Equal Pay Amendment (Regulations) 1983

This legislation added a further category to the Equal Pay Act 1970, that of equal value. It is therefore now possible for men and women who are doing totally different jobs and who are paid differently to bring a case against their employer if they feel that their job is of the same value to the organisation as the job done by the higher paid group. The legislation is complex, and most who have brought cases have been supported by their trade union or the Equal Opportunities Commission. Criteria such as the level of qualifications required, the level of effort or skill involved, and the amount of responsibility and decision making involved in each of the jobs are factors that are likely to be taken into account. In a tribunal hearing of this type, the person of the opposite sex with whom the claimant wishes to compare himself or herself must first be identified. If the tribunal decides that there are reasonable grounds for determining that the work is of equal value, a report will be commissioned by an independent expert as to the relative worth of each of the jobs. The tribunal will then convene once again after receiving the report of the independent expert, and will make a decision.

> ### Did you know?
>
> Thirty years after the Equal Pay Act made it illegal to pay women less than men, Payfinder.com has found that the average pay gap between the sexes now stands at 24% – and that it is continuing to grow. Between 2003 and 2004 it had risen by 9% in Wales, 8% in the West Midlands, 6% in the south-east and 4% in Scotland.
>
> (Jones 2004)

ACTIVITY 10.2

If you are in paid employment then check out your rate of pay to see if men and women are being paid equally in your region by using **www.payfinder.com** or **https://secure.payfinder.com/EO/** (web sites accessed 24.6.04).

The Employment Rights Act 1996

The Employment Rights Act 1996 is a consolidation act which consolidates previous legislation relating to employment rights. Under the Employment Rights Act 1996 an employer is not allowed to make deductions from an employee's wages except in the following circumstances:

● When deductions are authorised by law, such as tax or national insurance contributions or orders such as a court order relating to the provision of maintenance.
● When there is a statement in the employee's written contract which specifies that certain deductions may be made from wages and when the worker has already given consent in writing to the deduction, e.g. to pay membership fees for a sports or social club or when deductions are agreed for lateness or poor work.
● Accidental overpayment of wages, or of expenses, even though this is likely to be the fault of the employer.

- When the employee has been absent from work due to strike or other industrial action it is permissible for the employer to deduct money from the employee's wages.
- In retail organisations, employers may also deduct money from wages to make good any cash deficiency in the till or any shortfall in stock. This deduction should not exceed 10% of the wages due to the employee concerned on a particular day and the deduction must also be made within 12 months from the date that the discrepancy or shortfall in stock was discovered.

The National Minimum Wage Act 1998

The National Minimum Wage Act 1998 established a single national minimum rate with no variation for regions, jobs, size of organisation or industrial sector. Differences will be allowed, however, based on age. The National Minimum Wage provides some protection for the lowest paid groups of workers but at a lower rate, at least initially, for those who are aged between 18 and 21. From 1 October 2004 the adult national minimum wage rate for workers aged 22 and over is £4.85 per hour while the development rate for workers aged 18–21 inclusive is £4.10 per hour. A further new rate for 16- and 17-year-old workers of £3.00 per hour has been added, although 16- and 17-year-old apprentices remain exempt from this.

After 1 October 2004 employers who pay their employees on a piece-work basis also have to ensure they pay them the minimum wage for every hour worked and in April 2005 the Government proposes that home workers, traditionally a very badly paid group, should also receive the minimum wage.

These rates are subject to the continuation of favourable economic conditions. Employers will have to keep records for National Minimum Wage purposes and employees should have access to these records with a right to complain to an employment tribunal if the employer fails to give them the required access to the records.

Trade union and employee demands

Under the last Conservative Government a framework of legislation was introduced to curb the power of the unions and ensure that they were a less powerful force in bargaining on wages. Although under the Labour Government some of this legislation has been relaxed a little, it is not the pay of mainstream workers which is rising, but that of their senior managers and chief executives. Nevertheless it is important to consider the views of both trade unions and employees in general, and any payment system that an organisation may design needs to be introduced after full discussion and consultation with employees and trade unions. The most effective payment systems will have been selected to meet the needs of both the organisation and the workforce, will have the commitment of all groups and will have been developed, introduced and updated with the participation of employee representatives, whether or not they are members of a trade union.

Did you know?

According to the Equal Opportunities Commission (2005), women students can expect to be earning 15% less than men within five years of leaving college.

'Equal pay is an important issue for all students, not just the women. An employer who can demonstrate they value their women employees is likely to be a good employer to work for in other respects. If you go to work for a company which short changes women, what else might you find?'

Government initiatives

The Government can have an effect on the supply of labour as it introduces various training initiatives for adults or young people who are facing unemployment. This should have the effect of providing people with relevant skills that employers need, but it also has an effect on wage expectations, since if people are used to receiving a very low training allowance they are likely to feel pleased if they get a job that pays more than this, even if it is still a comparatively low wage.

The scarcity of particular skills

Even in years where there has been high unemployment, there has also been a scarcity in some industries of particular types of skilled workers. This may be due to failure in the past to train people adequately, but it appears that there is often a mismatch between the skills that employers require and the skills that those who are without jobs can offer. In a situation such as this, the relatively small number of people who do have the necessary skills can command high wages or salaries and may move from one organisation to another as different employers try to outbid each other for their scarce skills.

The state of the economy

We have already mentioned that the availability of labour and the scarcity of particular skills will have an effect on the wages paid. Other economic factors such as inflation will also have an effect, as in times of high levels of inflation there will be increasing pressure from workers to increase salaries to keep pace with, or get ahead of, inflation.

New technology

The relative pay levels of people in different jobs can change over time, for example, when new skills have to be learnt with the introduction of new technology, so that a particular group of workers change from being of low skill level to needing a high level of technical expertise. This change in skill level is likely to be reflected in a demand for higher wages.

The relative worth of each job as rated by a job evaluation exercise

Job evaluation is a way of rating the value to the organisation of the jobs that people do. It does not in itself decide what pay should be awarded to each job, but it is a systematic way of comparing different jobs so that this can be used as the basis for a payment system. The various ways in which job evaluation can be carried out and the different types of scheme will be discussed later in this chapter.

The performance of the individual employee in the job

In many organisations it will also be important to assess the effectiveness of the person doing the job. Whether this happens will depend on the type of payment system used and the organisation's views on collectivism or individualism with regard to payments. Organisations that favour collectivism will want to minimise differences in pay between employees as this may avoid costly or time-wasting disputes, while other organisations will want to pay everyone individual rates as far as possible in order to reward each person for his or her efforts, and these two perspectives will result in a variety of differing types of payment system.

It is clear that the last two factors are of great importance to payment systems, so we shall now go on to discuss each in detail.

Job evaluation schemes

Very few organisations will pay all the people who work for them exactly the same regardless of the job they do or how well they do that job. Most organisations therefore seek to find ways to compare the worth of different jobs to the organisation, as well as a person's performance in each job. We considered in the previous chapter the ways in which individual performance may be assessed, but here we shall concentrate on ways of comparing the relative worth of different jobs. If organisations were to base decisions about the relative worth of different jobs on managerial whims, they would be accused, quite rightly, of being unfair. That is why many organisations use a system for assessing the worth of different jobs based on job evaluation.

Job evaluation does not determine the correct payment level for a job, but rather provides a possible ranking of a job relative to other jobs. This has the merit of being systematic and of appearing objective, although in reality there is normally some degree of subjectivity in all job evaluation schemes. There are normally three stages involved when an organisation is deciding how much to pay for each job:

- evaluate the jobs in the organisation and get a ranking for them
- decide which jobs are similar in terms of the job evaluation exercise and group them together
- decide what pay to attach to these jobs, partially on the basis of market value.

There are a variety of job evaluation schemes in existence, and discussion of these could occupy a full chapter in its own right. We shall seek to give a brief outline of some of the more commonly used types of job evaluation scheme. They can be divided into non-analytical and analytical schemes, and we shall consider each of these groups in turn.

Non-analytical schemes

Non-analytical job evaluation schemes compare whole jobs rather than analysing the components of each job and assessing them factor by factor. There are three main types of non-analytical scheme:

- whole job ranking
- paired comparisons
- job classification.

In order to understand the basics of each of these approaches, you should complete the following activities. For both activities you need to consider the job descriptions we have provided and imagine that you had to evaluate the jobs as part of a job evaluation exercise, which will ultimately be used as the basis of the organisation's payment system. You are being asked to evaluate only three jobs, whereas in reality there would be far more jobs than this in most organisations.

Whole job ranking

ACTIVITY 10.3

(a) Consider each of the three job descriptions given below and decide which job you feel is worth most to the organisation, which is the next in value and which is of least value to the organisation.

Job description A

Job title:	Receptionist
Reports to:	Office Services Manager
Responsible for:	Assistant Receptionists (2)
Purpose of post:	To ensure that visitors to the company are received in a welcoming fashion, answer routine queries and ensure that all other queries are handled expeditiously by the appropriate staff member. To ensure that all telephone queries are handled in the same manner.
	As the first point of contact for the company, the receptionist must maintain high standards of customer care.
Contacts:	All customers and other visitors, to deal with initial and routine queries. All members of staff, to pass on queries as appropriate.

Major duties:

- Greet walk-in visitors and ascertain purpose of their visit. Handle or redirect queries as appropriate.
- Answer phone queries as above.
- Answer all initial queries about receipt of payments using the on-line payment receipts system.
- Open and sort incoming post by department. Organise delivery of post by assistant receptionists.
- Perform clerical tasks assigned by departments in agreement with the Office Services Manager.
- Supervise assistant receptionists and delegate work as appropriate.
- Perform other duties as assigned by the Office Services Manager or other authorised manager.

Job description B

Job title:	Human Resource Assistant
Reports to:	Human Resource Manager
Responsible for:	No one

Purpose of post:	To provide a day-to-day advisory service for the managers in the company on matters of human resource management policy and procedures, and to monitor and implement procedures.
Contacts:	Managers from head office and throughout the branches. Employees, to deal with initial and routine queries. Prospective employees, to deal with initial enquiries regarding job vacancies. Outside organisations such as employment agencies, training organisations and newspapers.

Major duties:

- Greet visitors and ascertain purpose of their visit. Handle or redirect queries as appropriate.
- Answer phone queries as above.
- Answer all initial queries about applications for employment.
- Pass all rejected applications to typist for standard rejection letters and check and sign these letters.
- Monitor application for employment forms submitted by line managers on behalf of candidates selected by them.
- Agree salary details, in accordance with company pay scales, with line manager.
- Enter agreed salary, contract, job title and joining details on successful applications and pass to typist for documentation.
- Sign joining documentation on behalf of the company.
- Advise line managers on the interpretation of the organisation's human resource policies and procedures.
- Advise line managers on the interpretation and implementation of the organisation's sickness pay and pension schemes.
- Advise line managers on the interpretation of relevant employment legislation.
- Advise line managers on employees' salary entitlements.
- Ensure that the human resource management records are kept up to date on the computerised information system, and that there is no unauthorised access to these and any manually produced records.
- Provide up-to-date reports or data for use by managers.

Job description C

Job title:	Sales Assistant
Reports to:	Buyer of China Department
Responsible for:	No one
Purpose of post:	To sell china goods and assist customers with their purchases and with any queries or problems that they might have.
Contacts:	All customers and other visitors to make sales of china and deal with routine queries.

Major duties:

- Sell china goods to customers.
- Provide expert advice about the various products on sale.
- Provide a high standard of service and customer care.
- Unpack with care valuable merchandise and pack customers' purchases carefully, including packing them for export.
- Display products attractively to encourage sales and promote certain special offers.

- Perform clerical duties associated with the work of the department, e.g. completion of orders, forms for returns or breakages.
- Handle accurately and honestly cash and credit transactions.
- Total cash and credit transactions and deliver money to Cash Control Office.

When you have read the three job descriptions, rank the jobs in order with the job you feel is worth most to the organisation being ranked as number 1.

1 _____

2 _____

3 _____

(b) What are the advantages and disadvantages of this approach?

Discussion of Activity 10.3

This is the simplest form of job evaluation exercise and we have ranked the three jobs in the following order: 1, Human Resources Assistant 2, Sales Assistant in China Department; 3, Receptionist. You may have reached a different rank order to us or to other students. This is because this is a very subjective way of ranking the jobs, and the criteria we took into account may be different to those that you have used. There is nothing in this method to indicate what criteria have been chosen. We have asked you to make decisions about only three jobs, and it would be more difficult to use the whole job ranking system in a large organisation where there were many different jobs to rank. In that case, the jobs would probably have to be grouped into categories first for ease of comparison and so that the appropriate criteria were used, e.g. for clerical jobs, as it could be a problem to identify suitable criteria if the jobs were very dissimilar.

We could make this system slightly more objective by agreeing the criteria to be considered in advance of the exercise, but even this would not help us to identify the extent of difference in the value of the different jobs to the organisation, so we would still have difficulty deciding how much more to pay the job that was ranked first compared to the job that was ranked second. In reality, job evaluation schemes should not depend on the subjective judgements of just one person. It would be better to involve more people in an exercise such as this and then get a consensus view from this job evaluation panel about the ranking of each job.

Advantages of whole job ranking

- simple
- cheap to operate
- easy to understand.

Disadvantages of whole job ranking

- subjective
- no analysis of jobs to explain reason for ranked order
- difficult to use with large number of jobs.

ACTIVITY 10.4

(a) Refer to the three job descriptions given in Activity 10.3, but this time compare pairs of jobs and decide which you feel is worth more to the organisation, so that each job is compared with the other jobs in turn. Use the following points system to work through this exercise.

- If you feel that a job is worth more than the job it is being compared with, give it 2 points.
- If you feel it is worth the same as the job it is compared with, give them both 1 point.
- If you feel it is worth less than the other job, give it zero points.

Enter the values that you give each job in the chart below, and then add the scores for each job. The job with the highest value will be the one that you decide to pay the most, followed with the job with the next highest value and the job with the lowest value.

We'll start by examining Job A, the job of the receptionist, and will compare our view of its value to the organisation with the value of the other two jobs to the organisation. Place all your scores for Job A in the vertical column below the heading Job A so that at the end of the exercise you can add up all the points for this job.

For example, if you think that Job A, the receptionist's job, is of more value to the organisation than Job B, the Human Resources Assistant's job, then on the chart below you should write '2' in the vertical column below Job A and on the horizontal line next to Job B.

Now compare Job A with Job C and, for example, if you decide that Job A is perhaps of less value to the organisation than Job C, you should write '0' in the next space down in column A, on the horizontal line next to Job C. Then add the total points in this column to gain a total score for Job A. Now complete this exercise for yourself and add up the total score in each column for each of the jobs in turn.

	JOB A	JOB B	JOB C
JOB A	No score in this section as Job A cannot be compared with itself		
JOB B		No score in this section as Job B cannot be compared with itself	
JOB C			No score in this section as Job C cannot be compared with itself
TOTAL SCORES FOR EACH JOB			

Total points for each job   A =   B =   C =

1st job _____

2nd job _____

3rd job _____

(b) Did you rank the jobs in the same order as before? What are the advantages and disadvantages of this approach?

Discussion of Activity 10.4

This is also a simple method of job evaluation, but it is slightly more systematic than whole job ranking. It still does not analyse particular jobs in detail and, although the numerical values attached to each job create an impression of objectivity, this is really not the case as again there is nothing to indicate what the criteria used might be. A large number of calculations may need to be made – for an organisation that intends to analyse 50 or more jobs, 1,225 calculations would need to be made. There are, however, computerised systems that work on this basis and solve this particular problem. Once again, an improvement to this approach would be to involve a job evaluation panel, drawn from various sections of the workforce, and then try to get agreement about the rating of various jobs.

Advantages of paired comparisons

- simple
- easy to understand
- slightly more systematic than whole job ranking
- it is easy to fit new jobs into this system.

Disadvantages of paired comparisons

- subjective
- no analysis of jobs to explain reason for ranked order
- the need for an enormous number of calculations if it is to be used with a large number of jobs.

Job classification

The exercises you have just completed indicate in a very simple way the main stages and the main problems with two forms of non-analytical job evaluation. The third non-analytical form of job evaluation is known as job classification. It is similar to job ranking but uses a different approach. In this case the number of groups of jobs, or pay grades, is decided first and a general job description is then produced for all the jobs in each of these groups. An individual job that is considered to typify this group of jobs is then used as a benchmark. Each job is compared with the benchmark jobs and the general job description, and placed in an appropriate grade.

Advantages of job classification

- simple to operate
- easy to understand
- it is easy to fit new jobs into job classification structure.

Disadvantages of job classification

- difficult to use with a wide range of jobs
- not analytical.

Analytical methods of job evaluation

Points rating

This is probably the most commonly used type of job evaluation scheme, and is regarded as analytical because instead of comparing whole jobs, the jobs are broken down into a number of factors such as skills, responsibility, physical requirements, mental requirements, working conditions. Each of the factors is awarded points based on a predetermined scale, and the total points determine the position of that job in the rank order. A weighting is often attached to the particular importance of each attribute to the organisation.

Although this scheme is analytical, there is, as we said earlier, an element of subjectivity in all job evaluation schemes, as subjective decisions are made about which factors will be weighted most highly to show their importance to the organisation. Care should be taken to avoid sex bias in the choice of factors for high weighting. Many older schemes based on this system were biased against women as characteristics such as physical strength, normally associated more with male employees, were given higher weighting than factors such as dexterity, which is more often associated with women.

Points rating schemes are easy to understand and are more objective than the non-analytical schemes. Because they are analytical, they can be used to explain the extent of differences between jobs and hence to justify subsequent differences in pay. They can, however, be time-consuming and costly to develop. Once again a panel of people is likely to be involved. An example of this type of scheme is given at the end of this chapter so that you can apply the concepts you have read about.

Did you know?

These methods of job evaluation are not just used in the UK. In May 2000 the Hong Kong Equal Opportunities Commission (2003) established a task force to encourage the implementation of equal pay for work of equal value in two pilot areas: The Hong Kong Civil Service and the Hospital Authority. They chose to base their approach to equal value on work done in both the UK and Canada. The factors chosen for this job evaluation exercise were typical of a points rating approach: skill, responsibility, effort and working conditions, although different weightings were given to each factor.

Proprietary schemes

Faced with the time and costs involved in designing and validating their own job evaluation scheme and checking that it is free of unfair bias, many organisations decide to buy a proprietary scheme or employ a consultant to design a scheme specifically for them. A scheme designed specifically for one organisation is obviously a good idea and is likely to have a great deal of credibility with the workforce, but buying a proprietary scheme has the advantage of giving access to extensive comparative data on job markets and rates of pay which designers of proprietary schemes also collect. This can provide much more comprehensive data on which to base decisions about payment levels to relate to jobs than any one organisation could collect.

Different types of payment system

There are, as we have shown, many factors that affect what the organisation pays its workforce, but whatever payment system is chosen will give a different message to the workforce about the issues and values that the organisation feels are important. In this section we shall consider some of the different payment systems that the organisation might choose. There are many variations in systems of payment: some of the more common types will be considered here.

- time rates
- individual payment by results (piece work)
- group incentives

- individual time saving
- measured day work
- profit sharing
- performance-related pay or merit rating
- non-monetary awards
- cafeteria-style payments or flexible pay
- total reward.

Time rates

This is the simplest of all payment systems: as the name implies, people are paid according to the time they spend at work. This may be based on an hourly rate, a weekly rate or an annual salary. In spite of all the talk of incentive schemes and movement towards a human resource management approach with performance-related pay systems, this is still an extremely popular way for many organisations to pay people. This is largely because it is a simple system that is easy to understand and does not result in a great many industrial relations disputes. On the other hand, organisations that have moved away from this system of payment have done so because it provides little incentive to improve productivity or efficiency.

As we said earlier, employers vary in their beliefs about what motivates employees. Those who say that employees can be motivated by the satisfaction gained from the job itself will be concerned to provide a reasonably competitive level of pay for all employees and won't want to pay bonuses or divide the workforce by performance-related pay systems, so that time rates and harmonisation of terms and conditions of employment are likely to appeal to them. The basic rate paid must be sufficiently high that it is adequate for most people's needs. If the rate of pay falls behind this level then the workforce are likely to be demotivated.

Pause for thought 10.1   What do you think about this philosophy? Does it link with anything you have studied on other modules about motivation theory?

The idea that pay is necessary at a certain level to provide for an employee's basic needs, but that to increase pay beyond this is not likely to result in increased performance at work, links very clearly with the work of another motivation theorist, Frederick Herzberg (1966), whose ideas you may have studied, and with his motivation/hygiene theories. Herzberg said that certain things, such as pay and good conditions at work, which he referred to as hygiene factors, were necessary to prevent employees from becoming dissatisfied with work, but that an improvement in these things would not necessarily motivate employees to work harder although it would remove the dissatisfaction. He said that these were the sort of things that people moan about, but that when the dissatisfaction had been removed and the pay or working conditions improved, these people would still not be actually motivated to work harder. The motivators, according to Herzberg, were factors such as making the job more interesting or giving the employee more responsibility.

Payments on time rates, as we have said, don't normally vary from week to week and people are paid for going to work, regardless of how hard they actually work when they are there. In the next Activity we would like you to consider a particular example of a time rate payment system, where there are some variations in the payments people receive.

ACTIVITY 10.5

Imagine that you are a branch manager in a large building society. You are talking to one of your staff, a graduate who is regarded as being bright and a hard worker and who should have an excellent future with the organisation. You ask how things are going and are rather dismayed when she replies, 'OK, but I'm getting a bit disillusioned. I seem to work hard and yet it will take me at least six years to get to the top of the pay scale. Most people around here seem to be at or near to the top of the pay scale already and they seem to take life easy and don't work nearly as hard as I do. I'm thinking seriously about looking for another job.'

1 What is an incremental pay scale supposed to achieve for the organisation?
2 What are the advantages and disadvantages of this type of payment system?
3 How does this payment system relate to what you know about motivation theory?

Discussion of Activity 10.5

1 An incremental pay scale is a form of time rate payment system, as people are still paid for the time that they spend at work regardless of the amount of effort they put into their work. In this case they are also paid an extra amount or increment for each year that they work for the employer. This is supposed to encourage employees to stay with the same employer for a long period of time, and so result in a stable workforce. There is also an implication that people will become more knowledgeable and effective in their job as they work for more years and gain more experience. This is not necessarily true, and although some people do learn from experience and will become more valuable employees the longer they are employed, you may be able to think of people that you know who have done the same job for years and who seem to have stopped learning from experience, and who do not appear to be any more effective in their job than they were on the day they started.

2 Advantages of incremental payment schemes:

   ● simple
   ● easy to calculate wages
   ● reward long service and lead to stable workforce.

   Disadvantages of incremental payment schemes:

   ● no incentive to work harder
   ● slow progress for high fliers
   ● no incentive at top of the scale.

3 This approach tends, like other forms of time rates, to reflect a collectivist view that everyone should be treated the same and that to pay people differently would be divisive. With incremental pay scales such as this, differences that are taken into account are usually about non-contentious things such as length of service. Everyone can see that people are treated fairly and that they will get the same treatment.

This approach tends to be favoured in relatively large, impersonal, bureau-cratic organisations, which place emphasis in determining pay on the jobs rather than the people. This form of payment system will also work best where the pace of change is slow and where there is little scope for individual initiative. An incremental pay system doesn't tend to work well in a fast moving organ-isation where it is likely to stifle initiative and innovation.

We shall now examine a group of payment systems that reflect a more individ-ualised approach, where individuals are rewarded for their contribution. We shall consider both individual payment by results and performance-related pay.

Individual payment by results (piece-work)

This approach, based on individualism, reflects the view that since some peo-ple work harder than others they should be paid different amounts to reflect the differences in effort that they have made. In this system the amount that people are paid depends on how much they produce, so there are very clear criteria and a strong link between earnings and effort. This system is most common in types of manufacturing environment where it is easy to identify the products that each individual has made, or to identify clearly an individ-ual's contribution to a manufactured product.

The main advantages to the employer of payment by results can be sum-marised as follows:

- there is a strong incentive to increase effort, as there is a very clear link with earnings
- if an increased number of tasks are completed in the same amount of time, using the same equipment, the costs per unit of output will be lower.

Like all payment systems, there are disadvantages as well as advantages. The main disadvantages are that:

- it can be expensive to install and maintain
- it can result in many disagreements about standards or levels of production
- production may increase at the expense of quality
- the emphasis on personal performance can cause friction between employees.

This payment system is expensive to install and maintain, as there needs to be a fair system for assessing the norm for levels of production so that production over and above this level can be paid. Work study engineers are often employed to find the most efficient method of carrying out a task, and managers and trade union officials may spend a great deal of time timing different stages in the production process. There is an emphasis in the payment by results system on providing an incentive, but also on control and measurement. Even with controls in place there can be problems, as Activity 10.6 shows.

ACTIVITY 10.6

Imagine that you are the human resource manager in a knitwear manufacturing company. You are about to negotiate with the trade union on the current round of pay talks. The sewing machinists are paid on a piece-work system but there is a great deal of absenteeism, particularly on Fridays. It seems to you that many workers increase their levels of production on the other days of the week so that they can have Fridays off. The company wants to ensure regular high levels of production on every day of the week in order to meet its full order books.

1 What is the underlying message that a piece work system, such as this one, intends to give to the employees?

2 Why is this system not working as well as the organisation wants?

3 How does the situation within this organisation link with motivation theories?

Discussion of Activity 10.6

1 The underlying message that a piece work system is intended to give is that a person will be rewarded for working hard, and the more they produce, the more they will be paid.

2 The system is not working as well as management had hoped because management have assumed that the workforce are only motivated to work harder for money, and that they will continue to work harder and harder for more and more money. Remember the factors that Herzberg (1966), for example, suggested as motivating factors.

3 This situation relates to the view that people may be motivated by a variety of things. In this case the workers wanted a high level of income, but they also wanted some time to relax and spend that income. Some people may be motivated by the opportunity of earning more money, especially if they are saving for some large expenditure. However, not everyone will attach the same degree of importance to financial rewards all the time, and the organisation needs to find out what its employees will value. The employees here seem to be sending a message that leisure is something they value, but other people might be motivated by promotion, a company car, increased responsibility or the increased respect of colleagues.

Individual payment by results is not always particularly appropriate, as we have seen in Activity 10.6. This payment system is most appropriate where:

- it is possible to measure work
- it is easy to attribute it to individuals
- the pace of work is under the employee's control
- management can provide a steady flow of work for the employee to do
- the work is not subject to constant changes in method, materials or equipment.

There are a variety of payment by results schemes. These include:

- group incentives
- individual time saving
- measured day work.

Group incentives

These are based on the same principles as the individual payment by results system, but are used when the individualistic approach is not wanted by the organisation. For example, in order to try to encourage teamworking or to take into account support workers who contribute to overall output, but whose contribution may be difficult to assess, some organisations introduce a system of group payment by results.

The size of the group may vary from small teams or work units to the whole plant or enterprise.

ACTIVITY 10.7

Make a list of the advantages and disadvantages of plant- and enterprise-wide payment by results schemes.

Discussion of Activity 10.7

You may have suggested some of the following advantages and disadvantages.

Advantages

- Employees see how they contribute to the whole organisation's effectiveness.
- Employees are usually encouraged to find ways to improve performance and productivity.
- Employees become interested in how the organisation is managed.
- It is cheaper to install plant- or enterprise-wide payment by results schemes than individual payment by results schemes.
- There is usually a need to discuss financial information with employee representatives and this can result in an improved understanding of how the organisation is run.

Disadvantages

- There is a weaker link in employees' minds between the bonus and the level of their effort, so it may not be a strong incentive.
- Schemes can be difficult to understand.
- Bonus payments could be affected by factors such as inflation which the workforce can do nothing about.

Individual time saving

Individual time saving is a further example of an individualised payment scheme. In this case, instead of basing payment on *x* pence per piece produced, an incentive is paid for the amount of time saved by the worker when he or she performs a specific task. There is normally a standard amount of time allowed for the workers to perform a particular task or sequence of tasks, and they get an extra payment when they manage to improve on this time. This has the advantage of being able to take account of situations where the worker is not able to complete tasks because there is no work to do, for example, because of a machine breakdown. In this situation the time involved is not counted in the calculations for the incentive payment.

Measured day work

Measured day work is another individualised payment scheme. In this case pay rates are agreed at a higher rate than would normally have been paid for a time worker doing the same job, but there is an agreement that the workers will work at a specified level of performance. These levels of performance are agreed using work study techniques and then management carefully monitors the actual level of performance. A further variation of this is the stepped measured day work system, where a number of levels of performance are specified and workers can choose at which level to work. If their work improves they can progress to higher levels and increased pay. These systems have the advantage that the employees' pay will not fluctuate wildly on a daily or weekly basis, and so they provide for stability, but they do not allow individual workers as much flexibility as to how hard they want to work each day.

Profit sharing

This is a form of payment scheme where the focus is on the group rather than the individual. Employees all receive a bonus, and its whose size depends on the profits made by the organisation that year. Once again there is little direct incentive for individuals to work harder, as it is difficult to see how their contribution actually relates to the profit made, but many profit-sharing schemes encourage employees to get involved with how the scheme is run. Sometimes, bonus payments are made in shares rather than cash. This is also intended to give employees an interest in the enterprise, but can result in a risk to both shares and job if the organisation does not do as well in the future. It is difficult to see this as a strong motivational force.

Performance-related pay or merit rating

Performance-related pay, which is sometimes referred to as merit rating, is also a way of linking an individual's pay progression to his or her level of performance or to a rating of competence. It is once again an individualistic approach which favours rewarding people differently according to level of performance or competence, and it aims to motivate all employees and give clear indications of what the organisation expects from employees. Performance-related pay differs from payment by results as it doesn't relate just to the quantity of a product that is produced, and may apply to workers where there is not even any end product to measure.

Initially, performance-related pay was used as a motivational tool primarily for non-manual employees, but in recent years it has been extended to shop floor workers and has been discussed as a tool for use in the health service and in education. It is increasing in popularity, and is often introduced even when organisations are aware of the fact that money is not necessarily a motivator to all employees in all circumstances, as it is felt to be fair to pay people according to the contribution that they make to the organisation.

Performance-related pay is often regarded as a key feature of performance management, as outlined in the previous chapter, and although some performance management schemes do not operate performance-related pay, most do use it. While the motivational theorists cast doubt on the value of money as a motivator, many managers instinctively feel that money will motivate employees. Some organisations, even if they do not feel that it will have a strong motivational effect, introduce performance-related pay as a way of being fair and rewarding high performers' past performance, and so argue that equity is the rationale for the introduction of such a scheme. The fact that performance is considered at all can also have positive effects, in that it helps to create a culture in which performance is valued and recognition of good performance can be a reward in itself. It is important once again to emphasise that performance-related pay needs to be based on what can be seen to be a fair and just system of allocation, with clear objective criteria being used.

ACTIVITY 10.8

Imagine that you work in an organisation where performance-related pay has recently been introduced. You are appraising one of your subordinates, a man in his fifties who has been with the organisation for about 15 years. You have discussed most of the rating criteria, which have all been satisfactory. You say, 'Your work has been good but are there any areas where you feel there could be improvements?' He replies, 'I'm happy in the job but I don't really see much point in working a great deal harder. The mortgage is paid off now, the children have finished their education and if I earn more money I will only have to pay more tax on it. I want to take life a bit easier now and spend more time at home or away in the caravan. I don't always want to be taking work home with me.'

1 What are the advantages and disadvantages of performance-related pay?

2 How does the situation here link with what you know about theories of motivation?

3 Suggest alternative ways of motivating this employee to work to his full potential.

Discussion of Activity 10.8

1   *Advantages* of performance-related pay:

- Rewards the individual by linking systematic assessment of their performance to their level of pay or to a bonus.
- The factors taken into account may be weighted to reflect their relative importance to the organisation.
- It can be used where an incentive is needed but the actual work rate is difficult to measure.
- It can reward factors not easily taken into account in other payment systems.

Disadvantages of performance-related pay:

- There may be disagreements about the performance factors to be assessed, and if great care is not taken in the choice of the factors there may be claims that they are too subjective or even of sex bias.
- Bonus payments may be too infrequent to provide a direct incentive.

2   This is another example of the view that individuals will be motivated by different things and that we value different things. This would link with Maslow's (1954) hierarchy of needs mentioned in the next chapter.

3   The situation described reflects the view that there needs to be a range of different forms of incentive so that individuals can choose what will motivate them. In this case the employee might well be motivated if he was offered the opportunity to work for increased holidays.

Performance-related pay can be paid in several ways, and may even involve non-financial rewards. The most commonly used financial rewards are:

- salary increases within the normal salary scale
- salary increases above the maximum point of the normal pay scale
- where each employee is paid on an individual fixed rate, with good performers getting something above the normal rate
- lump sum payments that are not included in salary.

Salary increases within the normal salary scale

This is a commonly used form of performance-related pay, and gives a clear message that although there is a fixed scale for the job and everyone's pay depends on performance, exceptional performers can progress through this scale more rapidly than others.

Salary increases above the maximum point of the normal pay scale

This is sometimes used when the organisation wants to maintain its existing incremental pay scales but also wants to reward excellent performance. In this case high performers benefit as everyone else progresses along the normal scale until they reach the maximum, but it is of no benefit to average employees who have reached the top of the scale because of the length of their employment.

Each employee is paid on an individual fixed rate, with good performers getting something above the normal rate

In this case the individual is paid on a particular rate, but there is no automatic annual salary increase. The organisation budgets for a percentage increase each year, but then allocates this money according to assessments of employee performance, with excellent performers receiving most, good performers getting some allocation of award and poor performers receiving nothing at all. This gives a very clear message to all concerned, and may result in those who are assessed as being poor performers leaving the organisation.

Lump sum payments that are not included in salary

This can be added to most payment systems, and it can be argued that a lump sum payment will have more impact than if the same amount were included in normal salary. This provides the opportunity to draw attention to the organisation's policy for rewarding excellence, especially if the opportunity is used for a special presentation ceremony.

Non-monetary awards

As shown in Activity 10.8, people may be motivated by a range of different factors and may not always be motivated by being paid more money directly in their pay, especially if they lose a great deal in tax. Although we are all pleased to get more money, there is no public recognition of a job well done in that approach. This view is recognised in many organisations, which now seek to provide both monetary and non-monetary awards. Some of the non-financial awards we have selected will also have a monetary value. We have included them as non-monetary awards as the fact of an award being special, in recognition of a job well done or special effort made, may have a motivating effect larger than purely monetary value. Saying 'thank you' is a much overlooked form of non-monetary award in many organisations. The most commonly used non-financial rewards are:

- commendation
- overseas travel
- gifts
- gift vouchers.

Commendation

The opportunity to commend someone for the efforts that they have made can be extremely important as a way of rewarding and motivating them, whether this is done through the normal performance appraisal interview or at a public ceremony at which a letter or certificate of commendation is presented. The latter situation, with the attendant publicity, will serve as a reinforcement of the values that the organisation wishes to encourage and may also motivate others to improve their work performance.

Overseas travel

This type of reward used to be used primarily to reward sales staff for improvements in sales, but in recent years it has become an incentive on offer to many other individuals. Sometimes overseas travel is used as an incentive for team effort, with the whole team being rewarded with a trip abroad.

This type of reward can be in the form of overseas holidays or the opportunity to attend a high profile training course held at an exotic destination.

Gifts

Other gifts awarded to people who have made significant improvements in their performance include consumer items such as cameras, microwave ovens or jewellery. Once again there is the problem of choosing an appropriate range of gifts, as individuals are not likely to be motivated by the opportunity to acquire a new microwave oven, for example, if they already own one.

Gift vouchers

Gift vouchers are perhaps the most flexible form of incentive payment and are also very popular with individuals, as they offer real choice. Many high street stores promote the use of their gift vouchers to organisations that are thinking of establishing this type of scheme.

Cafeteria–style payments or flexible pay

An even more flexible approach to pay is sometimes referred to as the 'cafeteria approach' or 'flex pay', because employees can choose their own preferred reward or combination of rewards. It gives an opportunity for employers to find a pay package that will suit a diverse range of staff, whether male or female, full time or part time, and who come from a wide age range. This can prove attractive for recruiting and retaining labour. In the cafeteria approach the workforce are told what rewards or benefits they can choose from each year. This could mean that they select from gift vouchers, gifts or holidays or they may prefer to choose from other benefits such as improved health care options, health or life insurance, an improved pension scheme, longer holidays or even additional cash.

Companies that have introduced flexible schemes such as this have done so not to cut costs but to tailor their benefits to the needs of their workforce, and they have found that younger staff prefer cash or a second car, older staff often prefer to improve their pensions or health cover, while staff with young families may prefer longer holidays.

In order for a flexible system to work there has to be an excellent system established for administration, and improvements in computer technology help here. There must also be an appropriate culture within the organisation and excellent communication with members of the workforce and their representatives. Not all organisations have moved towards a complete menu of options: some have felt that staff might be confused by too much choice and have gone for schemes that offer core benefits to all staff with some additional choice over certain options.

Total reward

Total reward is a newer concept than flexible pay that some organisations are starting to develop. This idea, like that of flexible pay, recognises that pay is not the only motivating force for people but it goes even further to include other aspects of employment in the total reward package. Total reward schemes normally do offer flexible benefits but also include aspects of work such as career and personal development, flex-time, a challenging job at work, opportunities for individual growth and development and recognition for achievements. Sometimes they even allow for individual preferences for type of office layout, space and equipment as well as for administrative support. Total reward schemes aim to align employers' HR and business strategies with employees needs in order to ultimately achieve improved performance.

Total reward is a new idea that employers are experimenting with, but many experts say it should only be tried once flexible pay and benefits have been successfully implemented and established. At the moment there are not many employers that have reached this stage and there is much debate about whether issues such as choice of office workspace or computer are actually suitable choices for individuals to make or whether they should remain purely business decisions. It is an interesting new concept but could be difficult to apply in practice within an organisation.

The Equal Opportunities Commission revised Code of Practice on Equal Pay

The Equal Opportunities Commission's (EOC's) revised Code of Practice on Equal Pay (2003b) came into force in December 2003. Like other codes of practice, such as that for discipline and grievance (discussed in Chapter 14) an employment tribunal may take into account any failure by the employer to act on its provisions. This code is admissible in evidence in any cases relating to the Sex Discrimination Act 1975 and to the Equal Pay Act 1970 (each as amended) so is very important and it aims to provide practical guidance on ways of achieving equal pay without sex discrimination.

Regular, transparent equal pay reviews are recommended as a key means of ensuring that equal pay is achieved. Other recommendations include the establishment of a clear, transparent pay system that is regularly monitored to ensure it achieves what it sets out to achieve and regular consultation with the workforce or their representatives.

The Equal Opportunities Commission (2003a) says that the foundations of a good review are:

- to compare the pay of men and women doing equal work and that employers must examine like work, work that has been rated as equivalent under a job evaluation scheme and work which is of equal value
- to identify any pay gaps
- to eliminate any pay gaps that cannot be explained on grounds other than sex.

Although there is no legal compulsion for employers to conduct an equal pay review, the EOC says that this is the most appropriate way of delivering equal pay that is free of sex bias. It further outlines a five-step model to achieve this. The five stages in the EOC's pay review model are:

1 Deciding the scope of the review and identifying the data required.
2 Determining where men and women are doing equal work.
3 Collecting pay data to identify pay gaps.
4 Establishing the causes of any significant pay gaps.
5 Developing an equal pay action plan and/or reviewing and monitoring (EOCb 2003).

Some of the issues can be very difficult as it is necessary both to have a transparent review so workers can see that everything is being treated in a fair manner and at the same time to be aware of the need to keep personal data confidential, as is required under the Data Protection Act(1998). Each of the stages in the EOC pay review model is discussed below.

1 Deciding the scope of the review and identifying the data required

This involves making decisions about who should be included in the review and also the type of information about pay that needs to be included. There will need to be an analysis of the workforce according to criteria such as gender, hours worked and qualifications. All aspects of pay and benefits such as pensions will also need to be examined.

Another crucial question is: Who will actually conduct the review and how much involvement should the workforce have? Certainly there are many people with specialised information, such as payroll managers or HR specialists, that are likely to be involved at different stages and in some instances it may be necessary to call on independent expert help. In a study for the Institute of Employment Studies (2003), quoted in the Code of Practice on Equal Pay (2003a), it was shown that 73% of employers carried out equal pay reviews of the whole of their workforce.

2 Determining where men and women are doing equal work

This will involve examining whether men and women are doing work that may be considered to be 'like work' or 'work that has been rated as equivalent under a job evaluation scheme' or even whether men and women are doing work which is of 'equal value' to the organisation. This can be difficult to establish.

Analytical job evaluation schemes, discussed earlier in this chapter, will be very useful in establishing whether men and women are doing equal work.

Of course, as we stated earlier, such schemes should have been designed to ensure that they contain no unfair bias so they do not discriminate on the grounds of sex. The Equal Opportunities Commission has produced the EOC Pay Review Kit to help organisations with this.

3 Collecting pay data to identify pay gaps

The third stage in the equal pay review should be to gather data relating to actual pay rates of men and women doing equal work. Information is needed relating to the average basic pay and total earnings of men and women, and this should also include an analysis of the component parts of the pay package.

Any gaps should then be identified and reviewed to establish whether they are significant enough to merit further investigation and whether or not they seem to be based on gender. The EOC recommends that records are kept of all significant gaps even if they do not seem to be gender based.

4 Establishing the causes of any significant pay gaps

Once any gaps have been identified, employers need to establish whether they are due to some genuine reason, other than the sex of the jobholders, and then they should examine their pay systems to try to discover which pay policies or practices are contributing to pay gaps based on gender.

5 Developing an equal pay action plan and/or reviewing and monitoring

If differences based on gender are discovered within the pay system then the employer must tackle this, for both the existing and future workforce. An action plan to tackle things in stages may be needed, and a system for monitoring and reviewing whether the changes have worked would also be necessary.

Even when the employer has established that there are no problems, it should continue to review and monitor its pay systems at regular intervals.

Developing an equal pay policy

It is obviously in everyone's interests that employees do not end up being dissatisfied with their pay, for whatever reason, as organisations normally want to motivate people to work well. One way to try to ensure this does not happen is for employers to think about the issues and develop an equal pay policy that clearly states what they are doing to tackle this issue and how they are going about it and monitoring it.

Possible penalties

If employees are unhappy with their pay because they feel they have been discriminated against on the grounds of their sex, they may bring a case before an employment tribunal, and any failure to take into account the EOC's Revised Code of Practice on Equal Pay is likely to count against the employer.

Employment tribunals can make awards to remedy any gender-based inequality in pay, if someone is still employed by the organisation. They may also award compensation for arrears of pay and/or damages. In England, five years' worth of back pay can be awarded while in Scotland an even bigger award of up to six years' back pay can be made to a person who succeeds in proving they have been underpaid for many years and that this was based on their sex. In addition, the employment tribunal may award interest on the award of compensation, and this alone could be a substantial amount.

Equal Pay 1970 (Amendment) Regulations 2004

This amendment to the Equal Pay Act increases a tribunal's powers when dealing with equal value cases. The amendment creates a strong presumption that where a job evaluation exercise has been conducted and has attributed different values to the work of the applicant and the comparator jobs, then these jobs are not of equal value. A tribunal can only decide that the jobs are of equal value if it establishes that the job evaluation exercise itself was flawed in some way or that the job evaluation exercise itself discriminated unfairly on sex discrimination grounds.

The euro

Although Britain has no commitment at present to join the single European currency and has to hold a referendum before any decision is made, the fact that other European countries are using the euro does have an impact. UK organisations need to consider the strategic implications of this as there may be increased competition and greater transparency on pricing and easier comparison of wages and benefits between those countries within the euro zone. The introduction of the euro in these countries brings both opportunities and threats which organisations should examine.

Wages and pensions departments have had to review their practices if their workforce covers several European countries. Data relating to pay in those countries using the euro are easier to compare but historical data on pay may also need to be converted to ease comparisons. For ex-pats working abroad, life is easier if both their home country and host country are in the euro zone, as there will be no exchange rate fluctuations to alter the value of their salaries.

The adoption of the single currency may result in increasing levels of movement of workers between countries within the euro zone as people find it easier to compare wages and conditions. This may also help trade unions when negotiating pay deals for workers in several countries and may even lead to a greater harmonisation of not only wages but also terms and conditions. Pension plans, share option schemes and profit-related pay schemes are likely to have to be reviewed.

HR departments have a very important role to play in examining the strategic implications of the euro for their organisation and may need to develop, in some cases, into a Europe-wide function. In multinational organisations, particularly where some of the workforce work in euros but others are outside the zone, communications and training will be particularly important. The HR department may also need to review their organisation's payment systems, pensions scheme, expatriate programmes and procedures for union negotiations and consider the cultural implications of the single currency and possible need for harmonisation of pay and conditions. They will also be involved in any practical issues relating to actual payments to some workers in euros.

Conclusion

We have examined some of the types of payment systems that are available to employers and related them briefly to motivation theory. No scheme is perfect for all organisations, and all schemes have advantages and disadvantages. Each scheme gives a clear message about the values of the organisation and should be a reflection of its mission statement. The choice of payment scheme will depend on the wishes of the workforce as well as the culture of the organisation, and these should be taken into account before any scheme is introduced. The workforce should be involved in discussion, design, implementation and review of whatever payment scheme is introduced. With the increasingly diverse workforce at the start of the twenty-first century, and moves towards a flexible workforce, many organisations have introduced flexible approaches to the pay and benefits that they provide for employees, using their payment systems as one mechanism for achieving their strategic goals.

Particular care should be taken to ensure that: the basis for the chosen payment system is transparent and understood by the workforce; full consultation with the workforce has occurred; and the selected pay system does not lead to unfair discrimination based on gender. This is still as necessary today as it was more than 30 years ago when the Equal Pay Act 1970 was first introduced. All organisations should review the basis of their pay systems in light of the Equal Opportunities Commission's revised Code of Practice on Equal Pay to ensure that they are rewarding and motivating all members of their workforce, regardless of their sex, in a fair way. A modern workforce has to be based on fair reward.

REVIEW QUESTIONS

You will find brief answers to these review questions on pages 493–494.

1 Imagine that you are the human resource manager for an organisation that is considering the introduction of a points rating system of job evaluation. The job evaluation committee with whom you are working has specified that the following criteria should be used in evaluating jobs:

- skill
- responsibility for people, e.g. in a job caring for children
- responsibility for equipment and materials
- responsibility for other employees
- mental effort
- physical effort
- working conditions.

Rate the three jobs, as described in their job descriptions (see pages 310–312), according to these criteria. You can give up to 10 points for each of these factors for each job:

10 exceptional
7–9 high
4–6 medium
1–3 low
0 negligible

Then add the total scores for Job A, Job B and Job C.

For example, if you feel that a medium level of skill is required by a receptionist as described in job description A you will give that job between 4 and 6 points in that category. If you feel that Job B, the human resource assistant, shows a high level of responsibility for people, you will give it between 7 and 9 points.

Remember that in job evaluation it is the *job* you are evaluating, not the person, so you do not need to know how effective a person actually is in that job.

Compare your evaluation of the three jobs using this points rating method, with your evaluations of the same jobs completed earlier in this chapter, using the whole job ranking method and then the paired comparison method.

Were your rankings of the jobs the same or different in all three cases? Why was this?

2 Find out how much the minimum wage actually is at the present time. How much is the rate for adults aged over 21?

How much is the rate for those aged 18–21?

What are the rates being paid to those who are on Government training schemes such as apprenticeships or New Deal?

3 Interview managers or employees from three organisations of your choice from different industrial sectors to establish what effect, if any, the introduction of the National Minimum Wage has had on that organisation/industrial sector.

4 Explain the process of job evaluation and comment on how a points rating job evaluation scheme can contribute to perceptions of fairness from the point of view of employees.

5 Fairness in pay is an objective of both employers and employees. Describe briefly the issues that need to be considered with reference to fairness, and evaluate critically the approaches that employers could adopt to achieve fairness.

6 Imagine that you are a consultant employed to select a job evaluation scheme for an organisation that employs 500 employees in a large range of clerical jobs. Write a report to the human resource manager in which you outline the advantages and disadvantages of the various types of job evaluation scheme and recommend what you consider to be a suitable job evaluation scheme for this organisation.

SELF-CHECK QUESTIONS

Answer the following multiple-choice questions. The correct responses are given on page 494 for you to check your understanding of this chapter.

(a) Does harmonisation of wages and conditions of employment mean that managers and other employees and workers in the same organisation in different countries get different payment systems and conditions of employment to each other? YES or NO

(b) Does job evaluation determine the amount of pay for a person doing a particular job? YES or NO

(c) Are the following all types of non-analytical job evaluation schemes: whole job ranking, paired comparisons, points rating? YES or NO

(d) Are all of the following advantages of the whole job ranking method of job evaluation: it is simple, cheap to operate and easy to understand? YES or NO

(e) Is the points rating system of job evaluation an analytical method of job evaluation? YES or NO

(f) Does job evaluation take account of the individual's performance in the job? YES or NO

(g) Does an incremental pay scheme provide an incentive for people to work harder? YES or NO

(h) Does a payment system based on time rates reflect an individualistic approach to the way people are paid? YES or NO

(i) Is piece work another name for individual payment by results? YES or NO

(j) Is performance-related pay a way of linking an individual's pay progression to their length of employment with the organisation? YES or NO

WHAT NEXT?

This chapter aimed to introduce you to the topic of payment systems and by this stage you should be able to meet the objectives stated at the beginning. You may now want to go further with the subject and the resources listed in the references and further study sections will help you to do this. There are lots more activities for you to check your understanding of Chapter 10 on our student web site at:

http://www.pearsoned.co.uk/foothook

You may also be interested in looking at research studies and articles. The CIPD carries out regular surveys of reward management; its latest survey conducted in November 2003 was of 572 organisations that employed between them about 1.5 million people. One of the key features of this survey is the prominence given to pensions as part of the overall reward strategy, with many CIPD members regarding it as a crucial reward issue.

If you are a full-time student, or at the start of your career, pensions may not seem the most exciting or relevant topic to you but it is going to be a key issue in relation to reward, particularly in view of the Equal Treatment Framework Directive due to come into effect in October 2006. While the proposed legislation is likely to mean that fixed retirement ages become unlawful, it may result in retirement age and the age at which pension can be drawn being different. According to Income Data Services (IDS 2003):

> It is likely that employers will struggle to show that it is appropriate and necessary to operate a mandatory retirement age rather than rely on normal performance management practices. However, the Government may intervene to a certain extent with the consultation document mooting the possibility of having a default retirement age at which employers could lawfully require staff to retire. The suggested age is 70: which would bring about a substantial change for many organisations and would mean that the retirement ages and pensionable ages would be out of kilter. In the future organisations will have to be much clearer about distinguishing between pensionable ages and retirement ages. In many organisations it could be that the former survives, while the latter is no longer relevant.

Some pay schemes also reward length of service (refer again to incremental pay schemes discussed on pages 316–318). Under the proposed legislation, these could in future be regarded as indirectly discriminating against younger workers.

What are your views on these issues? The CIPD survey (2004) *Reward Management 2004: A Survey of Policy and Practice* can be downloaded free from **www.cipd.co.uk/surveys**. IDS briefs can be found in libraries or downloaded from **www.ids.brief.co.uk** but you will need an Athens Username (usually available from university libraries) to access this in full.

References

Advisory, Conciliation and Arbitration Service (2003) *Job Evaluation: An Introduction*, ACAS (available at **www.acas.org.uk**; accessed 23.6.03)

Chartered Institute of Personnel and Development (2004) *Reward Management 2004: A Survey of Policy and Practice*, CIPD (**www.cipd.co.uk/surveys**; accessed 28.6.04)

Equal Opportunities Commission (2003a) *Campaign: 15% Off – Why are Women Workers still Going Cheap?* EOC (**http://www.eoc.org.uk/EOCeng/dynpages/camp_pay.asp**; accessed 24.6.04)

Equal Opportunities Commission (2003b) *Code of Practice on Equal Pay*, EOC (**www.eoc.org.uk**; accessed 24.6.04)

Equal Opportunities Commission (2004) *Conducting an Equal Pay Review in Accordance with Data Protection Principles*, EOC (**www.eoc.org.uk**; accessed 24.6.04)

Equal Opportunities Commission Hong Kong (2003) Eliminating discrimination: systems and policy reviews, equal pay for work of equal value, *Equal Opportunities Commission Hong Kong Annual Report 2001–2*, HKEOC (**www.eoc.org.hk/ME/annual/01-02/report/eliminate.htm**; accessed 24.6.04)

Herzberg, F. (1966) *Work and the Nature of Man*, Staples Press

Income Data Services (2003) *Editorial, Brief 739*, IDS (**www.idsbrief.co.uk**; accessed 28.6.04)

Jones, C. (2004) The great pay packet racket, *The Guardian: Office Hours*, 21 June, 2–3

Maslow, A. (1954) *Motivation and Personality*, Harper & Row

McGregor, D. (1960) *The Human Side of Enterprise*, McGraw-Hill

Neathey, Dench and Thomson, case study taken from *Monitoring Progress towards pay equality*, Institute of Employment Studies, EOC 2003.

Further study

Books

ACAS Advisory Booklets, particularly *Introduction to Payment Systems* (2003), *Job Evaluation: An Introduction* (2003) and *Appraisal-Related Pay* (2003).

Armstrong, M. (2002) *Employee Reward*, 3rd edition, CIPD. (This provides an in-depth coverage of all aspects of employee reward.)

Chartered Institute of Personnel and Development (2000) *The CIPD Guide on Team Reward*. CIPD, revised edition, July. (An excellent source of information for organisations which are seeking to find ways to reward teams in the workplace.)

Chartered Institute of Personnel and Development (November 2001; revised February 2004) *Total Reward*, CIPD. (An excellent introduction to the topic of total reward.)

Equal Opportunities Commission (2003a) *Code of Practice on Equal Pay*, EOC (**www.eoc.org.uk**; accessed 24.6.04). (Practical guidelines aimed at employers and others about implementing equal pay.)

Equal Opportunities Commission (2003b) *Conducting an Equal Pay Review in Accordance with Data Protection Principles*, EOC (**www.eoc.org.uk**; accessed 24.6.04). (More practical guidance to help employers and others review the extent to which they have achieved equal pay in their organisation.)

Equal Opportunities Commission (2004) *Good Practice Guide: Job Evaluation Schemes Free of Sex Bias*, EOC (**www.eoc.org.uk**; accessed 24.6.04). (More practical advice and guidance to help eliminate sex bias in job evaluation schemes.)

Equal Opportunities Commission (2005) *Campaign: 15% Off – Why are Women Workers still Going Cheap?* EOC (**http://www.eoc.org.uk/EOCeng/dynpages/camp_pay.asp**; accessed 21.02.05). (The EOC has joined with the National Union of Students to raise awareness among students about pay issues.)

Articles

Berry, M. (2004) Do benefits packages score with staff? *Personnel Today*, 23 March, 12. (Review of findings from a survey of employers and the benefits packages they use.)

Daugherty, C. (2002) How to introduce flexible benefits, *People Management*, Vol. 8, No. 1, 42–43. (A step-by-step approach to introducing flexible benefits into an organisation.)

Fisher, J. (2001) How to design incentive schemes, *People Management*, Vol. 7, No. 1, 11 January, 38–39. (Discussion of ways to design incentive schemes to improve employee motivation at work.)

Fowler, A. (1991) How to reward performance, *Personnel Management Plus*, July. (Two extremely useful short articles giving practical suggestions for job evaluation and reward management.)

Fowler, A. (1992) How to choose a job evaluation scheme, *Personnel Management Plus*, October.

Freeman, R. (2001) Upping the stakes, *People Management*, Vol. 7, No. 3, 8 February, 25–29. (Discusses studies to show whether giving employees a financial share in the business makes a difference to their performance and productivity.)

Haslett, P. and S. Palmer (2001) Hard to contain, *People Management*, Vol. 7, No. 11, 31 May, 30–34. (A review of the effects of skills and labour shortages on pay levels.)

Hogg, C. (ed) (1990) Incentive programmes, *Personnel Management*, Factsheet 33, September.

Jenkins, L. (2000) How to set up a share ownership scheme, *People Management*, Vol. 6, No. 19, 28 September, 44–45. (A short article which gives practical advice on this issue.)

Johnson, R. (2001) Import duty, *People Management*, Vol. 7, No. 5, 8 March, 25–29. (Discusses issues relating to the recruitment of overseas workers to fill skills gaps in Britain.)

Milsome, S. (2001) Distaff development, *People Management*, Vol. 7, No. 16, 9 August, 27–28. (A report on equal opportunities and salary within the Biotechnology and Biological Sciences Research Council.)

Paddison, L. (2001) How to conduct an equal pay review, *People Management*, Vol. 7, No. 12, 14 June, 58–59. (Suggestions for ways to help employers establish whether or not they have pay gaps based on gender, ethnicity or disability.)

Pay and Benefits Bulletin. (This is published twice a month and is in the *IRS Employment Review*. It provides a useful source of information about pay and benefits in various sectors and organisations.)

Roberts, Z. (2004) On the plus side, *People Management*, Vol. 10 No. 3, 12–13. (This briefly describes the ways in which three organisations are using a mix of existing reward practice and innovatory ideas to produce their own reward strategies.)

Shonfield, D. (2003) Spoilt for choice, *People Management*, Vol. 9, No. 2, 36–38. (Article about the way successful organisations differentiate themselves from the rest by their clever use of reward strategies.)

Smethurst, S. (2003) A slice of the cake, *People Management*, Vol. 9, No. 3, 32–34. (Article about the pros and cons of using shares in the company as a part of the employee reward package.)

Woolnough, R. (2004) How to set up an incentive scheme, *Personnel Today*, 17 February, 22. (A quick guide to the key steps to rewarding staff.)

Internet

The Advisory, Conciliation and Arbitration Service   **www.acas.org.uk**
(This site has guidance on various aspects of pay and texts of leaflets that can be downloaded directly or ordered.)

The Equal Opportunities Commission   **www.eoc.org.uk**
(There is plenty of advice and guidance about equal pay on this site. The EOC site contains sections on equal opportunities issues in Scotland and Wales. It also has on-line quizzes so you can test your knowledge about men and women at work.)

Department for Trade and Industry   **www.dti.gov.uk/er/nmw/index.htm**
(Up-to-date information about the minimum wage at this site.)

Incomes Data Services (IDS)   **www.incomesdata.co.uk**
(Abstracts from articles in the section on pay and labour market data.)

Payfinder   **www.payfinder.com** and **http://secure.payfinder.com/EO/**

(Two ways to check out your rate of pay to see if men and women are being paid equally in your job and region.)

CHAPTER 11

Managing employee welfare

OBJECTIVES

After you have studied this chapter you will be able to:

- explain the need to manage employee well-being
- describe the Health and Safety Executive's approach to stress management
- explain the need for counselling in the workplace
- identify the considerations that a workplace policy on counselling should address
- describe the major elements of the interpersonal communication model
- explain the concept of reflective responses
- describe the techniques involved in providing counselling
- understand and use basic counselling skills.

As described in Chapter 1, the main focus of personnel management has changed over the years. One of the earliest roles for personnel specialists included that of the welfare officer (Fowler 1994). The focus of this role was on the well-being of employees and it sometimes meant taking a paternalistic viewpoint, i.e. adopting a moral stance and telling people what was best for them. The personnel function has changed and become more complex, adopting a more strategic and integrated approach to human resource management, a theme taken up by a number of the subsequent chapters. Chapter 13, for example, will deal with the need for a high performance workplace culture where employees are encouraged to give of their best through management approaches involving partnership, a high level of communication through information sharing and consultation, and various bundles of HRM practices associated with employee involvement. Another factor, however, which has an obvious impact on employees' ability to function at high levels and add value to their organisation is their individual well-being. Employees who cannot concentrate at work or who may even stay away from work because of physical or psychological health problems obviously cannot contribute to their full potential, which has a negative impact on the goal of high performance working (IDS 2002b). In this context, the Engineering Employers' Federation (EEF 2001, p.1) identifies effective stress management as 'a key part of a positive, proactive human resources policy'.

There is evidence then that a concern for employee welfare is still an important aspect of human resource management. Even if the aforementioned paternalistic elements are not acceptable in our modern culture, employers are expected to care about their employees, and responsibility for this may be held by line managers as well as human resource and other specialists. There is a range of business and legal reasons for saying that an employer has not just an obligation but also a right to be involved in employee welfare.

A major focus of this chapter will be on the provision of counselling as a response to employee welfare problems, although other possible responses will also be discussed. To develop an understanding of the need for counselling and how it should be provided, we shall address the following issues:

- the role of the employer with regard to employee welfare
- the types of problem involved and their sources
- the implications of these problems for the workplace
- what to consider when drawing up policies and procedures
- who should be involved in providing counselling
- counselling skills and techniques.

The role of the employer in employee well-being

One area of debate on the subject of welfare is whether this is a personal and private matter. Should an employer have a right to enquire into the well-being of employees?

Pause for thought 11.1

Before you read on, take a few minutes to think about your position on this issue. Make a list of arguments for saying that employers should be concerned about the personal welfare of their employees, and a list of reasons why they should not.

The major argument for employers to concern themselves with the welfare of individuals is that personal problems may affect an individual's performance at work. These may be problems in their private lives, but also problems that arise in the workplace. When people are upset, angry or suffering from anxiety, this can manifest itself in a variety of behaviours, such as:

- tiredness due to lack of sleep or poor diet
- loss of appetite or eating more (particularly chocolate and cream cakes!)
- drinking more alcohol or coffee
- smoking more
- mood swings, particularly a tendency to be more irritable
- changed attitudes, loss of interest in work
- inability to concentrate.

These are just some examples of the changes in behaviour you might expect to see, and further examples can be found in documents prepared by the CIPD (**www.cipd.co.uk/subjects/health/stress**; accessed 09.09.04) and the EEF (2001). Their impact on work standards is obvious: productivity may decrease; standards of work are likely to fall; there is an increased probability of absenteeism and turnover.

Even if personal problems are affecting work performance, the question remains as to what the employer's role is and how far the employer should go in assisting people to solve these problems. Many feel that it is intrusive, an invasion of privacy, to ask about events in a person's life outside work; they consider that this is not the employer's business even if the effects are being felt within the workplace. One must also be mindful of a person's right to respect for their private and family life under the Human Rights Act 1998.

Pause for thought 11.2	Where do you think the balance lies between these two points of view?

Employers do have some responsibility for ensuring employee health, as discussed more fully in Chapter 12. This responsibility is partly addressed in the Health and Safety at Work Act 1974 which is intended to ensure the health, safety and welfare of persons at work. Much of this Act is directed at the prevention of accidents and physical injury to people in the workplace, and it could be argued that an employee distracted by personal problems is more likely to cause or be the victim of accidents. This, then, would be one argument for an employer's right and obligation to pursue a resolution of an employee's problems.

The principles of common law are also relevant. These dictate some of the factors that are implicit in a contract of employment. You will find a full discussion of this in Chapter 6. The issue that is important here is the expectation that employers will show due care for their employees. This obligation entails not exposing employees to known hazards. Historically, most discussion of this issue has centred around the physical environment and work methods that might have a direct impact on physical health. A court case in 1994, however, brought the issue of employee stress into the limelight.

In November 1994, John Walker, a senior social worker with Northumberland County Council, won his case in a high court, claiming that the employer had been negligent in its handling of this employee's stress. Mr Walker had returned to work after suffering a nervous breakdown. After his return to work the employer failed to make adjustments in his workload, and Mr Walker was dismissed on ill-health grounds after he had a second nervous breakdown. The fact that Mr Walker had suffered a first nervous breakdown meant that it could reasonably have been foreseen that the workload was a potential hazard for this employee. Mr Walker received an out of court settlement of £175,000 (Midgley 1997, p.36).

In recent years, the Health and Safety Executive (HSE) has played a major role in the development of guidelines for employers on various aspects of stress management. The duty of care addressed in the Health and Safety at Work Act 1974 applies to employees' physical and mental well-being, and since these can be affected by stress caused by workplace factors, the duty of care constitutes an obvious legal obligation to pay attention to stress management. The Management of Health and Safety at Work Regulations 1999 also impose a duty on employers to conduct a risk audit on potential hazards in the workplace, which also applies in this area as the effects of stress can be regarded as a hazard (see Chapter 12 for a detailed description of risk audits). The main focus of the Health and Safety Executive has been on the development of standards for employers to achieve in terms of stress management, and after a series of consultation and pilot exercises, the intention is to launch an official set of standards at the end of 2004. Organisations will be able to use these standards to measure their achievements in terms of stress management. The stress management standards are not legally enforceable on organisations, but the HSE may use them as evidence that an organisation is not fulfilling its duty with regard to stress management. The HSE has already issued an improvement order against one organisation for failing to manage stress adequately, West Dorset Hospitals NHS Trust in 2003 (reported by Hayden-Smith and Simms 2003), though the IDS (2004) reports that the Trust has since remedied the situation with suitable interventions.

Did you know?

Occupations where employees have reported high levels of work-related stress include: teaching and nursing; protective service providers, government administrators, certain managerial jobs; social workers, police officers, armed forces personnel, and medical practitioners.

(**www.hse.gov.uk/statistics/causdis/stress.htm**; accessed 03.02.04)

The draft standards addressed six areas of work that should be audited. These are laid out with a brief description of what each entails in Table 11.1. The basic idea was to ascertain what percentage of staff feel that they are able to cope with any work situations in these six areas. The proposed acceptable standard of achievement for demands, control and support was 85% of staff responding positively to questions about these aspects of their work, and the standard for relationships, role and change was 65% of staff. Organisations must also be able to show that they have 'systems in place locally to respond to any individual concerns' (**www.hse.gov.uk**; accessed 03.02.04). As Quinn (2004) points out, the identification of stress factors through such an audit makes the eventuality of stress foreseeable, so employers would be obligated to take some action in such an instance.

Table 11.1   **HSE draft stress management standards**

Area of work	Description
Demands	The range of tasks and requirements in a job; possibility of work overload. Demands should be well matched with employees in terms of their competencies. Good job design principles should be applied to ensure that jobs are not monotonous and boring.
Control	The extent to which employees have control over, and input into, decision making related to their own work.
Support	Provision of, or lack of, support mechanisms from colleagues, line managers, and others such as HR staff. Employee awareness of the people and systems they can call on for support when it is needed.
Relationships	Relationships with colleagues and line managers are important and can have a major impact on employees' motivation and sense of well-being. Systems for resolving conflict, and policies for dealing with unacceptable behaviour such as harassment.
Role	How well defined is each person's role and are employees helped to understand their role and how it fits in with others, for instance through a good induction programme? Is there role ambiguity because the role has not been well explained? Is there role conflict where the behaviours expected in the performance of one task are very different from the behaviours expected in other tasks? Do different colleagues expect different things?
Change	How much change are employees expected to cope with, and how well prepared are they when they do have to deal with change? Are the arrangements for information sharing and consultation adequate?

In addition, organisations should be aiming for a 5% improvement year on year until a target of 20% reduction of work-related illness has been achieved. Further HSE targets to be met by 2010 are 'a 30% reduction in the number of work days lost due to work-related ill health' and the provision of assistance with rehabilitation for employees after a bout of illness (**www.hse.gov.uk**; accessed 03.02.04).

An additional factor to do with employer obligations is that employment tribunals hearing cases of unfair dismissal would expect employers to have conducted a full investigation of the circumstances surrounding an incident of misconduct or incompetence, particularly in the case of a person who previously had a good work record, and to take any extenuating circumstances into consideration. You can read more about this in Chapter 14. The point about legal obligations could be summarised in the statement that employers have a duty of care.

A further point should be made here about the link between counselling and discipline. If an employee's personal problems result in falling standards at work, or even in an event that could be construed as misconduct, this could result in formal disciplinary action. On the whole, managers prefer to handle conflict in an informal manner to preserve good working relationships, and regard formal discipline as an action to be taken if the informal approach fails. This approach is encouraged by the ACAS guidelines on discipline (2004). Again, you will find a fuller discussion of this in Chapter 14. It should suffice to make the point here that the proper use of counselling may obviate the need to embark on formal disciplinary action.

Finally, we can justify an employer's interest in the well-being of employees with reference to the basic need to develop good working relationships, on the part of individual employees, individual managers, and from a corporate point of view. Abraham Maslow (1954) was one of the first writers to describe motivation in terms of human needs, and these concepts have often been applied to the workplace. One of the needs that Maslow identified is the social need for relationships, and indeed the importance of relationships has been reinforced by the inclusion of this factor in the HSE's list of aspects of stress management. A number of surveys on motivation have identified the importance of good relationships at work, and specifically the relationship between supervisor and subordinate. It is not inappropriate to care about the people we work with. Much has also been written about corporate image, and many employers wish to be recognised as 'good employers', especially since corporate image can affect an organisation's ability to attract and retain good employees and can therefore have a major impact on the success of the organisation.

The reasons for employers to be involved with employees' problems can be summarised as follows:

- to address problems with productivity, standards of work, attendance and turnover
- to meet legal obligations to ensure the health, safety and welfare of employees
- to avoid the development of disciplinary problems
- to maintain good employee relations.

Types of problem and their sources

Stress has already been identified as a major area of concern, and can be regarded as an umbrella term for a range of problems. Stress is manifested when people are dealing with so many pressures that their normal behaviour patterns become affected. Hans Selye (1956 and 1974), a noted writer on stress, used the terms 'eustress' and 'distress' to explain that stress is not always a negative concept. Sometimes people are stimulated by having to deal with a number of issues; this can be exciting and motivating. When it becomes too much and one cannot cope and at the same time continue to behave within the range of one's normal behaviour patterns, this is what Selye refers to as distress. This is what we normally mean when we refer to stress these days (Le Fevre *et al.* 2003).

What are the causes of stress? There are a wide range of factors that cause stress both in personal relationships and health and in work relationships (see Figure 11.1); these factors are referred to as stressors. Holmes and Rahe (1967) identified a number of life events as being sources of stress. Ranked at number one as a source of stress was the death of one's spouse, and other factors identified included divorce, taking on a high mortgage and taking a holiday.

It is also recognised that circumstances at work such as poor relationships, especially with one's manager or supervisor, and overwork or underemployment can contribute to stress. The case of John Walker mentioned earlier is an example of too high a workload combined with the demanding nature of the work contributing to stress.

The symptoms of stress include the behavioural changes we previously identified that might alert you to the fact that a colleague is under pressure. If not dealt with, the end result can be physical or mental illness leading to mental breakdown.

Figure 11.1   **Some causes of stress**

Implications of personal problems for the workplace

People who are worried, stressed or upset because of problems in their personal lives cannot automatically put these emotions to one side when they enter their organisations' premises. Being at work might sometimes provide some relief from having to think about personal problems, but more often it will be the case that an individual's powers of concentration are disturbed by the existence of personal worries. These preoccupations may manifest themselves in several ways, including:

- short temper and impatience
- emotional outbursts
- lack of attention to duties
- decreased productivity
- increase in number of accidents
- increased absence, lateness and turnover.

All of these obviously have a deleterious effect on a person's work and an organisation's performance.

Organisational policy and procedures

Did you know?

According to the HSE, 13.4 million days were lost from work in 2001 in Britain because of stress-related problems. This is more than double the number estimated in 1995/96 when the cost of such absences was put at around £381 million to employers and £3.8 billion to society.

(**www.hse.gov.uk**; accessed 03.02.04)

Policy statements and procedures provide guidelines for all employees. They let managers know how to handle problems, and inform everyone about the help, assistance and support they can expect to receive. There is a dual role for policies as far as situations requiring counselling are concerned. First there is a need for policies relating directly to the provision of counselling, and second an organisation should have policies dealing with workplace behaviours or events that have been identified as causing distress. For instance, in a *Guardian* Careers Section article, Professor Cary Cooper was quoted as saying that bullying probably accounted for a third to a half of all stress-related illness (Venning 1995).

Policies on bullying and sexual/racial harassment can help to eliminate these unwanted behaviours and promote a less stressful working environment. Many organisations such as banks and retail outlets, where staff handle cash and at the same time have direct contact with the public, have recognised that specialised counselling is necessary to deal with the trauma their employees can suffer after an episode involving violence or a threat of violence. This is true when they have either been directly threatened or witnessed an incident. Employers will obviously have to decide which issues are most important for their organisations, and this may involve surveying employees to discover which issues are of concern to them, and which solutions the employees would most like to take advantage of. The package of welfare policies, procedures and benefits an employer offers to employees is often referred to as an 'employee assistance programme'.

Policies should also address the following issues:

- who will be involved in providing counselling, and what are the parameters of their roles
- what type of services will be offered
- issues of confidentiality.

Who should be involved in providing counselling

Pause for thought 11.3

Before you read on, stop to consider who might be involved in providing counselling to employees, and why. Make a list of at least three potential sources of counselling, and compare it with lists made by other students in your class.

Did you know?

Rolls-Royce found a 21% decrease in stress-related absence in one unit after 75% of the line managers had attended a workshop on stress awareness and risk assessment.

(*Stress Essentials: Practical Solutions that Work*, reported from a conference held in Spring 2002; available on the EEF web site)

A number of people can be identified as providers of counselling within an organisation's employee assistance programme. They may themselves be employees of the organisation or the assistance may be available from external agencies. The possibilities include the following:

- *Direct line managers*. Line managers know their subordinates well and are in a good position to spot the initial signs of stress. They should be the first to observe or be affected by the existence of a problem in their work area. It is a fundamental part of a manager's job to ensure the smooth running of the organisation, so it is reasonable to expect that line managers should take appropriate action when counselling is needed.
- *Human resource managers*. Human resource specialists are often identified in organisations as capable of providing counselling and the natural choice to do so. Employees may prefer to talk to personnel staff, regarding them as disinterested parties who understand the organisation but have some distance, being outside their own department.
- *Occupational health unit/trained counsellors*. An employer may decide to employ professional staff to provide a dedicated service within the organisation's formal structure.
- *Trained volunteers*. One possibility is to develop a network of trained volunteer contacts throughout the organisation. Interested contacts with aptitude can be trained to provide initial counselling. This has the advantage of employees being able to talk to someone outside of their own work area, but within the organisation. Such a system is, however, probably feasible only in large organisations.
- *External agencies*. Provision of counselling can be contracted out to an external agency specialising in employee assistance programmes. Contracts can specify a range of services, and these variations are discussed in more detail later.

With the methods of providing employee assistance that involve non-specialists, there is a need for training for anyone involved at any level, at least in the basics of counselling (Shuttleworth 2004). As well as covering counselling skills, this training should enable people to recognise when the boundaries of their capabilities have been reached. That is, although we are maintaining that people throughout an organisation should be capable of offering initial counselling, we recognise that this is only one part of their job; they will not become professional counsellors. Part of the skill of basic counselling is knowing when to refer someone for further help and how to do this. It should also be recognised that providing help to others to deal with their stress can be stressful in itself, so non-specialists involved in this kind of activity should themselves be assured of on-going support in addition to training (Kiefer and Briner 2003).

In deciding for any particular organisation which particular methods of providing counselling are appropriate, you may wish to draw up a table showing the advantages and disadvantages of each, and indicating key issues to be considered. Table 11.2 presents an example of a generic assessment, but this could, of course, be tailored to the circumstances in an individual organisation.

Types of service

Employers need to decide what level of employee assistance they wish to offer, particularly if they are negotiating a contract with a specialist agency. Options include:

- telephone consultations
- referrals to specialist agencies such as Alcoholics Anonymous, debt counsellors, Relate (for guidance on marriage and other intimate relationships)
- face-to-face consultations
- agreement on the number of times any individual may use the service.

Usually the cost of an external service is based on a flat fee per employee with a service contract for an agreed array of services.

Table 11.2   **Assessment of methods of counselling provision**

Provider	Advantages	Disadvantages	Key issues
Line manager	Low cost/duty is part of job Knows employees well Knowledge of organisation	Employees may be reluctant to open up to someone they work with	Need for training and development of skills Need for support Organisation's culture and employee relations
Human resource specialist	Low cost/duty is part of job Knowledge of organisation	Employees may not wish to be seen approaching HRM office	Need for training and development of skills Need for support
Volunteer counsellor	Low cost	Employees may doubt confidentiality Suitable only for large organisations	Need for training and development of skills Need for support
Internal specialist	Availability of person dedicated to task Confidentiality	Higher cost Employees may not wish to be seen approaching internal specialist	Range of expertise required
External specialist	Confidentiality Distance from workplace Flexible choice between telephone and face-to-face counselling	Higher cost Reluctance to admit need for specialist help	Determine selection criteria and selection process

Confidentiality

Obviously there must be guarantees of confidentiality if any counselling system is to work. No one will reveal details of their personal lives to someone who they suspect will go away and reveal the information to other people, and anyone who provides counselling should be aware of the need to respect confidences. However, the decision about what can be treated confidentially versus the right to disclose or act on information obtained during a counselling session is not necessarily straightforward. What if someone admits within the framework of a counselling session to theft from the organisation, and the penalty for theft in the disciplinary code is instant dismissal?

There is a need to clarify what can be handled confidentially and what cannot. This should be addressed explicitly in the relevant policy statement and communicated to all employees.

Counselling skills

Before you read about the range of skills and techniques required for effective counselling, you may benefit from carrying out the following Activity to assess your approach to counselling.

ACTIVITY 11.1

You are the personnel manager in a large company with many divisions. An administrative assistant asks to see you about a problem at work. She tells you that her manager is always picking on her, criticising her work and the way she talks to clients. She has asked him to be specific, but she can never tie him down. The criticism always takes the form of throwaway, sarcastic comments. She also complains that this manager is totally disorganised, which creates a lot of work for other people as he does not plan ahead, so people in his department are always rushing to meet deadlines. Inevitably this leads to mistakes. The administrative assistant tells you that she is so distressed by this that she feels unwell most of the time and is often close to tears.

Think about how you would handle this situation and then choose from the following actions the one that most closely resembles what you would do.

(a) Refer the administrative assistant to the grievance procedure, and suggest that she either discuss the situation with her manager or put it in writing to him. Agree a date to review progress.

(b) Tell the administrative assistant about stress management techniques and suggest that she gives them a try. Agree a date to review progress.

(c) (a) and (b) together.

(d) Ask questions to get a clearer picture and ask the administrative assistant what she thinks the solutions are. Agree actions to be taken and fix a date to review progress.

After you have read more about counselling techniques you can look at this scenario again and consider whether you have adopted the most effective approach.

The importance of communication skills in counselling

The techniques that are emphasised for effective counselling are all to do with some aspect of communication such as listening, questioning, providing feedback. To ensure a full understanding of the impact of these techniques, it is a good idea to review a general model of interpersonal communication first. You can later examine how the counselling techniques fit into the communication model.

Figure 11.2 is a simplified model of the major stages of interpersonal communication, using terms developed by Berlo (1960), among others.

If one simply reads this model as a representation of the communication process, it gives the impression that the process is very uncomplicated. Someone, the sender, has some information to communicate. The sender decides how to formulate the message (encoding) and how to pass it on to the receiver (choosing a channel). The target person, the receiver, gets the message, interprets it, and takes appropriate action which provides feedback to the sender of the message. This seems very straightforward, but a more detailed examination of what is happening at each stage of the model will reveal its hidden complexities, highlighting why communications so often fail and how an understanding of the process can help you to improve your communication skills.

Figure 11.2   **A model of interpersonal communication**

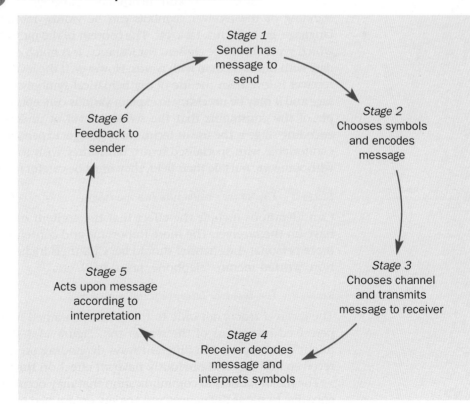

We shall examine the processes that occur at each stage of the communication process, paying particular attention to two things:

- the barriers to communication that can arise at each stage
- considerations that will help you to avoid these barriers.

Stage 1 – The sender has a message to send

Usually in discussions about the communication model it is assumed that the sender wishes to inform, persuade or give direction to the recipient of the message. In the case of counselling, the initiator of the communication will probably have recognised a need to elicit information rather than a need to pass information on. The same principles of communication apply, however, whether it is a matter of framing questions or statements.

Many people who have something to communicate focus exclusively on what it is they wish to say. That is, they concentrate on the content of the message when they formulate it. This is the first source of failure in communication. The model shows that every communication involves at least two parties; every message is intended for the person who will receive it. It makes sense, therefore, to take the receiver into consideration when you formulate a message. If you do not, you run the risk of putting together a message that although objectively correct will not be understood. Your knowledge of the receiver should be the major influence on the decisions made in the next two stages of the communication model.

Stage 2 – The sender encodes the message

At this stage the sender has to choose symbols that are appropriate to the message, but he or she must also incorporate knowledge about the level of understanding of the receiver. Symbols can be words, mathematical symbols, sign language, gestures, tick-tack, etc. The content of the message obviously influences which symbols will be chosen. For instance, it is much easier to describe financial data with numbers than with words. However, if the level of understanding of the receiver is low, then the use of mathematical symbols will not convey the message and it may be necessary to explain various concepts in words. Another example of the constraints that the sender's level of understanding places on the encoding stage is the use of technical language. Experts in any field become very comfortable with specialised terms, but if they wish to communicate effectively with someone outside their field, they must be careful not to overuse such terms.

Stage 3 – The sender transmits the message

Considerations include the effect that the content of the message is likely to have on the receiver. The more important and contentious the message is, the more personal the channel should be. Channels include face-to-face conversation, written memo, telephone, fax, e-mail, etc.

Stage 4 – The receiver interprets the message

The receiver reacts not only to the words contained in the message but to the perceived intentions of the sender too. Figure 11.3 shows how one message might be interpreted in different ways depending on the perceptual set of the receiver, and this will obviously have an effect on the receiver's response.

The major barriers to communication that may occur at this stage are interference due to status differences and anxiety occasioned by the content or expected content of the message. Anxiety makes people hear what they expect to hear.

| Figure 11.3 | **The receiver interprets the message** |

Stage 5 – The receiver reacts to the message

This reaction can take many forms, including spoken or written responses or actions.

Stage 6 – The feedback loop

This is a very important part of the communication process for two reasons:

- It shows that communication is not a one-way process; it is dynamic, two-way and on-going.
- It highlights the fact that the sender should receive information about whether or not the communication was successful.

It is important to understand that feedback does not only mean a verbal message sent back to the original sender. Any reaction on the part of the receiver can provide feedback to the sender. Physical reactions such as frowning, laughing, crying, shaking of the head or fist send obvious signals that the message has been understood or misunderstood. If the original message was a request to do something and the receiver fails to do it, this lack of action too provides feedback to the sender about how the message has been interpreted.

This understanding of the role of feedback in the communication model places the major responsibility for the success of communication firmly on the shoulders of the sender. The sender should actively look for signs of whether or not the message has been understood, and take further action if necessary.

The communication model requires you to allocate the roles of an initiator of the communication and a recipient of the communication. This raises the question in the counselling context as to who is the initiator of the communication. You may feel that this depends on whether a person decides they have a problem and seeks help with it, which would mean that the counsellee was the initiator of the process. An alternative scenario would be that a manager, for example, notices that an employee has a problem and decides to broach the topic. This would make the manager the initiator. There is another way of looking at these situations, however, and that is to say that whoever initiates the counselling, it will be the person with the counselling skills, i.e. the person in the counselling role, who will actively seek to structure the communication towards a successful outcome. In terms of the communication model, then, this puts the counsellor in the position of the sender, even if the event that starts the process off is the counsellee's sending a message requesting help.

As you read more about counselling skills, you will become aware that a counsellor's role is fulfilled much more by careful use of questioning techniques, soliciting rather than giving information, seeking to understand rather than providing input for another person to understand. This almost suggests a need for a redesigned model that shows that communication often starts with the need to obtain more information. Many concepts from the model still apply, particularly:

- the need to gear communication to the receiver
- the need to eliminate barriers to communication
- the need to look for, interpret and react to feedback.

We can return to an examination of these issues within the framework of a communication model after we have examined specific counselling techniques in more detail.

Counselling techniques

Now that we have a general understanding of the communication process, we can turn our attention specifically to the counselling process. Although most basic counselling in the workplace may be provided by people who are not professional counsellors, some of the concepts of clinical counselling provide the basis for an understanding of what might be an appropriate approach to any situation requiring counselling. One of the major contributions to our understanding of effective counselling is the work of Carl Rogers, and two of his articles are listed at the end of this chapter as suggestions for further study. Rogers is identified with a client-centred approach to counselling; he emphasised that there are two components that counsellors must master, and these are to adopt an appropriate general approach to counselling and then within this framework to utilise a specific method of questioning. The major concepts of importance to anyone providing counselling at any level are the need for empathy and the use of reflective responses.

◯ The counsellor's approach and attitude

Rogers explored three concepts that must be contained in the general approach to counselling if it is to be effective. In general, the counsellor must wish to help and the counsellee must perceive this. To achieve this, the counsellor must display empathy, acceptance and congruence.

Empathy

Empathy is displayed when the counsellor attempts to understand the situation from the point of view of the person with the problem. This means not superimposing one's own views and avoiding being judgemental, both in trying to understand and in one's response. Let us apply this concept to an example to understand it better.

A problem situation

You have always been very ambitious, and have worked your way through the ranks to a senior position. You have also acted as a mentor to a junior colleague and have promoted him as you have progressed. Now you are moving with the company to a new location, and you want your colleague to go with you. You foresee brilliant opportunities for both of you in the future. Your colleague tells you, however, that he is not happy with this, and he is worried about moving his family to another part of the country.

From *your* perspective this is wrong. If you respond by saying: 'You'd be a fool to give up this chance', what reaction would you be likely to get? This response is judgemental and superimposes your view. Your colleague is likely to be defensive; feeling that he is being judged, he may try to justify himself, or alternatively he may decline to discuss the issue further. Either way, it is not likely that the problem will be discussed further.

> **Pause for thought 11.4**
>
> What would be a more empathic response? How would the conversation be likely to continue following a display of empathy?

An empathic response would be anything that focuses on trying to understand the situation from the other person's point of view. You might say: 'What is it that worries you about moving the family?', or 'So you're not happy about moving with the company?' Such responses would encourage further discussion of the problem and might lead to the discovery of underlying reasons that have not yet been expressed.

Acceptance

Acceptance means showing that whatever the person decides to do, you accept the person's right to make these decisions. This does not mean that you necessarily agree, but you accept without making judgements. Again, the statement above, 'You'd be a fool ...', shows a lack of acceptance of another person's right to think and act differently from you.

Congruence

Congruence means showing that you are genuine in your concern. If the counsellee felt you were faking interest, the relationship of trust would be destroyed. Congruence occurs when there is agreement between the way you feel and your outer behaviour. This may be difficult to achieve if, for instance, you feel angry or disappointed. Showing this would be being judgemental and would inhibit the other person from opening up. It is obviously difficult to combine congruence with acceptance and empathy in all circumstances; the way to achieve it is to focus on your underlying genuine interest in the person, even if your own ultimate aim is the smooth running of the workplace.

Athos and Gabarro (1978) developed aspects of Rogers' work specifically for the use of managers, and highlighted the fact that at that time this caring attitude was not necessarily encouraged in the development of managers. In fact many of you may be thinking that you have not chosen to go into a caring profession, and that what is valued in the occupation of your choice is 'hard-headed business skills'. Counselling certainly requires the use of a specific attitude and specific communication skills that may vary from the day-to-day skills used by managers. Business efficiency, however, for reasons outlined earlier in this chapter, does require that these skills and attitudes be a part of the manager's repertoire, and ACAS (2004) refers to the informal investigation of workplace problems as counselling. Athos and Gabarro provide reassurances that an understanding of the techniques of reflective responses will reinforce the manager's ability to adopt an empathic stance.

Reflective and directive responses

Essentially, directive responses are those that reflect the viewpoint of the person directing the conversation, let us say for our purposes the manager, and reflective responses are used when the manager is trying to gain a better understanding of his or her subordinate. Interview skills are important in a range of circumstances; for instance, this text discusses interviewing in selection, performance appraisal and discipline. Different circumstances may call for different responses, but the counselling situation calls predominantly for reflective responses.

In order to explore and fully understand the types of responses one may make in a counselling situation, let us design a scenario to which we can apply each type of response and evaluate the usefulness of the potential reaction each may engender.

Imagine you are a manager in a bank. One of the cashiers has asked to speak to you privately. She tells you that she is having problems concentrating at work and is afraid she is going to make mistakes. What she does not tell you is that she has just left her husband and is living with her sister, although she doesn't get on with her sister's husband and this is causing a lot of arguments and bad feelings.

As we review the types of responses you might make, consider what effect each of them is likely to have in the above scenario. Remember that all the cashier has said is 'I am having problems concentrating at work and I'm afraid I'm going to make mistakes' and that at this stage you know nothing of the underlying problems.

Reflective responses

Reflective responses, focusing on gaining a better understanding of the cashier's point of view, include: silence; non-committal conversational sounds; paraphrase; clarification. It is also important to respond to apparent feelings and emotions expressed by the cashier and not just to her words.

Silence; conversational sounds; non-verbal cues

These techniques are meant to encourage the other person to continue talking so he or she may go on to tell you what the problem really is. Consciously practising these techniques also ensures that you do not do too much of the talking. Silence must be used judiciously, since a prolonged silence could lead to embarrassment and would inhibit communication rather than promoting it. Using silences merely means not jumping in too quickly to fill a pause; allow the other person to gather his or her thoughts. The term 'conversational sounds' refers to those companionable sounds we make to reassure someone who is talking that we are in fact listening. We use phrases such as: 'Yes, I see', 'Mmm', 'Oh, right', often accompanied by a nod of the head, a questioning frown or a smile.

Paraphrase

'So you think because you're thinking of something else, you might make mistakes.' This might lead the cashier into talking about what the something else is.

Clarification

'So there's something that's bothering you and making you afraid it's going to make you make mistakes?' The response should clarify whether there is something specific that is disturbing the concentration.

Respond to feelings

'You seem upset by something that's affecting your concentration.' The cashier may respond by revealing what it is that is upsetting her. Note that in responding to feelings, you have to sense what is the most important underlying emotion. Whatever is upsetting the cashier is more important, in terms of understanding the problem, than her fear of making errors.

Many inexperienced people feel a natural reluctance to 'pry into other people's affairs' and deal with sensitive situations, especially if it means picking up on emotional cues. If you wish to become a good counsellor, you must conquer these inhibitions. You can develop greater ease with such situations by taking part in role play exercises.

Directive responses

Directive responses shift the focus from trying to understand the perspective of the counsellee to expressing the viewpoint of the counsellor. Directive responses include: making suggestions; expressing approval or disapproval; trying to persuade or sell a course of action. These are more likely to occur once some of the hidden problems are revealed, so some of the examples below address this situation.

Making suggestions

'You're probably drinking too much coffee and not getting enough exercise.' This kind of response reflects the manager's interpretation of the situation and doesn't attempt at all to encourage further revelations about the true problem. It is not a solution to the core problem.

Approving/disapproving

Let us now assume in this case that the cashier has now told you about leaving her husband, and you respond, 'Well, I think it's a good job you left your husband since you weren't getting on with each other.' This does not encourage further exploration of the problem that now exists and needs to be solved.

Trying to persuade

'Why don't you take a week off to find your own apartment. You'll be all right when you have your own place. Go on, why don't you try that?' This has the same effect as making a suggestion, but is an even more effective communication barrier as the counsellor is obviously committed to this solution and not ready to explore others.

It is also important to avoid challenging questions that make a person defensive, particularly questions beginning with 'why': 'Why can't you concentrate?'; 'Why are you having arguments with your sister's husband?' In response to questions of this nature, people usually become very defensive and attempt to justify their actions. This does not help people to be open about their problems and diverts them from trying to find solutions.

ACTIVITY 11.2

Practise responding to counselling situations by creating a clarifying and a directive response in the following situations:

1 My partner has been offered a good position 200 miles away. It would mean finding new schools for the children and I would have to give up my job here.

2 My teenage son/daughter has started staying out late at night and I think he/she may be taking drugs. What do you think I should do?

3 My father has just died and my mother is now living on her own. She's getting on in years, and I don't think she'll be able to cope on her own for much longer.

4 My boyfriend/girlfriend has just told me that he/she is HIV positive. What would you do in my position?

5 I just can't get on with this new colleague in the office. You've got to do something about it.

6 A colleague tells you that her husband has been becoming more and more violent, and she admits that the bruises you have noticed on her arms and face resulted from his hitting her. (You feel very strongly that battered women should leave their husbands.)

ACTIVITY 11.3

1 Assess the usefulness of each of the responses you created for the situations described above. How is each response likely to help or otherwise affect the person seeking assistance?

2 Compare your responses with those of other students in your class, and choose those that you think would be most helpful in counselling.

A final word is necessary about the choice between directive responses and reflective responses to a request for advice. Activity 11.3 should have led you to choose and recognise the value of reflective response, and that it is usually counterproductive to offer your own opinions and solutions. It is much better to encourage the persons seeking advice to think the problem through themselves and arrive at their own solutions.

This is sound advice, but a more directive response may sometimes be called for to solve workplace problems. This is particularly the case if there is a policy setting out the procedures to be followed to resolve certain issues. Examples of this include instances of sexual or racial harassment, where an employee would rightly expect the employer to handle the issue rather than expecting the complainant to find a suitable solution. In these instances, it may be more appropriate to explain what the steps in the procedure are and recommend action to the person being counselled.

ACTIVITY 11.4

You should take the role of the Human Resources Manager in the following two scenarios. Examine each of the scenarios, and decide which one you feel calls for a reflective response and which calls for a more directive response. List your reasons for each choice, and compose suitable responses.

Scenario 1
A male cook who works in a company restaurant kitchen is quite open about the fact that he lives in a homosexual relationship. Most of the other people who work in the kitchen are women. One day the cook jokingly said in the kitchen that they'd better not kiss him under the mistletoe or they might get infected with HIV. Now the women will not speak to him, and he has heard that some of them would like him to be dismissed. He has come to ask you, as HR Manager, what he can do about it.

Scenario 2
One of the secretaries from the wages department has been newly promoted to the post of Administrative Assistant, supervising 15 office staff in the invoicing unit. She calls you at home one evening to ask how much notice she needs to give in order to leave her job.

Discussion of Activity 11.4

Scenario 1 would probably call for a more directive answer, since employees could expect an organisation to have a policy on how to deal with issues related to HIV and AIDS. This is especially so since these conditions are covered by the Disability Discrimination Act 1995. Since it is the behaviour of other employees that is causing the problem, it is the responsibility of the organisation to take appropriate action. A reflective response such as 'So you feel uncomfortable with the atmosphere in the kitchen?', aiming to get the cook to explore the situation more fully, would not be helpful in these circumstances. A directive response, outlining the steps recommended in the relevant policy, would be more appropriate.

Although it would be possible to respond to Scenario 2 with direct information about notice requirements, the situation seems to require a more reflective response to uncover the underlying problem. A suitable response might be 'Does this mean you're unhappy with the new job?'

◯ Practical counselling techniques

The abilities to be empathic and to use reflective responses are two mainstays of counselling. There are, however, a number of other techniques you can use in combination with these to ensure your effectiveness as a counsellor. Many of these are similar to skills we have identified in other interviewing situations and for effective communication in general. First we have set out guidelines for counselling, followed by more detailed discussion of the major techniques:

- Create the right environment.
- Listen actively.
- Identify the real problem.
- Clarify expectations and roles.
- Get the person to:
  - talk
  - recognise the existence of a problem
  - identify solutions
  - identify the preferred solution
  - accept responsibility
  - decide what to do.
- Follow up on actions agreed.

Create the right environment

As in other interview situations, the right environment is important to reassure the counsellee that you are prepared to give your full attention to the matter in hand and to ensure privacy and confidentiality. You will want to find a quiet room, ensure that there will be no interruptions, and arrange the seating to create an informal atmosphere.

Listen actively

Active listening is another concept that is connected with the work of Rogers and Farson (1976). In general, active listening refers to the development of listening skills to promote better communication. It includes the use of reflective responses to develop and check understanding, but also involves a range of techniques to reassure the partner in conversation that he or she is being listened to. These techniques include: looking for clues in facial expressions and general demeanour; eye contact; body language such as leaning forward and appearing relaxed.

Identify the real problem

Even if a person actively seeks help, it may be necessary to investigate what the real problem is. The core of the problem may be hidden for several reasons:

- People often suffer from what is known as free-floating anxiety. They know that something is making them unhappy, but they are unable to pinpoint exactly what it is.
- In information services it is a well-known fact that people do not know how to ask for exactly what they want. A person in Wakefield wanting to arrive in

Did you know?

The Samaritans handle questions by e-mail as well as over the phone and offer guarantees of confidentiality as far as it is within their control. Find out more by visiting their web site at **www.samaritans.org.**

Huddersfield in time for a job interview at 10.30 a.m. may call railway enquiry services and ask how frequently the trains run from Wakefield to Huddersfield. If the answer to this question were 'once an hour', the enquirer would still not have adequate information to plan the journey. For this person to get the information he or she really wants, the information provider would have to ask a series of questions to ascertain what the true query is.

- Even when people recognise that they need help, it may be difficult for them to talk about their problems. A popular TV series about a doctor's practice ran an episode which showed that people very often only reveal the true reason for their visit to the doctor when they have their hand on the door knob as they are about to leave the room.

Counsellors should be alert to signals given at any time in a counselling interview, and they should develop skills in questioning, listening and reacting to consciously or subconsciously revealed cues in order to reach the true nature of the problem.

Clarify expectations and roles

It is natural to feel that you should come up with solutions, especially if someone has approached you with a problem. Most counselling guidelines, as you now know, will urge you very firmly to resist this temptation. One way to help relieve this tension is to ask persons seeking counselling what they expect from you, how you might help them in solving their problem. The answer to this question may very often clarify the situation for both the counsellor and the person being counselled. If the person responds that you cannot do anything, they simply need someone to talk to, then this diminishes that natural inclination to come up with solutions. If the person asks you for direct action or to offer solutions, you can begin a discussion about what the appropriate role for you is, and again this will clarify for both parties what the options are and may lead towards the formulation of acceptable solutions.

Get the person to

- talk
- recognise the existence of a problem
- identify solutions
- identify the preferred solution
- accept responsibility
- decide what to do.

Again, it cannot be stressed too strongly that ultimately the solution to a problem has to be owned and pursued by the person with the problem. In terms of technique, as with most interview situations, the interviewer should be sure not to do most of the talking.

Follow up actions agreed

Although the emphasis has very definitely been on the counsellor not taking responsibility for the solution to a problem, he or she should still want to know that the problem has been resolved satisfactorily. Just because a solution is agreed in discussion doesn't guarantee that someone will go away and actually take action. There may be hesitation to take the action agreed, there may be a change of heart . . . any number of things might happen to impede progress. The counsellor should check on progress to ensure that agreed improvements are being achieved. This will also be further evidence of genuine concern, but any queries made after a counselling session must be carried out in a discreet and sensitive fashion; the counsellor must not give the impression of interfering or wishing to force the issue.

Pause for thought 11.5

Think about the interview skills we have identified in other chapters, for instance with reference to selection or performance appraisal. There is one important factor that we have omitted in the case of counselling interviews. What is it?

If you cannot remember, you should refer to Chapters 4 and 9 before you read on.

In other applications of interviewing and communication skills one of the major factors emphasised over and over again is preparation. In a counselling situation, however, a more spontaneous reaction is often called for. Also, if you adopt the reflective approach you cannot really prepare before a conversation, as the emphasis is on finding out what the other person thinks and feels and responding to this rather than following your own prepared agenda. You cannot prepare for these revelations. The only form of preparation you can undertake is to practise the techniques so that you will be more at ease with them when you are called on to use them.

A further reason for practising your counselling skills is to overcome the inhibitions that most of us feel when confronted with a person in obvious emotional distress. This is why much of the training provided to counsellors consists of role play exercises. Your lecturer will have access to a number of practical exercises and two major role play exercises contained in the Lecturer's Guide companion to this textbook. The more you practise, the better your counselling skills should become.

Cost and evaluation

As with any other human resource management programme, the provision of employee assistance should be costed and then monitored and evaluated for its effectiveness. A cost–benefit analysis can then be performed, and an assessment of the contribution of the programme to the organisation's effectiveness can be made. This is a difficult exercise, as the benefit from counselling is an absence of secondary problems. It is hard to account for savings achieved through the avoidance of problems. However, after the introduction of a counselling service 'before and after' measures of absenteeism, turnover, etc. can be used, and at least a proportion of improvements in these areas can be attributed to counselling. Employee opinion surveys can also be used judiciously to monitor the value that employees place on the availability of such services. It must be borne in mind, however, that existing benefits are sometimes taken for granted and people do not always value them at their true worth.

The costs of an employee assistance programme can be fairly easily estimated and would take into account the following factors:

- time of internal counsellors and counsellees spent in counselling sessions
- training costs
- administrative costs
- fees to external employee assistance providers.

Conclusion

As with any organisational problem, there is probably not just one solution to the range of problems identified in this chapter. Counselling is not a panacea, and providing a counselling service once a problem is identified may not be sufficient to eradicate or alleviate the problem: a range of complementary solutions should be considered.

Pause for thought 11.6

What initiatives do you think an organisation could undertake to complement counselling services in resolving human problems in the workplace?

Some suggestions are:

- training in areas such as stress management, time management, dealing with conflict
- development of policies to cover areas such as sexual and racial harassment, bullying
- management programmes to deal with absenteeism
- culture change programmes aimed at management style, employee empowerment
- job design related to reasonable workloads and expectations; flexible work patterns
- performance management systems
- communication and consultation systems to lessen the stress associated with insecurity
- employee opinion surveys followed by action in response to areas of concern identified by employees.

Effective human resource management necessitates an integrated approach towards best practice in all these activities. The provision of appropriate employee assistance programmes to enhance the personal effectiveness of every employee is just one facet of a complex picture. It should be remembered that counselling can play a vital part in maintaining the morale of employees, and consequently makes an important contribution to helping the organisation to achieve its objectives. And last but not least, proper attention must be paid to the re-integration of employees who, in spite of all efforts made to resolve problems, have had to have some time away from work due to illness (IRS 2003).

SELF-CHECK QUESTIONS

Answer the following multiple-choice questions. The correct responses are given on page 494 for you to check your understanding of this chapter.

1 Which of the following has not been identified as a justification for employer involvement in employee welfare and counselling?

(a) improved productivity

(b) decreased absenteeism

(c) improved discipline

(d) reduced wage demands.

2 What are the six areas in which the Health and Safety Executive has set draft standards for stress management?

3 Which of the following describes encoding?

(a) The sender telephones the recipient of the message.

(b) The sender chooses words to frame the message.

(c) The receiver interprets the meaning of the message.

(d) The receiver acts on the message.

4 Which of the following issues is NOT likely to be addressed in a policy on counselling?

(a) whether to respond directively or reflectively

(b) issues of confidentiality

(c) who is responsible for providing counselling.

5 Which of the following are components of the interpersonal communication model?

(a) encoding, reflection, feedback

(b) description, reflection, interpretation

(c) direction, transmission, feedback

(d) encoding, transmission, feedback.

6 Which of the following comes after the encoding stage of the communication model?

(a) interpretation

(b) feedback

(c) transmission

(d) direction.

7 Carl Rogers' term for trying to understand another person's point of view is:

(a) sympathetic listening

(b) active listening

(c) empathy

(d) reflection.

8 Joan tells you that she cannot manage with the new machines in the packing unit. A paraphrasing response would be:

(a) Well, why don't you ask for a transfer?

(b) I see. So you don't want to work there any more?

(c) What exactly is causing you a problem?

(d) So you're having problems with the new machines?

9 Tom tells you he has been very unhappy with his work. You respond by saying: 'So you're saying that you'd like to look for another post?' This is an example of:

(a) clarification

(b) paraphrasing

(c) a directive response

(d) a suggestion.

10 According to this text, is the following statement true or false? A directive response is never appropriate in a counselling situation.

MAJOR ASSIGNMENT: PERSONAL PROBLEMS AND PRODUCTIVITY

It has long been recognised that personal problems that employees experience either at work or at home can have an impact on their effectiveness and productivity in the workplace. Problems of this nature arise from a wide range of sources and include issues such as alcohol or drug dependence, gambling, debt, care duties, sexual/racial harassment, and aspects of personal relationships. Employers can respond to this with a variety of policies, procedures and programmes.

You are a personnel assistant working at the regional headquarters of an insurance company. The senior managers of the company recognise that they have never investigated the possible effect of such problems on the productivity of employees either at headquarters or in the branches. They have asked your personnel management team to write a report and make a presentation about one or more of these problem areas. They have asked you to report on how other employers are tackling them and to make recommendations for your own company.

Your report should include evidence from published materials and from analysis of primary data that your team of four or five personnel management professionals have collected yourselves. You should take a critical, analytical stance, and you may wish to address one or more of the following factors:

- what employers should consider when deciding which issues to pursue
- range of issues/specific issue
- role of policies, managerial attitudes, employee attitudes
- benefits/costs
- available programmes/support mechanisms
- personnel/line manager/other roles
- innovative solutions.

Your team will produce a report of approximately 5,000 words excluding appendices and prepare a presentation of the major points. Your presentation should last approximately 15 minutes to allow time for questions, and each person should take an active part in the delivery of the presentation. This will test your ability to produce a polished and focused presentation, and you will be penalised for overrunning.

WHAT NEXT?

Arthur (2004) suggests that the study of stress needs to move away from the examination of individuals to a more integrated analysis of what causes stress in general in organisations and how this might be dealt with. He writes in his concluding statement about 'inherently demanding and harmful work practices' and asks whether trying to get people to cope with these is the right approach (page 167). What does he mean by 'inherently demanding and harmful work practices'? Why do these raise questions about current approaches to stress management?

Arthur, A. R. (2004) Work-related stress, the blind men and the elephant, *British Journal of Guidance and Counselling*, Vol. 32, No. 2, May, 157–169

References

Advisory, Conciliation and Arbitration Service (2004) *Discipline and Grievances at Work. The ACAS Advisory Handbook*, ACAS

Athos, A. G. and J. J. Gabarro (1978) *Communication and Understanding in Relationships*, Prentice Hall

Berlo, D. K. (1960) *The Process of Communication*, Holt, Rinehart and Winston

Engineering Employers' Federation (2001) *Managing Stress at Work*, EEF

Fowler, A. (1994) Personnel's model army, *Personnel Management*, September, 34–37

Hayden-Smith, J. and R. Simms (2003) Pressure points, *People Management*, 25 September, 17

Holmes, T. H. and R. H. Rahe (1967) The social readjustment rating scale, *Journal of Psychosomatic Research*, August, 216

Incomes Data Services (2002a) *IDS Studies 732: Stress Management*, IDS

Incomes Data Services (2002b) *IDS Studies Plus: Employee Assistance Programmes*, IDS

Incomes Data Services (2004) *IDS HR Studies 775: Managing Stress*, IDS

Industrial Relations Services (IRS) (2003) Best-practice firms show way to manage stress, *IRS Employment Review 784*, 19 September, 18

Institute of Personnel and Development (1998) *IPD Guide on Counselling at Work*, IPD

Kiefer, T. and R. Briner (2003) Handle with care, *People Management*, 23 October, 48–50

Le Fevre, M., J. Matheny and G. S. Kolt (2003) Eustress, distress, and interpretation in occupational stress, *Journal of Managerial Psychology*, Vol. 18, No. 7, 726–744

Maslow, A. (1954) *Motivation and Personality*, 2nd edition, Harper & Row

Midgley, S. (1997) Pressure points, *People Management*, 10 July, 36–39

Quinn, J. (2004) Dodging the draft, *People Management*, 30 June, 17

Rogers, C. R. and R. E. Farson (1976) *Active Listening*, Industrial Relations Center of the University of Chicago

Selye, H. (1956) *The Stress of Life*, McGraw-Hill

Selye, H. (1974) *Stress without Distress*, Lippincott

Shuttleworth, A. (2004) Managing workplace stress: how training can help, *Industrial and Commercial Training*, Vol. 36, No. 2, 61–65

Venning, N. (1995) Taking the bull by the horns, *Guardian* Careers Section, 15 April, 2–3.

www.cipd.co.uk; accessed 09.09.04

www.eef.org.uk; accessed 06.02.04

www.hse.gov.uk; accessed 03.02.04

Further study

Books

Advisory, Conciliation and Arbitration Service (2004) *Health and Employment*, ACAS. (Outlines good practice for employers in dealing with health problems at work, and focuses specifically on issues to do with smoking, alcohol, drugs, AIDS and stress.)

Athos, A. G. and J. J. Gabarro (1978) *Communication and Understanding in Relationships*, Prentice Hall. (Chapters 8–11 deal with counselling techniques, including an in-depth discussion of Carl Rogers' concepts. Two interviews are reproduced as case studies, giving some excellent examples of the reflective technique.)

Beehr, T. A. (1995) *Psychological Stress in the Workplace*, Routledge. (An in-depth examination of stress emanating from issues in the workplace. Beehr examines stressors such as role ambiguity and role conflict, the workplace outcomes of stress, and methods of treatment.)

Burley-Allen, M. (1995) *Listening: the Forgotten Skill. A Self-Teaching Guide*, 2nd edition, Wiley. (An easy-to-read guide on how to improve your listening skills to promote better communication. Includes self-assessment exercises, cases and anecdotes.)

Cooper, C. L. (1994) *Creating Healthy Work Organizations*, Wiley.

Fisher, D. (1993) *Communication in Organizations*, 2nd edition, West Publishing Company. (A good introduction to the topic of communication in general and various aspects of workplace communications in particular. Chapter 15 deals with counselling, listening and feedback skills.)

Health and Safety Executive (2001) *Tackling Work-Related Stress: A Managers' Guide to Improving and Maintaining Employee Health and Well-Being*, HSE Books.

Institute of Personnel and Development (1998) *Stress and Bullying in the Workplace*, IPD.

Rasberry, R. W. and L. F. Lemoine (1986) *Effective Managerial Communication*, Kent Publishing Company. (A thorough introduction to the topic of communication and an examination of its importance in a variety of managerial roles.)

Summerfield, J. and L. Van Oudtshoom (1995) *Counselling in the Workplace*, Institute of Personnel and Development.

Thomson, L., F. Neathey and J. Rick (2003) *Best Practice in Rehabilitating Employees following Absence due to Work-Related Stress*, Institute for Employment Studies.

Articles

Arkin, A. (2004) The drugs don't work, *People Management*, 12 August, 25–28. (An example of the type of article you might search out for background reading if you undertake the major assignment described in this chapter, and if you decide to focus on employer interventions with regard to drug and alcohol problems.)

British Journal of Guidance and Counselling. (Volume 32, Number 2, May 2004 is an issue devoted to papers from a symposium on work stress and coping.)

Rogers, C. R. (1985) The characteristics of a helping relationship, *Personnel and Guidance Journal*, Vol. 37, No. 1, September, 6–16.

Rogers, C. R. and F. J. Roethlisberger (1952) Barriers and gateways to communication, *Harvard Business Review*, August, 46–50.

Internet

Bully OnLine   **www.successunlimited.co.uk**
(A very informative site on bullying in the workplace with numerous links to other sites.)

Chartered Institute of Personnel and Development   **www.cipd.co.uk**
(The CIPD has a number of informative items on health and stress.)

Health and Safety Executive   **www.hse.gov.uk**
(A number of leaflets, booklets and guidelines for employers can be downloaded at this site.)

International Stress Management Association (UK)   **www.isma.org.uk**
(A registered charity dedicated to best practice in the management of stress. A selection of
recent articles from ISMA's publication *Stress News* can be accessed at this web site.)

Health and safety

OBJECTIVES

By the end of this chapter you will be able to:

● explain what is meant by the terms 'health', 'safety', 'hazard' and 'risk'

● explain the human resource management approach to health and safety at work

● explain the key points in the main legislation relating to health and safety at work

● explain the role of various people and groups in health and safety at work

● design a health and safety policy

● demonstrate the need for occupational health programmes

● undertake a simple risk assessment exercise

● explain the main health and safety issues in an international context.

In Chapter 1 we traced the history of personnel management and examined several approaches to welfare. Some people who have adopted the 'hard' human resource management approach have tried to distance themselves from all these welfare approaches, as they felt that these approaches show a lack of business awareness.

In Chapter 11 we showed that even though the focus of the work of the personnel department has changed over the years, from the earlier welfare approaches to the more cost-conscious, hard-headed approach of the human resource manager of today, the importance of counselling and employee welfare remains. Welfare can be defined as 'well-being', and health and safety are both aspects of welfare as they are both important to the employee's well-being. In the past many employers merely reacted to issues about health and safety without appreciating the benefits that adopting a more proactive approach could bring them. Many still operate in this way. However, some more progressive employers are adopting a much more proactive approach to health and safety to prevent problems arising in the first place.

The Health and Safety Executive (HSE) has also been focusing on ways to draw all employers' attention to the benefits to be gained from a more proactive approach and has launched a series of initiatives called Revitalising Health and Safety. Organisations are increasingly operating in new ways with increasingly flexible ways of working and the HSE has been consulting and involving employers to demonstrate the business case for improved health and safety measures.

In this chapter we shall examine the topics of health and safety in the workplace and discuss the reasons why we feel that health and safety are important in the management of people.

Definitions

Safety

We define safety as absence from danger and avoidance of injury.

According to this definition, we should expect employers to do everything in their power to keep employees away from danger and free of injury while at work. This does not sound like a great deal to expect from an employer, but there is often a conflict in the employer's mind between increased production, which sometimes may involve some risk taking, and the necessity to keep employees safe and uninjured, which may cost money. Legislation has developed over a number of years to protect workers, and was initially designed to protect those who were weak and particularly vulnerable to exploitation from any employers who, tempted by the lure of increased production, might put their employees at risk of injury. Nowadays, with increasingly flexible patterns of work being available, many employees may work from home, or even from their car, for all or part of their working week, so employers will also have to consider the health and safety issues arising from this.

Health

Here the concern is for good health. We define good health as being physically and mentally well with body and mind in excellent working order.

This goes further than safety in that the employer is no longer just expected not to do anything to injure his or her employees, but should seek to promote activities that encourage the good health of the employees. We shall return to a discussion of health promotion activities later in this chapter.

Nowadays it is not enough for employers to merely react to issues relating to our health and safety: they have to be proactive about it too. In order to do this they need also to be concerned with hazards and risks and these two terms also have specific meanings.

Hazard

A hazard is something that could cause harm to someone. Employers who are being proactive about health and safety therefore have to try to identify potential hazards before they actually do cause any harm. Stranks (1994) says that hazards have been defined in various ways. He lists the following definitions:

> A situation of risk or danger.
>
> A situation that may give rise to personal injury.

Risk

The term risk relates to the chances of the hazard actually resulting in harm being done to someone. Once the employer has identified a potential hazard then they have to estimate the chances or risk of someone being harmed by it.

We shall discuss the idea of risk assessment later in this chapter. The emphasis in health and safety today is on the prevention of accidents if possible by eliminating anything that could be a hazard and by predicting the level of risk in various situations. It is not, of course, always possible to eliminate all hazards or minimise all risks in a workplace, but employers are expected to predict potentially dangerous situations and then do something about them to ensure they become less dangerous. The emphasis in modern health and safety is to encourage those who own, manage or work in organisations to take responsibility for health and safety in them. For this to happen, both the workforce and safety representatives also need to be involved, risks need to be assessed and action need to be taken to reduce these where possible.

Did you know?

In 2004 a senior pilot was forced to resign and two senior cabin crew were dismissed by Ryanair after the two off-duty crew members travelled on a full plane from Gerona to Dublin. Since there were no seats available for them, they sat in the rear toilets of the plane for both take-off and landing. The captain had allowed them to do this even though it contravened aviation regulations and was obviously potentially hazardous.

(Seenan 2004)

Safety

According to the Health and Safety Commission's (HSC's) *Health and Safety Statistics Highlights 2002/03* (HSC 2004b) there were 226 workers fatally injured at work during 2002/03. While this is still a high number of work-based deaths, it is part of a trend that has shown a steady decrease in the numbers of fatalities in the workplace each year since the 1990s, resulting in the current rate being one-third of the number of work-based fatalities reported in 1981.

However, the number of major injuries to employees that were reported rose during 2002/03 to 28,426 with 37% of all major injuries being the result of slipping or tripping. A further 14% of the major injuries were caused by people being struck by moving or falling objects, a further 14% were a result of the person falling from a height and a further 12% were gained as a result of handling, lifting or carrying objects.

The numbers of injuries that caused workers to be absent from work for three days or more fell to 126,004 in 2002/03 from 129,655 during 2001/02, with the most common cause of three-day injuries being handling, lifting or carrying goods. This category of accidents accounted for 39% of all three-day injuries while accidents due to slipping and tripping accounted for a further 25% of these injuries.

ACTIVITY 12.1

Sometimes employers are reluctant to spend money on safety improvements as they don't feel this is justified. There are, however, costs associated with accidents. List the possible costs to the employer of accidents at work.

Discussion of Activity 12.1

Obviously, depending on the severity of the injury, there are costs to the injured person in terms of pain and suffering, and possible loss of earnings. There are also costs to the employer, and your list is likely to include at least some of the following:

- cost of lost time and production due to absence caused by injury
- cost of lost time and production due to dealing with the injury
- cost of replacement worker or of training the replacement
- cost of replacing broken machinery or unsafe machinery or equipment
- cost of compensation to injured employee
- higher insurance premiums if the organisation's accident record is not good
- cost involved in carrying out a full investigation into the causes of the accident
- cost of paying fines or even facing imprisonment if the employer was to blame for the accident
- cost of poor morale within the workforce
- cost of people not being willing to work for the organisation because of its poor reputation for safety.

You may have found some other costs involved in accidents as well. Employers should be aware of the hidden costs of accidents; if they carried out a cost–benefit analysis they would probably be amazed at how much accidents were costing them and be more prepared to spend money on accident prevention. In their studies of accidents, the Health and Safety Executive (1995) identified one organisation where the costs of accidents amounted to as much as 37% of profits. This organisation did not have a particularly bad record on health and safety, nor had it suffered any major disasters, fatalities or prosecutions.

The human resource management approach has tended to distance itself from the topics of health and safety, even though, as we have shown, the costs of this lack of interest can be high. We feel that this neglect of health and safety issues is not wise, especially since the organisation's objectives will not be attained if the workforce are not in good shape or suffer from poor morale. We believe that health and safety is an important area of concern for all HRM practitioners, since it is in the organisation's interest to pursue any initiatives that will provide benefits and services which the employees will want and value but that will also fit with the strategic needs of the organisation by enhancing levels of employee performance.

Employers can check for themselves the actual costs of both accidents and work-related incidents in their organisations by using the accident and incident calculators provided by the Health and Safety Executive. They allow employers the choice of three different ways to calculate the annual costs of accidents in their organisation and also of using an interactive tool to calculate costs of other work-related incidents. Now there is really no excuse for employer ignorance of the cost of accidents or work-related incidents in their organisations. If you would like to see how easy it is for employers to calculate the costs of accidents and work-based incidents by examining these tools for yourself, go to **www.hse.gov.uk/costs/accidentcost_calc/accident_costs_intro.asp** (accessed 8.7.04).

Legislation

Did you know?

In the lower courts, penalties for a failure to comply with an improvement notice, a prohibition notice or a court remedy order can result in a fine of up to £20,000, or six months' imprisonment, or both. For a case heard in the higher courts, failure to comply with any of these things could result in two years' imprisonment, or an unlimited fine or both.

(HSC 2002)

In 1998, in a case against R F Howe and Son (Engineers) Ltd, the Court of Appeal said that fines being imposed for health and safety offences were too low. The Court of Appeal also set out guidance on future sentencing in health and safety cases. The Health and Safety Commission (HSC) is trying to ensure that all judges, magistrates and magistrates' clerks are fully aware of the penalties and sentences available for breaches of health and safety law.

(HSC 2001)

Much of the early development of legislation to protect employees at work was closely linked to the historical development of personnel management. The more enlightened employers were concerned to improve working conditions for their employees and appointed industrial welfare workers to help with this. Less enlightened employers were compelled to pay some attention to the protection of selected groups of employees, and as early as 1840 legislation designed to limit the hours that children worked was passed. In more recent times several new Acts have been passed and regulations issued, which were designed to protect employees.

The Health and Safety at Work Act 1974 (HASAWA)

In Great Britain the foundation for the system of regulating health and safety at work was introduced by the Health and Safety at Work Act 1974. HASAWA is mainly an enabling measure which states general principles of safety but also provides the power for the Secretary of State to make detailed safety regulations, based on advice from the Health and Safety Commission. This power may be used to update previous health and safety legislation and streamline it. One of the intentions was to enable older laws to be progressively replaced by a system of regulations and approved codes of practice which would operate in conjunction with the Act itself. It also enables future legislation to be incorporated into HASAWA. Since the Health and Safety at Work Act in 1974, the Health and Safety Commission has been involved in constantly reviewing and updating legislation. It encourages an approach which tries to modernise and replace detailed pieces of industry-specific legislation with legislation which expresses more generalised goals and where the detail is included in codes of practice or in notes for guidance. The Management of Health and Safety at Work Regulations (MHSWR) 1999 is a piece of legislation that typifies this approach. Before HASAWA, the legislation that could be used to protect employees at work was patchy and applied to vulnerable groups such as women or children, or to particular industries where there were thought to be high risks. The vast majority of the working population before 1974 were not actually protected by any health or safety legislation. The Health and Safety at Work Act 1974 set up some new bodies and reinforced the power of others:

- the Health and Safety Commission (HSC)
- the Health and Safety Executive (HSE)
- the enforcing authorities.

HASAWA was the first piece of legislation designed to protect everyone at work, and also to protect others who were not at work, such as customers or even passers-by. It is estimated that it brought an extra 3 million people under the scope of protective safety legislation for the first time.

The main aim of the Act was to provide a comprehensive system of law which would raise standards of safety and health for all persons at work and also protect members of the public who might be affected by their actions.

The Health and Safety Commission (HSC)

The Commission was set up under the Health and Safety at Work Act 1974 and is a quango responsible for carrying out the policy of the Act and for providing advice to local authorities and others about how to implement the provisions of the Act. It is largely independent and acts on behalf of the Crown, but reports to Parliament primarily through the Secretary of State for Work and Pensions. It has a chairman and nine other members drawn from bodies representing employers, employees and local authorities, who are appointed by the Secretary of State for Transport, Local Government and the Regions.

In 1999 John Prescott, the Deputy Prime Minister, announced a new impetus for health and safety called Revitalising Health and Safety. He said that the Health and Safety at Work Act 1974 had done its job as evidenced by the fact that the 'number of deaths at work today is a quarter of the 1971 level'. However, he wanted a strategic appraisal of the health and safety framework in order to build on the work of the previous 25 years and to establish a new agenda for the first 25 years of the new century (Prescott 2000).

The HSC, after consulting widely about ways of revitalising health and safety, has produced targets for health and safety in Great Britain and a Strategy Statement and Action Plan. The HSC (2000) says that targets for health and safety in Great Britain are needed because:

Health and safety is central to sustainable development and securing a better quality of life for all.

- Raising workplace standards will promote better public health and *social progress which recognises the needs of everyone.*
- Reducing the £18 billion bill for health and safety failures will contribute to *maintaining high and stable levels of economic growth and employment.*
- Controlling harmful substances in the workplace will help to *protect our environment.*

In order to achieve these general aims the HSC then outlined its strategic plan for 2001–4. The Chair of the Commission, Bill Callaghan, in the Foreword to the *Strategic Plan 2001–4* (HSC 2001) firstly talks of creating a strategy that will modernise health and safety and that focuses directly on objectives, not just on plans or intentions, but on real achievable objectives. Secondly, he says that the emphasis should be about moving away from concern just with the mere prevention of harm to a wider role of ensuring that every type of workplace should become a 'better, safer and healthier place to be'. Thirdly, he says that the HSC must be committed to analysing its own work by regularly scrutinising its own effectiveness and evaluating what types of initiative are most successful and cost-effective. Finally he emphasises the point that the HSC's strategy for the future also involves working closely with many other stakeholders in health and safety.

The Health and Safety Commission's Strategic Plan for 1999–2002 (2000) had five strategic themes which in turn were supported by key programmes. These were:

- to raise the profile of occupational health
- to improve health and safety performance in key risk areas
- to develop health and safety aspects of the competitiveness and social equality agencies
- to increase the engagement of others and promote full participation in improving health and safety
- to improve the Health and Safety Commission and Executive's openness and accountability (HSC 2000).

The 10-point Strategy Statement that supports the Action Plan also emphasises the need for a partnership approach towards health and safety between government, employers, employees and unions. It is not just a question of relying on a framework of legislation and enforcement, although laws will still provide a framework. (Partnership is discussed in more detail in the next chapter.) The strategy statement also stresses the point that a new approach is required to meet the changing needs of the modern workplace and that the health and safety systems should be complementary to the Government's vision for a competitive, knowledge-based economy. (Knowledge-based workplaces were discussed in Chapter 8.)

Remember that at the start of this chapter we defined safety as 'absence from danger and avoidance of injury'. This 10-point Strategy Statement and Action Plan show how far our views of health and safety are moving from this simple definition towards a view nowadays that health and safety clearly contributes to the success or failure of businesses, is clearly integrated with other HRM strategies and involves stakeholders in both the discussion and the implementation of the strategies. It is, after all, no good having a knowledge-based business with lots of potential for growth and success if the workforce has a poor level of attendance because of absences due to ill health or injuries. Health and safety has to be seen as an integral part of the modern successful business and to contribute to the bottom line.

As part of this drive to involve various stakeholders with health and safety there is also an emphasis on trying to get more involvement from small businesses, where traditionally there have been higher than average levels of accidents, and of motivating employers to improve their own performance in health and safety by setting themselves targets and working out strategies to achieve them. The emphasis on stakeholder involvement starts early with education about health and safety being encouraged at every level, even within primary schools. This should ensure increasingly knowledgeable stakeholders in the future.

There is also a recognition, in the 10-point Strategy Statement that workers carry out their work under a wide range of different terms and conditions and different contracts and that it can be difficult to police their safety. Employers are strongly encouraged to think about how they can improve health and safety for everyone, not just by relying on protective clothing or equipment to protect the workforce but also by designing safety into both products and processes so that they do not need additional protection.

To achieve the targets, the HSC has also set out a 44-step Action Plan as the start of this process. For example, as part of the target to motivate employers, the HSC published and promoted a ready reckoner, supported by case studies, to ensure employers realise exactly how much having poor systems of health and safety actually cost them and to promote the fact that there is a strong business case for excellent management of health and safety. (This ready reckoner was mentioned earlier in this chapter; you may already have checked it for yourself or you can do so now by going to **www.hse.gov.uk/costs/accidentcost_calc/accident_costs_ino.asp** (accessed 8.7.04).

The Health and Safety Executive (HSE)

The Health and Safety Executive (HSE) consists of three people who advise and assist the HSC. The executive also has a staff of approximately 4,000 to help carry out all its responsibilities in relation to its day-to-day functions and they are collectively referred to as the HSE. The HSE consists of policy advisors, inspectors and experts in medicine, science and technology. They are responsible for making provision for enforcing the legislation, for dealing with daily administration and conducting research, and for identifying the range of information necessary to enable the HSC to remain properly informed.

Local authorities also have responsibility for enforcement of health and safety in approximately 194,000 workplaces. Under HASAWA, the Secretary of State for Work and Pensions (DWP) can make regulations for local authorities to take on responsibility for certain activities and to ensure that there is no duplication of effort between them and the Health and Safety Executive. The local authority inspectors, normally known as environmental health officers, are responsible for health and safety mainly in the services sector, while the HSE tends to concentrate on the more hazard-prone industries. There is a liaison committee which ensures consistency of approach between the HSE and local authorities. The HSE publishes a wide range of material each year explaining its role and the practical implications of legislation.

The Health and Safety Executive can provide guidance, approved codes of practice and regulations.

Guidance

This fulfils three main purposes:

1 To help people to understand the law by explaining it in a clear way.
2 To ensure they then comply with the law.
   and
3 To provide rather more specialist advice.

Approved codes of practice

These give examples of good practice and help employers and workers understand what they should do to comply with the legislation. Failure to comply with a code of practice would not in itself mean that the individual or organisation would be prosecuted but, in any legal proceeding brought against them, failure to comply with an approved code of practice would be used as part of the evidence against them.

Regulations

Regulations can be made under HASAWA 1974 to identify specific risks in specific situations and the actions that need to be taken.

As well as enforcing health and safety legislation the, HSC and HSE have also been given the following tasks by the Government:

- Modernise and simplify the regulatory framework.
- Provide appropriate information and advice.
- Promote risk assessment and technical knowledge.
- Operate statutory schemes (HSC 2001).

The enforcing authorities

We shall now discuss how the inspection of workplaces and investigation of accidents is shared between HSE inspectors and local authority enforcement officers. Basically the HSE inspectors cover work conducted primarily in factories, building sites, mines, fairgrounds, quarries, railways, chemical plants, offshore and nuclear installations, schools or hospitals. The local authority enforcement officers cover retailing, some warehouses, most offices, hotels, catering, consumer services, sports and leisure activities and places of worship. Both have similar powers of enforcement. These include a right to:

- enter employers' premises
- carry out inspections/investigations
- take equipment or materials on to premises
- take measurements, photographs or recordings
- carry out tests on articles or substances
- examine books and documents
- issue improvement notices
- issue prohibition notices.

The last two points are very important and we shall consider each in turn. However, sometimes when an enforcing inspector finds a breach of the law which is relatively minor he or she may feel that improvement notices and prohibition notices are not appropriate.

Informal methods

In the case of a minor breach in legislation the inspector may choose to use informal methods and may simply give the employer or contractor advice about what they should do to comply with the law, and explain the reasons.

Improvement notices

If the inspector feels that an organisation is contravening one of the relevant provisions of legislation then he or she can issue an improvement notice which will specify that improvements must be made within a specified time limit to bring the equipment or process up to the required standard of safety.

Prohibition notices

If when the inspector visits he or she feels that there is serious danger or risk of injury to employees, he or she can issue a prohibition notice which will stop work activity immediately until the risk has been dealt with. In some circumstances a deferred prohibition order may be issued: this would occur, for example, if it would be difficult to stop a process in mid-cycle or if there was no immediate risk of injury. The Health and Safety Commission's Enforcement Policy Statement (2001) states the approach which both the Health and Safety Executive and local authorities should take in relation to law enforcement. The overall aims of the HSC are to protect the health, safety and welfare of employees and to safeguard others such as members of the public who may be exposed to risk from the workplace or activity.

> **Did you know?**
>
> In 2002/03 there were a total of 8,104 improvement notices and 5,159 prohibition notices issued. As the HSC is now trying to focus on priority areas, these figures were also provided for differing sectors. The largest number of improvement notices, 4,088, were issued to manufacturing organisations, while the service sector was issued with 1,573 and organisations in agriculture received 1,503.
>
> However, the sector in which by far the highest number of prohibition notices was issued was the construction sector, which received 2,788 during 2002/03. Manufacturing organisations were issued with 1,238 prohibition notices during this period, but only 602 were issued in agriculture. These are a result to some extent of the inspectors focusing their attention on areas of potential high risk and targeting them for improvement.
>
> (HSE 2003)

In more serious cases they could prosecute. Normally in England and Wales this would go to a magistrates' court but more serious cases are referred to the Crown courts. Under the Scottish judicial system the majority of cases go to a sheriff court or before a jury. Both organisations and individuals can face prosecution, and prison sentences and unlimited fines can also be given by the Crown courts.

Any accidents at work that result in death are treated as manslaughter. The police are involved in these cases and have over all responsibility for them.

In 2002 the HSC (HSC 2002) revised its Enforcement Policy Statement and set out the criteria for whether or not particular incidents or complaints should be investigated. This Policy Statement stresses four main things:

1 *The principle of proportionality*. This means that the severity of the action taken should be in proportion to the level of risk and the seriousness of the breach of law.
2 *Targeting*. The people/organisations who cause the most serious risks or who have failed to control hazards in the workplace adequately should be the ones to be targeted by the inspectors.
3 *Consistent*. For people to have faith in the system and the inspectors they need to feel that they will be treated in a consistently fair way.
4 *Transparent*. Every action taken should be clear, with explanations given for any action that is taken.

As well as the Policy Statement, in 2002 the HSE also devised the Enforcement Management Model to provide a framework for the way that inspectors should enforce health and safety legislation, and this should also guide them in any action they take. This is due to be revised in 2005.

Prosecution

If the case is very serious then the inspector may also need to initiate a prosecution. Any decision about whether or not to prosecute will be taken after considering the HSC's Enforcement Policy Statement.

Effects of health and safety legislation

More than 30 years after the Health and Safety at Work Act 1974 became law it still forms the foundation of health and safety legislation in the UK as it is still being used to update legislation. Therefore it is important to understand some of the fundamental principles that underpin this important piece of legislation.

ACTIVITY 12.2

Both employers and employees have responsibilities under HASAWA. List what you would expect to be the duties of employers and employees with regard to health and safety.

Duties of employers	Duties of employees

Compare your lists with the following duties summarised from the Health and Safety at Work Act 1974.

Discussion of Activity 12.2

Your list probably included some indication that employers were to take responsibility for having a safe workplace with safe equipment that would not injure anyone, and you also probably thought that employees too should take care not to harm anyone at work. There are no specific rules about lighting or temperature in the way that there are in the earlier Acts. Instead the Act is trying to involve people and make everyone take some responsibility for his or her actions. This approach is therefore moving towards a human resource management approach, and health and safety is not just in the domain of the human resource specialist but is shared with others. Sometimes the human resource specialist does have some aspects of health and safety included in his or her job description, and he or she may, for example, be expected to chair the safety committee if there is one.

The responsibilities of employers under the Health and Safety at Work Act

Employers have a basic duty of care to their employees to ensure their health, safety and welfare. As well as this rather general duty, they have five other duties. These are:

- to ensure that the workplace itself is safe; that equipment has been maintained correctly and work is safely organised
- that accidents do not occur because of incorrect handling, storage or transportation within the workplace
- that there is training, supervision and information relating to health and safety
- that the workplace itself is maintained adequately and that there are safe ways to get into and out of the buildings
- that welfare provisions are adequate.

All of these duties are expressed in quite general terms and there is nothing in the Act to specify, for example, how much training or information should be given. The words 'so far as is reasonably practicable' are used frequently within HASAWA. The exact meaning of this phrase will be discussed later in this chapter. The employer also has a further specific duty to produce a safety policy statement.

As we said earlier, HASAWA was designed to gain involvement in health and safety from as many sources as possible, so the responsibility was not just one way. Employees also have responsibilities.

The responsibilities of employees under the Health and Safety at Work Act

As you might expect, there are fewer responsibilities for the employees than for the employers. They have three main areas of responsibility under HASAWA in relation to health and safety. These are:

- to take responsibility for their own health and safety, and for any health and safety problems which might be caused to colleagues by their actions or in some cases their failure to act
- not to recklessly interfere with or misuse any machinery, equipment or processes
- to cooperate with employers about health and safety initiatives.

Although these may not seem very onerous responsibilities, they are important since employees who do not follow these guidelines could be disciplined or even face prosecution themselves if an accident occurred for which they were responsible. They should cooperate about health and safety issues, such as wearing protective clothing, if the employer provides it. Since they must take responsibility for their own health and safety and that of others, they must also not do anything to interfere with safety guards, as this could result in injuries to themselves or to other people.

Safety representatives

As we said earlier, there is a duty for employers to consult with and involve safety representatives in the workplace. In October 1978 the Safety Representatives and Safety Committees Regulations came into effect. These regulations form part of the Health and Safety at Work Act, and within a year over 100,000 safety representatives were in post. The regulations provide that any recognised trade union can appoint safety representatives, and they recommend that in general the people who are appointed should have worked for that employer for at least two years so that they have a reasonable range of experience from which to draw. In some trade unions the shop stewards take on the role of safety representatives, while in others the safety representative is a separate post. The people to fill these positions are, however, selected by the trade union, not by the management. Organisations where there are no recognised trade unions can still appoint safety representatives, and they are normally elected by the workforce.

The safety representative's main function is to represent the employee in consultation with the employer on issues relating to health and safety in the workplace, and they can investigate hazards or potential hazards as well as carrying out inspections of the workplace. They are entitled to paid time off to perform their duties and for training to enable them to carry out their duties effectively, and they may also require some facilities such as the use of a telephone, a filing cabinet and a room to conduct interviews. If two or more safety representatives make a written request to management for a safety committee to be established, then the employer is legally obliged to do so.

The Management of Health and Safety at Work Regulations 1992 (MHSWR) amended 1999 add to the Safety Representatives and Safety Committees Regulations 1977 and specify that every employer shall consult safety representatives in good time with regard to:

- the introduction of any measure at the workplace which may substantially affect health or safety of the workforce
- arrangements for appointing or nominating a 'competent person' who is able to assist the employer to carry out risk assessment exercises and help him or her in carrying out duties in relation to health and safety
- the health and safety information that the employer is supposed to provide to employees
- the planning and organisation of health and safety training
- the health and safety consequences of the introduction of new technology at work.

There are, as you can see, a wide range of duties performed by safety representatives. Safety representatives usually receive excellent training for this demanding role and those who take on these roles can also choose to take the training further and use it as part of a professional qualification in health and safety.

◯ Safety officer or safety adviser

None of the legislation actually specifies the need for a safety officer but, as the law has grown in complexity, many organisations have felt that it is necessary to appoint a person to specialise in this area of work. This is a management appointment and must not be confused with the trade union/employee-appointed safety representative. Safety officers are sometimes appointed to advise senior management without being part of any other department and report directly to the board, but in many organisations they form part of the human resource management department. Smaller organisations may not wish to appoint a full-time safety officer and may instead call on the expertise provided by independent consultants to act as safety advisers.

The Framework Directive (Article 7), which is discussed later, says that employers must designate 'a competent person' who has practical and theoretical knowledge of particular equipment and who is able to identify any problems that may occur with it. The provision of this directive is reflected in Regulation 6 of the Management of Health and Safety at Work Regulations 1992 and clearly refers to a management nominee, although not necessarily to the safety officer but to someone who because of his or her knowledge and experience of particular machinery, plant or equipment is able to identify problems or defects in it. That person needs to be able to carry out risk assessment for health and safety for employees and the public, and must monitor and review protective and preventive measures. A safety officer may fulfil this role but is not likely to be the only designated competent person, as she or he is unlikely to have the required level of knowledge or experience for all machinery.

It is important that anyone appointed as safety officer or safety adviser has the status and level of competence to provide authoritative advice to management and the workforce on aspects of health and safety.

Safety committees

Safety committees have to be established, as we said earlier, if two or more safety representatives request the organisation to do so, but many organisations do not wait for this request, and it is good practice to set up a safety committee in any case. The main objective of a safety committee is to promote cooperation between employers and employees in instigating, developing and carrying out measures to ensure the health and safety at work of employees. They are likely to provide some or all of the following functions:

- study figures and trends for accidents and notifiable diseases
- examine safety audit reports
- consider reports and factual information provided by inspectors
- consider the reports of safety representatives
- assist in development of safety rules and safe systems of work
- monitor the effectiveness of safety training in the workplace
- monitor the effectiveness of the safety and health communication in the workplace
- encourage publicity for health and safety programmes in the workplace
- provide a link with the appropriate inspectorates.

Membership of the health and safety committee

The membership of the committee should be agreed between management and the employees. The committee should normally include equal numbers of people from management and the workforce and should have representation from different areas of the workforce and different grades of management. People such as the organisation's doctor, nurse or safety officer should also be invited to attend as ex officio members. It is a good idea for the person who chairs the committee to have sufficient status within the organisation that they can authorise money to be spent on necessary aspects of health and safety without having to refer all such decisions to higher authority. A senior member of the management team would fulfil this role well, although in many organisations the chair of the safety committee may also alternate between management and the workforce.

The phrase 'as far as is reasonably practicable' is used several times in HASAWA. What factors do you think should be considered in determining whether or not something is 'reasonably practicable'?

This phrase means that circumstances, risks and cost need to be considered when an employer is endeavouring to make the workplace safe for employees. It would be very difficult to make anywhere completely safe and eliminate all accidents. Accidents are by definition something that you cannot predict; nevertheless, many situations do occur where it is possible to predict that someone could be injured if improvements are not made, and employers should try to anticipate the likelihood of these types of accident and take steps to prevent them from occurring. 'Reasonably practicable' means that a calculation must be made in which the risk is compared with the sacrifices, cost and level of effort needed to avert that risk. If there is a very slim chance that a comparatively minor accident might occur, but this chance could be eliminated by spending thousands of pounds on new equipment and also by disrupting the workforce, it might not be considered to be reasonably practicable to do so. If, however, the risk was of a serious injury or possibly death, then it would be reasonable to take every step and spend any amount of money to eliminate this risk. The term 'as far as is reasonably practicable' therefore means that the employer should do as much as they can to try to eliminate risks but that they need to review the balance between the risk and the amount of effort required to eliminate that risk.

Control of Substances Hazardous to Health Regulations (COSHH) 1988

These regulations were made under the Health and Safety at Work Act 1974 and came into effect on 1 October 1989. This is another far-reaching piece of legislation comprising 19 regulations and 4 approved codes of practice. The COSHH 1999 Regulations have been modified by COSHH Regulations 2002 and also by the COSHH (Amendment) Regulations 2003. Apart from some minor changes to tidy up the 1999 Regulations, both relate to fairly specialised areas and do not alter the main thrust of this legislation. (The 2002 regulations relate to the Chemical Agents Directive and the 2003 COSHH (Amendment) Regulations to definitions of carcinogens and mutagens, both of which are far too specialised for a chapter on health and safety in an introductory HRM textbook.) COSHH is designed to protect anyone who works with substances that could be hazardous to health. The regulations apply to all workplaces and include all substances with the exception of asbestos, lead, materials that produce ionising radiations and substances underground, which all have their own separate legislation. The legislation basically applies to any substances that can cause harm by being inhaled, ingested, coming into contact with the skin, or being injected or introduced into the body, so they do cover a very wide range of substances.

COSHH regulations require all employers to carry out an assessment of risks to their employees from substances that are identified in the workplace as being potentially hazardous to either their employees or others who might be affected. Any risks that are identified must then be controlled. While it would be easy to assume that these regulations would not have much effect on ordinary workplaces, this is not in fact the case, as many of the substances identified as potentially hazardous will be found in any workplace – e.g. fluid for photocopiers or cleaning products – so in reality all workplaces are affected. The main areas that employers should focus on are:

- assessing the risk of substances used and identifying the required precautions
- introducing appropriate measures to control or prevent the risk
- ensuring the correct use of the control measures, and that equipment is regularly maintained
- conducting health surveillance to monitor health of employees where there is a known identifiable risk
- informing and training employees about risks that may arise from their work, and informing them of the necessary precautions to take.

The Framework Directive

The European Union Framework Directive has broad objectives which were implemented in EU member states by 31 December 1992. This established in general terms the European Commission's approach to health and safety. The main objectives of the directive were to introduce measures to encourage improvements in safety and health of workers at work. In order to do this it contains general principles concerning the prevention of occupational risks, the protection of health and safety, the elimination of risk and accident factors, as well as informing, consultation and providing balanced participation in accordance with national laws.

The British response to the EU directive was made in the Management of Health and Safety at Work Regulations 1992, which were accompanied by an approved Code of Practice which came into effect on 1 January 1993. Five further sets of regulations were also implemented in Britain on 1 January 1993 and these have become known as the 'six-pack'. The 'six-pack' comprised:

- Management of Health and Safety at Work Regulations 1992
- Workplace (Health, Safety & Welfare) Regulations 1992
- Provision and Use of Work Equipment Regulations 1992
- Personal Protective Equipment at Work Regulations 1992
- Health and Safety (Display Screen Equipment) Regulations 1992
- Manual Handling Operations Regulations 1992.

Legislation becomes out of date and does not always meet the requirements of modern organisations, so amendments are often necessary. All of the original 'six-pack' regulations have recently been amended and updated so the new dates and any significant changes will be included with the regulations as they are discussed. The Provision and Use of Work Equipment was amended in 1998 and the Management of Health and Safety at Work Regulations in 1999. The remaining four regulations were also amended later under the Health and Safety (Miscellaneous Amendments) Regulations 2002.

The Management of Health and Safety at Work Regulations 1999

This is the law in the UK that implemented the Framework Directive. The HASAWA covered some parts of the directive but there were also new things that employers needed to do, such as carrying out certain detailed procedures, assessing risks, implementing certain safety measures and communicating with staff on health and safety. The Act was incorporated into law under the 1974 HASAWA. The key features of this regulation include the following.

Employers shall:

- carry out assessment of health and safety risks to both employees and the public (this may be done in writing or on computer)
- monitor and review protective and preventive measures
- appoint a competent person or persons to be responsible for protective and preventive measures
- establish emergency procedures
- give comprehensible and relevant information and training to employees (the training can be provided by a suitable training provider other than the employer)
- cooperate with any other employers who may share the same work site.

Employees shall:

- use equipment in the way in which they have been trained to use it
- report any dangerous situations or any problem areas that they spot in the arrangements that the employer has made for health and safety.

These regulations are intended for use in cases of criminal action against an employer, and may not be used in any civil cases as evidence of negligence.

Pause for thought 12.2   To what extent do you feel that the Management of Health and Safety at Work Regulations 1999 differ from the HASAWA 1974?

These regulations are more forceful than HASAWA and specify that employers 'shall' do certain things, whereas HASAWA only expected employers to carry out its provisions 'so far as it is reasonably practicable' to do so. You have already seen in our discussion of the role of safety representatives and safety officers how the original 1992 regulations strengthened their roles.

The new regulations also mean that employers have a legal duty to predict what could go wrong, before it actually happens, and to take preventive action to avoid it happening. They must record the preventive action that they have taken. This is referred to as risk assessment and is the same principle as under COSHH, but it is now applied more widely. This will be discussed more fully later in the chapter.

The new regulations require employers to be proactive and actively manage activities aimed at protecting the health and safety of their employees. This is more in line than previous legislative measures with the human resource approach of being proactive and actively managing human resources.

Workplace (Health, Safety and Welfare) Regulations 1992, amended by the Health and Safety (Miscellaneous Amendments) Regulations 2002

This law is intended to rationalise older pieces of legislation and provide clearer ruling as to exactly what facilities the employer should provide for the employee.
Employers shall:

- provide a good working environment with appropriate temperature, ventilation and level of lighting
- carry out maintenance and be responsible for keeping the workplace clean.

The 2002 amendments include further guidance for employers about achieving this, primarily in relation to rest rooms and rest areas. The amendments specify that there should be sufficient seats (with backs) and tables for the number of people likely to use them at any one time. According to the regulations, employers also need to devise an appropriate way to protect non-smokers from having to breathe in other people's tobacco smoke while they are in the rest areas.
The 2002 amendment regulations state that employers must ensure they meet the needs of any disabled workers by also providing suitable rest areas for them. Other equipment and facilities, such as workstations, passageways, doors, and washroom facilities, should also be designed to meet the specific needs of disabled workers.

Provision and Use of Work Equipment Regulations 1998, amended by the Health and Safety (Miscellaneous Amendments) Regulations 2002

This law aims to bring together many older laws governing equipment used at work.
Employers shall:

- consider when they purchase new equipment the working condition of the equipment and risks that it may pose to employees
- ensure the provision of appropriate levels of lighting and warnings about the safe use of the equipment
- ensure that the equipment is suitable for the use to which it will be put
- provide adequate information and training
- provide adequate protection from any potentially dangerous parts of the equipment or machinery.

Personal Protective Equipment at Work Regulations 1992, amended by the Health and Safety (Miscellaneous Amendments) Regulations 2002

These regulations replace part of more than 20 old pieces of legislation which were concerned with provision of protective equipment for employees. They aim to ensure suitable provision of protective equipment such as head protection, high visibility clothing or safety harnesses. Employers must ensure the equipment is appropriate for the likely type of risks, the specific working conditions in the workplace and the duration for which it is likely to be worn. In addition, they should consider the ergonomic requirements of the job, state of health of the person employed and any particular characteristics of their workstation that might affect the use of the personal protective equipment. Particular attention should also be paid to ensuring that the equipment provided is hygienic and compatible with any additional personal protective equipment that the worker may need to wear simultaneously.

Employers shall:

- ensure that equipment used is suitable for the job to be done
- adequately maintain, clean and replace equipment as necessary
- store it safely when it is not in use
- ensure correct use of the equipment
- inform and train employees in the correct use of the equipment.

Health and Safety (Display Screen Equipment) Regulations 1992, amended by the Health and Safety (Miscellaneous Amendments) Regulations 2002

This law implements the EU's Visual Display Unit Directive and specifies minimum levels of health and safety for people who spend a large part of their time at work working in front of computer screens or who are about to become employed in that capacity. It is primarily aimed at the prevention of damage to their upper limbs, and to prevent eye strain, fatigue and stress.

Employers shall:

- assess the risks and reduce any that are found
- ensure that workstations meet at least the minimum requirements
- ensure that the work is planned to include breaks and changes of activity
- arrange for employees to have their eyes tested regularly at time limits designated by the optician appointed by the employer and provide spectacles if necessary
- provide appropriate training for users or those about to become users of visual display units.

Eyesight tests should be completed as soon as possible after any request, or in the case of someone who is about to start work, before he or she becomes a computer user.

Manual Handling Operations Regulations 1992, amended by the Health and Safety (Miscellaneous Amendments) Regulations 2002

This aims to reduce the levels of injury and ill-health associated with manual handling of loads at work.

Employers shall:

- ensure, as far as is practicable, that employees do not need to use risky techniques when handling loads
- assess whether any risks are inherent in the manual handling that has to be done

- take necessary steps to reduce risks by introducing mechanical help, ensuring loads are lighter and assessing the capabilities of the individual
- ensure the provision of information to all employees
- if employees sometimes work on another employer's premises, liaise closely with the other employer.

When trying to determine whether each specific manual handling activity involves any risk, employers should pay particular attention to the following:

- the physical suitability of the employee for safely completing the particular form of manual handling required
- what the person is wearing and its suitability for the job
- the amount of knowledge and training that the person has received
- the results of any risk assessments that have already been completed that relate to the job
- whether the employee has been identified as being one of a group of employees who are particularly at risk
- the results of any health surveillance that has been undertaken.

This legislation is far reaching in its scope although its effects will vary from one organisation to another, depending on the nature of the work undertaken.

Reporting of Injuries, Diseases and Dangerous Occurrences Regulations (RIDDOR) 1995

RIDDOR 1995 came into effect on 1 April 1996 and requires employers to report certain work-related accidents, diseases and dangerous occurrences to the enforcing authorities so that they can identify risks and investigate serious accidents. The following briefly describes some of the circumstances in which reporting should occur:

- The death or major injury of an employee, or of a self-employed person working in the organisation, or of a member of the public must all be reported to the enforcing authorities immediately and this must be followed within 10 days by a completed accident report. Reportable major injuries include fractures, amputation, dislocation, loss of sight.
- If an employee or self-employed person working on your premises suffers an accident or injury which requires that person to be absent from work for at least three days, then a completed accident form must be sent to the enforcing authorities.
- Some work-related diseases, such as occupational dermatitis, skin cancer or occupational asthma have also to be reported on a disease report form to the enforcing authority, as do infections such as hepatitis, tetanus or tuberculosis.
- There may be instances where something occurs which does not actually result in a reportable injury but which could have done. For example, the collapse of a lift or an explosion in a closed vessel are likely to constitute a dangerous occurrence, even if no one is injured. Any dangerous occurrence has to be reported immediately by telephone to the enforcing authorities. An accident report form should also be completed within 10 days of the dangerous occurrence. (Details of where to find more information are given in further study at the end of the chapter.)

The enforcing authority will be the environmental health department of the local authority if the type of the business is an office, retail or wholesale, warehousing, hotel or catering, sports or leisure, a residential home or place of worship. Accidents or dangerous occurrences which happen in any other type of business will need to be reported to the area office of the Health and Safety Executive. Nowadays accidents and dangerous occurrences can even be reported using the Internet. Have a look at the web sites at the end of this chapter for more details of how to do this.

The Working Time Regulations 1998

We discussed the Working Time Regulations 1998 briefly in Chapter 6, but have also included them here, since the hours people work can have a big impact on both their health and safety in the workplace.

It is often claimed that the UK is the 'long hours capital' of Europe and that working such long hours adversely affects workers' health. In some organisations there is a culture of 'presenteeism', where people are expected to arrive early for work and leave late, forgoing home and social life. While some workers thrive in a long hours culture and live to work, such a culture is likely to hide a great deal of inefficiency and result in increased levels of stress and ill-health for many other workers. These regulations attempt to control the hours worked and control the way the hours are organised. They also establish minimum holiday levels for employees in the UK, although it is frequently claimed that a large number of UK employees actually fail to take all the holiday they are entitled to, either because they are too busy or are too frightened to be away from work for their whole holiday entitlement.

Although the regulations emanate from the Working Time Directive, adopted by the EU Council of Ministers in 1993, and therefore apply to all EU countries, there is some flexibility available for countries to implement European directives in their own way. Other European countries, for example France with its 35-hour working week, have implemented the directive differently. The main features for adult workers in the UK were outlined in Chapter 6.

Although the 48-hour working week means workers in the UK still work much longer hours than their counterparts in France, it is nevertheless considerably better than the expectation in countries such as Japan. In Japan it has been documented that many workers regularly work for over 100 hours per week, for many weeks, or even years at a time and that this frequently leads, not surprisingly, to ill-health or even death. Since we work increasingly in a global economy, where people are constantly accessible via mobile phones or e-mail, these long hour work practices are spreading to the USA and the UK.

> **Did you know?**
>
> Death from overwork is so common in Japan that they even have a special word for it, Karoshi. The first documented case of Karoshi occurred in Japan in 1969 but there have been many cases since. In Japan the spouses of those who have died from Karoshi have won claims for compensation from the companies concerned and each year between 20 and 60 claims for compensation are brought. This is still probably a gross underestimate of the real number of cases of Karoshi in Japan.
>
> (Nishiyama and Johnson 1977)

⬤ Safety policy statement

You will remember that under HASAWA one of the duties of an employer is to provide a safety policy statement to show each person's responsibilities and the arrangements they have made to carry out the policy. The safety policy applies to all organisations that employ more than five employees. This is supposed to be a document that can be used to show in a practical way how the arrangements for health and safety are to be carried out in the workplace, and it should be designed to have a genuine effect on health and safety working practices. This means that it should be clearly written and should be easily available to any employee, and a copy should preferably be given to each employee. It does not mean that it is a secret document, as some organisations in our experience seem to think, kept locked in a filing cabinet well away from the gaze of employees. In order to encourage awareness of health and safety and produce an effective safety policy document, it is also advisable that a range of people should be involved in its design and that key decision makers have been involved fully in these discussions. In some organisations a person will be chosen to champion the policy and targets for improvements in specific areas of health and safety may also be set. Arrangements should also be made to review the health and safety policy regularly, at least annually, since what is important is whether the policy is having an effect on health and safety in the workplace, rather than how well written it is.

The HSE recommends that the following two issues should be addressed in a safety policy statement.

- Who has responsibility for health and safety?
- What are the arrangements made for health and safety?

Responsibility for health and safety

The safety policy should show management's approach to health and safety and who is actually responsible for specific tasks. The safety policy is basically concerned with people, their duties and their accountability. It should include a management chart showing the chain of command in respect of health and safety, with a clear statement that the ultimate responsibility for health and safety rests with the board or chief executive or equivalent. The safety policy document should carry at the end the signature of the person with the ultimate responsibility for health and safety at work. There should be a clearly defined role for the safety adviser, if such a position exists, and clear explanation of his/her relationship to senior management and line management. This part of the document should also indicate the role of those appointed as 'competent persons' to assist the employer in implementing the safety policy.

According to David Morris (2001), Head of the HSE's Strategy and Management Branch:

> In principle, small firms will have much the same policy statements as larger firms, and their risk assessments will cover much the same ground. But there are differences. The policy statement is likely to show that there is less scope for delegation in a small firm, where many responsibilities are exercised directly by the owner. Equally, small firms may have relatively few, or simple, hazards, meaning that risk assessment will be less complex.

The health and safety arrangements

This section should establish systems and procedures and the practical arrangements for their implementation. It should also show the system for monitoring safety and for publishing results. The section of the safety policy covering arrangements should be a practical section that is regularly reviewed and updated.

The HSE (2003), in a booklet, *Stating Your Business*, suggests that small organisations organise their arrangements for managing health and safety under the sections listed below.

- health and safety risks arising from our work activities
- consultation with employees
- safe plant and equipment
- safe handling and use of substances
- information, instruction and supervision
- competency for tasks and training
- accidents, first aid and work-related ill-health
- monitoring
- emergency procedures – fire and evacuation
- key areas of risk.

Health and safety risks arising from work activities

This means that the arrangements for carrying out risk assessments, the results of the risk assessments and the actions taken will all need to be shown, although the findings and resulting actions will need to be shown in a separate document. Risk assessments will be discussed in more detail later in the chapter.

Consultation with employees

We have already discussed the fact that if there is a recognised trade union which has appointed safety representatives then by law they must be consulted about any changes likely to affect the health and safety of their members. If there is not a recognised trade union then the employers must consult their employees directly or through a works council.

Safe plant and equipment

This requirement is taken directly from HASAWA and means that employers must keep vehicles, machinery and equipment in good working order. In the safety policy, the names of people responsible for this should be stated, as should arrangements to deal with problems. Those responsible for checking that new machinery and equipment meets the required standards should also be listed here. Records of maintenance and service history of vehicles should be kept, perhaps separately in a log book.

Safe handling and use of substances

This section relates to those responsible for identifying substances that need a COSHH assessment. (If you cannot remember what COSHH refers to then re-read the section about it earlier in this chapter.) Once again the names of people with responsibilities should be listed here. This includes the names of those carrying out the assessments, those responsible for ensuring that any actions needed are taken, those who have to tell employees about the results of the assessments as well as the names of those people who have responsibility for checking the safety of new substances prior to purchase. There should also be an indication as to the frequency of assessments.

Information, instruction and supervision

This should show where health and safety law posters are displayed or where leaflets relating to health and safety are kept. It should also detail where health and safety advice can be obtained and the names of those responsible for supervising the work of trainees or young employees.

Competency for tasks and training

The names of people who provide induction training and job-specific training should be listed here. Some jobs may pose particular risks, for example the risk of back injury to workers involved in the manual handling of heavy or awkwardly shaped goods. Both the jobs and the training needed should also be identified. Training records should be kept for all health and safety training as well as other training and the safety policy should indicate where the records are stored and by whom.

Accidents, first aid and work-related ill-health

In this section any health surveillance required for certain jobs, such as work with flour, asbestos or some chemicals, needs to be identified. This should mean any problems in a worker's health caused by the job will be identified at an early stage so that action can be taken to prevent their health becoming worse. It shows who is responsible for health surveillance and where records are kept.

The locations of first aid boxes need to be shown and first aiders should be listed. Records of all accidents, however trivial, and instances of work-related ill-health should be recorded in the accident book and the location of this book should also be given in the health and safety policy.

Monitoring

It is very important that the policy is used and that good practices are checked regularly. Those who have responsibility for checking that working conditions are safe and that safe practices are being followed should be listed here, as should those who are responsible for carrying out investigations of accidents or investigating work-related causes of sickness absence.

Emergency procedures – fire and evacuation

Obviously it is important that there are adequate safety procedures in place in case there is a need to evacuate the building in an emergency. In this section it is important to state who checks the escape routes and the frequency of these checks. Safety equipment such as fire extinguishers has to be maintained and checked, alarms need to be tested, emergency evacuation drills need to be carried out and records of these must be kept.

Key areas of risk

These will vary depending on the organisation and the type of work undertaken but might include risks relating to particularly dangerous substances such as asbestos, or to stress or potential violence to staff from members of the public. Each organisation will need to carry out its own risk assessments relating to the areas of risk which are identified.

People need to be aware of their responsibilities as, if something goes wrong and a serious accident occurs, the relevant enforcement officers will want to know who was responsible. These enforcement officers would carry out a full investigation and would also want to examine the safety policy document. If a supervisor did not know that he or she was responsible for checking that a protective guard was in place, then the employer would have to be able to prove that he or she had informed the supervisor of his or her responsibilities and had also trained him or her adequately in the fulfilment of these responsibilities. Many tasks will of course be delegated to different levels of management and employees do, as we have seen, have some responsibility for their own actions. Senior management cannot, however, abdicate their ultimate responsibility for overall safety within the organisation, and must try to ensure the health and safety of their employees and others affected by their employees' actions. Those who carry the ultimate responsibility for this, such as the board of directors, could face prosecution and possibly a large fine or even a spell in prison for individual directors if their organisation is found to be at fault. Similarly, others with specific responsibilities such as safety officers, human resource managers, line managers or training officers could be charged and convicted of an offence.

Read the following Case study and carry out Activity 12.3. The Case study will be used later in the chapter as the basis for Activities 12.4 and 12.5.

CASE STUDY

The Sheffley Company employs nearly 330 employees and specialises in the production of steel castings. The organisation has a Director, Mr Jones, whose great-grandfather founded the business. There is a new Production Manager, Mr Tandy; an Import and Export Manager, Ms Jeffries; and an Administration Manager, Mrs Groves. Mr Tandy has eight line managers reporting to him, who have a total of 280 employees working for them. Mrs Groves has a Payroll Manager, a Canteen Manager and a Personnel Officer reporting to her and Ms Jeffries runs the Purchasing, Goods Inward and Goods Outward Departments, and the Warehouse and Export Sections.

The work involved in the production of steel castings is hazardous and the company has not had a good record with regard to health and safety. It is not only in the production areas that there have been problems – the offices also have suffered rather a large number of accidents which have required employees to have more than three days off work to recover.

The new Production Manager decides that something must be done about the record for safety, and in the weekly meeting with the production supervisors he informs them that from next week any employee who does not wear the protective equipment provided will be dismissed. The safety equipment comprises safety boots, safety goggles and overalls.

During the lead-up to the introduction of the safety equipment, notices are put up to explain the disciplinary penalty for non-compliance with the regulation, but information about the use and location of some of the equipment is not provided. Neither the safety representatives nor the safety committee have the opportunity to inspect the new protective equipment or to advise employees on its suitability.

The employees prove to be reluctant to wear the protective goggles which, they complain, pinch their skin and impair their vision. The Production Manager realises that the enforcement of safety is going to be problematic, and at the next week's meeting informs the supervisors that they do not have to be too rigid in their enforcement of the rules.

Two serious accidents occur just a month later in the production area and a further serious accident occurs in the offices. In the first incident molten metal splashes on to the foot of an employee, causing serious burns. In a separate accident a few days later an employee slips, splashing molten metal close to his eyes. Luckily his sight is saved, but he suffers severe burns and scarring. The accident record in the offices is also unsatisfactory, and one employee is injured when chemicals used in the photocopier spill on her leg causing a severe itchy rash to develop. Other employees in the wages office complain of backaches and headaches which they say are caused by poor lighting, uncomfortable chairs and badly adjusted screens on their visual display units.

ACTIVITY 12.3

Design a safety policy statement for the Sheffley Company. Remember that this should be a practical document that can be used by people in the organisation. Use the sections and main headings that we have given earlier (see pages 384–387).

Risk assessment

The idea of assessing and controlling risks was introduced to Britain with the Control of Substances Hazardous to Health Regulations 1988, when employers had to assess the risk of harm to people from certain substances being used at work. This was developed further in the 'six-pack' regulations in 1992. The 1992 Code of Practice for the Management of Health and Safety at Work made it a legal duty for employers to assess and record health and safety risks, and to appoint a 'competent person', i.e. a person who has been suitably trained and who is allowed adequate time and facilities to perform this role should assist in this and other safety tasks.

Every organisation has to carry out its own risk assessment, and strategies for this should be devised by management after consultation with all interested groups in the workforce.

According to the HSE in the booklet *Five Steps to Risk Assessment* (2000), the five main steps involved in assessing risks and hazards in the workplace are:

1 Look for the hazards.
2 Decide who might be harmed and how.
3 Evaluate the risks and decide whether the existing precautions are adequate or whether more should be done.
4 Record your findings.
5 Review your assessment and revise it if necessary.

Assessments do not have to be carried out by health and safety experts and small organisations may choose to undertake the initial assessment of risk by themselves: alternatively, they may prefer to employ a consultant.

Most organisations are likely to be able to carry out the first two steps quite easily and identify sources of risk and then identify those who may be harmed by the risks. One simple method used by some organisations to evaluate the risks is to rate each hazard against three scales – likelihood, severity and extent of harm – using a points system to assess these. To get some idea of how this might work in practice, try the following Activity.

ACTIVITY 12.4

Think of the three accidents that occurred in the Sheffley Company case study. The organisation should obviously have carried out a risk assessment before these accidents occurred and should, as the first stage in the risk assessment process, have already identified these three situations as being potentially hazardous. The second stage is to assess the likelihood or risk that each of the situations will cause harm. Using the scale given in Table 12.1, assess the potential risks in these three situations and see which, according to your assessment, has the highest score and hence the most potential risk of causing harm:

1 the risk of injury from transporting molten metal
2 the risk of injury from employees slipping or falling in the production area
3 the risk of injury from handling or transporting chemicals used in the photocopier.

Table 12.1

Risk assessment

	Risk 1	Risk 2	Risk 3
Likelihood of harm Certain 4 pts Probable 3 pts Possible 2 pts Slight 1 pt			
Severity of harm Major 4 pts Serious 3 pts Minor 2 pts Slight 1 pt			
Extent of harm V. extensive 4 pts Extensive 3 pts Limited 2 pts V. limited 1 pt			

Total score risk 1 = _____

Total score risk 2 = _____

Total score risk 3 = _____

Discussion of Activity 12.4

This is a very easy way of completing the second stage of risk assessment but is perhaps a little too simplistic. Activity 12.5. will ask you to focus on its problems.

ACTIVITY 12.5

What problems can you identify with this method of assessing risks?

Discussion of Activity 12.5

In Table 12.1, all three categories are rated in the same way. It is likely that an organisation would need to develop its own weighted scales, with clear descriptions of what is meant by each category, and that normally the severity rating should be weighted more heavily than the other two categories. After all, any risk of death should be treated very seriously and given a high rating even if there is a very slim chance of this ever happening.

Other factors may also need to be taken into account, such as the vulnerability of particular employees or whether the risk exists only in particular circumstances. However, an exercise such as this will provide the opportunity for systematically assessing risks and may help to indicate a priority for action.

Assessing the risk is not the end, as something must then be done to control or minimise the risk. This is the third stage in the process of assessing risk.

○ Control measures

The Code of Practice for the Management of Health and Safety at Work 1992 suggests a hierarchy of control measures in order to eliminate or minimise the risk. These are the measures in the suggested order of priority:

1 Substitute safer equipment or materials.
2 Tackle risk at source by improving design features, e.g. use remote control mechanisms, or protective barriers or guard machines.
3 Replan work procedures, e.g. minimise weights to be lifted or introduce mechanical lifting devices.
4 Use protective clothing.

The substitution of safer equipment or materials is considered to be the first priority here, even though other alternatives may be possible. This is because a safe system will not need constant monitoring, whereas using protective clothing or replanning work systems is likely to involve frequent checks and constant supervision, and so is less certain in its effectiveness.

ACTIVITY 12.6

Look once again at Activity 12.4 and the three situations where you assessed the risks. Make a list of the control measures that might be considered for each of these risks. Whatever the method chosen to eliminate or minimise risk, it will still be necessary to monitor the effectiveness of this method as accidents may still happen. The employer would not have a good case if he knew of the hazard's existence, took some steps to try to eliminate it, but then forgot to carry out maintenance to keep the safety equipment in good order.

Health

So far, we have focused primarily on approaches to safety in response to legal requirements. It is important for employers not only to try to prevent accidents and ill-health as encouraged by the legislation but also to be proactive and take measures to promote improvements in safety and encourage developments to ensure good health.

Did you know?

A survey of absence conducted by the CIPD in 2004 showed that sickness absenteeism accounted for 4% of working time. According to the CIPD this is the equivalent of 9.1 working days per employee per year and costs approximately £588 per person per year.
(CIPD 2004)

The high cost of absenteeism is a strong financial reason for taking measures to promote and improve health. Many employers have provided health screening services and membership of private health insurance schemes for their managers, and some are extending this provision to the workforce as a whole. Increasingly, organisations are actively trying to promote a healthier life style among their employees. Among the measures that have been tried are:

- help for smokers to quit, with support/self-help groups and psychologists giving advice and support
- a healthy diet, with a wider choice of health foods on the menu at work
- membership of a health club or purchase of multi-gym exercise equipment for employees to use to get fitter
- stress management programmes
- policies and education programmes on HIV/Aids
- policies and education on substance abuse.

In organisations where these programmes have been made available to all the workforce on a long-term basis, there have been benefits to employees' health, with weight reduction and improvements in blood cholesterol and blood pressure levels, and also improvements in absenteeism rates. It is claimed that the cost of the introduction of this type of programme is more than offset by the savings from lower rates of absenteeism. The CIPD (2000) stated that 'a survey of 97 organisations showed that employees who were participating in "wellness" programmes each incurred between £1,335 and £2,910 less per year in healthcare and absenteeism costs than colleagues who were not participating.'

Various studies have shown that those who are unemployed tend to have worse health than those in employment. However, those in employment may also suffer from ill-health and can suffer from work-related ill-health. A study by the HSE in 1995 suggested that more than 2 million people were suffering from illness caused by their work, or that had been made worse because of their work. While the numbers of accidents in the workplace has dropped steadily, there is now a focus on achieving the same effect for work-related illness.

In 2000 one of the priorities of the HSE was to improve this situation and an Occupational Health Strategy was devised to:

1 Stop people from becoming ill because of work.
2 Help those who are absent due to long-term illness to get back into work.

3 Improve work opportunities for those who are not currently in employment because of their ill-health or disability.

4 Use the workplace to encourage people to maintain or improve their health.

This approach is based once again on the idea of partnership between Government, the HSE and employers, workers and trade unions. Targets were set to
inspire action and five key programmes were started to complement other
Government initiatives, such as the Welfare to Work schemes. The five programmes of work which were established were about:

1 compliance
2 continuous improvement
3 knowledge
4 skills
5 support.

Targets were also set and it is hoped that all interested parties will be involved
in working towards their achievement. It is hoped that by 2010 the following
targets will be achieved:

- A 20% reduction in the incidence of work-related ill-health.
- A 20% reduction in the ill-health of members of the public that has been
  caused by work activity.
- A 30% reduction in the numbers of days absence caused by work-related
  ill-health.
- All who are employed but who are unable to work because of their ill-health
  or disability should be made aware of opportunities for speedy rehabilitation
  back into work.
- Everyone who is not employed because of their ill-health or disability
  should be offered opportunities to prepare for and find work.

It has been estimated that if just three of these targets are achieved, the value
to the UK could be huge and worth somewhere between £8.6 and £21.8 billion, although it is obviously very difficult to calculate such figures with any
degree of accuracy.

A Partnership Board was established, not only to oversee the implementation and delivery of the strategy but also as a way of drawing on ideas from a
range of interested parties. The roles of the Partnership Board are to:

- be strategic
- act as a champion
- use contacts to network and solve problems
- review progress overall
- make sure that sound management practices, such as evaluation, are fully
  used
- provide regular reports on progress to the HSC.

Did you know?

A casino worker, Michael Dunn, received £50,000 in an out-of-
court settlement after he developed asthma as a result of passive
smoking at work.
(Cacanas, Z. (2004) *The Guardian*, 24 July)

Failure to take steps to reduce risks in the
workplace is likely in the future to lead to
higher insurance payments for organisations
as insurance companies start to link premiums
to the way that organisations manage risks of
accidents and ill-health. Smokers generally
suffer worse health than non-smokers and the

charity Action on Smoking and Health (ASH) claims that 34 million working days are lost in Britain each year, just because of smoking. Some employers are becoming more proactive about their employees' health and are introducing measures such as bonuses to encourage smokers to quit. These can, however, prove controversial as non-smokers may then also want to benefit from bonuses.

International issues in health and safety

Although British health and safety legislation does not apply to workers based outside Britain, employers still have a duty of care towards their employees, no matter where they work. Employees who operate in a global scene need additional knowledge relating to the particular country in which they are working, and this also applies to health and safety. The HR departments in those organisations need to check on health and safety legislation in the countries concerned, and should also carry out a risk assessment of not only the job but also the country, and should evaluate the employee's health. This would help ensure, for example, that they are not sending an asthmatic employee into a very dusty desert environment that would probably make the employee's health worse.

Even within Europe we have seen that individual countries can interpret European directives in different ways so the actual health and safety legislation in countries may vary. Attitudes to safety can be different and vary from one culture to another. In cultures where people tend to sue for damages, such as America, people are used to having lots of rules even when they are relaxing, away from work, so on beaches they only swim in the designated areas and obey the lifeguards. In the Greek islands, tourists would seek their own sheltered cove and swim from their own secluded beach so would have to take more responsibility for their own safety. Such differences in cultural expectations do shape attitudes to health and safety, so it is important to take into account the culture of the country and consider this in relation to health and safety. When Disney first opened in Paris some of the instructions on rides such as the requirement 'to exit the ride using your left foot first' jarred a little with Europeans who were used to making such decisions for themselves!

Some employees are sent to work in countries which may be regarded as high risk and where dangers such as kidnapping could occur. Staff need to be briefed as to precautions to take in these countries, as do the local staff, who may actually be more at risk than the ex-pat staff, who probably live in a secure compound and have a driver to transport them safely. Some groups such as humanitarian aid workers are also likely to be at risk, since the nature of their jobs ensures that they are likely to be working in high risk areas. However, they should still not be exposed to unnecessary risks.

HR departments who have staff working in potentially high risk countries should carry out risk assessments, relating both to the dangers to health and to potential threats to safety, and should devise suitable emergency plans which can be put in place quickly. They should also devise suitable training programmes, perhaps drawing on local knowledge and expertise, for people undertaking these jobs. The workforce could even be involved in analysing the

Did you know?

In response to the killings of three UN workers in West Timor on 6 September 2000, humanitarian workers from around the world marched in protest for better protection. They sent a petition to the UN headquarters demanding 'greater pressure from the UN on national governments to guarantee the safety of humanitarian workers, together with internal measures addressing management accountability, risk assessment and more funding for security provision'.

(*People Management*, 31 May 2001, pp. 26–27)

hazards and designing their own security plans for the compounds in which they live. Training in potential high risk countries is likely to cover specific issues such as personal safety, office security, compound security, threats to convoys, risk analysis, first aid and emergency evacuation plans.

If this is done the workers are likely to feel and be safer and since health and safety will be perceived as being important, it is likely that they will take more care themselves. Measures such as these can do a great deal to eliminate unnecessary risks, although it is impossible to eliminate all risks completely.

The HRM approach to health and safety

We said at the beginning of this chapter that it is not enough for employers just to be concerned about preventing accidents in order to comply with legislation, although that in itself is a good start. The human resource management approach has tended to emphasise the need for individuality, flexibility and adaptability, although it is true that one cannot be flexible about whether or not to implement laws. Clearly employers have to act within the law or face prosecution. We have shown in this chapter that there has been a change of approach within the law, from mere compliance with minimum legal requirements in the legislation prior to HASAWA to the encouragement of increased involvement of all, and from compliance with legal requirements 'so far as it is reasonably practicable' under HASAWA to placing the duty on managers that they must introduce management systems, implement these systems and monitor the effectiveness of them.

Although the newer legislation is more forceful and hence more prescriptive, in some respects it is more in tune with the human resource management approach, since there is an emphasis on the need for managers to manage, on the development of strategies, procedures and systems for improving health and safety, as well as on a need for monitoring the implementation of these systems. This approach to health and safety should link with the overall business objectives of maximising efficiency and effectiveness by improving morale and reducing costs, and also allows for some scope for individuality and flexibility in how this is to be achieved. It is the approach to health and safety that we would advocate, and it is a very different approach to the purely legalistic one of just being concerned with not breaking the law. The HRM approach to health and safety involves the following features:

● The need to create a culture in which health and safety are seen to be important to the organisation. The safety policy statement will contribute to this if it is effectively written, known about and acted upon. The legal requirements must be complied with and risk assessments carried out, as well as gathering information about health and safety and carrying out a cost–benefit analysis. If there is to be a culture of health and safety aware-ness, there also need to be campaigns and publicity, and involvement of top management, individuals and teams. There need to be regular commu-nications and discussion of health and safety and the contribution that improvements will make to the organisation's overall effectiveness, so that all members of the organisation realise that health and safety are impor-tant to the way it operates.

- Commitment from the top to the achievement of progressively higher standards as expressed in the mission statement and safety policy. Top management must not only sign the policy documents but also set a good example in relation to health and safety, and emphasise that it is an area of importance to them and to the future of the organisation by showing their interest and by setting up new systems and monitoring the effective-ness of these systems.
- Commitment throughout the organisation, with all parties clear about their own responsibilities for health and safety, the targets they have to meet and the contribution these make to the organisation's objectives. This should be considered as an aspect of performance management, as individuals and teams would be encouraged to take responsibility for their own actions and to agree and work towards targets when making improvements.
- Managers to demonstrate by their example their commitment to the importance of a safer and healthier work environment. They should also find ways to motivate everyone to make a contribution to health and safe-ty improvements. Prizes and awards to individuals and teams can have an important effect.
- Policies and procedures designed to take account of the importance of a safer and healthier environment. There should also be effective systems to monitor their effectiveness.
- Policies to be backed by adequate resources for equipment and training. Provision of good health and safety costs money but the cost of not pro-viding these can be higher, as any cost–benefit analysis is likely to prove.
- The setting of realistic and attainable targets for everyone in the organisation.
- Encouragement of all to take responsibility for their own actions and involvement of all in health and safety.

The approach of the HSE to revitalising health and safety also reinforces these points. They encourage employers to become aware of health and safety issues by emphasising the business case for health and safety. They also encourage managers to be proactive about managing both the health and safety of their workforce. National targets have been set as part of the process to reduce both the number of accidents and the number of days of sickness absence. Involvement and partnership are both approaches which are strongly encouraged and these methods are typical of the HRM approach.

REVIEW QUESTIONS

1 Interview people (friends, family or work colleagues from a range of organisations) about their own responsibilities in relation to health and safety and then about their perceptions of other people's roles in their particular organisation. Try to establish how the roles relating to health and safety differ for managers, other employees, human resource managers, safety officers, safety representatives and someone designated to be a 'competent person'. Are these roles the same in different types of organisation? How do they compare with what we said earlier in the chapter about these roles?

2 Obtain a copy of the safety policy for either your college or your workplace.
   (a) Use this to identify the roles of various people in the organisation in relation to health and safety.
   (b) Use the safety policy to assess whether health and safety are linked to the organisation's strategic objectives.

3 Design a checklist for carrying out a safety inspection in the workplace. Use your checklist to actually carry out an inspection of a designated area either at work or in your college. Write a report about your findings for the safety officer.

4 Write a short report in which you assess the impact of one piece of health and safety legislation on an organisation of your choice.

5 Prepare arguments and then debate the following statements in two teams. Try to persuade the members of the other team to your point of view.

TEAM A: There is much too much legislation regarding health and safety at work and this is unnecessary as it is in the employers' interests to look after their employees. Legislation merely hinders employers in their ability to run their businesses effectively.

TEAM B: Legislation is necessary to control employers who would otherwise ignore health and safety issues at the expense of their employees' health, safety and welfare.

SELF-CHECK QUESTIONS

Answer the following multiple-choice and short-answer questions. The correct responses are given on page 494 for you to check your understanding of this chapter.

1 Which of the following was the first piece of legislation designed to protect everyone at work, and also to protect others who were not at work, such as customers or passers-by?
   (a) the Factories Act 1961
   (b) the Offices Shops and Railways Premises Act 1963
   (c) the Fire Precautions Act 1971
   (d) the Health and Safety at Work Act 1974
   (e) the Control of Substances Hazardous to Health Regulations 1988.

2 Which of the following pieces of legislation established the Health and Safety Commission?

(a) the Factories Act 1961

(b) the Offices Shops and Railways Premises Act 1963

(c) the Fire Precautions Act 1971

(d) the Health and Safety at Work Act 1974

(e) the Control of Substances Hazardous to Health Regulations 1988.

3 An improvement notice is issued when:

(a) something is found to be so dangerous that the factory inspectorate feels it necessary to stop work immediately

(b) improvements are required by the factory inspectorate but the employer can decide when these should take place

(c) improvements are required by the factory inspectorate within a specified period to bring the equipment or process up to the required standard

(d) the required improvement has been made by the employer

(e) improvements are required by the safety committee to be made within a specified period.

4 The term 'so far as it is reasonably practicable to do so' means:

(a) that employers must do everything in their power to make the workplace safe

(b) that employers may weigh up the costs of a safety improvement against the risks when deciding whether to make the improvement

(c) that employers must assess the risks of substances used and identify the required precautions to be taken

(d) that employers have a legal duty to predict what may go wrong before it happens

(e) that employers should be proactive and actively manage health and safety issues.

5 The Management of Health and Safety at Work Regulations contain the following legal requirement:

(a) that employers must do the best that they can to make the workplace safe

(b) that employers may weigh up the costs of a safety improvement against the risks when deciding whether to make a safety improvement

(c) that employers must assess the risks of any substances used by employees and identify the required precautions to be taken

(d) that employers should carry out an assessment of health and safety risks to both employees and the public

(e) that employers should carry out an assessment of health and safety risks for their employees only.

6 The term 'six-pack' refers to the following six pieces of legislation:

(a) the Factories Act 1961, the Offices Shops and Railways Premises Act 1963, the Fire Precautions Act 1971, the Health and Safety at Work Act 1974, the Control of Substances Hazardous to Health Regulations 1988, Manual Handling Operations Regulations 1992

(b) the Factories Act 1961, the Offices Shops and Railways Premises Act 1963, the Fire Precautions Act 1971, the Health and Safety at Work Act 1974, the Control of Substances Hazardous to Health Regulations 1988, the Management of Health and Safety at Work Regulations 1992

(c) the Factories Act 1961, the Health and Safety at Work Act 1974, the Control of Substances Hazardous to Health Regulations 1988, the Management of Health and Safety at Work Regulations 1992, Workplace (Health, Safety and Welfare) Regulations 1992, Provision and Use of Work Equipment Regulations 1992

(d) Management of Health and Safety at Work Regulations 1992, Workplace (Health, Safety and Welfare) Regulations 1992, Provision and Use of Work Equipment Regulations 1992, Personal Protective Equipment at Work Regulations 1992, Health and Safety (Display Screen Equipment) Regulations 1992, Manual Handling Operations Regulations 1992

(e) the Health and Safety at Work Act 1974, the Control of Substances Hazardous to Health Regulations 1988, Management of Health and Safety at Work Regulations 1992, Workplace (Health, Safety and Welfare) Regulations 1992, Provision and Use of Work Equipment Regulations 1992, Personal Protective Equipment at Work Regulations 1992.

Refer back to the Case study in this chapter (pages 387–388) and answer the following questions. Suggested answers for these are included in the tutor's pack.

7 Describe what the role of the safety committee should have been within the Sheffley Company.

8 Imagine that you are a consultant brought in to advise about health and safety at the Sheffley Company. Write a report to the Director in which you outline the improvements that should be made in health and safety at Sheffley, and recommend how these improvements should be introduced.

WHAT NEXT?

Do you remember the balanced scorecard that we discussed in Chapter 1? Research conducted by Aberdeen University on 13 offshore oil installations applies the balanced scorecard to occupational health. The article also discusses the results of interviews with UK and Norwegian managers on health and safety performance indicators and the reasons for including occupational health and safety as one measure of performance within the balanced scorecard. What do you think about the idea that measures of occupational health should be included in an assessment of an organisation's performance?

Mearns, K. and J. I. Havold (2003) Occupational health and safety and the balanced scorecard, *The TQM Magazine*, Vol. 15, No. 6, 408–423

References

Chartered Institute of Personnel and Development (2000) *Quick Facts. Occupational Health and Organisational Effectiveness*, CIPD (available at **www.cipd.co.uk**; accessed 04.09.01)

Chartered Institute of Personnel and Development (2004) *Occupational Health and Organisational Effectiveness*, CIPD (**www.cipd.co.uk/subjects/health/occpnhlth/**; accessed on 27.07.04)

Department of the Environment, Transport and the Regions (2000) *Revitalising Health and Safety Strategy Statement*, DETR

Health and Safety Commission (2000) *Revitalising Health and Safety: Strategy Statement*, HSE

Health and Safety Commission (2001) *Strategic Plan 2001–4,* HSE (**www.hse.gov.uk/ aboutus/plans/hscplans/plan0104-07.htm**; accessed 8.07.04)

Health and Safety Commission (2002) *Enforcement Policy Statement,* HSE (**www.hse.gov.uk/pubns/hsc15.pdf**; accessed 30.07.04)

Health and Safety Commission (2003) *Health and Safety Offences and Penalties 2002/2003,* HSE (**www.hse.gov.uk**; accessed 8.07.04)

Health and Safety Commission (2004a) *Accident Costs: Work Out Yours, Revitalising Health and Safety,* HSE (**www.hse.gov.uk/costs/accidentcost_calc/accident_costs_intro.asp**; accessed 27.07.04)

Health and Safety Commission (2004b) *Health and Safety Statistics Highlights 2002/03,* HSE (**www.hse.gov.uk/statistics/overall/hssh0203.pdf**; accessed 27.07.04)

Health and Safety Executive (1995) *Be Safe: Save Money. The Costs of Accidents: A Guide for Small Firms,* HSE Books, 4

Health and Safety Executive (1996) HSE announces new procedures when inspectors issue improvement notices, HSE Press Release: C10:96, 5 February

Health and Safety Executive (2000) *Five Steps to Risk Assessment,* HSE, INDG 163 revised (available at **www.hse.gov.uk**; accessed 04.09.01)

Health and Safety Executive (2002) *Enforcement Management Model,* HSE

Health and Safety Executive (2003) *Stating Your Business. Guidance on Preparing a Health and Safety Policy Document for Small Firms,* HSE, INDG 324 (available at **www.hse.gov.uk**; accessed 20.07.04)

Johnson, R. (2001) Security counsel, *People Management,* Vol. 7, No. 11, 31 May

Morris, D. (2001) How to draw up a health and safety policy, *People Management,* Vol. 7, No. 10, 17 May

Nishiyama, K. and J. Johnson (1997) *Karoshi – Death from Overwork: Occupational Health Consequences of the Japanese Production Management,* 6th Draft for International Journal of Health Services, 4 February (available at **www.workhealth.org/whatsnew/1pkarosh.html**; accessed 20.07.04)

Prescott. J. (2000) *Foreword to Revitalising Health and Safety: Strategy Statement June 2000,* Department of the Environment, Transport and the Regions (**www.hse.gov.uk**; accessed 8.7.04)

Seenan, G. (2004) No frills – and no travelling toilet class, *The Guardian,* 24 July

Stranks, J. (1994) *Management Systems for Safety,* Pitman

Further study

Books

Advisory, Conciliation and Arbitration Service (2000) *Health and Employment,* ACAS.

HSE publications exist on a wide range of topics, too numerous to include here, from general books to detailed explanations of legislation. Some of its leaflets are also available on the web page listed at the end of this chapter.

Stranks, J. (2003) *A Manager's Guide to Health and Safety at Work.* 7th edition, Kogan Page. (Clear guidance for managers and others who are interested in health and safety.)

Articles

Bibby, A. (2001) Mind your manors, *People Management,* Vol. 7, No. 16, 9 August, 30–32. (This article draws attention to the health and safety issues for employees who work from home.)

Chartered Institute of Personnel and Development (2004) *Health and Safety at Work Factsheet,* CIPD (**www.cipd.co.uk**; accessed 1.10.04).

Fowler, A. (1995) How to make the workplace safer, *People Management,* 26 January. (An excellent introduction to the topic of risk assessment.)

Geelmuyden, C. (2002) How to deal with alcohol and drug misuse, *People Management,* Vol. 8, No. 15, 46–47. (A good introduction to ways of dealing with this difficult issue.)

Hammond, D. (2001) Dangerous liaisons, *People Management*, Vol. 7, No. 11, 31 May, 24–29. (This article reviews some of the health and safety implications of sending employees to work in what may turn out to be dangerous countries. Suggestions are made for ways in which employers can protect employees and their families.)

Health and safety – six danger zones (1992) *Personnel Today*, 8 December. (An excellent short summary of the 'six-pack' regulations.)

Morris, D. (2001) How to draw up a health and safety policy, *People Management*, Vol. 7, No. 10, 17 May, 50–51. (A clear explanation of the key points which organisations should consider when designing a health and safety policy.)

Sheppard, G. (1995) Sick notes. Special report on health and safety, *Personnel Today*, 18 July. (Provides an account of the costs of occupational ill-health.)

Stevens, P. and E. FitzGibbons (2001) How to tackle long-term sick leave, *People Management*, Vol. 7, No. 14, 12 July, 42–43. (A short article outlining practical issues relating to discipline and dismissal involving long-term absence due to ill-health.)

Temperton, E. (2000) Time to simplify things, *People Management*, Vol. 6, No. 12, 8 June, 20–21. (This article explores some of the issues raised by the Government's *Guide to the Working Time Regulations*.)

Internet

Control Risks Group   **www.crg.com**

Department of Trade and Industry booklet   **www.dti.gov.uk/bestpractice**
Working Anywhere

Employment Conditions Abroad   **www.eca-international.com**

The Health and Safety Executive   **www.hse.gov.uk**

The International Labour Organization's report on   **www.ilo.org/safework/telework**
teleworking which includes health and safety issues

The Job Stress Network   **www.workhealth.org**
(Site with articles about many work and health issues including stress and *karoshi*.)

RIDDOR   **www.riddor.gov.uk**
(The site gives information about RIDDOR and has forms which can be downloaded to report accidents and dangerous occurrences, or these can now be reported directly on-line.)

Signup web   **www.signupweb.net**
(This site aims to be a one-stop site for everything relating to workplace health.)

CHAPTER **13**

Partnership, employee involvement and high performance working

---

OBJECTIVES

When you have studied this chapter you will be able to:

- explain what is meant by the terms 'unitarism' and 'pluralism'
- describe the concepts of participation, employee involvement, partnership, and high performance working
- describe developments in EU legislation relating to employee rights to information and consultation
- appreciate the importance of communication and consultation in the employment relations arena
- name and describe the techniques that can be used to enhance employee involvement
- describe the concepts of commitment and empowerment, and explain how they are connected to employee involvement and high performance working
- design an action plan for a work organisation to implement a programme of employee involvement.

Chapter 1 established that the HRM approach to managing employees, especially the part of it known as soft HRM, entails developing strategies and using techniques that result in employees giving their best efforts for the success of the organisation and reaching their full potential. This approach to management recognises that the contribution of the human resource is critical to the creation of a competitive advantage. Subsequent chapters have examined specific functions that can be performed in such a way as to acquire such employees (HR planning, recruitment and selection), retain them (payment systems), and develop them (performance management, training), HR practices which ought to result in the desired high performance workplace (EEF/CIPD 2003). The willingness of employees to contribute their best efforts, however, can be affected pervasively by the way they are treated on a day-to-day basis, by their relationships with managers and by the attitude they perceive management in general to have towards them. This is a matter of organisational culture which develops in part from the philosophical stance of senior managers and the owners of enterprises as to the role they expect employees throughout the organisation to play in the life of the organisation.

This chapter examines the basic stances that managers can adopt towards the workforce and the likely reaction of employees. We look in particular at the philosophy of partnership and at the techniques of employee involvement which are believed to enhance the willingness and ability of employees to contribute to the achievement of their organisation's goals, thus creating a high performance workplace.

Pause for thought 13.1

Given that the aim of human resource management is to use the potential of employees, how would you expect this to be achieved in terms of general management attitude towards employees and their place in the decision-making process?

In keeping with basic concepts of motivation theory, you have probably stated that employees are more likely to produce greater effort if they have a sense of responsibility and a feeling of achievement from their work. According to Frederick Herzberg *et al.* (1959) and later work by Richard Hackman and Greg Oldham (1980), one of the ways to achieve this is by job enrichment. One method of enriching jobs is to shift responsibility for making some decisions from supervisors to more junior employees. This is known as a vertical job loading factor, designed to improve motivation. Employee empowerment became a business buzzword in the 1990s, and this too involves devolving the responsibility for decision-making through all levels in the organisation.

The fact that we can talk about the *devolution* of decision making implies that it lay elsewhere before it was devolved. Traditionally owners and managers have regarded the right to make decisions as being theirs, an attitude reflected in the ideas of Frederick Winslow Taylor (1911). In Taylor's concept of Scientific Management, managers were to plan and control the work and give orders, while other employees were meant simply to carry out these orders. Taylor's ideas were underpinned by a view that workmen (at that time Taylor's work was primarily involved with men rather than men and women together in the workplace) were motivated only by money and the possibility of gaining financial incentives for producing more work.

Later theories of motivation, such as those of Herzberg, moved away from this concept of money being the only motivating factor for employees, but in spite of a growing acceptance of the fact that people look for responsibility, achievement and a sense of autonomy at work, the debate over the managerial prerogative to make decisions has continued. The ability or willingness of managers to share their decision-making powers with employees at a lower level in the organisation's hierarchical structure will be very much influenced by those managers' general attitude towards management–workforce relationships. The two major philosophical stances have been described as unitarism and pluralism, and latterly the focus of debate on employee relations has shifted to the concept of partnership. Recent and on-going legislative developments emanating from the EU have also meant that there is a heightened need to address employees' rights to information and consultation about what is happening in their workplace.

The unitary and pluralist perspectives

The type of relationship that will develop between employer (as represented by managers) and employee, and the techniques that are utilised to regulate this relationship, are influenced by the beliefs of the employer. You will see that a unitary stance is likely to result in a workplace culture that is different from what you would expect to find in an organisation headed by pluralists. These concepts were developed in the work of Alan Fox (1974).

The unitary perspective

Unitarists believe that all members of an organisation have the same interests, that they will all accept the organisation's goals and direct all their efforts towards the achievement of these goals. This implies that there is no conflict in such organisations; if conflict were to arise, it would be attributed to some misunderstanding of what the goals are or to deliberate trouble making on the part of some individual. The unitarist stance also implies that the person or persons leading the organisation have decided what the goals are, and there is an expectation that everyone who joins the organisation will internalise those goals. Unitarist organisations, therefore, depend on strong leadership from the top and are likely to purposefully recruit like-minded members. The signature of this philosophy is the belief that there is a common goal and that everyone is directing his or her efforts towards the achievement of this goal.

The pluralist perspective

Pluralists, on the other hand, believe that in any organisation a range of interests are likely to be represented among the members. One example of this is that employees are likely to be interested in increasing the pay they receive for a unit of work, whereas managers and owners will be concerned to increase profits. This is a clear example of differing objectives or a plurality of interests in the workplace. The existence of different interests means that conflicts are likely to arise as the various parties pursue their interests, and pluralists accept that this is natural and needs to be managed. These conflicts should be managed in such a way that they do not disrupt the running of the organisation, or even so that they potentially contribute to its success.

Pause for thought 13.2 Considering what you have just read about the unitary and pluralist approaches to employee relations, which would you consider to be more likely to accept unionisation of the workforce and which more likely to resist it? Give reasons for your choice.

Unitary employers are more likely to resist unionisation; pluralist employers are likely to accept unionisation more readily. Unionisation implies the existence of different sets of interests and the will to set up mechanisms for resolving these differences. Pluralists accept the existence of these differences and the need to work towards their resolution, whereas unitarists expect everyone to have the same goals. According to unitarists there should be no conflict, and therefore no need to have mechanisms for representing differing points of view and resolving conflict. Pluralists recognise from the outset that differing interests in the workplace will have an impact on the achievement of organisational goals, and therefore need to be incorporated into the decision-making process. This is an important point to bear in mind when you read about the methods employers can adopt for involving employees in decisions.

Partnership, participation and employee involvement

As well as the effects that involvement in decision making has on employee motivation, as discussed earlier, there is also a broader philosophical debate about the role of owners, managers and employees as players in the industrial relations scene. Are owners the only participants in industry with the right to make decisions? Are the providers of capital the only ones with a vested interest in the success of an enterprise? The concept of stakeholders suggests that the success of an organisation does not affect only those who have a financial stake in it, but that a range of people have a direct interest in what an organisation does. Everyone who is affected in any way by the actions and decisions of an enterprise is a stakeholder, including:

- employees, who depend on their organisation for their livelihood and for the pleasantness or otherwise of their work life
- customers, who have their own requirements of the organisation and who expect organisations to take their concerns into consideration
- suppliers, who depend for their own livelihood on the success of client organisations
- the community, which depends on organisations to protect the environment.

This raises again the question of managerial prerogative in deciding what should happen in the workplace versus the right or the desire of employees to have their interests represented. Arguments for maximising employees' input include their democratic right to have a say in any decisions that will affect them directly, their vested interest in the success of the organisation, and, on another level, the fact that it makes sense to use the expertise that is available throughout the organisation.

The above discussion touches on major political and ethical questions to which there are no easy answers, and certainly no one answer that everyone will accept. In the discussion of the role that employees should play in an enterprise there is often perceived to be a tension between economic and social imperatives (McGlynn 1995). Improvements in employee consultation, especially if they are legislated and therefore compulsory, are frequently seen as essentially social measures that impose unnecessary costs on businesses. But it is congruent with HRM thinking to see these improvements as measures leading to economic success; that is, you can attain a competitive edge by maximising the contribution of your employees, and the contribution of employees is greater the more they are consulted on, and therefore involved in, what is happening in the organisation. These arguments lead us into a discussion of the concept of partnership and the Labour Government's support for it.

Partnership

Coupar and Stevens (1998) make some interesting comments about the long-established pedigree of partnership, but the partnership concept in modern times emerged more clearly as part of the employee relations agenda in 1997, and the terminology appeared with increasing frequency throughout 1998, although an IPA (Involvement and Participation Association) paper on the benefits of partnership had already appeared earlier, in 1992. A clear link can be seen between a strategic goal of innovation and partnership as a method of engaging the full commitment of employees (Allen 1998), and the Labour Government, first elected in 1997, quickly aligned itself with the idea of partnership (*Fairness at Work 1998*, Chapters 1 and 2), presenting it as one of the 'three pillars' which supported its 'strategy for achieving competitiveness' (s1.3). So obviously, partnership was placed well and truly on the employee relations agenda for the foreseeable future.

As with HRM, partnership is an evolving concept and several commentators in the late 1990s observed that there was as yet no accepted definition of what partnership is and what it encompasses (Beardwell 1998; Marchington 1998). As the Government pointed out in its *Fairness at Work* paper, businesses should be free to adopt a contingency approach and develop whatever programmes suit their particular circumstances and indeed the IRS (2004) assert that companies tend to adopt their own definition of partnership. It may be, then, that the search for an authoritative definition of partnership is not a productive exercise.

We have gathered a number of descriptions of partnership from several publications, and present them here followed by a comment on the similarities that emerge.

Employers and employees working together jointly to solve problems.
(ACAS 1997, p. 13)

Key components might include high degrees of communication, personal development, employment security and an emphasis on ethical people management.
(Beardwell 1998, p. 36)

Individual representation; consultation and communication; values; and understanding and promoting the business.
(Allen 1998, p. 41, describing the partnership deal agreed between Tesco and Usdaw)

- Employment security and new working practices.
- Giving employees a voice in how the company is run.
- Fair financial rewards.
- Investment in training.

(Monks 1998, p. 176)

1 A commitment to working together to make a business more successful.
2 Understanding the employee security conundrum and trying to do something about it.
3 Building relationships at the workplace which maximise employee influence through total communication and a robust and effective employee voice.

(Coupar and Stevens 1998, p. 157)

- Commitment to the success of the enterprise.
- Building trust.
- Recognising legitimate roles and interests.
- Employment security.
- Information and consultation.
- Sharing success.
- Training and development.

Industrial Relations Services (2003a, p. 9 and 2004, p. 15)

Common themes that emerge among these definitions are the importance of security, the common aim of business success and the concept of employee voice.

Of these three components, the one which is probably the most contentious is security, implying, as it seems to, that employees are promised their jobs will be safe no matter what happens. The numbers of redundancies declared in the early years of this century are an indicator of how difficult it has been for many organisations to comply with such a promise (ACAS 2001). On the other hand, as John Monks points out: 'Security in exchange for positive work flexibility is at the heart of the partnership approach' (1998, p. 176). The Government also originally commented on 'job security with redundancy only as a last resort' as being a 'key element of the partnership approach' (**www.dti.gov.uk/partnershipfund/guidance. htm**; accessed 14.06.01). You will note, however, that Monks and Beardwell, as cited above, both refer to *employment* security rather than *job* security, and this distinction is important to the concept of partnership and the modern psychological contract. Employment security implies that employees will be developed in such a way that, should an employer ultimately have to declare redundancies, the employees affected will be highly skilled and therefore their chances of employment elsewhere will be enhanced.

The combination of a 'common aim of business success' and the concept of 'employee voice' is interesting, given our previous discussion of unitarism and pluralism. Working in partnership calls for the recognition of a mutually desirable goal (business success), but seems to imply at the same time that employees may have different opinions from management and that therefore some mechanism is needed to facilitate 'employee voice'. We shall return to this point after the discussion of participation and involvement.

Some further interesting points to note about partnership before investigating ways in which it can be achieved are as follows:

- The Government emphasises the development of a satisfactory work/life balance for employees as being another key feature of effective partnership.
- Partnership can be achieved in both a unionised and non-unionised environment. There is nothing to stop a non-unionised organisation from making arrangements with its employees to consult with elected representatives on a wide range of issues and indeed, as described in more detail later in this chapter, the scope of all employees' statutory rights to information and consultation is increasing. On the other hand, the Government obviously feels that if the majority of employees in an organisation wish to be represented by a union, employers should not be obstructive. The Employment Relations Act 1999 introduced new regulations to facilitate union recognition where an appropriate majority of the workforce desire it.
- In support of partnership development, the Government set up a Partnership at Work Fund which was to run until 2004. Initially, £5 million

was made available, and this was boosted in 2001 by a share of an additional £20 million which was allocated to DTI schemes including Partnership at Work projects. Organisations were able to apply for up to £50,000 to contribute towards the costs of a project related to developing or improving partnership in the workplace. Organisations that benefited from the 2003 round of awards include Norfolk County Council (together with the unions UNISON and the GMB), Avon Cosmetics Ltd, and easyJet. (See the DTI web site for more information.)

- The Government also intends, in its periodic review of ACAS, to examine ways in which the service can expand the good work it already does in this area of endeavour.

There is a definitive link between partnership and employee participation which can be the channel for employee voice, and between partnership and employee involvement initiatives in that these can represent the way to achieve partnership. Coupar and Stevens (1998, p. 157) state that 'the IPA sees partnership as a unique combination of employee involvement processes which has the potential to maximise the benefits to the company and to employees in the process of change'. They also comment (1998, p. 151) on the previously mentioned phenomenon, that 'companies typically use a very wide range of differing activities to develop the mix needed to gain staff commitment and achieve success in the marketplace'. The CIPD (IPD 1997, p. 8) also sees employer and trade union commitment to partnership as 'supported by mechanisms for communication and involvement'. We shall now review the concept of worker participation, developments with regard to regulatory information and consultation rights, and a variety of employee involvement practices that have been identified in various companies.

Participation and involvement

The word 'participation' is often used as an umbrella term for all forms of worker participation and employee involvement, and sometimes participation and involvement are used interchangeably. The mechanisms for encouraging employees to participate in decisions do, however, differ in their intent and effect, so we shall distinguish between participation and involvement.

Farnham and Pimlott (1995) define the terms 'worker participation' and 'employee involvement' as different aspects of the relationship between authority and decision making in organisations. They describe these concepts as follows:

> Worker participation 'aims at changing the basic authority structures of enterprises . . . by legislating for employee representation on company boards'. 'The law gives rights to employees or places restrictions on managerial power and authority.'
>
> Employee involvement aims 'to get the support and commitment of all employees in an organisation to managerial objectives and goals, thereby reinforcing a sense of common purpose between management and employees'. 'Employers and management are prepared to share decisions with or devolve them to employees or their representatives.'
>
> (Farnham and Pimlott 1995, p. 83)

A further definition of involvement, which will help to give some clarity, comes from the IPM/IPA code (1990, p. 11) which states that it is:

> a range of processes designed to engage the support, understanding, optimum contribution of all employees in an organization and their commitment to its objectives.

Pause for thought 13.3

How would you distinguish between the concepts of participation and involvement?

The definition of worker participation refers specifically to a relationship regulated by legal statute, and there is an element of protecting employees' interests, potentially in the face of resistance from management. The concept of involvement, in contrast, is defined as a management desire to inculcate organisational values in employees. The major differences, then, relate to a tension between a reliance on regulation (participation) versus a flexible and voluntary approach (involvement), and between management's initiating action (involvement) or being constrained in their decision making by having to take others' views into consideration (participation).

You should now be able to connect these definitions of participation and involvement with the previous discussion of the unitary and pluralist approaches to employee relations. Since the attitudes and philosophy of owners determine their relationships with their employees and the framework they will choose to adopt, it can be stated that each type of employer is more likely to favour either participation or involvement.

Pause for thought 13.4

Consider the definitions of employee involvement and employee participation. Which one is a unitary employer likely to adopt? Which one is a pluralist employer likely to adopt?

The wording of the definitions of involvement may have given you a clue. Since this entails everyone accepting the common aim of the organisation, albeit then being involved in deciding how to achieve this aim, employee involvement corresponds to the unitary viewpoint. Employee participation recognises that groups within an organisation will have different points of view, and allows for input on those differences to decisions before the major decisions are made at board level. In accepting the validity of the existence of differing interests, employee participation is pluralist in nature.

The concept of partnership, however, allows for the development of both participation and involvement. This is exemplified by the Government's urging businesses to voluntarily develop a range of techniques to empower employees and by the signing of the Social Chapter, which includes the adoption of the Directive on European Works Councils (EWC). The EWCs entail setting up legislated participative mechanisms, as will be described more fully in the next section. The Government has historically resisted legislation on national works councils, preferring employees, probably, though not exclusively, through union representation, to develop mutually agreed partnership with their employers, i.e.

on a voluntary, not a legislated basis, but that too is most likely to change, as will also be addressed in more detail in the next section. We have noted that partnership means that there is a common goal for employers and employees alike to recognise and pursue, but the notion of employee voice suggests that employees may at times differ with employers and may wish to be represented by a trade union or in some other structured fashion. With partnership, then, there is the possibility of a blend of some aspects of unitarism with some aspects of pluralism: we can have the pursuit of the unitarist common goal within a pluralist framework.

EU rights to information and consultation

European Works Councils

Participative structures have been a subject of debate for many years among the member states of the European Union, and a number of proposed directives have failed to be adopted. These include the Vredeling Directive and the Fifth Company Law Directive, which each contained broad proposals on consultation and information. On 22 September 1994 a Directive of more limited scope was adopted, and this is the European Council Directive on the establishment of a European Works Council or other procedure in Community-scale undertakings or Community-scale groups of undertakings for the purposes of informing and consulting employees. The main background details of the Directive and features of the works councils are described in the following paragraphs, and a fuller outline of events that preceded the adoption of the Directive and of the development of European thought on employee consultation and information can be found in Gold and Hall (1994) and Mill (1991).

The key issues in the Directive are that employees should be properly informed and consulted about major issues that will have an impact on them. The Directive refers to transnational undertakings where decisions could be made in one country that would affect employees in another country. In such circumstances, it seemed essential to most member states in the European Union that proper mechanisms should be in place in order to ensure that employees in the different countries of a transnational operation receive equal treatment with regard to information and consultation. This is the objective of the European Works Council Directive.

When the Maastricht Treaty on European Union was ratified in 1993, the UK Government opted out of the agreements on social policy, but the Protocol on Social Policy and Agreement on Social Policy, which are annexed to the treaty, allowed the other member states to adopt social policy measures without having to consult or gain agreement from the UK. This was the background against which the Directive on European Works Councils was developed.

Approximately 100 UK-owned undertakings were affected by the Directive because they have establishments in other member states that meet the threshold requirements. They were obliged to adhere to the Directive for employees located in other member states, but this obligation did not extend to employees located in the UK. That is, they did not have to establish works councils in relevant UK establishments, but they could do so if they chose to.

Two UK-owned multinationals that quickly decided to establish works councils in their undertakings in the UK were BP Europe and United Biscuits (see *Industrial Relations Review and Report*, December 1994, for more details).

The date set for the implementation of the Directive was 22 September 1996. If companies established a transnational agreement on information and consultation covering the whole workforce before this date, the Directive would not apply; i.e. companies that made an agreement by then would not be constrained by the terms of the Directive. This is, in fact, what companies such as BP Europe and United Biscuits opted to do.

By the end of 1997, this scenario had changed, when the Labour Government ended the UK's opt-out from the Social Chapter by signing the Treaty of Amsterdam. This meant that the Directive on European Works Councils now applied fully to relevant companies in the UK. The Directive was implemented in the UK as the Transnational Information and Consultation of Employees Regulations 1999.

The essential characteristics of the Directive/regulations and the prescribed process for developing and implementing a European Works Council (EWC) are listed below.

Characteristics

- The threshold at which employers come under the terms of the regulations is that they have at least 1,000 employees within the member states and at least 150 employees in each of any two member states.
- The terms of the regulations come into effect either when management initiates action or when a written request is made by at least 100 employees or their representatives in at least two undertakings in at least two member states.

Process

- Management and labour meet each other in order to establish a procedure for consultation about the issue of an EWC.
- There are four possible outcomes of this consultation process:
  - the parties establish an EWC
  - if they decide against an EWC, they may establish an alternative procedure for information and consultation on transnational issues
  - the parties agree not to have a specific procedure relating to transnational issues
  - the parties fail to reach agreement.
- The regulations establish a framework for handling confidential information.
- If the parties fail to reach agreement, there are minimum standards that will be applied: an EWC will be established and will meet management once a year, or more often if necessary, to be informed and consulted on any matters that will significantly affect the employees. Matters that the EWC will consider include the structure of the undertaking, its financial situation and the future development of the business. These issues set down in the minimum standards are a good indicator of the kinds of issues the ministers from the member states felt employees should be consulted on.

Information and Consultation of Employees: Company Councils and Committees

The EU Directive on Information and Consultation of Employees was finally adopted and came into force on 23 March 2002 after many years of discussion about its content and wording. The Department of Trade and Industry engaged in extensive consultation to establish the context of communication and consultation that already exists in the UK in order to provide a suitable framework for the national regulations. These will come into force on 6 April 2005 as the Information and Consultation of Employees (ICE) Regulations.

There is to be a phased introduction of the regulations, which will take effect as follows:

- 2005 – establishments with 150 or more employees
- 2007 – establishments with 100 or more employees
- 2008 – establishments with 50 or more employees.

The establishment of these regulations introduces employee rights to consultation on matters likely to affect the economic status of their employer, and any proposed changes that might affect their employment status. Consultation should include the provision of timely and accurate information to employees from management, opportunities for employees to put forward their views, a managerial response to these views together with reasons for their response, and an attempt to reach agreement on decisions. A request from 10% of the workforce will trigger the obligation for management to set some formal mechanism for the provision of information and consultation. The mechanisms have been variously referred to as national works councils (IRS 2001; IDS 2002a), works councils, consultation committees, company councils (IDS 2002b), forums, and staff councils (IDS 2004c).

In spite of the imminence of this legislation (at the time of writing), and the fact that organisations can to some extent forestall being bound by the structures contained in the regulations by setting up acceptable voluntary arrangements before they come into force or before they receive a formal request for a consultation committee, there is reportedly a lack of volition on the part of many organisations to move forward in this area (IDS 2004a; Pickard 2004), but there are also a number of examples of organisations cited where strides towards good systems of information and consultation have already been made (IDS 2004a; Pickard 2004).

Employee involvement and high performance working

A number of commentators on the economy note that productivity in the UK continues to lag behind that of the United States (EEF/CIPD 2003) and of some other European Union countries, notably Germany and France (DTI 2002). Such commentators, and employers in general, are keenly aware of the need to find a way of improving the productivity of UK workers. Much of the debate on this issue centres around the so-called 'high performance workplace', and the proposed methods of achieving high performance working are variously referred to as 'new working practices' (IRS 2003b), 'bundles of HRM practices' and 'employee involvement' (EEF/CIPD 2003). Some writers use a combination of these to refer to the same set of practices. In keeping with the DTI's (2002) continuing use of the term, we have opted to refer to these practices in the main as 'employee involvement', but we shall use the other terms when appropriate in referring to the work of others.

The purpose of employee involvement

As intimated above, the reason for pursuing a programme of employee involvement is the expectation that improvements in productivity levels will follow. By informing and consulting with employees and using other techniques to make them feel more involved in the workplace, workers will be enabled and feel empowered to add more value to their organisations. An important concept in terms of the expected motivational outcomes of employee involvement is employee commitment. The direct effect of involvement in the organisation is expected to be an increase in the individual employee's commitment to the workplace or the job, which will be reflected in increased productivity, lower labour turnover and reduced absenteeism. This constitutes the economic argument for encouraging employee involvement initiatives, and the ACAS Annual Report (1997) mentions research by Dr Mari Sako which offers some evidence that improvements in business performance are in fact an outcome of employee involvement. The Industrial Relations Services (1999) also report from their survey of 49 organisations that 50% of the sample noted an improvement in employee performance which they attributed to employee involvement measures.

The human resource management approach is intent on maximising the contribution of employees as a critical success factor, and increasing employee commitment through involvement is seen as a way to do this. There may, however, be some problems with the contention that involvement arrangements result in increased commitment. Commitment is an attitude, and the connection between attitudes and behaviour is not a straightforward one. Behaviour depends on a variety of influencing factors, including values and beliefs and what each individual sees as motivating factors, so attitudes are not always reflected in behaviour. For instance, if a person has a positive emotional reaction to a management innovation, we could say that that person may feel greater commitment to the job or the organisation. If, however, that person is influenced by co-workers who are not like minded, and the person values his or her relationship with those co-workers, then the positive attitude may not be reflected in subsequent behaviour. In fact, the person may attempt to rationalise the positive feelings away. Employee involvement could therefore engender a positive attitude in some people and not in others, and even where it does result in positive attitudes, it is only one feature of the workplace and other influences could result in this positive attitude not being reflected in the behaviour managers are hoping for. You will find a fuller explanation of these concepts in Cascio (1998).

This discussion of attitudes and behaviour is included just to sound a cautionary note that increases in commitment and productivity are not a foregone conclusion. In general, however, the introduction of employee involvement initiatives is welcomed by the workforce and results in a positive response. Some reactions will depend on the culture and relations that have traditionally existed either in organisation or in a particular industry. If employees do not trust management, they will greet management initiatives with scepticism. If employers wish to encourage change in these circumstances, they will have to build trust, which can only be achieved in the long term. Organisations should choose arrangements that best suit their individual situation (DTI 2002), which is one of the reasons for the Government's preference not to impose schemes, but rather to depend on encouraging employers to develop programmes voluntarily.

Employee involvement techniques

Our focus in the rest of this chapter is on a detailed overview of employee involvement techniques.

Pause for thought 13.5

Make a list of at least three techniques that could be used to promote the involvement of employees in decisions relating directly to their work or in general to make employees feel more that they are an equal partner in the workplace. As you read through the next section you can check your list against the mechanisms that are discussed here.

In 1994, the Department of Employment (DoE), as it was then called, used six categories, each with a range of initiatives, to describe employee involvement. These are summarised in Table 13.1, updated to include more recent developments, and discussed in more detail below. The practices listed by the DoE remain representative of the bundles of HRM practices described by later commentators such as the EEF and the CIPD (2003), Incomes Data Services (2002c, 2004a and 2004b) and the DTI (2002). The Department of Employment's categorisation is not an all-inclusive definition, i.e. you do not have to be involved in all the listed activities at the same time to say you are practising employee involvement. The DTI (2002) also lays great emphasis on the fact that different combinations of practices will be suitable for different businesses.

It must be stressed again that various combinations of these measures are taken up by organisations at different times (IRS 2003b). Research conducted by Marchington *et al.* (1993) revealed that individual managers tended to adopt their preferred measures, which might well be dropped when they moved on. This is an unfortunate aspect of the voluntary and flexible nature of involvement arrangements. As you will see in the discussion of the initiatives, a longer-term commitment on the part of managers is needed if the techniques are to work to best effect. Formal partnership deals agreed between managers and employees may introduce an element of continuity into this scenario.

Sharing information

- team briefing
- employer and employee publications
- company videos
- electronic news systems
- roadshows.

| Table 13.1 | **Employee involvement categories and areas for action** |

Category	Areas for action
Sharing information	Team briefing
	Employer and employee publications
	Company videos
	Electronic news systems
	Roadshows
Consultation	Staff suggestion schemes
	Staff opinion surveys
	Works committees
	Health and safety committees
Financial participation	Profit-related pay
	Employee share schemes
	Share incentive plans
Commitment to quality	Continuous improvement
	Teamwork
	Total quality management
	Quality circles
	Self-managed project groups
	Employee award schemes
Developing the individual	Performance management
	Staff appraisal schemes
	Employee development programmes
	Investors in People
	A qualified workforce
Beyond the workplace	The community
	The environment

Keeping people informed is often described as one of the cornerstones of employee involvement, and in fact provides the foundation on which many of the individual techniques can be built. Without information it is impossible for people to develop and contribute their own ideas. The will to share information is an essential component of involvement, and the list above gives an indication of some of the vehicles that can be used to get information to employees: face to face in small, regular meetings (team briefing), materials that could use the written word, graphics or electronic systems such as a company's intranet (company and staff newsletters, notices, posters), and video film. The IDS (2003) give Safeway as an example where senior managers often go on the road to ensure that information about major changes is disseminated effectively. Careful consideration should be given to choosing the form of communication most appropriate to the type of message.

In their survey of employee involvement in 49 organisations, the Industrial Relations Services (1999) found briefing sessions and company journals to be the techniques used by the largest number of employers, with 92% of the organisations indicating that they use them. With increasing legal pressures to inform and consult employees, we can expect to see even more attention being paid to this area of employment relations.

Consultation

- staff suggestion schemes
- staff opinion surveys
- works committees
- health and safety committees.

Along with sharing information, consultation is a key concept in developing good employee relations, and much of the on-going debate about the development of mechanisms to improve the employer–employee relationship centres on the employee's right to information and consultation. Of the information-sharing techniques we have discussed in the preceding section, briefing sessions allow for some immediate feedback from employees, but most of the other vehicles encourage only one-way communication. Remember that effective communication requires feedback. The consultation mechanisms named in this section essentially provide a route for employees to feed ideas back to their employers. These vehicles only represent true consultation, however, if there is an honest willingness to consider the ideas proffered and to incorporate reasonable suggestions into the decision-making process. As the regulations on information and consultation bed in, the use of those of the consultation mechanisms described here which are voluntary will be further supported by regulatory measures.

Most staff suggestion schemes are linked with a reward for successful suggestions, especially those where a cost saving for the organisation or other improvements in productivity can be identified. The reward does not, however, have to be financial for people to feel encouraged to contribute their ideas. Often people wish merely to see their expertise recognised, gaining a sense of achievement from this, and they need only to be encouraged by the introduction of a recognised scheme. The reward for successful suggestions could be linked to information vehicles from the first category, i.e. a mention in the company or staff newsletter.

Staff opinion surveys will be dealt with later in this chapter when we look at ways of developing and monitoring the success of employee involvement initiatives. You will find information about health and safety committees in Chapter 12.

Works committees to promote information and consultation involve meetings of management and employee representatives who may be elected directly or nominated through the trade unions. Their terms of reference can be tailored to the requirements of individual organisations, and may vary widely from one organisation to another. In its work with companies, ACAS very often establishes joint working committees to solve a variety of problems. These works committees are not to be confused with the works councils in countries such as Germany, which are established within the legislative framework in place for participative structures, and as councils become established under the relevant regulations in the UK, they will no doubt reflect the employee relations environment that is prevalent here. Employers who have already established information-sharing and consultation committees in their organisation may apply to the Central Arbitration Committee to have them recognised as valid arrangements under the ICE regulations. One caveat, however, is that such arrangements must apply to all employees (Pickard 2004).

Financial participation

- profit-related pay
- employee share schemes
- share incentive plans.

A number of schemes, often with tax relief approved by the Inland Revenue, exist to provide employees with financial participation in their organisations. These include group or individual bonuses (which *are* subject to income tax) linked to the company's profit performance, and ownership of shares.

Again, various schemes exist in relation to share ownership. In some schemes, known as all-employee share ownership plans or AESOPs, shares may be bought by a trust for employees, usually at no direct cost to them, and are later distributed to them; other schemes give employees the opportunity to buy shares directly. A variety of arrangements exist regarding the percentage of shares that employees can hold, what happens to the shares when an employee leaves the company, and, very importantly, whether the shares are voting or non-voting shares. If ownership of the shares gives employees a voice at shareholders' meetings, this is essentially a form of employee participation as it has been defined in this chapter. The Incomes Data Services study on all-employee share schemes (2001) contains excellent information on the types of plan brought in by the Finance Act 2000. The IDS (2004b, p. 1) also reports that the number of companies operating Share Incentive Plans 'had risen to 435 by April 2003'.

Commitment to quality

- continuous improvement
- teamwork
- total quality management
- quality circles
- self-managed project groups
- employee award schemes.

The human resource management approach and modern ideas about employee motivation go hand-in-hand with an emphasis on the social aspects of work. Human beings on the whole work better in groups, they respond to the stimulation of feedback on their achievements, and there are synergies in terms of improved ideas and methods of working to be gained from having people work in teams rather than as isolated individuals. All these factors are reflected in the techniques listed above.

The idea that benefits can be gained from the formation of teams and self-managed groups is addressed in the work done by Trist and Murray at the Tavistock Institute (1993). You may have encountered their concept of sociotechnical systems in your course on organisational behaviour. Basically this theory says that organisations must pay attention to the social systems in the workplace as well as the technical systems when designing jobs.

Total quality management emphasises the responsibility of each individual for ensuring the quality of his or her work and de-emphasises the role of supervision or inspection. This puts responsibility firmly with each individual employee. If this is combined with employee award schemes, it heightens an individual's awareness of the contribution he or she can make to the organisation and of the extent to which this is valued. The term 'quality circles' is linked with an approach adopted by Japanese companies, but the method stems from the work and thinking of an American, Dr W. Edward Deming. Essentially, quality circles involve having a group of people, usually from one work area, meet away from the shop floor to discuss improvements that could be made in the work systems. The group analyses data and sets up proposals which are presented to senior managers who consider the new ideas and report back to the quality circle, either accepting the proposal or explaining why it is rejected. Since this requires a greater level of analytical skill than the employees may need for their jobs, quality circles often have a facilitator who provides assistance in the presentational aspects but does not contribute ideas as far as content is concerned.

Continuous improvement is an umbrella term for any programme that focuses on identifying and solving problems or exploring opportunities to improve the organisation's performance. These programmes often focus on an improved response to customer requirements or a reduced rate of errors which can be targeted by a combination of initiatives such as teamwork, quality management and problem-solving groups.

Marchington *et al.* (1993) found total quality management/customer care programmes to be among the most frequently identified employee involvement arrangements: these practices were present in 19 of the 25 companies they surveyed.

Developing the individual

- performance management
- staff appraisal schemes
- employee development programmes
- Investors in People
- a qualified workforce.

All the employee involvement techniques that we have discussed contribute to the development of employees: better communication means that people are well informed; encouragement to share ideas through consultation equates with encouragement to develop ideas rather than accept the status quo; financial participation increases awareness and knowledge of the economic performance of the organisation. Employee development extends the boundaries of knowledge, interest and understanding and enables each employee to feel more involved and more able to participate in decisions. Chapters 8 and 9 explore in detail all the practices listed above related to developing people and the contribution that these practices make to the organisation.

Beyond the workplace

- the community
- the environment.

Did you know?

The management consulting firm, KPMG, runs a volunteering programme where some of its consultants provide free services to the crime reduction charity Nacro.

(*Guardian Society*, 4 July 2001, p. 12)

The Department of Employment (1994) proposed that attempts to make employees feel more committed should not be limited to activities at work. We have stated in other contexts, for instance with regard to human resource planning, that employers need to be aware of the community within which they operate, and this can mean the global community as well as the local community. A number of employers have empowered their staff to become involved in community initiatives such as working with schools or with disabled persons. This has the effect of increasing the loyalty of employees and strengthening the organisation's public image.

A similar argument is extended to environmental issues. If employers show concern for the environment and enlist employees in methods of protecting the environment, this is likely to gain loyalty and make employees proud to be associated with the organisation.

Implications of employee involvement for management

It is obvious from what we have said above that the introduction of employee involvement has implications for organisational culture and the managerial role. In its booklet *Effective Organisations: The People Factor*, ACAS (2003) recommends an approach it calls 'quality of work life' (QWL), which is very similar to employee involvement. It describes the essential message of the booklet to be that:

> improved levels of organisational effectiveness and hence competitive edge can be achieved by further developing the contribution of people in organisations. This requires the development of more rewarding, satisfying, effective jobs and work environments both rooted in the active encouragement of involvement at all organisational levels.

The booklet goes on to contrast QWL values, culture and job design with control values, culture and job design. Essentially the QWL approach equates with a programme of the initiatives we have described as employee involvement, whereas control implies that managers adopt a theory X approach (which you will remember from Chapter 10), retain decision-making powers, and use Taylor's approach to job design. We should emphasise, however, that the ACAS view of QWL would entail a *programme* of involvement initiatives and not the pick-and-mix approach that Marchington *et al.* (1993) felt they sometimes encountered. The development of QWL requires commitment and a long-term perspective, a factor that is also emphasised in the EEF/CIPD (2003) report, and ACAS is prepared to assist employers in developing these systems as part of its mandate to improve industrial relations.

The empowerment of employees also calls for new skills on the part of both managers and employees. Managers who have been used to a control style may need training in the techniques of participative management, and employees may need confidence-building sessions and training in decision making. A move away from a control culture and close supervision can also have an impact on organisational structures, and the traditional tall hierarchies with many reporting levels give way to the more modern, flatter structures towards which many organisations have moved.

ACTIVITY 13.1

You are the Head of Personnel at the headquarters of a national chain of supermarkets. The stores have always operated with a very hierarchical structure and a set of rigid rules. Major decisions about the business are made centrally by a board of senior executives, and only information that is deemed necessary is passed down the line to the next level of staff. The normal chain of command consists of a regional manager, a store manager, department managers and unit supervisors. Personnel at each level deal only with the level above them. Shop assistants expect explicit instructions from their supervisors, and will refer all matters to a supervisor if a question arises on which they have not been briefed. The extent of each person's authority is strictly defined, e.g. shop assistants cannot deal with returned items; unit supervisors are responsible for deciding when displays will change, what to display, and for maintaining the general tidiness of their area. All employees know their role and their limits, and managers and supervisors do not ask for opinions from their subordinates. This is accepted by all staff members, and everyone who has been with the company for any length of time is used to the way things are done.

A new chief executive has recently joined the company, and she is not pleased with the current way of running things. She asks you to investigate ways of changing the culture to improve the contribution from every employee, and to prepare a confidential report for her.

1 Draw up a list of the changes that could be made and how these changes would be implemented.

2 List the benefits to be gained if you try to implement your suggested changes, and the problems that may be encountered.

Developing, implementing and evaluating an employee involvement programme

The IPM/IPA code (1990) provides an action plan for implementing involvement practices, and ACAS (2003) provides a very useful generic model for implementing change which can be adapted and applied directly to involvement arrangements. An extended model adapted from the ACAS booklet is shown below.

Stage 1

Arrange initial meetings between management and employee representatives (elected by the workforce or designated by recognised trade unions) to explore ways of improving the current situation through employee involvement initiatives.

Stage 2

Reach agreement on the approach to be used, using a third-party facilitator such as ACAS if necessary. Ensure that issues of communication to the workforce are included in the details agreed at this stage.

Stage 3

Set up a joint steering committee to develop a plan covering the selection, development, introduction and coordination of the employee involvement practices.

Stage 4

Through the steering committee, extend the planning stage to involve individuals and work groups to analyse problems and deal with particular issues.

Stage 5

Develop alternative solutions and approaches; evaluate feasibility; select the optimum solution.

Stage 6

Implement the practices, and provide any necessary preparation and training.

Stage 7

Evaluate the success of the new arrangements, and review the arrangements.

In stages 3–5 of the model there will inevitably be much emphasis on choosing which initiatives to pursue. There is no set model of employee involvement, so various combinations of techniques will be found in different organisations. Stage 5 of the model will probably be concerned with problems of the acceptability of various bundles of practices and employee attitudes towards them, particularly if the past culture means that there is a fair amount of scepticism on the part of the workforce towards new measures.

Pause for thought 13.6   What factors will affect the choice of employee involvement initiatives in any particular organisation?

Some of the factors that ought to be included when choosing the appropriate practices are:

- the preferences of the owners and managers
- the preferences of employees ascertained through consultation
- the past and desired culture of the organisation
- the suitability of certain measures to the type of organisation – non-profit organisations, for instance, would have to devise alternatives to share ownership schemes.

Whatever choices are made, there should be wholehearted acceptance and commitment on the part of all involved, but particularly on the part of management, to making the new practices work. ACAS (2003) stresses that there has to be a long-term commitment; change will not happen overnight and a period of consultation, training and adjustment will be necessary.

Stage 2 mentions the possibility of involving a third party to help develop plans and solve problems. ACAS has a continuing mandate to work towards the improvement of industrial relations, and its officers have broad experience in helping organisations to promote employee involvement initiatives.

As you have seen, communication is both an employee involvement practice and a crucial component of the development, implementation and review stages. If you remember the communication model we discussed in Chapter 11 (pp. 345–348), you will recall the important role that feedback plays in effective communication. One way of getting feedback is to use employee opinion surveys. This is especially appropriate to evaluate the effectiveness of employee involvement practices, since what employers are looking for are more productive attitudes, and surveys of this nature have themselves been identified as an involvement practice. They are appropriate both for identifying which kinds of initiatives employees would like to have and for monitoring the success of those initiatives once implemented. The survey should ask for employee opinions about what is most important and what should be done first, i.e. it should result in a prioritised list of what concerns employees.

ACTIVITY 13.2

Examine the change model for developing, implementing and evaluating employee involvement initiatives. Review the communication model described in Chapter 11. Consider the issues addressed in the communication model as you review each step in the change model, and comment on what the communication model should alert you to when considered alongside the steps to be taken in the change model.

A further factor to be considered in implementing change of any kind is the training needed if managers and employees are to develop new roles and relationships. A range of additional skills might be required for some involvement practices, e.g. facilitators of, and participants in, quality circles need skills in the analysis and presentation of data, as already mentioned; team leaders need skills in eliciting input from people who are not used to sharing their views and who may therefore initially be hesitant to do so.

Conclusion

We have discussed a range of management approaches to the workforce, and the implications that different philosophies have for the ways in which, and the extent to which, employees might be encouraged to participate in the decisions made in the workplace. The development of employee involvement initiatives and partnership deals is likely to be found in organisations that espouse the tenets of human resource management. Through the use of involvement and partnership practices, these organisations will attempt to maximise their employees' contribution to the achievement of organisational goals and their ability to add value through high performance working while also directly benefiting the employees themselves.

REVIEW QUESTIONS

Brief answers to these review questions are provided on pages 494–495.

1 Describe the two main philosophical approaches underlying management–employee relations, and comment on the likelihood of each of these espousing worker participation or employee involvement initiatives.

2 Explain the connection between employee involvement and employee commitment and high performance working.

3 Describe the history of initiatives to improve employee consultation and information in the European Union.

4 Name the major components of partnership, and comment on its aims.

SELF-CHECK QUESTIONS

Answer the following multiple-choice and short-answer questions. The answers are provided on page 495 for you to check your understanding of this chapter.

1 Which of the following statements best describes the unitary perspective?
   (a) Managers expect all employees to espouse the organisation's goals. There are occasional conflicts of interest which managers settle by negotiation.
   (b) Managers espouse the organisation's goals and recognise that employees are likely to have their own set of interests. Differences in interests are regulated by negotiated agreements.
   (c) Managers expect all employees to espouse the organisation's goals. There are no conflicts of interest.

2 Participation and involvement are both ways of involving employees in the decisions made in the workplace. Match each term with the correct statement below.
   (a) _____ means that employees have input into decisions that affect their own jobs.
   (b) _____ means that employees have input through representatives to decisions made at a strategic level.

3 Participation is the method that you are most likely to find in unitarist organisations. TRUE or FALSE?

4 What is the threshold number of employees at which the Transnational Information and Consultation of Employees Regulations 1999 obliges a community-scale company to establish a European Works Council?

5 Which of the following statements are NOT true?
   (a) The Labour Government actively promotes partnership deals in the workplace.
   (b) Partnership deals can only be made when the workforce is not unionised.
   (c) Partnership deals can be made in both unionised and non-unionised companies.
   (d) Partnership deals can only be made in a unionised environment.

6 Which of the following was not named specifically by the Department of Employment as a technique for promoting employee involvement?
   (a) quality circles
   (b) peer appraisal
   (c) team briefing
   (d) profit-related pay.

7 Managers can confidently expect that employee commitment to work will be a direct result of employee involvement initiatives and will lead to improved motivation and productivity. TRUE or FALSE?

8 What does the acronym AESOP stand for?

9 Which techniques are listed in your text book as being part of sharing information?

10 Which of the following has NOT specifically been identified as a standard component of partnership agreements.
   (a) improvements in employment security
   (b) fair wages for employees
   (c) consultation on matters affecting employees
   (d) provision of flexible benefits.

WHAT NEXT?

The major message in this chapter has been about the important role that communication and consultation and other HRM practices play in the development of good employment relations. But do these practices necessarily result in the high performance workplace that employers desire (see Godard 2004)? And are HR practitioners equipped to bring about the changes required to implement the practices (see Caldwell 2004)? What are the reasons for the apparently slow uptake of these practices in the UK (see Caldwell 2004 and Guy 2003)? The articles listed below examine these questions in depth.

Caldwell, R. (2004) Rhetoric, facts and self-fulfilling prophecies: exploring practitioners' perceptions of progress in implementing HRM, *Industrial Relations Journal*, Vol. 35, No. 3, 196–215

Godard, J. (2004) A critical assessment of the high-performance paradigm, *British Journal of Industrial Relations*, Vol. 42, No. 2, June, 349–378

Guy, F. (2003) High-involvement work practices and employee bargaining power, *Employee Relations*, Vol. 25, No. 5, 453–469

References

Advisory, Conciliation and Arbitration Service (1997 and 2001) *Annual Report*, ACAS

Advisory, Conciliation and Arbitration Service (2003) *Effective Organisations: The People Factor*, ACAS

Allen, M. (1998) All-inclusive, *People Management*, 11 June, 36–42

Beardwell, I. (1998) Voices on, *People Management*, 28 May, 32–36

Cascio, W. F. (1998) *Applied Psychology in Personnel Management*, 5th edition, Prentice Hall

Coupar, W. and B. Stevens (1998) Towards a new model of industrial partnership: Beyond the 'HRM versus industrial relations' argument, in Sparrow, P. and M. Marchington (eds) *Human Resource Management: The New Agenda*, Financial Times Pitman

Department of Employment (1994) *The Competitive Edge: Employee Involvement in Britain*, Department of Employment

Department of Trade and Industry (2002) *High Performance Workplaces: The Role of Employee Involvement in a Modern Economy*, DTI (discussion paper available, at **www.dti.gov.uk**; accessed 03.10.03)

EEF/CIPD (2003) *Maximising Employee Potential and Business Performance: the Role of High Performance Working*, EEF/CIPD

Fairness at Work, Government White Paper, May 1998 (paper available at **http://www.dti.gov.uk/er/fairness**; accessed 16.02.05)

Farnham, D. and J. Pimlott (1995) *Understanding Industrial Relations*, 5th edition, Cassell

Fox, A. (1974) *Beyond Contract: Work Power and Trust Relations*, Faber and Faber

Gold, M. and M. Hall (1994) Statutory European Works Councils: The final countdown? *Industrial Relations Journal*, Vol. 5, No. 3, September, 177–186

Hackman, J. R. and G. R. Oldham (1980) *Work Redesign*, Addison Wesley

Herzberg, F., B. Mausner, and B. Snyderman (1959) *The Motivation to Work*, Wiley

Incomes Data Services (2001) *IDS Study 712: All-Employee Share Schemes*, IDS

Incomes Data Services (2002a) *IDS Studies 722: European Works Councils*, IDS

Incomes Data Services (2002b) *IDS Studies 730: Company Councils*, IDS

Incomes Data Services (2002c) *IDS Studies 752: Suggestion Schemes*, IDS

Incomes Data Services (2003) *IDS Studies 741: Internal Communications*, IDS

Incomes Data Services (2004a) *IDS HR Studies Plus 777: Employee Attitude Surveys + Guide to Suppliers*, IDS

Incomes Data Services (2004b) *IDS HR Studies 781: Share Incentive Plans*, IDS

Incomes Data Services (2004c) Information and consultation: nine months to go, *IDS HR Studies Update 776*, June, 1–9

Industrial Relations Services (1999) Trends in employee involvement, *IRS Employment Trends 683*, July, 6–16

Industrial Relations Services (2001) Common position reached on national works councils text, *European Industrial Relations Review 330*, July, 13–15.

Industrial Relations Services (2003a) An open relationship, *IRS Employment Review 779*, 4 July, 8–21

Industrial Relations Services (2003b) Raising productivity: policy and practice, *IRS Employment Review 776*, 23 May, 10–15

Industrial Relations Services (2004) We're all in this together – partnership at work, *IRS Employment Review 801*, 4 June, 15–17

Institute of Personnel and Development (1997) *Employee Relations into the 21st Century: An IPD Position Paper*, IPD

Institute of Personnel Management (IPM) and Involvement and Participation Association (IPA) (1990) *Employee Involvement and Participation in the United Kingdom: The IPA/IPM Code*, IPM and IPA

Marchington, M. (1998) Partnership in context: towards a European model?, in Sparrow, P. and M. Marchington (eds) *Human Resource Management: The New Agenda*, Financial Times Pitman

Marchington, M., A. Wilkinson and P. Ackers (1993) Waving or drowning in participation? *Personnel Management*, March, 46–50

McGlynn, C. (1995) European Works Councils: towards industrial democracy?, *Industrial Law Journal*, Vol. 24, No. 1, March, 78–84

Mill, C. (1991) The long road to employee involvement, *Personnel Management*, February, 26–27

Monks, J. (1998) Trade unions, enterprise and the future, in Sparrow, P. and M. Marchington (eds) *Human Resource Management: The New Agenda*, Financial Times Pitman

Pickard, J. (2004) Informed decision, *People Management*, 16 September, 31–34

Taylor, F. W. (1911) *The Principles of Scientific Management*, Harper

Trist, E. and H. Murray (eds) (1993) *The Social Engagement of Social Science: A Tavistock Anthology*, Vol. II: The Socio-Technical Perspective, University of Pennsylvania Press (**www.dti.gov.uk/partnershipfund/guidance.htm**; accessed 14.06.01).

Further study

Books

Advisory, Conciliation and Arbitration Service (2004) *Employee Communications and Consultation*, ACAS (available at **www.acas.org.uk**; accessed 20.09.04).

Guest, D. and R. Peccei (1998) *The Partnership Company: Benchmarks for the Future*, Involvement and Participation Association. (The report summarises the results of research into companies that use the partnership approach.)

Hollinshead, G., P. Nicholls and S. Tailby (eds) (1999) *Employee Relations*, Financial Times Pitman Publishing. (Comprehensive coverage of theoretical and practical aspects of employee relations in the UK and Europe. Chapter 11 deals with employee participation and involvement.)

Incomes Data Services (2002) *IDS Studies 722: European Works Councils*, IDS. (A review of EWCs five years on, with comment on likely future developments and case studies of six organisations.)

Incomes Data Services (2002) *IDS Studies 752: Suggestion Schemes*, IDS. (Practical advice on how to run an effective suggestion scheme, with case studies of seven organisations.)

Incomes Data Services (2004) *IDS HR Studies Plus 777: Employee Attitude Surveys + Guide to Suppliers*, IDS. (Practical advice on how to design, conduct, analyse and use employee attitude surveys, with case studies of six organisations and a guide to suppliers.)

Institute of Personnel Management (1993) *Quality: People Management Matters*, IPM. (Reviews the techniques used to achieve quality and provides several case studies of UK companies.)

Involvement and Participation Association (1993) *Towards Industrial Partnership: A New Approach to Relationships at Work*, IPA.

Sparrow, P. and M. Marchington (eds) (1998) *Human Resource Management: The New Agenda*, Financial Times Pitman Publishing. (Part 2 of this book, 'Developing partnership and employee voice', contains six excellent chapters giving different perspectives on partnership.)

Articles

Arkin, A. (1992) Personnel management in Germany: At work in the powerhouse of Europe, *Personnel Management*, February, 32–35. (Includes a brief review of the structures for employee participation in German companies. First in a series about personnel management in the EC member states at that time, apart from the UK.)

First British European Works Councils established (1994) *Industrial Relations Review and Report*, No. 574, December, 4–7. (A description of the EWCs set up by BP Oil Europe and United Biscuits, involving UK employees even before the directive was adopted by the UK.)

Fowler, A. (1993) How to manage cultural change, *Personnel Management Plus*, November, 25–26.

Fowler, A. (1994) How to manage suggestion schemes, *Personnel Management Plus,* July, 28–29.

Fowler, A. (1993) How to plan and use attitude surveys, *Personnel Management Plus*, June, 25–26. (The 'How to . . .' articles provide some helpful practical advice on activities that might be included in starting up an employee involvement programme.)

Hilton, P. (1993) The key to staff commitment, *Personnel Management Plus*, June, 18–19. (Examines the relationship between involvement and commitment.)

Incomes Data Services (2000) *IDS Study 699: Suggestion Schemes*, IDS, November.

Incomes Data Services (2001) *IDS Study 704: Secondments and Volunteering*, IDS, February. (Outlines the benefits to be gained from company support of employee secondments or volunteering, including fulfilling expectations of social responsibility, enhancement of employee competencies, and provides some case studies of existing programmes.)

Incomes Data Services (2001) *IDS Study 705: Bonus Schemes*, IDS, March.

Industrial Relations Services (2000) Buy in or sell out?, *IRS Employment Trends 716*, November, 6–11. (A review of what happens after union–management partnership agreements. Provides references to 12 IRS case studies.)

Industrial Relations Services (2000) Towards commercial consciousness raising, *IRS Employment Trends 718*, December, 12–16. (HR specialists' views on the link between enhanced communication with employees and improved performance.)

Industrial Relations Services (2003) Raising productivity: policy and practice, *IRS Employment Review 776*, 23 May, 10–15. (An overview of what various companies have done to improve productivity, with profiles of 12 organisations.)

Industrial Relations Services (2003) Sharing the spoils: profit share and bonus schemes, *IRS Employment Review 784*, 19 September, 28–32.

McGlynn, C. (1995) European Works Councils: towards industrial democracy?, *Industrial Law Journal*, Vol. 24, No. 1, March, 78–84. (An explanatory note outlining the background to the European Works Council Directive and the position of companies in Britain. This issue of the journal is a special issue entitled 'Towards 1996: A Review of European Labour Law'.)

O'Reilly, N. (1994) Question time, *Personnel Today*, 6 December, 22–23. (Describes how companies are using opinion surveys to involve employees and manage change.)

We're in this together: profit-sharing schemes (1998) *IRS Employment Review*, March. (Report of a survey of the financial participation schemes in 40 organisations.)

Internet

Advisory, Conciliation and Arbitration Service   **www.acas.org.uk**
(Provides good practice advice on how to implement the ICE regulations. Also has a download-able advisory booklet on communications in the workplace.)

Chartered Institute of Personnel and Development   **www.cipd.co.uk**
(Information on consultation and information, and high performance working.)

Department of Trade and Industry   **www.dti.gov.uk**
(Provides masses of information on consultation and information, including brief summaries of current and pending legislation, discussion papers, consultation documents, and summaries of responses to consultation.)

Involvement and Participation Association   **www.partnership-at-work.com**
(A rich source of information on partnership, employee involvement, high performance working, information and consultation. Includes a concise overview of the history and development of the concept of partnership.)

CHAPTER 14

Discipline and grievance

OBJECTIVES

By the end of this chapter you will be able to:

- understand the meaning of the terms 'discipline' and 'grievance'
- understand the role of human resource managers and line managers in discipline and grievance handling
- explain the importance of the ACAS *Code of Practice on Disciplinary and Grievance Procedures* (2004)
- describe the main stages in a disciplinary procedure and in a grievance procedure
- write appropriate letters for a disciplinary procedure
- design a simple disciplinary and grievance procedure.

In any organisation, however good the management and however highly motivated the workforce, there will be occasions when problems or difficulties occur between management and employees. In order that employees are able to work to their optimum performance and that these problems do not turn into even bigger issues, suitable ways of dealing with them need to be devised before they occur. If the problem has arisen from something that management has done, this may result in the employee concerned having a grievance. If, however, it is a problem arising from the behaviour or attitude of an employee, then disciplinary action may be called for.

Human resource managers are concerned to get the best out of people, and although the human resource approach tends towards a dislike of rules and procedures, in favour of a more individualised approach, there are times when this is not possible because of the need to comply with legislation or codes of practice. This is the case where discipline and grievance are concerned. While discipline and grievances are individual issues, it would be unfair to treat each case in a totally different way, and to do so might result in a claim for unfair dismissal against the organisation, or dissatisfaction among the workforce. Human resource managers need to consider these issues and design suitable procedures in order to enhance both the performance management process within the organisation and to enable employees to contribute fully to the strategic objectives of the organisation.

Discipline: introduction and definitions

The *Shorter Oxford English Dictionary* defines discipline in the following ways: 'To subject to discipline; in earlier use, to educate or train; later, to bring under control.' The term 'discipline', as we can see from this definition, can be used in various ways. It can refer to self-discipline, where an individual as a result of practice and training works in a ordered, self-controlled way, or is trained by others to work in a certain way, or it can be used to refer to the need to discipline someone by pointing out to them the error of their ways or by punishing them for mistakes that they have made. Human resource managers are concerned to motivate people to ensure they reach their maximum potential, and the adoption of a punitive approach is unlikely to facilitate much motivation.

Students dealing with case studies about disciplinary situations often tend to respond initially by enjoying the power to punish and often want to dismiss the alleged offenders. Sometimes new, inexperienced managers may adopt the same approach. In reality this approach is likely to prove counterproductive, as valuable staff who have been costly to recruit and train would be lost, and the motivation of everyone concerned would be low. Handling a disciplinary situation in an unfair way may result in the employee being dismissed, but this might also result in a case for unfair dismissal being brought against the organisation. This could be expensive if the organisation lost, and in any case would be expensive in terms of:

- the time needed to prepare for the tribunal
- the time lost
- disruption caused as witnesses are called
- the bad publicity for the organisation itself
- the poor employee relations likely to ensue because of unfair handling of a disciplinary situation.

In order to try to minimise these problems and to encourage employers to handle disciplinary offences in a fair and reasonable manner, ACAS published a code of practice in 1977 and ten years later an advisory handbook, *Discipline at Work*. In 1997 ACAS published a self-help guide to producing discipline and grievance procedures and in 2000, published a further *Code of Practice on Disciplinary and Grievance Procedures*. This was revised again to take into account the new statutory discipline and grievance procedure that was introduced by the Employment Act 2002.

Disciplinary procedures and practices

The ACAS Code of Practice on disciplinary and grievance procedures

Since the Employment Protection Act 1975, the Advisory, Conciliation and Arbitration Service (ACAS) has had the right to publish codes of practice, and in June 2004 it published a new Draft *Code of Practice on Disciplinary and*

Grievance Procedures which came into effect in October 2004. This aims to help all who may be concerned with this topic by providing practical advice about handling disciplinary and grievance procedures. A code of practice has an interesting status in law. An employer cannot have an unfair dismissal case brought against it in an employment tribunal just because it has not carried out a procedure as stated in the code of practice, but it would ignore the code of practice at its peril, as failure to comply with it is likely to be used as part of the evidence against it in an unfair dismissal case.

In the code, ACAS clearly states that although disciplinary rules are likely to be mainly designed by management, other groups such as trade unions, line managers, workers and employees should also have a part to play in formulating them. ACAS emphasises the fact that the main reason for having disciplinary rules is to promote fairness and set standards of conduct, and to provide a fair and consistent method of dealing with alleged offences. According to ACAS, one of the main reasons for having procedures is to ensure there are orderly employment relations so that everyone knows what is expected of them. If the rules have been designed solely by management without the involvement of other interested parties, employees and workers may be more cynical about management's motives and individuals may feel that when they are disciplined it is because of victimisation, or because their supervisor dislikes them. In order for the disciplinary procedure to be credible to employees and other workers, it is clearly in management's interests to involve them in its design. Good employers will certainly appreciate this need.

Other employers, however, may merely be motivated in their provision of a disciplinary procedure by the need to comply with the legislation. The Employment Rights Act 1996 requires employers who employ 20 or more employees to provide them with a copy of their disciplinary procedure within two months of the commencement of their employment or provide access for the workers to an accessible document, which gives appropriate information. Although smaller employers do not have same the legal compulsion as large employers to provide their employees with a copy of their discipline and grievance procedure, it is still clearly good practice for them to do so. Employment tribunals will take into account the size of the organisation and the administrative resources that are available to the organisation when they consider cases. Small organisations do need to ensure that everyone is aware of the procedures and if they are unable to provide everyone with their own individual copy then they must ensure that there are copies on notice boards or in other easily accessible places such as on a company intranet site. It is good practice to go through such a procedure with all new employees and ensure that they understand it. It is vital that all employers, regardless of their size, do follow the minimum statutory dismissal and discipline procedures.

These factors should prove sufficient to motivate the employer to provide a disciplinary procedure but, if not, in the last resort some employers may be motivated by the fact that they may need evidence that they have acted fairly and followed a fair procedure in the event of an alleged unfair dismissal claim before an employment tribunal. For whatever reason, it is obviously important to adopt a clear disciplinary procedure so that both the employer and the workforce know what standards of conduct are expected and what may happen if these standards are not achieved.

Pause for thought 14.1

Consider for a moment the word 'worker' and the word 'employee'. What is the difference between the two?

'Worker' applies to all workers whether they are employed on a contract of employment or not. As such it is much broader term than 'employee' since it could apply also to workers who were employed by an agency or who worked as volunteers in a charity. In the ACAS Code of Disciplinary and Grievance Procedures both these words are used. Some of the provisions in the Code of Practice refer to just employees while others, in particular the right to be accompanied at disciplinary and grievance hearings, apply to all workers.

The essential features of a disciplinary procedure

The ACAS Code of Practice (2004) lists the following as essential features of a disciplinary procedure.

According to ACAS, 'good disciplinary procedures should:

1 be in writing;
2 specify to whom they apply;
3 be non-discriminatory;
4 ensure matters are dealt with without unnecessary delay;
5 allow for information about proceedings, witness statements and records to be kept confidential;
6 state the disciplinary actions which may be taken;
7 specify the levels of management which have the authority to take the various forms of disciplinary action;
8 provide for workers to be informed of complaints against them and where possible all relevant evidence before any hearing;
9 give workers an opportunity to state their case before a decision is reached;
10 provide for workers to be accompanied;
11 ensure that, except for gross misconduct, no worker is dismissed for a first breach of discipline;
12 ensure that disciplinary action is not taken until the case has been carefully investigated by management;
13 ensure that workers are given an explanation for any penalty imposed;
14 provide a right of appeal – normally to a more senior manager – and specify the procedure to be followed.' (Code of Practice on Disciplinary and Grievance Procedures, ACAS 2004)

It may seem obvious that rules should be in writing and should specify to whom they apply, and that disciplinary issues should be dealt with quickly. If they are not written down people will remember the rules differently, and varying approaches to discipline will occur. Many organisations nowadays will put disciplinary rules on their intranet sites, as well as in their organisational handbooks. Since the management must ensure that these rules are available to everyone, the rules may also need to be translated into other languages where English is not the first language of some of the workers. They should also be explained orally, perhaps for new workers during the induction period. This will be of help to those with a disability such as a visual impairment, who may also require a large print, Braille or audio-tape version of the procedure, but will also ensure any workers who are unable to read will know of the rules. Employees may otherwise be uncertain as to what they may and may not do, and supervisors and managers may adopt different approaches to discipline between different departments, with some supervisors unsure of what action they have the power to take.

In some rare cases it may be legitimate to have different rules for different departments. A catering department is likely to have additional rules about hygiene that are not likely to be as relevant to a transport department. So the rules should specify to whom they apply.

It is necessary to indicate what disciplinary actions may be taken so that there is a level of consistency and employees know what misdemeanours are regarded as serious by management. In order to be fair, the worker should know of the case against them and have an opportunity to state their case and, if they want, have a trade union official or a friend accompany them.

Workers can make genuine mistakes, and it is extremely expensive to recruit and train staff. On these grounds alone it pays to be fair to workers and to avoid dismissing them wherever possible. In order to give workers a fair chance it is important not to dismiss anyone for a first breach of discipline, unless it is a case of gross misconduct. This ensures that the individual has a chance to learn from his or her mistake.

Management may also occasionally make mistakes, and the worker may not have committed a disciplinary offence at all. To prevent someone being disciplined for something they did not do, it is important to ensure that no disciplinary action is taken before a full investigation into the alleged offence has been carried out.

If workers are to learn from their mistakes, then they need to be very clear about what they did wrong, how to do it right, and also to have a clear explanation of any penalties imposed. It is still possible that in spite of all these precautions occasionally management may make a mistake in disciplining a person. In order to remedy this and to ensure that people don't feel that they are being disciplined just because their supervisor doesn't like them, it is important to have an appeal procedure that is made known to them.

The Code of Practice also makes clear that, as well as the 14 features listed, a disciplinary procedure should follow what ACAS regards as core principles for reasonable behaviour by:

- using the procedures to help and encourage better standards of work rather than as a punishment
- ensuring that the worker knows of the case against them and has a chance to give their side of the story before any decision is made
- ensuring workers are accompanied by a colleague or trade union official at the hearing itself
- making sure that all the facts of the case are established before any disciplinary action is taken, and that whatever action results is reasonable in the unique circumstances of that case
- ensuring that no one is dismissed for a first offence, unless for a case of gross misconduct
- giving the worker a written explanation for whatever disciplinary action is taken and ensuring they know exactly what improvement is required from them

● providing an opportunity for appeal
● dealing with all issues as thoroughly and promptly as possible
● acting consistently.

It is also vital to follow the requirements of natural justice so employees should be given the chance to talk with someone who has not been, and will not be, involved at all in this issue. They should then be informed of allegations and the evidence against them prior to any meeting. Opportunities for them to challenge the allegations before decisions are reached should also be ensured and, as already mentioned, there should be a right of appeal.

Disciplinary offences

It would be impossible to itemise fully the range of behaviour that might result in disciplinary action being taken. Employers seem to regard the more common offences as being issues about absenteeism, timekeeping or poor performance at work. There may also be concern about a range of issues including failure to obey organisation rules, such as rules about health and safety, e-mail abuse, theft, sexism, racism, problems arising from fighting or threatening behaviour, and alcohol or drug abuse. Many employers divide offences into two categories depending on the seriousness with which they are viewed within that organisation. They list issues that they regard as disciplinary offences, and then itemise as gross misconduct further offences that they consider to be more serious. These offences may be handled in different ways, depending on the seriousness with which the organisation views them.

Pause for thought 14.2

Consider any organisation that you know reasonably well, perhaps one where you have worked yourself.

1 What disciplinary rules did the organisation have?
2 How were these disciplinary rules made known to you?
3 What were considered to be disciplinary offences?
4 Were there any offences that were regarded as particularly serious in this organisation and that constituted gross misconduct? List these.
5 Compare your list with the list made by someone who has experience in a different organisation. Can you find reasons for the differences and similarities?

It is probable that there were disciplinary rules in most organisations and these were made known to you, either informally by your supervisor telling you about them or, more likely, by you being given or shown a copy of them as part of your induction to your new job. It is likely that in most organisations there will also be a list of offences that might constitute gross misconduct. When you compare your list with that of a friend who has worked in a different organisation, you will probably have listed many of the same offences as ones that constituted gross misconduct. Theft, dishonesty, verbal or physical abuse are likely to be regarded as serious in most organisations. It is also probable that there will then be some variation in your lists as to what else constitutes an offence, depending on the attitudes in that particular organisation and the nature of the work done there. If there is a serious concern about fire hazards, then smoking in an unauthorised place may constitute gross misconduct. This is often of concern in retail organisations, where there might be a danger to large numbers of staff and customers and where some goods sold may be easily flammable. Organisations involved in food preparation may be particularly concerned with hygiene, and may list offences concerning lack of personal hygiene as ones that could constitute gross misconduct. Organisations such as banks or building societies, where there is a need for a high degree of security, may be very concerned with e-mail abuse and have extremely strict rules about what is acceptable for workers to both send and receive. Other organisations, such as universities, may be much more concerned with freedom of information and ensuring access to information, so may have very different rules. Offences also change with time, fashion and new technology. Many organisations now have specific policies regarding both e-mail and appropriate use of the Internet at work and some have also had to introduce policies to control the use of mobile phones at work.

Pause for thought 14.3

Tim Hancock has worked for your organisation for nearly a year. He has in general been a good employee, but you have noticed that recently he has started to arrive about 10 minutes late for work each morning. You are his supervisor. Describe the action you would take.

The way in which you, as Tim's supervisor, choose to deal with this situation depends on a number of factors. First there is your own attitude to this issue, but there is also the attitude of the organisation to issues of poor timekeeping to consider. You may have personal views about this but you need to act in a way that is consistent with the organisation's views. Personally you may not feel too concerned about this issue as long as the work gets done, or you may take the view that it is a form of dishonesty when an employee steals time from an employer. In some organisations this may not be viewed as a problem at all. Employees may have the opportunity to create their own flexi-time system without management worrying unduly about this. However, the views of the organisation will be expressed in its disciplinary procedure, and it is likely that poor timekeeping will be an area of concern. If that is the case you, as Tim's manager, have to do something about Tim's lateness. It is not as yet a particularly serious offence, but it has the potential to become more serious if left unchecked. There may of course be a perfectly good reason why Tim has suddenly started to arrive slightly late for work. The first thing that needs to be done is for you to have a chat with Tim about it and try to find out the reason for this change in behaviour. This can be informal. It gives Tim the opportunity to explain, and also lets him know that you are aware of his lateness and are concerned about it. If he has a good reason then you will have to consider your reaction. If there is illness at home, this is likely to be a temporary situation, and you may reach an arrangement with Tim about his time of arrival for a limited period of time which can be reviewed at a later date. If the problem is related to a change in a public transport timetable, you may have to consider whether you can be flexible or not.

Pause for thought 14.4

Jasmine has worked for your organisation for nearly five years. Her work has always been good, but recently you have received many complaints from customers about the goods that they have ordered being late or not being received at all. You check through the records and find that all these delays can be traced back to orders that Jasmine has dealt with. You are Jasmine's manager. How will you deal with this situation?

As Jasmine's manager you will have to take some action about her poor quality of work since it is causing problems to customers, and there have been complaints. However, you know that Jasmine has always been a good worker so you need to talk to her about the problem and try to find out what the cause is. Once again, you need to have an informal chat with her to find out the cause of the problem and then decide on the action to take. You may find that there is a perfectly good reason, such as a problem relating to home life, for the change in the standard of her work. If this is the case then a counselling interview is likely to be most appropriate. If, however, there doesn't appear to be a clear reason, an informal discussion which lets Jasmine know of your concerns and reaches agreement about expected improvements should suffice.

The disciplinary procedure

This will be set out in writing and needs to fulfil the criteria already discussed as essential features of a disciplinary procedure. The self-help guide produced by ACAS (2002) suggests that there should be several sections to the procedure itself. These will vary according to the size of the organisation, but are likely to include:

1 the purpose of the procedure
2 the principles that underlie the procedure
3 informal actions
4 formal actions
5 the nature of gross misconduct
6 the appeals procedure.

1 The purpose of the procedure

The disciplinary procedure is likely first of all to explain why a disciplinary procedure is needed. It will probably indicate that the aim of the procedure is to help all employees to achieve high standards of conduct, attendance and job performance. It will also indicate what action should be taken if there is a breach of disciplinary rules, and refer to the need for fairness and consistency for all. It would also be useful to emphasise here the fact that the formal disciplinary procedure should only be started if discussions under the informal procedure have failed to bring about the requisite change in behaviour.

2 The principles that underlie the procedure

This section is likely to include a list of several of the essential principles that ACAS gives for a disciplinary procedure. This may vary in detail according to the size and nature of the organisation concerned. For example, in a small organisation where a simple disciplinary procedure is required, the principles might be stated as follows:

1 The procedure is to investigate fully the offence, to deal consistently with any disciplinary issues that arise and to ensure that no action will be taken until this investigation has been completed.
2 At every stage, the individual should be advised of the type of complaint.
3 To ensure fairness, the employee concerned will have an opportunity to state his or her case and be represented by a trade union representative or friend if so desired.

4 For a first breach of discipline, then the individual should not be dismissed unless it is a serious case that counts as gross misconduct.

5 The employee will have a right of appeal at any stage against disciplinary action that may be taken.

6 The procedure may be implemented at any stage if the alleged misconduct justifies this.

3 Informal actions

Informal action is normally the most appropriate way of dealing with alleged minor misconduct or unsatisfactory performance. This may just involve the supervisor or manager having a quiet word with the individual and can be a quick and easy way of sorting out a problem. This type of informal action was exactly what we recommended in both the situations in the Pause for thought exercises 14.3 and 14.4 which you examined earlier in this chapter. However, if this doesn't work, or if the alleged offence is regarded as being rather more serious in nature, then it is time for the employer to show his or her dissatisfaction and to take some formal action.

Pause for thought 14.5

Consider once again Pause for thought 14.3. If after the informal chat or chats there were still no improvement in Tim's timekeeping his manager would be likely to start the formal disciplinary process.

4 Formal actions

Inform employee of the alleged misconduct in writing

Once the informal action has been taken, if the misconduct reoccurs or the unsatisfactory performance fails to improve, it may be necessary for the employer to try a more formalised approach.

The first stage in the formal process is to ensure that the individual realises that there actually still is a problem, and to do this the employer first needs to write to them stating the nature of the alleged misconduct and explaining why this is not acceptable within their organisation. The letter should also invite the individual to a meeting and inform them of their right to be accompanied at this meeting, and copies of documents that will be used at that meeting should be given to them.

Arrange a meeting to discuss the situation with them

The date, time and place of the meeting should, if possible, be agreed with the individual concerned and should also be timed to allow them sufficient time to prepare adequately for this meeting. The meeting should be held somewhere private where there will not be any interruptions.

At this meeting the employer should first explain the complaint and go through the evidence. Then the individual should go through his or her case and answer any allegations that have been made against them. They can also ask questions, call witnesses, present evidence and raise any points about witness information.

If there is a problem in holding this meeting at the agreed time due to a legitimate reason, e.g. employee illness or unavailability of their chosen companion on that date, then the employer can arrange another date. This should normally be within five working days but this can be extended by mutual agreement. However, if the individual simply fails to attend the meeting, without giving any good reason, then the employer could hold the meeting and even reach a decision in their absence.

Decide on whether disciplinary action is justified

a. If it is decided that disciplinary action is not justified, the worker should be informed of this. If no further action needs to be taken then the employer must notify the individual in writing of this fact so they no longer worry.

b. If, however, disciplinary action is decided upon then the employer has to decide the form of the action, taking into account the individual's explanations, their past employment record and length of service, any actions that have been taken in similar cases in the past, and whether the proposed disciplinary action is reasonable in the circumstances. It is normally good practice to give all employees at least one chance to improve before issuing them with a final written warning.

Slightly different forms of action may be appropriate for cases of misconduct or for those involving unsatisfactory performance.

The first forms of formal action in a case of alleged *misconduct* could include the following:

- A first written warning stating the nature of the misconduct and stating what change in behaviour is required.
- The individual being told that this is part of a formal disciplinary process and the consequences if they fail to change their behaviour.
- The likely consequences, such as a final written warning which could ultimately lead to their dismissal or some other sanction, but that this would only happen after they had been given the chance to present their case at another formally convened meeting. (If the employer considers dismissal or an action other than a warning or suspension on full pay, then they need to take into account the statutory minimum procedure which will be discussed in Chapter 15 where we discuss dismissals.)
- A right to appeal against this decision.
- Records of this decision being kept for a specified period of time, e.g. six months, after which it should be disregarded.

The first forms of formal action in a case of alleged *unsatisfactory performance* may be slightly different but could include a written improvement note being given to any individual who is performing in an unsatisfactory way which states:

- the nature of the performance problem
- the required improvement
- the timescale within which the improvement should occur
- a review date and
- the support, if any, that the employer will provide to help the individual to reach the required level of performance
- notification that failure to improve, if this is what has been decided upon, could result in a final written warning and ultimately dismissal.

Final written warnings

When the requisite improvement in either performance or behaviour has not been made within the stated timescale, or if the alleged offence is sufficiently serious, the employee should normally be issued with a written warning. Once again, before this stage of the process they should be given the opportunity to present their case at a meeting.

Any final written warning that is issued should once again make the following clear to the individual:

● the grounds for the complaint
● that failure to make the required improvement within a specified time may result in dismissal or another penalty
● that there is a right of appeal.

Final written warnings should be disregarded once the specified time limit has elapsed.

Dismissal or other penalty

The subject of dismissal will be considered in more detail in the next chapter. However, we shall mention it briefly here as it is sometimes the final stage in the disciplinary process. Any decision to dismiss must be taken by a manager who has the necessary authority. The employee must be told as soon as possible of the decision to dismiss them, the reasons for the dismissal, the date on which their employment contract will end and their notice period and right of appeal.

Some organisations may choose to use alternative forms of sanction against the individual rather than dismissal. These could include demotion to another job, loss of seniority or pay, or a disciplinary transfer. These types of sanction may only be used if the employee's contract specifies these as alternatives or if agreement is reached with the individual concerned to allow them to be used.

The statutory discipline and dismissal procedure

In cases where employers dismiss someone, or take some other action against them such as demoting them, the employer must also comply with what is known as the statutory discipline and dismissal procedure. In most cases this involves three stages:

1　The employer must write to the employee telling them of the allegations against them.
2　They must hold a meeting with the employee to discuss the allegations. At this meeting they must allow the employee to be accompanied by a suitable companion, if the employee requires this. The employee must be told of the decision.
3　If the employee decides to appeal against this decision then the employer must hold a further meeting and once again allow the employee to be accompanied by someone appropriate. Once again the employer must inform the employee about the final appeal decision.

In the case of gross misconduct a modified procedure may be used. However, failure to comply with the standard statutory procedure in this or any other dismissal case will mean that if an employee is eligible to apply for unfair dismissal then the employment tribunal will automatically find the dismissal unfair. Not only that but it will also increase the level of compensation awarded by between 10% and 50%. Employers certainly need to heed this requirement. This will be discussed in more detail in Chapter 15.

5 The nature of gross misconduct

As we said earlier, organisations will have different ideas as to what constitutes gross misconduct. The employee should be given some indication of this also in the disciplinary procedure. It is impossible to design a list that covers all possibilities, but the organisation should list some of them. For example, the procedure may say that the following constitute gross misconduct and if any employee, after a full investigation, is found guilty of any of these offences he or she will be dismissed, even for a first offence:

● theft
● deliberate damage to the organisation's property
● fraud
● incapacity to work because of the influence of illegal drugs or alcohol
● physical assault
● sexual harassment
● racial harassment
● serious infringement of health and safety rules.

These are examples of offences that normally constitute gross misconduct, but it is not an exhaustive list and other serious offences may also constitute gross misconduct and merit dismissal.

It is also a good idea to state the organisation's position on criminal offences committed outside employment. There should be a statement in the disciplinary procedure indicating that a criminal offence which occurs outside of employment may be considered as gross misconduct and may result in dismissal. The word 'may' should be stressed here, as this is not an automatic reason for dismissal. The main considerations should be the nature of the offence and the type of work that the employee normally does, and whether the offence makes the employee unsuitable for his or her job.

In these cases, the employee concerned will normally be suspended from work on full pay, while a full investigation is being carried out. Suspension on full pay does not imply any guilt.

6 The appeals procedure

The last section of the disciplinary procedure should indicate what the employee should do if he or she is not happy with the action taken against him or her. There should be a clear appeal procedure, with time limits for the submission of appeals stated. The appeal procedure should of course meet the requirements set in the standard statutory procedure. Once again there should be the opportunity for a meeting to discuss the appeal and the person once again has the right to choose to be accompanied at this meeting.

The need for a record of warnings issued

All warning letters should state that the warning will be recorded on the employee's file for a set period of time. The period of time will vary between organisations. It may perhaps be three months for a written warning and six months for a final written warning. Once that period of time has elapsed, if the worker's conduct or performance has improved to the employer's satisfaction, the letter and note of the offence should be removed from that person's record. If he or she later commits the same or a different breach of disciplinary procedure, then the procedure must be started again. So if the employee who has been given a warning for an infringement concerning timekeeping then commits a different infringement, for example, by carrying out poor quality work, the employer should not go to the next stage of the disciplinary procedure but should start with an informal talk and issue a separate warning if that proves necessary.

If the employer ignored the fact that the warning was out of date or was about a different type of disciplinary offence, then it could hardly expect to win its case if it eventually dismissed the worker and he or she later decided to go to an employment tribunal to claim unfair dismissal. Such actions would be regarded as procedurally incorrect.

If records of warnings are kept on a worker's file indefinitely, then this could prejudice the person reading the file at a later date against this employee. The employee may well have changed over the years and so an unfair impression of this person would be given. The employee has the right, under the Data Protection Act 1998, to check his or her records to ensure that erroneous or out-of-date information is not being held and possibly used against them. Refer to the section on Data Protection in Chapter 6 for more information.

Groups that may pose particular problems

The ACAS Code of Practice also advises that certain situations may require special consideration. They list as particularly difficult cases:

- workers to whom the full procedure is not available
- trade union officials
- criminal charges or convictions outside employment
- cases involving statutory registration authorities, e.g. in the case of doctors the General Medical Council or for solicitors the Law Society.

The case studies in Pause for thought 14.6 and 14.7 serve to illustrate some of these areas of concern. How would you handle each of these cases?

Pause for thought 14.6

Paul has worked for Shepley Computers for four years, and for the past six months has worked on the night shift. He has a blemish-free record and is a highly regarded member of the workforce. One hot night in summer he leaves work after signing in at nine o'clock and goes to the pub. He returns to work under the influence of alcohol, and his supervisor, who has noticed his absence, tells him that he is suspended and must go home immediately. Paul becomes abusive and threatens to punch his supervisor. He takes his supervisor by the shoulders and shakes him while all the time threatening to punch him. His supervisor tells him that he is dismissed and should collect all his money and documents at the end of the week.

Do you feel that Paul's supervisor acted correctly in this case? If not, how would you have handled this situation?

Offences that occur when the human resources department is not available to give advice, as in this case, need particular attention. Supervisors and managers who work on the night shift are not likely to have the human resource manager to turn to for advice if a potential disciplinary situation suddenly occurs. They need to be very clear in their own minds exactly what powers are available to them, and to be extremely well trained. The supervisor initially acted well in suspending the employee. Paul was drunk and abusive and was behaving in a threatening manner towards him. Suspension with pay is a useful technique when there needs to be an opportunity to calm the situation or when time is needed to complete an investigation into whether or not an offence has occurred. He then acted rather rashly in telling Paul that he had been dismissed. No one should be dismissed unless a proper investigation has been carried out. Taking away someone's livelihood is a serious matter which could result in an employment tribunal case for unfair dismissal being brought against the organisation.

Even though some of Paul's actions, such as being drunk at work and acting in an abusive and threatening manner, could clearly be classified as gross misconduct, there still needs to be a full investigation with an opportunity for Paul and his superior to state their cases and for union representation, before a disciplinary decision is reached.

Pause for thought 14.7

Jane has been employed by your organisation for 10 years. She works as the assistant manager in the wages office and has always been an excellent worker. You hear, on the grapevine, that she has been accused of stealing £100 from the funds of the local youth club, where she acts as treasurer.

Imagine that you are the manager of the wages office. What will you do when:

1 you first hear the rumours
2 she is subsequently convicted but given a conditional discharge for this offence?

This is perhaps one of the most difficult situations for a manager to deal with. If the offence had happened at work it would have been a clear case of theft from work and, after going through the disciplinary procedure, may have been considered gross misconduct with the possibility of dismissal. As it is, should the manager consider this to be a disciplinary issue or not? ACAS (2002) says that being charged with a criminal offence, and even being convicted of one, does not necessarily warrant disciplinary action being taken. Even if the employee is convicted of the offence and is absent from work because they are being remanded in custody, there is no automatic reason for disciplinary action or dismissal.

Initially when you, the manager, hear of the alleged theft from youth club funds you will need to establish the facts of the case as best you can. You are likely to need to talk to Jane as part of this process. The main question that you as an employer must decide is whether the matter is sufficiently serious to warrant starting the disciplinary procedure. The main consideration should be whether the offence, or the alleged offence, makes the employee unsuitable for the type of work they are currently doing. You then have three options:

1 You could do nothing, if you are satisfied with Jane's explanation and decide that the matter is not sufficiently serious to be taken further within the disciplinary procedure.

2 You might consider suspending her on full pay pending the result of the court case. This would remove her from the situation at work where there would be gossip and rumours, and would also ensure that if anything went missing from work she would not be automatically accused. In many ways this is an attractive option, but the manager would need to be aware that the organisation may be paying Jane for several months before her case is heard.

3 You could consider moving her to another section where she would not deal with cash handling, although of course many wages offices do not necessarily deal with money anyway. This would have the same advantages as in 2, but she would be earning her wages. She still might be accused, however, every time anything went missing. You may of course not have any other suitable post to which she could transfer, and depending on her contract you may need her agreement to the transfer.

If she is found guilty, then there are once again a variety of appropriate responses. The main guidance is given in the ACAS Code of Practice, which states that offences which occur away from the workplace should not be treated as automatic reasons for dismissal. It goes on to say that the most important factor will be whether the nature of the offence makes the employee unsuitable for their particular job.

In the case of Jane, it would be possible to say that since she was found guilty of theft, this would affect people's view of her in a position of trust and so she may be dismissed for gross misconduct. Most disciplinary procedures follow ACAS's guidelines and include a section which states that offences which occur outside work may constitute gross misconduct. Dismissal should not be automatic, however. Other options are available and it depends on the circumstances.

These two case studies, concerning potential disciplinary offences that occur away from the place of work or outside normal working hours, help to illustrate some of the more difficult cases that may arise and show how useful it is to refer to the ACAS Code of Practice on Disciplinary Procedures for guidance in these areas.

Absence control

Absences are often another area of particular concern to employers. Here what is important is to find out exactly what the reasons are for the absence. In many organisations an absence control procedure is used, and this may result in the disciplinary procedure being used less frequently. Absence control systems usually require the employee to telephone the supervisor on the first day of absence, and the supervisor will go through a checklist of points with him or her. If the supervisor is not available there will be a second or a third designated person with whom the absent person will have to speak. An interview will be held with the supervisor or other designated person when the absentee returns to work.

There will also be a system of visits for people who are absent on a long-term basis to ensure that the organisation stays up to date with their current situation and knows when to expect them to return to work. Supervisors and managers will be aware of the level of absenteeism in their sections and will encourage good attendance.

The aim of an absence control procedure is to minimise the need for the use of the disciplinary procedure, by creating a culture in which everyone is aware of the importance of good attendance and of their value to the organisation. The danger is that some employees may feel pressurised into returning to work before they are really fit, and this may prove to be counterproductive, resulting in their needing more time off later to recover fully.

Disciplinary procedures and ill-health

If there is not a good reason for the absence then this is likely to be an issue considered to be misconduct. If a person has a record of short-term absences without suitable explanations or adequate medical evidence, then they can be dealt with under the organisation's normal disciplinary procedure. There is usually a specified level of absence, e.g. 10 days in three months, after which more formal controls will be introduced, leading to counselling or disciplinary action as appropriate. If employees are away on a long-term absence due to a genuine illness then the situation needs to be dealt with in an entirely differ-ent way. You cannot warn someone that there must be an improvement in their attendance if you know that this is impossible because of the nature of their illness. Instead, regular contact needs to be maintained with such employ-ees to establish the likelihood of their return, and medical evidence needs to be sought. A company doctor's advice may be needed. In the end it may be that the person is unable to return to work in the foreseeable future, and it may be necessary to consider whether there are any other suitable jobs that they may be able to undertake, or whether their employment needs to be terminated. Other factors, such as whether they have exhausted the organisation's sickness pay scheme, the age of the person, whether the illness is as a result of a dis-ability as defined by the Disability Discrimination Act 1995, and whether they could take early retirement under the organisation's pension scheme, will need to be considered here in order to find the best solution for both the employee and the organisation. There is also likely to be a need for employee counselling and advice, and this process, if handled with the sensitivity it deserves, is likely to be extremely lengthy.

Disciplinary hearings

The actual disciplinary is similar in many ways to the hearing interviews dis-cussed in Chapter 4. The manager who is conducting the hearing will need to prepare thoroughly, have the relevant information to hand and arrange for a quiet room with no disturbances and with an appropriate layout in which to hold the interview. The disciplinary hearing should be conducted in a system-atic and fair way in order to ensure that all the relevant information is consid-ered. The manager chairing it should explain clearly the purpose, who is present and why they are there, and the sequence.

Although there are many similarities between disciplinary hearings and interviews, and one would expect them to be conducted in a similar way, there are some specific legal definitions that apply to disciplinary hearings. It is important to consider these as there is a legal right for workers to be accom-panied at a disciplinary hearing and this is not something that would normally apply at most other interviews, with the exception of the grievance interview which will be discussed later in this chapter.

Disciplinary hearings are defined as all meetings where either disciplinary action or some other action could be taken against a worker. This includes any meeting that might result in actions such as a warning, final written warning, suspension without pay, demotion or dismissal being taken against the worker. It also applies to meetings to confirm warnings or other disciplinary action and to appeal hearings, even if they are held after the worker has left the employment concerned.

The right to be accompanied at a disciplinary interview

The Employment Relations Act 1999 gave workers the right to request a companion to accompany them at disciplinary or grievance hearings. This can be a fellow worker or a trade union official or even, in certain circumstances, a lay trade union official. The companion can address the hearing and advise workers, but is not supposed to answer questions on behalf of the worker. It is in order for a worker to request an alternative date for a hearing if the companion of their choice is unavailable on the designated date for the hearing.

The ACAS Code of Practice on Disciplinary and Grievance Procedures 2004 was written to take into account the statutory discipline and grievance procedures set out in the Employment Act 2002 and so gives practical guidance about workers being accompanied at disciplinary hearings. It explains that as well as the rights to be accompanied already mentioned, some workers may have other additional rights to be accompanied by different people specified in their contracts of employment. Employers should also consider sympathetically any specific needs raised by disabled workers or by a disabled companion.

Trade unions are supposed to ensure that there are suitable training and refresher courses for all their officials, so that they can confidently take on the role of companion if requested. However, ACAS explains that although workers can request a trade union official or a fellow worker to accompany them at any disciplinary hearing, the person selected for this role does not have to agree to do this and should not be pressurised to take on the role if they do not want to do it.

Before the hearing the worker should inform the employer of the name of their companion so that the companion can also be involved in discussions about choosing a convenient date and time for the hearing. The companion may carry out the following roles:

- state the worker's case for them
- summarise the worker's case
- respond on behalf of the worker to any views expressed at the hearing
- discuss points with the worker during the hearing
- ask witnesses questions.

However, the role of companion will depend on what the worker wants them to do and the worker may choose not to allow them to do some of these things.

If an employer fails to comply with a reasonable request for a worker to be accompanied at a disciplinary hearing then the worker may complain about this to an employment tribunal. If the worker's companion cannot attend the hearing on a specific date and the employer fails to re-arrange a hearing to take account of this then this can also be the cause for a complaint to an employment tribunal. Two weeks pay can be awarded by a tribunal in these cases and this could be increased if the tribunal also decides that the worker has been unfairly dismissed.

Grievance: introduction and definitions

The *Shorter Oxford English Dictionary* defines grievance as: 'The infliction of wrong or hardship on a person; injury, oppression; a cause or source of injury.' When referring to grievances it is useful to follow the approach of Pigors and Myers (1977) and identify the strength of the feeling about the behaviour or attitude of management that has resulted in injury, and how this is then expressed. Pigors and Myers distinguish between dissatisfaction, complaint and grievance:

- *Dissatisfaction*: anything that disturbs an employee, whether or not he expresses his unrest in words.

- *Complaint*: a spoken or written dissatisfaction, brought to the attention of the supervisor and/or shop steward.

- *Grievance*: a complaint which has been formally presented to a management representative or to a union official. (Pigors and Myers 1977, p. 229)

We shall use the term 'grievance' in this way as a form of dissatisfaction about which the employee feels sufficiently strongly that he or she formally raises the issue with his or her management representative or shop steward.

The ACAS Code of Practice on Disciplinary and Grievance Procedures (2004) provides guidance on grievance handling. Grievances may arise for a multitude of reasons. An employee may become dissatisfied with his or her hours of work or working conditions, he or she may feel a supervisor shows unfair favouritism to others, or may feel dissatisfaction about pay or sexual harassment. Some grievances may appear trivial and others, such as alleged sexual harassment, may be very serious, but to the employee concerned they will all have been serious enough to raise formally.

Anyone in an organisation could have a grievance, even a member of management. Some grievances may become a collective issue, with negotiations between management and a trade union arising over an issue such as a collective grievance about pay or working conditions. This chapter will focus solely on grievance as an individual issue.

Grievance procedures and practices

Reasons for having a grievance procedure

Employees need to know how they can raise a grievance and seek redress for any grievance that they might have. They need to feel confident that their grievance will be treated in a fair way and that they will get to know the result of raising this grievance within a short period of time. It is also important to settle the grievance quickly, to prevent it becoming a larger grievance that involves more people and takes longer to resolve.

It is regarded as good employment practice for employers to have a grievance procedure and the government has also introduced statutory grievance procedures for all workers, not just employees.

If there were no procedure for raising and resolving grievances, it would be likely that employees would grumble to colleagues, and not only their work but the work of the department would be liable to suffer as a result. Therefore the main aim of the grievance procedure is to settle disputes fairly and as near to the source of grievance as possible. If there were a grievance over an issue such as safety or harassment, failure to provide a mechanism to deal with the grievance could result in serious repercussions, with perhaps accidents or a sexual or racial harassment case occurring. A grievance procedure in effect provides a safety mechanism to prevent issues from getting out of control. It also ensures that management have a channel to hear about issues that may be worrying their staff.

Discipline versus grievance

Disciplinary action is, as we have seen, normally initiated by management to express dissatisfaction with, and bring about changes in, employee behaviour; grievance, on the other hand, is normally initiated by employees for similar reasons, but in respect of management's, or perhaps co-workers', behaviour. There is a need for fairness and justice in both procedures although they are initiated by different parties. Because of this it is sometimes claimed that they are the opposites of each other, and should be viewed as complementary processes in industrial justice.

Pause for thought 14.8 Consider what you have just learned about grievance and discipline. In what ways do you consider discipline and grievance to be opposites? Are there any facts which make you think that they are not truly opposites?

As we have shown, discipline and grievance are both concerned with fairness and justice. They differ in that the people who initiate the action in each case differ. The management initiates disciplinary action against employees, and employees initiate grievances mainly against their supervisors and managers. In this way they may be considered to be opposite faces of industrial justice. However, this disregards the balance of power in these cases. To consider them to be true opposites would entail the assumption that when an employee initiates a grievance they have the same amount of power as management, which is clearly not the case. An employee who has a grievance will not be able to insist that action is taken against the person who has caused the grievance, and will have to rely on management's willingness to take action.

The role of the human resource manager and the line manager

Discipline and grievances are sensitive issues requiring skilful handling, and in many organisations they have traditionally been an area that has been left to human resource managers. This has been partly due to the fact that the human resource managers were likely to be trained in skilful handling of sensitive interpersonal issues, but also many managers and supervisors were often unwilling to tackle something that might result in their unpopularity and cause difficulties in maintaining a suitable relationship with someone they had to work with on a daily basis. This attitude has changed considerably in recent years, as more and more of the human resource function has been devolved to line management; line managers in many organisations are nowadays expected to handle any discipline or grievance situations that arise in their section, at least in the early stages. Human resource managers still have several important roles to play, however:

- in devising the procedures
- in providing specialist advice
- in ensuring that everyone is aware of the procedures and acts consistently
- in ensuring that line managers are suitably trained
- in monitoring the effectiveness of the procedures.

The ACAS Code of Practice recommends that grievance and disciplinary machinery should be kept separate, although some organisations do provide for an appeal against a disciplinary action being handled through the general grievance procedure.

The informal grievance procedure

The Labour Research Department (1995) conducted a survey of the grievance procedures of 85 organisations. It found that the majority of complaints are resolved in an informal way, making it unnecessary to raise them as a formal grievance. Informal grievance procedures seem to be just as important in organisations as informal disciplinary procedures. However, a small number of complaints will not be resolved informally, and for these it is necessary to have a grievance procedure.

These findings are supported by Cully *et al.* (1999) in their study of Britain at Work as depicted by the 1998 Workplace Employee Relations Survey. This showed that while 91% of employees had access to grievance procedures in the organisations which were surveyed, in only 30% of the organisations had the formal grievance procedure actually been used during that year. According to Cully *et al.* (1999), 'One reason for this might be that employees had nothing to complain about. Another might be that the procedure is not a particularly effective mechanism for resolving problems.'

We have already outlined the reasons for having a grievance procedure, and in the next section will consider the form that the grievance procedure should take and the main points to be considered when designing a grievance procedure, before considering the way in which the grievance interview should be handled.

The formal grievance procedure

In order that both workers and managers are clear about how to handle grievances and to ensure grievances are resolved quickly and fairly, a grievance procedure should be designed and issued to all employees and other workers. It is a good idea, once again, to involve various groups in the design of a procedure to suit a particular organisation.

A suitable format for the grievance procedure might be to use similar headings to those used in the design of a disciplinary procedure. Suitable headings could be:

1 the purpose and scope of the grievance procedure
2 the principles that underlie the procedure

3 the stages in the grievance procedure
4 exceptional circumstances
5 the appeals procedure.

The purpose and scope of the procedure

This section is likely to indicate which employees are covered by this particular procedure if there are slightly different procedures for different groups. It should also state that the aim of the procedure is to settle any grievances in a fair manner and as near to the source of the grievance as possible. In order to minimise problems at work and ensure a happy and productive working environment, the procedure should be simple to use and rapid in operation.

The principles that underlie the procedure

This is likely to include some statements concerning the employer's views on fairness and justice and how these will be achieved, for example:

- All workers have a right to raise a grievance that they may feel with their supervisor or manager without fear of recrimination against themselves.
- Grievances will be investigated within specified time limits and the person with the grievance will be notified of the outcome.
- At each stage of the procedure they will have the right to be accompanied by a trade union representative or a friend.
- If the worker is not satisfied with the outcome of raising their grievance they will have a right of appeal.

The stages in the grievance procedure

The Labour Research Department (1995) found that 80% of the grievance procedures that it reviewed had between three and six stages after the informal stage. ACAS (2004) in its code of Practice says that: 'In most organisations it should be possible to have at least a two-stage procedure. However, where there is only one stage, for instance in very small firms where there is only a single owner/manager, it is especially important that the person dealing with the grievance acts impartially.' We do not feel that there is any advantage in having more levels than three in the procedure, even if there are more levels in the management hierarchy. We would suggest that three main levels should prove adequate for most organisations. Outlined below are the possible main stages in the grievance procedure.

Stage 1

The worker should raise the grievance, preferably in writing, with the immediate supervisor, who will reply within a specified time, e.g. three days. If the grievance is about the line manager, there needs to be an opportunity to bypass this stage and to raise the grievance with a manager at the next highest level. If there is a disagreement about the facts of the grievance then the manager should invite the worker to attend a grievance hearing in order to discuss it. The worker has, depending on the nature of the grievance, a statutory right to be accompanied at a grievance hearing and the manager should make him or her aware of this right. The statutory right applies if the grievance relates to something that concerns the performance of 'the duty of the employer in relation to a worker'. For example, this could apply in relation to a grievance raised about equal pay, because the employer has a clear duty to provide equal pay to all workers. Ultimately it will be the employment tribunals that will decide in which cases the worker should have been given the right to be accompanied at the grievance hearing, so it would be good practice to allow any worker raising a grievance to be accompanied, if they request it.

Stage 2

If it has not been resolved, the individual should request in writing an interview with a more senior manager. This manager should then arrange to hear the grievance within a specified time period, e.g. within five working days. The worker should be informed of their statutory right to be accompanied and a date set for them to present their case at a meeting. The manager should make a decision about the grievance within a specified time period and the worker should be informed of this. If there is likely to be a delay in reaching a decision then the worker should also be given a clear reason for this and told when he or she can expect a decision.

Stage 3

If it has not been resolved at stage 2, the individual should raise the grievance with the general manager or director or the next most senior person. Once again, the worker should be told of his or her statutory rights to be accompanied at a hearing at which they present their case. As in the earlier stages, an indication about the time it will take to reach a decision should be given to the worker, as should explanations about any unavoidable delay.

Time limits

You will have noted that fairly strict time limits were specified in the section on stages in the procedure. If there is not a satisfactory response to the grievance within a specified time limit, then the employee should be able to raise the grievance with the supervisor's immediate management. There should be a clear time limit for each stage of the grievance procedure, as without this there is a danger that, although a manager or supervisor may have good intentions to deal with a grievance, it will nevertheless be overlooked.

Representation

At each stage in the formal grievance procedure the worker should be informed of their statutory right to be accompanied by a companion who is another employee or who is a trade union representative. This right, once again, applies to all workers and not just employees, so agency workers, home workers, the self-employed or those doing voluntary work could all raise grievances and have the right to be accompanied. As we said earlier in this chapter, the right applies specifically when there is a requirement to attend a grievance hearing which relates to legal or contractual commitments such as grievances relating to grading or promotion, if they arise out of a contract. Some other grievances may not relate to contractual or legal matters but it may be safer for employers to allow workers to be accompanied rather than finding themselves testing the interpretation of the law at an employment tribunal.

Exceptional circumstances and special considerations

In exceptional circumstances it may not be practicable to raise the grievance with the immediate manager. This may be because the grievance is caused by the manager or because the manager will not be available, perhaps because of illness, to deal with the grievance with the urgency that it deserves. In those exceptional circumstances the grievance may be taken to the next level of supervision.

Some organisations may also want to establish special additional procedures to deal with specific types of grievances relating, for example, to discrimination, harassment or bullying and may design policies specific to these issues. The organisation may feel the need to have separate procedures as these are all very difficult areas that may need extra-sensitive handling.

Appeals

A right of appeal should be specified for each stage, with time limits within which the appeal should be heard.

Records

Records of grievances raised and the responses made to them should be kept. They should, in accordance with the Data Protection Act 1998, be kept confidential but certain information or data should normally be available to the individual concerned on request.

Pause for thought 14.9

Shazia, the shop steward, asks you for time off to make a complaint to the general manager about something in your department. You are the manager of that department: what will you do?

Shazia, as the shop steward, is entitled to reasonable time off to carry out her trade union duties, so she is in order to request time off. However, as we said earlier, a grievance should be settled as near to the source of the problem as possible. You need to remind Shazia, who as a shop steward should certainly be aware of this, that if she has a grievance herself, or if she is acting on behalf of one of your department, then you are the person with whom the grievance should first be raised. You should point out that if you cannot deal with this satisfactorily within the specified time period then of course she may then raise the grievance, in line with the grievance procedure, with the general manager.

Although there is a need for grievances to be settled as near to the source of grievance as possible, this becomes difficult if the grievance is about the manager or supervisor concerned, so if the grievance is about you as the supervisor, Shazia may be unwilling to discuss it with you. Nevertheless, if it is about you, you will need to know about it sooner or later, so at least you should try to ascertain the nature of the grievance before allowing it to go further.

Grievance interviews

Many of the features of a grievance interview are the same as for other types of interview. There is a need for a quiet, private room arranged to facilitate ease of communication. The employee or his or her companion is likely to do most of the talking, since they are raising the grievance. There may be a need to call witnesses, and after hearing all the evidence from both sides the manager may wish to adjourn before reaching a decision. The manager must ensure a fair hearing and that everyone concerned is aware of the purpose of the meeting, who is to be called as witnesses, the time limits within which a decision will be reached, and the way in which the decision will be announced to the employee or worker concerned. If there is not a swift and fair resolution of grievances, the grievances may tend to build up and the work of the section is likely to suffer. At worst this could ultimately result in a high labour turnover or a high level of absenteeism as people remove themselves from a situation where they feel unhappy, or it might escalate into an industrial dispute.

Some organisations may, in addition to these procedures, decide to have a whistleblowing procedure. This will then provide additional protection for workers who raise grievances about issues that involve some form of wrongdoing within the organisation, e.g. workplace hazards or fraud.

Conclusion

We have shown in this chapter the meaning and the importance of grievance and disciplinary procedures to the organisation. Both specialist human resource managers and line managers have an extremely important role to play in the design of procedures that are fair to all; it is also important that cases of grievance or discipline are dealt with in accordance with the organisation's procedures. Knowledge and understanding of the ACAS Code of Practice, and the ACAS self-help guide for producing discipline and grievance procedures are valuable aids to help ensure that fair procedures are designed and that disciplinary and grievance interviews are handled well. Good procedures and clear policies for dealing with both discipline and grievance issues should result in fewer of this type of problem for the organisation. Any issues that do arise are dealt with in a fair way that everyone understands. Organisations should at the design stage involve representatives from different levels and types of work to ensure policies and procedures really do meet the requirements of both the organisation and the workers. The chosen form of their policies and procedures should also be guided by advice in the ACAS Code of Practice (2004) and include the statutory right to be accompanied for workers at both discipline and grievance hearings. Organisations must also be clear about whether they are interpreting the right to be accompanied in its strict legal sense at specific types of discipline or grievance hearings, or whether they are extending this right to workers in any discipline or grievance situation. In the next chapter we examine the consequences of getting a disciplinary case wrong, and discuss unfair dismissal and redundancy.

The mind maps shown in Figures 14.1 and 14.2 summarise the key points covered in this chapter. When you have examined these, test your understanding of the chapter with the review questions and self-check questions.

Figure 14.1 Mind map: discipline

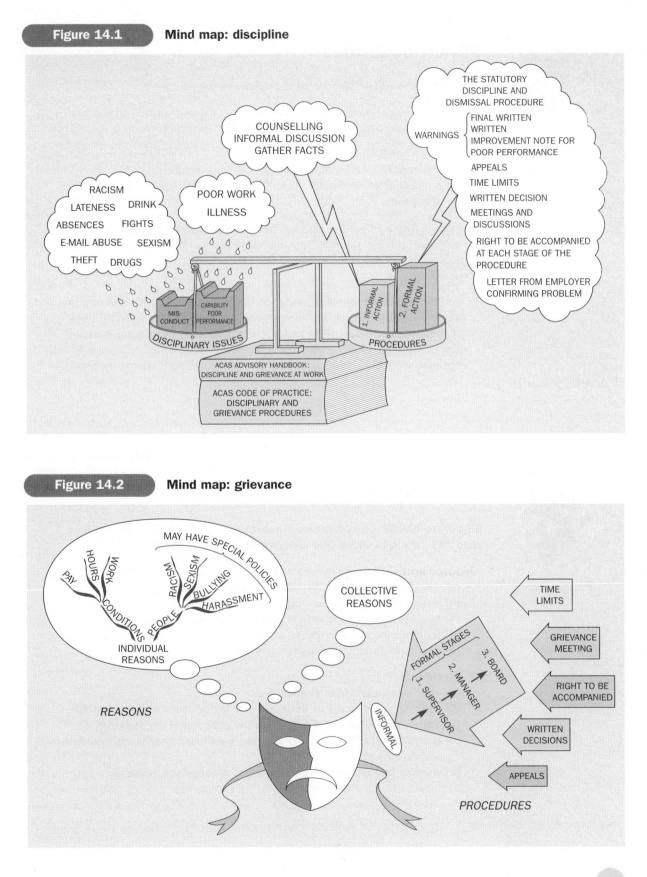

Figure 14.2 Mind map: grievance

REVIEW QUESTIONS

Brief answers to review questions 4 is provided on page 495.

1 Interview both a line manager and a personnel manager and try to establish what roles they play in relation to grievance and discipline handling in the workplace. How do your findings compare with what we have said in this chapter?

2 Obtain a copy of an organisation's discipline or grievance procedure and compare it to our suggested outline for these. Identify and comment on the similarities and differences.

3 Obtain a copy of the ACAS *Code of Practice on Disciplinary and Grievance Procedures* (2004). Use this, and our suggestions in this chapter, to rewrite or modify either of the procedures you used for question 2, if you find that this is necessary.

4 You have joined an organisation which has expanded recently and now has 100 employees. This organisation started as a small undertaking with only 18 employees and has never had a formal grievance procedure. Write a report for the general manager outlining why it is important to have a formal grievance procedure and suggesting what the procedure should contain.

SELF-CHECK QUESTIONS

Answer the following multiple-choice questions. The answers are provided on page 495 for you to check your understanding of this chapter.

1 According to ACAS, disciplinary procedures should be designed to:
   (a) provide a fair way to gather evidence against the offender
   (b) ensure that someone is caught for the offence
   (c) promote fairness and set standards of conduct
   (d) point out the mistake that has been made
   (e) provide fair methods of punishing the offender.

2 According to Pigors and Myers, a grievance is:
   (a) anything that disturbs an employee
   (b) anything that disturbs an employee and is discussed with the manager
   (c) a spoken dissatisfaction brought to the attention of the manager
   (d) a complaint that has been formally presented to a management representative or shop steward
   (e) anything that disturbs an employee and is expressed in words.

3 Which of the following are listed as essential features of a disciplinary procedure in the ACAS Code of Practice?
  (a) Be in writing, provide for fair punishment, specify to whom the rules should apply.
  (b) Be in writing, specify to whom the rules should apply, ensure that (except for cases of gross misconduct) no one is dismissed for a first disciplinary offence.
  (c) Provide for the matter to be dealt with quickly, provide for witnesses to give evidence, ensure that (except for cases of gross culpability), no one is dismissed for a first disciplinary offence.
  (d) Be in writing, provide for a fair system of punishment, specify all the offences that constitute gross misconduct.
  (e) Provide for the matter to be dealt with quickly, specify all the offences that constitute gross misconduct, ensure that except for gross misconduct, no one is dismissed for a first offence.

4 The Employment Act 2002 states which of the following:
  (a) That only employees have the right to be accompanied at disciplinary hearings.
  (b) That only employees have the right to be accompanied at grievance hearings.
  (c) That workers have the right to be accompanied, in certain circumstances, at formal disciplinary or formal grievance hearings.
  (d) That workers have the right to be accompanied, in certain circumstances, at informal discussions or counselling relating to discipline.
  (e) That workers have the right to be accompanied, in certain circumstances, at informal discussions relating to grievances they raise.

5 Once the time limit for a written warning has elapsed:
  (a) the warning should still be kept on the employee's personal record file
  (b) the warning should be removed from the employee's personal record file and placed in a central file in which records of all disciplinary offences are kept
  (c) the warning should be removed from the employee's personal record file only if the data are stored on computer
  (d) the warning should be removed completely from the employee's personal record file
  (e) the warning should be removed from the employee's personal record file after a further three months has elapsed.

6 According to ACAS, if a serious criminal offence occurs outside employment:
  (a) this is automatically considered to be gross misconduct and dismissal is justifiable
  (b) this is automatically considered to be gross misconduct and dismissal may be justifiable
  (c) this should not be treated as an automatic reason for dismissal – the main consideration should be whether or not the offence makes the employee unsuitable for his or her type of work
  (d) this should not be treated as an automatic reason for dismissal – the main consideration is whether you think that the employee is likely to commit the offence again
  (e) this should not be treated as automatic reason for dismissal – the main consideration should be the length of service the employee has had with your organisation.

7 The recommended first stage in a grievance procedure is:
(a) to raise the grievance with the top management immediately
(b) to grumble to your colleagues about your grievance
(c) to raise the grievance with your supervisor's manager
(d) to raise the grievance with the area manager
(e) to raise the grievance with your immediate supervisor.

8 The first Code of Practice about discipline at work was published by ACAS in:
(a) 1925
(b) 1944
(c) 1977
(d) 1987
(e) 2000.

9 Nowadays the role of human resource managers in handling discipline and grievance situations is:
(a) always purely advisory
(b) non-existent, as line managers deal with these topics
(c) purely to check on line managers and ensure they handle things correctly
(d) only to design the procedures themselves
(e) a mixture of things, including advice and guidance.

10 The initials ACAS stand for:
(a) Advisory, Counselling and Aid Service
(b) Aid, Counselling and Arbitration Service
(c) Aid, Conciliation and Arbitration Service
(d) Advice, Conciliation and Arbitration Service
(e) Advisory, Conciliation and Arbitration Service.

WHAT NEXT?

Find some good examples of disciplinary and grievance letters and forms by going to the ACAS web site:

www.acas.org.uk/emp_forms.html

Still on the ACAS web site, test your knowledge and understanding of discipline and grievance issues by taking its on-line course. This is designed for managers but if you have studied this chapter and answered the questions as you have gone through it you should have a good basis for developing your knowledge and understanding further by using these on-line materials:

www.acas.org.uk/elearning

References

Advisory, Conciliation and Arbitration Service (2002) *Producing Disciplinary and Grievance Procedures: Self-Help Guide*, ACAS

Advisory, Conciliation and Arbitration Service (2004) *Draft Code of Practice on Disciplinary and Grievance Procedures*, ACAS, June

Cully, M., S. Woodland, A. O'Reilly and G. Dix (1999) *Britain at Work as Depicted by the 1998 Workplace Employee Relations Survey*, Routledge

Labour Research Department (1995) *Bargaining. Report 149*, Labour Research Department, April

Pigors, P. and C. S. Myers (1977) *Personnel Administration*, 8th edition, McGraw-Hill

Further study

Advisory, Conciliation and Arbitration Service (2002) *Draft Code of Practice on Disciplinary and Grievance Procedures*, ACAS, June. (This provides extremely useful guidance for anyone involved in discipline or grievance cases at work.)

Advisory, Conciliation and Arbitration Service (2002) *Producing Disciplinary and Grievance Procedures: Self-Help Guide*, ACAS. (Clear practical guidance is provided to help in designing both discipline and grievance procedures.)

Fowler, A. (1968) *The Disciplinary Interview*, CIPD. (A small book with excellent clear advice about the ways in which to conduct disciplinary interviews.)

Jackson, T. (2000) *Handling Grievances*, CIPD. (An excellent little book which provides up-to-date information about everything relating to grievances including what they are, the legislation and how to handle grievances.)

James, P. and D. Lewis (1992) *Discipline*, IPM. (A specialist book written purely about discipline. It is clearly written and gives a great deal of information, especially about the legal issues relating to disciplinary procedures.)

Redman, T. and A. Wilkinson (eds) (2001) *Contemporary Human Resource Management*, Financial Times/Prentice Hall. Chapter 6 'Grievance and discipline handling', by D. Renwick and J. Gennard. (This chapter provides an up-to-date review of research in this area.)

Youngman, N. (1996) *Disciplinary Procedures, a Practical Guide*, Technical Communications (Publishing) Limited. (This book, which forms part of The Busy Manager series of Best Practice Management Reports, provides clear guidance on all aspects of disciplinary procedures except the recent changes in legislation about workers' right to be accompanied at disciplinary and grievance hearings. In spite of this it is still a very useful book, particularly since it has lots of examples of procedures and letters.)

Articles

Fowler, A. (1990) How to handle disciplinary interviews, *Personnel Management Plus*, November, 20–21. (A short article which gives clear information about disciplinary interviews.)

Fowler, A. (1994) How to handle employee grievances, *Personnel Management Plus*, October, 24–25. (Another excellent short article in the 'How to' series.)

Hook, C., D. Rollinson, M. Foot and J. Handley (1996) Supervisor and manager styles in handling discipline and grievance. Part one – comparing styles in handling discipline and grievance, *Personnel Review*, Vol. 25, No. 3. (An article about the ways managers deal with discipline and grievances.)

Rollinson, D., C. Hook, M. Foot and J. Handley (1996) Supervisor and manager styles in handling discipline and grievance. Part two – approaches to handling discipline and grievance, *Personnel Review*, Vol. 25, No. 4. (An article which provides more detail on some of the research findings mentioned in the previous article.)

Stevens, P. and E. FitzGibbons (2001) How to tackle long term sick leave, *People Management*, Vol. 7, No. 14, 12 July, 42–43. (A short article outlining practical issues relating to discipline and dismissal involving long-term absence due to ill-health.)

Internet

The Advisory, Conciliation and Arbitration Service   **www.acas.org.uk**
(Another source of information for ACAS publications, some of which are published in full on this site.)

The Department of Trade and Industry   **www.dti.gov.uk**
(Many useful DTI publications, discussion documents and some pieces of legislation can be found on this site.)

The TUC   **www.tuc.org.uk**
(This gives the TUC's views on many current issues and new legislation.)

Dismissal, redundancy and outplacement

OBJECTIVES

By the end of this chapter you will be able to:

● explain what is meant by the term 'fair dismissal'

● explain what is meant by 'redundancy'

● define the term 'outplacement'

● describe the services that an outplacement consultancy may provide.

In Chapter 14 we explained that there may be occasions when not everything in the relationship between employer and worker goes smoothly: the employee or worker may be dissatisfied with the employer and raise a grievance, or the employer may have to use a disciplinary procedure against an individual who is proving to be unsatisfactory. Human resource managers want to get the best from the people they employ: people are, as we have shown, very expensive to recruit and train, and HRM specialists will not wish to waste these resources. However, there will be occasions when it becomes inevitable that the organisation will have to end the employment of one or more employees, and line managers as well as human resource specialists will need to know something about this process.

This chapter will examine ways in which employment may be ended fairly. We shall then consider one particular type of dismissal – redundancy – and examine ways in which the effects of redundancy may be lessened by the provision of an outplacement service.

The chapter presents general guidance only, and is intended to provide not a complete or authoritative guide to employment law, but rather an appreciation of general principles with which students of HRM should be familiar and which they may use to guide them in dealing with people who are dismissed from an organisation.

It is important for a number of reasons that any dismissal should be fair. The workforce will be better able to trust and work effectively for a management that operates fair procedures and the reputation of the organisation in general will also benefit from this.

Fairness is both a moral and a legal issue, and sometimes organisations that have tried very hard to be fair in their procedures and practices will still be found in the eyes of the law to have acted unfairly. This may be because individual managers or supervisors have made errors in the way they handled an issue, or failed to document their actions adequately, or because of some legal technicality. HRM practitioners, therefore, need to be aware of the importance of legislation and must endeavour to have systems, procedures and training in place so that everyone involved in the dismissal process acts in a fair way. They also need to know where to find detailed guidance, as they cannot know in minute detail every aspect of the law: there are many specialist texts that can help with this. Although the HRM practitioner needs to be sufficiently aware of legislation and the need for fair procedures to be able to deal with issues that arise on a day-to-day basis, it may be that, faced with an unusual problem, he or she will also need the advice of the organisation's solicitor.

Legislation changes constantly, which means that you should be aware of general principles with regard to dismissal but you should always be prepared to check for the most recent legislation and the most recent interpretation of it, and not just rely on notes that you made years earlier. Textbooks become out of date, and you should always look for the most recent edition to guide you, although even this may not be enough to take account of the latest changes in law. We have listed some useful sources of information at the end of the chapter.

People leave organisations for a host of reasons, and of course not all who leave are dismissed. Resignations and retirements do not normally cause any legal problems to the organisation, but employers need to take great care in the case of dismissals that they abide by the law, and ensure not only that they dismiss for a potentially fair reason, but that the way they handle the dismissal and the whole dismissal process is also fair. As we said in Chapter 14, this means that employers who are dismissing someone must also take into account the statutory discipline and grievance procedures that were introduced by the Employment Act 2002.

Organisations, in particular, which employ people abroad, need also to ensure that they are fully aware of the legislation which applies within the countries in which they operate.

Dismissal

Usually both employers and employees understand when a dismissal has occurred as it results in a person's employment being ended. That person may have to work their notice period or the employer may prefer to pay them for this time, but terminate their employment immediately. This is often referred to as payment in lieu of notice. In circumstances where the dismissal has occurred because of the employee's gross misconduct, the employee is not entitled to any notice or payment in lieu of notice. There are, however, other circumstances in which dismissal may occur which may be less well known, such as the non-renewal of a fixed-term contract or constructive dismissal. We shall consider each of these in turn.

Fixed-term contract

This sounds straightforward enough, and occurs when there is a fixed-term contract for a particular period of employment. If the contract is not renewed, this technically counts as a dismissal although it is normally expected by both the employer and the employee. Sometimes in the past, organisations insisted that individuals whom they employed on fixed-term contracts gave up their rights to claim unfair dismissal by making them sign a waiver clause at the start of their employment. Waiver clauses in fixed-term contracts were abolished under the Employment Relations Act 1999 from 25 October 1999 so an individual can no longer be made to sign away their right to claim for unfair dismissal.

Constructive dismissal

The second definition given here is a little more complicated, and is known as constructive dismissal. It is often hard to prove that the dismissal was unfair, as the person has normally resigned and given some other reason for leaving. It is later, when he or she realises that the resignation was because of the employer's conduct, that he or she might decide to bring a case of constructive dismissal. For a case to succeed, the employer normally has to have done something so seriously wrong that the employee was justified in feeling that he or she could no longer work in that workplace, as the employer's action would be regarded as a significant breach of the employment contract. A possible example is an employer who bullied the employee so that his or her life was a total misery and the person felt obliged to leave.

Pause for thought 15.1 We said earlier that dismissal should be for a potentially fair reason and that a fair dismissal procedure should also be followed. What do you consider to be potentially fair reasons for dismissal?

Potentially fair reasons for dismissal

You have probably listed offences such as theft, poor attendance, assault, fraud, being under the influence of drugs or alcohol, sexual harassment or racial harassment, or perhaps a serious breach of a safety rule. If you refer back to Chapter 14, you will see that these are all examples of misconduct or of gross misconduct, although poor attendance, if it is due to ill-health, may be an example of lack of capability. There are three other potentially valid reasons for dismissal besides misconduct and lack of capability, and each of these covers a wide range of situations. For a dismissal to be fair, an employer must first be able to prove it was for one of these five reasons:

- conduct
- capability
- a statutory requirement
- some other substantial reason
- redundancy.

The need to act reasonably

Do you think that if an employee is guilty, for example, of misconduct or proves incapable of doing the job, this means that if the employer dismisses him or her it will automatically be fair? In Chapter 14 we said that it was important for an organisation to have a fair disciplinary procedure modelled on the ACAS Code of Practice. It is important, if an organisation is considering dismissing someone, that it not only has potentially fair grounds for dismissing them (i.e. it is dismissing them for one of the reasons listed earlier), but it also acts fairly in the way that it carries out this dismissal. The organisation needs to have a fair procedure for handling dismissals and should have followed its own procedure in a fair way. This also means, as we have already said, that the employer must have complied with the statutory discipline and dismissal procedures. This is what we mean by the condition that the dismissal also has to be actually fair. An employer should strive to be fair but may still face a claim for unfair dismissal, as dismissed employees may have a different perception of whether their treatment was fair.

Employment tribunals examine dismissal cases from two points of view. One is whether employers have acted reasonably in treating the grounds as sufficient reason to justify dismissal. The other is that they must satisfy the tribunal that they acted reasonably in the dismissal procedure. If an employee brings a claim for unfair dismissal, the tribunal will have to make a judgement about what happened after considering evidence from both parties; consequently it is important for employers to follow their own procedure and have clear records and documentary evidence.

ACTIVITY 15.1

Susan has been employed by your organisation for three years as a clerical assistant. During the past year there have been many problems with poor attendance and timekeeping. Susan's manager has tried to establish whether there is a problem underlying this poor attendance and timekeeping, but has found no clear explanation. Susan has been counselled about this situation and has gone through the disciplinary procedure, and she has been issued in the presence of her trade union representative with a written warning and a final written warning. The organisation has done everything required under the statutory discipline and dismissal procedures. The final written warning was issued only three weeks ago, and yet since then Susan has already had one day absent from work and has been late twice. She has not provided any good explanation for this, but simply says that she overslept and then did not feel like coming to work.

Do you think that the employer has potentially fair reasons for dismissing Susan? Give reasons for your answer. Which category of dismissal would this fall into?

If the employer does decide to dismiss Susan, do you think that it is being fair in the way that it is handling this dismissal?

Discussion of Activity 15.1

From the evidence given, this case looks to be a potentially fair dismissal on the grounds of misconduct, as Susan does appear to have behaved badly and the employer does appear to have a valid reason for dismissal. In this case, the management appear to have a disciplinary procedure which they followed and seem, from the evidence given here, to have acted reasonably and fairly. A case such as this would probably not go to an employment tribunal, but there may be other circumstances not given here that might lead Susan to feel her dismissal was unfair and to pursue a tribunal case.

Conduct

Conduct is the most common reason for dismissal and results in the most claims of unfair dismissal at employment tribunals. Both serious acts of misconduct, such as gross misconduct, and more minor but frequently repeated acts of misconduct result in dismissals that fall into this category. In Activity 15.1 Susan's dismissal was for a series of minor but repeated lapses in her conduct.

Capability

Lack of capability could arise for several reasons. We discussed the problems of absenteeism in the last chapter, and clearly not all absenteeism would fall into the category of misconduct as Susan's behaviour did. Many absentees are genuinely ill but the organisation, as we said in Chapter 14, may reluctantly, having exhausted all its procedures, have to consider whether or not to dismiss. This needs to be handled in a totally different way, but such a dismissal would be on the grounds of the person not being capable of doing the job.

Particular attention, however, should be paid to the requirements of the Disability Discrimination Act (1995) before making any decision to dismiss on ill-health grounds. If many of the absences are directly attributable to a disability the employer may have to discount these from their calculations when considering whether or not the employee's attendance record is satisfactory. This was the case in *Cox* v. *the Post Office* (IT/1301162/97) where it was decided that the Post Office should have discounted Cox's absences due to asthma, since this is classed as a disability, from the figures for his attendance which they had used to justify his dismissal.

It is also important to note that if the illness itself leads to a disability the employer should first try to establish whether reasonable adjustments could be made to enable them to keep their job, before considering dismissal. According to Gill Sage, an employment law specialist, 'No decision to terminate an employee's contract on the grounds of ill-health or to subject someone to any other detriment should now be taken solely on the basis of absence from the workplace' (Sage 1998, p. 24).

Some people may prove to be incapable of doing the job required because they lack the required level of skill or ability. This could be a reflection on the organisation's selection techniques or training, but if training and opportunities to improve have been given, it may be necessary to dismiss the person if he or she still proves to be incapable.

Lack of qualification is another potentially fair reason for dismissal. Although good selection procedures should mean that people who do not have the desired qualifications are not employed, there are many well-publicised examples of people who have lied about their qualifications and who have worked for an organisation for a number of years before being found out and dismissed. There have even been cases of doctors who have practised for many years without people realising that they did not have any medical qualification. In a case such as this there would be a potentially fair reason for dismissal.

A statutory requirement

This is a rarer reason for dismissal, which deals with the situation where the employer would be breaking the law if it continued to employ that person. Possible examples of this would be employing a person who did not have a work permit, or employing a person who was legally too young to work full time in that particular work environment, or possibly employing a driver who had lost his or her licence and was disqualified from driving.

Some other substantial reason

This category is to cover eventualities not listed already, where there is a genuinely fair reason for dismissal that does not fit neatly into any of the listed categories. One example of this is where the contract is only temporary and is not renewed. Legally the person has been dismissed. They have not been dismissed because of their misconduct or because of lack of capability or lack of qualification, or even because of some legal requirement, so this form of dismissal would fall into the category of some other substantial reason.

Redundancy

Many employers dislike discussing redundancies and invent other names for this type of dismissal. They refer to it as 'downsizing' or 'delayering', or even as being 'forced to let someone go'. It is certainly a very unpleasant form of dismissal for all concerned, as the person involved is not normally being dismissed because of anything that he or she has done wrong but as a result of the organisation's need to streamline its operations or cut back in some areas because of an unforeseen crisis, or perhaps through poor human resource planning. Many organisations are striving to be increasingly flexible in their deployment of people and often employ temporary or agency staff, with the result that redundancy affects more and more people in an increasingly wide range of jobs as these organisations move from traditional employment patterns to new ones.

Redundancy can occur because of three main circumstances:

- the whole business closes
- part of the business or a particular workplace closes
- there is less need for a particular type of work, which results in some employees being surplus to requirements.

We shall return to the topic of redundancy later in this chapter.

Who can bring a case for unfair dismissal

It is obviously important that all dismissals should be fair, but the law provides the opportunity for only some employees (those who have sufficient length of service), to bring a case claiming unfair dismissal before an employment tribunal. There are also other circumstances, which will be discussed later, in which dismissal will be automatically unfair, and where this qualification period does not apply. If you remember our discussion of equal opportunities issues in Chapter 3, you will recall that there was no mention of a qualification period for cases of sex discrimination, racial discrimination or discrimination on grounds of disability. This is because many cases of discrimination occur before people are actually employed at all. However, for most cases of unfair dismissal to be brought before a tribunal, employees do have to have been employed for a certain length of time, although the actual length of employment required has varied over the years. This means that some unscrupulous employers may be tempted to treat people who do not have sufficient length of service with them in an unfair way, as they know that a case for unfair dismissal cannot be brought against them. Clearly this is not good practice and employers should treat all workers in a fair way.

Since 1 June 1999, one year of service is required to bring a claim for unfair dismissal to an employment tribunal. For some forms of dismissals there is no service requirement at all. Dismissals which are called automatically unfair will be discussed later.

Did you know?

In 2003 there were 102,559 applications to employment tribunals compared with 94,453 in the previous years; 76,919 were settled or withdrawn compared with 72,728 in 2002. Unfair dismissal is always the largest category of complaint to the employment tribunals and accounts for more than a third of all cases.
(ACAS 2004)

ACAS tries to get both parties to reach a settlement about the claim. This is a free service that it provides to try and resolve differences. It will usually arrange meetings with each side separately and use conciliation to try to get a settlement before the case goes to a tribunal. Complete Activity 15.2 on page 464 and decide for yourself whether you feel it has been successful in this or not.

How to bring a case for unfair dismissal

Any employee with the required one year of service who feels that they were dismissed unfairly can complete an application for the case to be decided by an employment tribunal. Forms are easy to obtain and available from Job Centres, Law Centres or Citizens Advice Bureaux, or the process can be started by applying on-line at **www.employmenttribunals.gov.uk**. The tribunal system was overhauled in October 2004 and one result of this is that a new user-friendly application form (ET1) will be used from April 2005. Once the claimant has completed their application it should be sent to the relevant employment tribunal office or it can now be completed on-line.

For acceptance of unfair dismissal cases, and most other types of case, the time limit is usually three months from the date the employment ended. Employment tribunals do not usually accept cases outside the relevant time limit, but this does depend on the reason for the delay and in some exceptional circumstances late cases may still be considered. Tribunals will not consider claims unless they are assured that the organisation's grievance procedure has been exhausted.

The application form is allocated a case number by the tribunal office and a copy is sent to the respondent within five days of the tribunal receiving the application. (The respondent is the person the case is brought against. In most cases it will be the employer.) The respondent will be sent a response form (ET3) which they are asked to complete indicating whether they agree with or are resisting the claim against them. They must complete this form within 28 days in order to be allowed to answer the claim against them. Usually copies of both forms are also sent to ACAS, the Advisory, Conciliation and Arbitration Service.

ACAS has been using conciliation for several years but the concept of a conciliation period was changed in October 2004 to encourage employees and employers to try to reach a settlement at an earlier stage. Conciliation by ACAS will now normally be concentrated into a short, fixed period of between 7 and 13 weeks, depending on the nature of the claim, and once this time has ended ACAS is no longer able to be involved. In its role as conciliator, ACAS may repeat information provided by one side to the other side to try and bring about a settlement, but this information is not normally repeated at the tribunal itself, unless all parties give their permission.

In most cases the tribunal does not know about any of the correspondence between the parties and ACAS, so the tribunal will review the case on the evidence presented to it in writing and by witnesses at the tribunal hearing.

Since 2001 there has been an alternative way to resolve unfair dismissal disputes. This is the ACAS arbitration service which operates as a voluntary alternative to employment tribunal hearings. People who choose this option have to agree to accept the decision of the arbitrator, who is able to make exactly the same awards as an employment tribunal. The aims of this scheme are to cut the number of expensive tribunal cases and to create a quicker and simpler system that is free of much legal jargon. However, this has not proved to be a very popular alternative to employment tribunals and only seven cases were made to this scheme during 2003–04.

The tribunal itself normally comprises three people: the chair, who has to be legally qualified and have worked as either a solicitor or a barrister for at least seven years, and two wing members. One of the wing members will be chosen from a list of names submitted by employers' organisations and the other will be chosen from a similar list submitted by workers' organisations. All are there because of their knowledge and experience, in their different ways, of employment issues and work-related problems and their aim is to ensure a fair hearing for all concerned. They will probably ask questions to clarify any points they are unsure of during the course of the tribunal hearing.

ACTIVITY 15.2

Find out how many cases of alleged unfair dismissal have been brought during the last year.

a How many of these cases have been heard at employment tribunals?

b How many of these cases have been taken to ACAS voluntary arbitration?

c What was the success rates in each category?

Automatically fair reasons for dismissal

There are a very small number of situations in which dismissal is likely to be viewed as automatically fair. These include situations where the reason or main reason for the dismissal involved the employee:

- in problems of national security
- taking part in an unofficial strike or some other type of unofficial action (this does not apply in all circumstances)
- taking part in an official strike or some other form of official action and where all the relevant employees who participated in the same action were also dismissed and not re-employed during the next three months.

National security is obviously a serious concern, so someone who endangered national security, perhaps by selling secrets, would obviously come into this category. Taking part in unofficial strikes and even official strikes can also be a very risky undertaking for the employee, even though these actions do not seem to be in quite the same category as endangering national security.

Automatically unfair reasons for dismissal

Some reasons for dismissal are likely to be automatically unfair, and in these cases an employment tribunal does not need to go through the process of establishing whether there was a fair reason for the dismissal before it assesses whether or not the employer acted reasonably. These include dismissal related to discrimination on grounds of sex, race, disability or a spent conviction, as these areas are covered by the Sex Discrimination Act 1975, the Race Relations Act 1976, the Disability Discrimination Act 1995 or the Rehabilitation of Offenders Act 1974, and in all of these there is no requirement for a length of service qualification for bringing a claim before an employment tribunal. Similarly, it is also automatically unfair to use any of these as the basis for selection for redundancy.

Some examples of automatically unfair dismissal are given next but this is not an exhaustive list:

- trade union-related dismissals
- dismissal on maternity- or pregnancy-related grounds
- dismissal for taking, or proposing to take, some action on health and safety grounds
- dismissal for having sought in good faith to exercise a statutory employment right
- dismissal of a shop worker or betting shop worker for refusing, or proposing to refuse, to do shop work on Sundays
- acting as a representative for consultation about redundancy or business transfer or presenting oneself as a candidate to be this type of representative performing or proposing to perform duties in connection with an employee's role as an employee occupational pension trustee
- dismissal of the employee because they try to make the employer pay them the minimum wage
- a statutory discipline and dismissal procedure has not been completed by the employer and this is due to the fault of the employer.

In cases where there are automatically unfair reasons for dismissal, the employment tribunal does not have to go through the two-stage process, firstly establishing that there was a fair reason for the dismissal, then investigating whether the employer acted reasonably. In these cases the employment tribunal has to find the dismissal fair or unfair solely with regard to the reasonableness of the actions of the employer and the reason for the dismissal.

Trade union-related dismissals

It is an automatically unfair reason for dismissal if the dismissal is for trade union membership or activities. This will apply whether the employee is dismissed because of expressing his or her intention to join a trade union or not to join a trade union, or for his or her actual membership or non-membership of a trade union. It also applies if someone is dismissed just because of their trade union activities, such as handing out leaflets or going to a trade union meeting.

Dismissal on maternity- or pregnancy-related grounds

The law relating to pregnancy is complex but it obviously does not make very good business sense to dismiss someone in whom an organisation has invested time and training, just because she is pregnant. This is another automatically unfair reason for dismissal. An unfair dismissal of this type could also prove to be potentially very expensive for an employer as many claims of this type are also brought under sex discrimination legislation and there is no upper limit set on the amount of compensation that the woman could claim.

Dismissal on health and safety grounds

Once again the dismissal will be automatically unfair if the employer dismisses the employee or selects him or her for redundancy because he or she tried to bring health and safety issues to the attention of the employer. It would also be an automatically unfair dismissal if it was because the employee carried out or even just tried to carry out designated duties relating to health and safety or prevention of accidents at work, or because of his or her activities as a safety representative or on a safety committee.

Dismissal for wishing to exercise a statutory right

The dismissal will be automatically unfair if it occurs as a result of the employee bringing proceedings against the employer or alleging that an employer has infringed a statutory employment right such as a right to a minimum period of notice or the right of a trade union official for paid time off to carry out duties.

Dismissal of a shop worker for refusing to work on Sundays

Shop workers or betting office workers who are dismissed for refusal to work on a Sunday are also able to claim this as an automatically unfair reason for dismissal. When Sunday trading was introduced, some workers feared that they would be dismissed if they were unwilling to work on a Sunday so this is designed to afford them some protection.

Dismissal of a person because of his or her actions as a representative of the workforce for consultation about redundancy or business transfer

Another automatically unfair reason for dismissal occurs if the employer dismisses a person who was acting on behalf of the workforce, or who is proposing to act as their representative in connection with negotiations about redundancy or business transfer. This is to prevent unscrupulous employers from effectively 'shooting the messenger' by dismissing unfairly those who try to help or act on behalf of the employees.

Dismissal of a person because he or she is carrying out their role on an occupational pension scheme

It is also automatically unfair to dismiss employees because, in their role as an occupational pension trustee, they may have to perform certain duties such as to question their employer about payments, accounts or actions that have taken place. Once again, in the light of various alleged occupational pension scandals, such as the Maxwell case, which have occurred in recent years, one can see that it is necessary to afford protection to employees who may have to challenge unscrupulous employers with regard to occupational pensions.

Dismissal of the employee because they try to make the employer to pay the minimum wage

In this instance the employee may have been trying to ensure that the employer pays the minimum wage to him or herself or to other employees. If they have not been paid the minimum wage it is against the law, and if the employee who raises this issue is dismissed because they have raised it, then it will be an automatic dismissal.

A statutory discipline and dismissal procedure has not been completed by the employer and this is due to the fault of the employer

Introduced in October 2004, this is a new addition to the list of automatically unfair dismissals and reinforces the fact that the government wants employers to take seriously the need to complete disciplinary procedures and dismissals in a fair way and to comply with the statutory procedure.

Wrongful dismissal

Wrongful dismissal is based on contract law and relates to instances when the employer has broken the contract. One of the most common examples of breach of contract is when the employee is dismissed without notice in circumstances where this is clearly not deserved because of any wrong-doing on the part of the employee, or where the employee is dismissed but with the incorrect period of notice. Unlike claims of unfair dismissal, there is no qualifying length of service required for eligibility to bring a case of wrongful dismissal.

Compensation for unfair dismissal

If a former employee wins his or her case for unfair dismissal at an employment tribunal the compensation awarded may take several forms.

Reinstatement

In this case the employment tribunal or ACAS arbitrator says that the employer must give the former employee their old job back on exactly the same terms and conditions as before and pay compensation for any loss of wages while not employed. Failure on the part of the employer to comply with this order is likely to result in additional financial awards, known as an Additional or Special Award, being made to the employee.

Re-engagement

This means that the employment tribunal or ACAS arbitrator states that the employer must re-employ their former employee but it may be in a different job or on different terms and conditions of employment. For example, it may not be possible to give them back their old job as the vacancy may already have been filled by a new employee.

Compensation

This means financial compensation and is divided into the basic award and the compensatory award. The basic award is calculated in the same way as the statutory redundancy payment which is discussed later in this chapter. It is calculated by taking into account the age, number of years in that employer's service and amount of the average weekly wage. At February 2004 the weekly wage included in the calculation is subject to a weekly maximum of £270 per week. The DTI publishes an easy table for calculating these figures but amounts do change each year.

In some circumstances there may be deductions taken from the amount awarded by the employment tribunal — for example, if the employment tribunal feels that the employee partially contributed to his or her own dismissal or if the employer offered to reinstate the employee and he or she refused unreasonably.

A compensatory award may also be made and this is to take account of factors such as loss of earnings, loss of pension rights or loss of benefits, such as company car or house. There are unlimited awards made, as mentioned earlier, in cases of dismissal related to sex, race or disability discrimination. An additional award may also be made if the dismissal was for trade unionism.

Redundancy

We discussed earlier the fact that redundancy can be a potentially fair reason for dismissal. However, great care must be taken in the selection of those who are to be made redundant, and a large number of employment tribunal cases are brought each year where employees feel that they have been unfairly selected for redundancy.

Steps to preclude the need for redundancies

Any organisation should choose first to take various steps to try to preclude or minimise the need for redundancies. Good human resource planning should help to minimise this need, but however effective the human resource planning, there may still be a need for redundancies because of other problems, such as the unexpected loss of a large order or the failure of the business of a large debtor.

Consultation

Consultation is a very important stage in redundancies, both for legal reasons and in order to maintain morale. Morale is always likely to be low when there is a threat of redundancy, but rumour and uncertainty are only likely to make it worse. The law on redundancy in Britain is mainly derived from the Trade Union and Labour Relations (Consolidation) Act 1992, the Collective Redundancies and Transfer of Undertakings (Protection of Employment) Regulations 1995 and the Collective Redundancies and Transfer of Undertakings (Protection of Employment) (Amendment) Regulations 1999. This means that:

- If 20 or more employees at one establishment are to be made redundant, within a period of 90 days, consultation should start at least 30 days before the first dismissal.

- If 100 or more employees at one establishment are to be made redundant, within a period of 90 days, this consultation should start at least 90 days before the first dismissal is to occur.

In practice, in Britain, consultation frequently occurs at the same time as the notification of redundancies so that the redundant employees are often already working their notice when the consultation is supposed to be taking place. This has the effect of making it rather more difficult to achieve much by consultation in terms of avoiding dismissals or reducing the numbers since those to be made redundant have already been selected.

Groups to be consulted in collective redundancies

The following rules apply to those who should be consulted in collective redundancy situations. In this instance the definition of redundancy is slightly different to the one we used earlier for redundancy pay. Here it relates to a situation where an employer proposes to dismiss at least 20 employees at one establishment within a 90-day period. The dismissal is unrelated to the quality of work of the individual concerned as it could be due to the need for fewer employees to do a particular task or because of reorganisation or reallocation of work:

- Under the 1999 regulations, if there is a recognised independent trade union within the organisation, then the consultation must be with them.
- If there is no trade union recognition agreement in place then the employer has a choice and may consult either with a trade union or with employee representatives.
- Representatives of all employees affected should be consulted and not just those who are likely to be made redundant.
- Any organisation that has been obliged to collectively consult must also notify the Department of Trade and Industry.
- If those employees who are likely to be affected by the redundancies are not in a trade union, and there are no other suitable representatives for employees already in place in the organisation, then the employees must be given the opportunity to elect representatives. The employer should make arrangements to ensure the fairness of these elections and must also comply with the election rules set out by the Department of Trade and Industry.
- If the employees fail to elect representatives after being given opportunities to do so, then the employer will have to give the information direct to all relevant employees in order to fulfil its legal obligation to consult.

The information needed for consultation

The employee representatives will need sufficient information from the employer about its proposals to be able to fully participate in a meaningful way in the consultations. Certain information must be given to them in writing. This must be handed individually to each of them, sent by post to an address they have given the employer or, in the case of consultation with a trade union, sent to its head office.

The employer must provide the following information:

- the reasons for the proposed redundancies
- the numbers and types of jobs that are likely to be affected by the proposals
- the anticipated total number of employees who are likely to be affected in each job at the organisation
- the proposed selection methods for those to be made redundant
- the proposed method of actually dismissing people and the anticipated period over which dismissals will take place
- the proposed methods of calculating redundancy pay.

The penalties for inadequate consultation in Britain and in other European countries

The penalties for not consulting adequately may result in a fine for not notifying the DTI. The trade union representatives, employees' representatives or the employees themselves can apply to an employment tribunal which can make a protective award of up to 13 weeks' pay for each employee. Employers can, in their defence, claim that there were special circumstances which made it impossible to comply with the legislation and in many cases the consultation seems to amount to announcing the redundancies. The 1995 and 1999 regulations are the UK's response to a European ruling in 1994 from the European Court of Justice. However, the Government was not willing to sign up to a European Directive for Information and Consultation Rights. In spite of the fact that the British Government refused to sign this Directive, which would have given greater rights to consultation for the British worker, it still claimed to be furious about the lack of consultation from Corus, the giant steel producer, when the company announced redundancies in 2000.

The rules regarding redundancy in the other European countries do not appear at first sight to be very different to those of the UK, but the duty to consult starts sooner in France, Germany and Spain and usually applies when smaller numbers of employees are involved. Also, the duty to consult cannot be undertaken retrospectively in those countries, so the consultation has to occur before those selected for redundancy are told of the decision. It is often claimed that the laxer laws relating to redundancy in the UK make us the easiest European country in which to make staff redundant.

In spite of the British Government's initial refusal to sign these documents, it did eventually agree and the possible implications of the Information and Consultation Directive 2002 will be discussed later in this chapter.

Marks & Spencer found, to its cost, that expectations of the way redundancy should be handled are different in the rest of Europe, when in March 2001 it announced it was closing all its stores abroad. It probably felt it had consulted sufficiently, and possibly this would be true if British standards applied. However, it was undoubtedly surprised by the way its staff in France reacted with instant walk-outs in protest, TV and radio interviews with tearful staff and pictures in newspapers in France and Britain which depicted window displays in their Nice store in which a coffin appeared draped in black with mannequins dressed in mourning and bound in chains. Support from the Prime Minister, Lionel Jospin, followed and the Government in France supported the trade unions in court action against Marks & Spencer relating to lack of consultation, and Marks & Spencer was effectively stopped from making the redundancies, at least for a time.

In France, employers are obliged by law to establish a workers' council and the council must be consulted throughout any redundancy process with a view to finding suitable alternatives to the redundancies, rather than, as so often happens in Britain, the consultation process starting as the employees are given their notice. Moreover, in France, each individual employee must be spoken to personally before any public announcements are made and plans for training individuals should also be established. Decisions on redundancies should not be sent by fax or e-mail, as was alleged to have happened to Marks & Spencer's French employees. Trade unions, in France, can apply to the courts to stop redundancies from occurring, as happened in this case. John Monks, TUC General Secretary, said of the Marks & Spencer case, 'This welcome decision underlines the better protection available to workers across the Channel – French workers have shown they will not put up with such high-handed behaviour.'

> It may be the fashion in Britain to announce job losses to the media whenever a company needs a short term boost to its share price. But as this decision shows, in France employers need to act responsibly, taking into account the needs of their workforce as well as their shareholders. This shows why people at work in the UK need European proposals for wider information and consultation rights to become law as soon as possible.
>
> (Monks 2001)

As well as an order by the courts to prevent redundancies from taking place, there are also other penalties available in France for non-compliance with the law. This could, in theory at least, be prison for the directors of a company, although in reality this has never occurred. There is also a requirement in France, Germany and Spain for a social compensation plan and according to the European Industrial Relations Observatory (EIRO)(2001) this is common in most other European countries as a way of promoting redeployment and negotiating termination of employment through early retirement, redeployment and voluntary redundancy. According to the EIRO, 'The tangible outcome of redundancy negotiation tends to be:

- a reduction in the planned number of redundancies, the withdrawal of announced redundancies or the provision of employment guarantees
- the guaranteed safeguarding of wage and working conditions by the new employer
- a commitment to avoid compulsory redundancies.' (European Industrial Relations Observatory on-line February 2001)

A few days after the general election in 2001, the UK Government was in effect forced to drop its opposition to the Directive on Information and Consultation. Germany and Ireland had previously formed a minority with the UK in blocking this initiative but when Germany and Ireland withdrew their opposition to the Directive on 11 June, the UK Government had to agree to implement the Directive. Earlier in 2001, the Department of Trade and Industry had also stated that it would review the law on redundancy as a result primarily of the criticism levelled at some of the high profile firms such as Corus, which had failed to consult adequately when making staff redundant.

The actual form that the information and consultation legislation will take will depend on the government. Likely elements include:

- the right for employee representatives to be consulted on major developments in the business
- information to be given much earlier than at present to employee representatives so that they can make adequate preparations for a meaningful consultation
- if there is a danger that the information or consultation could result in harm to the organisation then there is likely to be a get-out clause to prevent the employer having to give this information.

The EU Information and Consultation Directive 2002 is also likely to have an effect on redundancy consultation. The Directive establishes, as we said in Chapter 13, a very general framework for information and consultation and applies to organisations with more than 50 employees. It will be implemented in stages and will apply to all organisations with more than 150 employees from 23 March 2005. Organisations that have over 100 staff will be affected from 23 March 2007 and small businesses with less than 50 employees will not be affected by this legislation until 23 March 2008.

Many EU states, as we showed earlier in relation to redundancy, already have legislation in place regarding information and consultation so this is likely to have the greatest effect on the UK and Eire, since they do not.

From the appropriate times, according to the size of the organisation concerned, it will be necessary for organisations to negotiate voluntary agreements about consultation and information with workers and whatever is agreed will need to be put in writing. The types of issue to be addressed should include information about the probable activities of the organisation and its financial situation, the employment situation within the organisation, especially where there is any likely threat to employment, such as in a redundancy situation. However, there should be information and consultation about any potential changes to the work situation, even if these do not go as far as actual redundancies.

ACTIVITY 15.3

This was the situation as we wrote this chapter. The requirement to consult will be brought into effect gradually and will apply to larger organisations first. Check what types and sizes of organisation the legislation relating to information and consultation actually applies to at the moment.

Steps to preclude the need for redundancies

While good employers should always be looking to the future and planning their manpower needs to suit their strategic objectives, there can also be changing economic situations caused by situations such as global events that are outside the employer's control and not easy to predict. Employers do need to be flexible and so have to develop a range of strategies to avoid or limit redundancies.

Even before the Information and Consultation Directive 2002 came into effect, organisations in the UK were supposed to consult in order to prevent or minimise the need for redundancies. It is foolish to contemplate making good employees redundant if a simpler solution is feasible, so a calm, objective review of the situation is called for and a consideration of all possible alternatives. The consultation must be undertaken with a view to reaching agreement with the appropriate representatives and should include the following:

- the actual numbers and job categories likely to be affected
- the reasons for the redundancies
- the criteria for selection
- the dismissal procedures and timescales during which the redundancies will occur
- the basis for the calculation of compensation if it is different from the statutory minimum.

According to the CIPD (2003b) 'case law indicates that discussion should include:

- why and how the individuals have been selected
- possible ways of avoiding redundancy
- possible alternative work'.

This sounds reasonable but, as stated earlier, there have been many occasions in the UK where consultation has only started after the redundancy period has been announced so although it is possible that dismissals may still be avoided, it seems less likely. Some bad employers also prefer to face the financial penalties rather than go through the process in the way in which it was intended.

The steps which can be taken to avoid redundancies will depend to some extent on the timescale available. Some employers are keen to look after their employees and to part company with them on as good terms as possible. Allowing for natural wastage is one possibility to consider, but for this to be effective one needs to be able to reduce the staff numbers over a period of time. Employers are supposed to consider alternatives to compulsory redundancy and ACAS suggests the following as ways of avoiding redundancies:

- natural wastage
- restrictions on recruitment
- retirement of employees who are already beyond the normal retirement age
- seek applications for early retirement or voluntary redundancy
- reductions in overtime
- short-time working
- retraining and redeployment to other jobs or parts of the organisation
- termination of the employment of temporary or contract workers.

According to the CIPD (2003b) 'other innovative practices within organisations have recently included:

- taking on no new graduate trainees or deferring their starting dates
- offering existing employees sabbaticals and secondments, or
- offering reduced-time working for full-time salary'.

The methods chosen will depend on the particular circumstances within the organisation. Natural wastage may work well if two organisations are combining and if there is sufficient time to allow for natural wastage to occur, but is unlikely to be the best solution if the organisation needs to reduce staff immediately. Most solutions also carry some costs to the organisation. Graduates who anticipated joining a specific organisation, only to find it is not taking on graduates in this particular area, are also likely to have some negative feelings about the organisation concerned.

Many organisations do already engage in meaningful negotiation with their employees and do take steps to minimise the needs for redundancies. Some go much further and provide outplacement services and these will be discussed later.

Selection for redundancy

If the consultations or measures chosen as a result of them fail to work, the employer needs to decide how to select and implement the redundancies. Ideally there should be an agreed procedure for handling redundancies but if not, then criteria which are fair need to be chosen and the pool of workers from among whom the redundancies are to occur also needs to be identified.

Selection criteria for redundancy

Employers need to choose criteria for selection carefully. They can use 'last in first out', sometimes referred to as LIFO, or other criteria such as level of competence or attendance record.

ACTIVITY 15.4

Read the following case study and answer the questions that follow.

The Spartan Insurance Company has decided that it is overstaffed and that it must cut back on its office staff. The departmental manager for administration recommends that the post room and print room, which between them employ seven staff, should be amalgamated into one section. This will eliminate the need for three members of staff.

The post room is run by Mr Arshad Mohammed, who is aged 34, is extremely efficient and has been with the organisation for three years. There are three other members of staff in this section – Mrs Sarah Sergeant, Ms Sandra Smythe and Mr Terry Gibbs. Mrs Sarah Sergeant, a widow aged 55, has worked for Spartan Insurance for 20 years. She has always been an extremely reliable employee, but since the death of her husband 18 months ago, she has suffered greatly from ill-health and has had a series of illnesses linked to depression.

Ms Sandra Smythe is a fairly recent recruit to the organisation. She is aged 25 and has been employed for six months. She has settled into the job well and is very efficient in everything she has to do, but is the first to admit that she still has a great deal to learn.

The most junior member of staff in this section is Terry Gibbs. He is only 20 and joined Spartan Insurance Company straight from school. He has been employed by the company for two years and seemed to have a few problems making the transition from school to work; Mr Mohammed has spoken to him informally once or twice about his attitude to work. More recently Mr Mohammed has had to warn him about his timekeeping, and he received a written warning about this. The written warning is still current and does not expire for a further month, but Terry has taken this warning extremely seriously and there has been a noticeable improvement in both his attitude and his timekeeping.

The print room has three staff – Mr George Brownlow, Mrs Rashida Ali and Ms Sally Wilson. Mr Brownlow, aged 44, is the supervisor of this section but in reality he does not actually perform any supervisory duties. Neither is he qualified to service any of the machines. He spends most of his time grumbling about the company and telling the other staff to get on with their work. He has been employed by the organisation for

10 years and it is generally thought that he was moved to his present job where he would be out of everyone's way, because of his generally uncooperative nature. It is believed that this situation was allowed to develop because he was a close personal friend of a former branch manager. This manager has long since left the organisation but Mr Brownlow is always clever enough not to do anything to warrant dismissal, and has not even received any warnings about his work. He is also a prominent local councillor and spends quite a bit of time attending council meetings.

Luckily for Mr Brownlow there are two very efficient employees who cover for his inefficiency and who do most of the work. Mrs Ali is 35 and has worked for Spartan Insurance for four years. She knows almost everything that there is to know about the machines and in effect runs the section. Sally Wilson is also extremely efficient; she is 17 years old and has been employed for a year, having started last summer straight from school.

1 What criteria would you propose for selection for redundancy here?
2 Which employees would you select for redundancy?
3 Who would be selected for redundancy if you agreed to use the LIFO method?
4 Who would be selected for redundancy if you chose criteria based on poor attendance or level of competence?

Discussion of Activity 15.4

You might have chosen criteria based on length of employment or factors such as level of competence or attendance and timekeeping.

If you chose to use LIFO then you would make the following people redundant: Ms Sandra Smythe (employed for 6 months), Mr Terry Gibbs (employed for 2 years) and Ms Sally Wilson (employed for 1 year).

If you chose criteria such as timekeeping and level of efficiency you are likely to have proposed the selection of Mr Brownlow, Mr Terry Gibbs and Mrs Sergeant.

The implications and importance of selection criteria are discussed below with further reference to this case study.

The importance of which selection criteria are used

You can see from Activity 15.4 that the criteria chosen when proposing the selection of people to be made redundant will make a big difference to who is actually selected. LIFO is often preferred by trade unions and it seems an objective method of selection, with those who have the shortest length of employment with the organisation being chosen for redundancy. This method also has the advantage of being easy to use and understand as well as being less costly in terms of redundancy pay. It may, however, as in this case, mean that those who are selected for redundancy are those who, although they have the shortest length of service, may be keen, enthusiastic employees who will have much to offer the organisation in the future. This might result in a stagnating, ageing workforce which lack the skills and versatility required for future business success.

Employers often choose to use other criteria so that they can retain such employees while making redundant others who may not have given such good service, even though they have been employed for a much longer period of time. Caution also has to be exercised in this case to ensure that the criteria chosen are objective and fair. Just saying that someone has, for example, 'a poor attitude to work' is not likely to prove adequate grounds for selection for redundancy, as this is rather vague and subjective. More objective criteria need to be used, and the ability to do this depends on whether the organisation has effective records of employee capability and competence. You would need to break job performance down into several areas such as level of skill, knowledge, experience, flexibility, productivity, appraisal records. If you selected Mr Brownlow for redundancy, you would need to have clear evidence about levels of efficiency and output. If, on the other hand, you chose Terry Gibbs for redundancy because of his poor attendance record, you would have to ensure that there are clear records for absence and that the pattern of absenteeism does not appear high because of an uncharacteristic level of ill-health just prior to the redundancy period. Criteria such as disciplinary warnings also need careful checks to ensure that they are still 'live'.

Some criteria may also make the redundancies potentially unlawful if, for example, they apply disproportionately to one sex, one ethnic group or to employees with disabilities. Whatever the selection criteria used, employers should take care to ensure that the criteria are neither directly nor indirectly discriminatory. Selection of part-time rather than full-time employees may, for instance, constitute indirect sex discrimination if the majority of part-time employees are women and the majority of full-time employees are men.

According to the CIPD (2003b) 'where there is a choice between employees, case law requires selection to be based on objective criteria. Subjective selection decisions, without objective evidence, have been found unfair by employment tribunals. Fair selection criteria include:

- length of service
- attendance records
- disciplinary records
- skills, competencies and qualifications
- work experience
- performance records.

Tribunals look favourably on selection procedures based on a points system. However, the fairness may be suspect if only one person has made the selection.' (CIPD 2003b)

Rights of redundant employees

Consultation with individual employees

Employers should also consult with each individual employee who is to be affected by the redundancies, even if there has also been consultation with the unions or with employee representatives. This consultation should:

- explain why the redundancies are needed
- explain why the particular employee has been selected
- show any relevant documentation
- explain why no suitable alternative work is currently available
- explain any requirements during the notice period such as whether normal working or part-time working is required, whether payment will be made in lieu of notice, and explain what time off is allowed to seek alternative work or for training.

Suitable alternative employment

The employer should offer a suitable alternative job if there is one, rather than making the employee redundant. If the employee's job title is broad, there may be sufficient flexibility to make an offer easily. If this is not the case, the employer should not automatically assume that any alternative employment that involved less pay or status would necessarily be unsuitable to the employee; it should still be discussed. The employees should, however, be given sufficient information about any alternative job so that they can realistically reach a decision, and they should also be offered the chance of a trial period. This should be of four weeks' duration, and will give both the employer and the employee the chance to assess the job's suitability. It should start as the old contract finishes. If a longer trial period is required because of the need for retraining, this should be agreed in writing before the date of commencement of the trial period. If either party finds the new job to be unsuitable during this period then the redundancy situation will still apply, and the redundant employee will still be entitled to his or her redundancy pay.

If the offer of suitable alternative employment is refused by the employee, then the employer has the option of withholding redundancy pay. Any claim to an employment tribunal will have to assess the suitability of the offer and the reasonableness of the refusal.

Right to time off for job searching or retraining

Employees who have worked for two years for the employer and are about to be made redundant have a statutory entitlement to a reasonable amount of time off from work to look for other jobs or to retrain in order to be able to improve their employment prospects. Any employee who is not allowed a reasonable amount of time off for these purposes can make a complaint to an employment tribunal.

Redundancy pay

Employers are expected to compensate any employee who has been made redundant, and who has worked for them for at least two years in continuous employment by paying them an amount of redundancy pay. The actual amount that the employee may be entitled to if they are redundant is calculated according to age, length of service and weekly pay. There is an upper earnings limit for the amount of weekly pay that may be included in this calculation, and this amount alters each year. Currently the limit on the weekly rate is £270. Redundancy pay is tax free and does not affect the right to unemployment benefit. Furthermore, the amount that the employee receives is not affected even if she or he starts another job immediately. The calculation of redundancy is based on the actual age of the employee at the date of dismissal, and takes account of each year of service in the appropriate age band as follows:

- for each complete year of employment in which the employee was aged 18 or over but was below the age of 22, half a week's pay
- for each complete year of employment in which the employee was aged 22 or over but was below the age of 41, one week's pay
- for each complete year of employment in which the employee was aged 41 or over but was below the age of 64, one and a half weeks' pay.

Did you know?

The reason redundancy pay increases with age is to compensate, to some extent, for the increased difficulty that older workers may experience when faced with finding a new job. A survey carried out by the Career Management Association on its web site found that people made redundant up to the age of 44 remained out of work for an average of 2.8 months. Those aged 45 or over had an average period of unemployment of 18.7 months. Robert Mackmurdo, the CMA secretary, said 'Our survey highlights the urgency with which the next government needs to outlaw age discrimination in employment.'

(Jobs and Money, page 24, *The Guardian*, 14 April 2001)

For employees who are over 64, but not yet 65, reductions in the amount of redundancy pay are made by reducing the amount received by one-twelfth for each month that the employee has worked after their sixty-fourth birthday. The maximum length of service taken into account when calculating redundancy pay is 20 years.

ACTIVITY 15.5

Consider once again the case study given in Activity 15.4 and the following information about the rates of pay of the individuals concerned. In order to simplify the calculation, imagine that each of the people concerned has worked for a whole number of years for the organisation.

Mr Brownlow: £300 per week
Mr Mohammed: £300 per week
Mrs Sergeant: £220 per week
Ms Smythe: £180 per week
Mr Gibbs: £130 per week
Mrs Ali: £210 per week
Ms Wilson: £120 per week

How much redundancy pay would each employee be entitled to?

Discussion of Activity 15.5

Mr Brownlow has worked for the organisation for 10 years and is aged 44. He has worked for 3 complete years since age 41, so is entitled to $3 \times 1\frac{1}{2}$ weeks' pay = $4\frac{1}{2}$ weeks' pay. He has also worked for 7 years between ages 22 and 40, so is entitled to 7×1 weeks' pay = 7 weeks' pay.

Therefore Mr Brownlow would be entitled to $11\frac{1}{2}$ weeks' redundancy pay if he were selected for redundancy. His weekly earnings are above the maximum allowed in this calculation, so he would actually be entitled to $11\frac{1}{2} \times £270 = £3,105$.

Mr Mohammed has worked for the organisation for only 3 years and he is aged 34. He would therefore be entitled to 3×1 week's pay. Thus he would receive $3 \times £270.00 = £810.00$.

Mrs Sergeant has worked for the organisation for 20 years and is aged 55. She has worked 14 years since the age of 41 and would be entitled to $14 \times 1\frac{1}{2}$ weeks' pay = 21 weeks' pay. She worked for a further 6 years before she was 41 and would be entitled to 6×1 weeks' pay = 6 weeks' pay.

The total number of weeks of redundancy pay she is due is therefore 27. Her weekly wage is £220 which is below the maximum entitlement. She would be entitled to $27 \times £220 = £5,940$.

Mr Gibbs is aged 20 and has worked for the organisation for 2 years. Since he is between the ages of 18 and 21 he will only be entitled to $2 \times \frac{1}{2}$ weeks' redundancy pay = 1 weeks' redundancy pay. His weekly wage is £130 and so he would be entitled only to £130 in redundancy pay.

Sally Wilson and Sandra Smythe would not be entitled to any redundancy pay as they have not worked for the required qualification period of two years, and Sally Wilson is also too young to be eligible for redundancy pay.

Tables are provided in the Department of Trade and Industry's (DTI) guide to redundancy payments which can be used so that this calculation does not have to be made in this way for every employee.

⬤ More favourable redundancy schemes

You will have noticed that the statutory levels for redundancy pay are not very high, especially if the person concerned is young or has not been employed by that employer for very long. This seems to contradict the huge amounts of redundancy pay that some people are rumoured to receive. This is because some employers have decided to make a more generous provision than is required by law. They may do this in some of the following ways:

- calculating entitlements based on actual pay rather than applying the upper earnings limit
- reducing the length of qualifying period necessary to receive redundancy pay from two years to one
- adding amounts to the statutory scheme
- making a more generous calculation such as two or three weeks' pay for each year of service.

They may also be concerned to help their employees in other ways through this difficult period, and may provide an outplacement service.

Outplacement

Did you know?

In the last ten years even communist and former communist countries which traditionally had enjoyed full employment and jobs for life have had to come to terms with redundancy. In many ways procedures are surprisingly similar to those in the West but there are often some quirky rules that HR managers would need to know. Even in Russia, according to Mike Madgewick, 'legislation is flexible enough to accommodate the enterprise that wishes to dispense with the services of one or a larger group of workers. As with so much in Russia paper rules: therefore the first and most important item is to issue a decree. Ideally one decree needs to be issued for each individual and a signed receipt obtained. The next task is to lodge a list of those affected with the local labour office. Timings are crucial and one must ensure that at least two months' notice is given before the actual terminations (under redundancy) are to be carried out.' According to Madgewick, when selecting for redundancy 'consistency is vital, the principal criteria being length of service, skills, performance and experience. In addition there are special category staff, ignored at one's peril! These include, but are not limited to, pregnant women, those already on maternity leave, single mothers and war veterans.' Two months is the statutory notice period which employees may elect to work. 'There is one small quirk that management needs to be aware of, that is the right to a third month's money if the person is still unemployed at the end of three months.'

(Madgewick, M. (1999) Russian redundancy: no longer a contradiction in terms, *Worldlink*, World Federation of Personnel Management Associations, Vol. 9, No. 6, 4–5)

This is the international name given to the process that many employers use to assist redundant employees. Outplacement can be defined as the process whereby the employer actively helps the employee to come to terms with the redundancy and assists them in the process of finding a new job or developing a new career. It is a type of aftercare service for employees who are facing redundancy, though it is by no means standard practice for all employers to provide such a service. It has been defined by Alan Jones (1994) as 'the provision of support to candidates during the transitional phase between involuntary/voluntary job loss and resettlement'. This is a useful definition as, although much of outplacement is concerned with job search skills and the finding of a new job or career, there are other avenues to explore such as further training or part-time or voluntary work, or perhaps self-employment. This definition also states that support is provided to the candidate, and this makes it clear that the responsibility for the resettlement process still rests with the candidate himself or herself but that help and active support will be given by the outplacement provider.

The CIPD (2003a) adopts a similar approach and defines outplacement as:

> Activities designed to enable individuals to develop awareness of their capacities, potential, skills and limitations, to help them to pursue the career opportunities open to them and to manage the transition through a career change or into re-employment following the loss of a job.

Once again the emphasis is on helping the individual during a difficult period but in many ways the fact that the employer provides an outplacement service also gives a very strong message to those who are still employed that they are working for a caring employer even though times may be hard. This is important as managing to keep morale high among the surviving employees can be a very difficult issue during a redundancy period.

Traditionally, employees who had been made redundant were left very much to fend for themselves, but large employers in particular have increasingly become concerned to provide an aftercare service for their former employees. Initially they concentrated on providing outplacement services just for senior managers as part of their redundancy package, but the provision of outplacement has spread and is now provided in many organisations to all staff who are made redundant. While outplacement is generally provided by or for employers, on occasions individuals whose organisation has not provided this facility may buy this provision for themselves, and a similar service is offered in many areas by the Department of Trade and Industry.

The consultancy firm Penna, Sanders and Sidney published in April 2001 the results of a survey it had conducted called 'Redefining Redundancy'. This 'highlighted a widespread belief that employers have a responsibility to help with the aftermath of redundancy. Yet only a third of respondents said that their employer had helped them to find another job or offered counselling' (*People Management* 5 April 2001, p. 11).

Pause for thought 15.2   What do you think are the main benefits to the employer of providing an outplacement service? Make a list before you read on.

The benefits of providing an outplacement service

Many human resource managers, when faced with making employees redundant, realise that it is important for the organisation to handle this difficult process as smoothly as possible, both for the sake of the individuals concerned and for the morale of the remaining employees, and in order to maintain or even enhance the good reputation of the organisation. In particular, the benefits to the organisation are likely to include:

- improved morale for remaining employees
- key staff are more likely to remain with the organisation if they see that other employees are treated well even in a redundancy situation
- good public relations with the local community will be less likely to be affected by the redundancies if they have been handled well
- there may be fewer problems with objections from trade unions if a good outplacement service is provided.

Individuals vary in the effect that redundancy has on them. For a few people it may provide a welcome opportunity to change direction in their careers, while others who have worked for a long time for an organisation may find redundancy a very traumatic experience with which they need help.

The outplacement process normally consists of provision of the following services:

- Counselling about the feelings brought about by the redundancy itself. This may sometimes involve also counselling the partner of the person who has been made redundant.
- Counselling about career or other options.
- Provision of facilities for conducting a job search.
- Provision of facilities for writing letters of application or curriculum vitae.
- Help with writing curriculum vitae and applications for jobs.
- Psychological tests to assist in career choice.
- Opportunities for practising interview skills.
- Possible direct contact with prospective employers.
- There may be provision of facilities in which interviews can be conducted.

An outplacement service can be provided either 'in-house', by the human resource department, or by external consultants.

ACTIVITY 15.6

List the advantages and the disadvantages of the provision of an in-house outplacement service and compare these with the advantages and disadvantages of external provision of an outplacement service.

Provision of in-house outplacement service

Advantages	Disadvantages

Provision of external outplacement service

Advantages	Disadvantages

Discussion of Activity 15.6

Your list probably indicates that provision of an internal outplacement service is likely to be cheaper than using a consultancy. Since many redundancies occur as part of a cost-cutting exercise, employers will be loath to spend additional money and cost may be a major concern. However, an organisation may not have sufficient facilities or levels of expertise to provide the standard of service that is required. Not only that, but it may be difficult, or even impossible, for redundant employees who have recently been told of their redundancy by their line manager or by the human resource manager to be helped by counselling from the same manager or any other manager within the organisation. Even identifying managers or others with suitable expertise may be a problem.

On the other hand, there may also be problems in finding a suitable consultancy with a high degree of expertise in this area. Anyone can establish themselves in business as an outplacement consultant, and they do not necessarily have to have any qualifications. This has been a cause for concern in recent years, with some people being charged high fees for an inadequate service, which resulted in the Chartered Institute of Personnel and Development issuing a *Code for Career and Outplacement Consultants* (2003a). This is a voluntary code of practice but gives some indication of the type of service and qualifications that an outplacement service should provide. It indicates that outplacement consultants should normally be able to demonstrate competence in 'the provision of career and outplacement consultancy services by possessing at least one of the following:

- chartered membership of the CIPD (Chartered MCIPD, Chartered FCIPD, Chartered CCIPD)
- registration with the British Psychological Society as a chartered psychologist
- other qualifications in psychology, vocational guidance or counselling recognised by a professional body
- psychometric testing and feedback must be conducted only by holders of the British Psychological Society Level A Statement of Certificate of Competence in Psychological testing. Those conducting personality testing should also hold the British Psychological Society Level B Statement or Certificate in Competence or the equivalent additional training specified by the supplier. Administration of psychological tests can also be carried out by members of the British Psychological Society Test Administration Certificate.' (CIPD 2003a)

Ideally a firm of consultants would want people who had a range of qualifications in these areas. The CIPD (2003a) differentiates between 'sponsored services where the client is an organisation paying for services provided to an individual or group of individuals' and 'private services where services are provided to clients as individuals for the services they personally receive'. All providers of whatever type of service should let the client know in advance, in writing, about the fees and terms of payment before the signing of any contract. They should also provide a written breakdown detailing exactly the service they will provide.

Conclusion

A discussion of dismissal and redundancy may seem a rather depressing topic but they are not inevitable stages if earlier advice for good human resource practices and procedures are followed.

WHAT NEXT?

The DTI (1998b) published an interesting research paper entitled 'Redundancy consultation: current practice and the effects of the 1995 regulations'. In 2003 it published a consultation paper on implementing the Information and Consultation Directive 2002 called 'High Performance Workplaces: Informing and Consulting Employees'. This is for consultation until October 2004 and it should then publish the results of the consultation exercise. Visit the DTI web site for current research in this area:

www.dti.gov.uk

References

Advisory, Conciliation and Arbitration Service (2004) *Annual Report 2003–2004*, ACAS

Chartered Institute of Personnel and Development (2003a) *Code for Career and Outplacement Consultants*, CIPD

Chartered Institute of Personnel and Development (2003b) *Redundancy Fact Sheet,* CIPD (**www.cipd.co.uk**; accessed 16.08.04)

Department of Trade and Industry (1998a) *Fairness at Work. Cm 3968*, DTI, May, Chapter 3 (**www.dti.gov.uk**)

Department of Trade and Industry (1998b) *Redundancy Consultation: Current Practice and the Effects of the 1995 Regulations,* DTI (**www.dti.gov.uk**; accessed 16.7.04)

Department of Trade and Industry (2003) *High Performance Workplaces: Informing and Consulting Employees*, DTI (**www.dti.gov.uk**; accessed 16.7.04)

European Industrial Relations Observatory on-line (2001) Industrial relations aspects of mergers and takeovers, February (**www.eirofound.ie**; accessed 16.06.04)

Jones, A. (1994) *Delivering In-House Outplacement. A Practical Guide for Trainers, Managers and Personnel Specialists*, McGraw-Hill

Monks, J. (2001) TUC welcomes French decision, TUC press release, 9 April (**www.tuc.org.uk**; accessed 11.04.01)

Sage, G. (1998) Health warning, *People Management*, 16 April, vol 4, no 8, p. 23.

Further study

Books

Advisory, Conciliation and Arbitrary Service (2002) Advisory booklet, *Redundancy Handling,* ACAS. (An excellent, clear guide to good practice.)

Advisory, Conciliation and Arbitratation Service (2001) *The ACAS Arbitration Scheme for the Resolution of Unfair Dismissal Disputes – A Guide to the Scheme*, ACAS (available at **www.acas.org.uk**; accessed 10.7.01).

Lewis, D. and M. Sargeant (2004) *Essentials of Employment Law*, 8th edition, CIPD. (An excellent guide to most aspects of employment law.)

Articles

Margolis, A. (2002) Implementation and connotation, *People Management,* Vol. 8, No. 18, 42–44.

Roberts, R. (2003) Informed discussion, *People Management,* Vol. 9, No. 15, 12–13.

Rothwell, J. (2000) How to break the news of redundancies, *People Management*, Vol. 6, No. 23, 23 November.

Stevens, P. and E. FitzGibbons (2001) How to tackle long term sick leave, *People Management*, Vol. 7, No. 14, 12 July. (A short article outlining practical issues relating to discipline and dismissal involving long-term absence to due ill-health.)

Other sources

ACAS telephone advice service. There are ACAS offices in most large towns and you should be able to find them in the telephone book. Alternatively, Department of Trade and Industry offices such as Job Centres should be able to give you their telephone number, which is also listed in DTI booklets.

Internet

Advisory, Conciliation and Arbitration Service   **www.acas.org.uk**
(A very useful source of information relating to dismissal and redundancy in Britain.)

Department of Trade and Industry   **www.dti.gov.uk**
(Many useful DTI publications relating to redundancy and dismissal in Britain can be found on this site.)

Employment tribunals   **www.employmenttribunals.gov.uk**
(A useful site for everything to do with tribunals.)

European Industrial Relations Observatory   **www.euro.eurofound.ie**
(This has up-to-date information about issues in industrial relations, including redundancy and dismissal, throughout the EU member states and Norway.)

European Trade Union Confederation   **www.etuc.org**
(This provides information from the unions' and workers' perspective but on a European dimension.)

Trades Union Congress (TUC)   **www.tuc.org.uk**
(Lots of information from the perspective of the unions and employees relating to redundancy and dismissal. This also has a useful section for students.)

Worldlink   **www.wfpma.com**
(A journal with articles on international aspects of managing people at work.)

Answers to review and self-check questions

We have provided a skeleton guide to issues you might address in answering review questions. In an exam or for an assignment, you would be expected to develop the ideas more fully to show your understanding of the topic. You can also enhance your response by making references to further reading.

Chapter 1 Introducing human resource management

Answers to review questions

It is not possible to provide model answers to the review questions for Chapter 1 because you will all have arrived at very individual answers to the activities suggested.

Answers to self-check questions

1 (*c*). **2** (*c*). **3** (*b*). **4** (*d*). **5** (*a*).

Chapter 2 Human resource strategy and planning

Answers to review questions

1 ● The levels of strategy are corporate, business and functional.
   ● You might wish to review the generic strategies associated with the corporate level (growth; stability; retrenchment) and the business level (cost competitiveness; differentiation of products or services; focus on a niche in the market).
   In general, it is expected that business strategies will grow out of corporate strategies and functional strategies will grow out of business strategies. However, each level can provide useful information for the others. Human resource strategies will have a direct impact on all the other functional strategies, and conversely cannot be formulated without knowledge of what the other functional goals are.
2 ● Define job analysis as the process of documenting the tasks performed in an organisation and the skills required to perform these tasks.
   ● Describe how job analysis results in job descriptions, person specifications and competency profiles.
   ● Comment on the range of functions that are supported by these documents.
   ● Explain how job analysis contributes to these functions: e.g. up-to-date, standardised information.
3 ● Name the major stages and describe how each is carried out.
   ● Development of the corporate plan: issues and information to be considered.
   ● Estimate demand for human resources: techniques such as work study.

- Estimate supply of human resources: skills inventory; effects of labour turnover. Labour force issues.
- Formulate human resource action plans: describe the functional areas.
- Comment on the need for evaluation and feedback into the corporate objectives.

4 ● Comment on the decisions made throughout the human resource planning process: what the corporate objectives are to be; what skills are required to achieve these objectives; how the organisation decides whether it has these skills; what action is to be taken.

- Describe the sources of information for each of these areas: knowledge of product and market developments; managerial judgement; CPIS; statistical information about the labour force.

Answers to self-check questions

1 Growth; stability; retrenchment. **2** Cost leadership; differentation, focus. **3** (b). **4** Job title; reports to; responsible for; purpose of job; major duties. **5** Recruitment and selection; day-to-day performance management; long-term performance management/performance appraisal; identification of training needs; job evaluation. **6** Job modelling. **7** 50%. **8** 80%. **9** Problems with keeping new employees. **10** Estimate the supply of human resources.

Chapter 3 Recruitment

Answers to review questions 1, 3 and 5

1 ● You should name and describe each relevant Act and Regulation, including: Sex Discrimination Act 1975; Race Relations Act 1976; Disability Discrimination Act 1995; Employment Equality (Sexual Orientation) Regulations 2003; Employment Equality (Religion or Belief) Regulations 2003; Rehabilitation of Offenders Act 1974; Equal Pay Act 1970.

- Can you give a good description of the protection that each of these Acts provides?
- Explain what is meant by direct discrimination, indirect discrimination, victimisation, and harassment.
- Discuss the need for equality policies, their integration into procedures, and the need for training and awareness throughout an organisation.
- You might also comment that some employers are looking to go beyond equality of opportunity by encouraging the active management of diversity in the workforce.

3 ● Explain how each section of these documents can help in designing a job advertisement.

- Comment on the need to give information of this kind so prospective applicants can engage in an informed process of self-selection.

5 ● Effects of an internal recruitment policy; the message that the employer rewards good performance.

- Adoption of, and commitment to, an equal opportunities policy.
- Treating people well and with respect in any telephone, written or personal contact.

Answers to self-check questions

1 (c). **2** (b). **3** (b). **4** (b). **5** The conviction is spent, so if you feel that John is otherwise qualified for the post, you have no good reason to reject him. He was entitled not to disclose his conviction since it was spent. **6** p. 79; **7** pp. 81-82; **8** p. 84; **9** No. **10** False.

Chapter 4 Selection: shortlisting and interviews

Answers to review questions

1 The aim of selection is to 'choose the best person for the job'. Selectors gather and analyse information in an attempt to predict the performance of applicants in the job. This must be done as objectively as possible by matching evidence of the knowledge, skills and personal qualities of applicants with the requirements outlined in the person specification. The selection process must also be fair, avoiding any unlawful discrimination in terms of sex, race and disability etc.

Methodical approaches include:
- having a selection policy and procedure which define the steps that will be followed in filling any vacancy
- using the person specification as a checklist when shortlisting applicants
- devising a set of standard questions to cover all the requirements on the person specification
- gathering a full set of information from all candidates and using this information to assess their suitability for the post.

Making sure that candidates can assess their own suitability for a post is also part of effective selection. Employers should therefore ensure that there is adequate opportunity for applicants to gather information about the organisation and the post during the selection process.

2 Validity and reliability are terms used in statistics to report on the results of tests. If a test consistently produces similar results when used at different times and administered by different people, then it would score high in reliability. Thus if an applicant was interviewed for a particular post by Mr Smith on Monday morning, and the same applicant was interviewed for the same post by Mr Jones on Friday afternoon, we would expect the same result if we thought that the interview was a reliable test. Research has, however, shown that interviews can be low in reliability.

Validity is an indicator of how well the test measures what it purports to measure. How well do interviews predict good performance on the job? Again, research has indicated that interviews can be low in validity. It must, however, be noted that a structured approach to interviewing can raise the level of both the reliability and the validity of employment interviews.

3 Employment interviews run a particular risk of being low in validity if they are approached in an unstructured fashion with the interviewers not properly prepared, and simply asking whatever they think is relevant in an impromptu manner. In these circumstances, interviewers are more likely to fall prey to perceptual errors than if they were conducting a structured interview.

Perceptual errors include the halo effect, the contrast effect, hiring in one's own image, and quite simply not gathering sufficient and relevant data.

These perceptual errors can be avoided simply by being aware of them and making a conscious effort to resist them. If a structured interview is conducted using a set of questions which is designed to elicit full information related to the person specification, and an attempt is made to assess all candidates objectively against these criteria, then the validity of the interview process should also increase.

4 The different types of questions that can be asked include open, closed, leading, probing, situational, and patterned behaviour description (or competency-based) questions. Each kind of question will typically elicit a different sort of response from applicants, so interviewers should carefully design their questions to gain the specific information they are seeking.

Closed questions can be used to confirm information. However, the interview is an opportunity to gain as much information as possible, and open questions are more likely to encourage applicants to talk freely. Most questions used in an interview should therefore be open questions. Probing questions can also be used to clarify points or seek more in-depth information.

Leading questions, which indicate to the interviewee what the expected response is, are not useful.

Experienced interviewers can make good use of situational and patterned behaviour description (or competency-based) questions. These require applicants to address their own behaviour in incidents which are typical of the post. Patterned behaviour description questions assume that applicants have previous related experience, whereas situational questions address what an applicant *would do* if faced with a particular situation in the future.

Answers to self-check questions

1 (*c*). **2** False. **3** (*b*). **4** (*d*). **5** (*d*). **6**(i) (*c*). **6**(ii) (*b*). **7** (*a*). **8** Patterned behaviour description. **9** Equal opportunities monitoring.

Chapter 5 Selection: supplementing the interview

Answers to self-check questions

1 (*b*). **2** Validity. **3** No. **4** True. **5** (*c*). **6** (*b*). **7** False. **8** (*b*). **9** False. **10** (*b*).

Chapter 6 The employment relationship

Answers to review questions 1 and 3

1 It is not possible to forecast what you may discover when perusing recent articles or court cases because although some issues remain contentious for many years, there are always new issues arising too. However, you will probably notice that some new issues can be directly linked to new legislation which needs to be interpreted. The meaning of new employment legislation is often tested in employment tribunals and the appeal courts.

Through doing this exercise, you will have further developed your competence in finding information. We hope you will also reflect on your learning. If you have done so, you may have realised a few implications, including the following:

● New issues are constantly arising in the HRM field, and practitioners need to stay abreast of developments by engaging in activities similar to the one you have just completed.

● You can adapt this activity to other issues too, such as unlawful discrimination, unfair dismissal, redundancy.

2 Annual leave; paternity leave: number of days/weeks allowed; may pay during paternity leave; may give more notice of termination of employment; maternity pay provisions may be more generous than the statutory minimum.

Answers to self-check questions

1 (*c*). **2** Express terms are those that are addressed directly; implied terms are those that are not expressed directly but are taken as assumed. **3** Fidelity; obedience of lawful and reasonable orders; and working with due diligence and care. **4** Nine weeks. **5** One week. **6** Employment Rights Act. **7** 26 weeks. **8** False. **9** False. **10** Isolation of employees; difficulties with supervision.

Chapter 7 Introduction to the learning process

Answers to review questions

It is impossible once again to give answers to the review questions in Chapter 7 as your answers will be individual to you.

Answers to self-check questions

1 (*a*) This effect is known as a *conditioned response*. (*b*) The cat food is the *stimulus* for Caroline's cats to make an appearance. (*c*) *Association*. The cats have started to associate the sound of the kettle with the cat food being put out. (*d*) In time the sound of the kettle becomes the *conditioned stimulus*, and the cats' response to it becomes the *conditioned response*. **2** (*b*). **3** (*c*). **4** (*a*). **5** (*e*). **6** (*b*). **7** (*d*).

Chapter 8 Learning and development programmes

Answers to review questions

1 A possible source of information would be a recent issue of the the IRS 'Employee development bulletin'. This is published monthly and is to be found within the *IRS Employment Review* which is published twice a month.

2 There is a huge amount of information on the Internet relating to these topics. Once you have chosen your topic and found information you will need to list all the key benefits from the introduction of that topic if you are to persuade a line manager about the topic. Consider the benefits to the organisation and the individual and particularly the potential benefits to the line manager, such as greater efficiency and higher productivity and an easier job with a more highly trained workforce.

3 If you interview someone from a large organisation you are likely to find that learning and development is tied in very clearly with the strategic plan and objectives of the organisation and there are likely to be clear objectives set for the learning and development department which clearly contribute to the overall objectives of the organisation. This is not the case in all organisations and some may still operate without making these links.

4 Answers should include comments on the cost involved in designing and running an induction programme, but should generally identify the benefits of easing a new employee into the workforce and how this is likely to result in a speedier route to full productivity, less labour turnover and fewer bad work habits being acquired. There should then be an outline of a suitable induction programme spread over some time.

5 Answers should define each concept and list the pros and cons of each, e.g. learning-by-doing in a realistic environment versus cost of errors and distractions. You should explain which technique you feel is the more successful overall.

Answers to self-check questions

1 No. **2** Yes. **3** No. **4** No. **5** No. **6** Yes. **7** No. **8** Yes.

Chapter 9 Performance appraisal and performance management

Answers to review questions

1 The main motivation theories that contribute to the philosophy of performance management are goal theory, reinforcement theory and expectancy theory. If you are not clear about these refer to a textbook on organisational behaviour for more detail.

2   Discussion of the main elements that are likely to cause appraisal to be done badly: poor planning and communication; poor attitudes; conflict of objectives (e.g. reward or development); lack of managerial ability; lack of training of appraiser and appraisee. These can cause bad feeling and therefore the appraisal will not achieve the benefits that it should.

Contrast this with a discussion of the main elements likely to result in appraisal being done well and which subsequently results in an improvement in motivation and performance. Explain the uses of appraisal for development for the individual and how this could literally transform someone's life. Explain also the huge benefits that can be gained for the organisation by the introduction of appraisal, e.g. by setting goals that tie in with the organisation's strategic objectives or by agreeing training provision that meets the needs of both the individual and the organisation. Feedback from the employees on goals is also important. Also explain how the introduction of appraisal can result in improved communication. You could also make the link between feedback and its role in motivational models. The fact that appraisal also focuses on the future and development towards it is also very important to both the individual and the organisation and ties in with the idea of strategic planning.

3   Outline how performance appraisal motivates employees and improves relations: provides better understanding of, and agreement on, goals; gives opportunities for praise/positive feedback; encourages agreement on training needs/use of appraisal for staff development; and results in improved communication. Performance appraisal should therefore help individuals and their team to contribute to the organisation's goals.

You will achieve an even better answer by linking these factors with concepts from motivation theories (growth, achievement, etc.).

Reasons for failure:
Lack of managerial skill and training. Explore typical managerial failures such as inability to give critical feedback. This could be in relation to lack of planning and preparation, poor interpersonal skills such as interview skills, poor communications skills, inability to build and develop teams and give feedback to individuals or team, etc. Also indicate that processes can be counterproductive, and comment on the need for managerial training and for commitment to the system.

Address the use of appraisal systems for conflicting purposes: development and pay decisions may conflict, and comment on the lack of employee involvement in the appraisal system.

4   Describe how performance appraisal systems are designed to provide feedback on past performance and how performance is measured in order to be able to do this; systems need to focus on future goals as well, and are used to identify training needs so that people can reach these goals; positive feedback is also given, and appraisal systems can be linked with pay awards (though this is problematic). Some comment on the link between goal setting and feedback and motivation should be made.

Link your answer to separate parts of the quote with a description of the performance management approach; use of performance goals and the use of feedback and recognition as a means of motivating people to their full potential.

The main benefits of performance appraisal are that people know where they stand and have opportunities to develop and be rewarded. There should also be a sense of feeling valued since organisations provide this opportunity and invest time in them. There should therefore be a direct impact on their performance through goal setting. (This is also a motivational technique.)

5 You should identify and describe three different approaches to performance apprais-al e.g. individual appraisal done by supervisor/manager, peer appraisal and 360°appraisal.

The general benefits relate to improved performance, motivation, communication and relationships. The actual nature of these benefits will need to be discussed in relation to the particular approach used.

Other general benefits include the opportunity to focus on future developments and to achieve organisational goals.

You might also mention the pitfalls, such as problems if there is lack of clarity in the purpose of the appraisal, e.g. reward or development. You may also mention skills needed in giving feedback and discuss in relation to approaches used, e.g. in peer appraisal, would everyone have the required level of skills and not have per-sonal vendettas to settle?

There is also, regardless of the approach chosen, a need to encourage owner-ship and participation.

Answers to self-check questions

1 (*c*). **2** (*b*). **3** (*c*). **4** (*a*). **5** (*b*). **6** (*a*).

◯ Chapter 10 Payment systems

Answers to review questions

1, **2** and **3** provide you with the opportunity to practise skills and seek relevant, up-to-date information for yourself and as such it is impossible to provide guideline answers here. The 'Pay and benefits bulletin', contained in the *IRS Employment Review*, is published twice a month and is an extremely useful source of articles and up-to-date information about pay and benefits in various sectors and organisations. This may be of help in getting the latest information on the minimum wage or rates paid to people on apprenticeships or New Deal. Publications such as *People Management* or *Personnel Today* may also prove useful, as should quality newspapers.

4 Your answer should define job evaluation as a method of deciding on the value of a job and address the need for a methodical approach. The points rating method and its main benefits should then be outlined. Benefits of the points rating approach to job evaluation include the fact that all jobs are rated using the same method and that these must be perceived to be fair. It is comparatively simple to use and understand and is analytical in nature.

The second part of your answer should examine perceptions of fairness. Involvement of representatives of the workforce in the design and implementation of job evaluation is likely to improve employees' perceptions of whether or not the system is fair. The points rating method is an analytical approach to job evaluation and so does break each job into parts rather than analysing the whole job. This is generally regarded as being more objective and hence fairer than non-analytical schemes. It is also more likely that this system could be justified in a tribunal if an equal pay/value claim was brought against the organisation. In order to be fair the Revised Code of Practice on Equal Pay should also be followed.

5 Your answer will describe issues such as internal and external relativities and dif-ferentials. You will also include and take account of the issues raised by legislation such as the Equal Pay Act 1970 and the Equal Pay (Amendment) Regulations 1983. Systems of job evaluation which try to ensure that fair systems of pay are in place need to be discussed. Those based on analytical methods of job evaluation are like-ly to result in fairer systems and it will be easier to prove the fairness, if necessary.

Involvement of representatives of the workforce in the design and implementation of job evaluation is likely to improve employees' perceptions of whether or not the system is fair.

Better answers will also comment on issues such as performance-related pay and how this may affect perceptions of fairness. They should also refer to the revised Code of Practice on Equal Pay, published by the Equal Opportunities Commission (2003) and to the Equal Pay 1970 (Amendment) Regulations 2004. The five stages of the EOC's pay review model should also be fully discussed.

6 Your answer should be in report form as if you are a consultant employed to advise this organisation. You need to describe various forms of both the analytical and non-analytical forms of job evaluation and outline the advantages and disadvantages of each. You should then decide on a scheme that you feel is most suitable for this organisation and make recommendations about its use. You are more likely to recommend an analytical form of job evaluation such as the points rating system. This would have benefits of being easy to justify but may be time-consuming to introduce. However, since we are making recommendations for a fairly small organisation, cost is also likely be an issue here and this form of analytical job evaluation will probably be cheaper to install than any designed or provided by a firm of consultants. Better answers would also refer to the need for fairness in whatever scheme is introduced and the need to involve members of the workforce in decisions about which scheme should be chosen. Reference should also be made to the need to take into account legislation, for example the Equal Pay (1970) (Amendment) Regulations 2004, and also the guidance provided in the EOC Code of Practice on Equal Pay (2003) and pay review model.

Answers to self-check questions

(a) No. **(b)** No. **(c)** No. **(d)** Yes. **(e)** Yes. **(f)** No. **(g)** No. **(h)** No. **(i)** Yes. **(j)** No.

Chapter 11 Counselling and employee welfare

Answers to self-check questions

1 (*d*). **2** Demands; control; support; relationships; role; change. **3** (*b*). **4** (*a*). **5** (*d*). **6** (*c*). **7** (*c*). **8** (*d*). **9** (*a*). **10** False.

Chapter 12 Health and safety

Answers to review questions

It is once again impossible to give ideal answers to the review questions here as your answers will depend on who you talk to or the organisations you analyse.

Answers to self-check questions

1 (*d*). **2** (*d*). **3** (*c*). **4** (*b*). **5** (*d*). **6** (*d*).

Chapter 13 Partnership, employee involvement and high performance working

Answers to review questions

1 ● Outline the concepts of unitarism and pluralism.
   ● Outline the concepts of participation and involvement; state how they differ from each other; identify each concept correctly as a unitary or pluralist idea.

2 ● Define employee involvement and give examples of individual techniques such as quality circles.

● Define commitment as an attitude; explain how this attitude might motivate towards more productive behaviour.

● Link the involvement initiatives you have described with motivation concepts; e.g. quality circles provide employees with feelings of responsibility and achievement because they see they can contribute their ideas. This in turn should contribute to the development of a high performance workplace.

3 ● You will have to read some of the references in order to gather more information for this question. Your answer should address developments on both a national and EU-wide scale.

4 ● You should have identified elements such as employment security, and information for employees and consultation with them to ensure an adequate channel for employee voice. Partnership recognises that employees are stakeholders in an organisation and have an interest in its success.

The aim of partnership is to improve productivity and competitiveness by fully engaging the capabilities of employees.

Answers to self-check questions

1 (*c*). **2** (*a*) Involvement. (*b*) Participation. **3** False. **4** At least 1,000 employees within the member states and at least 150 employees in each of any two member states. **5** (*b*) and (*d*). **6** (*b*). **7** False. **8** All Employee Share Ownership Plan. **9** Team briefing; employer and employee publications; company videos; electronic news systems; roadshows. **10** (*d*).

◯ Chapter 14 Discipline and grievance

Answers to review questions

It is impossible to give model answers for questions **1–3** as these require you to conduct your own research, so you may all have slightly different findings.

4   Your answer should be in the form of a report addressed to the general manager. When the organisation only employed 18 staff there was no legal requirement for it to have a grievance procedure, although it would still have been good practice to have had one. Now, since there are 100 employees there is a legal requirement to produce a grievance procedure (the Employment Rights Act 1996).

You should explain not only the importance of the legal situation to the general manager, but also make clear that grievance procedures provide a useful way for employees to express their grievances, rather than becoming dissatisfied and expressing the grievance by poor quality work or by leaving the organisation altogether.

A model grievance procedure should be described in order to show what the grievance procedure should contain. This should be modelled on the ACAS *Producing Discipline and Grievance Procedures: Self-help Guide* (2002). Key features should include: an informal stage before the formal procedure is reached; grievances should be settled as near to the source of grievance as possible, at the lowest level; a number of stages involving different people; time limits for responding at each stage and a right of appeal at each stage. There should also be a right to be accompanied by a friend or trade union official.

Answers to self-check questions

1 (*c*). **2** (*d*). **3** (*b*). **4** (*c*). **5** (*d*). **6** (*c*). **7** (*e*). **8** (*c*). **9** (*e*). **10** (*e*).

Chapter 15 Dismissal, redundancy and outplacement

Answers to review questions

1 Remember that offences that occur outside of work are not automatic reasons to dismiss an employee. ACAS advises that what is important is the nature of the offence and whether it destroys the employer's confidence in that employee. According to *The Guardian*, a CBI source described Mr Blair's comments as a legal minefield. Employers' organisations, civil servants and lawyers cautioned against the difficulties of sacking a worker for a conviction overseas, saying an employer would be open to legal challenge. The onus would be on proving that the organisation's reputation was being damaged. Even dismissing someone because they are not able to do their job because they are in prison has been found by many organisations to not necessarily be a good enough reason for dismissal.

2 You should outline the main grounds for dismissal as described in the Employment Rights Act 1996: incompetence, misconduct, redundancy, statutory bar, some other substantial reason. Better answers are likely to give examples of these types of potentially fair reasons for dismissal.

You should also explain that the process followed for dismissals is as important as the reason for the dismissal, and describe the need for a full investigation and hearing and the need to consider extenuating circumstances. Better answers are also likely to mention that some forms of dismissal are considered to be automatically unfair and for these there is only a one-stage process undertaken by the employment tribunals. You should outline some of the automatically unfair reasons for dismissal and indicate why these are designated as such.

You should express some considered opinion about the extent to which you feel that employers should try to avoid dismissals of employees. This is likely to include comment about managers taking early action to avoid the development of problems; the use of counselling skills by managers; the use of HRM planning to help avoid the need for redundancies; the training and development of employees if skills need change; a proper recruitment and selection processes to help minimise numbers of dismissals. Following good HRM policies and procedures should help to minimise costs involved. Sometimes, however, it is still necessary to dismiss and then it must be for a fair reason and must be handled reasonably in accordance with the statutory discipline and dismissal procedure.

Answers to self-check questions

1 (*c*). **2** (*e*). **3** (*b*). **4** (*c*). **5** (*a*).

Author index

Subject index